HOLOGRAPHIC MATERIALS AND OPTICAL SYSTEMS

Edited by **Izabela Naydenova, Dimana Nazarova** and **Tsvetanka Babeva**

Holographic Materials and Optical Systems

http://dx.doi.org/10.5772/63255
Edited by Izabela Naydenova, Dimana Nazarova and Tsvetanka Babeva

Contributors

Hiroshi Ono, Kotaro Kawai, Moritsugu Sakamoto, Kohei Noda, Tomoyuki Sasaki, Nobuhiro Kawatsuki, Tatsuki Tahara, Felix Buettner, Francisco Javier Martínez, Andrés Márquez, Sergi Gallego, Roberto Fernández, Jorge Francés, Manuel Ortuño, Inmaculada Pascual, Augusto Beléndez, Ana Arboleya, Jaime Laviada-Martinez, Yuri Álvarez, Fernando Las-Heras, Juha Ala-Laurinaho, Antti V. Räisänen, Dahi Ghareab Abdelsalam Ibrahim, Baoli Yao, Suzanne Martin, Hoda Akbari, Vincent Toal, Sanjay Kumar Keshri, Dennis Bade, Kevin Murphy, Izabela Naydenova, Alexander Ryskin, Aleksandr Angervaks, Andrey Veniaminov, Sergei Ivanov, Alexander Ignatiev, Nikolay Nikonorov, Viktor Dubrovin, Jean-Michel Desse, François Olchewsky, Anette Gjörloff Wingren, Zahra El-Schich, Sofia Kamlund, Birgit Janicke, Kersti Alm, Nam Kim, Yanling Piao, Huiying Wu, Zurab Vakhtang Wardosanidze, Ivan Divliansky, Xavier Allonas, Christian Ley, Christiane Carré, Ahmad Ibrahim, Tina Sabel, Marga Lensen, Maria Antonietta Ferrara, Gaetano Bianco, Fabio Borbone, Roberto Centore, Valerio Striano, Giuseppe Coppola, Miguel León-Rodríguez, Juan A. Rayas-Alvarez, Amalia Martínez-García, Raúl R. Cordero, Giuseppe Di Caprio, Gianfranco Coppola, Brian Dale, Elena Stoykova, Hoonjong Kang, Youngmin Kim, Joosup Park, Sung Hee Hong, Jisoo Hong, Vera Marinova, Shiuan Huei Lin, Ken Yuh Hsu

CBS, Edition **2018**

Published by InTech

Janeza Trdine 9, 51000 Rijeka, Croatia

Notice

Statements and opinions expressed in the chapters are these of the individual contributors and not necessarily those of the editors or publisher. No responsibility is accepted for the accuracy of information contained in the published chapters. The publisher assumes no responsibility for any damage or injury to persons or property arising out of the use of any materials, instructions, methods or ideas contained in the book.

Publishing Process Manager Iva Simcic

Technical Editor SPi Global

Cover Designer InTech Design Team

Additional hard copies can be obtained from orders@intechopen.com

Holographic Materials and Optical Systems, Edited by Izabela Naydenova, Dimana Nazarova and Tsvetanka Babeva
p. cm.
Print ISBN 978-953-51-3037-6
Online ISBN 978-953-51-3038-3

Contents

Preface

The book *Holographic Materials and Optical Systems* comprises three sections and twenty-one book chapters.

The first section has six chapters on volume holographic optical elements (HOE) and systems, including novel materials, methods, and applications (Chapter 1), holographic optical elements for solar concentrators (Chapter 2), volume Bragg gratings and their applications in laser beam combining and beam phase transformations (Chapter 3), low spatial frequency volume Bragg grating and holographic optical elements (Chapter 4), holographic optical elements and their applications (Chapter 5), and holographic data storage systems using parallel-aligned liquid crystals on silicon display (Chapter 6). Section 2 is dedicated to applications in holographic imaging and metrology. It has nine chapters focused on microtopography and thickness measurements (Chapter 7), 3D capture and 3D contents generation for holographic imaging (Chapter 8), multiwavelength digital holography (DH) and phase-shifting interferometry (Chapter 9), dynamic imaging with x-ray holography (Chapter 10), indirect off-axis holography for antenna metrology (Chapter 11), surface characterization by the use of digital holography (Chapter 12), digital holography for analyzing high-density gradients in fluid mechanics (Chapter 13), digital holographic microscopy (DHM) for clinical diagnostics (Chapter 14), and unlabeled semen analysis by means of the holographic imaging (Chapter 15). Section 3 is dedicated to holographic materials and systems for holographic recording and consists of six chapters describing materials suitable for holographic photoalignment for fabrication of twisted nematic liquid crystal gratings (Chapter 16), high-performance photoinitiating system for holographic grating recording (Chapter 17), fluorite crystals with color centers for recording extremely stable holograms (Chapter 18), new photo-thermo-refractive glasses for holographic optical elements (Chapter 19), materials for active holography (Chapter 20), and organic-inorganic hybrid structures for dynamic holography (Chapter 21).

The chapters describe a comprehensive review of the historical developments leading to the specific topic under discussion and will provide the reader with useful background information. The following paragraphs give a brief summary of chapters' contents.

"Volume Holography: Novel Materials, Methods, and Applications" provides basics on volume holography, specific material requirements for volume holography, and diffractive properties of the different types of volume holographic gratings. The interrelation between function and structure of volume holograms is investigated with a view to research on and develop novel materials, methods, and applications.

"Volume Holographic Optical Elements as Solar Concentrators" investigates holographic solar concentrator in a new photopolymer material as recording medium. Two different configurations of holographic lenses (with spherical and cylindrical symmetry) are described in terms of both recording process and optical response characterization. The possibility to use this new photopolymer to realize holographic solar concentrator for space applications is discussed.

"Volume Bragg Gratings: Fundamentals and Applications in Laser Beam Combining and Beam Phase Transformations" outlines the fundamentals of transmission and reflection volume gratings and compares their spectral properties. The applications of volume Bragg gratings for spectral and coherent laser beam combining and as holographic phase masks are demonstrated and discussed.

"Holographically Recorded Low Spatial Frequency Volume Bragg Grating and Holographic Optical Elements" presents examples of focusing elements and off-axis cylindrical lenses finding application for collection of solar energy. Some low spatial frequency diffusive elements and beam splitters were shown to illustrate the potential of low spatial frequency holographic elements in beam-shaping applications. The advantages of volume photopolymer holographic gratings are discussed in the context of existing research.

"Holographic Optical Elements and Their Applications" describes in detail the principles and characteristics of the holographic optical elements (HOE). A few typical holographic optical element–based applications such as head-mounted display, lens array, and solar concentrator are introduced. It has been demonstrated that the HOE is a much useful and an effective technique especially for simplified optical systems.

"Holographic Data Storage Using Parallel-Aligned Liquid Crystals on Silicon Display" explores the implementation of holographic data storage where a parallel-aligned liquid crystal on silicon microdisplay is utilized as the data entry point for a holographic data storage system. The authors demonstrate holographic data storage in a photopolymer as holographic recording material by utilizing a phase-only device as a data pager by using different modulation schemes.

"Microtopography and Thickness Measurements with Digital Holographic Microscopy Highlighting Its Tomographic Capacity" demonstrates the potential of digital holographic microscopy (DHM) by using a Mirau interferometric objective. The authors propose approaches for reduction of the noise by utilizing LED light and by performing an averaging process of phase and amplitude images reconstructed at different reconstruction distances. Ringing effect is reduced by using an ideal filter in off-axis digital holography.

"3D Capture and 3D Content Generation for Holographic Imaging" follows the two main tendencies in forming the 3D holographic content—direct feeding of optically recorded digital holograms to a holographic display and computer generation of interference fringes from directional, depth, and color information about the 3D objects. The focus is set on important issues that comprise encoding of 3D information for holographic imaging.

"Multiwavelength Digital Holography and Phase-Shifting Interferometry Selectively Extracting Wavelength Information: Phase Division Multiplexing of Wavelengths" proposes phase-shifting interferometry selectively extracting wavelength information as a novel type of multiwavelength imaging technique. In this technique, multiwavelength images and also the information of 3D space are simultaneously captured by the combination with holography. The proposed technique is experimentally validated.

"Dynamic Imaging with X-ray Holography" discusses the technical aspects of x-ray holography from an end user perspective, focusing on the requirements for obtaining a high-quality image in a short time. The chapter presents the key challenges of the techniques and gives ideas for their implementation.

"Indirect Off-Axis Holography for Antenna Metrology" studies the use of indirect off-axis holography in preventing the effect of errors related to phase acquisition. The aim is to develop new, efficient, and robust amplitude-only techniques while allowing for cost and complexity reduction of the measurement setup for antenna characterization.

"Surface Characterization by the Use of Digital Holography" studies numerical reconstruction algorithms and discusses the influence of slightly imperfect collimation of the reference wave in off-axis digital holography (DH). Two DH techniques for surface characterization are described and experimentally validated: (1) by using short coherent length, namely, high-brightness digital holographic microscope (DHM) and (2) by using long coherent length, namely, THz DH.

"Digital Holography Interferometry for Analyzing High-Density Gradients in Fluid Mechanics" presents the analysis of a small supersonic jet through comparison of three different optical techniques: (i) digital Michelson holography, (ii) digital holography using Wollaston prisms, and (iii) digital holography without reference wave. The advantages and challenges related to applying digital holography in analyzing high-density gradients in fluid mechanics are identified and discussed.

"Holography: The Usefulness of Digital Holographic Microscopy for Clinical Diagnostics" explores the implementation of digital holographic (DH) microscopy as a high-resolution imaging technique with the capacity of quantification of cellular conditions without any staining or labeling of cells. The unique measurable parameters are the cell number, cell area, thickness, and volume, which can be coupled to proliferation, migration, cell cycle analysis, viability, and cell death. The authors have used DH microscopy showing that the technique has the sensitivity to distinguish between different cells and treatments.

"Unlabeled Semen Analysis by Means of the Holographic Imaging" studies the morphology, the motility, and the biochemical structure of the spermatozoon and correlates these parameters with the outcome of in vitro fertilization. The chapter summarizes the recent achievements of digital holography as an efficient method for healthy and fertile sperm cell selection, without injuring the specimen, and explores new possible applications of digital holography in this field.

"One-Step Holographic Photoalignment for Twisted Nematic Liquid Crystal Gratings" describes an innovative method for fabrication of liquid crystal gratings, in which liquid crystal molecules are periodically aligned. Liquid crystal gratings are fabricated and characterized experimentally and theoretically. They exhibit potential for application as a diffractive optical element that can simultaneously control amplitude, polarization states, and propagation direction of light.

"Application of High-Performance Photoinitiating System for Holographic Grating Recording" presents a detailed analysis of widely used photoinitiators for polymerization reaction that takes place during holographic recording. The authors study three different components of photointiator systems and made conclusions about the main influencing factors in order to achieve the highest diffraction efficiency in a particular polymer system.

"Fluorite Crystals with Color Centers: A Medium for Recording Extremely Stable but Broadly Transformable Holograms" studies both the mechanisms of forming the photochromic color centers in fluorite crystals and the photochromism for recording and transforming of holograms. Possible applications as metrological elements and narrow-band transmission and reflection filters for the mid-IR spectral range based on the additively colored fluorite crystals are discussed.

"New Photo-Thermo-Refractive Glasses for Holographic Optical Elements: Properties and Applications" presents recent achievements of developing new holographic media based on fluoride, chloride, and bromide silicate photo-thermo-refractive glasses used for recording holographic optical elements for improving dramatically the parameters of laser systems of different types. The doping of photo-thermo-refractive glasses with rare earth ions was discussed as an opportunity for designing lasers with Bragg reflectors and distributed feedback.

"Active Holography" describes laser-active structures comprising dye-doped layers of cholesteric liquid crystal and polymer as a laser-active medium exhibiting spatial modulation of lasing controlled by the transversely distributed excitation located in the plane of the photosensitive layer. The influence of the parameters of the pumping interference pattern on the periodical character of the modulation of intensity of the lasing is studied, and the possible application is discussed.

"Two-Wave Mixing in Organic-Inorganic Hybrid Structures for Dynamic Holography" reviews recent progress of two-wave mixing and beam amplification in novel type of hybrid structures that combine photoconductive and photorefractive properties of inorganic crystals together with the high birefringence and anisotropy of LC (or PDLC) layers. The proposed organic-inorganic hybrid structures can control transmission, reflection, and scattering of light and are considered to play essential role in 3D holographic display technologies.

Prof. Izabela Naydenova
School of Physical and Clinical and Optometric Sciences,
Dublin Institute of Technology, Ireland

Dr. Dimana Nazarova
Institute for Optical Materials and Technologies,
Bulgarian Academy of Sciences, Bulgaria

Prof. Tsvetanka Babeva
Institute for Optical Materials and Technologies,
Bulgarian Academy of Sciences, Bulgaria

Volume Holographic Optical Elements and Systems

Chapter 1

Volume Holography: Novel Materials, Methods and Applications

Tina Sabel and Marga C. Lensen

Additional information is available at the end of the chapter

http://dx.doi.org/10.5772/67001

Abstract

This chapter aims to establish a link between material compositions, analytical methods and advanced applications for volume holography. It provides basics on volume holography, serving as a compendium on volume holographic grating formation, specific material requirements for volume holography and diffractive properties of the different types of volume holographic gratings. The particular significance of three-dimensional optical structuring for the final optical functionality is highlighted. In this context, the interrelation between function and structure of volume holograms is investigated with view to research on and development of novel materials, methods and applications. Particular emphasis will be placed on analytical methods, assuming that they provide access for a deeper understanding of volume holographic grating formation, which appears to be prerequisite for the design of novel material systems for advanced applications.

Keywords: volume holography, Bragg gratings, photonic crystals, refractive index contrast, photosensitive materials, polymers

1. Introduction

Impressive diffraction phenomena can be found in animate and inanimate nature: in the form of iridescence in birds, insects, shells, plants or muscle cells as well as in clouds and minerals. The fascination emanating from phenomena where light interacts with micro- and nano-structures may be traced back to the principle *from structure to function*, which is not limited to optical phenomena, but can be found in nature as a fundamental quality. In case of holography, light itself is capable to create the structures with which it subsequently interacts. The (optical) functionality of a holographic structure consists in its diffractive properties.

In turn, the principle *from structure to function* also comprises the possibility to understand function through structure. Taking advantage of this relation between structure and function culminates in the attempt of mimicking nature. Notable examples are functional surfaces with hierarchical structures based on the lotus effect to induce superhydrophobicity, the gecko effect for controlled adhesion or the moth's eye effect for anti-reflection coatings.

While the examples mentioned above remain limited to surface phenomena, the third dimension opens up entirely new possibilities with major relevance for many applications. Structures with a periodic modulation of the refractive index are of interest wherever light must be manipulated. Volume holographic gratings can be considered as such three-dimensional (3D) optical structures with diffractive properties.

Volume gratings made by nature can be found in the form of crystals wherever atoms are regularly arranged [1]. The dimensions of atomic and molecular structures usually result in interaction rather with a non-visible range of the electromagnetic spectrum, enabling access by means of X-ray crystallography. However, light-based photonic crystals (PCs), with functionality in the visible range, can be created artificially [2].

While holography allows three-dimensional imaging, the holographic structure itself extends not necessarily in three dimensions. Depending on the hologram formation technique as well as on the recording medium, the hologram itself takes shape as a surface pattern or rather emerges as a three-dimensional structure. A volume hologram or photonic crystal may only be formed if recording technique and recording medium allow modification of the optical properties in all three dimensions. The performance of such a grating with thickness in the range of 100 μm differ significantly from thin gratings or surface gratings: Volume Bragg gratings stand out due to their high diffraction efficiency, rigorous wavelength selectivity and the ability that multiple holograms may be superimposed by means of multiplexing.

There are many ways to create optical surface patterns by photolithography, self-assembly or other nano- and microfabrication methods with both, bottom-up and top-down approaches. However, entering the third dimension in optical structuring is accompanied with considerable challenges. Among existing techniques for three-dimensional optical structuring, such as direct laser writing [3] or self-assembly [4], volume holography provides the unique possibilities to create optical structures through the entire volume beyond a point-by-point, line-by-line or plane-by-plane fabrication, with high resolution and accuracy in a single step.

At the same time, the analysis of volume holographic structures emerges as a challenging task. Optical structures inside a volume may not readily be mapped by means of common microscopic methods [5]. This is where the mutuality of function and structure opens up new possibilities. In fact, the diffraction efficiency represents the only accessible parameter to entirely characterize a volume grating. Based on the optical functionality, conclusions may be drawn on grating parameters as well as on material parameters such as material response and energetic sensitivity.

Within this chapter, the interrelation between material compositions, analytical methods and advanced applications for volume holographic systems is investigated with particular emphasis on analytical methods. According to the leading idea of a correlation between function and structure, the deeper understanding of volume holographic grating formation appears prerequisite to design novel material systems for advanced applications.

2. Volume hologram formation in photosensitive materials

The mechanism of volume hologram formation in photosensitive materials, a complex process where several components are involved, is starting from the interference exposure. Holographic recording induces a generally three-dimensional spatial modulation in the optical properties. The final grating features optical functionality that consists in specific diffraction of light, to be characterized by means of its diffraction efficiency (defined as the ratio of the input readout power to the diffracted power), as well as angular response and frequency response. Different kinds of gratings are formed, according to the specific recording conditions. While the geometry clearly determines dimensionality and size of the grating, many factors influence how the material responds to light during the holographic exposure. The material response strongly depends on intrinsic material parameters, such as material composition or viscosity as well as on recording parameters, such as exposure duration and recording intensity [6].

2.1. Grating formation

Volume holographic grating formation can be attributed to different physico-chemical material transformations, depending on the type of photosensitive material. In case of polymers, an interplay of polymerization and diffusion, induced by the spatially modulated exposure, is responsible for hologram formation [7]. A light pattern is projected into the photosensitive medium, inducing local polymerization, proportional to the light intensity. Thereupon, a chemical gradient is induced, resulting in monomer diffusion and subsequent polymerization. As a consequence, the hologram is formed as a periodic modulation of optical properties, according to the recording light pattern. This grating formation mechanism is illustrated in **Figure 1**.

A special characteristic of volume gratings is that their optical functionality can be attributed to very small modulations of optical properties inside the holographic material. In case of phase gratings with a layer thickness of 200 μm, a refractive index contrast in the order of only 10^{-3} already results in diffraction efficiency close to 100%.

The contrast of such optical structures can be further enhanced with additives such as nanoparticles or quantum dots [8, 9]. It can also be combined with other mechanisms such as photochemical isomerization of optically anisotropic components or with polymer-dispersed liquid crystals (PDLCs) for switchable or tuneable optical devices [10, 11]. Furthermore, the light-induced mass transport may result in the formation of additional surface-relief gratings [12].

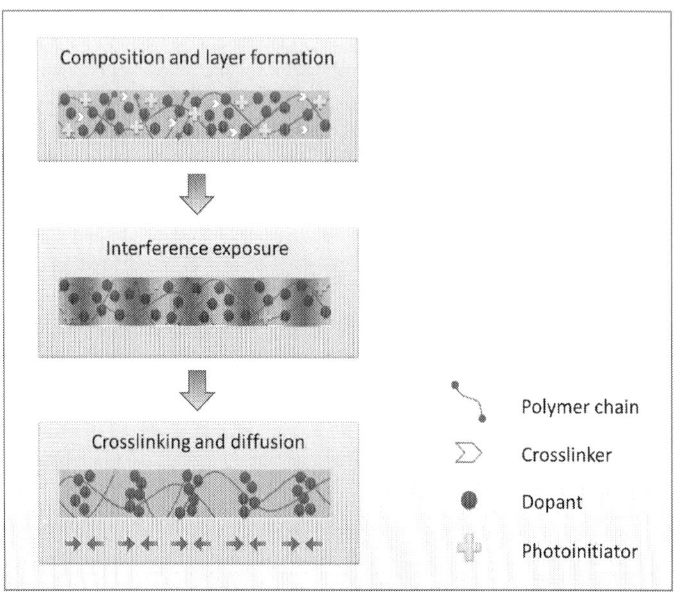

Figure 1. Schematic illustration of grating formation in photosensitive polymers: Unreacted polymer chains, cross-linker, dopant (e.g., monomers) and photoinitiator are needed for the material composition and layer formation (top). Interference exposure induces local polymerization (middle) and subsequent diffusion of components (either into the bright regions, as illustrated above, or into the dark regions) to form the permanent grating (below).

2.1.1. Specific material requirements

First of all, a photosensitive medium for volume holographic recording must be capable to undergo molecular or structural transformations with the result of a local, and in most cases, permanent change of the optical properties, as described in the previous section. In addition, and with focus on the functionality of volume holographic gratings, the medium must comply with high material standards. In this context, a number of material parameters must be optimized, namely sensitivity and dynamic range, resolution, transparency and stability. The following table gives an overview of important material parameters for volume holographic recording.

Parameter	Symbol	Unit	Target value
Layer thickness	d	[μm]	>50
Refractive index contrast	Δn	[-]	>0.001
Resolution	U	[lines/mm]	>5000
Sensitivity	S	[cm²/J]	>1
Transparency	T	[%]	>0.7

Table 1. Overview on volume holographic material parameters.

Indispensable prerequisite for the material composition is the ability to form stable layers with *thickness* d in the range of at least 50 μm where a *refractive index contrast* Δn in the order of 10^{-3} can be induced.

The material *resolution* U refers to the precision within the ability of a photosensitive material to transfer the interference pattern of exposure into a permanent modulation of optical properties during the recording process, depending on the smallest structure size of the exposure pattern. It is therefore related to the precision of the final recorded structure. With the objective to fully exploit the interference pattern of the exposure beams, high material resolution is required. With regard to the maximum spatial frequency response, that is, the highest frequency inducing a permanent refractive index modulation, a value in the range of 5000–10,000 lines per mm is aspired [13].

The *sensitivity* S provides information on how the input energy is converted into a certain holographic contrast. High sensitivity is required with respect to the possible application of low-power laser sources but also to ensure high recording speed [14]. In this context, the *dynamic range* M# refers to the total response of a medium, when divided up to n holograms. It determines how many holograms can be multiplexed in a single volume [15].

Highest *transparency* T of the material at the operating wavelength is required to achieve high diffraction efficiency. Low attenuation becomes particularly important in case of thick layers, desired for volume holographic applications. In general, losses arising from absorption and scattering should not exceed 30%. Although much lower values might be required, depending on the layer thickness, for certain specific applications [16].

Next to a high sensitivity, high spatial resolution and low losses, a high thermal stability and long-time stability of samples and systems are required [14].

Altogether, the diversity of material requirements is accompanied by a diversity of approaches to meet these needs.

2.1.2. Photosensitive media for volume holography

The range of photosensitive media used for volume holographic recording is as diverse as the spectrum of potential applications.

Although photographic emulsion, the original holographic recording material, is capable to form amplitude as well as phase holograms with good sensitivity and stability as well as high spatial resolution, it nevertheless appears inappropriate for volume holography [1]. This is due to the fact that the sample thickness is limited to only a few microns, a serious disadvantage in view of the aspired recording of thick gratings for volume holography.

Photosensitive polymers have been used as holographic media since 1969 [17]. Polymers combine many advantages, namely low cost, ease of fabrication, flexibility and the ability to be integrated in more complex systems, such as optical circuits. They fulfill the requirements for volume holographic recording with no need for solvent processing, good dimensional stability, variable thickness, high energetic sensitivity, large dynamic range and sharp angular selectivity [6, 15, 18, 19].

Among polymers for volume holographic recording, there are two material classes, differing in the mechanism of polymerization. The performances of free-radical (FRP) and cationic ring-opening polymerization (CROP) systems differ in many respects. Ranking among well-known FRP systems, glass-like polymer based on poly-(methyl methacrylate) (PMMA) with distributed phenanthrenequinone (PQ) is known as effective and thermally stable holographic recording material. Results on volume gratings within this chapter are based on investigations on gratings in free-surface epoxy-based polymer samples, prepared by microresist technology GmbH. High performance is achieved in volumetrically stable, free-surface samples with variable layer thickness [6]. The corresponding mechanism of polymerization is a cationic ring-opening polymerization. Similar to polyvinylalcohol/acrylamide (PVA/AA) material, grating formation occurs primarily as a consequence of photopolymerization and mass transport processes [20].

Photorefractive materials, such as lithium niobate, barium titanate or gallium arsenide, are capable to form temporary, erasable holograms as a result of a nonlinear optical effect [21]. Recorded data may be erased by flooding the crystal with uniform illumination. Improved properties with respect to the dynamic range, sensitivity and signal-to-noise-ratio have been demonstrated [22]. Drawbacks are partially slow response time and low stability.

2.2. Grating types

Volume holographic gratings can be categorized according to different criteria. The following section gives an overview on the different types of gratings, and how they can be distinguished with regard to their optical functionality such as diffraction efficiency and angular response.

2.2.1. Modulation

With regard to the modulated optical property, phase gratings can be differentiated from absorption gratings. Depending on the physico-chemical processes involved in the grating formation, the diffraction efficiency can be attributed to a refractive index contrast and/or to a modulation of the absorption, respectively. However, both can also be observed together [23]. In this case, the modulation of the refractive index yields a part of the total diffraction efficiency while the absorption modulation induces additional diffraction. As a consequence, it is not possible to distinguish between phase and absorption gratings, based on the diffraction efficiency. Nor can such information be derived from a microscopic image. However, it may be provided from local analysis of the optical properties, namely refractive index and absorption, respectively.

2.2.2. Dimensionality

The dimensionality of a volume holographic grating indicates in how many spatial directions the modulation spreads. This is determined by the recording interference pattern. **Figure 2** schematically illustrates how the dimensionality of a volume grating relates to the number and orientation of corresponding recording beams.

In case of a two-beam exposure, a one-dimensional volume grating is formed, illustrated by the grating planes on the left side of **Figure 2**. The grating vector $\vec{K}$ is defined by the two

wave vectors of the recording beams (this is also illustrated in **Figure 3**). At least three recording beams are needed to build a two-dimensional grating or rather optical pillars (center of
Figure 2). A three-dimensional grating, with a modulation in all three directions, results from
at least four exposure beams (right side in **Figure 2**).

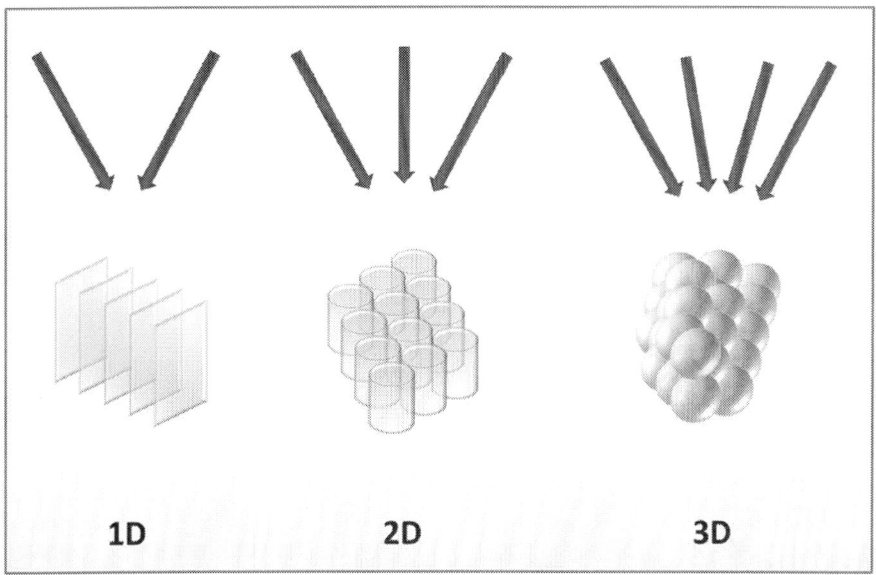

Figure 2. Schematic view of one- , two- and three-dimensional volume gratings formed by two, three and four recording
beams, respectively.

Higher dimensional gratings can also be obtained by means of superposition. The same applies
to the functionality of more complex structures. The diffraction pattern provides respective information according to the correlation of function and structure. A one-dimensional
grating shows diffraction with only one rotational degree of freedom (left side of **Figure 2**).
Each additional recording direction adds a spatial direction to the modulation of the grating
with the result of a higher dimension (middle and right side of **Figure 2**).

Microscopic images of one-dimensional and three-dimensional volume phase gratings are
shown in **Figure 8**.

2.2.3. Geometry

With regard to the geometry, transmission gratings can be distinguished from reflection gratings.
The geometry of a grating is determined by the recording geometry, as illustrated in **Figure 3**.

The transmission and reflection curves, respectively, are strongly peaked at the Bragg angle, which
is defined by Bragg's law. In case of unslanted transmission type gratings, the Bragg angle is equivalent to half the angle between reference and signal beam ($\Theta/2$). The grating period Λ is (where n is
the refractive index of the recording medium and λ is the free-space recording wavelength):

$$\Lambda_t = \frac{\lambda}{2n\sin\frac{\theta}{2}} \tag{1a}$$

$$\Lambda_r = \frac{\lambda}{2n\cos\frac{\theta}{2}} \tag{1b}$$

for transmission (Λ_t) and reflection gratings (Λ_r), respectively.

A grating is transmission type if the angle between incoming light wave vector $\vec{k}$ and grating vector $\vec{K}$ is less than 90 degrees, that is, $\angle\left(\vec{k}, \vec{K}\right) < \frac{\pi}{2}$. This is the case if both recording beams approach the sample from the same side (see left hand side of **Figure 3**). In contrast, the grating is reflection type if the recording beams come from both sides of the sample (see center of **Figure 3**). Again, transmission and reflection gratings may also be observed simultaneously. Beyond the possibilities to overlap gratings by means of multiplexing, superimposed holograms may also be formed due to the reflection of recording beams at the sample-substrate interface. This case of secondary gratings is illustrated on the right hand side of **Figure 3**.

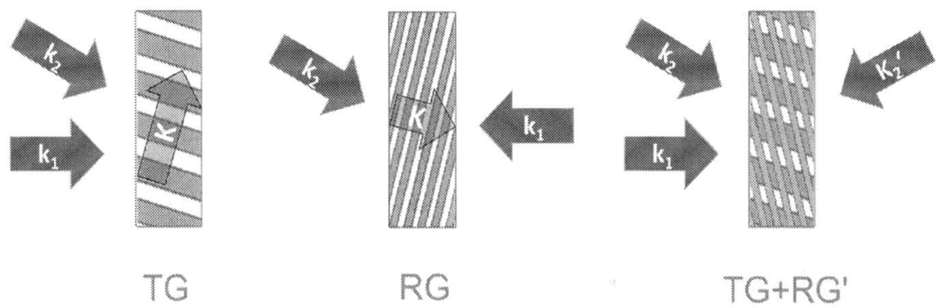

Figure 3. Recording geometries for transmission grating (TG) and reflection grating (RG). Wave vectors of recording beams $\vec{k}$ as well as grating vectors $\vec{K}$ are displayed. The reflected wave forms a secondary grating (RG') [5].

2.2.4. Selectivity

The selectivity of a volume phase grating serves as a criterion to classify the hologram with regard to the optical functionality. Therefore, it is indicated to define an important parameter with respect to the diffractive properties — the coupling constant κ:

$$\kappa = \frac{\pi\Delta n}{2\lambda} \tag{2}$$

where Δn is the refractive index contrast and λ is the recording wavelength. The coupling constant κ serves as a measure for the strength of a grating.

Holograms can be categorized into Raman-Nath type and Bragg type, respectively. A Raman-Nath hologram causes multiple diffraction orders, leading to low diffraction efficiency. A Bragg hologram shows single diffraction, enabling high diffraction efficiency and good selectivity. While Raman-Nath holograms may be recorded in a thin film, thick films are required to obtain Bragg holograms with good optical functionality [24].

With reference to the coupled wave analysis [25], the parameter:

$$\Omega = \frac{\left|\vec{K}\right|^2}{2k\kappa} \tag{3}$$

with κ the coupling constant, defined by Eq. 2, can serve as an indicator for the presence of volume-type gratings. For small Ω, multi-wave diffraction occurs and little selectivity is shown. If $\Omega \geq 10$ is fulfilled, only two diffraction orders are excited [26]. This is the case if the Bragg condition is satisfied (i.e. if the probe angle corresponds to the Bragg angle, defined by Eq. 1).

From a more general perspective, a Bragg grating, also called thick grating [14], satisfies the condition:

$$d \gg \frac{\Lambda^2}{\lambda} \tag{4}$$

with d the thickness of the grating or rather the layer thickness of the recording material.

The most important two-wave case or rather the Bragg regime, is illustrated in **Figure 4**.

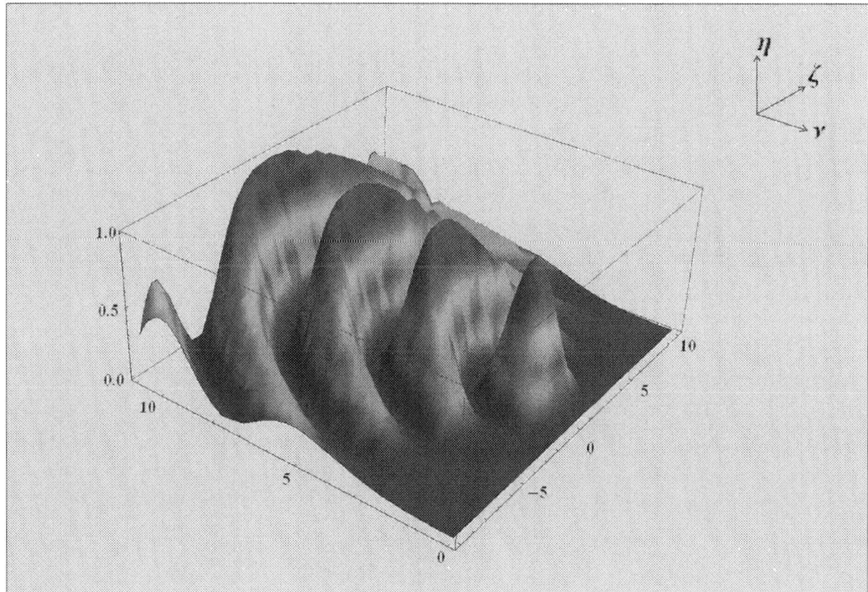

Figure 4. Diffraction efficiency η over normalized thickness ζ and normalized coupling constant v in Bragg regime. A grating is overmodulated in case of $v > \frac{\pi}{2}$.

In Bragg regime, the diffraction efficiency of the first diffraction order (η) is as follows:

$$\eta_1 = sin^2(v) \tag{5}$$

where $v = \frac{\kappa d}{\cos\theta_p}$ is the normalized coupling constant with θ_p the probe beam angle (depicted in **Figure 7**).

Figure 4 shows how the diffraction efficiency distributes over normalized thickness ζ and normalized coupling constant v. Hereby, the normalized thickness serves as off-Bragg parameter, accounting for small deviations from the Bragg condition either in terms of wavelength ($\Delta\lambda$) or in terms of angle ($\Delta\theta$) [27].

3. Analytical methods and corresponding results

The performance of volume holograms can be attributed to tiny modulations of optical properties inside the holographic material. As a consequence, direct analytical techniques, such as imaging by means of optical microscopy, are only partially appropriate for volume holograms. This is primarily due to the low optical contrast between the grating planes. But it also applies with regard to the most important three-dimensional structuring of volume holographic gratings.

3.1. Structure and function

A comprehensive analytical characterization of volume holographic gratings is possible based on the principle *from structure to function*. The idea of a correlation between structure and function for volume holograms is illustrated in **Figure 5**.

Figure 5 contrasts structural information and the related functionality for one-dimensional volume gratings. The structural information on the volume holographic grating is displayed on the left hand side. The holographic structure is described by its thickness d, the grating constant Λ and the refractive index contrast Δn. The (optical) functionality of a holographic structure consists in its diffractive properties, exemplarily displayed as angular resolved transmission on the right hand side of **Figure 5**. The link between structure and function consists in mutual determination: When the hologram is recorded, material response, exposure conditions and recording geometry determine the formation of the grating. For the final grating, the structural parameters {d, Λ, Δn} determine the diffractive properties or rather the angular resolved diffraction efficiency. In consequence, the diffraction efficiency can be utilized to access the characteristic parameters {d, Λ, Δn}. Corresponding analytical methods will be described below.

3.2. Real-time observation of grating formation

The dynamics of volume holographic grating formation may be accessed with the help of a time-resolved observation of the diffraction efficiency $\eta(t)$. However, to model the grating growth and to draw conclusions on the interplay of underlying mechanisms, such as polymerization and diffusion, the time evolution of the refractive index contrast $\Delta n(t)$ is needed. Potential factors, responsible for the change of the refractive index in the course of polymerization, are molecular polarizability, density and molar mass [28].

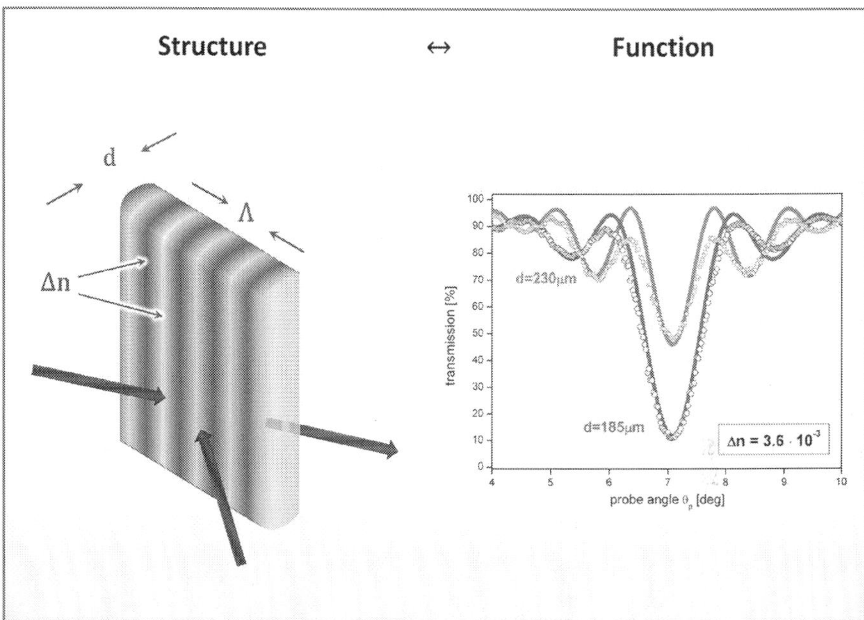

Figure 5. Relationship of structure and function for a volume holographic grating: The grating is determined by its thickness d, grating constant Λ and refractive index contrast Δn (left hand side). Those parameters determine the diffractive properties, exemplarily displayed as angular-resolved transmission (right hand side, from Ref. [6]).

Optical methods provide an elegant approach to study the kinetics of polymerization and diffusion in the course of grating formation [19]. Corresponding analysis setups feature in-situ parts for real-time, non-disturbing observation of the grating formation process and enable monitoring of the time evolution of the diffracted part of a probe beam from the very start of exposure. As a consequence, grating growth curves can be obtained.

Figure 6 shows recording and analysis setup plus corresponding grating growth curve. In this case, the growth curve reveals a transition of the refractive index contrast [29].

Figure 6 shows holographic exposure, performed by two freely propagating, s-polarized recording beams, 2 mm in diameter. Symmetric recording geometry results in unslanted gratings with periodicity of $\Lambda \approx 2\ \mu m$.

To ensure non-disturbing observation of the grating formation process, the wavelength for in-situ observation must be chosen outside of the absorption spectrum of the photosensitizer dye. In the above example, a fiber-guided 633 nm HeNe laser was used in combination with an adjustable collimator, allowing to probe with a slightly focused beam. This enables to steadily ensure a stable on-Bragg condition according to Eq. 1. A position sensitive device (PSD) was implemented to detect the diffracted light. The PSD provides time-resolved information on the diffraction efficiency as well as on the Bragg angle. The time-resolved information on the grating constant is derived from the position of the diffracted beam on the detector. This also enables to draw conclusions on time-resolved optical shrinkage [30, 31].

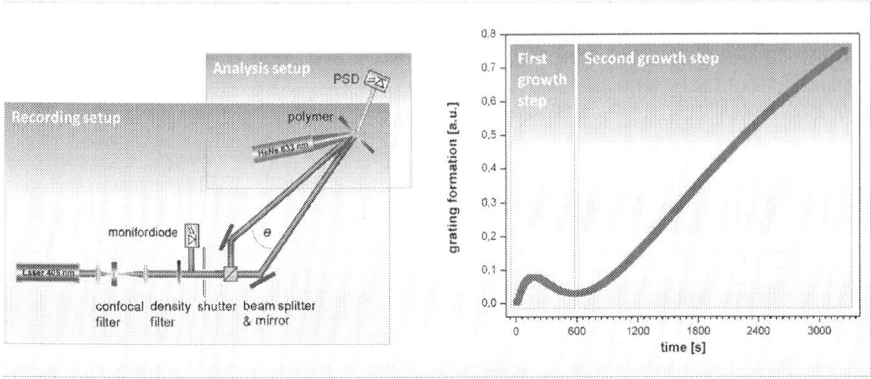

Figure 6. Recording and analysis setup for real-time observation of volume holographic grating formation: Holographic exposure is performed by two freely propagating, s-polarized recording beams with λ = 405 nm (left). The corresponding grating growth curve shows a two-step grating growth (right).

The grating growth curve shown in **Figure 6** belongs to a one-dimensional, plane-wave volume hologram of transmission type, recorded in epoxy-based polymer [29]. The characteristic two-step growth can be attributed to a transition of the refractive index contrast from positive to negative values, as a result of competing effects, taking place on overlapping time scales.

Investigations on the dynamics of volume holographic grating formation may also be applied to study the influence of important factors. This applies to material parameters, such as composition or viscosity, to grating parameters such as grating constant or geometry as well as to recording parameters, such as exposure duration or recording intensity [30].

3.3. Angular-resolved analysis

In the context of the leading idea *from structure to function*, the angular resolved analysis of volume holograms is of particular importance. Analysis of diffracted light provides basic access to the characteristic properties of the patterns causing the diffraction. Particularly, the angular-resolved diffraction efficiency provides information on the key features, such as grating constant, grating slant and, by comparison with coupled-wave-theory (RCWA) calculations, also about layer thickness, refractive index contrast and refractive index profile.

Analysis of the final holograms is usually accomplished in a rotation scan setup with collimated probe beam [32]. **Figure 7** shows a rotation scan setup plus corresponding transmission curve, that is, the angular response of a volume hologram (dots) and comparison with RCWA calculations (solid line).

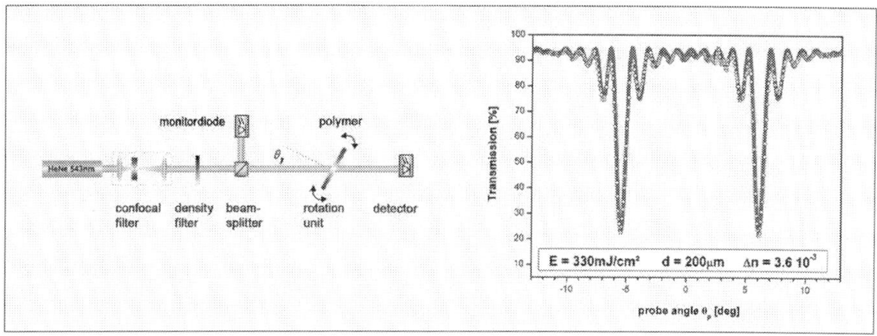

Figure 7. Rotation-scan setup (left) and corresponding angular response of a volume holographic grating, from which conclusions are drawn on grating parameters and material response (right).

The transmitted signal of a 543 nm HeNe laser is detected while the hologram under test is rotated. From the angularly resolved transmission, the following information is derived. First, the maximum diffraction efficiency can be obtained and can be correlated with the exposure energy density E to yield the material response [6]. Second, the grating constant Λ can be derived with the help of Eq. 1a. Finally, RCWA calculations can be used to derive values for the layer thickness d and the refractive index contrast Δn.

3.4. Microscopic techniques

As outlined above, low contrast is the main problem in imaging of volume holographic gratings. It might be proposed to apply fluorescent media or dyes as contrast agents to improve the image contrast. In this case, agglomeration of the contrast media along the grating planes would be prerequisite to achieve the desired effect, which cannot always be ensured. To achieve contrast in electron microscopy, conductive species are necessarily required. This is the case where nanoparticles are incorporated [33, 34]. Thus, transmission electron microscopy (TEM) is used to evaluate the degree of nanoparticle assembly [33, 35]. Scanning force microscopy (SFM) may be applied additionally, to map surface modulations [33, 36]. Nanocomposite materials are also the subject of investigations by luminescence microscopy [37]. However, mapping of nanoparticles yields only a limited description of lattice structures, not necessarily identical with the grating of interest, which is linked to the diffractive properties. In fact, it has been demonstrated that photoinsensitive nanoparticles experience counterdiffusion during grating buildup [38].

The imaging task is becoming increasingly complex without conductive species and with regard to the three dimensionality of volume phase gratings. However, it is the third dimension in particular to which the specific features of volume holograms can be assigned.

All the limitations notwithstanding, optical microscopy might nevertheless be applied to analyze volume holograms. Corresponding images are shown in **Figure 8**.

A one-dimensional volume phase grating is shown on the left side of **Figure 8**. In case of higher dimensional gratings, optical microscopy may only be applied to picture single planes of the structure. As an example, the middle and right hand side of **Figure 8** show two planes of a three-dimensional holographic grating with hexagonal close packing crystal structure. It was produced by four mutually coherent exposure beams. The lateral distance of neighboring crystal units is 2 μm, to be read from **Figure 8**. The grating constant perpendicular to the image plane amounts to 22 μm (not shown) [39].

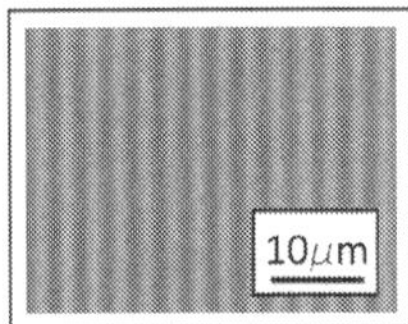

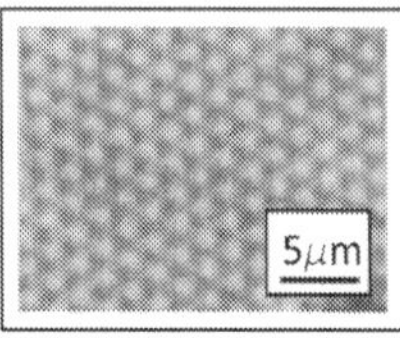

Figure 8. Optical microscopic imaging of volume phase gratings in photosensitive polymer: one-dimensional grating (left hand side) and 3D photonic grating under variation of the microscopic focal plane (middle and right hand side).

3.5. Spatially resolved diffraction analysis

Optical microscopy provides local information on the grating in the context of geometry and dimensionality. No information on the optical functionality, such as on the Bragg selectivity, is provided. However, this information is accessible according to the relation between structure and function and can be derived from spatial-resolved analysis. In case of transmission type gratings, this can be accomplished by means of scanning the lateral plane to obtain local values of the grating parameters. Local values of thickness d, refractive index contrast Δn, as well as grating period Λ and the grating slant Φ can be obtained. The lateral scan method is keeping track of the hologram shape, which is determined by the material response to the Gaussian intensity distribution of the recording beams [30].

Probing only a fraction of the exposed area is primarily for the purpose of measuring precision [29, 40]. However, it also enables scanning of the grating by moving the sample perpendicular to the optical axis. A sequence of rotation scans through the grating diameter constitutes a lateral scan. This analytical method allows the determination of the hologram characteristics along the sample surface. Thereupon, it is possible to compare and track respective properties from the center of the grating to the edges, corresponding to the areas of highest and lowest recording intensity. As a consequence, spatial sequences of the grating parameters are derived, providing insight into the local material characteristics.

Figure 9 illustrates the principle of lateral scanning. The ratio of probe beam to exposure beam diameter was 1:6. The local diffraction efficiency is displayed along the lateral position of five different volume holograms. The gratings were recorded with different exposure dose. The respective energy density of exposure (E) is displayed in **Figure 9**. The lateral scan reveals the material response, resulting in overmodulation ($v > \frac{\pi}{2}$) in case of E > 330 mJ/cm^2.

The results from spatially resolved investigations of the grating constant reveal the influence of the recording intensity and exposure duration on the Bragg selectivity [30]. The advantage of lateral scanning consists in the exploitation of the Gaussian intensity distribution of the recording beams. Thus, lateral scanning provides direct access to characterize the material response, based on one single exposure. As a result, other influential factors on the material response, such as pre-exposure, are eliminated.

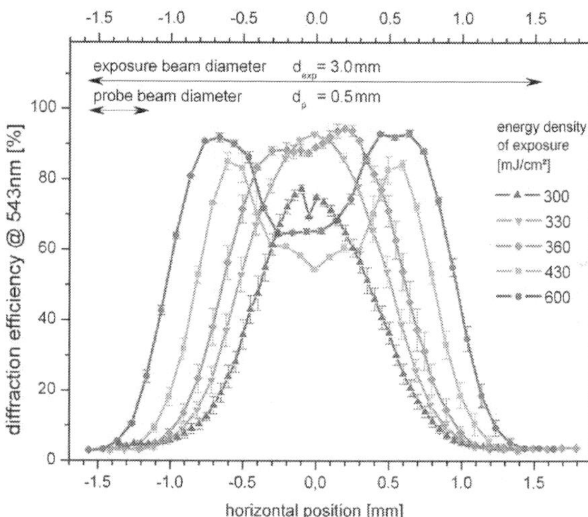

Figure 9. Principle of lateral scanning: Holograms were recorded with exposure beam diameter of 3mm and scanned step-by-step with a probe beam diameter of 0.5 mm. Five lateral scans are shown. The corresponding gratings were recorded with different exposure energy densities.

4. Volume holographic applications

The range of applications for volume holographic materials spreads wide across several disciplines. Holographic optical elements can perform the functions of mirrors, lenses, gratings or combinations of them to be applied for scanning, splitting, focusing and controlling of laser light in optical devices. The corresponding scope of applications reaches from light-guiding in general to more complex systems and operational areas, specific technologies, metrology such as holographic interferometry, through to potential use for consumer electronics such as for display technologies, as well as the many applications associated with the exploding bandwidth in meeting the demands of internet traffic and related data storage. Furthermore, holography and photolithography may arise in a powerful combination to create complex structures for micromechanical and photonic devices with potential applications not only in optics and electronics, but also in tissue engineering, cell biology and medical science as well.

Some selected application areas are described in more detail below.

4.1. Integrated optics

Photosensitive polymers are highly interesting materials for applications in integrated optics [6, 29]. This particularly applies with respect to the multi-functional applicability as well as the ability to optimize and miniaturize respective components.

Information and communication technologies are subject to a continuing shift toward optical solutions. All optical devices are needed to evade the current drawback of electro-optical chips, slowing down the whole process by forcing to work at the speed of electronics. Another objective is to reduce feature sizes in the course of miniaturization of components.

Future photonic devices such as electro-optical chips may incorporate micro-lasers and holographic optical elements (HOEs) for optical computations, interconnects and memory systems, possibly forming smaller and cheaper computer parts with higher performance [41]. Furthermore, HOEs may pave the way for the future of optical information technologies with all optical switchers, optical interconnects, (De-) multiplexers and narrow-spectral bandwidth filters, as well as photonic crystals with the potential to create integrated optical devices, capable of all optical signal processing.

The field of applications for integrated optics can further be enlarged. HOEs are also capable to efficiently redirecting light with the aim to improve light collection in solar cells [42]. Volume holographic optical elements (vHOEs) with tuneable angular and spectral Bragg selectivity, produced in instant developing photopolymer film, have recently been reported for use as lightweight, thin and flat optical elements for photovoltaic applications [43, 44].

4.2. Security technologies

Hologram encoding refers to the representation of the complex wavefield at the hologram plane, capable to encrypt information. The microscopic structure of a hologram is hard to replicate, constituting the particular applicability of holographic parts for security features. Embossed holograms are usually applied for mass production of cheap holograms for security applications, for instance on credit cards. But photopolymer holography and volume holographic parts in particular could provide considerable benefits for advanced security solutions. A volume hologram may not be copied by embossing.

Photopolymer holograms are expected to play an increasingly important role in security and authentication markets due to tight color control and strikingly realistic dimensions resulting in the unique looks of recorded images compared to embossed holograms. Photopolymer holograms can be individualized or serialized [41]. Furthermore, advanced holographic security labels could be used to fully exploit the capabilities of volume holographic systems. To further enhance the level of security, additional functionalities can be achieved by incorporation of nanoparticles. The nanoparticle-rich grating planes result in an additional security level of volume holographic labels, attained by means of specific characteristics, such as local photoluminescence in the patterned microscopic structure [37].

While two-dimensional surface holograms, currently in use, may in principle be copied by means of a point-by-point survey and imitation, the only possibility to reproduce three-dimensional volume holograms is optical reconstruction of the original hologram and interference with the reference wave. As a consequence, the exploitation of the photosensitive volume in all three dimensions could result in a considerable increase of the security level. Recently, 2.5D nanostructures based on holographic surface-relief Bragg gratings have been demonstrated, which show tuneable diffraction in the visible spectrum and can further be combined with additional functionalities for enhanced multilevel security [45].

4.3. Biomedicine

In tissue engineering, cell biology and medical science, many applications become accessible through explicit control over molecular structure and mechanical properties, such as elasticity, cross-linking degree or surface morphology of certain biomaterials [46, 47]. In view of such applications, a combination of holographic and photolithographic processing may be used to create complex structures for micromechanical and photonic devices [2, 48]. Here again, volume holography in photosensitive polymers is of high interest for practical applications, with respect to the high flexibility and optimization ability of subsequent devices [41]. The optical functionality can be applied for the use as holographic sensors [49]. Photonic crystals are promising candidates for biosensors and bioassays. With view to the interrelation of function and structure, functional structures of different PC materials are linked with respective sensing mechanisms [50]. Optical structures have already been incorporated in hydrogels for diagnostics. Bragg grating-based hydrogel sensors as well as hydrogel microlenses are utilized as optical sensors. In both cases, a significant change in the refractive index or rather high diffraction efficiency is required to ensure good functionality [51]. Substantial benefits of holographic patterning concern the fabrication flexibility. Furthermore, hydrogels can also be structured photolithographically, taking advantage of diffusion processes. Three-dimensional structuring at the microscale results in the ability to spatially tailor biomechanical and biochemical material properties [52].

Beyond the specific material characteristics, discussed in Section 2.1.1, there are additional requirements for the composition of novel biomedical material systems, such as biocompatibility and non-toxicity [53]. Investigations on cellular behavior on one- and two-dimensional surface topography may be used to evaluate cytotoxicity and cytocompatibility as a function of mechanical properties, such as the cross-linking degree. Selective cell adhesion and spreading can be observed, depending on the (bio)chemical, physical and mechanical properties [54].

For applications in tissue engineering and medical science, the desired functionality could be achieved with a combination of optical structuring of the volume and specific modification of the surface. With view to the possibilities of miniaturization, this could result in the design of advanced biomedical implants, sensing systems and diagnostic tools for in vivo studies. In particular, intra-ocular lenses (IOLs), implanted in place of the natural eye lens in ophthalmic surgery, open up the prospect of substantial improvement, such as to overcome the systematic induction of higher order aberrations or to enhance the approximation to the original function of the natural eye lens [55, 56]. This affects not only the visual ability but also some more complex abilities of the eye such as accommodation (the capability of the eye to focus sharply on close-up and distant objects) or brightness-darkness adaptation. With regard to the design, diffractive approaches are feasible and highly favorable in many respects compared with conventional refractive designs [57, 58]. Systems currently in use are limited to surface patterns, providing combined diffractive-refractive structures. Volume holographic systems, with potential special features involved, have not yet been applied. However, the use of refractive-diffractive optical properties by means of an integration of volume structuring, in combination with surface modification could provide highest possible functionality and applicability. Besides design, performance and functionality, biocompatibility, especially in case of foldable hydrogel lenses, must be ensured [59, 60]. Prospective IOLs could fulfill their function with an optically structured volume, leaving the surface free for other functionalities. Thus, late postoperative opacification of implanted lenses, resulting in glare and misty vision, might be addressed based on surface modifications for specific bio-interaction [60]. In any case, the integration of optical functionality into the volume of intra-ocular lenses might succeed according to the leading idea *from structure to function* and would be accompanied with considerable benefits.

5. Conclusion and outlook

In this chapter, the interrelation of structure and function for volume holographic gratings was investigated with view to materials, methods and applications for volume holography. Hereby, volume holograms were considered as three-dimensional optical structures with specific functionality in terms of diffractive properties. The mechanism of volume holographic grating formation in photosensitive polymers was described. Specific requirements for volume holographic materials and respective material systems were discussed. Different types of volume holographic gratings were characterized. Analytical methods for volume holograms were presented for the real-time observation of grating formation as well as for the analysis of the final optical functionality. In addition, imaging techniques were discussed and optical microscopy was applied to image 1D and 3D volume phase gratings. Lateral scanning was proposed to exploit the Gaussian intensity distribution of the recording beams, providing direct access to the material response, based on a single exposure. Finally, some selected application areas have been described with respect to the specific advantages of volume holographic materials for the respective applications. It could be demonstrated that the opening up of new applications for volume holography is accompanied with the design of novel, functionally tailored material systems. Therefore, a deeper understanding of volume holographic grating formation mechanisms remains required, driving the need for appropriate analytical methods. In this context, future opportunities and challenges related to the three dimensionality of volume holographic gratings have been highlighted.

Acknowledgements

This work was supported by the Deutsche Forschungsgemeinschaft (DFG, German Research Foundation) under grant number SA 2990/1-1.

Author details

Tina Sabel* and Marga C. Lensen

*Address all correspondence to: tina@physik.tu-berlin.de

Department of Chemistry, Technische Universität Berlin, Berlin, Germany

References

[1] Solymar L., Cooke D.J. Volume Holography and Volume Gratings. London: Academic Press; 1981.

[2] Lourtioz J.-M. Photonic crystals: Writing 3D photonic structures with light. Nature Materials. 2004;**3**:427–428.

[3] Deubel M., Freymann G., Wegener M., Pereira S., Busch K., Soukoulis C.M. Direct laser writing of three-dimensional photonic-crystal templates for telecommunications. Nature Materials. 2004;**3**:444–447.

[4] Cai Z., Smith N.L., Zhang J.-T., Asher S.A. Two-Dimensional Photonic Crystal Chemical and Biomolecular Sensors. Analytical Chemistry. 2015;**87**(10):5013–5025.

[5] Sabel T., Zschocher M. Imaging of Volume Phase Gratings in a Photosensitive Polymer, Recorded in Transmission and Reflection Geometry. Applied Sciences. 2014;**4**:19–27.

[6] Sabel T., Orlic S., Pfeiffer K., Ostrzinski U., Grützner G. Free-surface photopolymerizable recording material for volume holography. Optical Materials Express. 2012;**3**(3):329–338.

[7] Zhao G., Mouroulis P. Diffusion model of hologram formation in dry photopolymer materials. Journal of Modern Optics. 1994;**41**(10):1929–1939.

[8] Tomita Y., Urano H., Fukamizu T., Kametani Y., Nishimura N., Odoi K. Nanoparticle-polymer composite volume holographic gratings dispersed with ultrahigh-refractive-index hyperbranched polymer as organic nanoparticles. Optics Letters. 2016;**41**(6):1281–1284.

[9] Goourey G.G., de Sainte Claire P., Lavinia B., Israeli Y. Acrylate photopolymer doped with ZnO nanoparticles: an interesting candidate for photo-patterning applications. Journal of Materials Chemistry C. 2013;**1**(2):3430–3438.

[10] Priimagi A., Shevchenko A. Azopolymer-based micro- and nanopatterning for photonic applications. Journal of Polymer Science, Part B: Polymer Physics. 2014;**52**:163–182.

[11] Liu Y.J., Sun X.W. Holographic polymer-dispersed liquid crystals: materials, formation, and applications. Advances in OptoElectronics. 2008;**2008**:684349(52 pages).

[12] Sabat R.G. Superimposed surface-relief diffraction grating holographic lenses on azopolymer films. Optics Express. 2013;**21**(7):8711–8723.

[13] Andreeva O.V., Korzinin Yu.L., Manukhin B.G. Volume Transmission Hologram Gratings — Basic Properties, Energy Channelizing, Effect of Ambient Temperature and Humidity. In: Mihaylova E., editor. Holography - Basic Principles and Contemporary Applications. InTech, Rijeka, Croatia, 2013; 37–60.

[14] Criante L., Castagna R., Vita F., Lucchetta D. E., Simoni F. Nanocomposite polymeric materials for high density optical storage. Journal of Optics A: Pure and Applied Optics. 2009;**11**:024011.

[15] Shelby R.M. Media requirements for holographic data storage. In: Coufal H.J., Psaltis D., Sincerbox G.T., editors. Holographic Data Storage. Berlin: Springer; 2000.

[16] Mahmud M., Naydenova I., Pandey N., Babeva T., Jallapuram R., Martin S., Toal V. Holographic recording in acrylamide photopolymers: thickness limitations. Applied Optics. **2009**;48(14):2642–2648.

[17] Close D.H., Jacobson A.D., Magerum R.C., Brault R.G., McClung F.J. Hologram recording on photopolymer materials. Applied Physics Letters. 1969;**14**:159–160.

[18] Ingwall R.T., Waldmann D. Photopolymer Systems. In: Coufal H.J., Psaltis D., Sincerbox G.T., editors. Holographic Data Storage. Berlin: Springer; 2000.

[19] Gleeson M.R., Guo J., Sheridan J.T. Photopolymers for Use as Holographic Media. In: De Souza Gomes A. editor, New Polymers for Special Applications. InTech, Rijeka, Croatia, 2012; 165–200.

[20] Guo J., Gleeson M.R., Sheridan J.T. A Review of the Optimisation of Photopolymer Materials for Holographic Data Storage. Physics Research International. 2012;**2012**:80 3439(16 pages).

[21] Tsutsumi N. Recent advances in photorefractive and photoactive polymers for holographic applications. Polymer International. 2016. doi:10.1002/pi.5096.

[22] Guo Y., Liao Y., Cao L., Liu G., He Q., Jin G. Improvement of photorefractive properties and holographic applications of lithium niobate crystal. Optics Express. 2004;**12**(22):5556–5561.

[23] Matusevich V., Matusevich A., Kowarschik R., Matusevich Yu. I., Krul L. P. Holographic volume absorption grating in glass-like polymer. Optics Express. 2008;**16**(3):1552–1558.

[24] Shishido A. Rewritable holograms based on azobenzene-containing liquid-crystalline polymers. Polymer Journal. 2010;**42**:525–533.

[25] Kogelnik H. Coupled wave theory for thick hologram gratings. The Bell System Technical Journal. 1969;**48**(9):2909–2947.

[26] Syms R.R.A. Practical Volume Holography. Oxford: Clarendon Press; 1990.

[27] Brotherton-Ratcliffe D. Understanding Diffraction in Volume Gratings and Holograms. In: Mihaylova E., editor. Holography - Basic Principles and Contemporary Applications. InTech, Rijeka, Croatia, 2013; 3–36.

[28] D. W. van Krevelen, K. te Nijenhuis: Properties of Polymers. Amsterdam: Elsevier, 2009.

[29] Sabel T., Zschocher M. Transition of refractive index contrast in course of grating growth. Scientific Reports. 2013;**3**:2552(6 pages).

[30] Sabel T. Spatially resolved analysis of Bragg selectivity. Applied Sciences. 2015;**5**(4): 1064–1074.

[31] Sabel T., Zschocher M. Dynamic Bragg angle shift in the course of volume hologram formation. Materials Research Letters. 2013;**2**(2):76–81.

[32] Neipp C., Gallego S., Ortuno M., Marquez A., Belendez A., Pascual I. Characterization of a PVA/acrylamide photopolymer. Influence of a cross-linking monomer in the final characteristics of the hologram. Optics Communications. 2003;**224**:27–34.

[33] Del Monte F., Martínez O., Rodrigo J.A., Calvo M.L., Cheben P.A. Volume Holographic Sol-gel material with large enhancement of dynamic range by incorporation of high refractive index species. Advanced Materials. 2006;**18**:2014–2017.

[34] Smirnova T.N., Kokhtych L.M., Kutsenko A.S., Sakhno O.V., Stumpe J. The fabrication of periodic polymer/silver nanoparticle structures: In situ reduction of silver nanoparticles from precursor spatially distributed in polymer using holographic exposure. Nanotechnology. 2009;**20**:405301.

[35] Juhl A.T., Busbee J.D., Koval J.J., Natarajan L.V., Tondiglia V.P., Vaia R.A. et. al. Holographically directed assembly of polymer nanocomposites. ACS Nano. 2010;**4**:5953–5961.

[36] Castagna R., Milner A., Zyss J., Prior Y. Nanoscale poling of polymer films. Advanced Materials. 2013;**25**:2234–2238.

[37] Sakhno O.V., Goldenberg L.M., Smirnova T.N., Stumpe J. Holographic patterning of organic-inorganic photopolymerizable nanocomposites. In: Optical Materials in Defence Systems Technology; Berlin: Proc. of SPIE, **7487**; 2009.

[38] Suzuki N., Tomita Y. Real-time phase-shift measurement during formation of a volume holographic grating in nanoparticle-dispersed photopolymers. Applied Physics Letters. 2006;**88**:011105-1-01105-3.

[39] Bernstein F. Optische Erzeugung und Charakterisierung von 3D photonischen Kristallen in Photopolymeren Diploma thesis, Technische Universität Berlin, Institute for Optics and Atomic Physics, September 2012.

[40] Steckman G.J., Havermeyer F. High spatial resolution measurement of volume holographic gratings. In: Practical Holography XX: Materials and Applications; San Jose, CA, USA; Proceedings of SPIE; 27 February 2006.

[41] Trout T.J., Schmieg J.J., Gambogi W.J., Weber A.M. Optical Photopolymers: Design and Applications. Advanced Materials. 1998;**10**(15):1219–1224.

[42] Akbari H., Naydenova I., Martin S. Using acrylamide-based photopolymers for fabrication of holographic optical elements in solar energy applications. Applied Optics. 2014;**53**(7):1343–1353.

[43] Bruder F.-K., Bang H., Fäcke T., Hagen R., Hönel D., Orselli E. et al. Precision holographic optical elements in Bayfol HX photopolymer. Proceedings of SPIE; 9771, Practical Holography XXX: Materials and Applications, **977103**; 7 March 2016.

[44] Marín-Sáez J., Atencia J., Chemisana D., Collados M. Characterization of volume holographic optical elements recorded in Bayfol HX photopolymer for solar photovoltaic applications. Optics Express. 2016;**24**(6):A720–A730.

[45] Yetisen A. K., Butt H., Mikulchyk T., Ahmed R., Montelongo Y., Humar M., et.al. Color-Selective 2.5D Holograms on Large-Area Flexible Substrates for Sensing and Multilevel Security. Advanced Optical Materials. 2016;**4**(10):1589–1600.

[46] Nie Z., Kumacheva E. Patterning surfaces with functional polymers. Nature Materials. 2008;**7**:277–290.

[47] Lensen M.C., Schulte V.A., Salber J., Diez M., Menges F., Müller M. Cellular responses to novel, micropatterned biomaterials. Pure and Applied Chemistry. 2008;**80**(11):2479–2487.

[48] Campbell M., Sharp D. N., Harrison M. T., Denning R. G., Turberfield A.J. Fabrication of photonic crystals for the visible spectrum by holographic lithography. Nature. 2000;**404**:53–56.

[49] Naydenova I., Raghavendra J., Toal V., Martin S. Characterisation of the humidity and temperature responses of a reflection hologram recorded in acrylamide-based photopolymer. Sensors and Actuators B. 2009;**139**(1):35–38.

[50] Zhao Y., Zhao X., Gu Z. Photonic crystals in bioassays. Advanced Functional Materials. 2010;**20**(18):2970–2988.

[51] Yetisen A.K., Butt H., Volpatti L.R., Pavlichenko I., Humar M., Kwok S.J. et. al. Photonic hydrogel sensors. Biotechnology Advances. 2016;**34**(3):250–271.

[52] Hahn M.S., Miller J.S., West J.L. Three-dimensional biochemical and biomechanical patterning of hydrogels for guiding cell behavior. Advancedz Materials. 2006;**18**:2679–2684.

[53] Cody D., Gribbin S., Mihaylova E., Naydenova I. Low-toxicity photopolymer for reflection holography. ACS Applied Materials and Interfaces. 2016;**8**(28):18481–18487.

[54] Lensen M.C., Schulte V.A., Diez M. Cell Adhesion and Spreading on an Intrinsically Anti-Adhesive PEG Biomaterial. In: Pignatello R., editor. Biomaterials - Physics and Chemistry. InTech, 2011; 397-414.

[55] Christ F.R., Buchen S.Y., Deacon J., Cunanan C.M., Giamporcaro J.E., Knight P.M. Biomaterials used for intraocular lenses. In: Wise D.L., Trantolo D.J., Altobelli D.E., et. al., editors. Encyclopedic Handbook of Biomaterials and Bioengineering. 2nd ed. New York: Marcel Dekker; 1995.

[56] Chehade M., Elder M.J. Intraocular lens materials and styles: a review. Australian and New Zealand Journal of Ophthalmology. 1997;**25**:255–263.

[57] Percival S.P.B. Prospective study of the new diffractive bifocal intraocular lens. Eye. 1989;**3**:571–575.

[58] Davison J.A., Simpson M.J. History and development of the apodized diffractive intra-ocular lens. Journal of Cataract and Refractive Surgery. 2006;**32**(5):849–858.

[59] Hollick E.J., Spalton D.J., Ursell P.G. Surface cytologic features on intraocular lenses: can increased biocompatibility have disadvantages? Archives of Ophthalmology. 1999;**117**:872–878.

[60] Izak A.M., Werner L, Pandey S.K., Apple D.J. Calcification of modern foldable hydrogel intraocular lens designs. Eye. 2003;**17**(3):393–406.

Volume Holographic Optical Elements as Solar Concentrators

Maria Antonietta Ferrara, Gaetano Bianco,

Fabio Borbone, Roberto Centore,

Valerio Striano and Giuseppe Coppola

Additional information is available at the end of the chapter

http://dx.doi.org/10.5772/66200

Abstract

In this chapter, we investigate the possibility to realize a holographic solar concentrator by using a new photopolymeric material as recording medium. Therefore, two different configurations of holographic lenses (lenses with spherical and cylindrical symmetry) are described in terms of both recording process and optical response characterization. Finally, we propose the possibility to use this new photopolymer to realize holographic solar concentrator for space applications.

Keywords: holographic solar concentrator, holographic lens, volume-phase holographic optical elements

1. Introduction

Photovoltaic (PV) electrical energy generation is one of the most sustainable solar energy conversion processes, but its main drawback is the cost. With the current technology, the highest efficiency (37%) is from photovoltaic (PV) cells with triple-junction InGaAs; however, their high cost makes them unattractive. Nevertheless, it is possible to solve this problem by replacing a significant amount of expensive PV material with an optical concentrator. Consequently, in the last 15 years in many fields of application, from the aerospace industry to the domestic applications, people tried to use solar concentration technologies to direct all the exploitable light towards the solar cells. Indeed, solar concentrators, which focus the sun's rays onto the active solar cell area, enable to use solar power also when solar intensity is very weak allowing,

at the same time, smaller active areas of solar cells, reducing the size of the expensive portion of the solar power system [1]. However, so far concentrator systems have low spread in the market due to their high prices mostly induced by (i) complex designs — the small acceptance angle of standard CPVs (e.g. lenses or mirrors) forces to use active solar tracker and (ii) thermal management: the solar cell is excessively heated when illuminated with concentrated solar radiation, and an active or passive cooling system must be taken into account. Holographic optical elements (HOEs) could in part overcome the aforementioned limitations. Holographic PV concentrators were proposed for the first time in the 1980s [2–5]; indeed, holography as an optical technology is much more versatile and cheaper with respect to other concentrating optical systems (lenses or mirrors, for instance). It can also eliminate the need for solar tracking, thus allowing uniform levels of illumination during the course of a day or during different seasons without any moveable parts and so reducing the whole-system complexity [6].

Among holographic concentrators, volume holographic optical elements (V-HOEs) have been proposed for use as solar concentrators [2]. Compared with conventional refractive and reflective optics, V-HOEs can be thinner and more lightweight and have the potential for being very inexpensive in mass production. Moreover, the ability of light manipulation, shown by these diffractive devices, allows replacing standard concentrators with planar optical concentrators for high efficiency and low-cost photovoltaic modules [7]. HOEs have long been suggested for use (i) in a variety of solar collection applications [2–4, 6, 8–10], (ii) in spectral splitting applications to increase the conversion efficiency of PV cells [2, 8, 9] and (iii) in simultaneous concentration and spectral splitting applications [4]. Nevertheless, nowadays, there are only few commercial holographic concentrators, patented by Prism Solar Technologies [11], which work by total internal reflection by means of multiplexed gratings [12]. It has low cost (around 1 \$/W), and it is easy to be integrated into buildings, leading to a cost-effective solar building-integrated concentrating system [13].

The simplest V-HOE is a volume holographic grating (VHG), which consists in a photo-induced modulation of the refractive index in a photosensitive thick film and acts as non-focusing element; therefore, it simply redirects the light. VHGs are recorded by interference between two collimated light beams and are different from other diffraction gratings based on surface or amplitude modulation [14]. In particular, the most important advantages offered by VHG are:

- The peak efficiency can be theoretically 100% [15]. In practice, diffraction efficiency of the order of 90% can be easily reached.

- Transmission or reflection gratings can be recorded.

- They require a very rapid and low-cost effective manufacturing.

- The recorded device is easily customizable, and element with multiple optical response can be fabricated (multiplexing).

Additionally, their response can be customized in order to obtain not only grating but also lenses or other optical elements. Indeed, if during the recording process the wavefront of one collimated beam is replaced with a converging one, an interferometric pattern that replaces the response of the focusing optical systems can be generated, obtaining V-HOEs that act as focusing elements. These optical elements produce a converging wavefront, having the same effect as spherical or cylindrical lenses [16]. Furthermore, lenses can be recorded in off-axis configuration, allowing deflection and focusing of the light at the same time. These considerations led to the idea to use holographic gratings and lenses as light deflectors and concentrators. In the absence of holographic deflector devices, the useful conversion area of the sunlight into electrical energy is only the area occupied by the PV cell, as shown in **Figure 1(a)**.

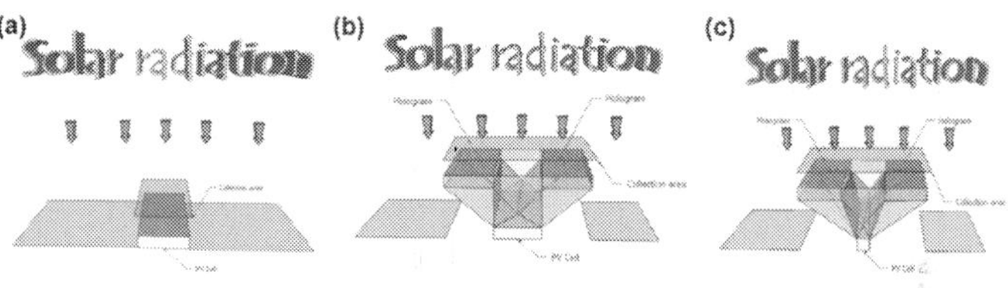

Figure 1. (a) PV module without deflector devices, (b) PV module in the presence of deflector devices and (c) PV module with deflection and concentration of the sunlight.

If a VHG is used as a device to redirect the light, and therefore as a deflector, it is possible to use a configuration like that shown in **Figure 1(b)**. In this arrangement, the incident light on two VHGs is deflected on the same PV cell. Therefore, the collecting surface of the single cell is increased (in this case is tripled), while keeping the constant area occupied by the PV material. To realize a high-efficient holographic solar concentrator, a V-HOE has to be capable not only to deflect the light of the sun but also to concentrate it; in this way the area used by a PV cell can be further reduced, as shown in **Figure 1(c)**.

However, V-HOEs have two characteristics that can affect their performance as solar concentrator: angular selectivity and chromatic selectivity. Due to the angular selectivity, volume holograms have high efficiency only when the incidence direction varies in the plane formed by the two recording beams, and this can be considered as a limitation. Additionally, the efficiency of the volume hologram is related to the wavelength: it is high for a bandwidth centred at a wavelength determined by both the refractive index modulation obtained in the recording material and the angle of incidence. V-HOEs have to be designed in order to present a high efficiency for the spectrum of the sunlight inside the PV conversion range. For multi-junction PV cells, the useful solar spectrum ranges from 350 to 1750 nm [17]. This requirement allows minimizing the amount of solar radiation beyond the conversion range (>1700 nm) that reaches the solar cell. Thus, one of the main problems of concentration refractive systems, namely, the heating of the cell, can be managed. Lower cell temperature results in a higher conversion efficiency and thus lower cost/watt [13, 18].

Regarding the aerospace applications, the solar power conversion is vital to the survival of the satellite, and loss of power, even temporarily, can have catastrophic consequences. With the succession of missions that use the technology of solar concentration, since the Galaxy 11 mission launched in 1999 that made use of mirrors, until contemporary missions, researchers tried to reduce the area, weight and footprint occupied by photovoltaic cells. Note that cost is a factor usually addressed by means of the mass (weight) of the system [16]. Additionally, among design parameters, some crucial points related to hostile space environment have to be taken into account. For example, it is important to consider the extreme temperature changes at which the concentrators are subject. However, in this field, only few works are reported in literature; therefore, our results could open the way to a new line of research [19, 20].

With this aim, in this chapter, we explore the opportunity to record a holographic solar concentrator by using a photopolymeric material as recording medium. In particular, two different configurations of holographic lenses, namely, a spherical lens and a cylindrical lens, are investigated in terms of both recording process and optical response characterization. As a final point, we suggest the possibility to use this photopolymer to realize holographic solar concentrator for space applications.

2. Theoretical background

A generic V-HOE-based solar concentrator system generates electrical power by using a V-HOE to concentrate a large area of sunlight onto a small PV cell. The efficiency of the whole system can be evaluated as

$$\eta_T = \frac{\iint S(\lambda, \zeta)\eta(\lambda, \zeta)\eta_{PV}(\lambda, \zeta)d\lambda\lambda d}{\iint S(\lambda, \zeta)d\lambda\lambda d} \tag{1}$$

where S is the solar spectrum (air mass (AM) coefficient, followed by a number, is commonly used to characterize the performance of solar cells. Generally, AM1.5 for earth, AM0 for space), η is the V-HOE diffraction efficiency and η_{PV} is the efficiency of the photovoltaic cells. All the terms are function of the wavelength (λ) and the sun illumination (ζ). The latter is function of the daily and seasonal sun trajectory and of the tilted angle between the V-HOE and PV cell. Thus, in order to evaluate, the performance of the whole system is instrumental to maximize the diffraction efficiency of the V-HOE. Since each point of a V-HOE can be locally seen as a plane holographic grating, the theoretical approach to evaluate the diffraction efficiency of a VHG has been examined.

Figure 2 illustrates the model of a transmission VHG, where a refractive index spatial sinusoidal modulation (Δn) with period Λ is recorded inside a material with a thickness d. The grating is slanted with an angle of φ. θ_i is the incident angle, and θ_d is the diffracted angle considered inside the holographic material. The use of Kogelnik's theory [15] is widely accepted for analytically modelling the behaviour of volume photopolymer holograms. This theory allows relating some volume gratings' physical characteristics, such as thickness, spatial frequency/fringe spacing and depth of refractive index modulation, to their diffraction efficiency and angular/chromatic selectivity.

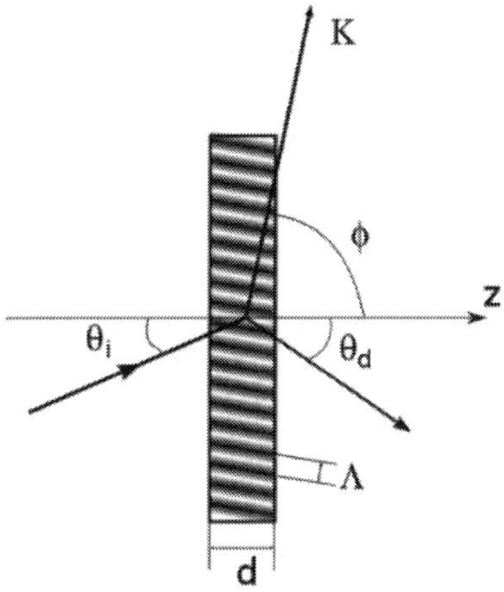

Figure 2. Model of a transmission VHG.

According to Kogelnik's theory, the diffraction efficiency (η) for a lossless material can be theoretically evaluated as

$$\eta = \left(\frac{\pi d \varDelta n}{\lambda \chi}\right)^{2} sinc^{2} \sqrt{\left(\frac{\pi d \varDelta n}{\lambda \chi}\right)^{2} + \left(\frac{d \cos \theta_{i}}{2 \chi^{2}}\right)^{2}} \tag{2}$$

where the parameters ϑ and χ are defined as

$$\vartheta = K \cos\left(\phi - \theta_{i}\right) - \frac{K^{2}}{4\pi n}\lambda \tag{3}$$

$$\chi = \sqrt{\cos\theta_{i}\left(\cos\theta_{i} - \frac{K}{\beta}\cos\phi\right)} \tag{4}$$

where $K = 2\pi/\Lambda$ is the length of the grating vector normal to the fringes (see **Figure 2**), while n is the average refractive index of the holographic medium (after the recording process) and $\beta = 2\pi n/\lambda$ is the average propagation constant. Eq. (2) allows designing gratings with high diffraction efficiency that operate over large angular and wavelength bandwidth ranges. In particular, when the Bragg condition is satisfied, i.e. $2\beta\cos(\Phi-\theta_{B}) = K$ (where $\theta_{i} = \theta_{B}$ is the Bragg angle), the parameter $\vartheta = 0$ and $\chi = \sqrt{-\cos\theta_{B}\cos\left(\theta_{B} - 2\phi\right)}$. Thus, the diffraction efficiency η can be theoretically evaluated as

$$\eta = sin^2\left(\frac{\pi\,d\,\Delta n}{\lambda\,\chi}\right) \tag{5}$$

As expected, the angle at which the diffraction intensity is maximum is strictly related to the incident wavelength [14]. While regarding the angular selectivity, hologram diffraction efficiency drops very quickly when the direction of the incident radiation does not fulfil the Bragg condition in the recording plane formed by the two recording beams [13].

For solar applications, a high efficiency is required for the whole useful solar spectrum (350–1750 nm) and for each position of the sun. Eq. (2) can be used to easily quantify how much the Bragg condition is violated either in terms of wavelength or in terms of incident angle (detuning analysis). This analysis is fundamental to design the VHG in terms of d and Δn. In particular, the detuning range can be extended minimizing the recording material thickness in combination with the maximum refractive index modulation Δn available.

It is useful to evaluate the so-called Q factor, defined as

$$Q = \frac{2\,\pi\lambda d}{n\varLambda^2} \tag{6}$$

This parameter allows to estimate if the recorded hologram is a volume and not a surface hologram. Indeed, a holographic grating is considered to be thin (surface hologram) when $Q \leq 1$, thick (volume hologram) when $Q \geq 10$ [21]. However, angular and chromatic selectivity increases when parameter Q increases; thereby, for solar application it is better to adopt a Q value close to the limit of 10. For a VHG, the behaviour is the same in all the points of the hologram. If the solar concentrator is realized by means of a V-HOE, the efficiency and its angular and chromatic selectivity vary at each point of the hologram. However, a V-HOE can be locally seen as a plane holographic grating, so the aforementioned approach can be employed to sample point by point the behaviour of the V-HOE [12, 22]. Obviously, for each local grating, the requirement $Q \geq 10$ has to be satisfied.

It is important to point out that if a V-HOE is used as solar concentrator, in order to determine the image ray direction, the grating equation has to be considered differently from the conventional optics where Snell's law is used [23].

The approach of Kogelnik can be also used to evaluate the dependence of the diffraction efficiency on the polarization. In fact, since solar illumination is randomly polarized, it is necessary to divide the incident optical power into both states of polarization and averaging the respective diffraction in order to evaluate the global efficiency of the concentrator [15, 16]. Thus, Kogelnik's coupled wave theory is enough to analytically predict the effect of the first useful parameters, such as wavelength, incident angle, grating thickness, index modulation and polarization state. However, a rigorous solution of the coupled wave equations is necessary for a completely accurate description of diffraction in gratings [18, 24–26].

3. Recording materials

The use of holographic solar concentrators for space or terrestrial photovoltaic applications is a still limited field of research, although the idea has been known for a long time [2]. Among the known materials are the classic substrates based on silver halide emulsions, recently used to obtain a panchromatic holographic material for the fabrication of wavelength-multiplexed holographic solar concentrators [27] and dichromatic gelatines [28–30], which have shown the best performance in terms of diffraction efficiency and tuning of the refractive index. The most studied holographic materials since the 1970s are those based on polymerization and cross-linking reactions induced by absorption of light, the so-called photopolymers, thanks to the numerous advantages they offer compared with silver halide and dichromatic gelatines. They show high diffraction efficiencies, allow an advantageous real-time monitoring of the recording process, do not require complicated development processes, can be produced from raw materials at low cost and give the possibility to modulate the properties through chemical synthesis. In these materials the grating is registered at a molecular level, and this has a high impact on the resolution. Typically, a photopolymerizable material is composed by a photoinitiator system (photoinitiator or photosensitizer), one or more polyfunctional monomers or oligomers and a polymeric binder. The binder is used to give mechanical stability and must ensure compatibility between all components in order to obtain a homogeneous, transparent material with good optical quality. The formulation can include plasticisers, additives, stabilizers and compounds that increase the photosensitivity of the writing medium. In a system based on radical polymerization, the initiation takes place during the illumination and leads to the production of radicals, which react with the monomers to produce chain initiators. This reaction gives way to the subsequent steps of propagation and growth of the polymer chains. In a writing process, using interference of two laser beams, radical initiation occurs faster in areas of constructive interference, i.e. where the illumination is more intense. Consequently, the polymerization proceeds more rapidly in these regions leading to an increased consumption of the monomers, while the polymerization is limited or absent in the areas of destructive interference (low-light intensity areas). The difference of monomer consumption rate creates a concentration gradient that drives monomer diffusion from dark to illuminated areas [31]. This mass transport proceeds until the monomer is exhausted or no longer able to diffuse through the material, due to the increased viscosity. The polymer concentration distribution will follow the sinusoidal pattern of light intensity. If the refractive index of polymer and binder are different, the result is a permanent modulation of the refractive index, that is, a volume-phase hologram. The refractive index variation is also determined by the density variation of the polymer. At the end of the writing process, a further irradiation of the layer with incoherent light is typically performed, leading to bleaching of the remaining photoinitiator. The first holographic photopolymers were based on liquid mixtures containing acrylamide [32]. Later, polymeric binder such as polyvinyl alcohol or gelatin was used, and diffraction efficiency greater than 80% could be reached [33–35]. This approach was recently used to demonstrate the fabrication of holographic solar concentrators [36]. Also, Sam and Kumar [37] demonstrated the fabrication of holographic solar concentrator in HoloMer 6A photopolymer material with an efficiency of 70% and an average efficiency of 56.6% for a wavelength range from 633 to 442 nm. The most common formulations include acrylic acid esters and amides, N-vinyl compounds and allyl esters. Holograms with efficiencies exceeding 95% and refractive index variation until 10^{-2} have been recorded using visible laser light [38, 39]. One of the best performing materials (DMP 128) was created by Polaroid Corporation and allows recording of reflection and transmission holograms with a spectral range from 442 to 647 nm. This material is a mixture of acrylic monomers such as acrylic acid and N,N'-methylenebisacrylamide in a matrix of poly-N-vinylpyrrolidone and showed 95% diffraction efficiency and a refractive index modulation of 0.03 in films with thickness up to 30 μm [40]. The radical polymerization has many advantages that it proceeds rapidly and the reaction is irreversible, which allows the realization of a single write. However, the main drawback is the high volumetric shrinkage of the material during polymerization. This shrinkage induces distortions of holograms by altering the characteristics of gratings. Several solutions have been adopted to solve this problem, such as the introduction of nanoparticles in the photopolymeric mixture [41]. An interesting solution is that of cationic ring-opening polymerization (CROP) systems, where the volume shrinkage following the polymerization is balanced by an effect of ring opening which produces instead a volume increase [42]. Aprilis HMD has recently commercialized a high-performance material of this type, characterized by two types of monomers that give rise to orthogonal, not interfering chemical reactions. The cationic polymerization is used to produce the cross-linked matrix, while the acrylic monomers polymerize during the hologram writing stage and diffuse according to the concentration gradient mechanism. A further interesting example is that of Reoxan [43], proposed in the late 1970s as a kind of alternative to the photopolymerizable materials because it contains no polymerizable monomers in the binder (usually polymethyl methacrylate (PMMA)) and a sensitizer of anthracene oxidation in place of a photoinitiator. The photosensitizer transfers the energy of the electronic excited state to oxygen which ends up in a singlet state and reacts with anthracene to form a peroxide. Since this transformation is accompanied by a strong change in the ultraviolet (UV) absorption spectrum, the refractive index of the material is reduced, to form a phase hologram. In the subsequent dark step, an increase of the refractive index modulation is observed due to the slow and uniform diffusion of the remaining anthracene molecules throughout the film and further irradiation and oxidation. These systems show excellent optical properties and high stability and can be obtained as films with thickness from a few microns to centimetres.

3.1. Holographic materials for solar concentrators

In view of possible applications of holographic elements as terrestrial and space solar concentrators, the holographic materials must be able to withstand harsh conditions such as high irradiation and temperatures. In the space they should also withstand much more drastic conditions, due to strong thermal excursions, high vacuum and the presence of high-energy gamma, electronic and protonic radiation originating from the solar wind. In particular high resistance to corrosion by atomic oxygen and a very low outgassing level are required to avoid contamination of the components, although the level of acceptance depends on the destination of use. Currently, no studies are known on the resistance of materials for holographic concentrators in these conditions, and their behaviour is therefore yet to be determined. However, there are durability tests on some of the most widely used materials in conventional Fresnel-type solar concentrators, such as elastomers based on silicone and acrylic polymers [44]. The latter represents a significant component of the photopolymer used for holography as a result of the process of photopolymerization of acrylic monomers typically dissolved in a matrix. Polymethyl methacrylate (PMMA) is widely used for the production of lenses for concentrators and protective layers for photovoltaic cells [45], as it guarantees an excellent resistance to UV radiation and a greater than 92% transmittance. The degradation of this type of material in response to UV irradiation mainly takes place with release of an ester radical and subsequent scission of the polymeric chain. Stabilization effects can be induced, for example, by the use of copolymers or through cross-linking of the material [46]. Alternatively, the ultraviolet sensitivity can be reduced by using protective layers or by adding radical scavengers or antioxidants to the formulation of the material. Silicones represent another important class of materials used for the fabrication of solar concentrators. They are characterized by a chemical structure that is less affected by radical photodegradation mechanisms triggered by UV light as in organic polymers. The most widely used polydimethylsiloxane (PDMS) is made of [Si-O]n-type polymeric chains with lateral methyl groups. Since the Si-O binding energy is much higher than that of the C–C bond, PDMS features an excellent stability against UV radiation and resulted very suitable for use in the extraterrestrial environment [47]. Furthermore, a great advantage of this material is the greater optical transmittance compared to PMMA and the tendency to cross-link after irradiation rather than degrade and produce volatile substances, as in the case of acrylic polymers. Starting from these evidences, a promising route towards solar compliant holographic materials is the synthesis of new photopolymers wherein part of the organic material would be replaced with inorganics or hybrid organic/inorganic components, which are less sensitive to thermal and photochemical degradation phenomena. One interesting category from this point of view is that of nanoparticle-polymer composites, that is, photopolymers containing nanoparticles of inorganic species such as SiO_2, ZrO_2 and TiO_2 [48]. The introduction of such nanoparticles was adopted to reduce the shrinkage caused by the polymerization but also helped to obtain higher refractive index modulation [49, 50]. This increase is due not only to the diffusion process of acrylic monomers during the writing process but also to the consequent counterdiffusion of nanoparticles which redistribute in the dark regions of the illumination pattern. Tomita et al. [51] showed that embedding nanoparticles of SiO_2 and ZrO_2 in photopolymers lead to an effective suppression of thermally induced refractive index and dimensional changes. Similar formulations containing zeolite nanocrystals as inorganic dopant are also reported with the aim to improve compatibility between inorganic particles and polymer and reduce the optical losses due to scattering [52]. Dramatic improvement of photostability can be induced on hybrid organic/inorganic materials by the use of similar inorganic porous components, as demonstrated by the case of Maya Blue pigment. This material is made of the organic blue indigo captured within the layers of a phyllosilicate. It remained unchanged for more than 12 centuries and was proved to resist against organic solvents, acids and alkalis [53]. Materials with a high level of interpenetration between the organic and inorganic networks, and no phase discontinuity can be obtained by exploiting the versatility of the sol-gel chemistry [54]. Although high-optical-quality glasses can be produced under mild conditions, the preparation (hydrolysis and condensation) requires relatively long times to produce a consolidated material [54]. The generic approach is to dissolve the photopolymerizable species in the liquid precursors (typically modified organoalkoxysilanes) of the glassy material in a single reaction mixture, followed by hydrolysis and gelification which lead to the formation of a glassy matrix. By this approach samples of high thickness with good mechanical properties, low shrinking and high thermal and chemical stability can be obtained [55]. Some variants have been proposed to increase the refractive index change after exposure, such as the addition of titanium or zirconium alcoholates to the initial mixture [56] or using low refractive index monomers [57]. A further alternative is to increase the refractive index of the photosensitive material by introducing reactive species with high refractive index species (HRIS) [58]. This solution led to refractive index modulations up to 0,015. A further advantage of this approach seems to be that high refractive index species are dispersed in molecular form with respect to systems containing nanoparticles [59].

4. VHOE-based solar concentrators

Since 1980, several scientific papers have been published to demonstrate that HOEs can provide improvements in solar energy collection over large incident angles and the entire solar spectrum range [2–4, 8, 10, 28, 60]. In particular, Ludman [3] described two configurations with multi-hologram lenses useful to concentrate the sunlight onto an absorber for different sun positions in the day. On the other hand, V-HOEs can be employed to obtain both a concentration and a spatial separation of the solar spectrum. This approach allowed employing different solar cell materials with optimized band gaps achieving high PV efficiency [2, 61].

Ludman et al. [5, 8] demonstrated that a well-designed holographic concentrating and spectral splitting systems can reduce the cooling requirements of the photovoltaic cells. As illustrated in **Figure 3**, PV cells were positioned at right angles with respect to the hologram orientation. This configuration allows eliminating shadow effects and facilitates cooling.

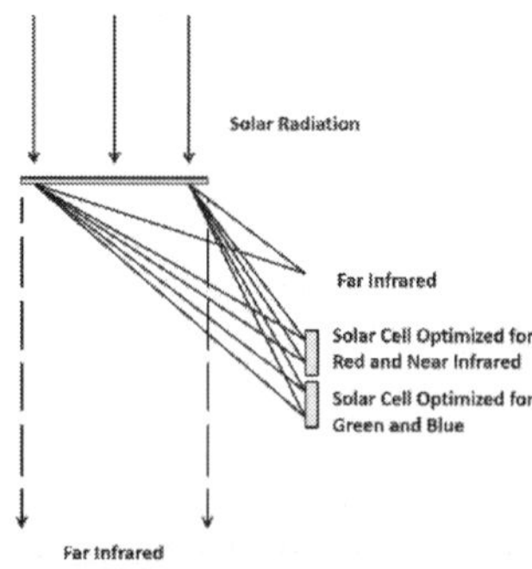

Figure 3. Holographic solar concentrator with spectral splitting systems [5, 8].

The holographic system was designed to direct and concentrate the red and near-infrared spectrum on one photocell and the green and blue spectrum on another one, 2hereas the far-infrared spectrum, which mainly contributes to the heating, is diffracted away from the cells. The authors compared the holographic systems with a Fresnel-based solar concentrator, demonstrating that the holographic system concentrates more total power than the Fresnel system and has a larger relative efficiency and that large heat sinks are not necessary allowing decreasing the bulk and cost.

Muller [62] showed a variety of potential applications in architecture for utilization of solar energy, improvement of room comfort as well as design of solar light and colour effects. The possibility to record more than one transmission hologram (superimposed holograms) on the same holographic medium was detailed described by Bainier et al. [4]. The authors estimated and experimentally measured the energy efficient of a system composed of a PV cell (Silicium- or GaAs-type cell) and a holographic concentrator. In particular, they compared two types of holographic systems: the first concentrator was with a single holographic element, where the maximum of reconstruction wavelength (620 nm) was chosen to be centred in the middle of the range of the PV cells (i.e. 500–800 nm). The second concentrator system was composed of two holographic recordings, where the two maximum of the reconstruction wavelengths (514.5 and 620 nm) were chosen both to well overlap the operating spectrum of the PV cells and to avoid coupling effect. The PV cell was a GaAs with an efficiency of 23%. The authors proposed both a reflecting and transmitting version for the double hologram system. For the transmission, one of the two holograms was superimposed on the same holographic medium. Estimation and experimental evaluation of the energy efficiency of the holographic systems were of 6 and 5% for the single holographic elements and of 11 and 9% for the double holographic element, respectively.

James and Bahaj [63] published a very interesting study on the application of V-HOE-based solar concentrator for solar control of domestic conservatories and sunrooms. They demonstrated that a well-designed V-HOE applied on the glasses of a domestic conservatory can allow keeping the daytime temperatures to an acceptable level. In particular, the authors estimated the temperature reduction inside a conservatory for different configurations of the V-HOEs. Moreover, the angular selectivity of the V-HOEs allows avoiding any actuation of the incident sunlight during the winter months. So, in the winter season, the temperature reduction due to the V-HOEs is inhibited allowing to obtain a comfortable temperature.

In 2010, Hung et al. [64] proposed a superimposed structure with a doubly slanted reflecting hologram fabricated by using 488 and 632 nm laser sources. The slanted structure with an inclination of 30° assures a total internal reflection at the surfaces of the holographic medium. Thus, light emerges at the edges of the holographic plate, where appropriate PV cells can be positioned. From a theoretical point of view, the structure was analyzed as a 1D photonic band gap material. **Figure 4(a)** shows a sketch of the experimental set-up for the doubly slanted layer structures, whereas the diffraction of normally incident white light for the doubly slanted structure is illustrated in **Figures 4(b)** and **(c)**.

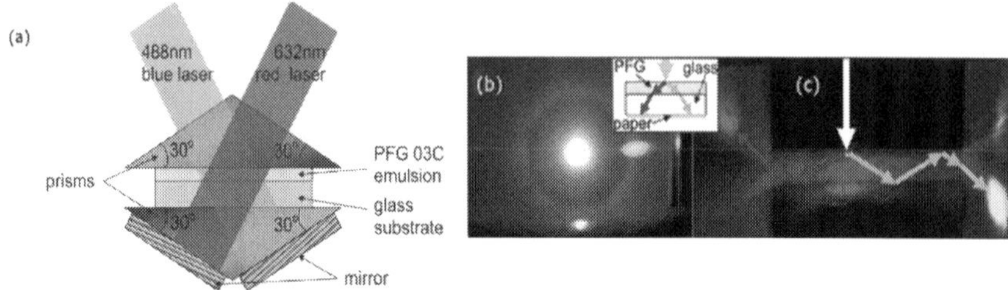

Figure 4. (a) Sketch of the experimental set-up used by Hung et al. [64] for the doubly slanted layer structure. Diffraction patterns evaluated taken from behind (b) and above (c).

Castro et al. [12] reported a detailed study on the design and characterization of a holographic grating used to address the direct sunlight on PV cell with the maximized energy efficiency possible. In particular, they analyzed the effects of incident spectra that vary hourly, daily and seasonally. To maximize the energy collection efficiency during the course of a year, the authors proposed the system based on the structure illustrated in **Figure 5(a)**.

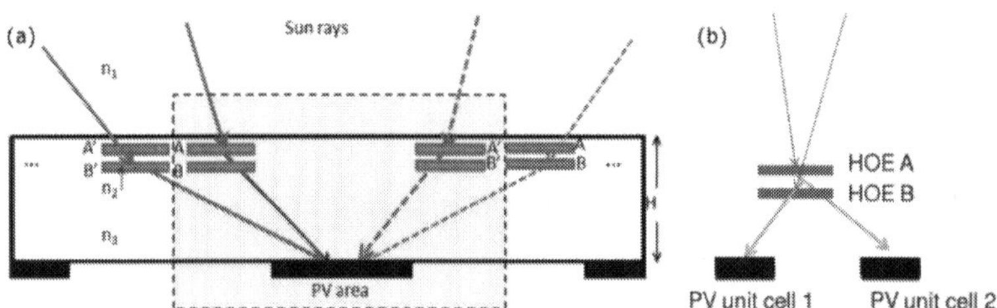

Figure 5. (a) Holographic solar concentrator structure proposed by Castro et al. [12]. Dashed box: unit cell. (b) Holographic design to reduce the optical crosstalk.

The unit cell includes two cascaded holographic grating on each side of the PV cell (holograms A and B). The holograms on each side of the PV cell are conjugated (i.e. A and A' or B and B') to provide peak energy collection at different seasons. In order to reduce the optical crosstalk of the V-HOEs, the two cascaded holograms are designed to diffract light in opposite directions with the incident angles in different quadrants of the Bragg circle (**Figure 5(b)**). Moreover, the geometrical parameters of the system (such as the hologram width and the distance hologram PV cell) are optimized to assure that maximum of the diffracted rays of the sunlight within the solar responsivity spectrum of PV cell can reach the surface of the cell independently of the incident angle. An energy increase due to the concentrator averaged over a particular day of 147% can be obtained, and nearly 50% of the available energy illuminating hologram areas can be collected by photovoltaic cells without the need of tracking.

Hsieh et al. presented a solar concentrator based on a so-called 90° hologram that allows obtaining a compact and wide-angle structure [60]. The conceptual recording set-up is illustrated in **Figure 6(a)**. In particular, the reference and object beam are an edge-lit and a cylindrical converging beam, respectively. Thus, a combination of a lens and a mirror can be simultaneously recorded in the holographic medium. Then, the medium is shifted, and the recording is repeated obtaining an array of V-HOEs that assure a large angular acceptance. In fact, when the sunlight, assumed as/like a plane wave, impinges on the solar concentrator with different incident angles, the diffracted wave is guided to the edge of the recording medium where a PV cell is positioned (**Figure 6(b)**). The author demonstrated that using a 2 mm thick holographic medium, the proposed architecture increases the collection angle from 0.01° to 6°.

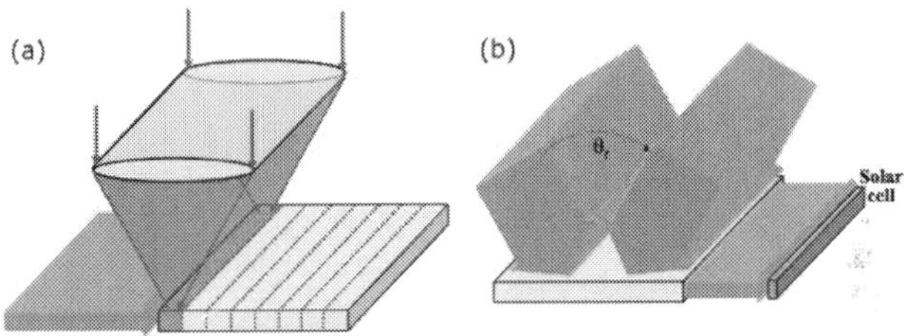

Figure 6. (a) Recording set-up and (b) configuration of volume holographic concentrator [60].

Atencia's group analyzed in detail the design and characterization of a solar PV linear concentrator based on a cylindrical holographic lens [13, 18]. In particular, a simulation tool has been developed to take into account a specific set of designed parameter, such as angular selectivity, bandwidth, optical polarization, PV cell size and so. The possibility to realize a high-efficient system that only requires one-axis tracking was demonstrated.

5. Experimental

5.1. Photopolymer

The recording material was a prototype of photopolymer sensitive to light at wavelength of 532 nm. It was obtained by sol-gel reaction of functionalized alkoxysilanes in acidic conditions and by adding a mixture of acrylic monomers and bis[2,6-difluoro-3-(1-hydropyrrol-1-yl) phenyl]titanocene photoinitiator before thin-film deposition. The mixture was made of halogenated high refractive index species dissolved in phenoxyethyl acrylate and methacrylic acid. Photopolymer was deposited through bar-coating method to obtain 30 μm thickness films. The films were exposed to green light pattern for hologram recording and subsequently to halogen lamp to bleach the unreacted photoinitiator. The final modulation of refractive index showed by this photopolymer is of about 0.02 [65].

In our previous paper, we experimentally demonstrated that this new photosensitive material allows to record volume, holographic diffraction gratings with a very good diffraction efficiency of about 94% [66].

5.2. Recording set-up

The dimensions of an individual HOE range from 1 cm × 1 cm to 10 cm × 10 cm. In a step-by-step exposure process by coherent and monochromatic light (laser), the holograms are produced in patterns on a film, which can have a maximum size of 1 m × 2 m at the present state of technology.

The experimental set-up used to record holographic in-line spherical lenses was a typical Michelson interferometer with a concave mirror with a focal length of 5 cm placed on the object beam. A recording light source emitting at 532 nm (green) with a maximum power of 750 mW in CW and a coherence length up to 100 m was used. The diameter of the hologram was about 4 cm. To record an off-axis holographic cylindrical lens, the experimental set-up was modified, and two beams of equal intensity interfere with an angle α at the surface of the recording medium. A commercial cylindrical lens, with a focal length of 5.08 cm, is placed on the object beam. Finally, to record a volume holographic grating (VHG), two collimated beams interfere with an angle α at the surface of the recording medium.

6. Results and discussions

6.1. Characterization of a volume holographic spherical lens

The volume holographic in-line spherical lens was characterized, and its efficiency η was calculated as the ratio between the power focused by the holographic lens ($P_{f\_Holo\_lens}$) and the power focused by a commercial Fresnel lens ($P_{f\_Fresnel}$) with the same focusing features:

$$\eta = P_{f\_Holo\_lens} / P_{f\_Fresnel} \tag{7}$$

In particular, both holographic and Fresnel lenses have been illuminated by a beam with a diameter comparable with that of the lenses ($\approx$4.5 cm), and a power metre was positioned at the focal length. The evaluated efficiency was 42%.

The angular selectivity was assessed by measuring the diffracted intensity from the holographic spherical lens as a function of the angle of incidence. Two different laser sources, emitting at 532 and 633 nm, were used in order to consider different behaviours of the lens at different wavelengths. Experimental results of the angular scan at different incident wavelengths are showed in **Figure 7(a)**. As expected, the angle at which the diffraction intensity is maximum increases as the wavelength increases [14]. Additionally, the lens chromatic aberration was investigated. Ideally, an optical lens should focus all of the component colours of white light to a single point. This means that the lens should refract all of the colours of white light in the same way, so they all intersect each other at the same location (or focus). The measurement of axial or longitudinal chromatic aberration is given by the difference of focal length between blue (442 nm), green (532 nm) and red (633 nm), caused by chromatic dispersion.

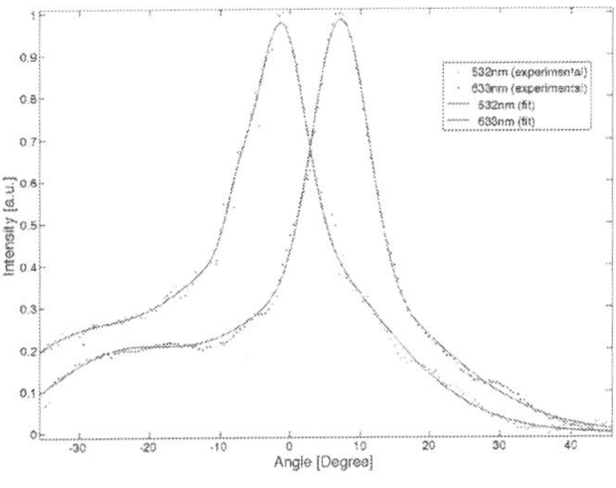
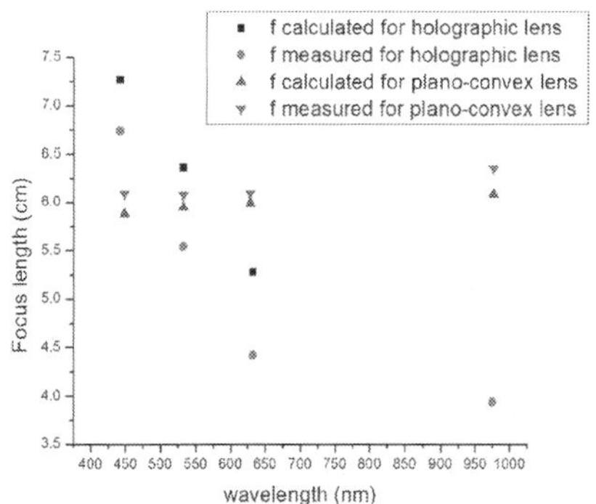

Figure 7. (a) Angular scan of the volume holographic lens at two different wavelengths and (b) focal length for different incident wavelengths both for conventional plano-convex lens and for holographic spherical lens.

The focal length was measured as function of wavelength both for a conventional lens and for a holographic spherical lens. Results are reported in **Figure 7(b)**. The conventional lens was a 2″ plano-convex lens with a focus distance of 6 cm. Its theoretical focal length was also evaluated by using a simplified thick lens equation:

$$f = R / (n-1)$$
(8)

where n is the index of refraction and R is the radius of curvature of the lens surface. The lens used in our experiments had $R = 30.9$ mm, and it was fabricated from N-BK7, so we used the index of refraction for N-BK7 at the wavelength of interest to approximate the wavelength-dependent focal length. Seeing **Figure 7(b)**, it is evident that, while for the conventional lens the focal length slightly increases by increasing the incident wavelength, the holographic lens shows a marked decrease of the focal length by increasing the incident wavelength. Also, this behaviour can be explained by considering the Bragg condition. Indeed, the Bragg angle θ_B increases when wavelength increases. In particular, the focal length is related to θ_B, and so to λ, by the geometrical relationship $f = \dfrac{D/2}{tan(\theta_B)}$, here D is the lens diameter.

Chromatic aberration of the holographic lenses can be reduced in the visible range designing an achromatic doublet by using two holographic elements: a holographic lens and a holographic grating, as proposed by Udupa et al. [67]. Therefore, the combined two holographic element systems behave like a single element holographic achromatic lens.

The beam profile in the focal point of the holographic optical lens was also characterized, and a comparison with the beam profiles both of a conventional lens and of a Fresnel lens was carried out. In **Table 1** the evaluated widths of the beam as four times the standard deviation (4-sigma) for the three different lenses characterized are summarized.

Beam width (4-sigma)	X [μm]	Y [μm]
Holographic spherical lens	4754.62	5279.20
Conventional optical lens	4171.23	4155.35
Fresnel lens	4007.91	4018.47

Table 1. Beam width 4-sigma evaluated for three different lenses.

It is clear that the holographic spherical lens shows a reduced ability to concentrate light at the focal distance with respect to the other two lenses considered. This result can depend from the chromatic aberration that affects the holographic lens.

6.2. Characterization of a volume holographic cylindrical lens

The volume holographic off-axis cylindrical lens was characterized, and its efficiency η was evaluated as the ratio between the power focused by the holographic lens ($P_{f\_Holo\_lens}$) and the power focused by a commercial in-line cylindrical lens (P_{f_Cyl}) with the same focusing features. A beam with a diameter comparable with that of the lenses (≈1.5 cm) was used, and the focused power was measured by a power metre positioned at the focal length. The obtained value for the efficiency was 25%.

Considering that both holographic spherical and holographic cylindrical lenses follow the same theoretical laws; also in the case of cylindrical holographic lenses, it is expected that the focal length as a function of the incident wavelengths follows the same behaviour of that observed for the holographic in-line spherical lens described in the previous section (**Figure 7(b)**). Therefore, a decrease in the focal length of the holographic cylindrical lens is expected by increasing the incident wavelength.

In **Table 2** the evaluated widths of the beam as 4-sigma obtained by the intensity profile of the wavefront acquired at the focal plane of the off-axis holographic cylindrical lens with focal length f = 5.08 cm are summarized.

Beam width (4-sigma)	X [μm]	Y [μm]
Holographic cylindrical lens off-axis	995.84	237.78

Table 2. Beam width 4-sigma evaluated for the off-axis cylindrical lens.

As can be noted from **Table 2**, in the case of the off-axis cylindrical lens, the beam width (4-sigma) along the y-axis is greatly reduced in the focus of the lens, thereby drastically reducing the width along the y-dimension. For that reason, cylindrical lenses are the most commonly suggested to avoid tracking in one direction; indeed, if the incidence direction varies in the perpendicular plane, the angular selectivity is lower, so it is possible to eliminate tracking in this direction [24].

6.3. Solar concentrators in the space

In order to utilize a material in space environment, an appropriate characterization of this material for these applications is required. The first problem is the large temperature range of operation. For this reason, a characterization in temperature was made to verify the possibility to use HOEs described before in the aerospace industry.

In order to characterize the behaviour of the new proposed photopolymer as a function of the temperature, a VHG was recorded with a diffraction angle α of 30° leading a VHG with 1000 lines per millimetre. Experimentally, the diffraction efficiency was evaluated by using the following relationship:

$$\eta = \frac{P_1}{\left(P_0 + P_1\right)} \tag{9}$$

where P_1 is the measured power of the first diffraction order and P_0 is the measured power of the zero diffraction order. With this aim, a He-Ne laser emitting at 633 nm, a motorized goniometer and a power metre were used. Measures were carried out at room temperature (TR = 24°) in a given point of the VHG that was rotated at the Bragg angle. Afterward, the VHG was exposed to a stress in temperature, to verify its behaviour in terms of diffraction efficiency. With this aim, the temperature of the photopolymer, and so of the grating, was increased at 150° for 2 h. Then, the temperature was reported at TR, and the diffraction efficiency at the same previous point of the VHG was measured again. Finally, the temperature was lowered at −80° for 23 h, and the diffraction efficiency was measured again in the same previous point of the grating when the temperature was reported to TR. In **Table 3** the efficiencies measured at TR in initial condition and after two different thermal stresses (increased and lowered of temperature of material) are summarized.

	At room temperature (24°C)	After exposure to +150°C	After exposure to −80°C
η [%]	96.5	93.5	94.3

Table 3. Diffraction efficiency measured as a function of temperature.

Preliminary results confirm that the diffraction efficiency of the VHG subjected to thermal stress does not change significantly. The little variations observed in the diffraction efficiency maybe are ascribed to errors in positioning the red laser for measurement in the same point. Therefore, we can conclude that VHGs do not lose efficiency after a single cycle of thermal stress, and so this very promising material could be successful used for aerospace applications. Of course, further study has to be performed to demonstrate that no changes in the VHG performance are observed even after several cycles of thermal stress.

To consolidate the previous results, a test of outgassing of the photopolymer was carried out. This characterization is very important to evaluate the behaviour of the photopolymer in the absence of pressure (space conditions). In this test, the grating was firstly cleaned with isopropanol and then was inserted in a chamber connected with a turbo pump variation. The chamber was also connected to a residual gas analyzer (RGA) consisting of a mass spectrometer. Two tests were performed at different pressures. The first one had a base pressure of 2×10^{-8} mbar after 6 days of pumping at room temperature. The results, acquired with a mass spectrometer, reported the presence only of main gas species known that are the contaminants based on the chamber.

The second test had a base pressure 7×10^{-8} mbar after 3 days of pumping at room temperature. Results acquired with the mass spectrometer highlighted the presence of unknown main gas species, with atomic mass units (AMU) up to 100. However, the intensity of the unknown gas is very small and comparable with the contaminants of the same chamber of the test.

Finally, the behaviour of the focal length for different incident wavelengths reported in **Figure 7** can be useful in aerospace application. Indeed, considering that in the infrared region the focal length is very far by the focal length in the visible region (where the PV cell will be placed), the thermal overheating of the photovoltaic cell due to the absorption of infrared radiation is avoided, reducing cooling requirements. All these results confirmed the possibility to use this photopolymer in spatial applications.

7. Conclusions

In this chapter, we experimentally demonstrated that a new photosensitive material can be used to realize holographic solar concentrators.

Two configurations of holographic lenses were investigated: spherical in-line lenses and cylindrical off-axis lenses. The chromatic aberration of the spherical lens was characterized, proving a decrease of the focal length as the incident wavelength increases. Furthermore, the beam profile was characterized for both the proposed holographic lens in their focus. Performances of holographic lenses were compared to those of conventional optics. Some lower performances of holographic lens highlighted with respect to conventional optics, such as higher axial chromatic aberration and lower ability to concentrate light in the focus, are rewarded with a lower size, lower weight and lower cost. However, chromatic aberration can be useful to reduce cooling requirements. Indeed, considering that the PV cell will be placed at the focal length in the visible region, the infrared region will be focalized very far, avoiding the thermal overheating of the photovoltaic cell due to the absorption of infrared radiation.

Finally, a preliminary study of the influence of the thermal stress and the behaviour of the photopolymer in the absence of pressure (space conditions) revealed that the proposed photosensitive material could be suitable in space environment. Therefore, we are quite optimistic that our experimental results can open the way to the fabrication of efficient, cheap and lightweight holographic solar compatible with space applications.

Author details

Maria Antonietta Ferrara[1*], Gaetano Bianco[1], Fabio Borbone[2], Roberto Centore[2],
Valerio Striano[3] and Giuseppe Coppola[1]

*Address all correspondence to: antonella.ferrara@na.imm.cnr.it

1 National Research Council, Institute for Microelectronics and Microsystems, Naples, Italy

2 Department of Chemical Sciences, University of Naples Federico II, Naples, Italy

3 CGS S.p.A., Benevento, Italy

References

[1] V.J. Lyons. Power and propulsion at NASA Glenn Research Center: historic perspective of major accomplishments. Journal of Aerospace Engineering. 2013; 26(2):288–299. DOI: http://dx.doi.org/10.1061/(ASCE)AS.1943-5525.0000304.

[2] W.H. Bloss, M. Griesinger, E.R. Reinhardt. Dispersive concentrating systems based on transmission phase holograms for solar applications. Applied Optics. 1982; 21:3739–3742.

[3] J. Ludman. Holographic solar concentrator. Applied Optics. 1982;21:3057–3058.

[4] C. Bainier, C. Hernandez, D. Courjon. Solar concentrating systems using holographic lenses. Solar & Wind Technology. 1988;5(4):395–404.

[5] J.E. Ludman, J. Riccobono, I.V. Semenova, N.O. Reinhand, W. Tai, X. Li, G. Syphers, E. Rallis, G. Sliker, J. Martín. The optimization of a holographic system for solar power generation. Solar Energy. 1997;60(1):1–9.

[6] M. Green. Third Generation Photovoltaics. 1st ed. Springer-Verlag Berlin Heidelberg; 2003. 126 p. DOI: 10.1007/b137807.

[7] I. Naydenova, H. Akbari, C. Dalton, M. Yahya, C.P. Tee Wei, V. Toal, S. Martin. Photopolymer holographic optical elements for application in solar energy concentrators. In: E. Mihaylova, editors. Holography – Basic Principles and Contemporary. InTech, Croatia (EU); 2013. pp. 129–145.

[8] J. Ludman, J. Riccobono, N. Reinhand, I. Semenova, J. Martin, W. Tai, X.L Li. Holographic solar concentrator for terrestrial photovoltaics. In: IEEE, editor. Conference Record of the 1994 IEEE First World Conference on Photovoltaic Energy Conversion; 5–9 Dec. 1994; IEEE Hawaii; 1994. 1212–1215.

[9]   A.G. Imenes, D.R. Mills. Spectral beam splitting technology for increased conversion efficiency in solar concentrating systems: a review. Solar Energy Materials and Solar Cells. 2004;84:19–69.

[10]   J.R. Riccobono and J.E. Ludman. Solar holography. In: J. Ludman, H.J. Caulfield, J. Riccobono, editors. Holography for the New Millennium. Springer New York; 2002. pp. 157–178. DOI: 10.1007/b97439.

[11]   Prismsolar. Available from: http://www.prismsolar.

[12]   J.M. Castro, D. Zhang, B. Myer, R.K. Kostuk. Energy collection efficiency of holographic planar solar concentrators. Applied Optics. 2010;49(5):858–870.

[13]   D. Chemisana, M.V. Collados, M. Quintanilla, J. Atencia. Holographic lenses for building integrated concentrating photovoltaics. Applied Energy. 2013;110:227–235.

[14]   S.C. Barden, J.A. Arns, W.S. Colburn. Volume-phase holographic gratings and their potential for astronomical applications. Proceedings of SPIE. 1988;3355:866. DOI: 10.1117/12.

[15]   H. Kogelnik. Coupled-wave theory of thick hologram gratings. Bell System Technical Journal. 1969;48:2909–2947.

[16]   R. Leutz, A. Suzuki. Solar concentration in space. In: Nonimaging Fresnel Lenses: Design and Performance of Solar Concentrators. Springer Verlag Heidelberg; 2001. pp. 246–256.

[17]   F. Dimroth, N.H. Karam, J.H. Ermer, M. Haddad, P. Colter, T. Isshiki, H. Yoon, H.L. Cotal, D.E. Joslin, D.D. Krut, R. Sudharsanan, K. Edmondson, B.T. Cavicchi, D.R. Lillingto. Next generation GaInP/GaInAs/Ge multi-junction space solar cells. In: Proceeding 17th European Photovoltaic Solar Energy Conference; 22–26 October 2001; Munich, Germany. Proceedings published by ETA-Florence, Italy and WIP-Munich, Germany 2001.

[18]   P.B. Palacios, S. Álvarez-Álvarez, J. Marín-Sáez, M. Victoria Collados, D. Chemisana, J. Artencia. Broadband behavior of transmission volume holographic optical elements for solar concentration. Optics Express. 2015;23(11):A671–A681. DOI: 10.1364/OE.23.

[19]   K. Renk, Y. Jacques, C. Felts, A. Chovit. Holographic Solar Energy Concentrators for Solar Thermal Rocket Engines. NTS Engineering, Long Beach, CA; 1988;No. NTS-6006.

[20]   J. Loicq, L.M. Venancio, Y. Stockman, M.P. Georges. Performances of volume phase holographic grating for space applications: study of the radiation effect. Applied Optics. 2013;52(34):8338–8346.

[21]   B.C. Kress, P. Meyrueis. Applied Digital Optics: From Micro-optics to Nanophotonics. John Wiley & Sons, United Kingdom 2009. pp. 638.

[22] Y. Luo, J. Castro, J.K. Barton, R.K. Kostuk, G. Barbastathis. Simulations and experiments of aperiodic and multiplexed gratings in volume holographic imaging systems. Optics Express. 2010;18(8):19273–19285.

[23] D.H. Close. Holographic optical elements. Optical Engineering. 1975;14:408–419.

[24] M.G. Moharam, T.K. Gaylord. Three-dimensional vector coupled-wave analysis of planar-grating diffraction. Journal of the Optical Society of America. 1983;73:1105–1112.

[25] E.N. Glytis, T.K. Gaylord. Rigorous 3D coupled wave diffraction analysis of multiple superposed graings in ansiotropic media. Applied Optics. 1989;28(12):2401–2421.

[26] P. Wissmann, O.S. Baek, G. Barbastathis. Simulation and optimization of volume holographic imaging systems in Zemax. Optics Express. 2008;16(10):7516–7524.

[27] V. Vadivelan. Recording of holographic solar concentrator in ultra fine grain visible wavelength sensitive silver halide emulsion. American Journal of Electronics & Communication. 2015;2(1):15–17. DOI: 10.15864/AJEC.V2I1.

[28] J. Hull, J. Lauer, D. Broadbent. Holographic solar concentrators. Energy. 1987;12(3): 209–215. DOI: 10.1016/0360-5442(87)90079-X.

[29] J.A. Quintana, P.G. Boj, J. Crespo, M. Pardo, M.A. Satorre. Line-focusing holographic mirrors for solar ultraviolet energy concentration. Applied Optics. 1997;36(16):3689–3693. DOI: 10.1364/AO.36.003689.

[30] R. Ranjan, A. Khan, N.R. Chakraborty, H.L. Yadav. Use of holographic lenses recorded in dichromated gelatin film for PV concentrator applications to minimize solar tracking. In: L. Perlovsky, D.D. Dionysiou, L.A. Zadeh, M.M. Kostic, C. Gonzalez-Concepcion, H. Jaberg, K. Sopian, editors. Energy Problems and Environmental Engineering; WSEAS Press Athens; 2009. p. 49–52.

[31] G. Zhao, P. Mouroulis. Diffusion model of hologram formation in dry photopolymer materials. Journal of Modern Optics. 1994;41(10):1929–1939. DOI: 10.1080/095003494 14551831.

[32] D.H. Close, A.D. Jacobson, J.D. Margerum, R.G. Brault, F.J. McClung. Hologram recording on photopolymer materials. Applied Physics Letters. 1969;14(5):159–160. DOI: 10.1063/1.

[33] S. Calixto. Dry polymer for holographic recording. Applied Optics. 1987;26:3904–3910. DOI: 10.1364/AO.26.003904.

[34] N. Sadlej, B. Smolinska. Stable photo-sensitive polymer layers for holography. Optics & Laser Technology. 1975;7(4):175–179. DOI: 10.1016/0030-3992(75)90056-0.

[35] S. Blaya, L. Carretero, R. Mallavia, A. Fimia, R.F. Madrigal, M. Ulibarrena, D. Levy. Optimization of an acrylamide-based dry film used for holographic recording. Applied Optics. 1998;37(32):7604–7610. DOI: 10.1364/ao.37.007604.

[36] H. Akbari, I. Naydenova, S. Martin. Using acrylamide-based photopolymers for fabrication of holographic optical elements in solar energy applications. Applied Optics. 2014;53(7):1343–1353. DOI: 10.1364/AO.53.001343.

[37] S.T.L. Sam, A.P.T. Kumar. Design and optimization of photopolymer based holographic solar concentrators. In: AIP Conference Proceedings Vol. 1391; AIP Publishing, New York (U.S.A.) 2011. pp. 248–250. DOI: 10.1063/1.3646844.

[38] W.J. Tomlinson, E.A. Chandross, H.P. Weber, G.D. Aumiller. Multicomponent photopolymer systems for volume phase holograms and grating devices. Applied Optics. 1976;15(2):534–541. DOI: 10.1364/AO.15.000534.

[39] A. Bianco, G. Coppola, M.A. Ferrara, G. Pariani, C. Bertarelli. Analysis of phase patterns in photochromic polyurethanes by a holographic approach. Optical Materials Express. 2015;5(10):247457. DOI: 10.1364/OME.5.00228.

[40] R.T. Ingwall, H.L. Fielding. Hologram recording with a new photopolymer system. Optical Engineering. 1985;24(5):808–8011. DOI: 10.1117/12.946298.

[41] I. Naydenova, H. Sherif, S. Mintova, S. Martin, V. Toal. Holographic recording in nanoparticle-doped photopolymer. Proceedings of SPIE 2006;6252:45–50. DOI: 10.1117/12.676503.

[42] D.A. Waldman, C.J. Butler, D.H. Raguin. CROP holographic storage media for optical data storage at greater than 100 bits/m2. Proceedings of SPIE 2003;5216. DOI: 10.1117/12.513614.

[43] A.V. Veniaminov, U.V. Mahilny. Holographic polymer materials with diffusion development: principles, arrangement, investigation, and applications. Optics and Spectroscopy. 2013;115(6):906–930. DOI: 10.1134/S0030400X13120199.

[44] D.C. Miller, S.R. Kurtz. Durability of Fresnel lenses: a review specific to the concentrating photovoltaic application. Solar Energy Materials and Solar Cells. 2011;95(8):2037–2068. DOI: 10.1016/j.solmat.2011.01.031.

[45] P. Schissel, G. Jorgensen, C. Kennedy, R. Goggin. Silvered-PMMA reflectors. Solar Energy Materials and Solar Cells. 1994;33(2):183–197. DOI: 10.1016/0927-0248(94)90207-0.

[46] S.M. Lomakin, J.E. Brown, R.S. Breese, M.R. Nyden. An investigation of the thermal stability and char-forming tendency of cross-linked poly(methyl methacrylate). Polymer Degradation and Stability. 1993;41(2):229–243. DOI: 10.1016/0141-3910(93)90048-N.

[47] J.A. Dever, B.A. Banks, L. Yan. Effects of vacuum ultraviolet radiation on DC93-500 silicone. Journal of Spacecraft and Rockets. 2006;43(2):386–392. DOI: 10.2514/1.15226.

[48] R.A. Vaia, C.L. Dennis, L.V. Natarajan, V.P. Tondiglia, D.W. Tomlin, T.J. Bunning. One-step, micrometer-scale organization of nano- and mesoparticles using holographic photopolymerization: a generic technique. Advanced Materials. 2001;13(20):1570.

[49] Z. Lei, H. Jun-He, L. Ruo-Ping, W. Long-Ge, H. Ming-Ju. Resisting shrinkage properties of volume holograms recorded in TiO_2 nanoparticle-dispersed acrylamide-based photopolymer. Chinese Physics B. 2013;22(12):124207. DOI: 10.1088/1674-1056/22/12/124207.

[50] N. Suzuki, Y. Tomita, K. Ohmori, M. Hidaka, K. Chikama. Highly transparent ZrO_2 nanoparticle-dispersed acrylate photopolymers for volume holographic recording. Optics Express. 2006;14(2):12712–12719. DOI: 10.1364/OE.14.012712.

[51] Y. Tomita, T. Nakamura, A. Tago. Improved thermal stability of volume holograms recorded in nanoparticle–polymer composite films. Optics Letters. 2008;33(15):1750. DOI: 10.1364/OL.33.001750.

[52] M. Moothanchery, I. Naydenova, S. Mintova, V. Toal. Nanozeolites doped photopolymer layers with reduced shrinkage. Optics Express. 2011;19(25):25786. DOI: 10.1364/OE.19.025786.

[53] C. Sanchez, B. Julián, P. Belleville, M. Popall. Applications of hybrid organic–inorganic nanocomposites. Journal of Materials Chemistry. 2005;15(35–36):3559. DOI: 10.1039/b509097k.

[54] P. Cheben, F. del Monte, D. Levy, T. Belenguer, A. Nuñez. Holographic diffraction gratings recording in organically modified silica gels. Optics Letters. 1996;21(22):1857. DOI: 10.1364/OL.21.001857.

[55] Y. Park, E. Kim. Preparation and characterization of organic-inorganic nanocomposite films for holographic recording. Key Engineering Materials. 2005;277–279:1039–1043. DOI: 10.4028/www.scientific.net/KEM.277-279.1039.

[56] N. Hayashida, A. Kosuda, J. Yoshinari. A new class of photopolymer for holographic data storage media based on organometallic matrix. Japanese Journal of Applied Physics. 2008;47:5895–5899. DOI: 10.1143/JJAP.47.5895.

[57] Y.M. Chang, S.C. Yoon, M. Han. Photopolymerization of aromatic acrylate containing phosphine oxide backbone and its application to holographic recording. Optical Materials. 2007;30(4):662–668. DOI: 10.1016/j.optmat.2007.02.050.

[58] M.L. Calvo, P. Cheben. Photopolymerizable sol–gel nanocomposites for holographic recording. Journal of Optics A: Pure and Applied Optics. 2009;11(2):024009. DOI: 10.1088/1464-4258/11/2/024009.

[59] F. del Monte, O. Martínez, J.A. Rodrigo, M.L. Calvo, P. Cheben. A volume holographic sol-gel material with large enhancement of dynamic range by incorporation of high refractive index species. Advanced Materials. 2006;18(15):2014–2017. DOI: 10.1002/adma.200502675.

[60] M. Hsieh, S. Lin, K.Y. Hsu, J. Burr, S. Lin. An efficient solar concentrator using volume hologram. In: CLEO:2011–Laser Applications to Photonic Applications, OSA Technical Digest; Optical Society of America, Baltimore, Maryland United States; 2011. paper PDPB8. DOI: http://www.opticsinfobase.org/abstract.cfm?URI=CLEO: A and T-2011-PDPB8.

[61] K. Frohlich, U. Wagemann, J. Schulat, H. Schutte, C.G. Stojanoff. Fabrication and test of a holographic concentrator for two color PV-operation. Proceedings of SPIE 1994;2255:812–821.

[62] H.F.O. Muller. Application of holographic optical elements in buildings for various purposes like daylighting, solar shading and photovoltaic power generation. Renewable Energy 1994;5:935–941.

[63] P.A.B. James, A.S. Bahaj. Holographic optical elements: various principles for solar control of conservatories and sunrooms. Solar Energy 2005;78:441–454.

[64] J. Hung, P.S. Chan, C. Sun, C.W. Ho, W.Y. Tam. Doubly slanted layer structures in holographic gelatin emulsions: solar concentrators. Journal of Optics. 2010;12:045104. DOI: 10.1088/2040-8978/12/4/045104.

[65] M.A. Ferrara, F. Borbone, V. Striano, G. Coppola. Characterization of photopolymers as optical recording materials by means of digital holography microscopy. Proceedings of SPIE. 2013;8792:87920Z. DOI: 10.1117/12.2021654.

[66] G. Bianco, M.A. Ferrara, F. Borbone, A. Roviello, V. Pagliarulo, S. Grilli, P. Ferraro, V. Striano, G. Coppola. Volume holographic gratings: fabrication and characterization. Proceedings of SPIE. 2015;9508:950807. DOI: 10.1117/12.2179121.

[67] D.Y. Udupa, R.P. Shukla, N.C. Das and M.V. Mantravadi. Theory of a holographic lens with a high efficiency. Journal of Optics. 2004;33(2):49–66.

Chapter 3

Volume Bragg Gratings: Fundamentals and Applications in Laser Beam Combining and Beam Phase Transformations

Ivan Divliansky

Additional information is available at the end of the chapter

http://dx.doi.org/10.5772/66958

Abstract

Two major volume Bragg grating (VBG) applications will be presented and in particular laser beam combining and holographically encoded phase masks. Laser beam combining is an approach where multiple lasers are combined to produce more power. Spectral beam combining is a technique in which different wavelengths are superimposed spatially (combined) using a dispersive element such as a volume Bragg grating. To reduce the complexity of such combining system instead of multiple individual VBGs, it will be demonstrated that a single holographic element with multiple VBGs recorded inside could be used for the same purpose. Similar multiplex volume holographic elements could be used for coherent beam combining. In this case, the gratings operate at the same wavelength and have degenerate output. Such coherent combining using gratings written in photothermo-refractive (PTR) glass will be discussed. The chapter also demonstrates that binary phase profiles may be encoded into volume Bragg gratings, and that for any probe beam capable of satisfying the Bragg condition of the hologram, this phase profile will be present in the diffracted beam. A multiplexed set of these holographic phase masks (HPMs) can simultaneously combine beams while also performing mode conversion. An approach for making HPMs fully achromatic by combining them with a pair of surface gratings will be outlined.

Keywords: holography, volume Bragg gratings, beam combining, phase plates, photothermo refractive glass, multiplexed volume gratings

1. Volume Bragg gratings

1.1. Description and properties

Volume grating as its name suggest is a grating that occupies the volume of a medium. Typically, for such gratings the term volume Bragg gratings (VBGs) is used in relation to Sir William Bragg who in 1915 used diffraction of light propagating through a crystal to determine the crystal's lattice structure [1]. What he found was that at certain conditions the light is strongly diffracted by the crystal. Such condition is called "resonant condition" or also "Bragg condition." Here is also the place to make the distinction between surface and volume Bragg gratings. If we start with a surface grating and start increasing its thickness at some point the different diffraction orders will reduce to a moment where there will be only one order. This defines the transition to a volume grating behavior [2].

There are two basic types of VBGs which is shown in **Figure 1**. The first one is a transmission Bragg grating (TBG) for which if the incident light satisfies the Bragg condition it is not transmitted but also diffracted. The second type is a reflection Bragg grating (RBG) which behaves like a mirror for incoming light that matches the Bragg condition.

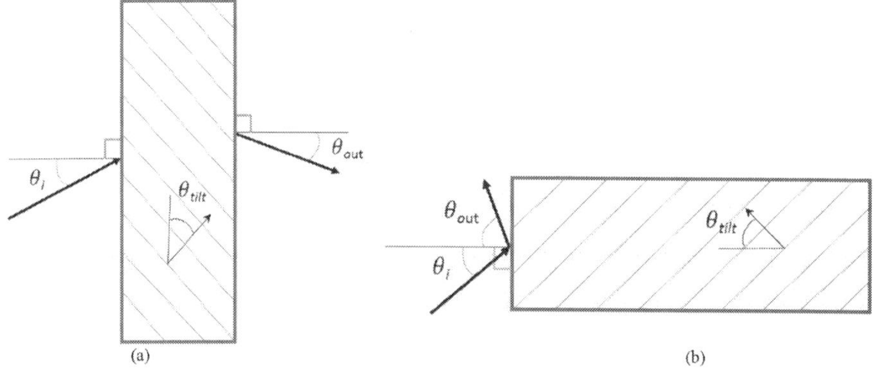

Figure 1. Beam geometries for transmission Bragg grating (a) and for reflective Bragg grating (b).

For simplicity, in **Figure 1**, for both types of volume gratings, the angle of incidence is the same θ_i and the tilt of the volume grating inside the medium is θ_{tilt}. Resonant diffraction from each of these VBGs occurs upon satisfaction of their Bragg conditions which are defined by Eqs. (1) and (2).

$$\lambda_{TBG} = 2\Lambda \sin(\theta_i + \theta_{tilt}) \tag{1}$$

$$\lambda_{RBG} = 2\Lambda \cos(\theta_i + \theta_{tilt}) \tag{2}$$

Here, Λ is the period of the VBG and λ_{VBG} is the wavelength of the incident light which for the particular θ_i and θ_{tilt} satisfies the Bragg condition. The gratings depicted in **Figure 1** are uniform VBGs that can be recorded in a photosensitive material by simple interference of two collimated laser beams. The recording wavelength, angle of interference, and the refractive index of the material determine the grating's parameters. There are techniques capable of recording more complex volume gratings which have nonuniform period and for which the Bragg condition will be different depending on the space coordinates [2]. Regardless, if the variation of the period is negligible when compared to the probe beam size used for characterization of the VBG; Eqs. (1) and (2) can still provide the resonance wavelength.

Figure 2 exhibits one example of beam geometry for recording uniform transmitting and reflecting volume gratings. In this recording approach, two plane waves (purple beams) illuminate the sample from one side at a half-angle of interference ϕ. Depending on the direction from which the grating is used, it can either work as a TBG (green beams) or as an RBG (orange beams). Before recording, the grating parameters such as period and modulation need to be calculated so the recording is carried out accordingly.

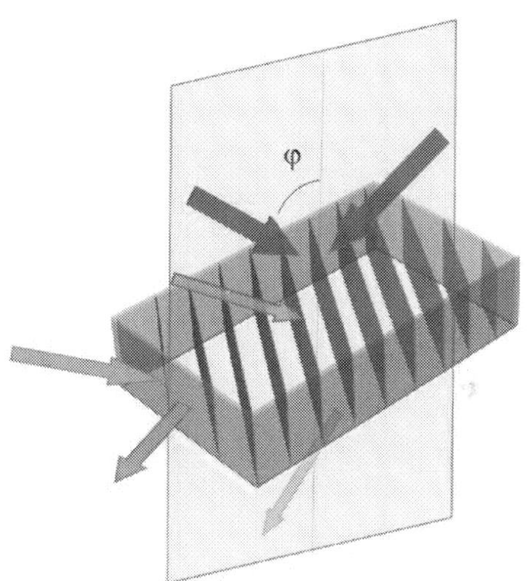

Figure 2. Recording geometry used for recording reflective and transmitting Bragg gratings. The recording beams are shown in purple and the half-angle of interference φ determines the properties of the grating. The VBG is utilized as an RBG if probed as the orange beams or as TBG if probed as the green beams.

The main model describing volume Bragg gratings was introduced by Kogelnik [3] in 1969. His model describes that diffraction from a VBG is based on coupled wave theory (CWT) and provides analytical solutions for RBGs and TBGs including tilted ones. **Figures 3(a, b)** and **4(a, b)** present examples of the wavelength and angular responses of an RBG and a TBG correspondingly, calculated using Kogelnik's theoretical approach.

Figures 3 and **4** give good overview of the main properties of TBGs and RBGs. In particular, RBGs are much more suited for implementation as narrow wavelength filters. For example, the full-width half-maximum (FWHM) wavelength selectivity of the reflective grating simulated in **Figure 3(a)** is around 225 pm but it can reach down to 15–20 pm if designed accordingly. TBGs, in contrast, have much wider wavelength acceptance starting at a few hundred picometers and reaching several nanometers. **Figure 4(a)** shows the spectral response of 1.5 mm thick TBG with nodulation of 330 ppm. For these parameters, its FWHM of 2.3 nm is close to an order magnitude larger if compared to the RBG one.

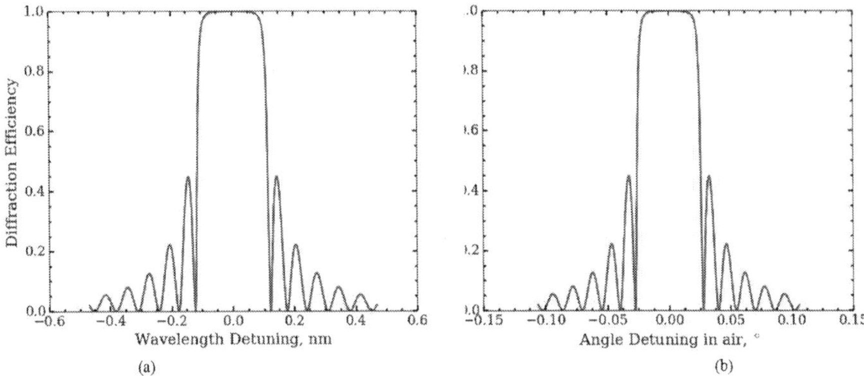

Figure 3. Wavelength (a) and angular (b) response for an RBG. The VBG is 5.5 mm thick, it is 20° tilted, and has a 240 ppm refractive index modulation.

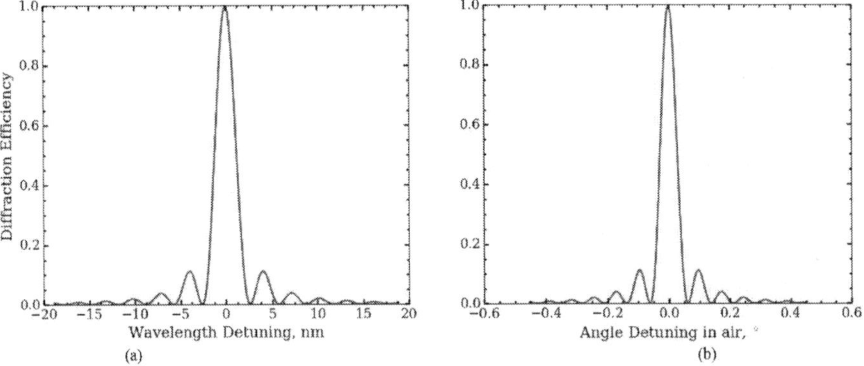

Figure 4. Wavelength (a) and angular (b) response for a TBG. The VBG is 1.5 mm thick, it is 20° tilted, and has a 333 ppm refractive index modulation.

TBGs, alternatively, can be used as narrow angular filters with acceptance values as low as 0.1 mrad, whereas RBGs have typical angular acceptance of more than 10 mrad all the way to 100 mrad. These properties of the two types of VBGs define their use in different applications. For example, the narrow angular selectivity of the TBGs makes them a great angular filter that can be used to suppress higher order modes generation in laser cavities while keeping them very compact [4]. Alternatively, RBGs with their narrow wavelength selectivity can be used for narrow wavelength beam combining where the diffracted by and the transmitted through an RBG beams can be separated by only a few hundred picometers [5]. Regardless of the close wavelength separation, the RBG does not diffract the transmitted beam even though both beams have a common propagating direction.

Table 1 summarizes the TBG's and RBG's characteristics and their typical range. Until now, we have discussed wavelength and angular selectivity of VBGs but the third very important parameter is the VBG's efficiency. There are two generally accepted ways to define a VBG's efficiency and the more widely used on is the so-called "relative diffraction efficiency." It is defined as normalization of the diffracted to the transmitted by a VBG power. Its advantage is that it removes any losses introduced by the medium. The second way is called "absolute diffraction efficiency," where the diffracted power is normalized to the incident power.

	Transmitting VBG (TBG)	Reflecting VBG (RBG)
Angular selectivity	0.1–10 mrad	10–100 mrad
Spectral selectivity	0.3–20 nm	0.02–2 nm
Diffraction efficiency	Up to 100%	>99.9%

Table 1. TBG and RBG characteristics.

1.2. Recording materials

Recoding of a volume grating requires the use of a material that is photosensitive. The modulation of the recording light intensity should create a corresponding refractive index change in the recording material which on a macroscopic level will be in fact the volume Bragg grating. There is a wide variety of photosensitive materials that can be used for recording VBGs [6, 7]. The main requirement that they need to fulfill is to have enough spatial resolution that will allow the recording of gratings with particular periods. The other two factors are the photosensitivity of the material and its dynamic range. The photosensitivity determines the exposure duration and given that VBGs are most commonly recorded by interference of light, it is of great benefit to keep the exposure time as short as possible. The material's dynamic range provides the maximum refractive index change that can be achieved. This property affects the VBGs thickness and the maximum number of volume gratings that can be multiplexed together in the same volume. Other properties that depending on the particular application may be important are the optical damage threshold, the maximum physical dimensions of the material, its losses, its environmental sensitivity, and others.

The most common recording materials are dichromated gelatins, photopolymers, photorefractive crystals, photosensitive fibers, and photothermo refractive glasses. We will not discuss in detail the properties of each of these materials because they have been well investigated in the literature [8–16]. The applications and experimental results shown further in the chapter are based on using photothermo-refractive glass (PTR) due to its capabilities of handling high-power laser radiation because of its low losses, its environmental robustness, and extremely high resolution [14–16].

Photothermo-refractive glass is a relatively new photosensitive material well suited for phase hologram recording. It combines high sensitivity achieved by two-step hologram formation process and high-optical quality resulting from its technological development. The PTR glass is a Na_2O-ZnO-Al_2O_3-SiO_2 glass doped with silver (Ag), cerium (Ce), and fluorine (F). It is transparent from 350 to 2500 nm. The chain of processes, which produce refractive index variation, is as follows: the first step is the exposure of the glass to UV radiation, somewhere in the range from 280 to 350 nm. This exposure results in photoreduction of silver ions Ag^+ to atomic state Ag^0. This stage is similar to formation of a latent image in a conventional photo film because no significant changes in the optical properties of the glass occur. The final formation of the holographic recording is secured by subjecting the glass to thermal development. During this step, at elevated temperatures, a number of silver containing clusters are formed in the exposed regions of the glass due to the increased mobility of Ag^0 atoms. These silver-containing clusters serve as nucleation centers for the growth of NaF crystals. Interaction of these nanocrystals with the surrounding glass matrix causes the decrease of refractive index. Refractive index change Δn of about 1.5×10^{-3} (1500 ppm) can be achieved and is enough to allow the recoding of high-efficiency hologram into glass wafers with thickness exceeding several hundred microns.

The second consequence of the crystalline phase precipitation in PTR glass is related to its physical properties and is extremely valuable. The NaF crystalline particles in the glass matrix are almost impossible to destroy by any type of radiation which makes PTR holograms stable under exposure to IR, visible, UV, X-ray, and gamma-ray irradiation. For example, laser damage threshold for 8 ns laser pulses at 1064 nm is in the range of 40 J/cm². Also, the nonlinear refractive index of PTR glass is the same as that for fused silica which allows the use of PTR diffractive elements in all types of pulsed lasers. Another PTR advantage is its very low losses—on the order of 10^{-5} cm^{-1}. Testing of VBG recorded in the PTR glass performed under irradiation of 9 kW CW with a 6-mm-diameter spot showed heating that did not exceed 15 K [17]. Even though small heating effects lead to thermal variations of the refractive index of the glass ($dn/dt = 5 \times 10^{-8}$ K^{-1}). In the case of Bragg grating written inside a PTR glass, this feature leads to thermal shift of the Bragg wavelength of around 10 pm/K. It is worth mentioning also that due to the melting temperature of the NaF crystals being almost 1000°C, PTR holograms are stable at elevated temperatures and could tolerate thermal cycling up to 400°C. This temperature is determined by the plasticity point of the glass matrix.

Typically, Bragg gratings in the PTR glass are recorded by an exposure to interference pattern of radiation from a He-Cd laser operating at 325 nm. The spatial frequency of the gratings can vary from 50 up to about 10,000 mm^{-1}, their thickness from 0.5 to 25 mm, and a diffraction efficiency of up to 99.9%.

2. Applications of volume Bragg gratings

2.1. Spectral and coherent laser beam combining by volume Bragg gratings

Single laser sources are limited in terms of maximum power by thermal and nonlinear effects and can achieve no more than few kW. Laser systems that can generate from 10 to 100 kW CW power integrate from several to tens of laser sources. There are several approaches for integrating/combining laser beams but the most common ones are using either volume Bragg gratings, diffractive optical elements, or surface diffraction gratings [18]. This chapter discusses the use of VBGs for laser beam combining including spectral and coherent combining.

Spectral beam combining (SBC) and coherent beam combining (CBC) are two complimentary methods leading toward multi-kilowatt diffraction limited laser sources. In SBC, multiple channels of different wavelengths are superimposed spatially to generate a single output beam. The main advantage of SBC if compared to CBC is the simplified optical setup due to the fact that there is no need to monitor and adjust the phase of the individual beams. The drawback of using SBC is the fact that the spectrum of the combined beam is much broader when compared to the individual input beams. Regardless of this, the final combined output could still have diffraction limited quality. To minimize the wider spectrum issue, it is necessary to use very narrow spectrally selective beam combining elements that will deliver an output beam with minimum spectral bandwidth.

Reflective volume Bragg gratings are holograms that are not angularly dispersive and depending on their design they can be made to be very wavelength selective. Also, they can have diffraction efficiencies close to 100%, and if recorded in a suitable material that can have very low losses, which makes them suitable for high power laser applications. All these facts together make them a very good optical element for implementation in the SBC system. **Figure 5** demonstrates the concept for using a VBG for spectral combining: diffraction efficiency is close to 100% when the Bragg condition is met and is close to 0% at wavelengths shifted away from the Bragg condition and corresponding to the grating's minima in its characteristic curve.

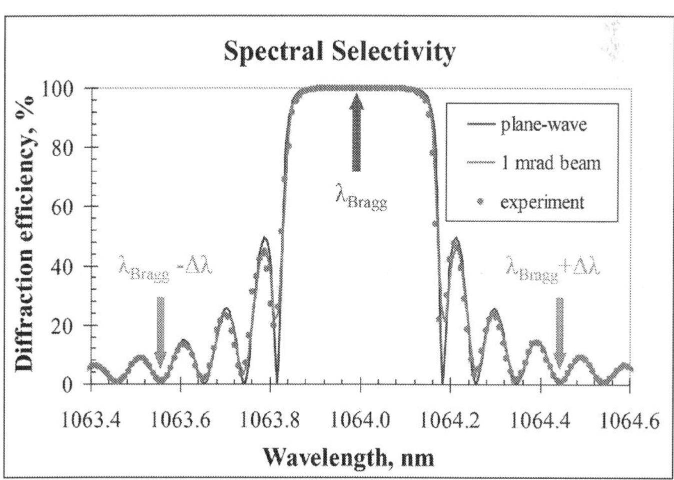

Figure 5. Spectral dependence of the diffraction efficiency of an RBG.

In the example shown in **Figure 6**, two beams with shifted wavelengths are brought to interact with a reflective VBG with characteristic efficiency versus wavelength curve shown in **Figure 5**. This VBG reflects wavelength λ_1 when it satisfies the Bragg condition at a given angle but transmits wavelength λ_2 with minimal losses if it matches with one the VBG's minima (e.g., the forth one). In this way, the diffracted beam λ_1 and the transmitted beam λ_2 can emerge overlapped and collinear. When using reflective VBGs for spectral beam combining, it is imperative to ensure as high as possible diffraction efficiency for the diffracted beam and minimal diffraction efficiency for the transmitted beam.

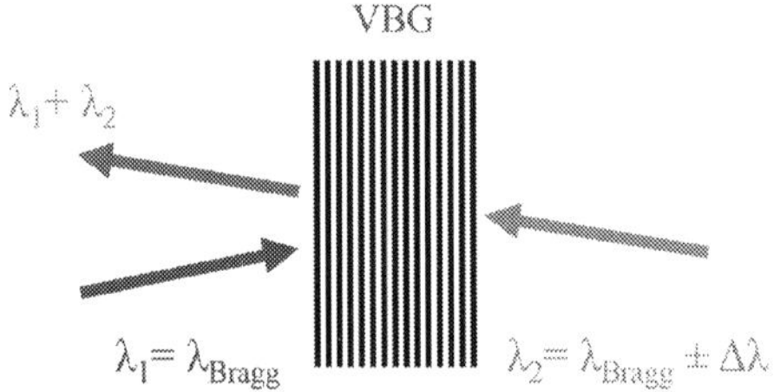

Figure 6. Schematic description of two-beam spectral combining setup using RBG as a combining element.

This approach for SBC can be extended where several VBGs are used to combine more than two laser beams. Such system was presented in [5] and demonstrated the combining of five lasers, each generating 150 W CW to give a total combined power of 750 W (**Figure 7**). Spectrally, the beams were 250 pm apart so the combined spectrum had width of 1 nm in total. For many applications, it is not only the total power that is of significance but also to final beam quality. In this particular example, the M^2 of the combined beam was 1.6 and the beam combining efficiency was greater than 90%. The VBGs were recorded in the PTR glass which, as already mentioned, possesses very low intrinsic losses and therefore can handle high power fluxes with minimal light being absorbed and converted to heat. Regardless, the authors had to implement a thermal tuning and compensation scheme in order to control the resonant conditions of each grating and to manage thermal distortions. As shown in **Figure 7**, the five-beam combining system is quite complex and scaling it to a larger number of channels will scale the mechanical and also thermal management complexity. In addition, the footprint of the systems will also be quite substantial and will make it impractical for use out of laboratory environment.

An approach where a single diffracting optical element that is capable of diffracting several beams simultaneously and substitutes several single beam reflecting elements can reduce the complexity and the space that the beam combining system occupies. Such element can be a computer-generated DOE or one consisting of several mutually aligned VBGs that occupy the same volume. We will discuss in detail the latter where several reflective VBGs are multiplexed such that each laser channel is redirected into a single, common output.

Figure 8 shows the design of a spectral beam combining system capable of combining five laser beams by using a multiplexed VBG (MVBG) element. The MVBG contains four volume Bragg gratins that reflect four beams with different wavelengths correspondingly while transmitting the fifth beam which is out of resonance with any of the four multiplexed VBGs. This system is fully analogous to the one shown in **Figure 7** but with the benefits of being more compact and simpler to align. The feasibility of the approach was proven and demonstrated in [20] where a double-multiplexed VBG recorded in the PTR glass was used to combine three laser beams. As a first step, the authors combined the two reflected by the MVBG beams to realize a total power of 282 W with combining efficiency of 99%. The M^2 of the combined beam was very close to the lasers' original M^2 of 1.05 and was measured to be 1.15 in the 'X' direction and 1.08 in the 'Y' direction. The MVBG was kept at constant temperature by a placing it in a copper housing in which thermo-electric elements attached to it. This approach allowed keeping the MVBG into resonance with the lasers in the case of heating due to absorption occurred. Heating leads to expansion of the glass and therefore to change of the gratings' periods which, on its own, leads to the lasers falling out of resonance with their corresponding VBGs. At the power density of approximately 3 kW/cm², the authors did not observe any heating problems and therefore no beam quality degradation. Next, the third beam, in this case the transmitted one, was added to the system to achieve a total combined power of 420 W. While the final three beam combining efficiency of 96.5 % was still very high, the total beam quality parameter got worse and reached 1.38 in the 'X' and 1.20 in the 'Y' directions. The worse M^2 was due to heating of the glass introduced by the transmitted beam. Such thermal effect was not observed when combining only reflected beams because they penetrated the MVBG significantly less and therefore much less of their power was absorbed and dissipated as heat into the glass. Using better cooling techniques such as surface air-flow can eliminate the thermal effect and the resulting beam quality degradation observed [17]. In conclusion, the use of multiplexed volume Bragg gratings for spectral beam combining is excellent alternative and addition to the current state of the art combining techniques. The capability of reducing the number of combining elements in the system while being able to manage the thermal load is especially valuable especially when combining kilowatt level laser sources.

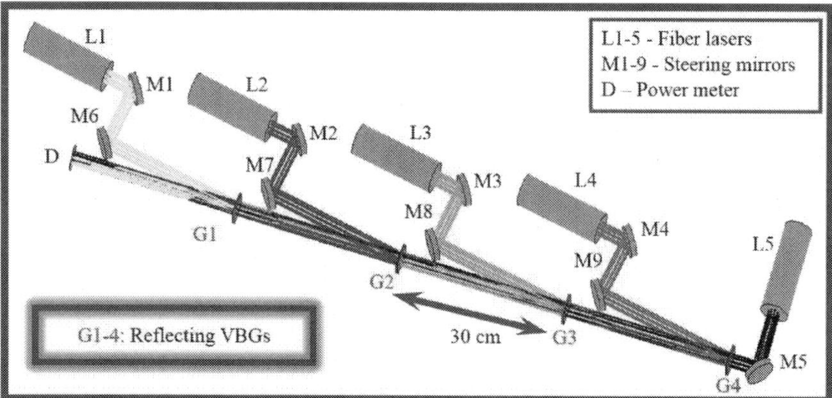

Figure 7. Five -beam combining setup using RBGs as combining elements [32].

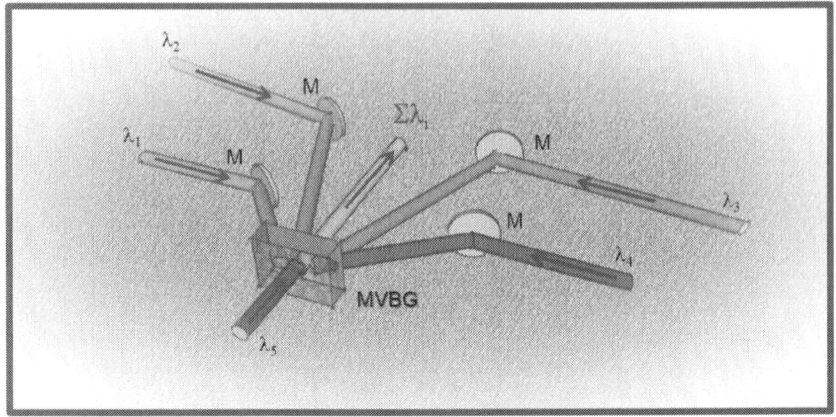

Figure 8. Five-beam combining setup using a single multiplexed VBG as combining element [19].

Volume Bragg gratings can be used for coherent beam combining (CBC) as well [21]. In coherent combining, the lasers are phased to emit coherently at the same wavelength and in phase. Depending on how the phase-locking of the lasers is achieved, CBC can be either passive or active. In the active case, the phase of each of the lasers that are being combined is controlled with high precision using feedback loop. This drastically complicates the whole system from optical and electronics perspective. In the passive approach, the sources share a common resonator and due to this they emit coherently without the need for external phase control. Such system is very simple and compact. Volume Bragg gratings and especially multiplexed ones are the ideal option for use in passive CBC because a system implementing such MVBG will have a single coherently combined output beam. The MVBG is used as 1:N splitter and combiner and it is important that there is equal radiation exchange between each laser.

Such approach was used by [22] where two lasers were coherently combined using a double MVBG. Two identical reflecting VBGs were symmetrically recorded in the PTR glass in such a way that they have a degenerate output. **Figure 9** presents the optical setup of the two-channel system. The output of each of the fiber lasers is reflected in the common/degenerate direction toward the output coupler (OC). The part of the combined output reflected by the OC is split by the MVBG for feedback to the two lasers. Small part of the emission that leaks through the MVBG is used to confirm the mutual coherence of the two lasers by interfering the two lasers. Using this scheme for CBC, the authors reported a combining efficiency of more than 90%, slope efficiency of almost 50%, and fringe contrast of 96%, which indicates a significant degree of coherence between the two channels. A similar scheme can be realized using multiplexed transmitting Bragg grating as well.

The design of the multiplexed VBG is quite important in order for the systems as whole to operate with high combining and slope efficiencies. For example, losses due to lower than 99% diffraction efficiency of the gratings lead to losses in both the combining and the splitting processes in a given resonator round trip.

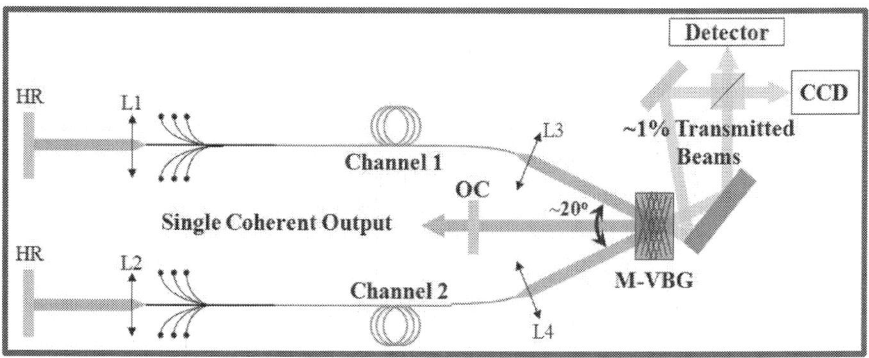

Figure 9. Coherent beam combining setup using double RBG as a combining element [22].

In conclusion, an approach for passive coherent beam combining capable of delivering from kW to tens of kW narrow-linewidth laser power is highly desired and sought after. Passive CBC using multiplexed volume Bragg gratings is a very promising technique that can deliver such power levels with great efficiency and minimal system complexity.

2.2. Holographic phase masks and their applications

Phase masks have found numerous applications in areas such as beam shaping, laser mode conversion, encryption, and others. The two most common ways to make phase masks are either by using a contoured surface where the path length for different parts of the beam is different or by using a bulk material inside which localized refractive index changes are made. In both cases, the phase shift is done by changing the local optical propagation path and therefore the phase masks are limited to use at a specific wavelength. This limits substantially their potential for use in different applications. The solution will be to make an achromatic phase mask and some attempts have been performed in the past [23–25]. For example, multiplexing many computer-generated holograms is one approach where arbitrary wavefronts can be generated if the mask is illuminated with a suitable beam. For this approach to work, a separate hologram needs to be recorded for every desired wavelength which makes the method quite complicated. A simpler and more flexible approach for making achromatic phase masks will be described in this section of the chapter.

The foundation of the approach is to encode phase mask profile into transmitting Bragg grating, which as whole works as a so-called "holographic phase mask" (HPM). This HPM can be implemented for a broad range of wavelengths and for each one of them it produces the desired diffracted phase profile, as long as the Bragg condition of the TBG is met for the given wavelength. As it will be shown, such HPM can be made fully achromatic by introducing two surface diffraction gratings with particular periods, before and after the HPM. In this way, no angular Bragg angle tuning is required. As expected, HPMs utilize the diffraction properties of regular TBGs and therefore they can diffract up to 100% of a beam into a single order.

Another specific property of TBGs is that they have relatively narrow angular selectivity and that allows the multiplexing several HPMs into one piece of recording materials, while having little or no cross-talk between them.

To help understand the way HPMs work, it is important to note that a volume Bragg grating is the simplest volume hologram that can diffract different wavelengths without distorting the initial beam profile (as long as they satisfy the Bragg condition) which sets it apart from more complex holograms, which are capable of changing the beam wavefront. Also, this leads to the fact that HPM can be tested with wavelength different or the same as the recording one.

The encoding of a phase profile into a TBG can be carried out by using a holographic setup shown in **Figure 10** [26]. In the setup, a standard binary phase mask (see **Figure 11**) is placed into one of the arms (object beam) of a two-beam-recording system. It is important to emphasize that the phase mask must have the desired phase transitions for the hologram recording wavelength and not for the reconstructing wavelength. The beams interfere at an angle θ relative to the normal of the sample to create a fringe pattern inside the sample following the equation:

$$I = I_1 + I_2 + 2\sqrt{I_1 I_2} \cos((\vec{k}_1 - \vec{k}_2) \cdot \vec{r} + \phi(x, y, z)), \tag{3}$$

where I is the intensity, $\vec{k}_i$ is the wavevector for each beam, and ϕ is the phase change introduced by the phase mask after the object beam has propagated to the recording material. As described in [26], the recorded hologram will have a refractive index profile described by:

$$n(x, y, z) = n_0 + n_1 \cos(\vec{K} \cdot \vec{r} + \phi(x, y)), \tag{4}$$

where n_0 is the background refractive index, n_1 is the refractive index modulation, and $\vec{K} = \vec{k}_1 - \vec{k}_2$ is the grating vector.

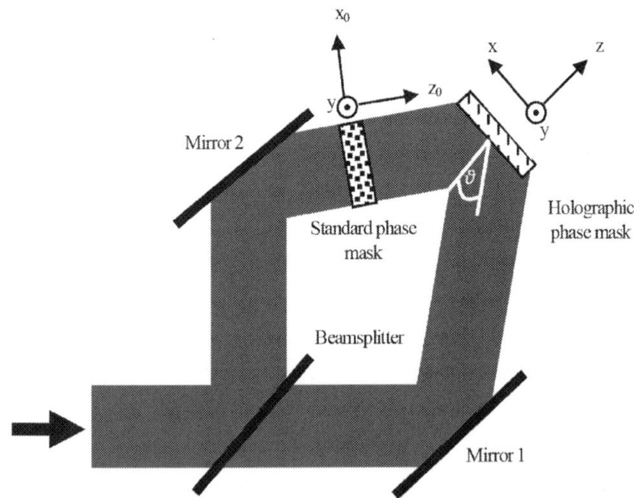

Figure 10. Recording setup used for encoding phase profile into a TBG [26].

By applying coupled wave theory, one can determine the diffracted beam phase profile and diffraction efficiency of a beam satisfying the Bragg condition of an HPM [3]. The model was applied for the binary phase profile encoded in a TBG as the one shown in **Figure 11**.

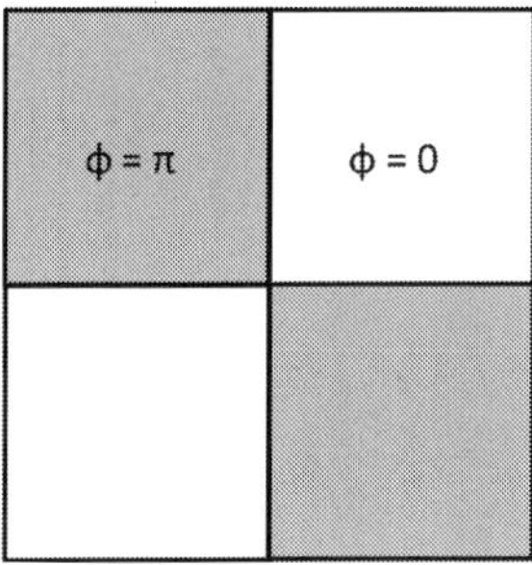

Figure 11. Binary phase distribution for a four-sector phase mask.

Applying binary π phase shift to a regular TBG along both the x- and the y-axis will determine if there are any orientation-dependent variations in the output beam's phase profile or diffraction efficiency. The performance of the HPM was simulated for 632 and 975 nm. The parameters of the TBG were the same for both wavelengths just the incident angle was adjusted in order to match the corresponding Bragg condition.

As shown in **Figure 12(b)**, the diffraction efficiency of an HPM can reach the one of a uniform TBG illuminated with a plane wave. The observed lower efficiency for smaller probe beam sizes is due to the fact that the parts of the beam that cross the phase discontinuity will not satisfy the Bragg condition and this affects smaller beams more when their area is comparable to the phase discontinuity total area. For larger beams, this effect is negligible and its influence on the diffraction efficiency is very little. **Figure 12(c)** shows that the π phase shift is present for all three wavelengths when it is along the x-axis. The slight offset of the phase shift from the origin is due to the propagation of the test beam through the HPM and the diffraction that occurs only in the x-direction. In the case when the phase jump is along the y-axis, as shown in **Figure 12(d)**, it is as well present for all wavelengths but the discontinuity is centered exactly at the origin because the test beam does not have a component propagating in the y-direction. In conclusion, HPMs have the wavelength and angular diffraction properties of regular TBGs, while capable of encoding a desired phase profile on to a test beam over its whole bandwidth as long as it satisfies the Bragg condition.

Experimentally, HPMs were fabricated and characterized using PTR glass and some of the results will be discussed here [27]. As a master phase mask was used a four-sector one, as shown in **Figure 11**. The mask was designed to give π phase shift for the hologram recording wavelength of 325 nm. For comparison purposes, a regular TBG was also recorded in the same piece of PTR glass by removing the phase mask and rotating the sample. Such multiplication guarantees that both diffractive elements share the same glass volume and therefore any localized glass inhomogeneity will influence both of them in the same way. **Figure 13** shows the measured diffraction efficiencies of the HPM and the standard TBG. The results match very well the theoretically predicted small difference in efficiency due to the phase shift areas and also show that HPMs behave as regular TBGs in terms of angular selectivity properties.

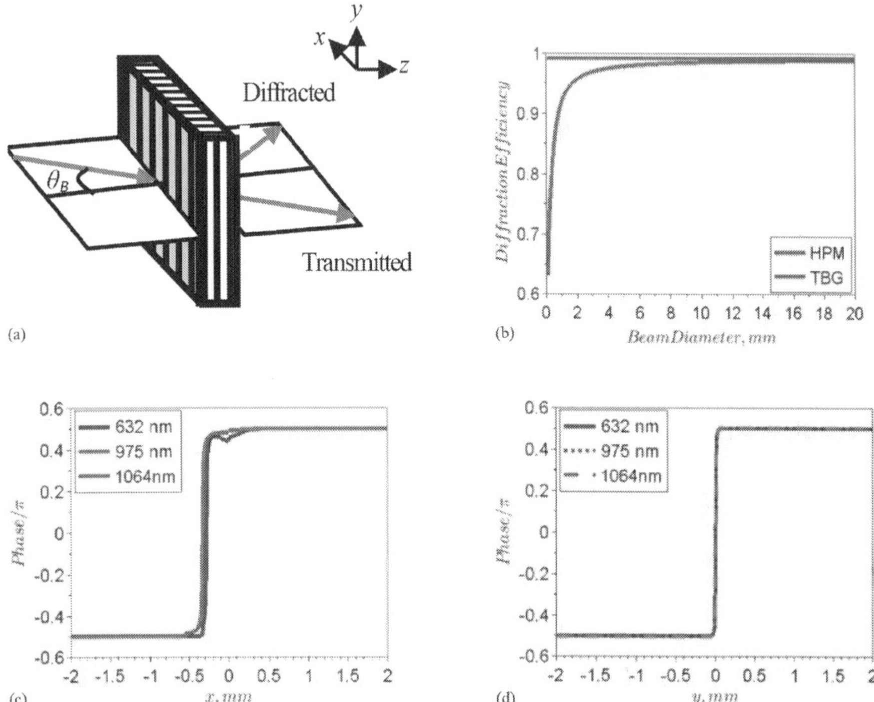

Figure 12. (a) Schematic representation of beam incident on HPM, (b) diffraction efficiency of an HPM at 1064 nm as a function of beam diameter when a binary phase dislocation is encoded along the x-axis, (c) the diffracted beam phase profile when a binary phase dislocation is encoded along the x-axis for beams of different wavelength, (d) the diffracted beam phase profile when a binary phase dislocation is encoded along the y-axis for beams of different wavelength.

HPM, as the one just theoretically discussed, was experimentally realized and used to demonstrate its capabilities as an optical mode converter that can operate at different wavelengths. To show the unique properties of HPMs, the fabricated element was tested with three different wavelengths (632.8, 975, and 1064 nm). A standard binary four-sector phase mask can convert a Gaussian beam to a TEM_{11} mode if properly aligned to the center of the phase jump boundaries. **Figure 14** demonstrates the far-field intensity pattern for a simulated mode conversion through a binary phase mask (a) and the patterns experimentally observed for three different wavelengths after diffraction by the HPM (b–d). The diffracted beam profiles clearly exhibit the four-lobed pattern which confirms the notion that the phase profile imprinted in the HPM is present in the diffracted beam and this fact applies for very broad range of wavelengths. Unlike standard phase masks which can only operate for one predetermined wavelength for which the corresponding phase shift is as required. This example demonstrates the great potential that HPMs possess given that laser and fiber modes are present in almost any optical system and their conversion to other modes is of great interest.

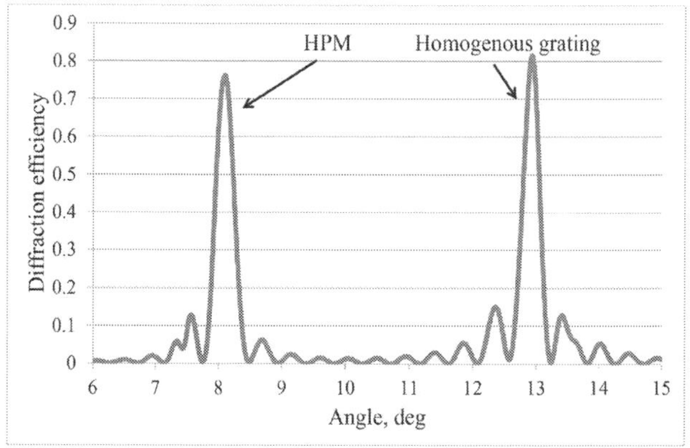

Figure 13. Diffraction efficiency angular spectrum of an HPM and homogenous grating.

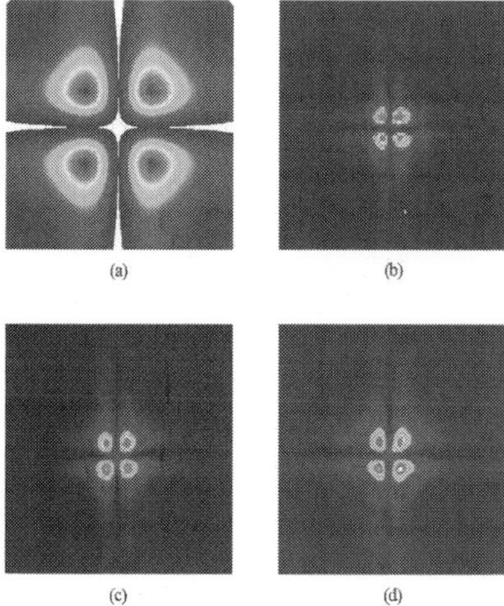

Figure 14. (a) Simulated far-field profile of a beam after passing through an ideal four-sector binary mask and the diffracted beam from a four-sector HPM at (b) 632.8 nm, (c) 975 nm, and (d) 1064 nm. The sizes shown here are not to scale [27].

We already described that multiplexing of volume Bragg gratings can be used for laser beam combining. The same approach can be applied to HPMs and as a result fabricate an element with unique functionality. The property of the HPMs to do mode conversion is not unique [28, 29], but if this is integrated with the capability of VBGs to do beam combining, an element will be created that can simultaneously convert multiple beams into different modes while combining them to a single beam. For example, fiber lasers that operate at higher order mode are of interest because they are considered to overcome the power limitations of fiber lasers operating at the fundamental mode. Therefore, beam combining several lasers operating at higher order modes into one high-power fundamental mode beam will be very beneficial and of interest as a power scaling approach.

As an example, **Figure 15** shows how a double multiplexed HPM can convert individually two TEM_{11} modes (**Figure 15a** and **15b**) to TEM_{00} modes (**Figure 15c** and **15d**) while also spectrally beam combining the beams into one beam (**Figure 15e**) [27]. The lasers were operating at 1061 and 1064 nm and the HPM consisted two four-sector phase masks integrated in two TBGs that had a generate output. The authors attributed the difference between the far-field profiles of the two laser beams after their conversion to different collimations. In the final combined beam, there are wings present but these were credited to the generation of the initial TEM_{11} modes which was done by a set of HPMs. This brought some alignment challenges as shown in **Figure 15(c)** and. Nevertheless, it is evident that the integration of VBGs and phase plates could open new optical design spaces in areas such as high-power beam combining, mode multiplexing in communication systems, and others.

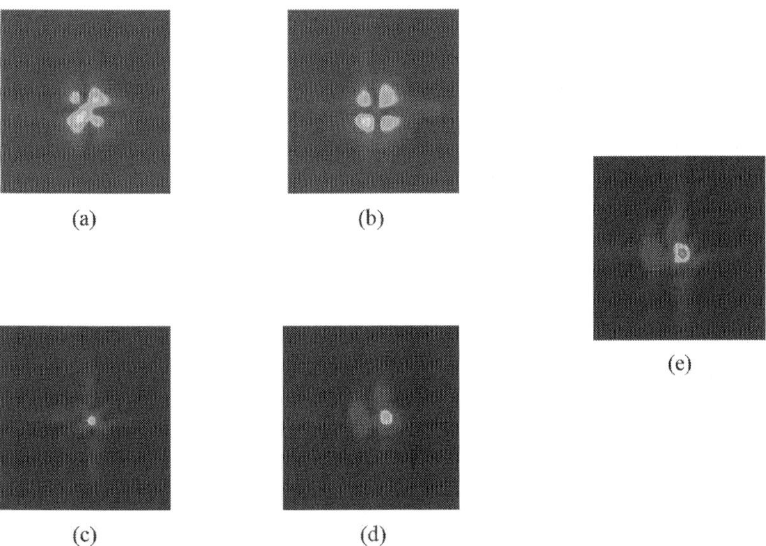

Figure 15. Demonstration of conversion from the TEM_{11} mode to TEM_{00} for 1061 and 1064 nm lasers separately (a, c and b, d); a multiplexed four-sector HPM spectrally combines the two beams and converts them to TEM_{00} (e).

3. Achromatization of HPM with surface diffraction gratings

As discussed, HPMs can successfully imprint their phase pattern as long as the wavelength satisfies the Bragg condition but to achieve this, the HPM needs to be angle tuned which cannot be considered pure achromatization. Such achromatization of HPMs can be accomplished with the concept of pairing the Bragg grating with two surface gratings [30]. According to the grating dispersion equation (Eq. (5)), a surface grating with a given period (Λ_{SG}) will diffract normally incident light at an angle (θ) as a function of its wavelength (λ):

$$\Lambda_{SG} \sin\theta = m\lambda \tag{5}$$

Based on coupled wave theory [2], a VBG will diffract light if the Bragg condition (Eq. (6)) is met and can reach diffraction efficiencies as high as $\approx$100% [3]:

$$2\,\Lambda_{VBG} \sin\theta_B = \lambda \tag{6}$$

Since both of these diffraction angles are dependent on the corresponding grating periods, if the surface grating period is double the period of the volume Bragg grating (Eq. (7)), then any first-order diffraction by normally incident light will be at the corresponding Bragg condition of the volume Bragg grating and that will hold for any wavelength [30]:

$$2\,\Lambda_{VBG} = \Lambda_{SG} \tag{7}$$

Therefore, a surface grating with twice the period of a TBG can make different wavelengths get diffracted by the TBG at the same time as long as they have the same incident angle. In order to recollimate the diffracted beams, an identical surface grating needs to be added in a mirror orientation to the transmitting volume Bragg grating, as shown in **Figure 16**. This grating completely cancels out the dispersion of the first surface grating and recollimates the outgoing beam. Applying this concept to an HPM will eliminate the need for angle tuning in order to meet the Bragg condition for different wavelengths, making, therefore, the device a fully achromatic phase element.

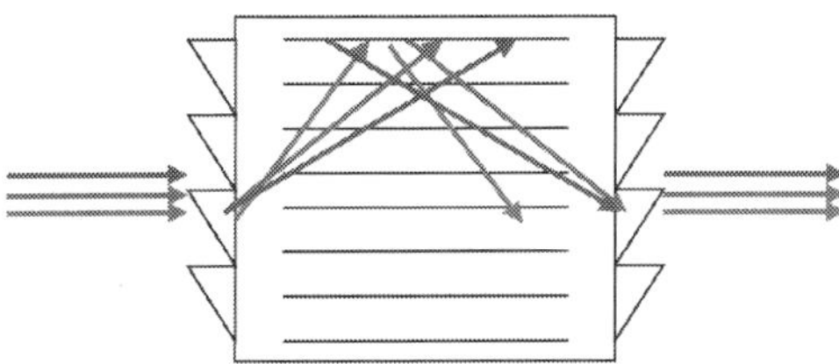

Figure 16. Concept of using surface grating pairs to meet the Bragg condition for various wavelengths regardless of angle tuning [30].

The experimental proof was carried out by using two surface gratings with a grove spacing of 150 lines/mm (a period of 6.66 µm) aligned to an HPM with a period of 3.4µm in setup shown in **Figure 17** [31]. The goal of the experiment was to achieve successful broadband mode conversion from a Gaussian to a TEM_{11} mode without the need to angularly tune the HPM. Three different TEM_{00} tunable diode laser sources were used in order to get a wavelength range of over 300 nm (765–1071 nm).

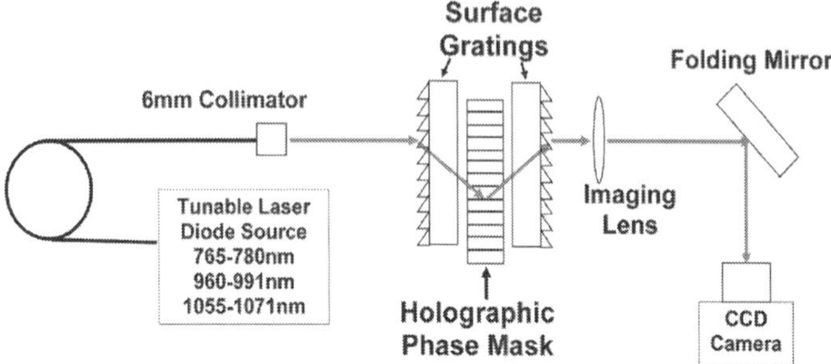

Figure 17. Experimental setup for observing Gaussian to TEM_{11} conversion of the HPM surface grating system with three different diode sources [31].

Figure 18 shows as an example, the far-field profiles of three different wavelengths ((a) 765, (b) 978, and (c) 1071 nm) that were converted to the TEM_{11} mode without any angular adjustment of the HPM. This successfully demonstrates that full achromatization of a holographic phase mask can be achieved with the combination of surface gratings and phase-encoded transmitting volume Bragg grating.

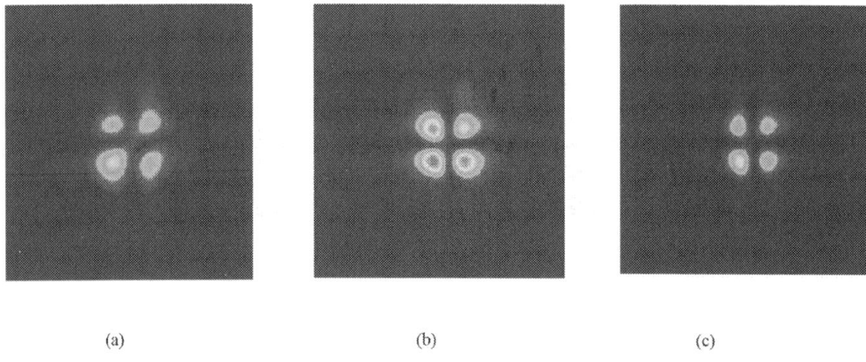

(a)   (b)   (c)

Figure 18. Far-field profile of the diffracted beam after propagating through a holographic four-sector mode converting mask aligned to two surface gratings at (a) 765 nm, (b) 978 nm, and (c) 1071 nm. The sizes shown are not to scale.

In conclusion, this is a demonstration of a way to make phase masks fully achromatic—something not possible until recently. This is achieved by the combination of surface gratings and phase-encoded transmitting volume Bragg grating.

4. Conclusion

The chapter discussed the nature and properties of volume Bragg gratings and presented several of the broad number of applications where VBGs find use. The opportunities to multiplex

VBGs and integrate them with specific phase profiles were shown to bring unique capabilities that are hard or impossible to achieve by other means. VBGs are and will continue to benefit the development and the abilities of many laser and optical systems.

Author details

Ivan Divliansky

Address all correspondence to: ibd1@creol.ucf.edu

The College of Optics & Photonics (CREOL), University of Central Florida, Orlando, FL, USA

References

[1] W. H. Bragg and W. L. Bragg, *X Rays and Crystal Structure*. London: G Bell and Sons, Ltd., 1915.

[2] R. R. Syms, *Practical Volume Holography*. Oxford, UK: Clarendon Press, pp. 48, 64, 132–162, 1990.

[3] H. Kogelnik, "Coupled Wave Theory for Thick Hologram Grating," *Bell Syst. Tech. J.*, vol. 48, no. 9, pp. 2909–2945, 1969.

[4] B. M. Anderson, G. Venus, D. Ott, E. Hale, I. Divliansky, D. R. Drachenberg, J. Dawson, M. J Messerly, P. H. Pax, J. B. Tassano, and L. B. Glebov, "Higher order mode selection for power scaling in laser resonators using transmitting Bragg gratings", Proc. SPIE 9466, Laser Technology for Defense and Security XI, 94660C, 2015.

[5] D. Drachenberg, I. Divliansky, G. Venus, V. Smirnov, and L. Glebov, "High-power spectral beam combining of fiber lasers with ultra high-spectral density by thermal tuning of volume Bragg gratings", SPIE Photonics West 2011, Proc. SPIE 7914, 79141F, 2011.

[6] L. H. Lin, "Method of Characterizing Hologram-Recording Materials," J. Opt. Soc. Am., vol. 61, no. 2, pp. 203–208, 1971.

[7] R. Collier, C. Burchardt, and L. Lin, *Optical Holography*. New York: Academic, 1971.

[8] B. J. Chang and C. D. Leonard, "Dichromated gelatin for the fabrication of holographic optical elements.," Appl. Opt., vol. 18, no. 14, pp. 2407–17, 1979.

[9] W. S. Colburn and K. A. Haines, "Volume hologram formation in photopolymer materials.," Appl. Opt., vol. 10, no. 7, pp. 1636–41, 1971.

[10] S.-D. Wu and E. N. Glytsis, "Holographic grating formation in photopolymers: analysis and experimental results based on a nonlocal diffusion model and rigorous coupled-wave analysis," J. Opt. Soc. Am. B, vol. 20, no. 6, p. 1177, 2003.

[11] F. S. Chen, J. T. LaMacchia, and D. B. Fraser, "Holographic Storage in Lithium Niobate," Appl. Phys. Lett., vol. 13, no. 7, pp. 223, 1968.

[12] S. I. Stepanov, "Applications of photorefractive crystals," Rep. Prog. Phys., vol. 57, pp. 39–116, 1994.

[13] S. Dewra, V. Grover, and A. Grover, "Fabrication and applications of fiber bragg grating — a review," Adv. Eng. Tec. Appl., vol. 4, no. 2, pp. 15–25, 2015.

[14] L. B. Glebov, "Kinetics modeling in photosensitive glass," Opt. Mater. (Amst)., vol. 25, no. 4, pp. 413–418, 2004.

[15] O. M. Efimov, L. B. Glebov, and V. I. Smirnov, "High-frequency Bragg gratings in a photothermorefractive glass," Opt. Lett., vol. 25, no. 23, pp. 1693–5, 2000.

[16] O. M. Efimov, L. B. Glebov, and V. I. Smirnov, "Diffractive optical elements in photosensitive inorganic glasses," Inorg. Opt. Mater., vol. 4452, pp. 39–47, 2001.

[17] B. Anderson, S. Kaim, G. Venus, J. Lumeau, V. Smirnov, B. Zeldovich, and L. Glebov, "Forced air cooling of volume Bragg gratings for spectral beam combination," Proc. SPIE. 8601, Fiber Lasers X: Technology, Systems, and Applications, 86013D. (March 22, 2013) doi: 10.1117/12.2005951.

[18] T. Y. Fan , "Laser beam combining for high-power, high-radiance sources," IEEE J. Sel. Top. Quantum Electron., vol. 11, no. 3, pp. 567–577, 2005.

[19] I. Divliansky, D. Ott, B. Anderson, D. Drachenberg, V. Rotar, G. Venus, and L. Glebov, "Multiplexed volume Bragg gratings for spectral beam combining of high power fiber lasers", SPIE Photonics West 2012, Proc. SPIE 8237, 823705, 2012.

[20] D. Ott, I. Divliansky, B. Anderson, G. Venus, and L. Glebov, "Scaling the spectral beam combining channels in a multiplexed volume Bragg grating", Opt. Express, vol. 21, no. 24, pp. 29620, 2013.

[21] A. Jain, D. Drachenberg, O. Andrusyak, G. Venus, V. Smirnov, and L. Glebov, "Coherent and spectral beam combining of fiber lasers using volume Bragg gratings," Proc. SPIE, vol. 7686, p. 768615, 2010.

[22] A. Jain, O. Andrusyak, G. Venus, V. Smirnov, and L. Glebov, "Passive coherent locking of fiber lasers using volume Bragg gratings," Proc. SPIE 7580, 2010, vol. 7580, p. 75801S.

[23] D. Mawet, C. Lenaerts, V. Moreau, Y. Renotte, D. Rouan and J. Surdej, "Achromatic four quadrant phase mask coronagraph using the dispersion of form birefringence," in Astronomy with High Contrast Imaging, C. Aime and R. Soummer, ed., EAS Publications Series, vol. 8, pp. 117–128, 2003.

[24] J. Rosen, M. Segev, and A. Yariv, "Wavelength-multiplexed computer-generated volume holography," Opt. Lett. Vol. 18, no. 9, pp. 744–746, 1993.

[25] T. D. Gerke and R. Piestun, "Aperiodic volume optics," Nat. Phot. vol. 4, pp. 188–193, 2010.

[26] M. SeGall, I. Divliansky, C. Jollivet, A. Schülzgen, and L.B. Glebov, "Holographically encoded volume phase masks", Optical Engineering, vol. 54, no. 7, pp. 076104–076104, 2015.

[27] M. SeGall, I. Divliansky, C. Jollivet, A. Schulzgen, and L. Glebov, "Simultaneous laser beam combining and mode conversion using multiplexed volume phase elements," SPIE LASE, Photonics West, 89601F-89601F-6, 2014.

[28] A. Shyouji, K. Kurihara, A. Otomo, and S. Saito, "Diffraction-grating-type phase converters for conversion of Hermite-Laguerre-Gaussian mode into Gaussian mode," Appl. Opt. vol. 49, no. 9, pp. 1513–1517, 2010.

[29] M. Beresna, M. Gecevičius, P. G. Kazansky, and T. Gertus, "Radially polarized optical vortex converter created by femtosecond laser nanostructuring of glass," Appl. Phys. Lett. vol. 98, pp. 201101, 2011.

[30] L. Glebov, V. Smirnov, N. Tabirian and B. Zeldovich, "Implementation of 3D angular selective achromatic diffraction optical grating device", Frontiers in Optics 2003, Talk WW3.

[31] I. Divliansky, E. Hale, M. SeGall, D. Ott, B. Y. Zeldovich, B. E. A. Saleh, and L. B. Glebov, "Achromatic phase elements based on a combination of surface and volume diffractive gratings", Proc. SPIE 9346, Photonics West: Components and Packaging for Laser Systems, 93460Q, 2015.

[32] I. Divliansky, A. Jain, D. Drachenberg, A. Podvyaznyy, V. Smirnov, G. Venus, L. Glebov, "Volume Bragg lasers," Proc. SPIE 7751, XVIII International Symposium on Gas Flow, Chemical Lasers, and High-Power Lasers, 77510Z, 2010.

Chapter 4

Holographically Recorded Low Spatial Frequency Volume Bragg Gratings and Holographic Optical Elements

Suzanne Martin, Hoda Akbari, Sanjay Keshri,

Dennis Bade, Izabela Naydenova, Kevin Murphy and

Vincent Toal

Additional information is available at the end of the chapter

http://dx.doi.org/10.5772/67296

Abstract

Low spatial frequency volume gratings (a few hundred lines per millimetre) are near the borderline of what can be considered Bragg gratings. Nevertheless, in some applications, their very low selectivity can be a benefit because it increases the angular and spectral working range of the holographic optical element. This chapter presents work carried out using an instantaneously selfdeveloping photopolymer recording material and examines holographic optical elements with spatial frequencies below 500 lines/mm. The advantages of volume photopolymer holographic gratings are discussed in the context of existing research. Specific examples explored include a combination of off-axis cylindrical lenses used to direct light from a solar simulator onto a c-Si solar cell, producing increases of up to 60% in the energy collected. A study of the microstructure of such elements is also presented. A good fit is obtained between the experimental and theoretical Bragg curves and the microstructure of the element is examined directly using microscopy. This is followed by a discussion of an unusual holographic recording approach that uses the nonlinearities inherent in low spatial frequency grating profiles to record gratings using a single beam. In conclusion, the properties of low spatial frequency volume gratings are summarized and future development discussed.

Keywords: Bragg gratings, low spatial frequency, photopolymer, holography

1. Introduction

Holographic optical elements (HOEs) are generally considered as either thin or thick gratings when their diffraction behaviour is modelled. Examples of thin gratings are commonplace because most commercially produced holograms, such as those on credit cards or banknotes, are surface relief holograms produced by a stamping process, and so the diffracting part of the structure is only a fraction of micron in thickness.

When a light beam passes through the grating, it obeys the classical grating equation given below, and orders are observed at the predicted angles

$$m\lambda = n\Lambda(\sin\alpha + \sin\beta) \tag{1}$$

where λ is the wavelength of light, Λ is the spatial period of grating, m is the order of diffraction, n is the refractive index of medium and α, β are the angles of incidence and diffraction, respectively.

Thick gratings, on the other hand, are usually volume gratings, distinct from surface gratings because the structures causing the diffraction are distributed through the full thickness of the material. Photopolymer gratings are one example. Some commercial photopolymer holograms have begun to appear on mobile phone batteries and other high value products. In these holograms, the refractive index variation is recorded through the full thickness, typically tens of microns, of the photopolymer layer. Light diffracted from this 'thick' Bragg structure also obeys the grating equation, but the greatest proportion of the light will be diffracted into the first order. This is because the light is effectively reflected from the planes of the fringes. This reflection combined with the grating equation gives the well-known Bragg condition which can be written as [1]

$$2n\Lambda\sin\theta = m\lambda \tag{2}$$

where θ is the angle of incidence.

The important factor determining whether 'thin' or 'thick' diffraction behaviour is observed is the size of the diffraction features in comparison to the thickness. Usually if the thickness of the recording material is smaller than the average spacing of the interference fringes, the holograms are considered to be thin holograms. The Q parameter, defined by Eq. (3), is derived from Kogelnik's equations for diffraction from volume gratings (discussed in the next section) and can be used in order to determine whether a hologram is 'thin' or 'thick' in its diffraction behaviour.

$$Q = \frac{2\pi\lambda d}{n\,\Lambda^2} \tag{3}$$

where λ is the wavelength, d is the thickness of the recording medium, n is the refractive index of the recording material and Λ is the fringe spacing.

Generally, gratings with the $Q < 1$ are considered thin gratings while those with values of $Q > 10$ are considered thick [2]. As can be seen from Eq. (3), for any given thickness and wavelength this depends on fringe spacing or spatial frequency. Low spatial frequency volume Bragg gratings, having grating spatial frequency of typically a few hundred lines/mm, are on the borderline of what can be considered Bragg gratings, but at typical photopolymer thicknesses 30–50 µm, they can be considered Bragg gratings for visible wavelengths. In some applications, their low selectivity can be a significant benefit because it increases the angular and spectral working range of the HOE. In materials that perform well at low spatial frequencies, it is interesting to examine the characteristics and applications of HOEs with spatial frequencies below 500 lines/mm.

Volume phase holograms have advantages over surface relief holograms because of their high efficiency and resistance to surface contaminants. Applications include spectroscopy, astronomy and ultrafast lasers [3], as well as solar concentrators [4]. A number of different materials are available for recording them including silver halide, dichromatic gelatin (DCG), photoresists and photopolymers. The primary advantages of thick volume holograms over thin surface holograms are the possible high efficiencies (theoretically 100%) and the fact that most of the energy is diffracted into a single direction (order). For most applications where the hologram is expected to perform some or all of the functions of a conventional optical element such as a lens, maximum efficiency and minimum additional beams are advantageous. Beam splitting applications are an exception, of course. Photopolymers are useful materials because of their ease of use and potential for very high diffraction efficiency, but their key advantage in optical device applications is their self-developing capability, because it removes the need for chemical or physical processing after exposure. Assuming shrinkage is not a significant problem in the photopolymer used, the avoidance of chemical and physical processing is very important in maintaining the original photonic structure written in the volume of the material during the exposure/recording step. The longer term shelf life of the recorded devices varies according to the photopolymer used. In the acrylamide-based photopolymer used in the examples in this chapter, long-term stability of recorded gratings is good when the photopolymer layer is laminated with a protective plastic layer. Recent studies of the shelf life of such gratings sealed in plastic showed varied results however [5] pointing to the need for improved protection and alternative more robust formulations [6].

For thick gratings and elements, Kogelnik's coupled wave theory [1] is a widely accepted model that relates diffraction efficiency and angular selectivity of gratings to the grating's physical characteristics (thickness, spatial frequency and refractive index modulation).

According to Kogelnik, the diffraction efficiency (η) can be calculated using Eq. (4), allowing us to model how the diffraction efficiency varies with the angle of incidence, near the Bragg angle. This allows us to observe how grating thickness and spatial frequency affect the angular selectivity of an individual grating:

$$\eta = \frac{\sin^2 \sqrt{(\xi^2 + \upsilon^2)}}{\left(1 + \frac{\xi^2}{\upsilon^2}\right)} \tag{4}$$

The parameters ξ and υ are defined as:

$$\xi = \Delta\theta \frac{kd}{2} \tag{5}$$

$$\upsilon = \frac{\pi n_1 d}{\lambda \cos\theta} \tag{6}$$

where d is the thickness of the grating, n_1 is the refractive index modulation, λ is the wavelength of the reconstructing beam, $\Delta\theta$ is the deviation from the Bragg angle and k is interference fringe vector, normal to the fringes with a magnitude $K = 2\pi/\text{spatial period}$. It can be seen from Eq. (4) that increasing the spatial period (reducing spatial frequency) is effective in controlling the angular selectivity. In materials where the refractive index modulation is small, significant thickness is required for high efficiency. Decreasing the spatial frequency (increasing the period) can be the better approach to control the angular selectivity as long as the gratings still behave as thick volume gratings [7].

2. Experimental arrangement for holographic elements

Holographic recording of diffractive optical elements involves careful spatial overlapping of two or more coherent beams so that the interference pattern they produce, once recorded into the material, will create a photonic structure capable of diffracting light in the desired way. For a simple diffractive device such as a two-way beam splitting element, the desired photonic structure may be a simple grating. For example, two coherent, collimated beams would be arranged to meet at the recording plane at a specific angle, producing a simple sinusoidal variation in intensity across, say, the horizontal axis of the recording medium. Once this is recorded in the material, a sinusoidal grating is produced which will act as a two-way beam splitter for a beam of the appropriate wavelength and incident angle.

The next step up in complexity is a shaped beam, such as a diverging beam, which when combined with the collimated reference beam produces an interference pattern consisting of a series of concentric rings. Once recorded, this pattern will produce a diffractive element with a similar variation in the refractive index, which, when illuminated correctly, produces a diverging beam. There are many types and variations of diffractive elements that can be produced in this way, especially when we consider recording with multiple beams, converging and diverging wavefronts, different inter-beam angles and different wavelengths. In this chapter, we discuss basic gratings and focusing/diverging elements with an angular offset.

The basic set-up for recording is shown in **Figure 1**; however, different adaptations are necessary for the work in each of the sections below. In order to make cylindrical lens elements, for example, a cylindrical lens is introduced into one of the interfering beams and for single-beam recording (Section 5) one beam is blocked completely during the second step. These alterations are mentioned in the relevant sections. Here, we show the standard optical arrangement for recording using the interference between two coherent beams.

The beam from a coherent laser source is spatially filtered, collimated and split in two and, after reflection of one of the beams of a plane mirror, the two beams are made to overlap at the photopolymer plate. The angle at which the beams meet can be altered by repositioning the mirror, allowing variation of the spatial frequency of the interference pattern and therefore the fringe period of the recorded grating. A grating has a single spatial frequency throughout, because two collimated beams are interfering so the inter-beam angle is constant across the polymer. The interference pattern at the photopolymer is recorded as a variation

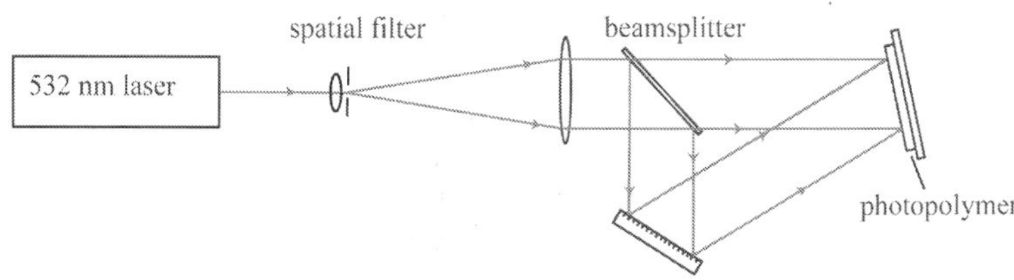

Figure 1. Basic optical arrangement for the recording of a holographic grating.

in the local refractive index inside the volume of the photosensitive material. The recording set-up includes a green laser of 532 nm wavelength, spatial filter, collimating lens, polarizing beam splitter, plane mirror, and for focusing elements, a conventional cylindrical lens (focal length 5 cm, ThorLabs, LJ182L2-A). The recording medium is the standard photopolymer used by researchers at the Centre for Industrial and Engineering Optics (IEO). It is an acrylamide-based formulation using acrylamide and bisacrylamide monomers, triethanolamine as the electron donor and polyvinylalchohol as the binder, as described elsewhere [7]. Layer thickness is controlled by the volume of liquid coating solution deposited on a known area of glass substrate.

3. Holographic low spatial frequency lens elements for light collection

The purpose of a diffractive solar collector is to gather sunlight from a large area and direct it onto a smaller area, where it can be converted to electric or thermal energy by, for example, using PV cells or thermal conversion. The advantage is that the light can be harvested cheaply from a larger area and the energy per unit area on the converter can be increased. As discussed previously, diffraction gratings can be used to change the direction of a light beam very efficiently, but they are only efficient over a small range of angles close to the Bragg angle, so they need to be used in combination if they are to be useful in collecting sunlight over most of the day.

Holographic optical elements (HOEs) have potential as solar concentrators because of their ability to diffract light at large offset angle and the potential for multiplexing a number of optical components in the same layer. Recent research has demonstrated different holographic elements in a variety of arrangements for solar applications to make diffractive elements that will re-direct and focus incoming light to the desired line using (cylindrical HOE) or spot (spherical HOE) for conversion [8–12].

A large number of researchers have demonstrated novel designs, for example, a planar concentrator using a low-cost holographic film that selects the most useful bands of the solar spectrum and concentrates them onto the surface of the photovoltaic cell, has been demonstrated by Kostuk et al. [13], and Sreebha et al. [14] have reported results on transmission holographic optical elements recorded in a silver halide material. Bianco et al. have recently reported successful concentration of solar light using an array of three spherical lenses recorded in a sol-gel photopolymer [15].

Photopolymers are excellent materials for producing such diffractive elements, being thin, lightweight, inexpensive and highly efficient, but challenges remain in reducing the angular selectivity of these relatively thick layers and in applying the technology to natural light in real-world applications.

High-efficiency diffractive optical elements have been recorded and multiplexed in photopolymer materials previously for this and other applications [16, 17]. Previous work by the authors addressed the issue of increasing the angular working range in photopolymers and demonstrated photopolymer spherical and cylindrical focusing elements that had very high efficiency when measured with monochromatic, linearly polarized laser sources [18]. In this section, the combination of pairs of elements with the same focus is demonstrated in photopolymer and tested with a solar simulator.

For these experiments, the electrical characterisation was carried out by measuring the current-voltage (I-V) characteristics of c-Si solar cells (Solar capture Technologies) with and without the DOE placed in front of the cell in such a way as to re-direct and focus additional light onto the solar cell. I-V measurements were performed using an Keithley 2400 SMU (source meter unit) with a LabVIEW interface, using the set-up shown in **Figure 2**. The light source used was a metal halide discharge lamp (Griven, GR0262).

The distance between the HOE and the silicon cells was the same as the focal length of the HOEs which in this case was 5 ± 0.1 cm. This arrangement tests the effect of two DOE elements; however applications could involve arrays of such elements surrounding the cell, each contributing additional light.

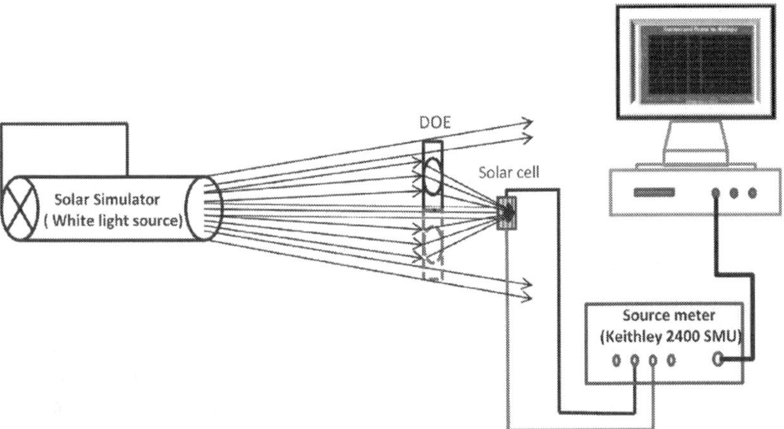

Figure 2. Diagram of the experimental setup for electrical measurements.

3.1. Recording high efficiency diffractive optical elements at low spatial frequency

Focusing HOEs were made by interfering a beam focused by a cylindrical lens beam with a collimated reference beam and placing the photopolymer layer at the area of overlap using the basic holographic set-up described in the experimental section. In such off-axis focusing DOEs, the spatial frequency of the grating planes will vary across the DOE, as will be discussed in the next section. In this example, the minimum and maximum spatial frequencies were 112 and 485 lines/mm, respectively.

A range of HOEs with an off-axis focusing effect was recorded in order to demonstrate that high efficiency could be achieved with low spatial frequency elements. Diffraction efficiency at Bragg incidence is over 95% (corrected for reflection at front and back surfaces). **Figure 3** shows how the diffraction efficiency changes with the angle of incidence. The full-width half-maximum (FWHM) is approximately 4°, which is a significant improvement on the working range for higher spatial frequencies [18]. The data were obtained by mounting the grating on a rotation stage keeping the laser and detector fixed.

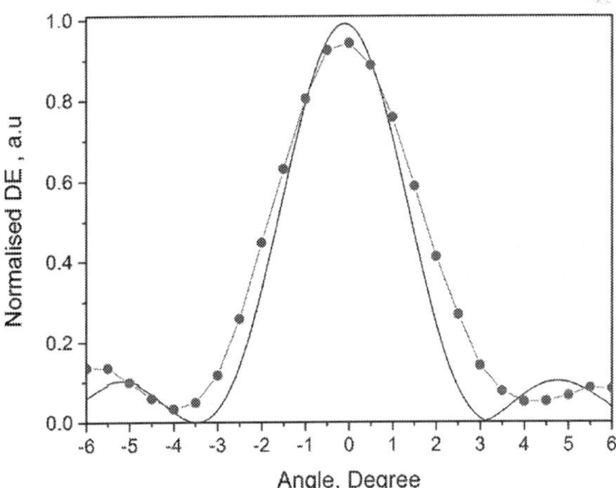

Figure 3. Diffraction efficiency versus angle for a cylindrical DOE at central spatial frequency of 300 lines/mm and recording intensity of 1 mW/cm². The dotted line shows the measured values and the smooth line is the theoretical curve for a 300 lines/mm volume grating of this diffraction efficiency in a 50 micron thick photopolymer layer.

3.2. Investigating the potential for multiplexing by stacking: three gratings with different slant angles

Photopolymer gratings were recorded with three different slant angles. **Figure 4** shows plots of the percentage of light falling on the fixed detector as the angle of incidence of the light is varied for the three individual gratings before stacking them together. In each case, the grating is fixed relative to the detector and only the angle of incidence is varied. This mimics the function of a passive (non-tracking) solar cell. The detector collects the light that would fall on

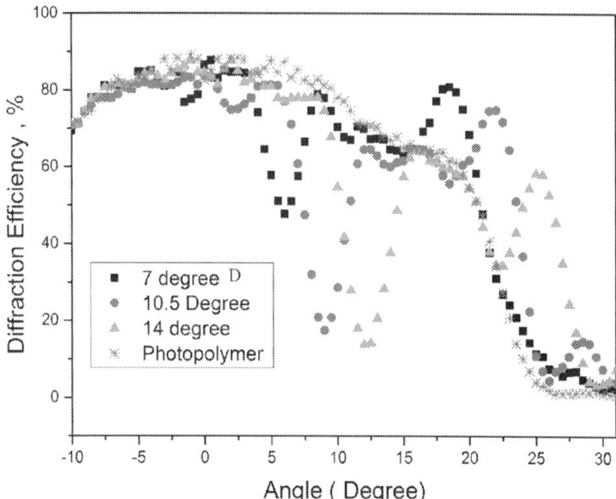

Figure 4. The variation of the percentage of light falling on the detector with angle of incidence for three individual gratings recorded at different slant angles with a spatial frequency of 300 lines/mm in layers with thickness of about 50 μm; the recording intensity was 1 mW/cm². A photopolymer layer with no grating is included for comparison.

the cell with and without the gratings in place. The 'photopolymer' line shows the variation in intensity at the detector without the presence of any grating (just a layer of clear photopolymer) for comparison. From these results, redirection of the incident beam by the gratings can clearly be observed at the appropriate angles. Light incident at over 25°, which would have otherwise missed the detector (or solar cell in a real application) is very efficiently captured using the gratings. However, a key issue is highlighted here. As well as directing the light from higher angles to a lower angle, each grating will also do the reverse. This is caused by the fact that each grating has two angles for which the light is 'on Bragg' for diffraction (corresponding to the two beams with which the grating was recorded).

The angular selectivity of the stack of the three gratings laminated together was then measured using the same method. The results are shown in **Figure 5**. The same effect was observed for the stacked device as in **Figure 4**. The results confirm that this method has improved the angular working range of the device. However, efficiency is reduced at the lower angles so that there is no net gain. Diffraction from higher angles would appear to be most useful in circumstances where the grating is offset from the main path to the solar cell, such as off-axis DOEs, in this way the direct light is unaffected, but the grating can usefully divert light from higher angles onto the solar cell.

3.3. Use of a combined device to increase the concentration ratio of solar cells

An alternative arrangement is to use off-axis elements to increase the area from which light is collected and focused onto the solar cell, thereby increasing the energy at the cell. For maximum concentration, the DOEs should be recorded so that their focal points overlap. Low

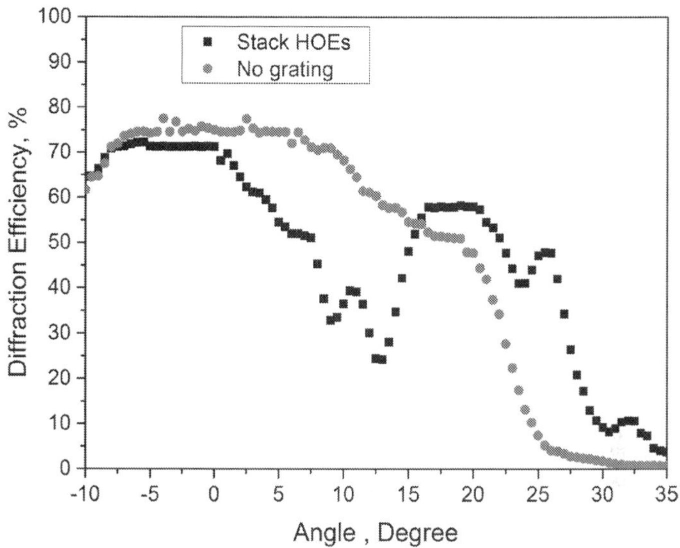

Figure 5. The variation of the percentage of light falling on the detector with angle of incidence for a stack of three laminated gratings (from **Figure 4**) and a clear photopolymer layer with no grating.

spatial frequency elements are used so that the wavelength selectivity is low and the elements can focus the full spectrum of white light onto the same solar cell. Tests were carried out using a solar simulator and a Si solar cell.

The current I, as a function of voltage applied, V, across the c-Si solar cell, was measured and the I-V curve was obtained (**Figure 6**). In this experiment, the area of the DOE was kept constant at 113 mm^2. In **Table 1**, I_{sc} represents the short circuit current for the solar cell, which is the maximum possible, produced when the cell impedance is low and is calculated when the voltage equals zero, i.e. at $V = 0$, $I = I_{sc}$. The short circuit current is due to the generation and collection of light-generated carriers within the cell. For an ideal solar cell, the short circuit current and the light-generated current are identical for moderate resistive loss. Therefore, an increase in the short circuit current is a reliable indicator of an increase in the light-generated current. J_{sc} is the short circuit current density, defined as $J_{sc} = I_{sc}$/area of the cell.

The short circuit current (I_{sc}) output of the reference cell, without the DOE in place, was approximately 3.7 ± 0.1 mA. When a single cylindrical DOE was included, an increase in I_{sc} of 16% was observed.

This measurement was then carried out for an array of two cylindrical DOEs, which resulted in an increase in the I_{sc} of 40%. These results suggest that the use of larger arrays of cylindrical and/or spherical DOEs can achieve higher relative increase in I_{sc} for smaller areas of solar cells. The value for the short circuit current density (J_{sc}) of the Si solar cell was estimated using the I-V data for a single cylindrical DOE and a pair of DOEs for a solar cell of area 60 mm^2. The results are presented in **Table 1**.

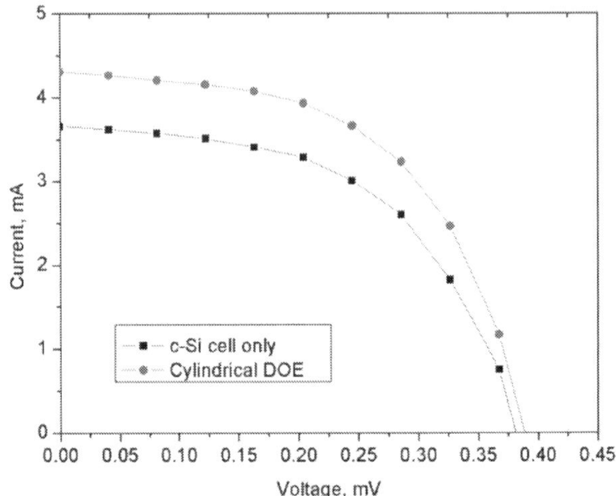

Figure 6. *I-V* curves for a c-Si solar cell (area = 60 mm^2) with and without a cylindrical DOE in place.

	I_{sc} mA/cm^2	ΔI_{sc}	ΔI_{sc} % ±0.03	J_{sc} mA/cm^2
Si cell	3.7			0.061
With cylindrical DOE	4.3	0.6	16	0.071
Array of two cylindrical DOE	5.2	1.5	40	0.086

Table 1. Calculated J_{sc} of the Si solar cell with a range of DOEs. I_{sc} is the short-circuit current and J_{sc} is the short circuit current density.

Figure 7 presents the relative increase in the I_{sc} for the c-Si solar cells versus the area of the solar cells. The illuminated area of the DOE remained constant at 113 mm^2 throughout the experiment while the solar cell area was varied between 9 and 100 mm^2. In order to optimize the concentration ratio, the preference is to use solar cells significantly smaller than the DOEs. These results show that there is a significant improvement in the output current obtained when using the holographic focusing elements.

It has been observed that for solar cells with an area of 9 mm^2, a 34% increase in the output current is achieved with a single DOE compared to 10% for a 100 mm^2 solar cell. This is because the smaller cell area makes better use of the focusing effect.

The relative increase for an array of two cylindrical DOEs was nearly double that of single cylindrical DOE. The device is capable of collecting light from a large incident angle and redirecting it onto the centre of the solar cell. Photographs of the light spots diffracted from holographically recorded diffractive lenses are shown in **Figure 8**. The first photograph shows a collimated green laser beam (circular spot) which is brought to a line focus by the DOE on the left of the picture. Additional beams to the left and right of these are also observed in the photograph; however, in reality they are very weak. Experimentally, for off-axis focusing DOE lenses, more than 90% of the incident light is typically measured in the focused beam. The second image in **Figure 8** is a photograph of the transparent diffractive lens viewed in room lighting.

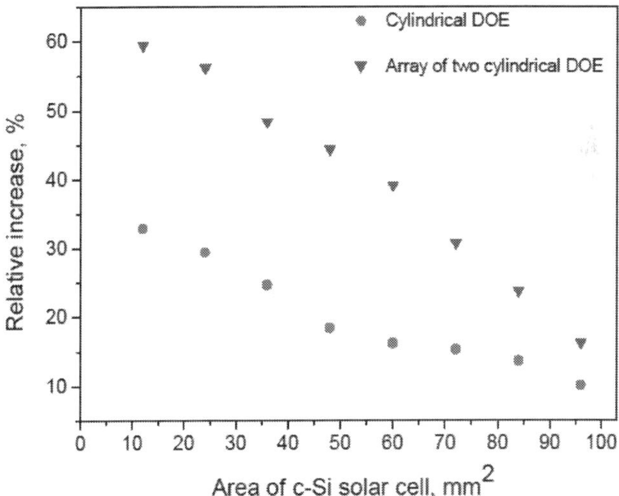

Figure 7. The percentage increase of output current of c-Si solar cells versus area of the c-Si cells for a single cylindrical DOE and an arrangement of two cylindrical DOEs.

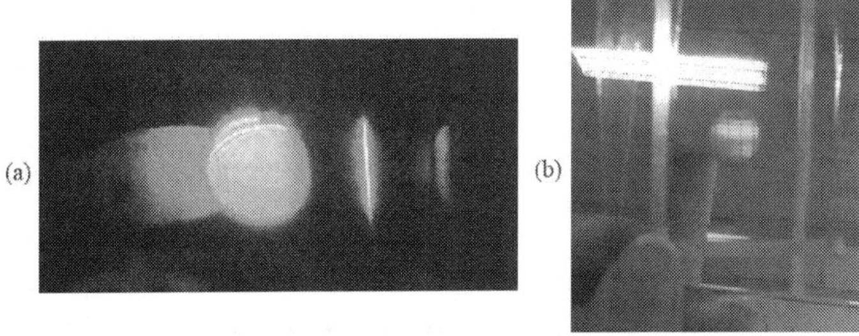

Figure 8. Photographs of the light diffracted by holographic lenses recorded in acrylamide photopolymer (a) illuminated with an expanded laser beam and (b) in room light.

4. Analysis of the photonic structure of low spatial frequency lens elements

Volume phase holographic (VPH) gratings can be recorded on different types of materials such as silver halide, dichromatic gelatin (DCG), photoresists, photopolymer, etc. However, photopolymer provides certain advantages [19] such as higher efficiency, self-development and cost effectiveness. In general, VPH gratings follow Bragg's law [20] for the propagation of light inside a volume in which periodic modulation of the refractive index forms the grating structure. In certain circumstances, for example thicker media, VPH gratings recorded at low spatial frequency can also be considered as Bragg gratings and they increase the angular and spectral range of VPH gratings [18]. In this section, we examine the photonic structure of the recorded lenses using microscopy in order to verify the model used to design the lens and calculate the spatial frequency and slant angle of the grating pattern at specific points on the recorded lens. We also use Kogelnik's coupled wave theory (KCWT) to predict the expected Bragg curves and compare them to the curves obtained experimentally measured at these locations.

The lens elements are recorded as described above by including a focusing lens into one arm of a standard two-beam optical arrangement for holographic recording at 532 nm. In this section, the analysis of the local diffraction behaviour using an unexpanded 633 nm laser beam and measuring the Bragg curve (intensity variation in the diffracted beam as the grating is rotated though a range of angles) is complemented by microscopic imaging at the same location.

4.1. Modelling the recorded holographic optical element

The focusing elements studied were 5 cm focal length off-axis cylindrical lenses, so the micro-structure was expected to vary significantly laterally across the recorded element. **Figure 9** shows a schematic of the recording arrangement. Clearly the angles at which the interfering beams meet varies from left to right and we would expect both slant angle and spatial frequency of the grating pattern to change.

Simple geometry allows us to calculate the inter-beam angle (which determines the spatial frequency) and the slant angle, i.e. the angle between the bisector of the angle between the two beams (inside the medium) and the normal to the recording plane). Since the lens is not spherical in this example there is no variation vertically (out of the plane of the page in **Figure 9**). The Bragg angle θ_o is related to the fringe spacing (Λ) recorded in the hologram by the relation

$$\sin \theta_o = \frac{\lambda}{2\Lambda} \tag{7}$$

In this work, we use equation (7) to predict the grating structure and verify it experimentally at three specific locations on the element, the centre and points 3 mm either side of the centre. For any local position across the element, the slant could be calculated using the recording geometry and compared to the experimentally observed position of the peak in the Bragg curve. Equally, the local grating period was calculated from knowledge of the inter-beam angle at that specific location during recording and this was compared with microscopic imaging results.

The shape of the Bragg curve was then modelled using those parameters in KCWT, and fitted to the experimental data (normalised to the measured diffraction efficiency value). **Figure 10(a)** shows the calculated spatial period across the lens element. The inverted red tri‐angles show the measured values obtained from the microscopy images, which are 2.66, 3.37, 6.59 μm at left, centre and right, respectively (left, right are 3 mm away from centre). **Figure 10(b)** shows the calculated slant angle at positions across the element.

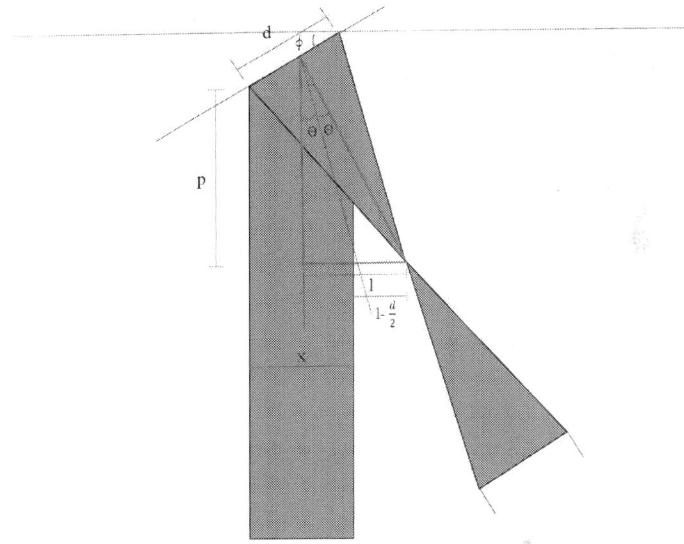

Figure 9. Schematic illustration of the geometry of the recording set-up showing the angles at which the interfering beams meet at the photopolymer plate of width d, at a slant angle ϕ.

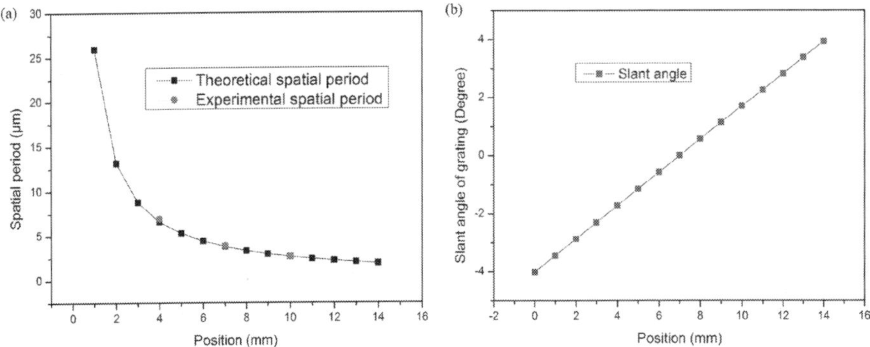

Figure 10. (a) Spatial period across the VPH lens: 0 corresponds to the right side and 14 corresponds to the left side of the lens and (b) slant angle across the VPH lens.

4.2. Local microstructure and diffraction behaviour

Figure 11 shows the experimental intensity data obtained by illuminating the three positions with an unexpanded 633 nm He-Ne beam and varying the angle of incidence. As expected, the three curves are shifted relative to one another, verifying that each location has a different slant angle and inter-beam angle. Each curve has a different FWHM because of the different grating periods.

The curves are fitted to theoretical curves generated by putting the parameters calculated using the geometry into the KCWT equations and setting the wavelength to 633 nm.

As can be seen from the figure very good agreement is obtained. The small broadening of the Bragg peaks can be accounted for by the fact that the incident beam had a finite width, and so in reality the result is not for a specific location but for an average over the beam width. The thickness of the photopolymer used was 70 ± 5 μm and was measured by white light interferometry.

In order to verify the theoretical calculation of spatial period of grating, the microscopic image of the gratings has been taken using a phase contrast microscope (Olympus DP72) at three different positions, centre and 3 mm away from the centre (right and left). These are shown in **Figure 12**. The spatial periods measured using the microscope are 2.6 ± 0.1, 3.9 ± 0.1 and 7.0 ± 0.1 μm at left, centre and right of the VPH cylindrical lens, respectively. The theoretical values for these positions can be seen from the graph of **Figure 12(a)** and are 2.66, 3.37, 6.59 μm, respectively.

It can be observed that the holographic recording has produced the predicted diffraction grating patterns. The experimental results for the diffraction characteristics of the local pattern fit well with the theoretical predictions for these spatial frequencies made with KCWT. A small

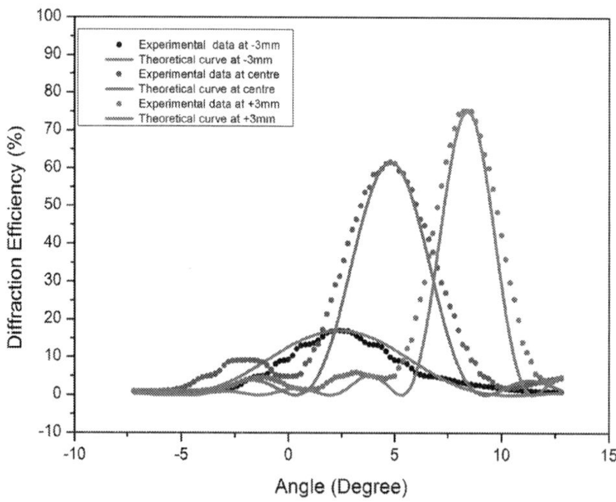

Figure 11. Theoretical and experimental angular selectivity curves for three different positions (centre and 3 mm left and right of centre) on the VPH cylindrical lens.

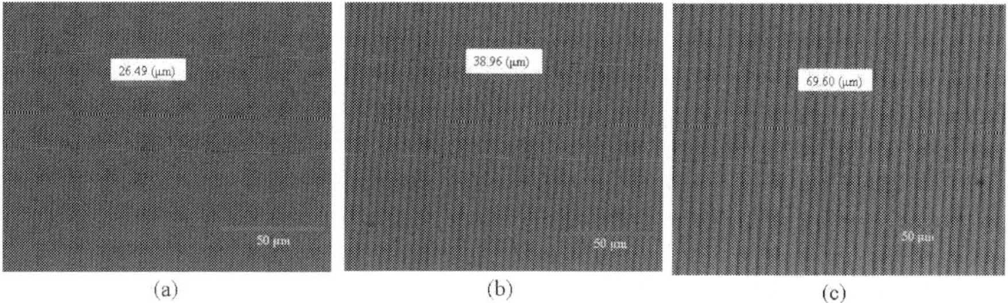

Figure 12. Microscopic image of the surface structure of the holographic lens at the (a) left position (3 mm from centre), (b) centre and (c) right position (3 mm from centre).

amount of broadening is observed in the experimental curves, but this is probably due to the size of the probe beam, beam walk off or scattering. The spatial periods obtained from the microscopic images agree with the theory, and it can be seen from the microscopic images that the spatial period is increasing from left to right of the VPH cylindrical lens. Future work will involve fabricating and modelling lens elements at different wavelengths.

5. Writing gratings with a single beam

Most standard holographic recording is, of course, achieved by interfering two coherent recording beams. The interference pattern they create is recorded in the medium as a diffractive structure in the medium. However, due to the challenges of stability and size associated with splitting and recombining beams, various methods have been employed in order to achieve recording with a single beam.

Early work by Kukhtarev et al. [21] demonstrated holographic recording using only one input beam in a photorefractive $BaTiO_3$ crystal using the photogalvanic coupling between orthogonal birefringent modes. Later, Naruse et al. [22] multiplexed ten gratings into a Fe-doped $LiNbO_3$ crystal with a single recording beam. They used the crystal edge in a wavefront splitting arrangement. Mitsuhashi and Obara [23], using a similar approach, demonstrated a compact holographic memory system using a single-beam geometry in Fe-doped $LiNbO_3$. At that time, they estimated a maximum total capacity of 23 GB based on beam diameter of 5 mm in a system using 635 nm light and a 10 mm crystal using both angular and spatial multiplexing. More recently, Yau et al. [24] have proposed another method that uses a single object beam to record images in a photorefractive $LiNbO_3$ crystal which allows imaging through a dynamically varying medium. Chiang et al. proposed a method that uses a single object beam to record multiple images in a medium without the need for a reference wave using a lenticular array [25]. This was demonstrated by recording four holograms in a $30 \times 30 \times 1$ mm^3 Fe-doped $LiNbO_3$ crystal with a single exposure.

Recent work by Kukhtarev and Kukhtareva develops a dynamic version of the early single-beam recording system, demonstrating dynamic holographic interferometry [26] and also holographic amplification of weak images without phase distortions [27].

In the commercial arena, Optware, a Japanese-based company, developed a new method of holographic storage called collinear holography. Instead of separate signal and reference beams to create the interference pattern, Optware are using a collinear approach by aligning the two laser beams into a single beam of coaxial light to create data fringes. This approach significantly simplified the recording set-up [28]. Optware released a prototype of this recording system operating at a wavelength of 532 nm with an overall storage capacity of 200 GB on a recording medium with a diameter of 120 mm (HVD Pro Series 1000). They also released a credit card-sized layer with a storage capacity of 30 GB and demonstrated a recording system with a storage capacity of 1 TB with a data transfer rate of 128 MB/s.

An example of the single-beam recording method described here was first reported by the authors in 1998 [29]. After first recording, weak diffraction gratings in the photopolymer were illuminated on Bragg, with just one of the recording beams. For gratings with initial diffraction efficiencies ranging from less than 1% to 64%, a further increase in diffraction efficiency was observed during the single-beam exposure. For example, a grating with 7.5% efficiency was observed to increase to 60% efficiency over several minutes of single-beam exposure. It was suggested at the time that the increase may be caused by either uniform polymerization of unreacted monomer in the grating, as had been observed in other photopolymers [30], or diffraction from the recorded grating. Further work [31] showed that the grating strength only increased significantly when the single writing beam was incident close to the Bragg angle of the pre-recorded grating.

In this section, this method of writing holographic gratings using weak pre-recorded gratings is explored further, because of its potential to allow the use of just one beam at the data writing stage. New gratings, angularly separated from the pre-written grating, are written using a single beam and the dependence on grating thickness is demonstrated. We demonstrate that this approach allows the writing of high diffraction efficiency gratings in unstable conditions due to the fact that the second beam is generated from within the photopolymer layer, in a manner similar to beam pumping in photorefractive crystals. We demonstrate that angular multiplexing is also possible, allowing one grating to be amplified without amplifying the other pre-recorded gratings.

5.1. Holographic recording process

A two-step process was used: (1) recording the weak 'seed' gratings with two recording beams and (2) exposure of the seed grating to one beam. There was a short delay between the two steps, during which both beams were blocked.

5.1.1. Two-beam recording

The first step was to record a grating, usually with a diffraction efficiency of approximately 1%, in the photopolymer medium. A standard holographic grating recording arrangement was used, with two coherent interfering beams (532 nm) using beam splitters and mirrors, as shown in **Figure 1**. The arrangement is for unslanted gratings. A He-Ne beam (633 nm) was used to monitor the diffraction efficiency throughout the initial recording and subsequent illumination. This was possible because, in the formulation used, the photopolymer is not sensitive to red light. A short exposure time (around 1 sec) was used for the initial recording in order to keep the efficiency of the initial grating low. The spatial frequency was controlled by adjusting the angle between the two interfering beams and is 500 lines/mm in the work reported here.

5.1.2. Single-beam recording

The next step was to illuminate the grating on Bragg, with a single beam and observe the change in diffraction efficiency. The simplest way to do this was to use an additional shutter to block one of the two recording beams. Usually a short interval with no writing beam illumination was allowed after the initial grating recording in order to allow the system to record any spontaneous change that may be occurring in the absence of illumination. Exposure times and writing beam illumination were controlled using Uniblitz electronic shutters. The photopolymer grating was mounted on a rotation stage so that angles of illumination could also be varied.

5.2. Single-beam holographic recording results

Figure 13 shows the diffraction efficiency changing during a typical exposure starting with a standard two-beam holographic recording of 2 sec followed by a 25 sec delay, during which there is no illumination. Then, at 27 sec, illumination with one of the writing beams commences. The diffraction efficiency increase obtained during the single-beam exposure is significant and diffraction efficiency of the final grating is much higher than at the point when single-beam exposure commences. In this case, the grating spatial frequency is 500 lines/mm, and the layer thickness is 135 μm. Each exposing beam has an intensity of 2.5 mW/cm^2. **Figure 13** shows typical diffraction efficiency increase observed upon exposure to a single on-Bragg recording beam. No dependence was found on the delay time between the two beams and single-beam exposure and weak gratings could be enhanced by single-beam exposure after 12 weeks, as long as the photopolymer was still sensitive.

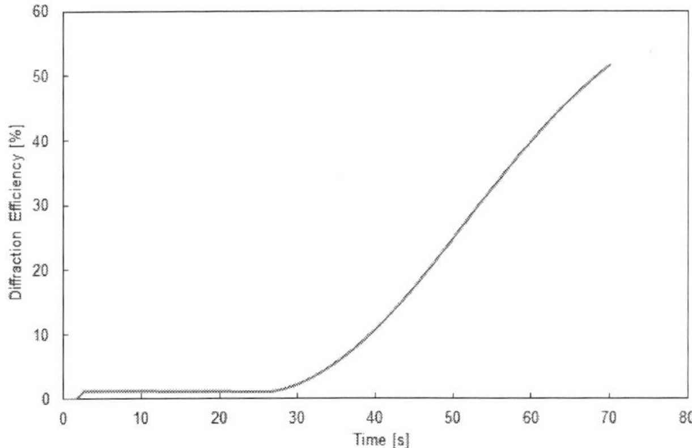

Figure 13. Diffraction efficiency versus exposure time. A standard two-beam holographic recording of 2 sec is followed by a 25 sec delay (no illumination) and then illumination with just one of the writing beams. Exposure intensity is 2.5 mW/cm^2 in each beam.

The increase in diffraction efficiency consistently observed under single-beam illumination in this photopolymer is due to a new grating formed by the interference between the single writing beam and the first-order beam generated by diffraction at the pre-recorded weak grating (see discussion below).

5.2.1. Single-beam recording with Bragg mismatch

The need for near-Bragg matching of the single writing beam rules out any bulk photochemical effect as the cause of the diffraction efficiency increase, supports the idea that diffraction is the main contributor. In order to study this further, and also assess the potential for multiplexing, the angle of incidence of the single writing beam was varied around the Bragg angle of the pre-recorded grating. The results are shown in **Figure 14**. The original seed grating diffraction efficiency was close to 1% in each case and the photopolymer thickness was 200 μm. The spatial frequency of the seed grating was 500 lines/mm. It can be seen from **Figure 14** that there is an optimum angle, close to the Bragg angle of the pre-recorded grating, that maximizes the strength of the grating recorded with the single-beam writing process. As the illuminating beam is moved further away from the optimal angle, the final diffraction efficiency is reduced under the same exposure conditions. This is probably due to the reduced coupling

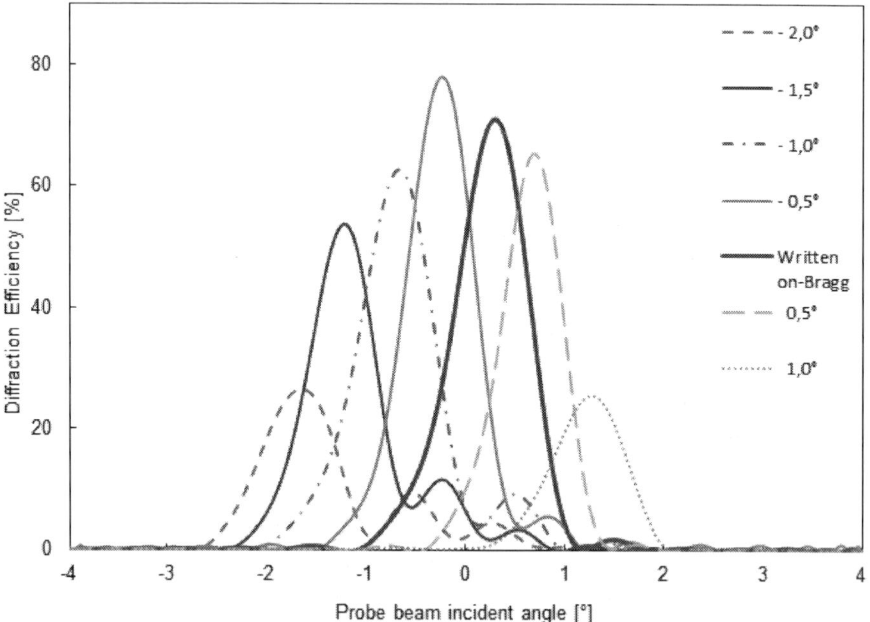

Figure 14. Bragg curves (the variation of diffraction efficiency with reading beam angle of incidence) for a series of gratings formed using the single beam process, using different angles of incidence of the single writing beam. The layer thickness is 200 μm. The arrows indicate the offset (in degrees) from the Bragg angle of the seed grating (0°).

between the single writing beam and the seed grating. In this example, the optimal angle is about 0.5° from the Bragg angle for the original grating. The asymmetry of the sidelobes is also a consistent feature. Both of these are thought to be due to fringe bending during the formation of the grating under single-beam exposure as discussed below.

This work demonstrates that the grating strength only increases significantly under single-beam illumination when the single writing beam is incident close to the Bragg angle of the pre-recorded grating.

As discussed in Ref. [31], the angular position of the Bragg peak for the gratings recorded in this way is linearly dependent on the angle of incidence of the single writing beam. This shows that the formation of a new grating formed by diffraction is responsible for the observed increases.

We propose that the weak diffracted beam interferes with the undiffracted beam to produce a low-contrast interference pattern which is immediately recorded in the material. If the new grating is in phase with the original grating, more light will then be diffracted into the weaker beam, reducing the beam ratio and increasing the contrast in the interference pattern, in turn producing an even stronger diffracted beam. In this way, quite weak gratings can rapidly 'seed' the growth of relatively high diffraction efficiency gratings. This growth of a new grating is analogous to the energy transfer between the strong beam and the weak beam in 'beam pumping' in photorefractive crystals, except that the refractive index modulation created is permanent.

A potential difficulty with the above explanation is the phase mismatch between the 'seed' grating and any grating created by diffraction at the 'seed' grating. This is due to the fact that there will be a phase difference ($\pi/2$) between the incident beam and the beam diffracted by the phase grating, which would cause any new grating to be out of phase with the original. Beam pumping in photorefractives, which is also initiated by diffraction at a weak grating, occurs only because the recorded grating in photorefractive crystals is laterally displaced with respect to the interference fringes that create it.

Unlike photorefractive crystals, photopolymers are usually considered to produce gratings that are not laterally shifted from the interference pattern that creates them. Thus we might not expect the interference pattern created by the incident beam and its diffracted beam to produce a grating that is in phase with the one that created it. However, such shifts and non-linear recording profiles have been observed in holographic recording materials such as acrylamide photopolymers [32], nanoparticle-doped photopolymers [33] and silver halide emulsions [34]. Murciano et al. [35] reported that effects such as beam bending and two wave mixing have been observed even with very small phase shifts, by them and other authors in similar materials. They analysed the origin and effects of fringe bending and Bragg detuning in holographic gratings recorded in rigid media such as photopolymerizable inorganic silica glass materials and proposed that they occurred as a result of the non-sinusoidal nature of the recorded pattern. Using an acrylamide photopolymer-doped sol gel, Murciano et al. observed two-wave mixing during two-beam recording and used a two-wave mixing model to explain the asymmetry and angular shift (fringe bending) observed in their angular selectivity (Bragg) curves. The reconstruction model used by Murciano et al. to analyse the gratings used coupled wave theory taking into account two wave mixing occurring during recording. Fringe bending becomes larger as thickness and refractive index modulation increase and, of course, depends greatly on the initial beam ratio. Good agreement was obtained between experimental and theoretical results of simulations with a shift of just 2.6° between the recorded grating and the light pattern, demonstrating that very small shifts can cause such effects.

It seems likely that our results described above would have a similar origin. That is the non-sinusoidal refractive index profile of the recorded grating provides enough of a phase shift to allow coupling from the strong beam to the weak diffracted beam during single-beam recording. It should also be borne in mind that the beam ratio is very large (typically 99:1) at the start of the single-beam recording step, so small amounts of energy transfer from the strong beam will have a significant effect and the fringe period is very much larger than the wavelength for these low spatial frequency gratings. In the case of these acrylamide-based photopolymers, gratings are recorded via photopolymerization and diffusion. Either of these processes can dominate depending on the recording intensity, spatial frequency and photopolymer formulation [36], and non-sinusoidal grating profiles are also common especially at low spatial frequencies [37]. It has been observed that the process of enhancing diffraction efficiency reported here is stronger at lower spatial frequencies.

5.2.2. Single-beam recording with different layer thickness

Experiments with different layer thicknesses ranging from 60 to 240 μm showed that the enhancement of the seed grating occurs much more in thicker layers. **Figure 15** shows the diffraction efficiency increasing under single-beam illumination from an initial diffraction efficiency of approximately 1% for thicknesses of 60, 130, 190 and 240 μm. These curves are each obtained in the same way as that in **Figure 13** but the delay between the two exposures was 110 sec in these experiments. The gratings were exposed to a single beam at the Bragg angle for 150 sec. The spatial frequency is 500 lines/mm and each exposing beam has an intensity of 2.5 mW/cm². It is observed that the increase in efficiency when recording with a single beam is much more pronounced in thicker layers and practically non-existent in the layer with thickness 60 μm It is probable that this dependence is due the increased distance over which energy can be transferred from the weaker beam to the stronger beam, as described above.

5.2.3. Single-beam recording at different spatial frequencies

Figure 16 shows the Bragg curves of a number of single-beam gratings recorded at different spatial frequencies. Although the diffraction efficiency of the 'seed' grating was approximately 1% in each case and the single-beam recording time is 30 sec for all gratings, a significant dependence on grating spatial frequency is observed. In this instance, the recording intensity is 1.8 mW/cm². The initial exposure time with two beams was 1 sec for 2000 and 1500 lines/mm and 0.75 sec for 1000–250 lines/mm in these examples but the diffraction efficiency was close to 1% in each case.

The pronounced increase observed for lower spatial frequencies indicates that fringe period may be a crucial factor. It was suggested above that the non-sinusoidal refractive index profile of the recorded grating could provide enough of a phase shift to allow coupling from the strong

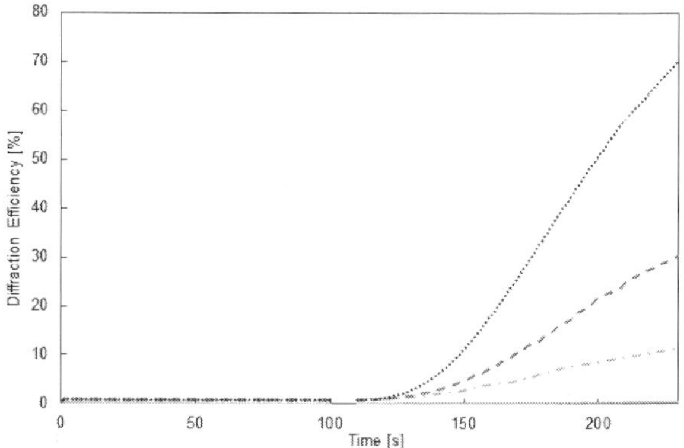

Figure 15. Growth in diffraction efficiency, under single beam illumination, of 'seed' gratings in samples prepared with different thicknesses. The grating spatial frequency is 500 lines/mm and the layer thicknesses are approximately 60 μm (solid), 130 μm (dotted-line), 190 μm (dashed line) and 240 μm (dotted line). Initial diffraction efficiency is approximately 1% for the two-beam grating.

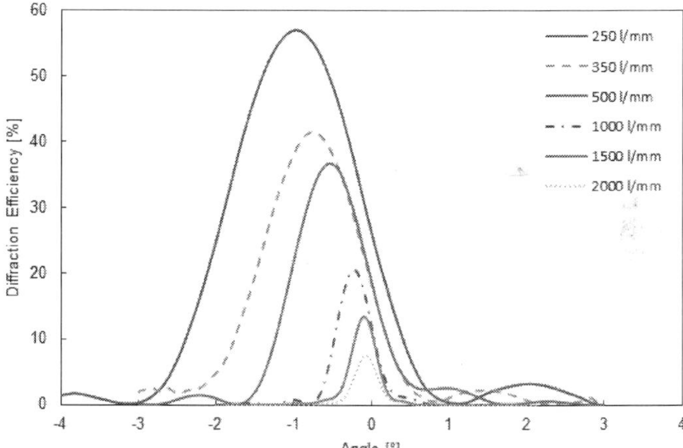

Figure 16. Bragg curves (the variation of diffraction efficiency with reading beam angle of incidence) for a series of gratings formed using the single beam process using different spatial frequency seed gratings. Layer thickness is approximately 140 μm.

beam to the weak diffracted beam during single-beam recording. It seems reasonable that this process will be more efficient when the fringe period is very much larger than the wavelength.

As well as the clear dependence of final on-Bragg diffraction efficiency on spatial frequency, the changes in the width of the Bragg curve are also obvious. In addition, we can see that the shift in the position of the Bragg peak increases as the spatial frequency decreases and the magnitude of the effect increases.

5.2.4. Angular multiplexing of data using a one beam system

In some applications, it may be necessary to obtain a diffraction efficiency increase in one grating selected from a number of gratings angularly multiplexed in the same region of the photopolymer layer, without affecting its neighbours. The selectivity demonstrated in **Figure 14** implies that this should be possible.

In order to investigate if it would be possible to selectively boost one grating from a series, a layer of photopolymer 135 µm in thickness was used and five seed gratings of equal strength were angularly multiplexed into it. One of the gratings was then illuminated at its Bragg angle in order to increase its efficiency. For separations up to 1.8°, illumination caused a significant increase in the diffraction efficiency of gratings on either side of the intended grating. **Figure 17** shows the result for gratings 2° apart. Although there are only five seed gratings in these examples, the principle is demonstrated that one of a set of angularly multiplexed gratings, separated by 2°, can be enhanced by illuminating it at the appropriate angle with a single beam of light. Working with higher spatial frequency and thickness would be likely to allow smaller angular separations between neighbouring gratings.

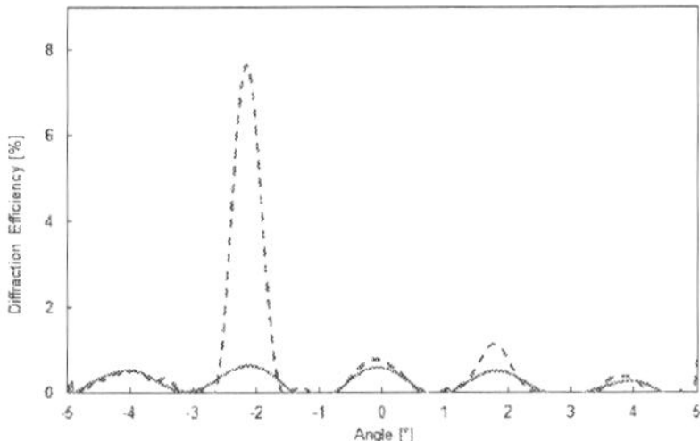

Figure 17. Variation of diffraction efficiency with the reading beam angle of incidence for a series of gratings, from which one individual grating has been enhanced by illuminating with a single on-Bragg beam of light. The angular separation between neighbouring gratings is 2°.

6. Conclusion

High efficiency diffractive optical elements have been recorded holographically with low spatial frequency. Three slanted gratings were successfully stacked using lamination and shown to increase significantly the range of angles from which light could be collected. However, positioning gratings in the path of the detector/cell meant that although light incident at large angles was coupled into the detector, an equivalent amount of light was deflected away from the detector at lower angles. When arranged off-axis, however, they increased the total light collected. The HOEs were then tested with a solar simulator and shown to improve the energy collected at a Si solar cell by up to 60% when used off-axis in pairs.

Modelling off-axis low spatial frequency focusing elements confirms that a range of gratings spatial frequencies and slant angles exists in the recorded elements and by simple geometry we can predict the grating spacing and slant angle at any point across the element and use coupled wave theory to predict the diffraction behaviour at a particular location. Good agreement is shown between theory and experiment and measurements made using phase contrast microscopic imaging of the photonic structure also agree closely.

A method of writing low spatial frequency holographic gratings with a single beam was also presented and shown to be capable of writing high diffraction efficiency gratings under unstable conditions. The technique is based on the exposure of very weak pre-recorded gratings to a single illuminating beam in order to write new high efficiency gratings in the photopolymer material. Strong spatial frequency dependence was shown. Diffraction efficiencies of 60% were obtained in just 30 sec with a 250 line/mm grating. With longer exposures up to 80% was achieved. The potential for angular multiplexing was shown by illuminating a single grating from among five multiplexed weak gratings and increasing its efficiency eightfold with a negligible effect on the other gratings.

In conclusion, these studies of low spatial frequency holographic optical elements have shown their potential for solar applications, their capacity to function as thick volume gratings and the success with which their microstructure can be controlled and modelled. Their particular potential for recording self-interference has also been exploited as a vibration-immune holographic recording method. The challenges that remain include modelling of the non-linear effects that occur during low spatial frequency holographic recording, development and modelling of more complex low spatial frequency elements and combinations of elements. Future work will focus on developing new diffractive elements and exploitation of these in practical applications.

Acknowledgements

The authors would like to acknowledge the IEO Centre's funding from Enterprise Ireland through its Commercialization Fund (which is co-funded by the European Union through the European Regional Development fund), the Dublin Institute of Technology's Fiosraigh Scholarship Fund, and the Irish Department of Education's Programme for Third Level Research Institutes Strand 1 scholarships.

Author details

Suzanne Martin*, Hoda Akbari, Sanjay Keshri, Dennis Bade, Izabela Naydenova, Kevin Murphy and Vincent Toal

*Address all correspondence to: suzanne.martin@dit.ie

Centre for Industrial and Engineering Optics, School of Physics, College of Sciences and Health, Dublin Institute of Technology, Dublin, Ireland

References

[1] H. Kogelnik. Coupled wave theory for thick hologram gratings. The Bell System Technical Journal. 1969; **48**(9):2909–47.

[2] P. Hariharan. Optical holography, principles techniques and applications. 2nd ed. New York: Cambridge University Press; 1996. 405 p.

[3] A. Bianco et al. The design of dispersing elements for a highly segmented, very wide field spectrograph. SPIE Proceeding. 2010; **7735**: 77357M-1. DOI: 10.1117/12.857689.

[4] J. Marín-Sáez, J. Atencia, D. Chemisana and M. V. Collados. Characterization of volume holographic optical elements recorded in Bayfol HX photopolymer for solar photovoltaic applications. Optics Express. 2016; **24**(6): 258–926. DOI: 10.1364/OE.24.00A720.

[5] H. Akbari. Investigation of photopolymer-based holographic optical elements for solar applications [thesis]. Dublin, Ireland: Dublin Institute of Technology; 2015.

[6] T. Mikulchyk, S. Martin and I. Naydenova. Investigation of the sensitivity to humidity of an acrylamide-based photopolymer containing N-phenylglycine as a photoinitiator. Optical Materials. 2014; **37**: 810–815. DOI: 10.1016/j.optmat.2014.09.012.

[7] H. Akbari, I. Naydenova and S. Martin. Using acrylamide-based photopolymers for fabrication of holographic optical elements in solar energy applications. Applied Optics. 2014; **53**: 1343–1353.

[8] S. T. L. Sam and A. P. T. Kumar. Design and Optimization of Photopolymer Based Holographic Solar Concentrators. AIP Conference Proceedings 1391, 2011; 248250, DOI: 10.1063/1.3646844.

[9] A. Ghosh, A. K. Nirala and H. L. Yadav. Dependence of wavelength selectivity of holographic PV concentrator on processing parameters. Optik—International Journal for Light and Electron Optics. 2015 Mar; **126**(6): 622–625.

[10] M. Hsieh, S. Lin, K. Y. Hsu, J. A. Burr and S. Lin. An efficient solar concentrator using volume hologram. Conference on Lasers and Electro-Optics. 2011; **1**: 4–5.

[11] D. Zhang, J. M. Castro and R. K. Kostuk. One-axis tracking holographic planar concentrator systems. Journal of Photonics Energy. 2011; **1**(1): 015505.

[12] J. Hung, P. S. Chan, C. Sun, C. W. Ho, W. Y. Tam. Doubly slanted layer structures in holographic gelatin emulsions: solar concentrators. Journal of Optics. 2010; **12**(4): 045104.

[13] R. K. Kostuk, J. Castillo, J. M. Russo and G. Rosenberg G. Spectral-shifting and holographic planar concentrators for use with photovoltaic solar cells. SPIE Proceeding. 2007; **6649**: 66490I–66490I-8.

[14] B. Sreebha, V. P. Mahadevan Pillai PTAK. Development of a window holographic lens to utilize solar energy, advances in optical science and engineering. V. Lakshminarayanan, I. Bhattacharya, editors. New Delhi: Springer India; 2015.

[15] G. Bianco, M. A. Ferrara, F. Borbone, A. Roviello, V. Striano, G. Coppola. Photopolymer-based volume holographic optical elements: design and possible applications. Journal of the European Optical Society—Rapid publications. 2015; **10**: 15057. DOI: 10.2971/jeos.2015.15057.

[16] I. Naydenova, H. Akbari, C. Dalton, M. Yahya so M. Ilyas, C. Pang Tee Wei, V. Toal and S. Martin. Photopolymer holographic optical elements for application in solar energy concentrators. In: E. Mihaylova, editor. Holography—basic principles and contemporary applications. InTech; 2013. DOI: 10.5772/55109.

[17] S. Altmeyer, Y. Hu*, P. Thiée, J. Matrisch, M. Wallentin and J. Silbermann. Multiplexing of transmission holograms in photopolymer. DGaO Proceedings ISSN: 16148436; 2013; urn:nbn:de:02872013B0099

[18] H. Akbari, I. Naydenova, L. Persechini, S. M. Garner, P. Cimo and S. Martin, Diffractive optical elements with a large angle of operation recorded in acrylamide based photopolymer on flexible substrates. International Journal of Polymer Science. Vol. **2014**; 2014.

[19] M. Ortuño, F. Fernández, S. Gallego, A. Beléndez and I. Pascual. New photopolymer holographic recording material with sustainable design. Optics Express. 2007; **15**(19): 12425–12435.

[20] I. K. Baldry, J. Bland-Hawthorn and J. G. Robertson. Volume phase holographic gratings: polarization properties and diffraction efficiency. Astronomical Society of Pacific. 2004; **116**(819): 403–414.

[21] N. Kukhtarev, G. Dovgalenko, G. C. Duree, Jr., G. Salamo, E. J. Sharp, B. A. Wechsler and M. B. Klein. Single beam polarization holographic grating recording. Physical Review Letter. 1993; **71**(26): 4330.

[22] S. Naruse, A. Shiratori and M. Obara. Holographic memory with one-beam geometry in photorefractive crystal. Applied Physics Letter. 1997; **71**(4).

[23] H. Mitsuhashi and M. Obara. Compact holographic memory system using a one-beam geometry in a photorefractive crystal. Applied Physics Letter. 2001; **79**(7).

[24] H. F. Yau, J. P. Liu, H. Y. Lee and Y. Z. Chen. Single beam one-way imaging through a thick dynamic turbulent medium. Applied Optics. 2006; **45**(19): 4625.

[25] C. S. Chiang, M. T. Shiu and W. H. Wu. Multiple-hologram recording with one-beam encoding. Optics Express. 2012; **20**(7): 6897.

[26] N. Kukhtarev and T. Kukhtareva. Single beam dynamic holographic interferometry. In: Photonic Fiber and Crystal Devices: Advances in Materials and Innovations in Device Applications IV; August 17th; SPIE; 2010. 77810H p.

[27] N. V. Kukhtarev, T. V. Kukhtareva and A. Chirita. Holographically amplified interferometry with coherent fringe projection for the oil on the water remote sensing and characterization. In: Photonic Fiber and Crystal Devices: Advances in Materials and Innovations in Device Applications VII; September 25th; SPIE; 2013. 88471J p.

[28] H. Horimai, X. Tan and J. Li. Collinear holography. Applied Optics. 2005; **44**(13): 2575.

[29] S. Martin, C. A. Feely, J. T. Sheridan and V. Toal. Applications of a self-developing photopolymer material: holographic interferometry and high efficiency diffractive optical elements. Optical Memory and Neural Networks. 1998; **7**(2): 79.

[30] B. L. Booth. Photopolymer material for holography. Applied Optics. 1975; **14**(3): 593.

[31] S. Martin, D. Bade, I. Naydenova and V. Toal. A single beam data writing process for holographic data storage. In: K. Kurtis, editor. IEEE LEOS Optical Data Storage; 10–13 May; Florida. IEEE; 2009. TuC5 p.

[32] M. R. Gleeson, J. V. Kelly, F. T. O'Neill and J. T. Sheridan. Recording beam modulation during grating formation. Applied Optics. 2005; **44**: 5475–5482.

[33] M. Kveton, A. Havranek, M. Skere and P. Fialia. Real-time measurements of diffraction grating growth in photopolymer recording materials. EPJ Web of Conferences. 2013; **48**: 00013. DOI: 10.1051/epjconf/20134800013.

[34] M. Ulibarrena, L. Carretero, R. Madrigal, S. Blaya and A. Fimia. Nonlinear effects on holographic reflection gratings recorded with BB640 emulsions. Optics Express. 2003; **11**(16): 1906–1917. DOI: 10.1364/OE.11.001906.

[35] A. Murciano, S. Blaya, L. Carretero, P. Acebal, M. Pérez-Molina, R. F. Madrigal and A Fimia. Analysis of nonuniform transmission gratings recorded in photopolymerizable silica glass materials. Journal of Applied Physics. 2008; **104**: 063109. DOI: 10.1063/1.2980332.

[36] I. Naydenova, R. Jallapuram, R. Howard, S. Martin and V. Toal. Investigation of the diffusion processes in self-processing acrylamide-based photopolymer system. Applied Optics. 2004; **43**(14): 2900.

[37] T. Babeva, I. Naydenova, R. Jallapuram, R. Howard, S. Martin and V. Toal. Study of the photoinduced surface relief modulation in photopolymers caused by illumination with a Gaussian beam of light. Journal of Optics. 2010; **12**: 124011.

Chapter 5

Holographic Optical Elements and Application

Nam Kim, Yan-Ling Piao and Hui-Ying Wu

Additional information is available at the end of the chapter

http://dx.doi.org/10.5772/67297

Abstract

Holographic optical element has a high diffraction efficiency and a narrow-band frequency characteristic, and it has a characteristic that is able to implement several features in a single flat device. It is widely applied in various fields. In this chapter, the principle and characteristics of the holographic optical elements are described in detail, and few typical holographic optical element-based applications, such as head-mounted display, lens array, and solar concentrator, are introduced. Finally, the futuristic research concepts for holographic optical element-based applications and contents are discussed.

Keywords: holography, holographic optical element (HOE), head-mounted display (HMD), lens-array HOE, solar concentrator

1. Introduction

The term of "holography" was proposed by Denies Gabor in 1948, and the invention has received a lot of interests since it was introduced first. Holography is the technique that deals with the interference and diffraction of the visible light in order to record the three-dimensional (3D) information of the objects into the amplitude or phase holograms on the holographic material and reconstruct the 3D visualization of the object. The holographic optical elements (HOEs) are the very interesting applications of the holography where many institutes work and develop for them. The first HOE concepts of holographic application, a holographic mirror, have been described by Denisyuk in 1962 [1]. Then, the point-source hologram which acts as lens was demonstrated by Schwar et al. in 1967 [2]. And, Latta et al. analyzed the compensate aberrations for HOE, the quantitative consideration [3]. Hence, a lot of institutes and companies work for the practical application of the HOE, and it is still a hot research topic in holography-based fields.

A HOE is the technique using a principle of holography, is a kind of diffraction optical elements (DOE), to replace heavy and complicated optical element has been highlighted as a useful technique. HOEs can be a mirror, lens, or directional diffuser, because it can implement various functions on a single material according to high diffraction efficiency and narrow-band frequency characteristics. Therefore, the HOEs are widely applied in many fields such as a hologram memory, holographic projection screen, holographic printer, 3D head-mounted display (HMD), and so on.

In this chapter, first, the principle of HOE, the basic concept of recording and reconstruction for HOE, and the characteristic of the HOE are described in detail. Then, several examples of applications of HOE such as waveguide and wedge-shaped waveguide-based HMD, HOE lens array, and solar concentration are reviewed.

2. Principle of HOE

2.1. Basic concept of HOE

The HOE is an optical element (such as a lens, filter, beam splitter, or diffraction grating), i.e., produced by using holographic imaging process or principles [4]. **Figure 1** shows the basic concept of HOE. The two beams from the laser are interfering in recording materials. One beam is the object beam reflected or scattered from the object, and another beam is reference beam. The object beam and the reference beam intersect and interfere with each other to record an interference pattern in recording materials. This interference pattern records the information of the object. When the object is a lens, the interference pattern reconstructs the optical element, which has function of lens as shown in **Figure 1**.

Generally, HOEs are classified into two main types, thin and volume HOEs. In the case of a thin HOE, the efficiency is low due to the incident light beams that are diffracted by grating in various directions, and the diffraction efficiency is changed so much when the incident angle is changed. Then, for the volume HOEs, the incident light beams are diffracted by grating only at the particular angle, so the high diffraction efficiency can be achieved. Also, HOEs can be classified into transmission and reflection types depending on the geometry of the recording, as shown in **Figure 2**.

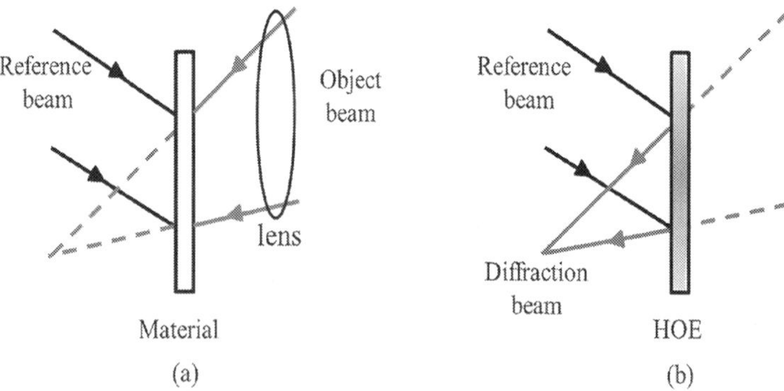

Figure 1. HOE principle: (a) recording and (b) reconstruction.

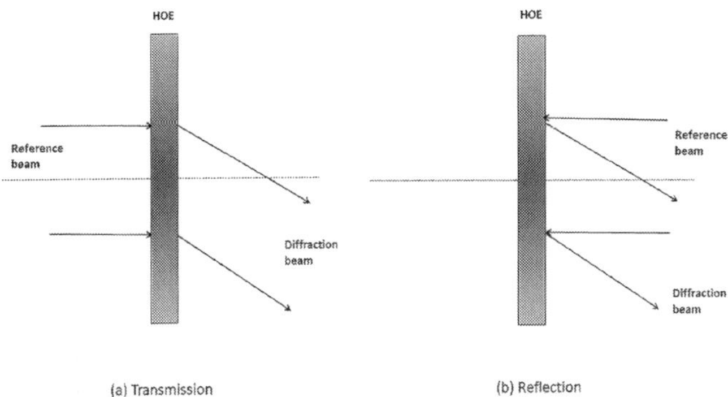

Figure 2. HOE classification: (a) transmission HOE and (b) reflection HOE.

In a transmission HOE, the object beam and the reference beam are on the same side of the recording material. The diffracted beam emerges on the opposite side from the incident beam; the beam goes through the entire thickness of the materials. In a reflection HOE, the object beam and the reference beam are on the different side of the recording material. The diffracted beam is on the same side as the incident beam. The fringes due to interference between the object beam and the reference beam are perpendicular to the grating plane for transmission gratings or parallel for reflection gratings.

HOEs have some characteristics as follows [5]. Multiple holograms can be recorded on a single recording material; spatially overlapping elements are possible. General optical elements are obtained by surface processing. However, HOEs are obtained by recording interference patterns from two coherent light beams on high-resolution photosensitive materials.

Therefore, it is easy to fabricate and duplicate, and it is possible to enter mass production. The production and functioning of HOEs are based on the implementation of the diffraction and interference of light; it is easy to utilize in the narrow bandwidth. Axial synthesized holograms serve the functions of standard, power, and compensating optical elements. The direction of the diffracted beam is determined by fringe of interference pattern on the surface, while the efficiency of diffracted beam is determined by the direction of interference pattern and refractive index in its inner structure. These characteristics and interactions provide both advantages and disadvantages for any particular application.

The characteristics of the recording material have significant effects on the many applications and the development of holography. The properties of ideal holographic material should be good light sensitivity, flat spatial frequency response, bright hologram, no haze, no absorption, no shrinkage or detuning, industrially available, fast hologram formation, unnecessary postprocessing, and stability (environmental and light). To fabricate the HOE, it is necessary to understand the optical characteristics of the recording material.

Typically, different materials, such as silver halide emulsion [6], dichromated gelatin [7], photoresist [8], photorefractive [9], or photopolymer [10], are used for manufacturing of HOEs. A photopolymer is one of the hologram recording materials, which has high diffraction efficiency, low cost, and excellent signal-to-noise ratio [10, 11]. Furthermore, it does not require any chemical or wet processing after recording the holograms. Because of such advantages, the photopolymer has been used widely in several research fields, which include optical elements [12, 13], holographic storage [14], holographic display [15], etc.

Bayer MaterialScience is developing its photopolymer to be easy to handle, with high diffraction efficiency, polychromatic, durable, and customizable. This material will be simple to expose, with no wet or heat processing. The ease of use and simple processing requirement allow these materials to be amenable to mass production of holographic optical elements [16–19].

Bayfol HX film 102 consists of a four-layer stack of a backside cover film of the substrate, the substrate itself, the light-sensitive photopolymer, and a protective cover film as shown in **Figure 3**. A polycarbonate (PC) substrate with a thickness of 175 ± 2 μm and polyethylene (PE) are used as backside cover foil and protective cover foil, which are both 40 μm in thickness. The protective cover film can be removed. The photopolymer layer itself has a thickness (d) of 16.8 μm.

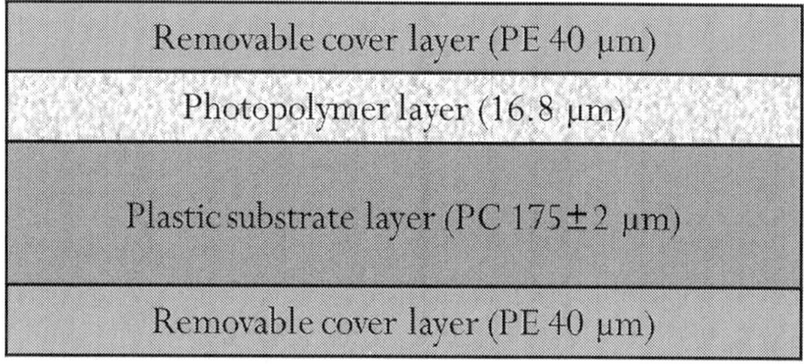

Figure 3. Bayfol HX 102 film structure.

Bayfol HX 102 photopolymer can be used to manufacture reflection and transmission volume-phase holograms with appropriate laser light within the spectral range of 440–660 nm.

In **Figure 4**, the basic product characteristics are depicted. The transmission spectrum of the unrecorded photopolymer film was recorded after removal of the protective cover film. In this material, the dye-related absorption peaks are located at 473, 532, and 633 nm, with associated transmittance of 56%, 45%, and 31%, respectively.

2.2. Characteristics of HOE

Generally, there are some important properties of a HOE that should be known. They are diffraction efficiency, wavelength selectivity, and angular selectivity. Of the many methods [20] to describe grating behavior, the couple wave theory as presented by Kogelnik [21, 22] will be the primary method used in this study, due to its simplicity and applicability.

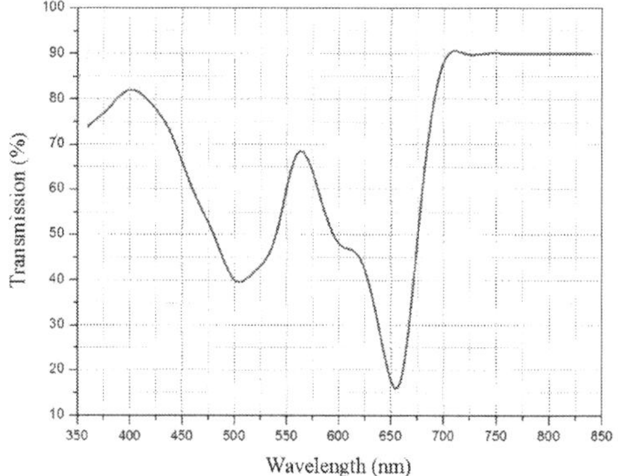

Figure 4. Transmission spectra of the unrecorded RGB-sensitive Bayfol HX 102 film.

In 1969, Herwig Kogelnik published the coupled wave theory, analyzing the diffraction of light by volume gratings. It assumes that monochromatic light is incident on the volume grating at or near the Bragg angle and polarized perpendicular to the plane of incidence. This theory can predict the maximum possible efficiencies of the various volume gratings and the angular and wavelength dependence at high diffraction efficiencies.

Figure 5 shows the model of a transmission volume hologram grating with slanted fringes. The x-axis is parallel to the recording material on the plane of incidence, the y-axis is perpendicular to the paper, and the z-axis is perpendicular to the surface of the recording material. The grating vector K is oriented perpendicular to the fringe planes and is of length $K = 2\pi/\Lambda$, where Λ is the period of the grating (spatial frequency $f = 1/\Lambda$). The angle of incidence measured in the material is θ_R. The fringe planes are oriented perpendicular to the plane of incidence and slanted with respect to the material boundaries at an angle ϕ.

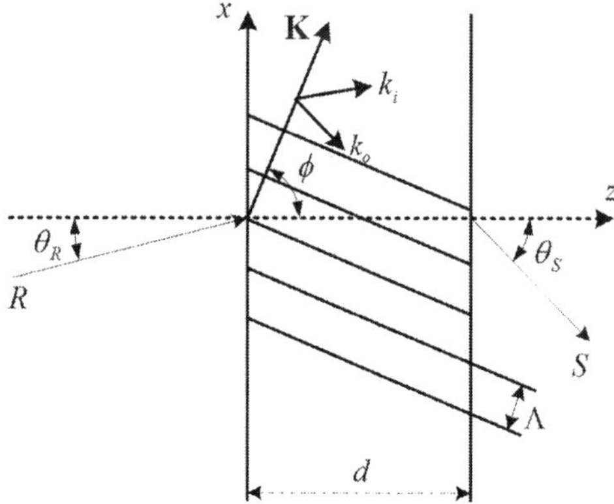

Figure 5. Model of a transmission volume grating with slanted fringes.

Figure 6 shows the fringe formations according to the recording process. The fringes are perpendicular to the grating plane for transmission gratings or parallel for reflection gratings.

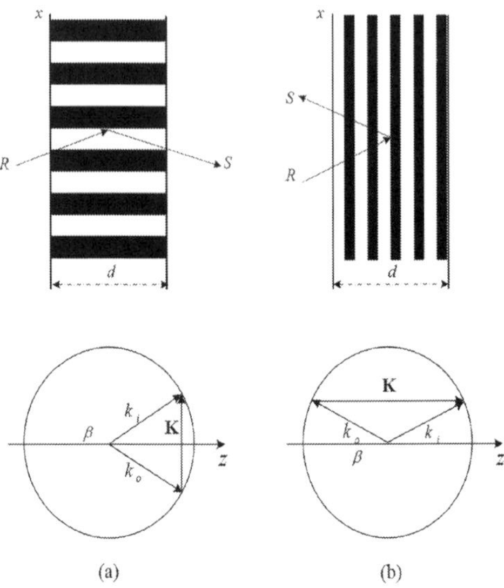

(a)   (b)

Figure 6. (a) Volume transmission gratings, (b) volume reflection gratings, and their associated vector diagrams for Bragg condition.

The volume record of the holographic interference pattern usually takes the form of a spatial modulation of the absorption coefficient or of the refractive index n(r) of the material, or both. For the sake of simplicity, here is the analysis restricted to the holographic record of sinusoidal fringe patterns. The grating is assumed dielectric, nonmagnetic, and isotropic. Hence, once the recording process has taken place, the resulting modulation may be described at the first order by the following relations:

$$n = n_0 + \Delta n \cos (K \cdot x) \tag{1}$$

$$\alpha = \alpha_0 + \Delta \alpha \cos (K \cdot x) \tag{2}$$

where x represents the radius vector x = (x, y, z), whereas n_0 is the average reflective index, α_0 is the average absorption coefficient, and Δn and $\Delta \alpha$ are the amplitudes of the spatial modulations of the index and absorption coefficient, respectively.

Generally, wave propagation in the grating is described by the scalar wave equation:

$$\nabla E + k^2 E = 0 \tag{3}$$

where E (x, z) is the complex amplitude of the y-component of the electric field, which is assumed to be independent of y and to have a wavelength λ. The wave number is equal to the average propagation constant β:

$$\beta = n_0 k_0 = \frac{2\pi n_0}{\lambda} \tag{4}$$

and the coupling constant κ can be simplified to

$$\kappa = \frac{\pi \Delta n}{\lambda} - i\frac{\Delta \alpha}{2} \tag{5}$$

The coupling constant is the central parameter in the couple wave theory as it describes the coupling between the "reference" wave (R) and the "signal" wave (S). If $\kappa = 0$, there is no coupling; therefore, there is no diffraction.

The propagation of two coupled waves through the grating can be described by their complex amplitudes: the incoming wave R(z) and the outgoing wave S(z), which vary along the z axis. The total field within the grating is written as follows:

$$E(x, z) = R(z)e^{-jk_i \cdot r} + S(z)e^{-jk_o \cdot r} \tag{6}$$

where r is the position vector and the symbols $\mathbf{k_i}$ and $\mathbf{k_o}$ are the wave vectors of the incoming and outgoing waves, respectively, which are related to each other by

$$\mathbf{k_o} = \mathbf{k_i} - \mathbf{K}. \tag{7}$$

The vector relation from Eq. (7) is shown in **Figure 7** together with the circle of radius β. **Figure 7(b)** shows the general case that the length of $\mathbf{k_o}$ differs from β and the Bragg condition is not met. **Figure 7(c)** shows the special case that the length of both $\mathbf{k_i}$ and $\mathbf{k_o}$ is equal to the average propagation constant β at the Bragg angle θ_0. And the Bragg condition is obeyed:

$$\cos\left(\phi - \theta_R\right) = \frac{K}{2\beta} = \frac{\lambda}{2n_0 \Lambda}. \tag{8}$$

For fixed wavelength, the Bragg condition may be broken by angular deviations $\Delta\theta$ from the Bragg angle θ_0. Analogously, for fixed angle of incidence, detuning takes place for changes $\Delta\lambda$ with respect to the Bragg wavelength λ_0. Differentiating the Bragg condition, we obtain

$$\frac{\Delta\theta}{\Delta\lambda} = \frac{K}{4\pi n_0 \sin\left(\phi - \theta_R\right)} = \frac{f}{2n_0 \sin\left(\phi - \theta_R\right)} \tag{9}$$

that relates the angular selectivity to the wavelength selectivity of a volume hologram grating; small changes in the angle of incidence or the wavelength have similar effects. High-performance devices, typically, should have a large selectivity and large diffraction efficiency.

Kogelnik introduced the parameter of mismatch constant Γ for evaluating the effects of deviations from the Bragg condition:

$$\Gamma = K \cos\left(\phi - \theta_R\right) - \frac{K^2 \lambda}{4\pi n_0} \tag{10}$$

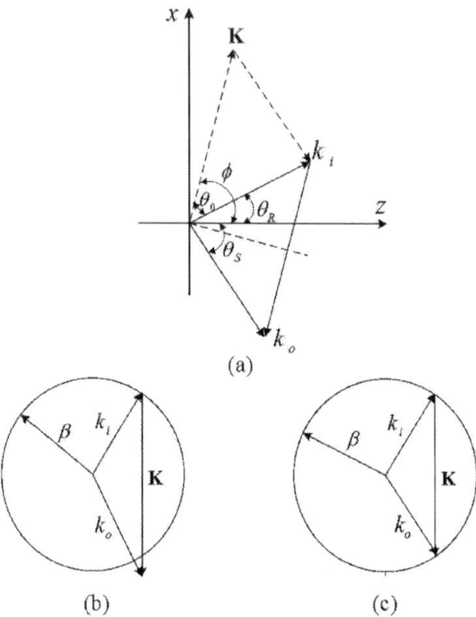

(a)

(b)　　　　　(c)

Figure 7. Vector diagram: (a) the relation between the propagation vector and the grating vector, (b) near at Bragg condition, and (c) exact Bragg incidence.

When the Bragg mismatch is due to the angular detuning $\Delta\theta$ and wavelength detuning $\Delta\lambda$, the mismatch constant expressed as

$$\Gamma = \Delta\theta \cdot K \sin\left(\phi - \theta_R\right) - \frac{\Delta\lambda \cdot K^2}{4\pi n_0} \tag{11}$$

Substituting Eqs. (1), (2), (4), and (6) into Eq. (3), R(z) and S(z) must individually satisfy the following equations in order for the wave equation to be satisfied:

$$\cos\theta_R \frac{dR}{dz} + \alpha R = -j\kappa S \tag{12}$$

$$\cos\theta_S \frac{dS}{dz} + (\alpha + j\Gamma)S = -j\kappa R \tag{13}$$

where the obliquity factor $\cos\theta_S = \cos\theta_R - K\cos\phi/\beta = -\cos(\theta_R - 2\phi)$. Solving Eqs. (12) and (13), the diffraction efficiency η is defined as

$$\eta = \frac{|\cos\theta_s|}{\cos\theta_R} SS^* \tag{14}$$

2.2.1. Transmission HOE

In transmission volume grating, the fringes are perpendicular to the surfaces of the recording material, and the incoming "reference" wave (R) and the outgoing "signal" wave (S) are on the opposite side of the recording material.

In lossless volume gratings, $\alpha_0 = \Delta\alpha = 0$, and the coupling constant is $\kappa = \pi\Delta n/\lambda$. Diffraction is caused by spatial variation of the refractive index; the diffraction efficiency of the slanted lossless transmission volume grating is as follows:

$$\eta_T = \frac{\sin^2\sqrt{v^2 + \xi^2}}{1 + \xi^2/v^2} \tag{15}$$

where v and ξ are given by

$$v = \frac{\pi d\Delta n}{\lambda\sqrt{\cos\theta_R \cdot \cos\theta_S}} \tag{16}$$

$$\xi = \frac{\Gamma d}{2\cos\theta_S} \tag{17}$$

Figure 8 shows the diffraction efficiency of the lossless transmission volume gratings as a function of the parameter ξ for three values of the parameter v. The diffraction efficiency of the volume grating is 100% for $v = \pi/2$, 50% for $v = \pi/4$ and $v = 3\pi/4$. It can be observed that for a fixed value of ξ the diffraction efficiency drops to zero if there is slight deviation from the Bragg condition.

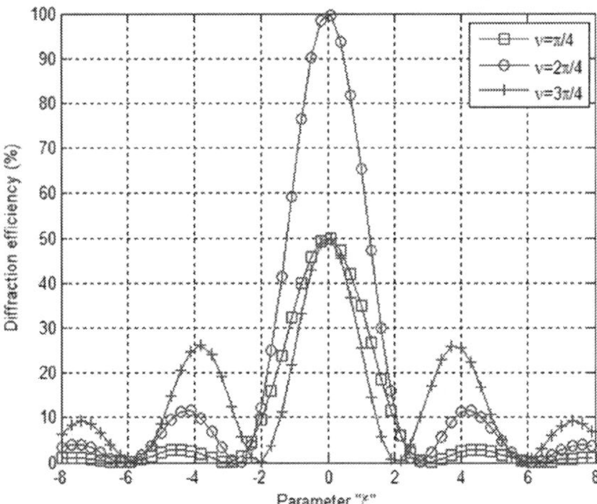

Figure 8. Transmission grating: diffraction efficiency η of lossless volume grating as a function.

When the wavelength and the angle are gradually out of the Bragg condition, the parameters ξ is obtained as follows:

$$\xi = \frac{\pi f d}{\cos\left(\phi - \theta_0\right) - (f\lambda_0/n_0)\cos\phi}\left(\Delta\theta\sin\theta_0 - \frac{f\Delta\lambda}{2n_0}\right) \tag{18}$$

From the above Eqs. (16), (17), and (18), it is clear that the diffraction efficiency of the volume grating is influenced by angular deviation $\Delta\theta$ and wavelength deviation $\Delta\lambda$ through the parameter ξ.

If there is no slant ($\phi = \pi/2$) and if the Bragg condition is obeyed, then $\cos\theta_R = \cos\theta_S = \cos\theta_0$, and Eq. (15) becomes

$$\eta_{\pi/2} = \sin^2 v = \sin^2\left(\frac{\pi d\Delta n}{\lambda\cos\theta_0}\right) \tag{19}$$

As thickness d or the variation of the refractive index Δn increases, the diffraction efficiency increases until the modulation parameter $v = \pi/2$. At this point $\eta = 100\ \%$, and all the energy goes into the diffracted light. When v increases beyond this point, the energy is back-coupled into the incident wave, and η decreases.

The angular selectivity of un-slanted transmission volume grating could be determined by substituting Eqs. (16), (17), and (18) into Eq. (15) at $\Delta\lambda = 0$:

$$\eta_T(\Delta\theta) = \frac{\sin^2\left(\pi d\sqrt{\left(\frac{\Delta n}{\lambda\sin\theta_0}\right)^2 + (f\Delta\theta)^2}\right)}{1 + \left(\frac{\lambda f\sin\theta_0\Delta\theta}{\Delta n}\right)^2} \tag{20}$$

It is important to note that Eq. (20) requires the following criterion for equalizing of diffraction efficiency to zero:

$$\sqrt{v^2 + \xi^2} = j\pi \tag{21}$$

where j = 1, 2, $\cdots$n, $\cdots$. Angular selectivity in the volume grating at the half width at first zero (HWFZ) level, $\Delta\theta^{HWFZ}$, as the angle between the central maximum and the first minimum at the diffraction efficiency curve. For the volume Bragg grating with 100% diffraction efficiency, the following expression for the HWFZ angular selectivity could be given at $j = 1$:

$$\Delta\theta_T^{HWFZ} = \frac{\sqrt{3}}{2}\frac{1}{d_0 f} \approx 0.87\frac{1}{d_0 f} \tag{22}$$

It should be noticed that the HWFZ angular selectivity $\Delta\theta_T^{HWFZ}$ is slightly lower than widely used grating parameter of HWFZ angular selectivity.

Figure 9 shows the angular selectivity of a transmitting volume Bragg grating. The parameters are varied from more than 100 mrad to less than 0.1 mrad. According to spatial frequency of grating, the value of refractive index modulation Δn can provide 100% diffraction efficiency. And, it should be optimized with equation $d_0 = \lambda \cos(\phi - \theta_0)/2\Delta n$.

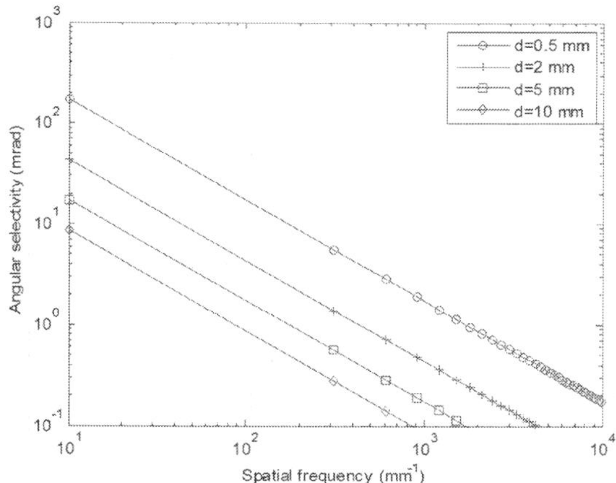

Figure 9. Angular selectivity (HWFZ) of transmitting volume gratings at $\lambda = 532$ nm and $n_0 = 1.5$ on spatial frequency for optimal refractive index modulation with grating thickness in 0.5, 2, 5, and 10 mm.

Just as the description for angular selectivity, the wavelength selectivity $\Delta\lambda^{HWFZ}$ can be determined as a distance between the central maximum and the first minimum in wavelength distribution of diffraction efficiency. It could be expressed by substitution of Eqs. (16), (17), and (18) into Eq. (15) at $\Delta\theta = 0$. In the case of un-slanted transmission volume grating, this expression is simplified by the use of Eq. (18) when $\phi = \pi/2$:

$$\eta_T(\Delta\lambda) = \frac{\sin^2\left(\frac{\pi d}{\sin\theta_0}\left(\sqrt{\left(\frac{\Delta n}{\lambda_0}\right)^2 + \left(\frac{f^2\Delta\lambda}{2n_0}\right)^2}\right)\right)}{1 + \left(\frac{f^2\lambda_0\Delta\lambda}{2n_0\Delta n}\right)^2} \tag{23}$$

Wavelength selectivity has the same structure as angular selectivity due to their linear interrelationship described by Eq. (9). For un-slanted transmitting volume gratings with 100% diffraction efficiency, $\Delta\lambda_T^{HWFZ}$ could be derived by substitution of Eq. (22) into Eq. (9):

$$\Delta\lambda_T^{HWFZ} = \sqrt{3}\frac{n_0}{d_0 f^2} \tag{24}$$

Figure 10 shows dependence of wavelength selectivity on spatial frequency for different grating thicknesses. HWFZ wavelength selectivity of transmitting volume grating could be easily varied from values below 0.1 nm to more than 100 nm by proper choosing of grating parameters.

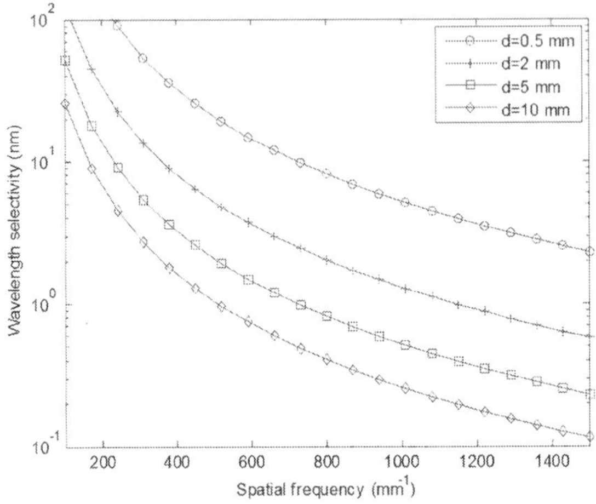

Figure 10. Wavelength selectivity (HWFZ) of transmitting volume gratings at λ = 532 nm and n_0 = 1.5 on spatial frequency for optimal refractive index modulation with grating thickness in 0.5, 2, 5, and 10 mm.

2.2.2. Reflection HOE

In reflection volume grating, the fringes are more or less parallel to the surfaces of the recording material, and the incoming "reference" wave (R) and the outgoing "signal" wave (S) are on the same side of the recording material. **Figure 11** shows the model of a reflection volume hologram grating with slanted fringes. It is expressed in the coupled wave analysis by negative values of the obliquity factor $\cos \theta_S (\cos \theta_S < 0)$.

The diffraction efficiency of slanted lossless reflection volume grating can be written as

$$\eta_R = \left[1 + \frac{1 - \xi^2/v^2}{\left(\sinh^2 \sqrt{v^2 - \xi^2} \right)} \right]^{-1} \tag{25}$$

where v and ξ are given by

$$v = \frac{i\pi d \Delta n}{\lambda \sqrt{\cos \theta_R \cos \theta_S}} \tag{26}$$

$$\xi = -\frac{\Gamma d}{2 \cos \theta_S} \tag{27}$$

Figure 12 shows the diffraction efficiency of the lossless volume gratings as a function of the ξ, for the values of $v = \pi/4$, $\pi/2$ and $3\pi/4$. The figure shows the sensitivity of a grating with $v = \pi/4$ and a peak efficiency of 43%, a grating with $v = \pi/2$ and η = 84 %, and the corresponding values for $3\pi/4$ and η = 96 %. For $v = \pi/2$, the diffraction efficiency drops to zero in all cases when $\xi \approx 3.5$.

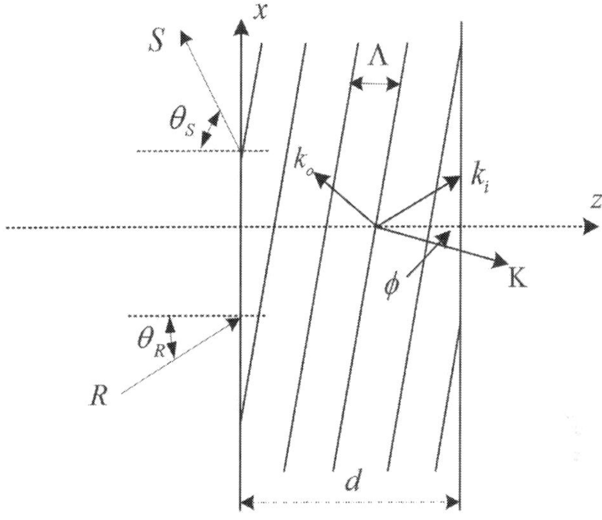

Figure 11. Model of a reflection volume grating with slanted fringes.

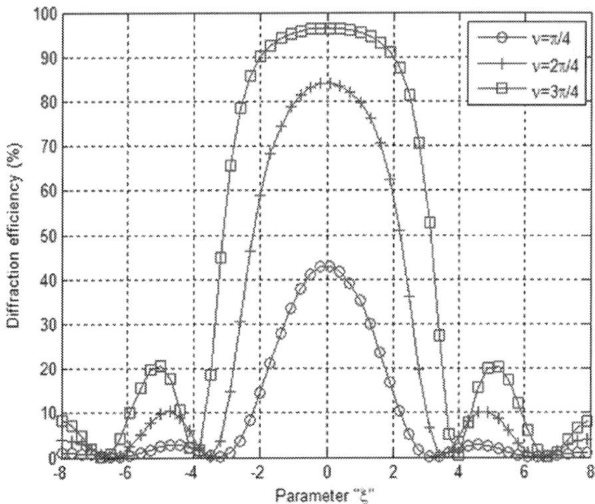

Figure 12. Reflection grating: diffraction efficiency η of lossless volume grating as a function of the parameter ξ for various values of the parameter v.

When the wavelength and the angle are gradually out of the Bragg condition, the parameters ξ is obtained as follows:

$$\xi = \frac{\pi f d}{\cos\left(\phi - \theta_0\right) - \left(f\lambda_0/n_0\right)\cos\phi}\left(\Delta\theta\sin\theta_0 + \frac{f\Delta\lambda}{2n_0}\right) \tag{28}$$

For an unslanted grating ($\phi = 0$), the Bragg condition is obeyed; then $\cos\theta_R = -\cos\theta_S = \cos\theta_0$, the Eq. (25) becomes to

$$\eta_0 = \tanh^2 v = \tanh^2\left(\frac{\pi d \Delta n}{\lambda\cos\theta_0}\right) \tag{29}$$

By increasing of grating thickness d or refractive index modulation Δn, the diffraction efficiency asymptotically approaches the 100% value with the hyperbolic tangent function.

If the diffraction efficiency η_0 could be predetermined at a certain level, the value could be used for designing a reflection volume grating. The interrelationships between refractive index modulation, thickness, and incident Bragg angle θ_0 could be expressed by Eq. (29):

$$\Delta n = \frac{\lambda\cos\theta_0\tanh^{-1}\sqrt{\eta_0}}{\pi d} \tag{30}$$

Figure 13 illustrates the interrelation between refractive index modulation, thickness, and predetermined diffraction efficiency η_0. The three values of predetermined diffraction efficiency are 90% which correspond to 10 dB transmitted beam attenuation, 99% (20 dB) and 99.9% (30 dB) at $\lambda = 532$ *nm*, respectively. As shown in **Figure 13**, refractive index modulation Δn is

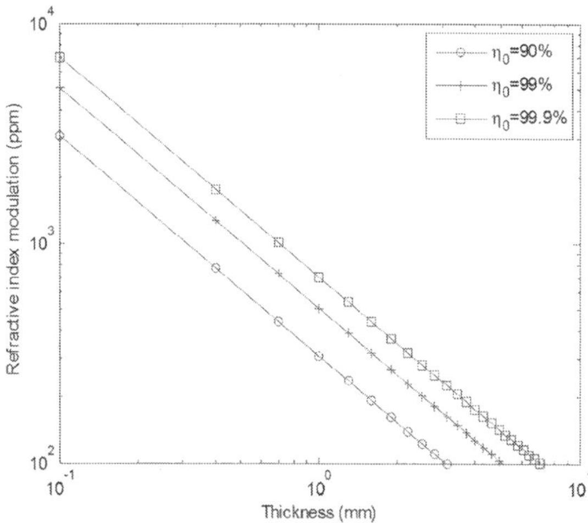

Figure 13. Dependence of refractive index modulation which secured predetermined diffraction efficiency on the grating thickness. Diffraction efficiency: η_0 = 90 %, 99%, and 99.9%. Normal incidence, λ = 532 *nm* and n_0 = 1.5.

less than 1000 ppm when the grating thickness is more than 1 mm with $\eta_0 = 99\ \%$. Therefore, reflecting volume gratings should be thick enough with relatively low values of refractive index modulation to secure predetermined diffraction efficiency.

The angular selectivity of unslanted reflection volume grating could be determined by substituting Eqs. (26) and (28) to Eq. (25) at $\Delta\lambda = 0$:

$$\eta_R(\Delta\theta) = \left[1 + \frac{1 - \left(\frac{\lambda f \sin\theta_0 \Delta\theta}{\Delta n}\right)^2}{\sinh^2\sqrt{\left(\frac{2\pi n_0 d \Delta n}{\lambda_0^2 f}\right)^2 - \left(\frac{2\pi n d \sin\theta_0 \Delta\theta}{\lambda}\right)^2}} \right]^{-1} \tag{31}$$

To determine angular selectivity $\Delta\theta^{HWFZ}$ at HWFZ level, the diffraction efficiency reaches zero value at multiple points when v is not equal to ξ:

$$\sqrt{v^2 - \xi^2} = j\pi \tag{32}$$

where j = 1, 2, $\cdots$ n, $\cdots$. The HWFZ angular selectivity could be considerably simplified for unslanted gratings with diffraction efficiency of Eq. (28) at $j = 1$:

$$\Delta\theta_R^{HWFZ} = \frac{\lambda\sqrt{\left(tan\,h^{-1}\sqrt{\eta_0}\right)^2 + \pi^2}}{2\pi n_0 d \sin\theta_0} \tag{33}$$

Figure 14 shows the dependence of angular selectivity on volume grating thickness at different incident Bragg angles θ_0 for a 99% efficiency grating. As one can see, the thicker the grating, the wider the angular selectivity is. For instance, 7 mrad HWFZ selectivity is secured at $\theta_0 = 2°$ for 1 mm thick grating or at $\theta_0 = 10°$ for 2.01 mm grating thickness.

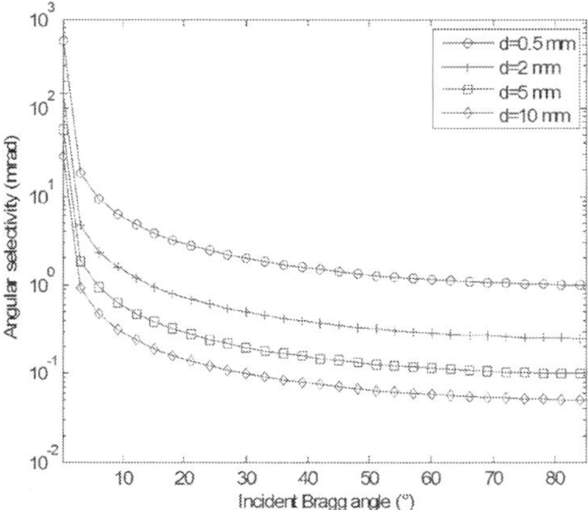

Figure 14. Angular selectivity (HWFZ) of reflecting volume grating with 99% diffraction efficiency at $\lambda = 532$ nm and $n_0 = 1.5$ on spatial frequency for optimal refractive index modulation with grating thickness in 0.5 mm, 2 mm, 5 mm, and 10 mm.

By the same way as it was described above for angular selectivity, spectral selectivity could be expressed by substitution of Eqs. (26) and (28) to Eq. (25) at $\Delta\theta = 0$:

$$\eta_R(\Delta\lambda) = \left[1 + \frac{1 - \left(\frac{\lambda_0 f^2 \Delta\lambda}{2n_0\Delta n}\right)^2}{\sinh^2\sqrt{\left(\frac{2\pi n_0 d \Delta n}{\lambda_0^2 f}\right)^2 - \left(\frac{\pi d f \Delta\lambda}{\lambda_0}\right)^2}} \right]^{-1} \tag{34}$$

The HWFZ wavelength selectivity also could be considerably simplified for un-slanted gratings with diffraction efficiency of Eq. (29):

$$\Delta\lambda_R^{HWFZ} = \frac{\lambda_0\sqrt{\left(\text{atanh}\sqrt{\eta_0}\right)^2 + \pi^2}}{\pi d f} \tag{35}$$

Figure 15 shows dependence of wavelength selectivity on spatial frequency for different grating thicknesses. HWFZ wavelength selectivity of reflection volume grating could be easily varied from values below 0.1 nm to more than a dozen nm by proper choosing of grating parameters.

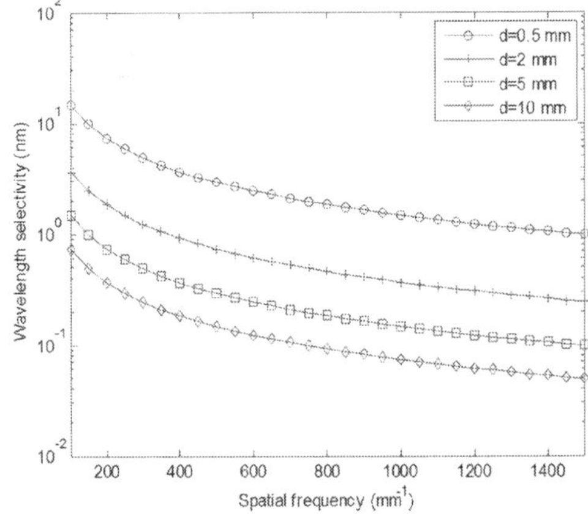

Figure 15. Wavelength selectivity (HWFZ) of reflecting volume grating with 99% diffraction efficiency at $\lambda = 532$ nm and $n_0 = 1.5$ on spatial frequency for optimal refractive index modulation with grating thickness in 0.5, 2, 5, and 10 mm.

3. Application of HOE

3.1. Waveguide and wedge-shaped holographic optical element (HOE) waveguide HMD

HMD is a display device, worn on the head or as part of a helmet that has a small display optic in front of one or each eye. HMD has been widely used in virtual reality and augmented reality applications [23–25]. There are two main kinds of HMD: "curved mirror"-based HMD and "waveguide"-based HMD. The curved mirror HMD uses semi-reflective curved mirrors placed in front of the eye with an off-axis optical projection system. This system suffers from a high mount of distortion which needs to be corrected optically or electronically adding cost and reducing image resolution. Moreover, a small heavy "eye motion box" will be needed, which is uncomfortable and requires mechanical adjustment, further adding to cost. The waveguide HMD removed the side electronics and display using a waveguide; it reduces the cumbersome display optics and provides a fully unobstructed view of the scenes. Among the waveguide techniques, the holographic waveguide method focuses on the advantage of having a small volume, low price, and command of angular and spectral selectivity of optical elements. In this chapter, we will mainly talk about the holographic waveguide HMD based on HOE. Note that among a lot of types of recording materials, these holographic waveguide HMD techniques are utilized the photopolymer which is high-efficiency material and most widely used in various research fields. In addition, other HOE-based techniques which will be reviewed in next sections, section 3.2 and 3.3, also used the photopolymer.

Ando et al. proposed and fabricated an HMD using HOEs instead of half mirror [26]. The benefit of this system is that all functions of lens, combiner, and binocular stereoscopy can be kept within single HOE. However, this method has limited size reduction, because they did not use waveguide-type HMD. As shown in **Figure 16**, two small LCD displays are replaced in both sides of the head and prevent the reflection light from the HOE to the human eyes. The HOE was recorded in 120° of recording angle between an object beam and a reference beam. The binocular images are modulated by illumine light for reconstruction.

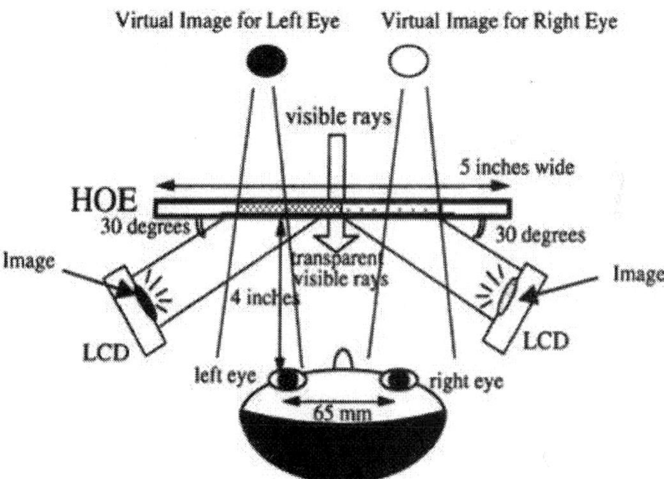

Figure 16. The optical specification of HOE for binocular stereoscopy-type HMD.

Amitai et al. and Kasai et al. reported a monochrome eye display using a volume hologram or grating [27] as the optical combiner in front of the eyes on a waveguide [28, 29]. Although the size of the optics is minimized, this method did not yield high diffraction efficiency. Subsequently, full-color eyewear display was proposed by Mukawa et al. [30]. In this method, the issue of color uniformity should be solved. **Figure 17** shows the basic structure of the HOE for waveguide-type HMD. As shown in this figure, the system has three optical parts, the couple-in part, couple-out part, and waveguide plate. In couple-in part, an image is magnified by micro-display, and the light is refracted into the waveguide; then the light was reflected by the first HOE guided in the waveguide plate with the total internal reflection. In couple-out part, the guided light refracted by the second HOE projects the image to the observers.

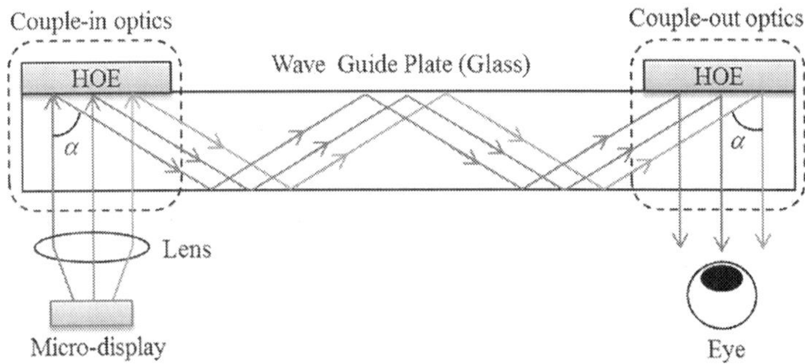

Figure 17. A basic structure of the HOE for waveguide-type HMD.

Recently, Piao et al. proposed a reflection-type HOE with high diffraction efficiency for a waveguide-type HMD using a photopolymer and present a laminated structure method for fabricating full-color HOE [31]. A photopolymer is one of the hologram recording materials that has high diffraction efficiency and low cost. Furthermore, it does not require any chemical or wet processing after recording the holograms. As mentioned earlier, the photopolymer is applied in various fields such as optical elements, holographic storage, holographic display and so on. Piao et al. analyzed the optical characteristic of the photopolymer using three lasers operated at 473, 532, and 633 nm, respectively. **Figure 18** shows the efficiency of full-color HOEs: (a) combined structure, (b) three-layer laminated structure, and (c) two-layer composited structure.

In this experiment, the diffraction efficiencies of the photopolymer were more than 90% for each R, G, and B color that provides wide angular selectivity. And, the output efficiencies of full-color HOEs are 40%, 44%, and 42% for R, G, and B colors. The proposed method reduced the volume of the system by using photopolymer, and the system also has good color uniformity, brightness performance, and high diffraction efficiency. **Figure 19** shows the experimental results for the full-color HOEs which were fabricated using the proposed two-layer composited structure.

However, based on the design configuration of the system, the thickness, weight, color uniformity, and field of view (FOV) issues of the system were not solved entirely.

According to the previous work, M. Piao et al. designed waveguide glass specifications for the HMD system in accordance with wedge-shaped waveguide design [32]. **Figure 20** is the designed waveguide structure. This system includes a lens positioned proximate to the micro-display and two reflection holographic volume gratings (HVGs) in HOEs attached on either side of a waveguide.

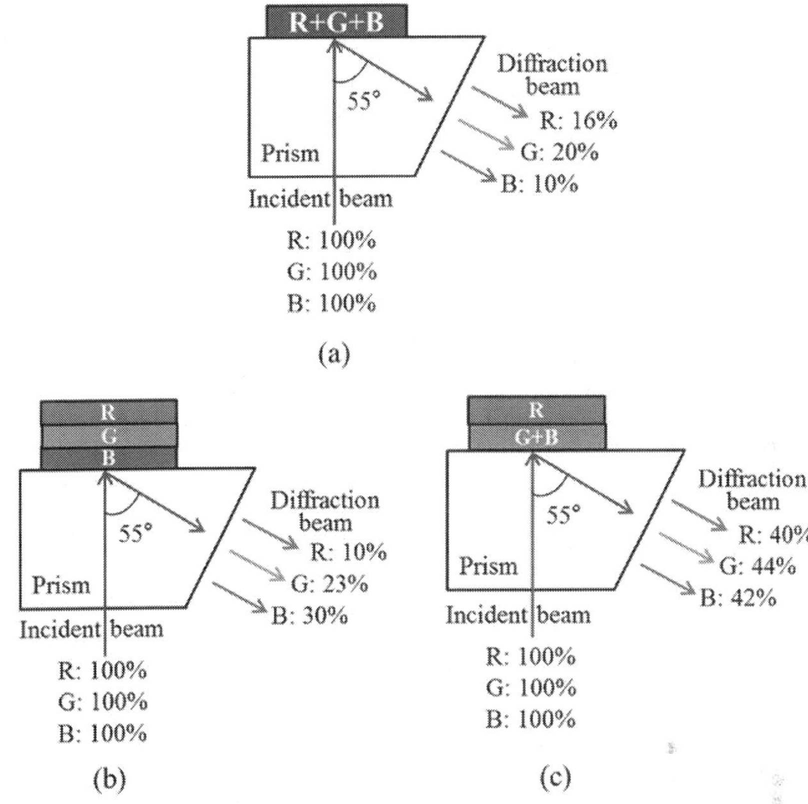

Figure 18. Efficiency of the full-color HOEs for (a) combined structure, (b) three-layer laminated structure, and (c) two-layer composited structure.

Unlike the previous method [31], the both ends of waveguide are wedge-shaped by the certain angle and the HOEs are mounted onto the wedge-shaped sides. Structurally, the thickness of the waveguide can be reduced by a large angle of total internal reflection. In addition, the wide angular selectivity of the HVGs allows for a large FOV, and the narrow spectral selectivity can be used with broad spectral sources, such as light-emitting diodes (LEDs). By observing the optical path of light in the waveguide, they theoretically analyzed the angular and spectral selectivity of the HVG, presented the correlation of the spatial frequencies of the HVG with the slope of the wedge-shaped waveguide, and determined the specific waveguide structure. According to the Bragg condition, Kogelnik's theory [21], their experiment shows $\theta_1 = 40°$ and $\theta_2 = 30°$ are suitable for recording the incident angle of the HVGs (**Figure 21**), which were attached on both sides of the wedge-shaped waveguide, because the large total internal reflection angle leads to a thin waveguide design.

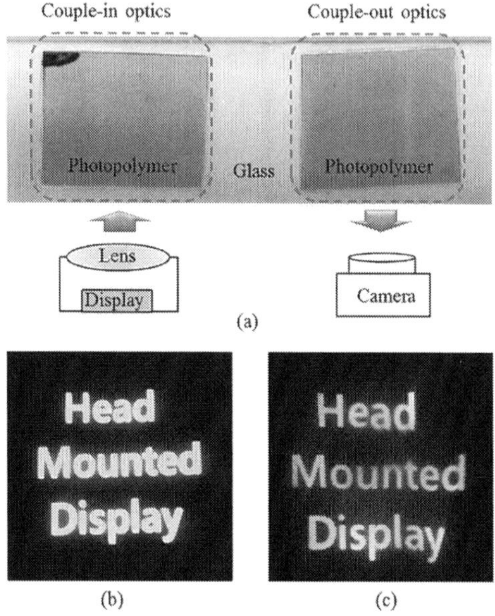

Figure 19. Experimental results (a) using full-color HOE for HMD system, (b) input image, and (c) output image.

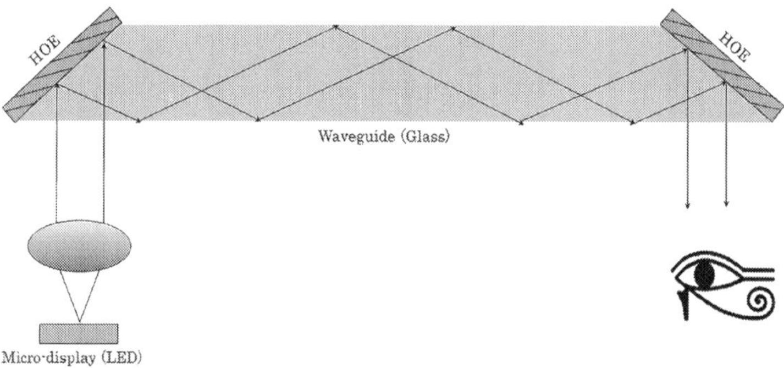

Figure 20. Structure of the wedge-shaped holographic waveguide wearable display.

The fabricated holographic waveguide using a photopolymer was tested using the optical setup shown in **Figure 22**. To confirm the light path in the designed waveguide, each monochromatic holographic waveguide HMD system was investigated. And the plane wave of the three combined beams (633 nm, 532 nm, 473 nm) illuminated a reflection-type spatial light modulator (SLM).

The image illuminated by an LED captured by the demonstration system is shown in **Figure 22**. **Figure 23(a)** shows the original test image. **Figure 23(b–d)** shows each monochromatic HVG of the input image with accurately guided in the designed waveguide. **Figure 23(e)** shows that the results of the full-color HVG fabricated using a GBR sequential recording on one photopolymer

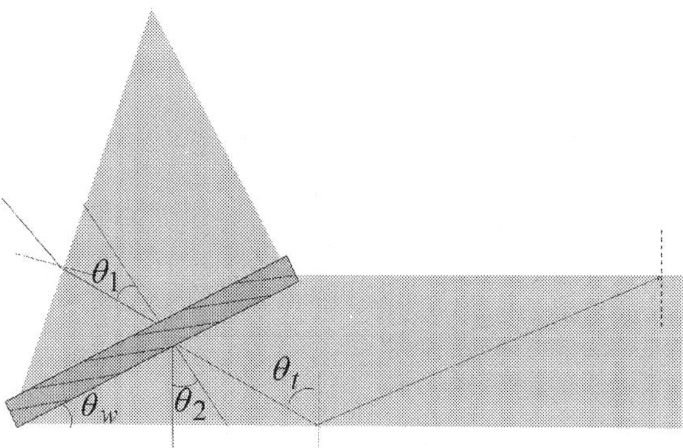

Figure 21. Designed angle of the light path in the waveguide.

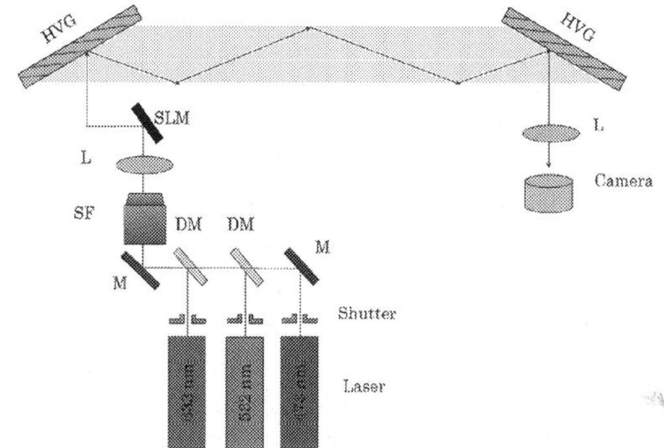

Figure 22. Experimental setup for testing the fabricated wedge-shaped holographic waveguide using SLM. M, mirror; DM, dichroic mirrors; SF, spatial filter; L, collimating lens; and PBS, polarizing beam splitter.

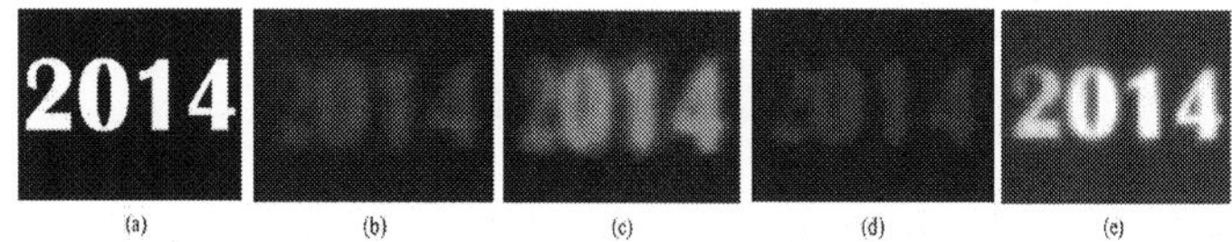

Figure 23. Experimental results captured from the wedge-shaped waveguide wearable display: (a) the original test image; output image fabricated by (b) 633 nm, (c) 532 nm, and (d) 473 nm; and (e) GBR sequential exposure in the DMD system.

layer with good quality. The image clearly was reproduced with a white color, the same as the ideal one shown in **Figure 23(e)**.

In addition, they successfully fabricated a compact full-color HVG, which performed with high levels of optical efficiency, using one layer of photopolymer based on a color analysis of the HVG.

Recently, Yeom et al. proposed a bar-type waveguide 3D holographic HMD using HOE with astigmatism aberration compensation [33]. Here, a conventional bar-type waveguide HMD structure is used, and 3D holographic images are displayed in both SLMs without the accommodation-vergence mismatch. Also, the ray tracing based on the H. Kogelnik-coupled wave theory has been analyzed. **Figures 24(a)** and **24(b)** show the simulated footprint image of in-coupling and out-coupling HOEs on the waveguide, respectively, where the light rays which come from the SLM are diffracted on the in-coupling HOE and go to the out-coupling HOE through the waveguide glass. When the light rays are transmitting between two HOEs, in-coupling and out-coupling, too much of distortion occurs due to the asymmetric diffraction of HOEs, i.e., the optical path length of the light ray experience in the waveguide. Naturally, this issue makes the astigmatism in the final images. In order to eliminate the distortion, a constant difference Δz parameter is added in the hologram generation process as the following:

$$H(u, v) = \sum_i A_i \exp\left\{\frac{jk_{o, air}}{2}\left(\frac{(x_i - u)^2}{z_i} + \frac{(y_i - v)^2}{z_i - \Delta z}\right)\right\} \tag{36}$$

Figure 25 shows the reconstructed image from the hologram which is applied in holographic compensation. **Figure 25(a)** shows the 3D image generated from the hologram without compensation; the aberration is visible. Then, in **Figure 25(b)**, the 3D image reconstructed from the hologram with compensation is presented. **Figure 26(a)** shows the experimental setup, and **Figure 26(b)** shows the combined visualization for real object and holographic images displayed on the HOE-based HMD.

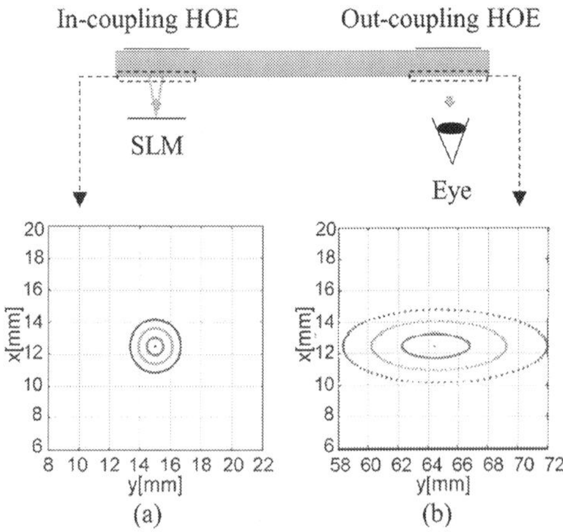

Figure 24. Footprint of ray on the bottom side of the waveguide: (a) in-coupling HOE and (b) out-coupling HOE.

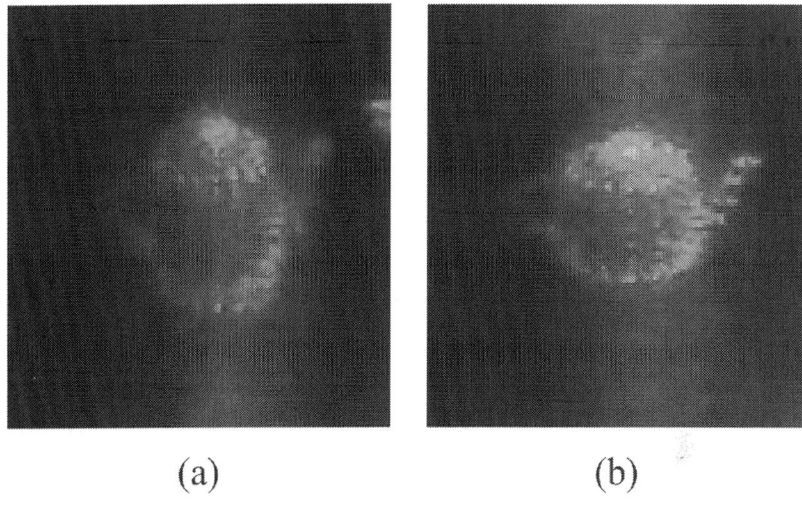

Figure 25. Reconstructed image of holographic compensation: (a) without compensation and (b) with compensation.

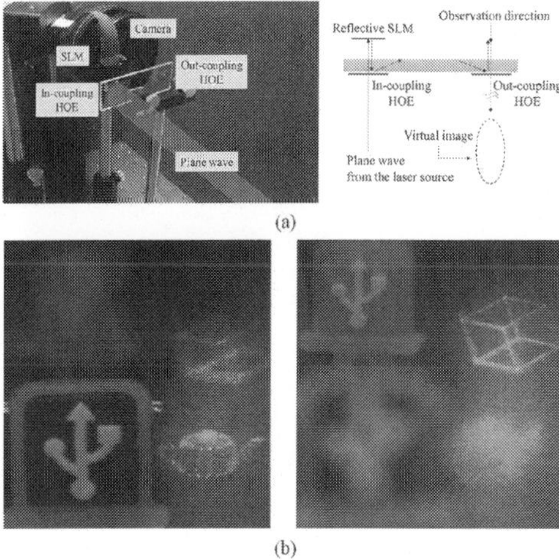

Figure 26. (a) Experimental setup and (b) real object and holographic images with the holographic compensation.

3.2. Lens-array HOE

Integral image is one of the most attractive ways to create autostereoscopic 3D display providing real-time full parallax information without requiring special glasses [34]. However, integral image still has a problem with limitation of resolution, viewing angle, and depth of field. Among these, the narrow viewing angle is the main disadvantage. Several methods have been proposed to increase the viewing angle of integral imaging displays. Curved lens array and curved screen can be one solution, though the necessary physical configurations make these systems difficult to implement.

A wide-viewing-angle 3D display system using HOE lens array is proposed by H. Takahashi et al. where the system consists of a projector and HOE lens array [35]. Here, the main role of HOE lens array is virtual curved lens that each individual axis is not perpendicular to HOE plane. The basic procedure of the display system is that the elemental images are projected as parallel beams to the corresponding elemental lens areas; the HOE lens array reconstructs the 3D image. As mentioned above, the HOE lens array has manufactured that all of the transmitted light rays through the elemental lenses can be crossed onto the single point, similar with the curved-type lens array, so the viewing angle of reconstructed image is much wider than original object's viewing angle acquired into the elemental images. **Figure 27** shows the schematic configuration of HOE lens array-based wide-viewing-angle 3D display system, where p is the pitch of elemental lens recorded onto HOE, r is the radius of virtual curvature of HOE lens array, and ψ is viewing angle of the reconstructed image.

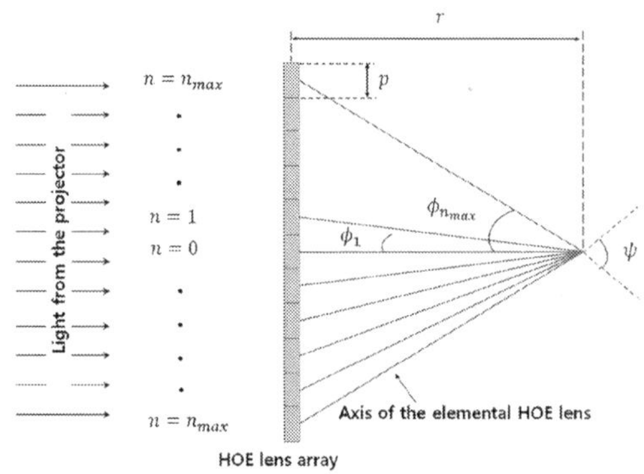

Figure 27. The scheme of HOE lens array-based 3D display system.

In the experiment, HOE lens array consists of 17 × 13 elemental lenses, as shown in **Figure 28**, where each of them is 4.4 × 4.4 mm, the focal length of the central elemental lens is 18.3 mm, and the radius of virtual curvature of HOE lens array, i.e., the distance from HOE lens array to reconstructed image, is 50 mm. Here, the viewing angle of central elemental lens is approximately 7° on each side of the individual axis, and the entire viewing angle of reconstructed image is much wider, approximately 35°, where the theoretical angle is 37°. Note that if the common lens array has been used in the reconstruction, the reconstructed image viewing angle would be approximately 7°, because the elemental lens axes are parallel with each other. Also, the HOE lens array reconstructs the flipped ray-free 3D images, and if the virtual curvature of HOE lens array is desired by 2D lens array configuration, the full viewing angle, horizontal and vertical, can be widened.

Figure 28. HOE virtual lens array in experimental system.

Recently, Hong et al. proposed a full-color 3D display on the basis of a projection-type integral imaging for the optical see-through AR by making use of a full-color lens-array HOE as the image combiner [36]. Here, the HOE lens array has been manufactured by the interference pattern which includes all of characteristics of the given common lens array recorded onto the photopolymer where the interference pattern is formed by spherical-wave-type object beam and plane-wave-type reference beam. The photopolymer is provided from Bayer MaterialScience AG, and the thickness of the photopolymer is 14–18 μm. Then, the wavelength multiplexing and spatial multiplexing methods in order to display the full-color virtual 3D images and record the large-sized HOE lens array are proposed [37]. **Figure 29** is showing the schematic diagram of experimental setup for recording the full-color lens-array HOE. And, experimental setup for displaying 3D virtual images in the proposed optical see-through AR system is shown in **Figure 30(a)**. **Figure 30(b)** shows the computer-generated elemental images of S, N, and U, which were used in experiment. They used a telecentric lens with the relay optics for collimated light of projection to avoid the Bragg mismatch.

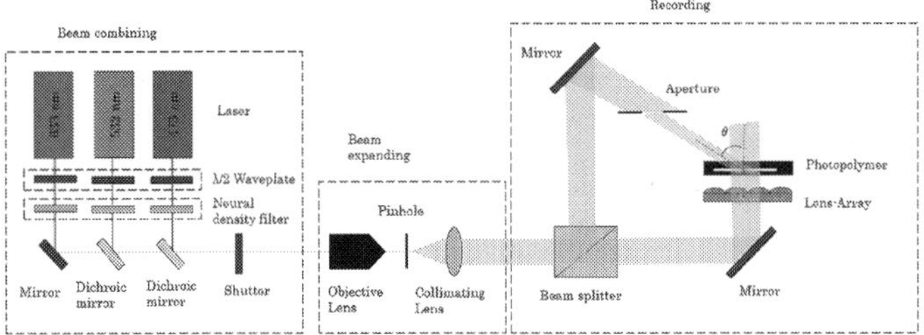

Figure 29. The schematic diagram of experimental setup for recording the full-color lens-array HOE.

The collimated reference beam in the recording setup and the imaging device for a display setup should also project collimated light on the full-color lens-array HOE to avoid the Bragg mismatch.

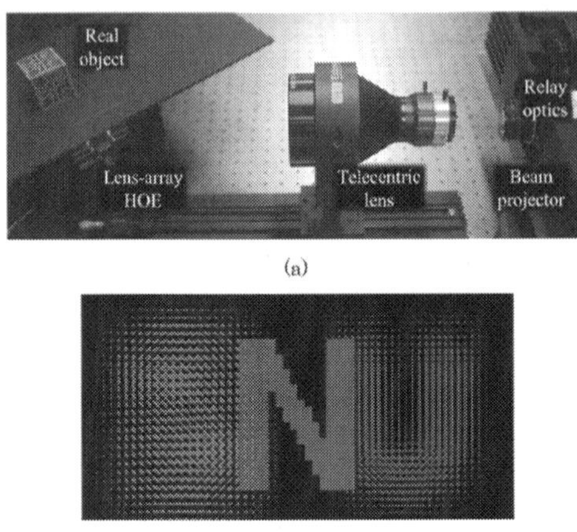

(a)

(b)

Figure 30. (a) Experimental setup for displaying 3D virtual images in the proposed optical see-through AR system. (b) The elemental images for three characters (S, N, and U) projected on the lens-array HOE for 3D virtual imaging.

Figure 31 shows the results of see-though 3D virtual images captured in the display experiments from five different viewing points relative to the proposed optical see-though AR system. It is clearly confirmed that the disparities among the images captured from top, left, center, right, and bottom provided a binocular disparity and give a 3D perception to the observer.

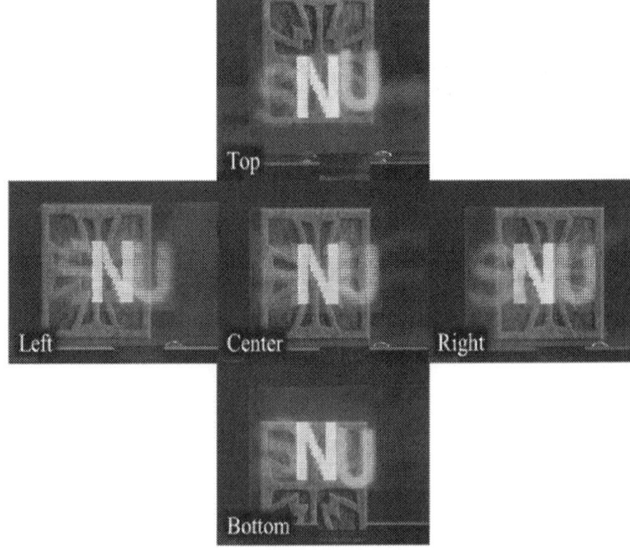

Figure 31. Perspective see-through 3D virtual images of three characters (S, N, and U) with a real object cube for a background, which were captured from five different view positions in the display experiment.

3.3. Holographic solar concentrator

Recently, HOEs have been studied for use in various solar applications to substitute optical mechanisms in solar concentrators [38–40]. The recording material of HOEs is usually flat and thin. It is possible to multiplex several holographic elements into the same material and collect solar energies with different incidence angles. Moreover, HOEs have the ability to diffract the light in a specific direction, and they also have the potential to provide angular or wavelength multiplexing. By applying the angular multiplexing method to the HOE recording, the angular multiplexing-based HOEs could act as the sun tracker. The HOEs that operate at specific wavelengths are able to diffract the desired specific wavelengths and remove other unwanted wavelengths, such as UV rays.

HOEs were suggested to be used in solar applications for the first time in 1982 [38]. The major attraction of holography is that it appears possible to make a holographic concentrator that has no moving parts and is able to track the daily movement of the sun and concentrate the sun's rays onto an absorber. Afterward, a variety of designs have been suggested over the years [41, 42]. For example, it was demonstrated that a volume holographic lens allows a single-axis tracking over 55° angular variation [43, 44].

Designs of multiplexed holographic lenses have been also proposed by Naydenova et al. [45]. Here, the multiplexed HOEs are recorded in the same photopolymer layer. **Figure 32** shows the optical setup for recording the holographic lens in the photopolymer plate with focusing lens. Then, the recorded HOE has the characteristic of focusing the light in the recording direction.

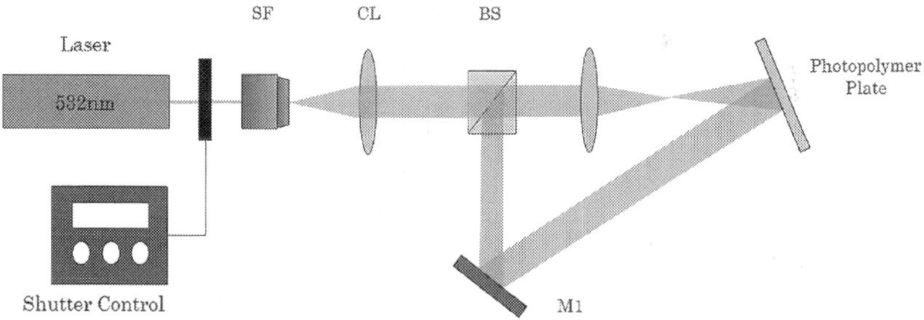

Figure 32. A schematic configuration of experimental setup for recording a holographic lens.

For focusing the light from the multiple directions, a schematic configuration for recording multiplexed HOEs is illustrated in **Figure 33**. The reference beam reflects the light in five different mirrors to record the multiplexed transmission gratings with the object beam. The object beam and the different reference beam are recorded by adjusting the photopolymer material to bisect the inner beam angle. By variability of exposure time and intensity, the multiplexed HOEs can obtain optimum diffraction efficiencies.

Recently, the angular multiplexed holographic solar condensing lens has been proposed by J. H. Lee et al. [46]. In order to combine the solar concentrator and sun tracking functions in a single photopolymer, a convex lens was used as a recording object while multiplexing the incident

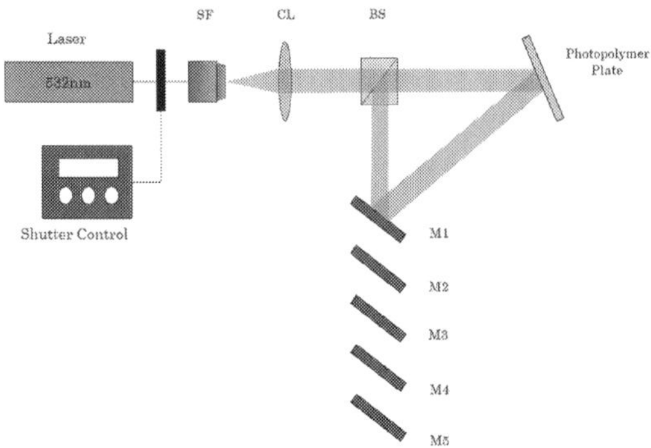

Figure 33. A schematic configuration of experimental setup for recording multiplexed HOEs.

beams of three angles. Generally, the performance of a HOE is determined by the diffraction efficiency. The diffraction efficiency is defined as the ratio of the intensity of the diffraction beam to the sum of the intensity of diffraction beam and transmission beam. However, it is difficult for the diffraction efficiency to evaluate the performance of the HOE as a solar concentrator. Therefore, they newly suggest the concentrated diffraction efficiency (CDE) calculation method that uses an effective concentration rate (ECR). ECR is a metric measure, i.e., already proposed for measuring the concentration rate of the solar concentrator. The ECR was calculated from the equation

$$ECR = \eta_{opt} \times R_c \tag{37}$$

where η_{opt} is the optical efficiency which is the ratio of condensed light intensity to incident light intensity and R_c is the geometric concentration rate which is the ratio of area of incident beam and condensed beam. The CDE, η_c, is defined by ECR_h of HOE and ECR_l of the convex lens as follows:

$$\eta_c = ECR_h / ECR_l \times 100(\%) \tag{38}$$

Eq. (2) shows the actual performance of the recorded HOE as a solar concentrator. **Figure 34** shows the schematic diagrams of the hologram recording for the solar concentrator. In this experiment, holograms are recorded by transmission geometry because it is advantageous for the HOE solar concentrator.

In solar concentrator systems, the sun tracking systems are necessary owing to the movement of the planet. In order to realize the effective sun tracking system, an interval within 10 am–2 pm is widely used, as shown in **Figure 35**. This scheme shows the schematic diagram that condenses the light coming from three different angles to a fixed single point. Note that the interval degrees between each angle are decided as 10° because it matches the movement interval of the sun at 10 am–2 pm.

The iterative recording method is used to improve efficiency and uniformity. The iterative method is applied to make holograms through repetitive exposure in one photopolymer that each of the N holograms is recorded with a series of short exposure time within the material's saturation time. At 0.5 second, 0.25 second and 0.125 second of the exposure time and from twice to six times of the iteration number were applied. And, the order of recording is A, B, and C. This schedule is laid out with consideration of saturating condition. And, the result is shown in **Figure 36**. It shows the possibility of increasing the efficiency by using iterative recording method.

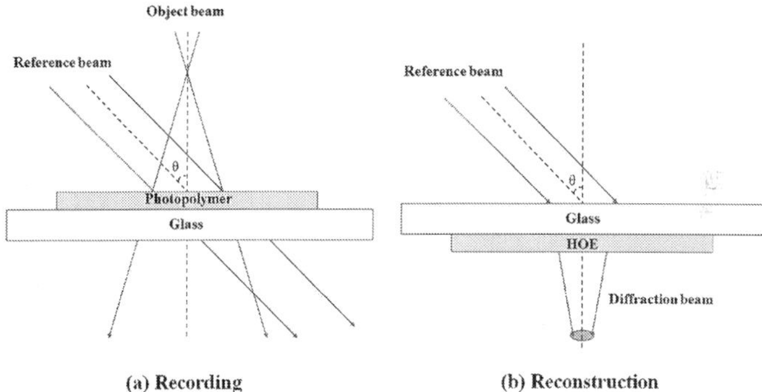

Figure 34. Schematic diagrams of the transmission hologram for the HOE solar concentrator on the photopolymer film.

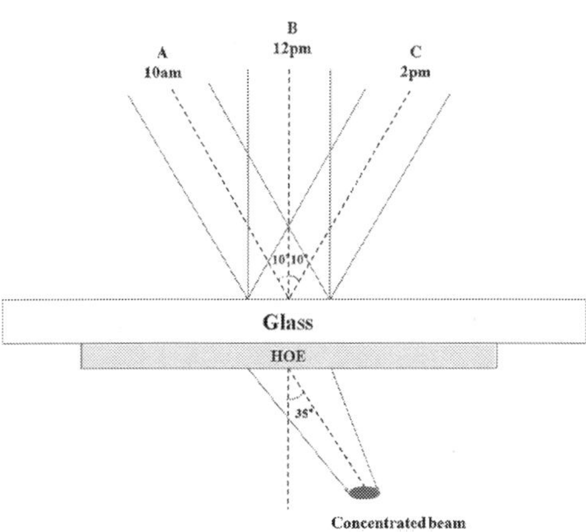

Figure 35. Schematic diagram for angular multiplexed holographic solar concentrator.

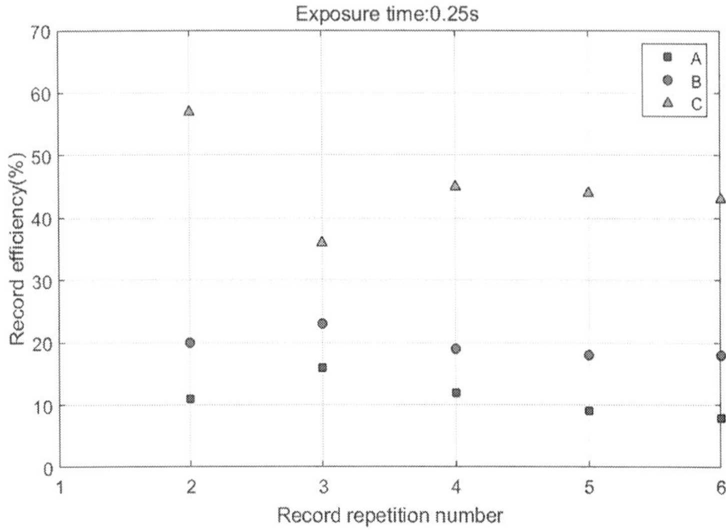

Figure 36. Result of iterative recording at 0.25 seconds of exposure time.

4. Conclusion

HOE is an optical device able to include a variety of features in a transparent thin film or plastic. The biggest advantage of HOE is that the traditional optical element or the multifunctional devices which does not exist can be produced on single HOE. Therefore, it is investigated in various fields, such as optical device, communication, and display. Nowadays, the usage of 2D holographic projection screen is increased in advertisement, performance, AR fields, and so on, and the development trend of holographic 3D screen is turned into HMD from 3D TV. It has been certified that the HOE is much useful and an effective technique especially for simplified optical systems. In order to develop the HOE more practical and applicable, the manufacturing system for recording medium and the lossless replication technology for mass production are required. However, only few materials that are applicable in replication technology are suggested, and the perfect solution for replication technology has not been completed yet. Therefore, the medium recording and replication technology should be developed continuously, and the main issues of the full-color HOE, color uniformity, and chromatic aberration need more researches.

Acknowledgements

This research was supported by the Ministry of Science, ICT and Future Planning (MSIP), Korea, under the Information Technology Research Center (ITRC) support program (IITP-2016-R0992-16-1008) supervised by the Institute for Information & communications Technology Promotion (IITP).

Author details

Nam Kim*, Yan-Ling Piao and Hui-Ying Wu

*Address all correspondence to: namkim@chungbuk.ac.kr

Chungbuk National University, South Korea

References

[1] Denisyuk, Y. N. Photographic reconstruction of the optical properties of an object in its own scattered radiation field. Sov. Phys. Dokl. 1962;**7**:543.

[2] Schwar M. J. R., Pandya T. P. & Weinberg F. J. Point holograms as optical elements. Nature. 1967;**215**:239–241. DOI: 10.1038/215239a0

[3] Latta J. N. Computer-based analysis of hologram imagery and aberrations. I. Hologram types and their nonchromatic aberrations. Applied Optics. 1971;**10**(3):599–608.; II: Aberrations induced by a wavelength shift. Appl. Optics. 1971;**10**(3):609–618.

[4] Wikipedia. Holographic Optical Element [Internet]. 9 June 2016. Available from: https://en.wikipedia.org/wiki/Holographic_optical_element

[5] Lukin V. Holographic optical elements. J. Opt. Technol. 2007;**74**:65–70.

[6] Kim J. M., Choi B. S., Choi Y. S., Bjelkhagen H. I., Phillips N. J. Holographic optical elements recorded in silver halide sensitized gelatin emulsions. Part 2. Reflection holographic optical elements. Appl. Opt. 2002;**41**:1522–1533.

[7] Kubota T., Ose T. Lippmann color holograms recorded in methylene-blue sensitized dichromated gelatin. Opt. Lett. 1979;**1**:8–9.

[8] Kozna. Effects of film-grain noise in holography. J. Opt. Soc. Amer. 1968;**58**:436–438.

[9] Gunter P., Huignard J. P. Photorefractive Materials and their Applications 3. In: Buse K., Havermeyer F., Liu W., Moser C., Psaltis D., editors. Holographic filters. Springer-Verlag, Berlin:2007. pp. 295–317.

[10] Berneth H., Bruder F. K., Fäcke T., Hagon T., Hönel D., Jurbergs D., Rölle T., Weiser M. S. Holographic Recording Aspects of High Resolution Bayfol HX Photopolymer. In: Proc. SPIE; 2011. p. 79570H.

[11] Jurbergs, D., Bruder, F. K., Deuber, F., Fäcke, T., Hagen, R., Hönel, T., Rölle, T., Weiser, M. S., Volkov, A. New Recording Materials for the Holographic Industry. In: Proc. SPIE; 2009. pp. 72330K–K10.

[12] Piao M. L., Kim N., Park J. H. Phase contrast projection display using photopolymer. J. Opt. Soc. Korea. 2008;**12**:319–325.

[13] Lee K. Y., Jeung S. H., Cho B. M., Kim N. Photopolymer-based surface-normal input/output volume holographic grating coupler for 1550-nm optical wavelength. J. Opt. Soc. Korea. 2012;**16**:17–21.

[14] Fernandez E., Marquez A., Gallego S., Fuentes R., García C., Pascual I. Hybrid ternary modulation applied to multiplexing holograms in photopolymers for data page storage. J. Lightwave Technol. 2010;**28**:776–783.

[15] Stevenson S. H., Armstrong M. L., O'Connor P. J., Tipton D. F. Advances in Photopolymer Films for Display Holography. In: Proc. SPIE; 1995. pp. 60–70.

[16] Tipton D. F., New hologram replicator for volume holograms and holographic optical elements. Proc. SPIE. 1998;vol. **3294**:136–144.

[17] Caulfield, H. J. Handbook of optical holography. 1st ed. New York: Academic Press; 1979. 638 p.

[18] Baldry I. K., Bland-Hawthorn J., and Robertson J. G., Volume phase holographic gratings: Polarization properties and diffraction efficiency. Publ. Astron. Soc. Pac. 2004;**116**:403–414.

[19] Johnston S. F., Holographic Visions. Oxford: Oxford University Press; 2006. 30–32 pp.

[20] Smith H. M., Principles of Holography. New York: Wiley; 1975. 58 p.

[21] Kogelnik H., Coupled wave theory for thick hologram gratings. The Bell Sys. Tech. J. 1969;**48**:2909–2947.

[22] Goodman J., Introduction to Fourier Optics. 2nd ed. New York: McGraw-Hill; 1996. 333–336 pp.

[23] Melzer J. E. and Moffitt K., Head Mounted Displays: Designing for the User. New York: McGraw Hill; 1997.

[24] Tomilin M. G. Head-mounted displays. J. Opt. Technol. 1999;**66**:528–533.

[25] Hua H., Girardot A., Gao C., and Rolland J. P. Engineering of head-mounted projective displays. Appl. Opt. 2000;**39**:3814–3824.

[26] Ando T., Matsumoto T., Takahashi H., and Shimizu E. Head mounted display for mixed reality using holographic optical elements. Mem. Fac. Eng. 1999;**40**:1–6.

[27] Oh Y. H., Lim S., and Go C. S. Alternative method of AWG phase measurement based on fitting interference intensity. J. Opt. Soc. Korea. 2012;**16**:91–94.

[28] Amitai Y., Reinhorn S., and Friesem A. A. Visor-display design based on planar holographic optics. Appl. Opt. 1995;**34**:1352–1356.

[29] Kasai I., Tanijiri Y., Endo T., and Ueda H. Actually wearable see-through display using HOE. Int. Conf. ODF. 2000;**2**:117–120.

[30] Mukawa H., Akutsu K., Matsumura I., Nakano S., Yoshida T., Kuwahara M., and Aiki K. A full-color eyewear display using planar waveguides with reflection volume holograms. J. Soc. Info. Disp. 2009;**17**:185–193.

[31] Piao J. A., Li G., Piao M. L., and Kim N. Full color holographic optical element fabrication for waveguide-type head mounted display using photopolymer. J. Opt. Soc. Korea. 2013;**17**:242–248.

[32] Piao M. L., Kim N. Achieving high levels of color uniformity and optical efficiency for a wedge-shaped waveguide head-mounted display using a photopolymer. Appl. Opt. 2014;**53**(10):2180–2186.

[33] Yeom H-J, Kim H-J, Kim S-B, Zhang H.J, Li B. N, Ji Y-M, Kim S-H, and Park J-H. 3D holographic head mounted display using holographic optical elements with astigmatism aberration compensation . Opt. Expr. 2015;**23**:32025–32034.

[34] Okoshi T. Three-dimensional displays. Proc. IEEE. 1980;**68**(5):548–564.

[35] Takahashi H., Hirooka S. Stereoscopic see-through retinal projection head-mounted display. In: Stereoscopic displays and applications XIX; January 27, 2008; San Jose, CA. SPIE; 2008. p. 68031N.

[36] Hong K., Yeom J., Jang C., Hong J., Lee B. Full-color lens-array holographic optical element for three-dimensional optical see-through augmented reality. Opt. Lett. 2014;**39**

[37] Coufal H. J., Sincerbox G. T., and Psaltis D. Holographic Data Storage. Springer-Verlag; 2000.

[38] Ludman J. E. Holographic solar concentrator. Appl. Opt. 1982;**21**(17):3057–3058.

[39] Castro J. M., Zhang D., Myer B., and Kostuk R. K. Energy collection efficiency of holographic planar solar concentrator. Appl. Opt. 2010;**49**:858–870.

[40] Kostuk R. K. and Rosenberg G. Analysis and Design of Holographic Solar Concentrators. In: 7043; SPIE; 2008. p. 70430I.

[41] Zhang Y. W., Ih C. S., Yan H. F., and Chang M. J. Photovoltaic concentrator using a holographic optical element. Appl. Opt. 1988;**27**:3556–3560.

[42] Quintana J. A., Boj P. G., Crespo J., Pardo M., and Satorre M. A. Line-focusing holographic mirrors for solar ultraviolet energy concentration. Appl. Opt. 1997;**36**:3689–3693.

[43] Chemisana D., Collados M. V., Quintanilla M., and Atencia J. Holographic lenses for building integrated concentrating photovoltaics. Appl. Energ. 2013;**110**:227–235.

[44] Ren X., Liu S., Zhang X., Chen X. Fabrication of Holographic Fresnel Lens used as Solar Concentrator. In: Holography and Diffractive Optics III; Beijing. SPIE; 2007. pp. 1–7.

[45] Photopolymer Holographic Optical Elements for Application in Solar Energy Concentrators. In: Mihaylova E., editor. Holography — Basic Principles and Contemporary Applications. InTech; 2012. pp. 129–145.

[46] Lee J. H., Bang L. T., Wu H. Y., and Kim N. Angular Multiplexed Holographic Solar Condensing lens using Iterative Record Method. In: S VII-3; ICGHIT; pp. 355–356.

Chapter 6

Holographic Data Storage Using Parallel-Aligned Liquid Crystal on Silicon Displays

Francisco J. Martínez Guardiola,
Andrés Márquez Ruiz, Sergi Gallego Rico,
Roberto Fernández Fernández,
Jorge Francés Monllor, Manuel Ortuño Sánchez,
Inmaculada Pascual Villalobos and
Augusto Beléndez Vázquez

Additional information is available at the end of the chapter

http://dx.doi.org/10.5772/67158

Abstract

The parallel-aligned liquid crystal on silicon (PA-LCoS) microdisplay has become a widely used device for the photonics community. It is a very versatile tool that can perform several tasks which transforms it into a key element in many different photonics applications. Since our group is interested in holography, in this chapter, we want to use these displays as the data entry point for a holographic data storage system (HDSS). Due to the novelty of this kind of device, we have done an intense work characterizing it. These efforts are reflected in this chapter where the reader will find two different characterization methods that will enable to predict the performance of the device in a specific application. Additionally, we present how a phase-only device can be used as a data pager using different modulation schemes and combined with a photopolymer as the holographic recording material.

Keywords: holographic data storage, PA-LCoS, modulation schemes, liquid crystal, photopolymer

1. Introduction

In this chapter, we present an analysis on the use of modern parallel-aligned liquid crystal on silicon displays (PA-LCoS) in diffractive optics and holographic data storage (HDS). The PA-LCoS acts as a spatial light modulator (SLM) in different roles: as data entry point,

state of polarization (SOP) converter, phase-only modulator, or amplitude-mostly modulator. All these roles are interesting in many research fields [1–3].

PA-LCoS devices have become widely used in diffractive optics due to its ease of operation and phase-only modulation capabilities, because of its high spatial resolution and high light efficiency [3]. The liquid crystal (LC) technology has achieved a high level of maturity and enables us to have a data entry point in HDS for a high data density recording, and it provides us with the ability to design different modulation schemes.

In order to incorporate this kind of microdisplays into a complete holographic data storage system (HDSS), we have done an intense work to characterize PA-LCoS devices. As a phase-only device, we need to know the retardance introduced for every gray level. The microdisplay is digitally addressed with a pulsed voltage signal. This fact implies a fluctuation in the phase that will be reflected in the optical response [4–7]. For that reason, for a full characterization, we need to obtain the average retardance and the fluctuation amplitude for every gray level. This enables us to select the best device configuration for our application.

Even though PA-LCoS are widely used by the photonics community, these phase-only devices have not been intensively applied in holographic data storage applications. These devices could be a key element for a phase multilevel data page coding. If the trend is to use this kind of coding scheme, a right characterization and a profound knowledge will be useful.

2. PA-LCoS characterization

In this section, we present two characterization methods for PA-LCoS microdisplays. One of them uses any equipment that is present in almost every optics laboratory. The other makes use of a commercial rotating wave plate polarimeter.

2.1. Extending the linear polarimetric method to characterize the PA-LCoS

Parallel-aligned devices are totally characterized by their linear retardance versus voltage values. For this reason, we can use methods typically used in the characterization of wave plates. All these methods assume that the retardance introduced does not change with time [8, 9]. So, we have to adapt the method for elements that present some levels of fluctuation in the retardance signal.

We use the linear polarimetric method to measure the retardance introduced by the wave plate (our PA-LCoS). We use the next scheme.

In **Figure 1**, we see a wave plate sandwiched between two linear polarizers. For the appropriate angles between wave plate and the linear polarizers, we can calculate the retardance as follows [7]:

$$\Gamma = \cos^{-1}\left(\frac{I_{OUT}^{//} - I_{OUT}^{\perp}}{I_{OUT}^{//} + I_{OUT}^{\perp}}\right) \tag{1}$$

where Γ is the measured retardance. $I_{OUT}^{\parallel}$ and $I_{OUT}^{\perp}$ are the intensity measured at the exit of the system when the two linear polarizers are oriented at +45° with respect to the slow axis of the wave plate, and when the input linear polarizer is oriented at +45° and the output polarizer is oriented at −45°. These are the so-called "parallel" intensity and "crossed" intensity. With just two measurements, we can calculate the retardance of the wave plate. These intensities are defined as follows:

$$I_{OUT}^{//} = \frac{I_0}{2}[1 + \cos\Gamma] \tag{2}$$

$$I_{OUT}^{\perp} = \frac{I_0}{2}[1 - \cos\Gamma] \tag{3}$$

where I_0 is the total light intensity introduced in the system.

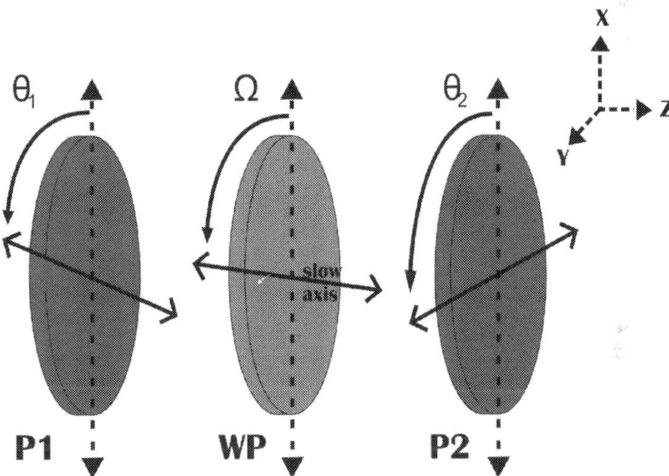

Figure 1. Linear polarimeter with the wave plate (WP) to be measured. P1 and P2 are linear polarizers.

As mentioned, the PA-LCoS device introduces a fluctuation due to its digital-addressing scheme. We see how this fact alters the equations described above. As a first approximation, we consider a triangular profile for the periodic variation of retardance with time, $\Gamma(t)$ described by Eq. (4)

$$\Gamma(t) = \begin{cases} \Gamma - a + \frac{2a}{T/2}t & 0 \leq t < T/2 \\ \Gamma + 3a - \frac{2a}{T/2}t & T/2 \leq t < T \end{cases} \tag{4}$$

where Γ is the average value of the retardance during a period T. This function is represented in **Figure 2**.

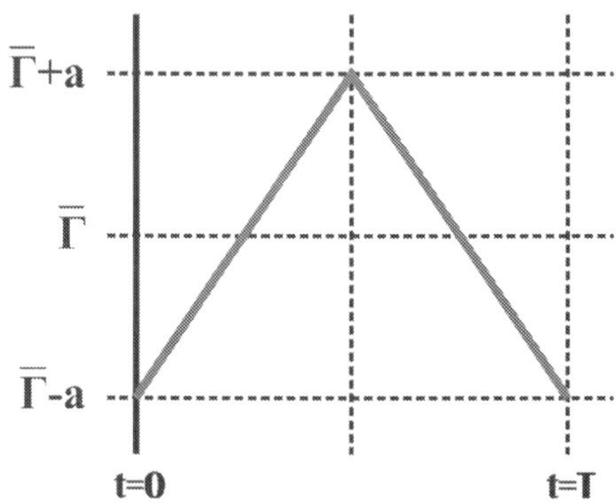

Figure 2. Triangular profile considered for the temporal fluctuation of the linear retardance.

Following the proposed model in Eq. (4), if we calculate the average value for a period of $\cos(\Gamma(t))$, we obtain,

$$\langle \cos(\Gamma - a + \tfrac{2a}{T/2}\, t) \rangle \;=\; \frac{\sin(a)}{a}\cos(\Gamma) \tag{5}$$

We can see how a *sinc* term appears modulating the cosine function. Taking into account Eq. (5), we can rewrite Eqs. (2) and (3) in terms of average intensity as follows:

$$\langle I_{OUT}^{//} \rangle \;=\; \frac{I_0}{2}\left[\,1 + \frac{\sin a}{a}\cos\Gamma\,\right] \tag{6}$$

$$\langle I_{OUT}^{\perp} \rangle \;=\; \frac{I_0}{2}\left[\,1 - \frac{\sin a}{a}\cos\Gamma\,\right] \tag{7}$$

We see how the intensity that we really measure is affected by the *sinc(a)* function when we are trying to measure the retardance introduced by a wave plate that presents instabilities. If we combine Eqs. (6) and (7), we obtain the next expression for the average retardance:

$$\frac{\langle I_{OUT}^{//} \rangle - \langle I_{OUT}^{\perp} \rangle}{\langle I_{OUT}^{//} \rangle + \langle I_{OUT}^{\perp} \rangle} \;=\; \frac{\sin a}{a}\cos\Gamma \tag{8}$$

$$\Gamma \;=\; \cos^{-1}\!\left(\frac{\left(\langle I_{OUT}^{//} \rangle - \langle I_{OUT}^{\perp} \rangle\right)/\left(\langle I_{OUT}^{//} \rangle + \langle I_{OUT}^{\perp} \rangle\right)}{\left(\sin a / a\right)}\right) \tag{9}$$

In the case when no fluctuation exist ($a = 0°$), we recover the classical result presented in Eq. (1). In essence, assuming a linear variation with time, as expressed in Eq. (4), this fluctuation is translated into a *sinc* function when averaging the cosine in a period.

To analyze how the fluctuations limit the classical linear polarimeter, we performed the next simulated experiment: using Eqs. (6) and (7), we simulate the intensity values measured in the presence of fluctuations in the retardance. Then, we consider Eq. (1) to obtain the retardance value as if we ignore the existence of these fluctuations.

In **Figure 3**, we show the calculated retardance values as a function of the true retardance ones used in the simulation and for different fluctuation amplitudes, indicated with the curves in the plot.

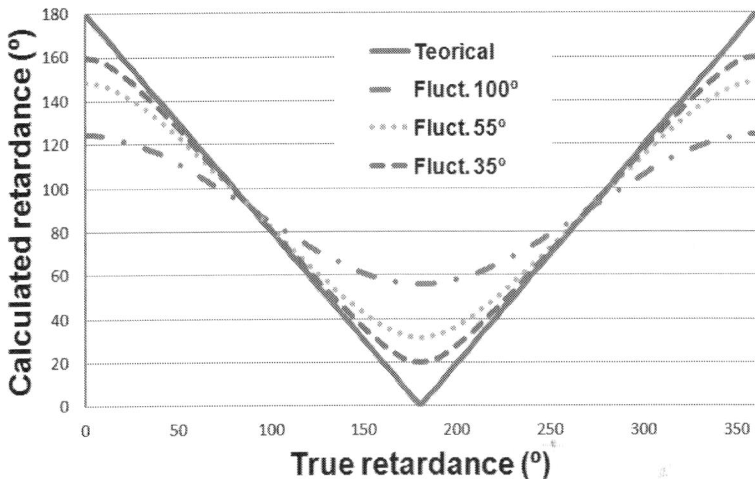

Figure 3. Simulation of the retardance measurement experiment in the presence of fluctuations. The calculated retardance uses the classical expression where fluctuations are not considered. Various fluctuation amplitudes are considered to be compared with the no-fluctuations case.

In **Figure 3**, we see how the fluctuations affect the calculated retardance. The maximum and the minimum measurements are produced at the same places of the theoretical wrapped retardance. This means that they are produced at values multiple of 180°. We also note that the deviation amount of deviation depends on the true retardance value. At true retardance, values multiple of 180° deviation are magnified. Outside of these points, if the fluctuation amplitude is not very large, we also find that the calculated values are very close to the true retardance values.

From the study of Eq. (8), it can be easily deduced that for average retardance values multiple of 180°, the calculated retardance only depends on the fluctuation amplitude a. So, in these cases we can uncouple the average retardance measurements from the fluctuation amplitude. These cases are the maximum and minimum points obtained from the measurements.

At those points, we can estimate the fluctuation amplitude. The fluctuation difference in these maximum and minimum points can be expressed as

$$\Gamma_{\text{diff}} = \cos^{-1}\left(\frac{\sin a}{a}\right) \tag{10}$$

Using Eq. (10) and the calculated retardance, for the maximum and minimum points, we obtain Γ_{diff}. Then, we estimate the fluctuation amplitude, and, eventually, we can correct the measurements of the retardance using the exact Eq. (9) instead of the classical one (Eq. (1)) [10].

2.2. Applying the method to a PA-LCoS microdisplay

To validate and test the method described in the previous section, we use the next experimental setup.

Figure 4 shows the experimental setup used to measure the average retardance versus the applied voltage (gray level) for a PA-LCoS device. It consists of a light source (He-Ne laser, $\lambda = 633$ nm), the LCoS, the necessary input and output linear polarizers which are in parallel or crossed configuration, and a radiometer to measure the intensity. For measuring time variations in the retardance, we need to measure the intensity in both cases (parallel and crossed) at the same time, for this reason we have introduced two high-quality nonpolarizing cube beam splitters (model 10BC16NP.4, from Newport): one of them to separate the incident and the reflected beams, and the other to enable synchronized measurement of the parallel and crossed intensities.

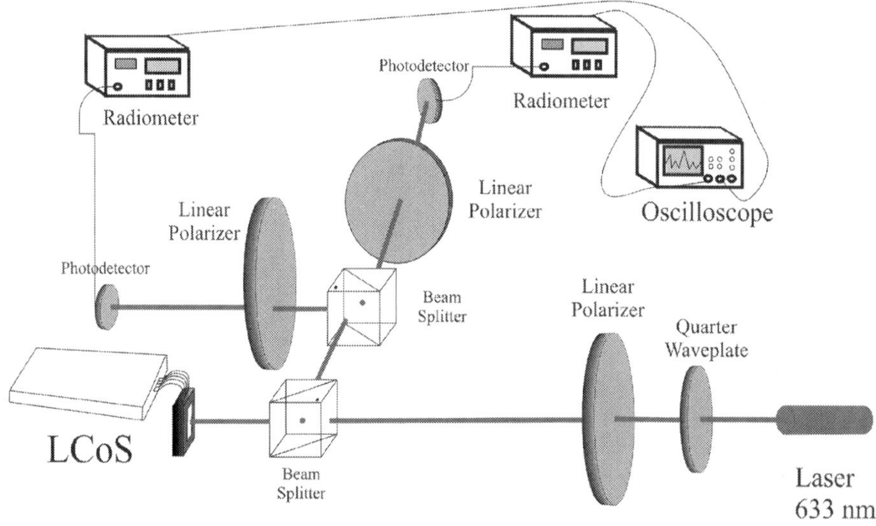

Figure 4. Experimental setup used to measure the linear retardance as a function of the applied voltage (gray level) for a PA-LCoS. The setup allows to measure both average and instantaneous values.

These simultaneous measurements when obtained with the help of an oscilloscope are used to validate the estimated fluctuation amplitude calculated with the previous method.

We demonstrated that the estimated values are in good agreement with the measurements done with the oscilloscope [10]. So, the oscilloscope is no longer necessary. This is the reason why we affirm that the method does not need special equipment (as the mentioned oscilloscope), which maybe is not found in an optical laboratory.

In our experiments, we have used and analyzed an LCoS display distributed by the company HOLOEYE. It is an active matrix reflective mode device with 1920 × 1080 pixels and 0.7" diagonal named PLUTO spatial light modulator. The pixel pitch is of 8.0 μm and the display has a fill factor of 87%. The signal is addressed via a standard digital visual interface (DVI) signal. Using an RS-232 interface and its provided software, we can perform gamma control to configure the modulator for different applications and wavelengths. The manufacturer provides some configuration files for the equipment. These configurations are designed for different applications. The configuration files are labeled as "18-6 default," "18-6 2pi linear 633 nm," and "5-5 2pi linear 633 nm." From the name, we can infer that the ones with "2pi linear 633 nm" are designed for a linear response in retardance for 633-nm wavelength. The labeled as "default" means that no gamma correction has been applied and the retardance response will be nonlinear. The other part of the label (18-6 and 5-5) makes reference to the configuration of the digital addressed signal. This part reflects the number of bits used in the signal, so the signal has different lengths depending on the configuration file. In principle, a shorter length presents less flicker. You can find more information about the digital signal and configuration in Refs. [10, 11].

The method presented in Section 2.1 enables us to correct the measures done for characterizing the PA-LCoS in order to know the exact average retardance introduced by each gray level. To do that, we extrapolate the fluctuation amplitude value calculated from the extremals (180° multiples) to a wider gray level range: the fluctuation amplitude value from the first extremal is consi dered to be roughly valid until half of the gray level distance between itself and the next extremal.

In **Figure 5**, we show the directly taken measurements ("Uncorrected" ones) that we obtain by applying Eq. (1) to the parallel and crossed intensities measured. We know that we are not taking into account the presence of fluctuations. From the extremal points, which are multiples of 180° in the retardance, we can calculate the fluctuation amplitude using Eq. (11). In this way, we obtain a fluctuation amplitude that we apply by intervals between the different extremals. Using Eq. (9), and knowing the value of the fluctuation, we recalculate the average retardance correcting the previous obtained curves ("Corrected" ones).

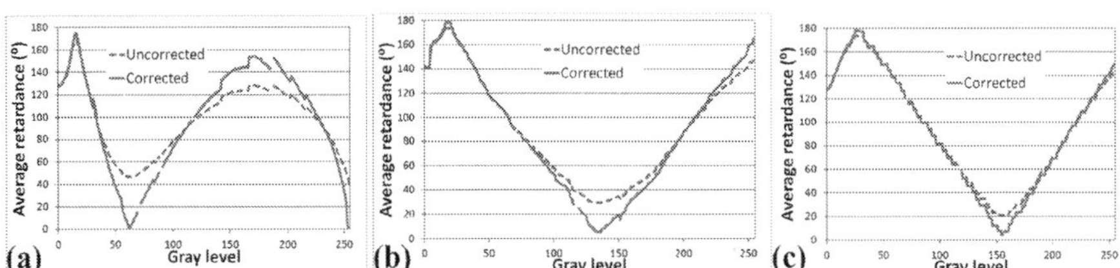

Figure 5. Average retardance versus gray level considering the existence of the fluctuation amplitude in the retardance, "corrected" curve, and considering the ideal $a = 0°$, "uncorrected" curve. (a) "18-6 default"; (b) "18-6 2pi linear 633 nm"; (c) "5-5 2pi linear 633 nm".

To sum up: we are able of obtain the corrected curves. With this information, we can change the gamma curve configuration to obtain a selected behavior. And we can just evaluate Γ_{diff} in the extremals to select the configuration that has less fluctuation amplitude [10, 12].

2.3. Characterization using averaged stokes polarimetry

The method showed in the previous section enables us to configure the device but it does not provide a full characterization. We only have information about the fluctuation amplitude in some points. In this section, we present a method that provides full information about the average retardance and the fluctuation amplitude for all gray levels.

We will use the Mueller-Stokes formalism [8], which enables to deal both with polarized and with unpolarized light. In this formalism, the retardance wave plate matrix is

$$M_R(\Gamma) = \begin{pmatrix} 1 & 0 & 0 & 0 \\ 0 & 1 & 0 & 0 \\ 0 & 0 & \cos\Gamma & \sin\Gamma \\ 0 & 0 & -\sin\Gamma & \cos\Gamma \end{pmatrix} \tag{11}$$

Eq. (11) describes a wave plate with the fast axis along the X-axis and a retardance Γ. Let us consider a unit intensity Stokes vector corresponding to a state of polarization linearly polarized at $+45°$ with respect to the X-axis impinging perpendicular onto the linear retarder. Then, the SOP at the exit is calculated as follows:

$$\begin{pmatrix} 1 \\ 0 \\ \cos\Gamma \\ -\sin\Gamma \end{pmatrix} = \begin{pmatrix} 1 & 0 & 0 & 0 \\ 0 & 1 & 0 & 0 \\ 0 & 0 & \cos\Gamma & \sin\Gamma \\ 0 & 0 & -\sin\Gamma & \cos\Gamma \end{pmatrix} \begin{pmatrix} 1 \\ 0 \\ 1 \\ 0 \end{pmatrix} \tag{12}$$

In Eq. (12), we see how the second element of the resultant Stokes vector is zero independently of the retardance introduced by the wave plate, and it does not depend on the possible temporal retardance fluctuations. If we introduce the signal variation model described in Eq. (4), we calculate the average value for S_2 and S_3 components as follows:

$$\langle S_2 \rangle = \frac{1}{T/2} \int_0^{T/2} \cos\left(\overline{\Gamma} - a + \frac{2a}{T/2}t\right)dt = \frac{\sin(a)}{a}\cos(\overline{\Gamma}) \tag{13}$$

$$\langle S_3 \rangle = \frac{-1}{T/2} \int_0^{T/2} \sin\left(\overline{\Gamma} - a + \frac{2a}{T/2}t\right)dt = \frac{-\sin(a)}{a}\sin(\overline{\Gamma}) \tag{14}$$

Therefore, the average exit vector S_{out} reflected by the PA-LCoS when a linear polarized beam impinges, and the angle between the slow axis and the polarizer is $45°$ is given by

$$\langle S_{out} \rangle = \left\langle \begin{pmatrix} 1 \\ 0 \\ \cos\Gamma(t) \\ -\sin\Gamma(t) \end{pmatrix} \right\rangle = \begin{pmatrix} 1 \\ 0 \\ \frac{\sin(a)}{a}\cos(\overline{\Gamma}) \\ -\frac{\sin(a)}{a}\sin(\overline{\Gamma}) \end{pmatrix} \tag{15}$$

From Eq. (15), we see how, when we calculate the degree of polarization (DoP), it depends only on the fluctuation amplitude

$$\mathrm{DoP} = \frac{\sqrt{\langle S_1\rangle^2 + \langle S_2\rangle^2 + \langle S_3\rangle^2}}{S_0} = \frac{\sin(a)}{a} \tag{16}$$

Eq. (16) shows that the DoP is produced by the fluctuation in the retardance and provides as a way to calculate the fluctuation amplitude for every gray level by measuring the DoP.

From Eq. (15), it is clear that the average retardance can be obtained by calculating the ration between third and fourth Stoke vector components,

$$-\langle S_3\rangle / \langle S_2\rangle = tg(\overline{\Gamma}) \tag{17}$$

We have presented a method that can be applied to any electro-optic element acting as a wave plate and presenting fluctuations in its optical response [10]. It is not only applicable to PA-LCoS devices. We have applied them to the mentioned PLUTO device obtaining a complete characterization [13].

2.3.1. Experimental setup for characterization

To use the method described above, we just need a polarimeter. In our case, we have used a commercial PAX5710VIS-T model from THORLABS. This is a rotating wave plate-based polarimeter, which belongs to time-division mode polarimeters. They are not able to provide instantaneous values if the state of polarization changes more rapidly than its measurement time interval. In our case, the THORLABS polarimeter has a measurement time interval of 3 ms (maximum rotation frequency is 333 Hz). But as long as we need an average value, and the software allows to enlarge the measurement time interval, we just select an appropriate time interval larger than the fluctuation time period of the PLUTO device, which is about 8.66 ms (120 Hz).

In **Figure 6**, we show the experimental setup used for characterizing our PA-LCoS, the first wave plate shown is used just to guarantee enough light intensity regardless of the polarizer angle, since the output light from the laser is linearly polarized. A quarter wave plate, as in the figure, with its neutral lines properly oriented can do the work, even though it is not the only possibility. As we show in the method the input polarizer has to be at 45° from the neutral lines of our PA-LCoS, in our case it is the x-y-axis.

We test the method with the "18-6 633 nm 2pi linear" and "5-5 633 nm 2pi linear" configurations, already introduced. We measure the Stokes vector and degree of polarization of each gray level. We have obtained the next results.

Figure 7 shows the data obtained for the two different configurations tested when linearly polarized light impinges onto the device at 45°. In dashed lines, we show the measurements for "5-5 633 nm 2pi linear" configuration. In continuous lines, we show the measurements for "18-6 633 nm 2pi linear." The first thing that we have to note is that parameter S_1 is close to zero for all gray levels, in clear confirmation of the result obtained in Eq. (15). To obtain the retardance value and the fluctuation amplitude, we have to apply Eqs. (17) and (16), respectively.

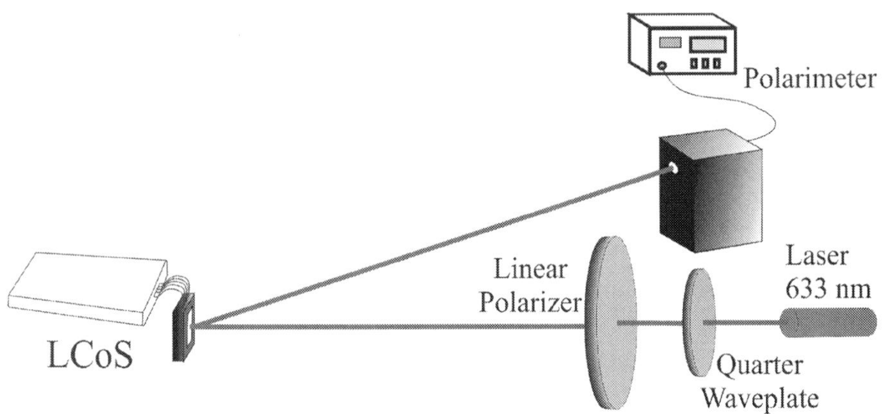

Figure 6. Experimental setup for characterizing a PA-LCoS.

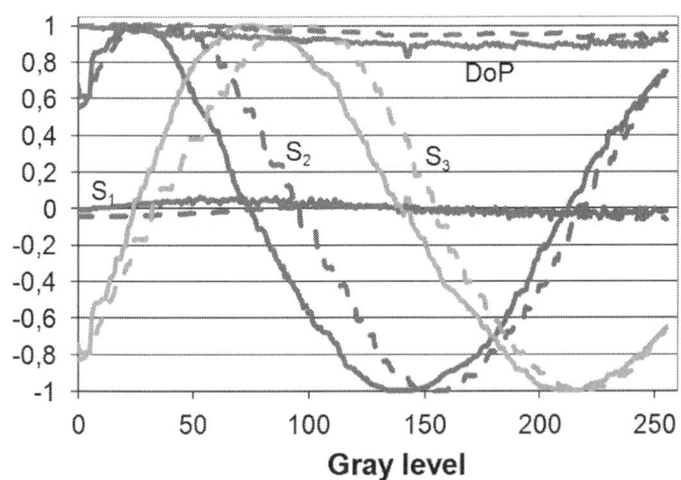

Figure 7. Measurements obtained from the PLUTO for "5-5 633 nm 2pi linear" (dashed line) and "18-6 633 nm 2pi linear" (continuous line).

In **Figure 8**, we have calculated the fluctuation amplitude and the average retardance. We have obtained a full characterization of the device. We observe that the retardance range is about 360° for both sequences with very good linearity. The fluctuation amplitude is clearly smaller for the 5-5 sequence.

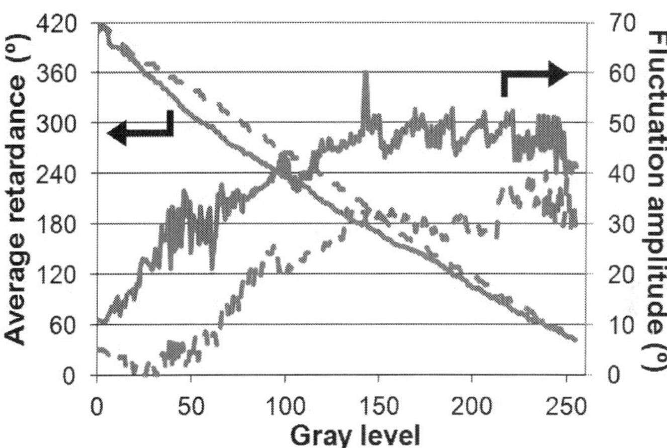

Figure 8. Calculated values for the average retardance and the fluctuation amplitude for $\lambda = 633$ nm, and for sequences "5-5 633 nm 2pi linear" (dashed) and "18-6 633 nm 2pi linear" (continuous).

This method has been validated with the direct measurements of the retardance fluctuations and with the predictive capability of the SOP at the exit regardless of the SOP at the input [13]. The direct measurements of the fluctuation amplitude have been done with the help of an oscilloscope [14], and we have also tested the predictive capability of the model when applied to a more complex diffractive optical element (DOE) as a blazed grating [15].

3. Using a PA-LCoS in a holographic data storage system

We have a good characterization method and control over the display that will act as a spatial light modulator in our holographic data storage system. We present how we can implement different modulation schemes with a phase-only device as our PA-LCoS.

HDSS enables true three-dimensional (3-D) storage of information and also associative memory retrieval [16]. There are many aspects that need to be addressed for HDSS to be commercially viable [2]. These systems are always taking advantage from the latest technological advances in the various components that form a complete system. In this sense, PA-LCoS microdisplays have replaced previous liquid-crystal display (LCD) technology in most photonics applications [17]; this fact makes PA-LCoS an interesting device to test in

HDSS. PA-LCoS are high-resolution reflective devices which enable phase-only operation. They are ideal for binary or multinary phase-only data pages [18, 19]. This leads to DC term cancellation when recording the Fourier transform of the data page, avoiding the premature saturation of the recording material.

3.1. Modulation schemes

We try to implement the well-known binary intensity modulation (BIM) and the hybrid ternary modulation (HTM) [20, 21]. PA-LCoS devices are designed for displaying phase-only elements without coupled amplitude. This is easily achieved by illuminating them with a linearly polarized light parallel to the director axis. We have investigated that the PA-LCoS can also be used to display the widely applied BIM data pages. We also try to implement the more demanding HTM data pages. HTM had not been studied with PA-LCoS devices. HTM has the advantage that combines the ease of detection of BIM data pages (that only needs to detect intensity) and it reduces the DC term of the Fourier transform. The reduction on the DC term is necessary to avoid saturation of the dynamic range of the recording material [20, 21].

We use the model and characterization technique presented in Section 2.3 that enable us to obtain the average retardance and fluctuation amplitude for every gray level. Before applying the configuration needed, we need to calculate the complex amplitude of the electric field at the exit. To do that, we use the Jones matrix formalism, so we present the basic elements involved,

$$P_X = \begin{pmatrix} 1 & 0 \\ 0 & 0 \end{pmatrix} \tag{18}$$

Eq. (18) is the matrix associated to a linear polarizer with its transmission axis along the X-axis,

$$W(\phi) = \begin{pmatrix} \exp(-j\phi/2) & 0 \\ 0 & \exp(+j\phi/2) \end{pmatrix} \tag{19}$$

Eq. (19) is the matrix for a linear retarder of linear retardance φ with its slow axis along the X-axis. When polarization elements are rotated an angle θ with respect to the X-axis, we need the two-dimensional rotation matrix,

$$R(\theta) = \begin{pmatrix} \cos\theta & \sin\theta \\ -\sin\theta & \cos\theta \end{pmatrix} \tag{20}$$

To produce both BIM and HTM with the PA-LCoS device, we need to insert the display between two rotated linear polarizers at angles θ_1 and θ_2, that is, the complex amplitude for the electric field at the output is given by the following equation:

$$\vec{E}_{OUT} = P_X \cdot R(\theta_2) \cdot W_{PA}(\Gamma) \cdot \begin{pmatrix} \cos\theta_1 \\ \sin\theta_1 \end{pmatrix} \tag{21}$$

where $\vec{E}_{OUT}$ corresponds to linearly polarized light at an angle θ_2, always with respect to the X-axis. $W_{PA}(\Gamma)$ is the matrix for the PA-LCoS which is given by Eq. (19), and whose average retardance varies with gray level, and it will be given by our characterization method. Its fluctuation amplitude will not be considered in the calculations: in the calibration we have taken care to select electrical configurations minimizing the existence of this flicker in the retardance [9, 10].

If we take into account the calculated values for the average retardance, we can calculate the trajectories in the complex plane. In **Figure 9**, we present the configurations used to implement the different modulation schemes.

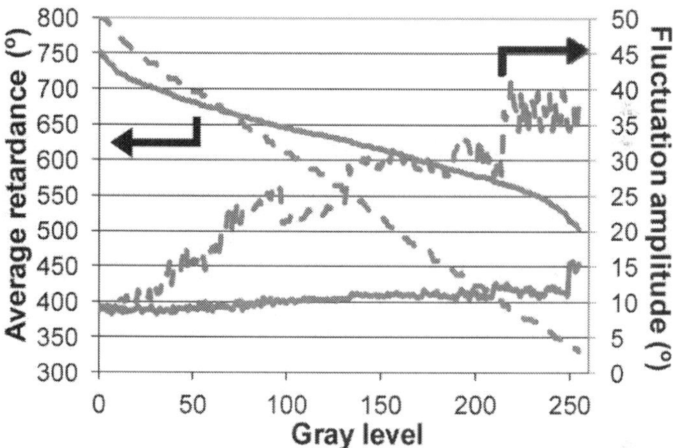

Figure 9. Calculated values of the average retardance and the fluctuation amplitude for λ = 532 nm at an angle of incidence of 11.5°, for two different device configurations that enables us to implement BIM (continuous) and HTM (dashed).

The configuration shown in **Figure 9** is obtained at an angle of incidence of 11.5°, which is the incidence angle presented in our setup for holographic data storage. The sequences used are both 5-5, but the voltages applied are changed for the BIM configuration (continuous lines in **Figure 9**). In this case, the voltage has been reduced to V_{bright} = 2.02 V and V_{dark} = 1.11 V. For BIM, we only need a phase depth of 180°, this is the reason that we can relax the requisites of the device. As shown in **Figure 9**, the fluctuation amplitude has been reduced, in comparison with the configuration used for HTM that is the configuration called "5-5 532 nm 2pi linear" provided by the manufacturer. For more information about the influence of V_{bright} and V_{dark}, reference [12] can be consulted.

After we have defined the average retardance, from Eq. (21) we can calculate the intensity transmission I_{OUT} that is given by the hermitic product of $\vec{E}_{OUT}$ and the phase shift φ_{OUT} will be given by the argument. We can optimize in the computer the angles θ_1 and θ_2 of the linear polarizers to produce the best BIM and HTM regimes.

In the case of BIM, we need to generate the maximum intensity contrast between the on and off values, that is, $I_{contrast} = I_{oOn}/I_{Ooff}$. We need at least a contrast of 1:20 for achieving an acceptable bit error rate (BER) [22]. Maximum contrast can be obtained with only polarizers, if they are parallel of crossed with each other at 45° with respect to the director axis of the PA-LCoS. Using the data from **Figure 9**, we obtain the intensity transmission and phase-shift curves as a function of the gray level. It is displayed in **Figure 10(a)**, which are also represented as a phasor in the complex plane in **Figure 10(b)**

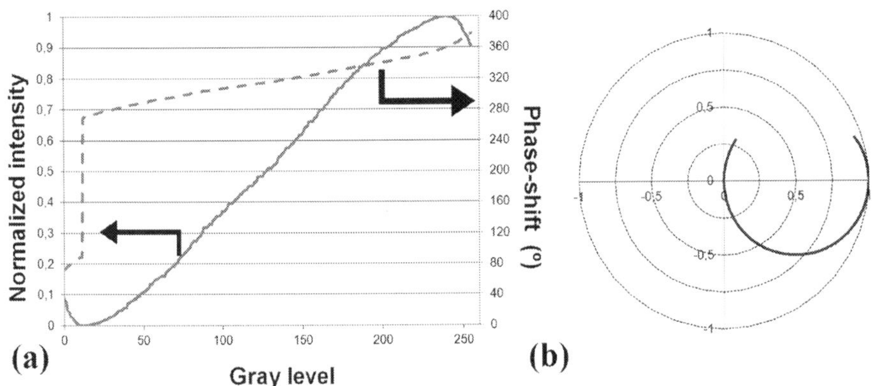

Figure 10. Simulation for BIM. (a) Intensity transmission and phase shift as a function of gray level; (b) phasor evolution in the complex plane. The PA-LCoS is sandwiched between linear polarizers at +45° with respect to the X-axis (neutral lines).

In **Figure 10(a)**, the lowest and highest intensity transmission points occur at gray levels 12 and 239, respectively. From the values, we calculate that the theoretical contrast tends to infinity, and the phase-shift values are 270° and 360°. From **Figure 9**, we see that the difference in the retardance value is very close to 180° between these two gray levels. In the experimental measurements, we obtain that the low and high transmission points occur slightly displaced at gray levels 14 and 248, and the contrast we measure is about 1:50. The theoretical contrast value is idealistic since the various degradation effects in the PA-LCoS have a direct impact on the minimum intensity.

The representation in the complex plane (**Figure 10(b)**) is useful to see the complex evolution and the trajectory described with the variation of gray level. We see that the 180° phase jump is produced at the vicinity of the origin (gray level 12). It can be verified that independently of the orientation of the transmission axis of the polarizers, we always obtain a circular trajectory. The same effect is produced when adding wave plates to the system, at the entrance or/and the exit of the PA-LCoS (it will be like adding an offset to the retardance; it will not vary the trajectory). This will be a problem when implementing the HTM scheme.

For HTM scheme, we need three gray level values, two of them with a 180° relative phase shift and an equal and high intensity level (On levels). The third level will be the Off level that has to block as much light as possible to obtain a good contrast. As long as the trajectories in the complex plane are always circular and the 180° phase jump is produced in the origin, we have found that the PA-LCoS device cannot fully meet these requirements. In the case of Twisted-Nematic (TN) LCDs, this is possible. TN LCDs provided a coupled amplitude and phase-shift modulation. This fact enables to produce arbitrary complex amplitude trajectories that can accomplish the requirements of HTM [20, 21].

Therefore, we can produce a compromise solution by slightly shifting the circular trajectory. At the cost of leaking some light intensity in the Off level, we can achieve two On levels with an appreciable transmitted intensity and a relative phase shift close to 180°. The closer these On levels are to a phase difference of 180° the lower the DC term is. We have named this modulation scheme as pseudo-HTM modulation (p-HTM). We want to know if this p-HTM scheme is still useful for its application in an HDSS.

In **Figure 11**, we show the complex amplitude for one of the possible p-HTM configurations. It corresponds to input and output polarizers at 55° and −45° with respect to the slow axis. In **Figure 11(a)**, we show the intensity and the phase-shift versus gray level, and in **Figure 11(b)** we plot the phasor evolution in the complex plane where we see that the circular trajectory is slightly displaced from the origin. The two On gray levels considered are 105 and 168 with amplitude transmission values of 0.28 and phase-shift difference of 206°. The Off gray level is 140 with an amplitude transmission of 0.03 and phase shift 170°. The intensity contrast is then 1:10. This is a low value; however, increasing the contrast means almost crossing the two polarizers. This produces that the 180° phase jump is closer to the origin and the difference in phase between On levels is increased rapidly producing a larger DC term, which is what we are trying to reduce [23].

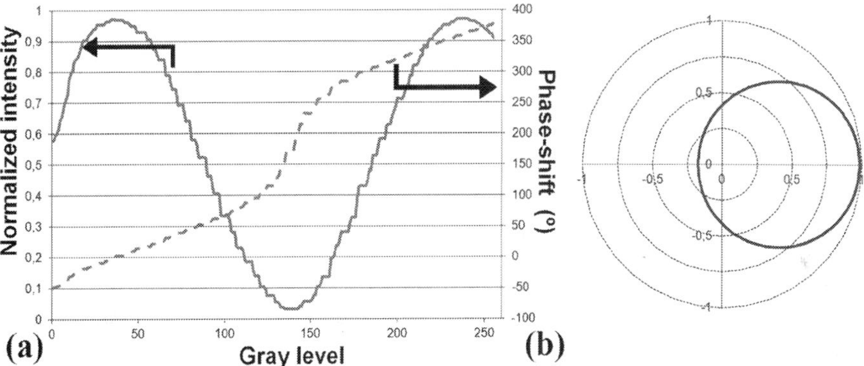

Figure 11. Simulation for p-HTM: (a) intensity transmission and phase shift; (b) phasor evolution in the complex plane. input and output polarizers are at +55° and −45° with respect to the slow axis.

3.2. Experimental results

To test the modulation schemes presented, we use the next experimental setup represented in **Figure 12**.

Figure 12 shows us the scheme for the experimental HDSS used. We consider a 532-nm laser beam, to which the PVA photopolymer is sensitized. We use PVA/AA because it is a well-studied photopolymer, and our group had done an intense work to characterize and model it. More information about the photopolymer can be found in references [24, 25]. We have inserted a half wave plate before the shutter and spatial filter to ensure that enough light intensity impinges onto the linear polarizers in the object and reference beam. The intensity ratio between both beams is controlled with one attenuator in reference beam. The linear polarizers LP are used to produce the appropriate SOP for the object and reference beam. In the reference beam, a stop limits the aperture of the beam to about a diameter of 1 cm. Lenses in the reference beam form an afocal system so that the rotating mirror and the recording material are at conjugate planes; this enables angular multiplexing simply by rotation of the mirror. In the object beam, we have combined a divergent and a convergent lens in order to control the curvature of the converging beam onto the PA-LCoS. At the convergence plane, we find the Fourier transform of the data page, in this plane we used a stop that will act as a Nyquist filter. Then we have built a relay system to image the Nyquist filter plane onto the recording plane. We can also introduce some defocusing degree by displacing the recording material plane. This system uses a convergent correlator setup, and finally we read the data saved with the help of a high dynamic CCD camera [25].

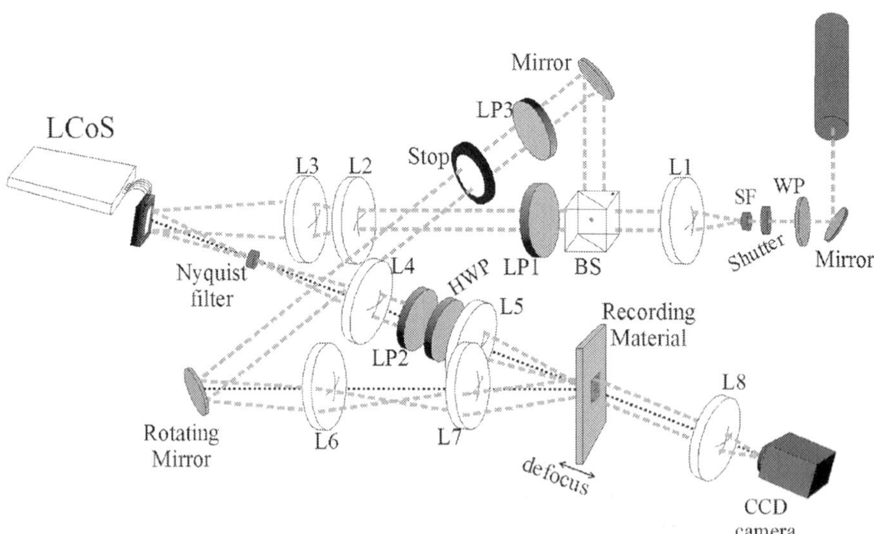

Figure 12. Schematic representation of our experimental HDSS testing platform.

In the present work, we focus on testing the modulation schemes implemented with our PA-LCoS. We address a data page formed with random data bits. Afterwards, in the reconstruction step, we retrieve the data saved with CCD camera. Compared with the original data, we make a count on the errors detected. This provides us with a measurement or the raw BER. We only apply a simple treatment consisting in looking for the best threshold level that minimizes the errors counted [26].

The data page is formed by 64 × 64 information bits, and each bit of information is formed by 8 × 8 pixels in the PA-LCoS. This is necessary to avoid interpixel cross-talk effects [16]. We have 4096 information bits of information in each data page.

In **Figure 13**, we present the first result for BIM scheme; in this case, we are not using material to register the hologram. This image enables us to evaluate the optics performance of our experimental setup (**Figure 12**). We see some interesting facts. In the first place, we see how the data page is perfectly reconstructed and the 1's and 0's distribution in gray levels is clearly separated. No errors in the reconstruction have been produced.

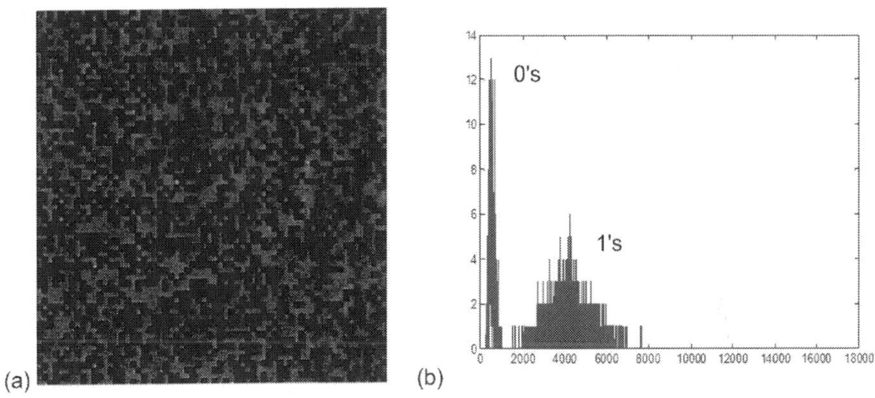

(a)   (b)

Figure 13. Experimental results for BIM scheme and no material. (a) Data page; (b) histograms.

In **Figure 14**, we present the results obtained for p-HTM scheme without using material. We see that the histograms are not clearly separated. This implies that some error will be produced in the reconstruction. We detect eight errors, which corresponds to a BER of 2.0×10^{-3}. This is due to the lower contrast of the data page, but we still can reconstruct the image with an acceptable BER.

Figure 15 shows us the results obtained when the data page is stored in a PVA/AA film. The beam intensity ratio used is about 1:400, where the intensity incident onto the recording material is 3.16 mW/cm^2 and 8 μW/cm^2, respectively, for the reference and object beam, and for an exposure time of 6 s. As we can see in the histograms, the 0's and 1's show a slight overlap. We detected 52 errors, that is, BER = 1.3×10^{-2}. The BER is still in the range that allow to retrieve the information without errors when applying error correction codes [26].

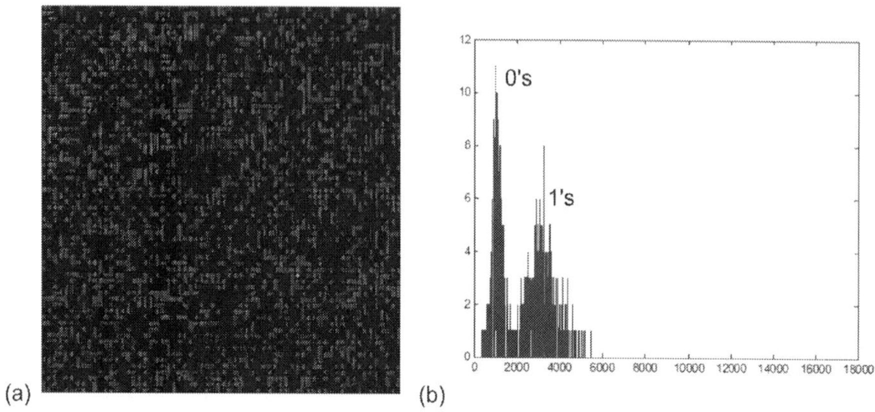

Figure 14. Experimental results for p-HTM scheme and no material. (a) Data page; (b) histograms.

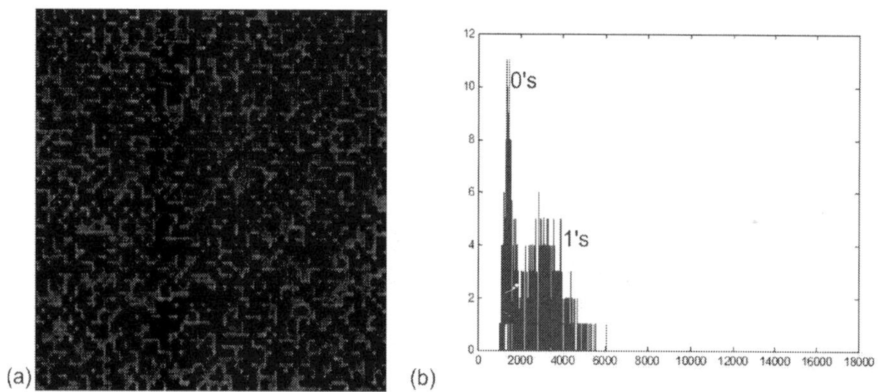

Figure 15. Experimental results for BIM scheme and PVA/AA. (a) Data page; (b) histograms.

In **Figure 16**, we see the results for a data page stored in PVA/AA using p-HTM scheme. Beam intensity ratio is about 1:800, where the intensity incident onto the recording material is 3.16 mW/cm^2 and 4 µW/cm^2, respectively, for the reference and object beam, and for an exposure time of 10 s. As we can see, and due to the lost of contrast, the results are a worse that in BIM case. There are 229 errors detected, that is, BER = 5.6 × 10^{-2}. BER is still in an acceptable range, and it is only five times larger than the BIM case.

We did some simulations to predict the results [23]. Our simulations predicted worse results for p-HTM, when we compare it with BIM, than the ones obtained experimentally. We believe that the better experimental ratio is due to the reduction in DC term, which is to not have into account in our simulations just because we considered a linear material. Further experimental work has to be done with PVA/AA photopolymer to study these saturation effects. In general, we can say that the p-HTM scheme can be used in an HDSS because of its promising results. Maybe, it can show all its potential when the multiplexing capability will be used.

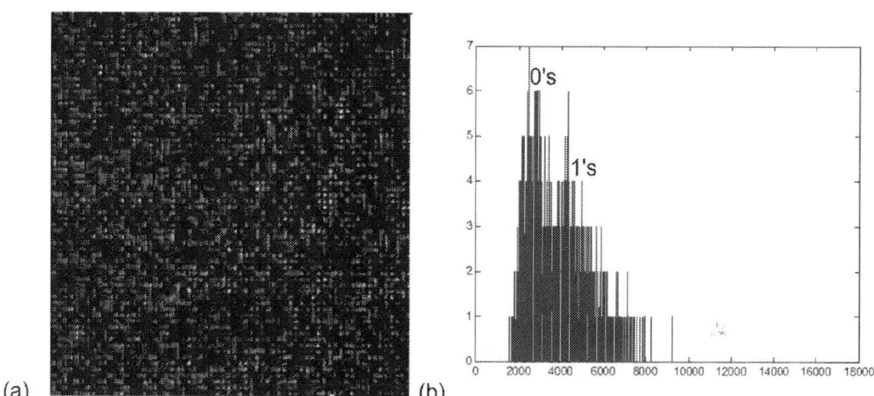

(a)   (b)

Figure 16. Experimental results for p-HTM scheme and PVA/AA. (a) Data page; (b) histograms.

4. Conclusions

This chapter presents how to apply a novel PA-LCoS microdisplay to an HDSS. To accomplish that, we presented two methods to characterize the device. The first method does not use any special equipment and permits us to customize the configuration of the PA-LCoS. The second one enables a complete characterization and presents a good prediction capability, which will be useful to test if the device can be applied in a specific setup or application. The method has been validated in different ways, and can be applied to any device that acts as a wave plate but present some fluctuation in the introduced retardance.

When we have characterized the PA-LCoS microdisplays, we have applied it in a complete HDSS. We have found that we can design some modulation schemes that can be used in HDSS. We present the promising p-HTM scheme that can be comparable with the widely used BIM scheme in terms of BER.

Acknowledgements

We want to acknowledge the financial support from the Spanish Ministerio de Trabajo y Competitividad under projects FIS2014-56100-C2-1-P and FIS2015-66570-P and by the Generalitat Valenciana of Spain under projects PROMETEOII/2015/015 and ISIC/2012/013 and by the University of Alicante with the project GRE12-14.

Author details

Francisco J. Martínez Guardiola*, Andrés Márquez Ruiz, Sergi Gallego Rico, Roberto Fernández Fernández, Jorge Francés Monllor, Manuel Ortuño Sánchez, Inmaculada Pascual Villalobos and Augusto Beléndez Vázquez

*Address all correspondence to: fj.martinez@ua.es

Instituto de Física Aplicada a las Ciencias y las Tecnologías, Universidad de Alicante, Alacant, Spain

References

[1] J. Turunen and F. Wyrowski, editors. Diffractive Optics for Industrial and Commercial Applications. Berlin: Akademie Verlag; 1997.

[2] H. J. Coufal, D. Psaltis, and B. T. Sincerbox, editors. Holographic Data Storage. Springer-Verlag ed. Berlin: Springer-Verlag; 2000.

[3] G. Lazarev, A. Hermerschmidt, S. Krüger, S. Osten. LCOS Spatial Light Modulators: Trends and Applications. in Optical Imaging and Metrology: Advanced Technologies: John Wiley & Sons; 2012.

[4] Z. Zhang, Z. You, D. Chu. Fundamentals of phase-only liquid crystal on silicon (LCoS) devices. Light Sci. Appl. 2014; **3**:1–10. DOI: 10.1038/lsa.2014.94

[5] S. T. Wu and D. K. Yang. Reflective Liquid Crystal Displays. Chichester: John Wiley & Sons Inc.; 2005.

[6] A. Lizana et al. Influence of the temporal fluctuations phenomena on the ECB LCoS performance. In: SPIE, editor. Proceeding of SPIE; 2012; EEUU: SPIE; 2012. p. 74420G.

[7] J. García-Márquez, V. López, A. González-Vega, E. Noé. Flicker minimization in a LCoS spatial light modulator. Opt. Express. 2012;**20**:8431–8441. DOI: 10.1364/OE.20.008431

[8] G. Goldstein. Polarized Light. New York, NY: Marcel Dekker; 2003.

[9] P. A. Williams, A. H. Rose, and C. M. Wang. Rotating-polarizer polarimeter for accurate retardance measurement. Appl. Optics. 1997;**36**:6466–6472.

[10] F. J. Martínez, A. Márquez, S. Gallego, J. Francés, I. Pascual. Extended linear polarimeter to measure retardance and flicker: application to liquid cystal on silicon devices in two working geometries. Opt. Eng. 2014;**53**(1):014105-1– 014105-9. DOI: http://dx.doi.org/10.1117/1.OE.53.1.014105

[11] A. Hermerschmidt, S. Osten, S. Krüger and T. Blümel. Wave front generation using a phase-only modulating liquid-crystal based micro-display with HDTV resolution. In: SPIE, editor. Proceedings of SPIE; 2007; EE.UU.: SPIE; 2007. p. 65840E.

[12] F. J. Martínez, A. Márquez, S. Gallego, M. Ortuño, J. Francés, A. Beléndez and I. Pascual. Electrical dependencies of optical modulation capabilities in digitally addressed parallel aligned liquid crystal on silicon devices. Opt. Eng. 2014;**53**(6):067104. DOI: http://dx.doi.org/10.1117/1.OE.53.6.067104

[13] F. J. Martínez, A. Márquez, S. Gallego, J. Francés, I. Pascual and A. Beléndez. Retardance and flicker modelling and characterization of electro-optic linear retarders by averaged Stokes polarimetry. Opt. Lett. 2014;**39**:1011–1014. DOI: http://dx.doi.org/10.1364/OL.39.001011

[14] F.J. Martínez, A. Márquez, S. Gallego, M. Ortuño, J. Francés, A. Beléndez and I. Pascual. Averaged Stokes polarimetry applied to evaluate retardance and flicker in PA-LCoS devices. Optics Express. 2014;**22**:15064–15074. DOI: http://dx.doi.org/10.1364/OE.22.015064

[15] F. J. Martínez, A. Márquez, S. Gallego, M. Ortuño, J. Francés, I. Pascual and A. Beléndez. Predictive capability of average Stokes polarimetry for simulation of phase multilevel elements onto LCoS devices. Appl. Optics. 2015;**54**(6):1379–1386. DOI: http://dx.doi.org/10.1364/AO.54.001379

[16] D. Sarid and B.H. Schechtman. A roadmap for data storage applications. Opt. Photonics News. 2007;**18**(5):32–37. DOI: https://doi.org/10.1364/OPN.18.5.000032

[17] G. Lazarev, A. hermerschmidt, S. Krüger and S. Osten. LCOS spatial light modulator: trends and applications. In: W. Osten and N. Reingand, editors. Optical Imaging and Metrology. Wiley-VCH Verlag GmbH & Co. KGaA; 2012. pp. 1–29. DOI: http://dx.doi.org/10.1002/9783527648443.ch1

[18] J. Joseph and D. A. Waldman. Homogenized Fourier transform holographic data storage using phase spatial light modulators and methods for recovery of data from the phase image. Appl. Optics. 2006;**45**(25):6374–6380. DOI: https://doi.org/10.1364/AO.45.006374

[19] B. Das, J. Joseph and K. Singh. Phase modulated gray-scale data pages for digital holographic data storage. Optics Commun. 2009;**282**(11):2147–2154. DOI: http://dx.doi.org/10.1016/j.optcom.2009.02.048

[20] A. Márquez, S. Gallego, D. Méndez, M. L. Álvarez, E. Fernández, M. Ortuño, C. Neipp, A. Beléndez and I. Pascual. Accurate control of a liquid-crystal display to produce a homogenized Fourier transform for holographic memories. Optics Lett. 2007;**32**(17):2511–2513. DOI: https://doi.org/10.1364/OL.32.002511

[21] E. Fernández, R. Fuentes, A. Márquez, A. Beléndez and I. Pascual. Binary intensity modulation and hybrid ternary modulation applied to multiplexing objects using holographic data storage on a PVA/AA photopolymer. Int. J. Poly. Sci. 2014;**2014**:356534. DOI: http://dx.doi.org/10.1155/2014/356534

[22] M. J. O'Callaghan. Sorting through the lore of phase mask options—performance measures and practical commercial designs. In: SPIE, editor. Advanced Optical and Quantum

Memories and Computing; 17 of June; San Jose, CA, United States. United States: SPIE; 2004. pp. 150–159. DOI: http://dx.doi.org/10.1117/12.529854

[23] F. J. Martínez, R. Fernández, A. Márquez, S. Gallego, M. L. Álvarez, I. Pascual and A. Beléndez. Exploring binary and ternary modulations on a PA-LCoS device for holographic data storage in a PVA/AA photopolymer. Optics Express. 2015;23:20459–2047. DOI: https://doi.org/10.1364/OE.23.02045

[24] H. Sherif, I. Naydenova, S. Martin, C. McGinn, V. Toal. Characterization of an acrylamide-based photopolymer for data storage utilizing holographic angular multiplexing. J. Opt. A, Pure Appl. Opt. 2005;7:255–260.

[25] C. E. Close, M. R. Gleeson, D. A. Mooney, J. T. Sheridan. Monomer diffusion rates in photopolymer material. Part II. High-frequency gratings and bulk diffusion. J. Opt. Soc. Am. B. 2011;28:842–850. DOI: 10.1364/JOSAB.28.000842

[26] Govind P. Agrawal, editor. Fiber-Optic Communication Systems. 4th ed. Rochester, New York, NY: John Wiley & Sons; 2012. 626 p. DOI: 10.1002/9780470918524

Holographic Imaging and Metrology

Microtopography and Thickness Measurement with Digital Holographic Microscopy Highlighting and Its Tomographic Capacity

Miguel León-Rodríguez, Juan A. Rayas-Alvarez, Amalia Martínez-García and Raúl R. Cordero

Additional information is available at the end of the chapter

http://dx.doi.org/10.5772/66750

Abstract

The refocusing capacity is a unique feature of digital holography. In this chapter, we show the capability of reconstructing digital holograms at different planes for different purposes. One of such purposes is to increase the focus depth of the microscope system. First, we show experimental results of the feasibility to perform digital holographic microscopy (DHM) using a Mirau interferometric objective. A profile phase comparison of a 4.2 µm high microlens using interferometry and DHM, extending the depth of focus of the microscope objective as proof of the proposal, is presented. Second, it is also useful in reducing shot noise when using an LED as a light source. In order to attain the reduction noise, we performed an averaging process of phase and amplitude images reconstructed at different reconstruction distances. This reconstruction range is performed within the focus depth of the optical system. We get a reduction of 50% shot noise. Finally, we show a strategy based on this tomographic capability of reducing a ringing effect by using an ideal filter in off-axis digital holography.

Keywords: digital holographic microscopy, phase-contrast imaging, optical metrology, tomography, phase-shifting

1. Introduction

Digital holographic microscopy (DHM) is a very popular noninvasive testing tool due to its optical nature [1–3]. Many applications use DHM and they have been demonstrated, showing its unique focusing capability; among those applications, micro-electro-mechanical systems (MEMS) and micro-opto-electromechanical systems (MOEMS) analysis demand

higher topographical resolution accuracy [4, 5]. In the inspections of test objects with microscopes presenting some nondesirable phenomena, such as a limited depth of field, aberrations due to defects of optical elements inside the arrangement, optical noise, and parasitic interferences by multiple internal reflections, among others. DHM is not an exception. The microscope has a depth of focus (DOF) limited and as in bright-field microscopy, the areas outside the DOF give out-of-focus and blurred amplitude. Ferraro et al. demonstrated that by DH it is possible to obtain an extended focused image (EFI) of a 3D object without any mechanical scanning, as occurs in conventional optical microscopy [6]. As the unique DHM feature of refocusing works normally, which Ferraro et al. and Colomb et al. demonstrated in their results [6, 7], we can put under inspection MEMS and MOEMS with thicknesses larger than microscope objective (MO) depth of focus. One of the most important challenges in DHM is the reduction of noise. This is because, the lower noise, the smaller will be the measurement error. Different methods have been applied to reduce noise in digital holography. Kang obtained multiple holograms from different angles of illumination by rotating the object or the illumination source. He obtained an improved image through an averaging process [8], similar to the process applied by Baumbach et al. [2]. On the other hand, Rong et al. [9] varied the polarization angle to get an improved image. Also, Charrière et al. [10] applied a method to reduce the shot noise that consisted of averaging multiple holograms in order to get an improved phase image. The noise is reduced by low partial coherence sources. These are usually used, such as laser diodes or light emitting diodes (LEDs) [11, 12]. A disadvantage is their inability to reconstruct the wavefront object for larger reconstruction distances [13]. Here, we present two methods to reduce measurement error in DHM and DH. These methods perform an averaging procedure of phase maps reconstructed at different distances. In addition, we show compensation in the topographical measurement of a 4.2 μm high microlens attained with classical interferometry. This error is due to the limited depth of focus of a Mirau interferometric objective (MIO). In this case, we extend the DOF of the MIO by using the numerical focusing capability of DHM. The last method is based on this tomographic capability of the DHM to reduce a ringing effect by using an ideal filter in off-axis digital holography. We use this capability to get an enhanced image, which is obtained from the spatial averaging method between the focused image at plane ($z = z_{hd0}$) and the first Talbot distance plane ($z = z_{hd1}$). This distance is determined by the period of the ringing phenomenon. Reductions of 50% of these anomalies are computed in simulation and 30% is obtained experimentally (nearly 2 nm). In addition, the simulation results show that the focusing resolution is related with the filter size.

2. Extending DOF of a Mirau interferometric objective by DHM

In this section, we present some experimental results to show how the DOF of a MIO is increased. We show a topographical measurement of a 4.2 μm high microlens attained with classical interferometry. A comparison with the proposal shows the existence of an error. This error is due to the limited depth of focus of the MO. We extend the DOF of the MO by using the tomographic capability of DHM.

2.1. Experimental configuration

The CCD camera records a hologram $I(x, y)$ on the recording plane (x, y). This hologram is the interference between the reference (R) and the object (O) waves. The hologram is magnified by the lens of the microscope (L) (**Figure 1**) and it is given by

$$I(x',y') \;=\; \left|O(x',y')\right|^2 + \left|R(x',y')\right|^2 + O(x',y')R^*(x',y') + O^*(x',y')R(x',y'), \tag{1}$$

where the first two terms are the DC term, and the last ones represent the real and the virtual images respectively, while * denotes the complex conjugated.

2.2. Reconstruction of the hologram

Some considerations we need to clarify for the proposal. We must avoid the use of object specimen of low reflectivity because the reference wave cannot be attenuated. The last consideration we have to care about is the dark zone due to obstruction of the reference mirror in the MIO [14].

The most common configurations to obtain $I(x, y)$ in DHM are from either on-line or off-axis. In both cases, we need to tilt the sample (OS) modifying the interference angle between (R) and (O). In the case when this angle is ~0°, the configuration is in-line. This alignment is more accurate than its off-axis counterpart but in the classical way, one needs more images recorded by the CCD camera. We eliminate DC term and the virtual image of Eq. (1), by applying the phase-shifting technique. The filtered hologram $I_F(x, y)$ and the wavefront of the object $U(x, y)$, respectively, calculated from four $\pi/2$ phase-shifted images I_1–I_4 with the four frame algorithm [15]:

$$I_F(x, y) \;=\; OR\,\exp\!\left[i\big(\phi_A + \phi_o\big)(x, y)\right], \tag{2}$$

$$U(x, y) = I_F(x, y)\left(R^*\,\exp\!\left[-i\phi_A(x, y)\right]\right), \tag{3}$$

where ϕ_A is a distribution of system aberrations. Once that remaining aberration of $U(x, y)$ is compensated for, the numerical object wavefront is reconstructed.

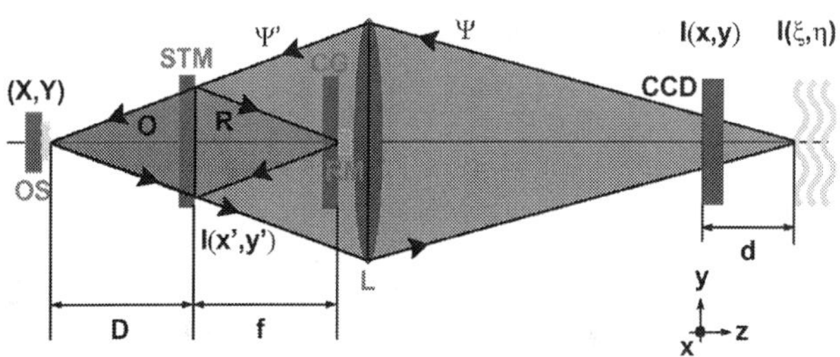

Figure 1. Scheme of the MIO which shows the optical path. L, lens of the microscope; STM, beam splitter mirror; OS, object; CG, compensating glass; RM, reference mirror.

2.2.1. Numerical reconstruction of the wavefront

The wavefront of object $U(x, y)$ is propagated numerically along the optical axis to the image plane (ξ, η), defined by the numerical distance d, according to the angular spectrum method [16].

$$U(\xi, \eta) = \Im^{-1} \left\{ \exp\left[ikd\,(1 - \alpha\lambda - \beta\lambda)^{1/2}\right] \left[\Im\, U_0(x, y)\right]_{(\alpha,\beta)} \right\}_{(\xi,\eta)}, \tag{4}$$

where (ξ, η) are the spatial variables, (α, β) are the spatial frequencies, and $\Im$ denotes a two-dimensional continuous Fourier transformation.

The discrete form of Eq. (4) is written as

$$U(m\Delta\xi, n\Delta\eta) = FFT^{-1} \left\{ \exp\left[ikd(1 - \lambda\,r^2 - \lambda\,s^2)\right] FFT\left[U_0(k, l)\right]_{(r,s)} \right\}_{(m,n)}, \tag{5}$$

where FFT is the fast Fourier transform operator, $\Delta\xi$ and $\Delta\eta$ are the sampling intervals at the observation plane (pixel size), and r, s, m, and n are integers ($-N/2 \leq m, n \leq N/2$).

The reconstructed wavefront $U(\xi, \eta) = O(\xi, \eta)\,\exp[i\phi_o(\xi, \eta)]$ provides the amplitude $O(\xi, \eta)$ and phase images $\phi_o(\xi, \eta)$ of the object. From the reconstructed phase distribution $\phi_o(\xi, \eta)$, the specimen topography is determined for the reflection configuration $T(\xi, \eta) = \phi_o(\xi, \eta)/2k$.

2.3. Experimental results

In **Figure 2** is presented the schematic of the digital holographic Mirau microscope (DHMM). The proposed method was carried out using a He-Ne laser of $\lambda = 633$ nm in wavelength. The beam is filtered spatially with a spatial filter (SP). The beam goes through a Nikon 50X MIO with a numeric aperture, NA = 0.55. The hologram of sample (S) is imaged on the CCD camera plane by the tube lens (TL). The intensity hologram is recorded by a Pixelink ™ digital camera of CMOS 1280 × 1024 pixels, 8 bits, with a pixel size of 6.7 μm × 6.7 μm. The sample holder is attached with a piezoelectric transducer (PZT) to perform the phase-shifting technique. In addition, this sample holder is attached on an x, y, z displacement and θ rotation stage to perform the sample tilt, which is necessary for the off-axis configuration recording.

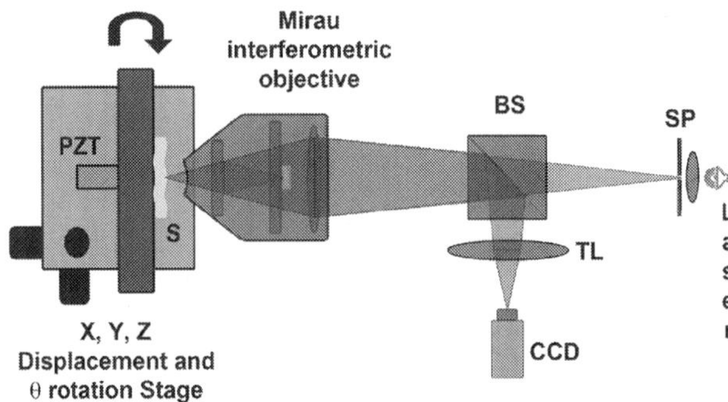

Figure 2. Schematic diagram of the digital holographic Mirau microscope (DHMM).

Now we present one real application of the usefulness of the tomographic capability of DHM. Typically, the MIO is used as a white light scanning and surface profiler in interferometry [14, 17]. In this section, we use this MIO with the DHM and compare the results with interferometry results.

As the tomographic feature of DHM works normally, which was demonstrated in [18], we can put under inspection MEMS and MOEMS with thicknesses larger than MO depth of focus (DOF), as Ferraro et al. and Colomb et al. have demonstrated in their results [6, 7], where this DOF is defined by DOF = $\lambda n_m / NA^2$, where n_m is the refractive index of the medium. We record four shifted holograms of a microlens of 100 μm in central diameter and 4.2 μm in height. **Figure 3(a)** shows a shifted hologram. The reconstruction distance at the top of

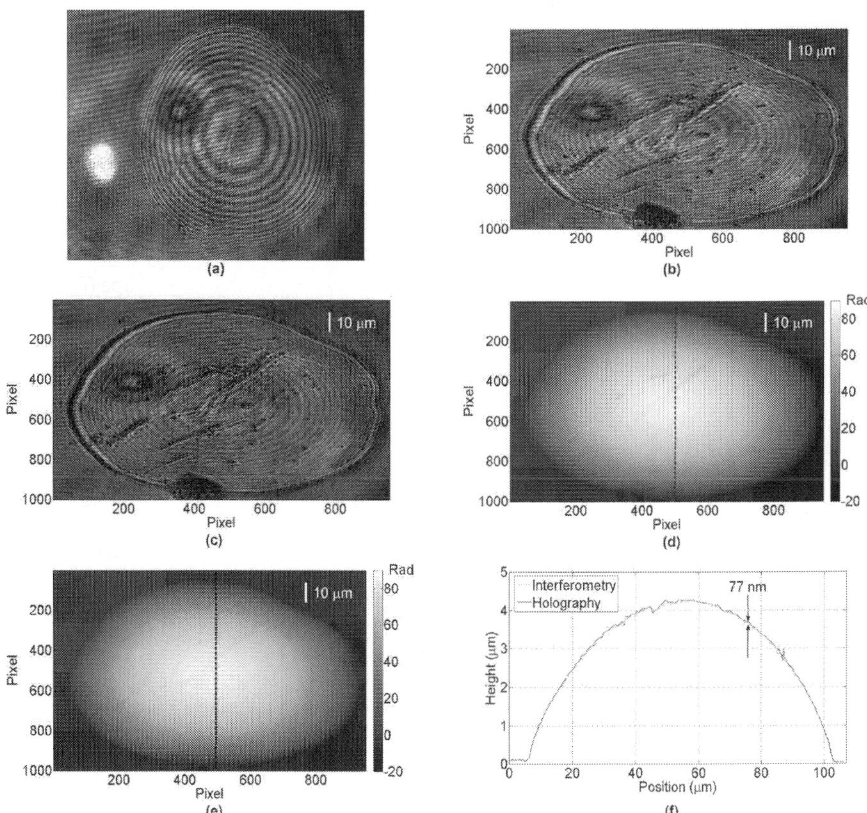

Figure 3. DHM using a MIO applied to a microlens topographic measurement. (a) One of the four-recorded holograms, (b) the reconstructed amplitude image focusing the bottom zone of the object, (c) the reconstructed amplitude image focusing the whole the object, (d) unwrapped phase map applying the phase shifting interferometry method, (e) unwrapped phase map of (c), (f) comparison between profiles measured along the black dash line in both methods, interferometry (d) and DHM (e).

the lens was of 0.4 μm (**Figure 3(b)**). Because the DOF is limited, the areas outside the DOF give out-of-focus and blurred amplitudes. **Figure 3(c)** shows the amplitude distribution map which was reconstructed with the different reconstruction distance method [6, 7] using the MIO and DHM. The initial DOF = 2.09 μm is increased by a factor of 2, as the height of the microlens is about 3.8 μm. **Figure 3(d)** and **(e)** shows both the unwrapped phase images of the specimen by using phase shifting interferometry and DHM methods, respectively. **Figure 3(f)** depicts profiles that compare the phase shifting interferometry result (**Figure 3(d)**) and DHM extending the DOF numerically (**Figure 3(e)**). These profiles correspond to the black-dashed line of the corresponding unwrapped phase map. A difference of about 77 nm is obtained between both measurement methods. The result is in agreement with the results obtained in references [6, 7] for an increased factor of 2. One has to keep in mind that the higher the factor is, the larger the measurement error (difference) will be. Here, we present a measurement system that uses DHM method in order to extend the DOF of the system. Our proposal produces better measurement accuracy due to extended DOF and the numerical reconstruction techniques. With these results, we have demonstrated that it is feasible to perform DHM with the MIO [18].

2.4. Conclusion

We have presented DHMM as a new reliable optical tool for performing DHM in-line reflection configuration. In the experimental results, we have principally proved the unique refocusing capability and the amplitude and phase images of DHM. The object under test sample was a microlens of 100 μm in diameter and 4.2 μm height. With these experimental results, we have also shown that it is possible to extend the DOF of the MO by using the numerical focusing capability of DHM. In addition, we have presented not only DHMM as an alternative to obtain digital holograms without spherical aberration, but also that an easier, well-aligned, and insensitive to external vibrations setup is reached, in comparison with the typical setups. Finally, a topographic measurement error attained with interferometry is demonstrated and compensated with DHM, which is due to the limited depth of focus of the MO.

3. Shot noise reduction in phase imaging of digital holograms

In this section, we show digital holograms with shot noise when they were recorded with a CCD camera. The illumination source used in the optical set up was a commercial LED. Here, we present a technique to reduce the shot noise of the phase and amplitude images coming from a single reconstructed wavefront of the object. To attain a shot noise reduction, an averaging procedure of reconstructed images at different reconstruction distances within the range determined by the focus depth is performed. With this tomographic capacity of DHM, we ensure an improved image without quality diminution, where a noise reduction of 50% is achieved. The results were compared with results from an atomic force microscope (AFM) in order to determine the system accuracy.

3.1. Experimental configuration

3.1.1. LED physical properties

Parasitic interferences and multiple reflections in optical setups are typical; one uses a low coherent source to reduce them. Here, we use a commercial ultrabrilliant LED of 5 mm in diameter, with emission in the red spectrum range. We used a calibrated i1Pro eye-one spectrophotometer of spectral range from 380 to 730 nm. The peak wavelength (λ) measured was of 630 nm, and a full width at half maximum (FWHM, $\Delta\lambda$) of its spectrum was of 24 nm. **Figure 4** shows the typical normalized spectrum of the LED that was used. Then, with the spectral data above mentioned ($\lambda^2/\Delta\lambda$), the coherence length was of 16.5 µm.

3.1.2. Reconstruction process

The experimental setup used was a modified Mach-Zehnder interferometer, as shown in **Figure 5**. When the beam is incident on the diaphragm D of a diameter of 300 µm, spatial coherence is increased. The spatial filter SP with an adjustable diaphragm to limit the source

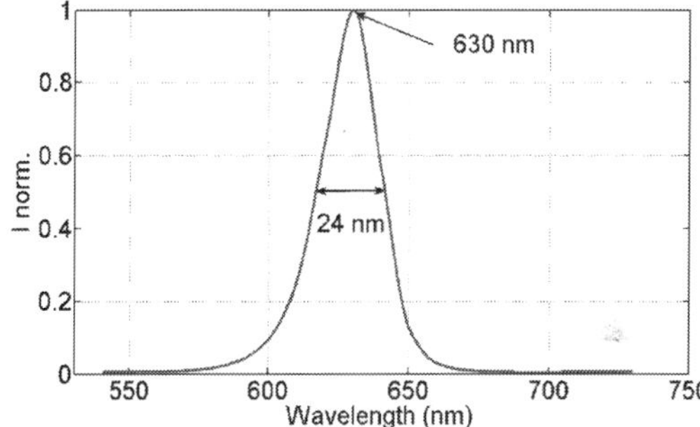

Figure 4. Normalized spectrum distribution of the light intensity emitted by the commercial ultrabrilliant LED.

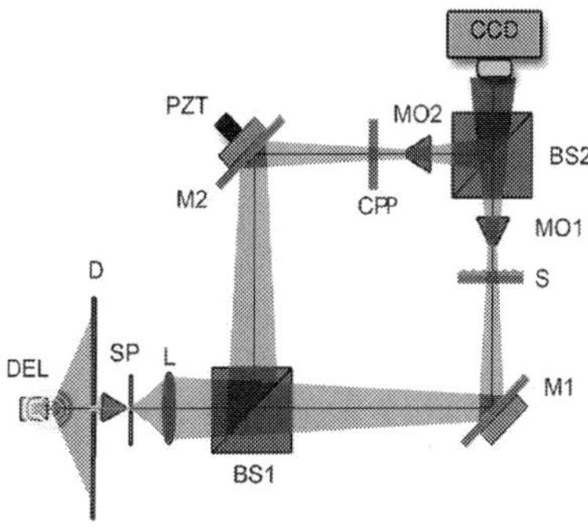

Figure 5. Optical setup implemented on a Mach-Zehnder interferometer with a low coherent source for digital holographic microscopy.

size creates a secondary source of low coherence. The lens L images D at the plane of the sample S and on the compensating plate (CP) when the beam is divided by BS1. The transmitted light through the specimen (S) is collected by a microscope objective (MO1) of 10× with 0.25 of numerical aperture (N.A.), which forms object wave O. The object wave interferes with a reference wave R when the light is collected by the microscope objective of 10× 0.25 N.A. (MO2) to produce a hologram. The hologram intensity (IH) is recorded by a camera; a CP was inserted in the setup to achieve interference between the two beams (Section 2.3). Also, mirror M1 was mounted on a linear displacement stage with step resolution of 1.25 μm. Mirror M2 was mounted on a piezoelectric transducer (PZT) to implement the phase-shifting technique.

The intensity $I(x,y)$ at the CCD sensor plane is formed by the interference of the object wave $O(x,y)$ and the reference wave $R(x,y)$ as Eq. (1). Mirror M2 is mounted on a PZT to calculate the phase of the initial object using the phase-shifting technique, and to eliminate the DC terms and the virtual image of Eq. (1). The 2π phase module is calculated with the four frame algorithm [15]:

$$\phi_0(x, y) = \tan^{-1}\left[\frac{\left(I_4(x, y; 3\pi/2) - I_2(x, y; \pi/2)\right)}{\left(I_1(x, y; 0) - I_3(x, y; \pi)\right)}\right].\tag{6}$$

The amplitude of the optical field $A_0(x,y)$ can be obtained by blocking the reference beam and recording only the diffraction object intensity in the CCD plane. Then, the object complex amplitude is as follows:

$$U_a(x, y) = A_0(x, y) \exp\left[i(\phi_0(x, y) + \phi(x, y))\right],\tag{7}$$

where the object wave is determined at the recording (x, y) plane, and ϕ is the phase aberration term.

To reduce phase aberrations induced by misalignment of the optical setup and MOs, we perform the reference conjugated hologram (RCH) method [19]. We obtain the phase aberration term without the presence of the test object, which can be subtracted from Eq. (7) to get the object complex amplitude:

$$U_0(x, y) = A_0(x, y) \times \exp\left[i(\phi_0(x, y) + \phi(x, y) - \phi(x, y))\right].\tag{8}$$

The angular spectrum method (AS) is performed to calculate the object wavefront at any other plane (ξ, η), in order to refocus it by Eqs. (4) and (5).

3.1.3. Focus depth and averaging method

A limitation in DHM is a limited depth of focus. High magnifications are achievable for investigating microobjects with this technique. However, higher is the required magnification, and lower is the focus depth system. As the geometrical DOF of an imaging system is related to the sampling rate, this DOF is defined as a function of the pixel size and the N.A. of the MO:

$$\mathrm{DOF} = \frac{\Delta\xi}{M^2\,\mathrm{N.A.}'}\tag{9}$$

where M is the magnification.

DHM has as a unique feature that is possible to refocus the object complex amplitude at any plane within the maximum refocus distance [6, 11]. We demonstrate that it is possible to refocus the complex amplitude at different distances within DOF (ΔDOF). The specimen physical thickness is given by

$$h = [\,\lambda(\Delta\phi/2\pi)/(n - n_0)\,], \qquad (10)$$

where λ is the wavelength, $\Delta\phi$ is the phase step, and $(n - n_0)$ is the index difference between the specimen's material and air.

Shot noise depends on optical power, and it follows a Poisson's statistics [20]. Then we say that a higher light intensity corresponds to a lower shot noise. A way to increase the amount of photons is performing an averaging of the reconstructed images in order to attain an improved image.

We performed an averaging process of the reconstructed images that are obtained from different reconstruction distances within the system's DOF in order to get an improved image. These reconstructed images are uncorrelated with each other at specific reconstruction distances, and computed from the same complex amplitude [21].

We think that if these reconstructed images are uncorrelated with similar standard deviations STD_c, one can write the following for the standard deviation of an averaged image $\sigma_{\bar{x}}$:

$$\sigma_{\bar{x}} = \frac{1}{\sqrt{C}}STD_c, \qquad (11)$$

where C is the number of images to average.

If four images are averaged, theoretically, noise reduction is of 50%.

3.2. Numerical and experimental results

In this part, the results of the recorded holograms are presented. The shutter camera enables us to reduce the exposure time down to 40 µs, with a variable gain from 0 to 17 dB in 14 increments. We do not reach a camera's full well capacity with a LED source in the setup presented, even with the maximum integration time and no electrical gain of camera parameters [21]. The optical power of the intensity was measured with a photo detector. First, a comparison between a blank experimental hologram and the simulated hologram results is shown. The intensity of the blank holograms was of 6.7×10^{-15} W/cm^2, and this corresponds to an average number of 5100 of photons per pixel. **Figure 6(a)** presents a blank phase image that is reconstructed without a phase aberration correction. A standard deviation (STD) $= 12°$ is computed in the black square area. On the other hand, **Figure 6(b)** presents the same reconstruction after the RCH method was applied, with a STD $= 0.7°$ in the same area.

We have noncorrelation among phase images reconstructed at different distances [21]. These images were obtained of the recorded experimental holograms from Eq. (4). **Figure 7** shows that when there is a difference of distance of 2 µm from one reconstructed phase image to

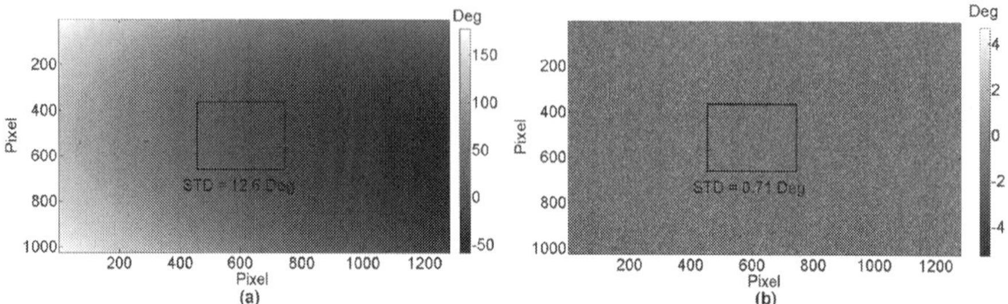

Figure 6. Reconstructed phase image from a recorded hologram without any sample. (a) Phase image without aberration correction and (b) phase image with aberration correction.

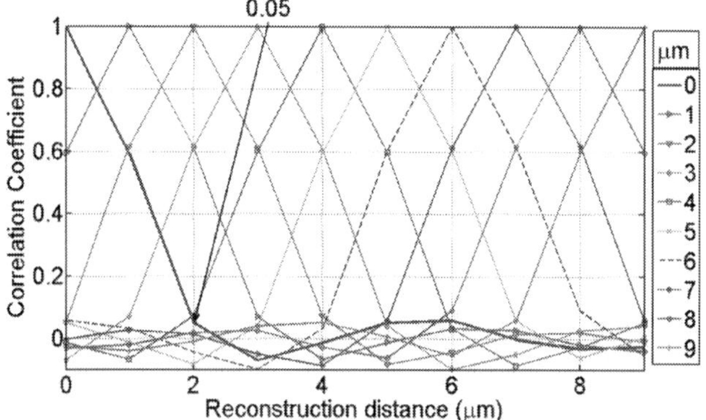

Figure 7. Correlation coefficient between reconstructed phase images at different reconstruction distances from the same wavefront of holograms recorded with low intensity (photons per pixel of 5100).

another one obtained from same complex wavefront, a noncorrelation exists between these images. In that case an averaging procedure can be performed of these noncorrelated images in order to get an improved image. These results validate the proposal previously demonstrated in reference [21].

With the $\Delta d = 2$ μm calculated, we can average C images. In **Figure 8(a)**, the phase image is shown without any averaging. This image was reconstructed within DOF of the system with $d = 30$ μm. The STD in this phase image is of 0.69°. On the other hand, **Figure 8(b)** shows a phase image after applying the proposed averaging procedure with 10 phase images. The STD of this image is of 0.231°. We get an image improvement of 68.4% of noise reduction. This is in agreement with Eq. (11). A profile comparison is shown in **Figure 9(a)**. The profiles were taken for the marked profile as a white line in the phase images in **Figure 8**.

Figure 9(b) presents the behavior of the STD as a function of the number of phase images C used in the averaging procedure. Also, a comparison between numerical simulation results and

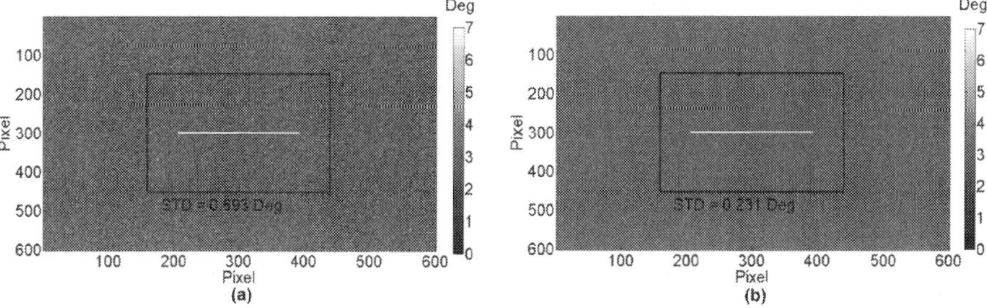

Figure 8. Improvement of phase image by the proposed averaging method in DHM. (a) Reconstructed phase image within DOF of the system and (b) phase image improved from 10 averaged phase images reconstructed.

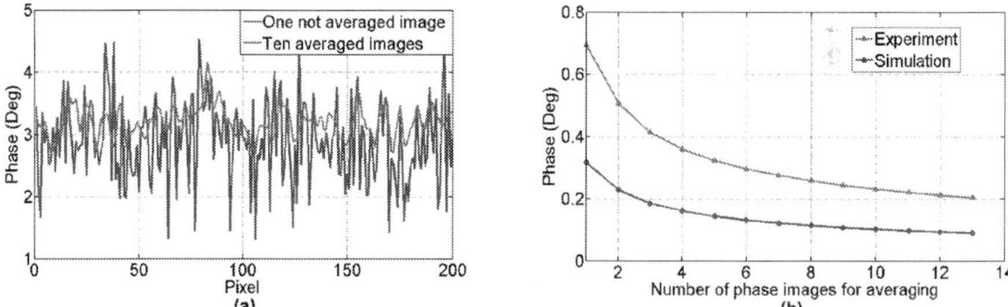

Figure 9. Behavior of noise phase reduction when, the averaging method is applied. (a) Profile of phase images in **Figure 8**, where a diminution of STD when 10 phase images are averaged and (b) profile of phase STD as a function of the number of phase images, where a behavior of $C^{-1/2}$ is shown in the STD reduction [21].

experimental results is presented. The simulation results were attained with a 5100 photons per pixel. The behavior of the shot noise reduction in experimental results follows the expected theoretical function defined in Eq. (11). Then we can say that the averaged images are noncorrelated. The difference, presented between experimental and simulations results, is due to the presence of sources of noise other than shot noise, quantum efficiency, and small optical defects in the optical components. One can see that if the number of averaged images increases, the offset also decreases. Noise sources should be speckle and thermal noise of CCD camera. Both the integration time during hologram recording is not the highest and the camera's well capacity is not reached due to low illumination, therefore the noise related to the quantum efficiency of the CCD detector is the main factor which is the difference between the experimental and simulated results.

3.2.1. Decrease of shot noise in amplitude images

A principal limitation in the proposal is limited DOF. As we have already seen in Section 3.1.3, DOF is related with the sampling distance and numerical aperture of the optical system. In the system described, the theoretical DOF is of about 0.268 μm. But, in the experimental

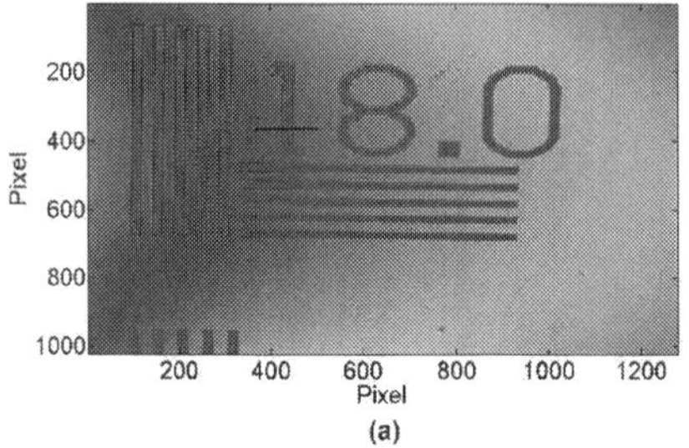

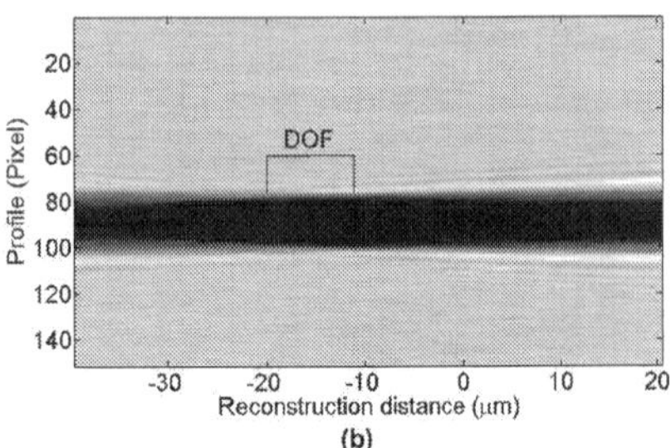

Figure 10. Determination of the DOF experimentally. (a) Recorded hologram and the profile zone taken to measure the DOF and (b) evolution of intensity when reconstruction distance is increased.

reconstruction, DOF is higher than would have been expected from Eq. (9). This is because the fact that the spatial resolution (pixel size) introduced by the optical setup is limited [13]. To experimentally attain the DOF, in **Figure 10(b)**, we have plotted a line profile shown in **Figure 10(a)**, where the profile is marked with a black line. The evolution of this plot starts at 40 μm before the image is focused. After zooming on the focus zone, we can determine that the DOF is 9 μm. The test object we used was an Edmund NBS 1963A resolution card. The zone of interest corresponds to 18 double lines per mm (lpmm). The reconstruction distance was of 15 μm.

If the DOF is 9 μm and Δd is of 2 μm, then we can average four images to carry out what we propose. These images have to be reconstructed at a distance within DOF to guarantee that image quality is not affected. **Figure 11** shows the image improved when the proposed method is applied. This evaluation is through STD in the area defined by the white square in each image. We attain a STD = 1.57 gray levels (GL) for an image focused without averaging (**Figure 11(a)**), and STD = 0.869 GL by applying the proposal method (**Figure 13(b)**). Then we say that the averaging process that we propose also improves the amplitude image.

In order to show that the lateral resolution is not affected by the averaging method that here is proposed, we have plotted a line profile marked by the white lines in **Figure 11**. **Figure 12**

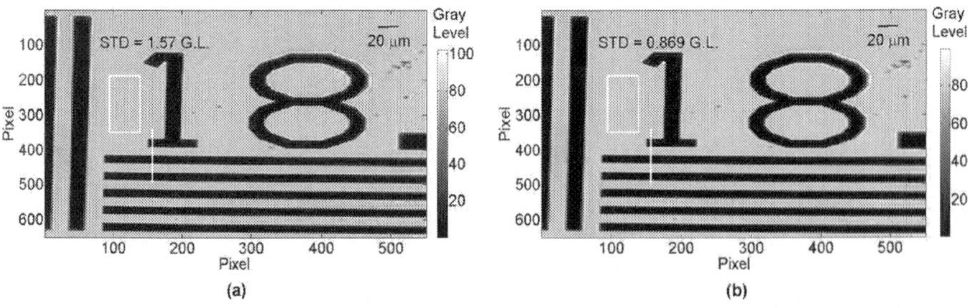

Figure 11. Reconstructed focused amplitude images. (a) Reconstructed focused amplitude image without averaging and (b) reconstructed amplitude image when the averaging process is performed with four focused amplitude images.

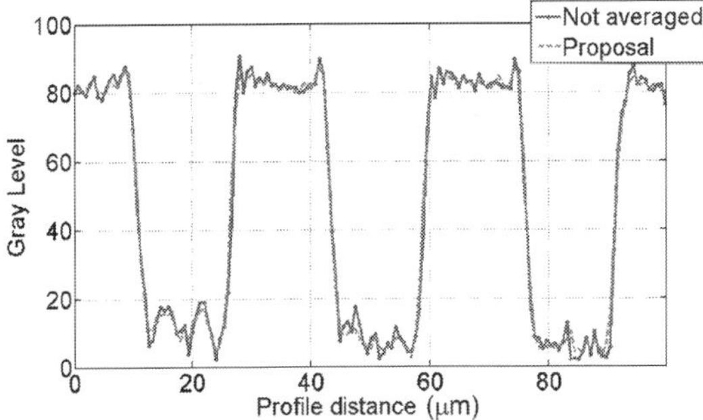

Figure 12. Comparison between profiles measured along the white lines defined in **Figure 11(a)** and **(b)**.

shows this plot and the comparison between the focused amplitude image without averaging and the improved image after applying the proposed method.

We can note, from this comparison in **Figure 12**, that there is no difference in the transition edges. On the other hand, we can clearly note the improvement on top and bottom areas from these profiles where the STD of the proposal clearly is the lowest.

3.2.2. Decrease of shot noise in phase images

First, we use a 100 nm step-wise specimen made at home of TiO_2 thin film, with a refraction index of 1.82 for a wavelength of 632.8 nm, as a phase-calibrating gauge. The specimen was made using a Balzer B-510 vapor deposition machine. To ensure a real and accurate measurement reference, the test object was measured with a Digital Instruments 3100 AFM. **Figure 13(a)** shows the reconstructed phase image of the step-wise, where the reconstruction distance was of 10 μm. The STD measured in the zone enclosed by the black square is of 3.44 nm. After applying the averaging proposal of four reconstructed phase images at $\Delta d = 2$ μm inside DOF, we compute a reduction of about 1.24 nm (corresponding to 0.57° of STD reduction). **Figure 13(b)** shows the improved phase image in comparison with the predicted value of the experimental results, where the STD reduction was of 0.35 deg (**Figure 9(b)**). This is because the higher than expected SDT reduction is mainly due to a lower intensity recording than the blank recorded holograms. This lower intensity is due to the glass plates thickness located in the arms of the interferometer (4.7 mm glass of each). There are some other causes that generate noise in the phase image, such as quantum efficiency of CCD and small optical defects in the optical components, Thermal noise of CCD, among others. The noise generated by these causes is also reduced in a percentage. The evaluation zone is marked in **Figure 13(b)** by the white solid square. In **Figure 13(d)**, we present the topography measurement, which was done by AFM. Normally, this measurement needs to correct it by a numerical procedure. This is due to a tilt contribution in one or both lateral directions. In **Figure 13(c)**, we present the zone where the comparing information was taken of the improved phase image by zooming in the white dashed rectangle of **Figure 13(b)**. A profile comparison extracted from the white lines in **Figure 13(c)** and **(d)** is presented in **Figure 14**. These profiles show their topographic

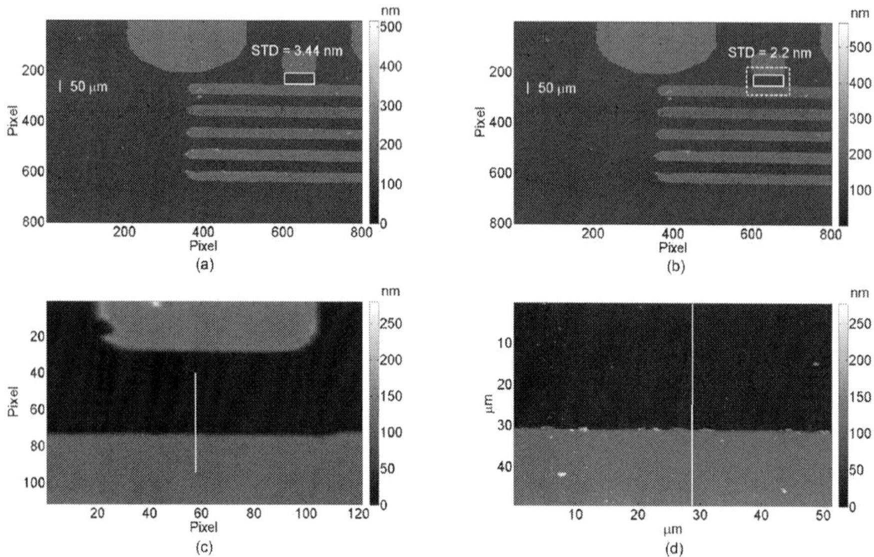

Figure 13. Topographic measurement of the TiO$_2$ step-wise specimen. (a) One reconstructed phase image, (b) improved phase image when the averaging process is performed, (c) corresponding zoomed area inside the white dashed rectangle in (b), and (d) numerical data extracted from AFM.

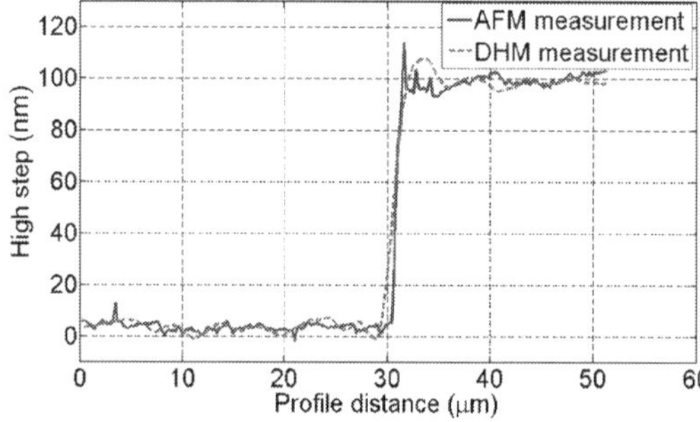

Figure 14. Comparison between profiles measured along the white lines defined in **Figure 13(c)** and **(d)**.

heights. The biggest difference is mainly located in the transition zones. This difference is due to differences in the lateral resolution between microscopes. It can also be improved in the upper and lower areas with topographic measured while the AFM (blue solid line), due to what has been discussed above. DHM must be reached in larger lateral resolution by using an MO with high NA., this makes our proposal is a comparable alternative method with AFM [21]. Furthermore, the method has some advantages DHM against AFM. One of them is the time to obtain topographic data, because while our proposal takes just seconds to perform the

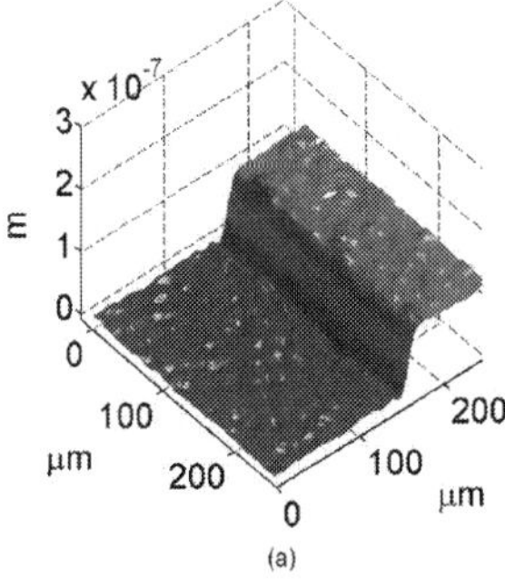
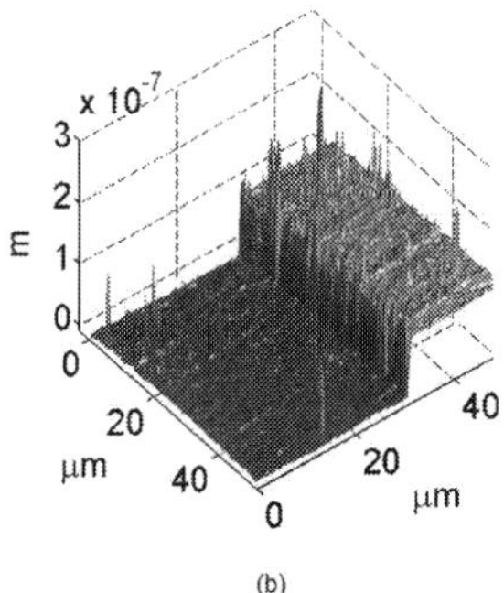

Figure 15. 3D TiO_2 step images. (a) Topographic measurement done by AFM and (b) topographic measurement enhanced through the averaging process done by DHM.

topography, AFM measurement takes several minutes to complete this task. Another advantage is the flexibility to test an area larger than the AFM method. A last important advantage of our proposal is that it is cheaper in their application that the AFM.

Finally, **Figure 15(a)** and **(b)** present the 3D topographic map of the TiO_2 step presented in **Figure 13(d)** and **(c)**, respectively. **Figure 15(a)** corresponds to the data provided by the AFM. The smaller sampling rate commented above has a better ability to detect defects in the sample. **Figure 15(b)** corresponds to an improved topographic data obtained by DHM.

3.3. Conclusion

In DHM the phase information has great importance for the analysis and characterization of materials, such as biological samples and microoptical systems. In this study we have shown a different way to get an improved topographic measurement. The proposal is based on the decrease of the shot noise in DHM. In this section, we show a proposal that is based on the averaging process of reconstructed images by the tomographic capacity of DHM within the range determined by the focus depth. We obtained an improved phase image without quality diminution, in which a noise reduction of 50% was achieved. In addition, we have been shown axial topographic measurements in agreement with the measurements made with a standard AFM.

4. A method to reduce the ringing effect in phase imaging in off-axis digital holograms

In this section, we present a method to reduce the ringing effect of discontinuous surfaces in the reconstruction process in off-axis digital holography. The method is based on the natural diffraction of light (Talbot effect). We previously showed that for variable grating, Talbot phenomenon is also present [22]. When you use a binary filter in order to attain the object-wave in off-axis digital holography, this allows an easy implementation of filtering mask in the filtering process. By using the binary filter the appearance of Gibbs phenomenon in discontinuous surfaces appear. However, such a phenomenon was possible to reduce (experimentally nearly to 2 nm) by using the unique feature that digital holography have, this is the tomographic capacity. In addition we show that the size of the binary low-pass filter in the holographic reconstruction process is related to the focus zone. The versatility by using binary low-pass filter allows us to fit size according to the sample under study. It is possible with the tomographic capability chose the interest zone in axial direction to inspect the sample. This allows us while applying the low-pass filtering process to avoid the defects that can occur on either the optical component or the sample container. The results should be of interest to readers in the areas of optical metrology, grating diffraction, digital holography, and digital holographic microscopy.

4.1. Proposal of the method

The optical setup used in the present study for recording off-axis digital holograms is a Michelson interferometer presented in **Figure 16**. The light source is from a laser diode with a wavelength of 643 nm, which is expanded by a beam expander system (BE). This source is linearly polarized plane wavefront with short coherence (coherence length about 0.1 mm). The beam is split by a beam splitter (BS) into a reference wave R and an object wave O. The CCD camera records an off-axis hologram at the exit of the interferometer. This hologram (H) is created by the interference between the $O(x,y)$ and $R(x,y)$, after they reflect on the sample (S) and mirror (M), respectively. To obtain off-axis holograms, the orientation of M is set in such a way that, the CCD is reached by $R(x,y)$, with an incident angle θ, while $O(x,y)$ is perpendicularly propagated with respect to the hologram plane. The distance z between the CCD and the object is 85 mm. The CCD is a standard black and white camera with pixel size of 4.4 μm and 8 bits of depth.

This off-axis digital hologram $H(x,y)$ can be expressed by the Eq. (1). A window function $W(f_x,f_y)$ is used to filter the term $O(x,y)R^*(x,y)$ of Eq. (1) in the frequency domain. On the other hand, the so-called frequency spectrum filtering method [23] is applied in order to retrieve the object wavefront $O(f_x,f_y)$. Here,

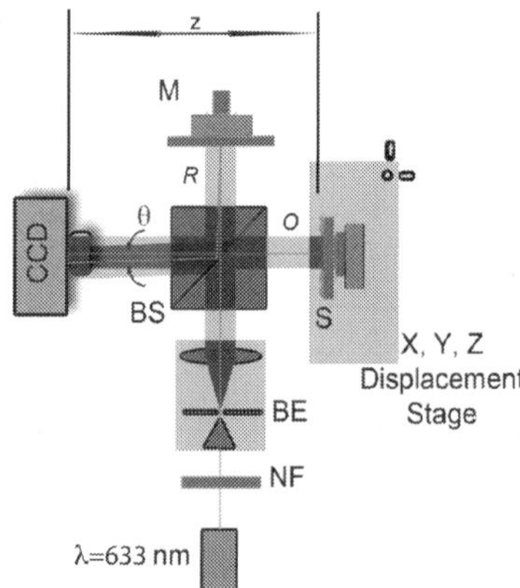

Figure 16. Optical system based on a Michelson interferometer. M is a mirror, NF is a neutral filter and BE is a beam expander.

$$O(f_x, f_y) = W(f_x, f_y)\ \Im^{\mp 1}\{H(x, y)\ R_D(x, y)\},\tag{12}$$

where R_D is a digital replica of R, and $\Im^{\mp 1}$ stands for either the direct continuous Fourier transform or its inverse counterpart, in other contexts. Hence, the object $O(f_x, f_y)$ can be propagated using the approximation of the Fresnel-Kirchhoff propagation integral as follows [16]:

$$O_i(x, y, z_i) = \Im^{+1}\left\{ \begin{array}{l} \left[O(f_x, f_y)\right]\exp(jk\,z_i) \\ \times \exp\left[-j\pi\lambda\,z_i\right]\left[(f_x)^2 + (f_y)^2\right] \end{array} \right\},\tag{13}$$

where λ is the wavelength, k is the wave number and z_i is the reconstruction distance. The reconstructed object wavefront $O(x,y)$ provides the amplitude image $A_i(x,\ y)=|O_i\ (x,y)|^2$ and the phase image $\phi_i(\ x,y)=tg^{-1}(imag(O_i\ (x,y))/real(O_i\ (x,y)))$ of the object. The topography $T(x,y)$ of the specimen is computed from the reconstructed phase $\phi(\ x,y)$, by the reflection configuration $T(x,y) = \phi(\ x,y)/2k$.

4.1.1. The Fourier filtering process

The filtering process is a well-known technique outlined by Cuche et al. [23]. However in this proposal the *DC* term is eliminated by the subtraction of the intensity of R and O, recorded independently, in Eq. (1). Edges and other sharp transitions (such as noise) in the digital hologram contribute significantly to the high-frequency content of its Fourier transform [16]. We considered three types of low-pass filters: ideal (ILPF), Butterworth (BtwLPF), and Gaussian (GLPF). These three filters cover the range from very sharp (ideal) to very smooth (Gaussian) filter functions. When we use the ILPF, a ringing effect appears at the sharp transitions zone of the reconstructed image due to transfer function W in Eq. (12); which is a *sinc* function. In addition, the filter size (cut-off frequency) is directly related to the period of the ringing [24, 25]. On the other hand, since the transfer function of the Gaussian filter is also a Gaussian function, it will have a blurring behavior, but no ringing effect. When you use the BtwLPF of second order, the ringing effect and the blurring is similar to that observed in the Gaussian filtering. Then the ringing increased, according to the order of the filter as we commented in [22].

4.1.2. The Talbot effect

When a monochromatic wavefront is plane and illuminates a linear grating of period p, multiple identical images of the original grating are observed along the propagation axis of the light. These images are formed without any lenses on multiples of the Rayleigh distance (z_{tdu}). This phenomenon is known as the Talbot effect or self-imaging and it is due to the diffraction of light when pass through the grating [26]. The Talbot distance is located at:

$$z_{tdu} = \frac{up^2}{\lambda},\tag{14}$$

where $u = 1, 2, 3,\ldots$ denotes the Talbot plane order (TPO) and λ is the illumination light wavelength. When u is odd the self-imaging has 180° phase shift and contrast reversal [16]. The same result can be present in a thin phase attenuated sinusoidal grating as we presented in [22].

4.2. Simulations

A simulation was performed to get an off-axis digital hologram. According to the optical scheme (**Figure 16**), two plane waves of equal intensities have been considered to interfere in a Michelson interferometer for attaining off-axis digital hologram. We design a synthetic object, which consists of three horizontal bars and three vertical bars etched on a thin chromium film (100% reflective) deposited in a glass substrate. The reflectance of the film is of 6.25% and the thickness of 0.7π rad. (**Figure 17(a)** and **(b)**). In real world the reflectivity of 100% of an object is not possibly reached, but the simulation allows us to design synthetic objects with 100% reflectivity. The size of this object is of 1200 × 1200 pixels; the distance between the object and the CCD plane is of z = 84.4 mm. We assumed a red wavelength of 643 nm from a laser, and pixel size of 4.4 μm × 4.4 μm of the CCD according to the real parameters. If we consider a wavelength of 643 nm then the sample thickness will be of 112.5 nm by applying the topographic formula that was mentioned at the end of Section 4.1. We have considered the standard deviation (STD) as a measure of the axial resolution and amplitude improvement (arbitrary unit [a.u.]) in all sections. **Figure 17(c)** present the synthetic off-axis digital hologram.

We start reconstructing the object wavefront by performing the Eq. (13) with a reconstruction distance (z = z_{td0}) of 84.4 mm. To remove the DC term and the virtual image, we perform the Fourier filtering process mentioned in Section 4.1.1. **Figure 18(a)** and **(b)** presents the amplitude and phase images, respectively, by using an ILPF with a cut-off frequency of radius of 100 pixels. As we have been mentioned, **Figure 18(a)** shows a profile where the ringing effect appear with a period of u = 53 μm. This profile is comparable to a variable transmittance function (VTF) grating simulated, according to Goodman [16] and confirmed in previous simulations [22] with the 180° phase shift and contrast reversal of the field distribution at the first TPO (z_{td1}) property. Next a second reconstruction was performed at $z = z + z_{td1}$ = 88.7 mm with the same size of the filter. It should be noted that normally the reconstruction of the object wavefront is done only at one distance; this is the focusing distance z. However, to reduce the ringing effect we need to perform an averaging operation between phase and amplitude reconstructed images at different distances z_{ht0} and z_{ht1} that is:

$$\phi(x, y) = [\phi_0(x, y) + \phi_1(x, y)]/2$$
$$A(x, y) = [A_0(x, y) + A_1(x, y)]/2. \tag{15}$$

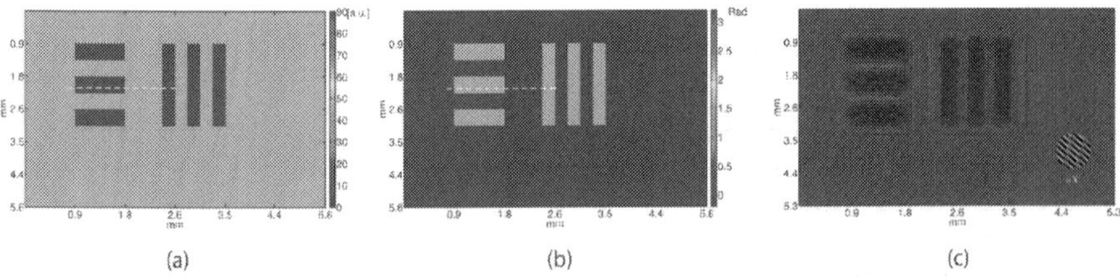

(a)

(b)

(c)

Figure 17. (a) Amplitude and (b) phase test object used to perform numerical simulation, and (c) off-axis digital hologram recorded at z = 84.4 mm from the object test.

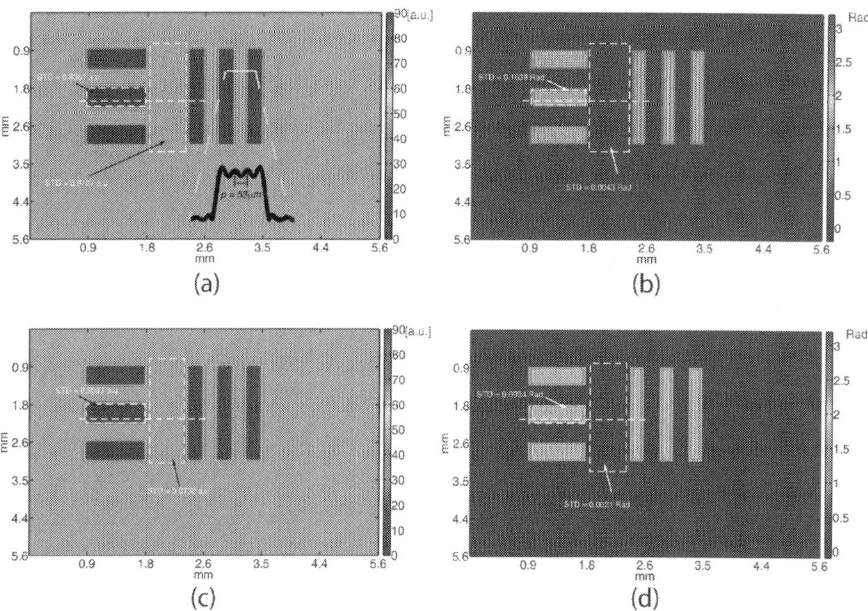

Figure 18. Reconstructed images from the hologram of **Figure 3(c)**. (a) and (b) Reconstructed amplitude and phase images at $z = z_{td0}$ respectively, (c) and (d) improved amplitude and phase images, respectively, after proposal is applied.

From **Figure 18(c)** and **(d)**, we can see the both improved images amplitude and phase map, obtained with this proposal. A comparison between the corresponding images obtained at a single distance of reconstruction z and our proposed method is done. We can note a clearly noiseless images reconstructed by our proposal. The improvement with this procedure is an average decrease of STD of 64% in the amplitude image and 47% in phase image. The percentage is an average between the two zones delimited by the dashed rectangles in **Figure 18**. The STD of the region of interest is represented in each reconstructed images. As far as we know this is a new and useful method to reduce the ringing phenomenon.

In **Figure 19(a)** and **(b)**, we show line profiles taken from white-dashed line shown in **Figures 17(a)–(b)** and **18(a)–(d)**. Also, we have included profiles from reconstructed images at the first TPO and profiles from reconstructed images when Gaussian and Butterworth filters were used in the filtering process. We can appreciate the periodic property as a result of using an ideal filter not only at z_{ht0} but also at z_{ht1}. We can note this behavior in both amplitude and phase distributions. Additionally, and in agreement with simulations performed in [22], we can observe not only a phase shift of 180° and reversal amplitude attained in the reconstruction at z_{ht1}. An unfavorable anomaly, but usual, phase, and amplitude variances are presented in boundaries (edges) due to single diffraction order that does not superpose with other diffraction orders [27]. Due to that, when the averaging is performed between reconstructed images at z_{ht0} and z_{ht1}, we cannot compensate the ringing in this zone. On

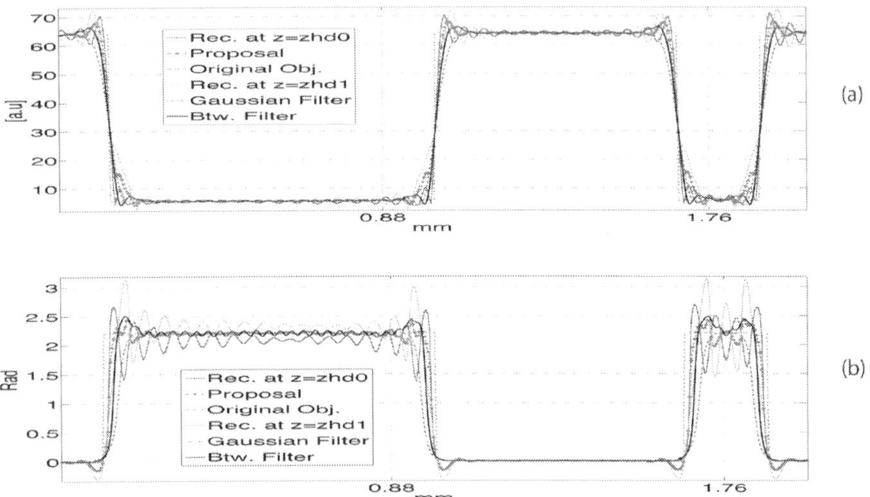

Figure 19. Comparison between profiles measured a long white dashed line of **Figures 3(a)**, **(b)** and **4(a)–(d)**. (a) Profiles of amplitude distributions and (b) profiles of phase distributions.

the other hand, we observe a loss of lateral resolution in reconstructed images (principally in phase distribution) when BtwLPF and GLPF are applied in the filtering process. This is important to know as phase distribution is directly related with thickness and, in our case, sample topography.

Nevertheless we can see a slight difference between proposal and the BtwLPF of second order in the profiles comparison. However, an advantage of ideal low-pass filter is that have the possibility to increase the tomographic resolution. This property is due to pixel size, magnification, and numerical aperture of the optical imaging system as demonstrated by Dubois et al. [13] and in our case, the filter size. To illustrate the determination of tomographic zone (TZ), in **Figure 20(a)** we have plotted the intensity evolution with the reconstruction distance on a line profile from the **Figure 18(a)**, where the profile zone is marked with a white-dashed line. The starting image is defocused by -10 to 10 mm. We can see that the TZ is of 3.2 mm by using the ideal filter and 16 mm by using the Butterworth one. Then we say that ideal filter is better to determine a focus zone than Butterworth. This result permit us not only to determine the best and most accuracy reconstruction distance zone to prevent measurement errors [28], but also to adjust the tomographic capability with respect to the sample thickness to reduce the defects that can occur on either the optical component or the sample container. Also this capacity helps us to control the resolution of plane scanning in a tomographic scheme [13]. **Figure 20(c)** presents the intensity evolution of the line profile in the zone marked with white-dashed line as **Figure 20(a)** but with filter size of 200 pixels of radius. This shows a smaller focus zone than a filter size of 100 pixels of radius (**Figure 20(a)**) evidencing the above mentioned.

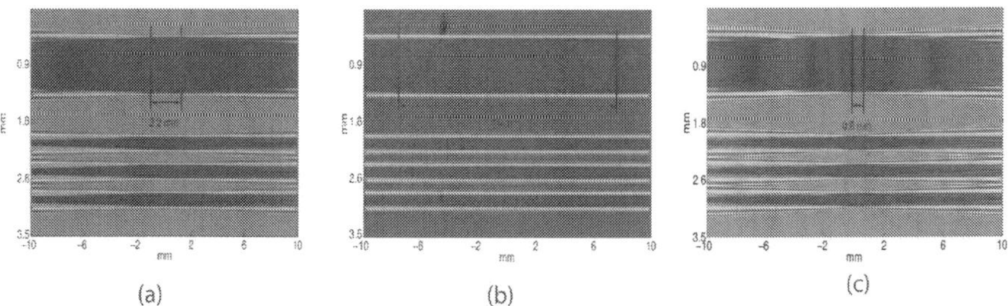

(a)   (b)   (c)

Figure 20. Evolution of intensities determined on a profile line when reconstruction distance is increased. Using (a) an ILPF of 100 pixels of radius, (b) a BtwLPF of 100 pixels of radius and (c) an ILPF of 200 pixels of radius.

4.3. Experimental results

In this section, we present experimental results of the recorded holograms of 1600 × 1200 pixels size. **Figure 15** shows the digital holographic setup that we implement. We use a laser diode of 643 nm in wavelength as light source. This source is a diode of low coherence (about 0.1 mm) linearly polarized plane wavefront to prevent parasitic interference and optical noise. The hologram is recorded by a CCD Pixelink™ digital camera of 1600 × 1200 pixels, 8 bits, with a pixel size of 4.4 μm × 4.4 μm. The sample holder is supporting on an x, y, z, displacement and θ rotation stage to perform the sample tilt, which is necessary for the off-axis configuration recording. We used an USAF 1951 resolution test target in the zone that corresponds to the 1-1 test group as the object test. In **Figure 21**, we show a recorded digital hologram [22].

At the beginning, we reconstructed the object wavefront by performing the Eq. (13) with a reconstruction distance ($z = z_{td0}$) of 85 mm. **Figure 22(a)** and **(b)** shows the amplitude and topography distributions, respectively, by using an ILPF with radius of 100 pixels (cut-off frequency). As ILPF size is the same, as used in simulations results, then a ringing artifact with a period of $u = 53$ μm appear in the reconstructed images. A second reconstruction was

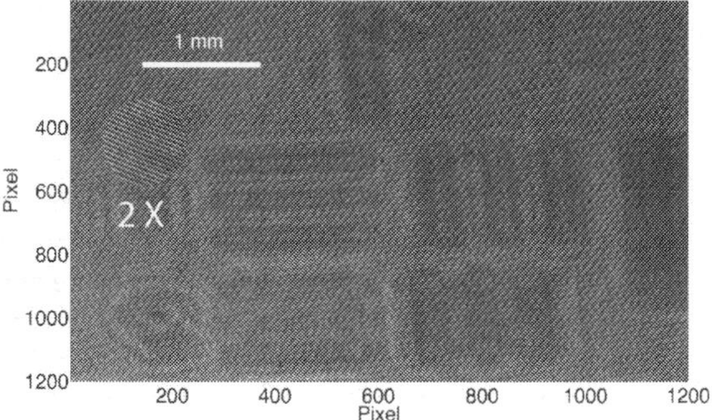

Figure 21. Digital experimental hologram of the USAF 1951 resolution test target.

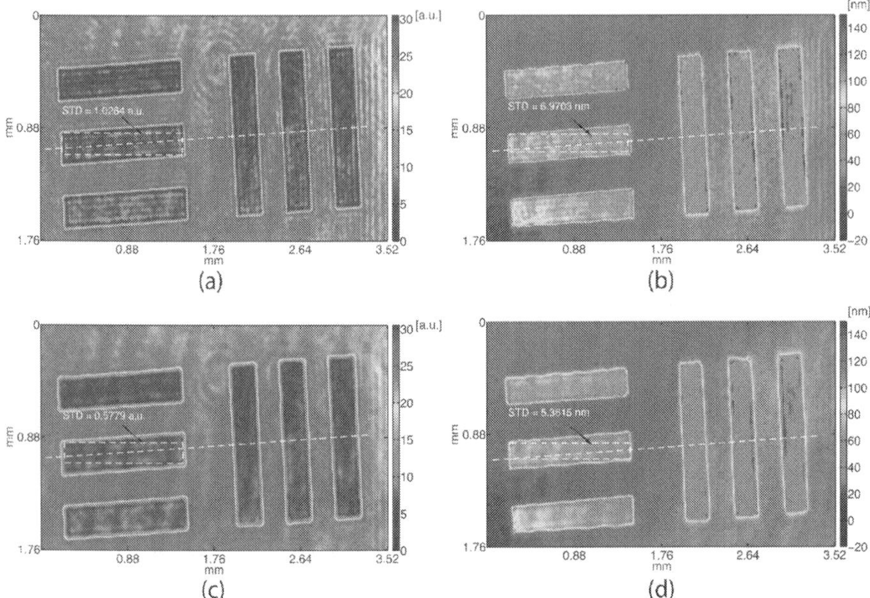

Figure 22. Reconstructed images from the hologram of **Figure 7**. (a) and (b) Reconstructed amplitude and topography distributions at $z = z_{td0}$ respectively, (c) and (d) improved amplitude and topography respectively after proposal is applied.

performed at $z = z + z_{td1} = 89.4$ mm. To reduce the ringing effect we perform the averaging proposal between phase and amplitude reconstructed images, as we previously mentioned. In **Figure 22(c)** and **(d)**, we present the enhanced images obtained with this proposal. The improved distributions contain nearly all the details of the original object. The reduction with this procedure is an average of 43.7% of STD in amplitude image and 23.1% in the topography. The percentage is an average between the two zones delimited by the dashed-white rectangles in **Figure 22**. **Figure 23(a)** and **(b)** presents line profiles where region is marked with a white-dashed line shown in **Figure 22(a)–(d)**. Also, as simulation results, we have included profiles from reconstructed images at the first TPO and profile from reconstructed images when Butterworth filter is used in the filtering process. We can note the periodic component as a result of using an ideal filter at z_{ht0}. This behavior is presented in both amplitude and phase distributions in agreement with simulation results. We assume that the percentage difference between simulation results and experimental results is principally due to an additional low frequency noises coming from optical devices defects, a nonperfect plane wave reference, aberrations noncompensated, and also a nonuniform thin film deposited on target. Nevertheless, we can see a difference between proposal and the BtwLPF of second order in the profiles plot exactly as in simulation performed in [22]. These differences are mainly at the transition edges, which are related to the lateral resolution.

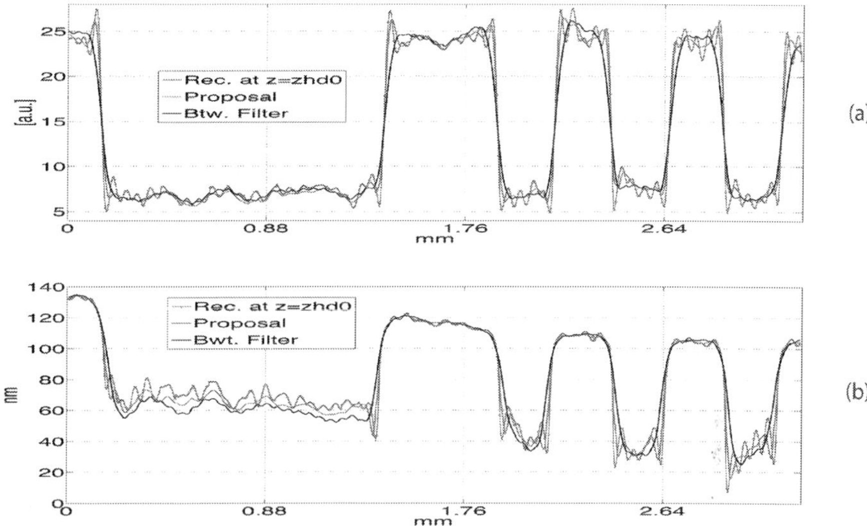

Figure 23. Comparison between profiles measured a long white dashed line of **Figure 8(a)–(d)**. (a) Profiles of amplitude distributions and (b) profiles of topography distributions.

4.4. Conclusions

In this work, we present a new method to reduce the ringing effect of discontinuous surfaces reconstruction in off-axis digital holography. The technique is based on the diffractive nature of light (Talbot effect). We use an ideal filter in the filtering process in digital off-axis holography, because it allows an easy implementation and versatility to choose frequencies of interest. The major disadvantage in using this filter is the appearance of Gibbs phenomenon in discontinuous surfaces. However, such a phenomenon was possible to reduce by using the unique feature that digital holography have, this is the tomographic capability. Experimental results have proved reductions of these anomalies, 30%. Also, we have demonstrated a better tomographic capacity by using an ideal filter than Butterworth. Numerical simulation evidenced that the Talbot effect can also be present in VTF grating from 0 to 2 TPO. Also, we have shown that the size of the ideal low-pass filter in the holographic reconstruction process is dependent on focus zone. The results should be of interest to readers in the areas of optical metrology, grating diffraction, digital holography, and digital holographic microscopy.

5. Summary

DHM give us the possibility to scan biological samples, semitransparent materials and tissues in axial direction with nanometric resolution. This is possible because the technique have a unique characteristic of numerical refocusing or tomographic capacity. In this chapter, we have shown three application of this capacity. First, we extend the DOF of the MIO in order to avoid topographical measurement error of a microlens of a 4.2 μm high. The compactness and easy-use of the MIO that we have presented not only DHMM as a new alternative to obtain digital holograms without spherical aberration and easy tilt correction in the phase image, but also that an easier, well-aligned, and insensitive to external vibrations setup is reached, in comparison with the typical setups. Second, we reduce the shot noise in phase and amplitude images coming from digital holograms. This reduction allows us to attain high topographic resolution comparable with an AFM results. Finally, we present a method to reduce noise in off-axis holograms when a Fourier filtering method is applied.

Acknowledgements

The support of FONDECYT (Preis 3140076, Preis 1140239 and Preis 1120764), FONDEF (Preis IT13I10034), CORFO (Preis 14BPC4-28651), USACH-DICYT ASOCIATIVO, SEP-PROMEP Preis 14146 F-38, and UTFSM-DGIP, CONICYT-PCHA/Doctorado Nacional 201363130065, is gratefully acknowledged. Some parts of the chapter are part of the previously published papers [18, 21, 22].

Author details

Miguel León-Rodríguez[1, 2*], Juan A. Rayas-Alvarez[1], Amalia Martínez-García[3] and Raúl R. Cordero[1]

*Address all correspondence to: y_migue@hotmail.com

1 Universidad de Santiago de Chile, Santiago, Chile

2 Universidad Politécnica de Guanajuato, Cortazar, Guanajuato, Mexico

3 Centro de Investigaciones en Óptica, A.C. Loma del Bosque, León, Guanajuato, México

References

[1] Schnars U, Jüptner W. Direct recording of holograms by a CCD target and numerical reconstruction. Appl Opt. 1994;33(2):179–81.

[2] Baumbach T, Kolenovic E, Kebbel V, Jüptner W. Improvement of accuracy in digital holography by use of multiple holograms. Appl Opt. 2006;45(24):6077–85.

[3] Mann CJ, Yu L, Kim MK. Movies of cellular and sub-cellular motion by digital holographic microscopy. Biomed Eng Online. 2006;5:21.

[4] Charrière F, Kühn J, Colomb T, Montfort F, Cuche E, Emery Y, et al. Characterization of microlenses by digital holographic microscopy. Appl Opt. 2006;45(5):829–35.

[5] Kemper B, Stürwald S, Remmersmann C, Langehanenberg P, von Bally G. Characterisation of light emitting diodes (LEDs) for application in digital holographic microscopy for inspection of micro and nanostructured surfaces. Opt Lasers Eng. 2008;46(7):499–507.

[6] Ferraro P, Grilli S, Alfieri D, De Nicola S, Finizio A, Pierattini G, et al. Extended focused image in microscopy by digital Holography. Opt Express. 2005;13(18):6738–49.

[7] Colomb T, Pavillon N, Kühn J, Cuche E, Depeursinge C, Emery Y. Extended depth-of-focus by digital holographic microscopy. Opt Lett. 2010;35(11):1840–2.

[8] Kang X 康 新. An effective method for reducing speckle noise in digital holography. Chinese Opt Lett. 2008;6(2):100–3.

[9] Rong L戎路, Xiao W 肖文, Pan F 潘锋, Liu S 刘烁, Li R 李瑞. Speckle noise reduction in digital holography by use of multiple polarization holograms. Chinese Opt Lett. 2010;8(7):653–5.

[10] Charrière F, Rappaz B, Kühn J, Colomb T, Marquet P, Depeursinge C. Influence of shot noise on phase measurement accuracy in digital holographic microscopy. Opt Express. 2007;15(14):8818–31.

[11] Dubois F, Requena MN, Minetti C, Monnom O, Istasse E. Partial spatial coherence effects in digital holographic microscopy with a laser source. Appl Opt [Internet]. 2004;43(5): 1131–9. Available from: http://www.opticsinfobase.org/abstract.cfm?URI=ao-43-5-1131

[12] Kühn J, Charrière F, Colomb T, Cuche E, Montfort F, Emery Y, et al. Axial sub-nanometer accuracy in digital holographic microscopy. Meas Sci Technol. 2008;19(7):074007.

[13] Dubois F, Joannes L, Legros JC. Improved three-dimensional imaging with a digital holography microscope with a source of partial spatial coherence. Appl Opt. 1999;38(34):7085–94.

[14] Malacara D. Optical Shop Testing. Third. New Jersey: Wiley; 2007. pp. 696–731.

[15] Zhang T, Yamaguchi I. Three-dimensional microscopy with phase-shifting digital holography. Opt Lett. 1998;23(15):1221–3.

[16] J.W. G. Introduction to Fourier Optics. Second. New York: McGraw-Hill; 1996. 441 p.

[17] Ma S, Quan C, Zhu R, Tay CJ, Chen L, Gao Z. Application of least-square estimation in white-light scanning interferometry. Opt Lasers Eng. 2011;49(7):1012–8.

[18] León-Rodríguez M, Rodríguez-Vera R, Rayas JA, Calixto S. Digital holographic microscopy through a Mirau interferometric objective. Opt Lasers Eng. 2013;51(3):240–5.

[19] Colomb T, Kühn J, Charrière F, Depeursinge C, Marquet P, Aspert N. Total aberrations compensation in digital holographic microscopy with a reference conjugated hologram. Opt Express. 2006;14(10):4300–6.

[20] Goodman JW. Statistical Optics. New York: John Wiley & Sons; 1985.

[21] León-Rodríguez M, Rodríguez-Vera R, Rayas J a., Calixto S. High topographical accuracy by optical shot noise reduction in digital holographic microscopy. J Opt Soc Am A. 2012;29(4):498.

[22] León-rodríguez M, Rayas JA, Martínez-garcía A, Martínez-gonzalez A, Téllez-quiñones A, Flores-muñoz V. Reduction of the ringing effect in off-axis digital holography reconstruction from two reconstruction distances based on Talbot effect. Opt Eng. 2015;54(10):1041101–9.

[23] Cuche E, Marquet P, Depeursinge C. Simultaneous amplitude-contrast and quantitative phase-contrast microscopy by numerical reconstruction of Fresnel off-axis holograms. Appl Opt. 1999;38(34):6994–7001.

[24] Gonzalez RC, Woods RE, Eddins SL. Digital image processing using Matlab. Upper Saddle River, NJ: Woods, & Eddins; 2009.

[25] Ream N. Discrete-Time Signal Processing. Electronics and Power. Upper Saddle River, NJ: Prentice-Hall; 1999. 157 p.

[26] Creath K, Wyant J. Moiré and fringe projection techniques. Optical shop testing. Third. New Yersey: Elsevier Ltd; 1993. 653–685 p.

[27] Kim MS, Scharf T, Menzel C, Rockstuhl C, Herzig HP. Phase anomalies in Talbot light carpets of self-images. Opt Express [Internet]. 2013;21(1):1287–300. Available from: http://www.ncbi.nlm.nih.gov/pubmed/23389022

[28] El Mallahi A, Dubois F. Dependency and precision of the refocusing criterion based on amplitude analysis in digital holographic microscopy. Opt Express. 2011;19(7):6684–98.

3D Capture and 3D Contents Generation for Holographic Imaging

Elena Stoykova, Hoonjong Kang, Youngmin Kim,
Joosup Park, Sunghee Hong and Jisoo Hong

Additional information is available at the end of the chapter

http://dx.doi.org/10.5772/65904

Abstract

The intrinsic properties of holograms make 3D holographic imaging the best candidate for a 3D display. The holographic display is an autostereoscopic display which provides highly realistic images with unique perspective for an arbitrary number of viewers, motion parallax both vertically and horizontally, and focusing at different depths. The 3D content generation for this display is carried out by means of digital holography. Digital holography implements the classic holographic principle as a two-step process of wavefront capture in the form of a 2D interference pattern and wavefront reconstruction by applying numerically or optically a reference wave. The chapter follows the two main tendencies in forming the 3D holographic content—direct feeding of optically recorded digital holograms to a holographic display and computer generation of interference fringes from directional, depth and colour information about the 3D objects. The focus is set on important issues that comprise encoding of 3D information for holographic imaging starting from conversion of optically captured holographic data to the display data format, going through different approaches for forming the content for computer generation of holograms from coherently or incoherently captured 3D data and finishing with methods for the accelerated computing of these holograms.

Keywords: holographic display, computer-generated holograms, phase-added stereogram, holographic printer, spatial light modulator

1. 3D capture and 3D content generation by digital holography

Three-dimensional (3D) displays are the next generation displays. The claim for 3D imaging is indisputable in mass television, game industry, medical imaging, computer-aided design, automated robotic systems, air traffic control, education and cultural heritage dissemination. The ultimate goal of 3D visual communication is 3D capture of a real-life scene that is followed

by creating its scaled exact optical duplicate at a remote site instantaneously or at a later time moment [1]. Tracking the development of 3D imaging devices from Wheatstone stereoscope designed in 1830 to modern full HD 3D displays with glasses (**Figure 1**) reveals some memorable periods of booming public interest to this area, e.g. the 3D theatres boom observed in 1950 as a counterpoint to the increasing popularity and commercialization of the television or the last years reaction to the 'Avatar' movie. Multiple parallax 3D display technology has evolved to full-parallax displays for a naked eye observation as integral imaging displays [2] and super-multi-view displays [3]. However, since invention of holography by Dennis Gabor in 1948 [4] and the first holographic 3D demonstration by Emmett Leith and Juris Upatnieks in 1964 [5], the consumer public has high expectations for a truly holographic display in view that holographic imaging is the best candidate for 3D displays.

Holography is the only imaging technique which can provide all depth cues. High quality of 3D imaging from analogue white-light viewable holograms is well known [6]. They provide a wide viewing angle due to the very fine grain size of the holographic emulsions. Realistic images can be viewed by an arbitrary number of viewers with unique perspectives. Motion parallax both vertically and horizontally and tilting of the head are possible. The viewer is capable of focusing at different depths. There are no convergence-accommodation conflict and discontinuities between different views as for multiple parallax displays. Holographic imaging allows for building autostereoscopic displays. To realize a holographic display, the 3D scene description should be encoded as two-dimensional (2D) holographic data. The 3D content generation is carried out by means of digital holography [7] based on the classical holographic principle. According to it, holography is a two-step process enabling storing and reconstruction of a wavefront diffracted by 3D objects. The hologram records as a 2D intensity pattern the

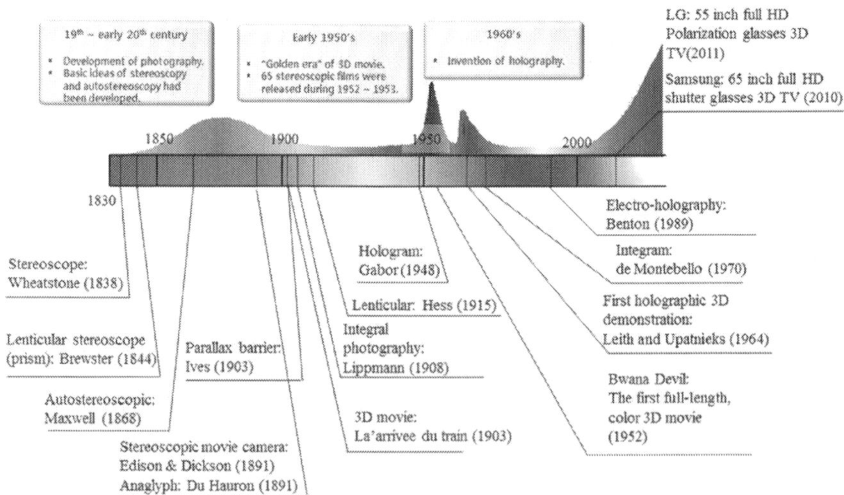

Figure 1. History of 3D displays with some of the major events depicted as a diagram with years along the horizontal axis and intensity of the public interest along the vertical axis.

interference of this wavefront with a mutually coherent reference wave as depicted schematically in **Figure 2**. The wave field from the object is characterized by a complex amplitude, $O(x,y) = a_O(x,y)\exp[j\varphi_O(x,y)]$, where $a_O(x,y)$ and $\varphi_O(x,y)$ are the amplitude and phase of the object beam, respectively. Interference of $O(x,y)$ and the mutually coherent reference beam $R(x,y) = a_R(x,y)\exp[j\varphi_R(x,y)]$ results in four terms superimposed in the hologram plane (x, y):

$$I_H(x,y) = |O(x,y) + R(x,y)|^2$$
$$= O(x,y)O^*(x,y) + R(x,y)R^*(x,y) + O(x,y)R^*(x,y) + R(x,y)O^*(x,y) \tag{1}$$

where the asterisk denotes a complex conjugation. The sum of intensities of the object and reference beams gives the zero-order term. The last two terms are the +1 and –1 diffraction orders and contain the object wavefront information. The object field $OR^*R = O$ or $O^*RR^* = O^*$ brings into focus the virtual or the real image when $I_H(x,y)$ is multiplied by $R(x,y)$ or its conjugate. These twin images are separated for the off-axis geometry where the object and reference beams subtend an angle θ, and overlap in inline geometry at $\theta = 0$.

Digital holography grew from a purely academic idea into a powerful tool after the recent progress in computers, digital photo-sensors (CCDs or CMOS sensors) and spatial light modulators (SLMs). The capability of digital holography for digital analysis and synthesis of a light field forms two mutually related branches. The branch dedicated to analysis comprises methods for optical recording of holograms using digital photo-sensors. The holograms are sampled and digitized by the photo-sensor, stored in the computer and numerically reconstructed using different approaches to describe diffraction of light from the hologram and free space propagation to the plane of the reconstructed image [8]. Thus, capture of both amplitude and phase becomes possible enabling numerical focusing at a variable depth and observation of transparent micro-objects without labelling [9]. The holographic data are in the

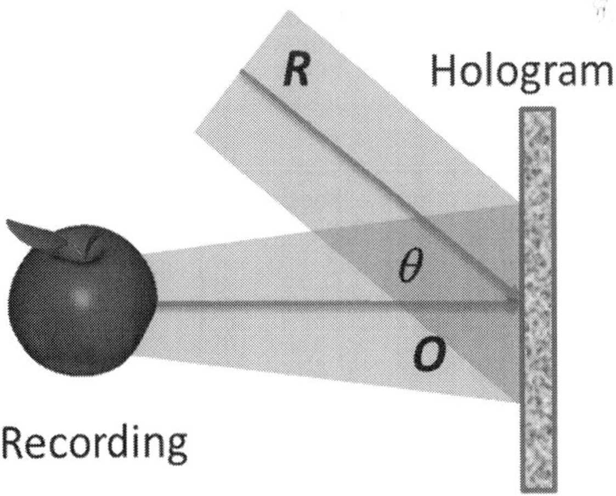

Figure 2. Schematic representation of holographic recording.

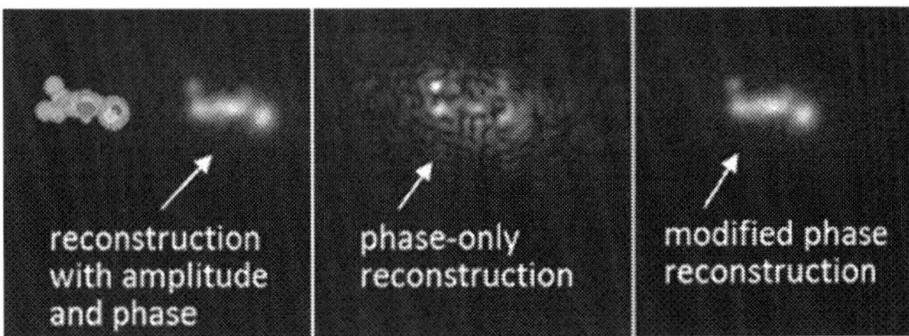

Figure 5. Numerical reconstructions of a virtual transparent object given in the left section of the figure as a 3D distribution of the refractive index n_O (green colour, n_O =1.001; red, n_O = 1.002; yellow, n_O =1.003; blue, n_O = 1.004 [31]).

holograms of weakly refracting transparent object with a size of 25 µm were recorded by a phase-shifting technique [31]. The object had refractive index variation from 1 to 1.004 but due to its small size it gave rise to a strong diffraction. The capture parameters were: $\lambda_c = 0.68$ µm, $\Delta_c = 2.4043$ µm, $N_c = 200 \times 200$, $z_o = 68$ µm [31]; the display parameters were as above. Direct optical reconstruction from the captured phase-only data failed. Usage of the full complex amplitude $O(x, y)$ provided numerical reconstruction as a concise 3D shape resembling closely the 3D refractive index distribution within the object (**Figure 5**). Omission of the amplitude, $a_O(x, y)$, destroyed entirely this 3D shape. The observed severe distortions showed the necessity for phase modification in the hologram plane. This was done iteratively by applying the Gerchberg-Saxton algorithm at known correct complex amplitude at the reconstruction plane. Quality of the numerical reconstruction from the modified phase was satisfactory. Thus the problem with optical reconstruction was solved. Introduction of a digital magnifying lens at the SLM plane enlarged the reconstructed object to 6 mm [31]. This gives about 240 times magnification in comparison with its original size.

3. Computer generation of 3D contents for holographic imaging

3.1. Methods for computer generation of holographic fringe patterns

A CGH is a fringe pattern that diffracts light into a wavefront with desired amplitude and phase distributions and seems to be the most appropriate choice for 3D content generation. This wavefront can be created both for real and virtual objects. The goal in developing the CGHs input data for a 3D holographic display is to have real-time generation of large-scale wide-viewing angle full-parallax colour holograms which provide photorealistic reconstruction that can be viewed with both eyes. These CGHs must support a motion parallax and the coupled occlusion effect expressed in the visible surface change according to the viewer position. For the purpose, a CGH must have a very large number of samples displayed on a device with high spatial resolution. So the most important requirements to CGH synthesis are computational efficiency and holographic image quality. The CGH computation involves digital representation of the 3D object which includes not only its geometrical shape but also texture and lighting conditions, simulation of light propagation from the object to the CGH plane, and encoding of the fringe pattern formed by the interference of the object light wavefront with a reference beam in the display data format.

There are two basic frameworks for CGH generation depending on the mathematical models of 3D target objects: (i) point cloud algorithms and (ii) polygon-based algorithms. In the point-cloud method [32], the 3D object is a collection of P self-luminous point sources. The method traces the ray from a source 'p' with spatial coordinates (x_p, y_p, z_p) to the point (ξ, η) on the hologram plane at $z = 0$ and is sometimes referred to as a ray-tracing approach; the distance between both points is $r_p = \left[(\xi - x_p)^2 + (\eta - y_p)^2 + z_p^2\right]^{1/2}$ (**Figure 6**). Each point source emits a spherical wave with an amplitude, a_p, and an initial phase, ϕ_p. The amplitude and phase distributions in the point cloud can be controlled individually. The fringe patterns for all object points are added up at the hologram plane to obtain the CGH. The method is highly flexible due to ability to represent surfaces with arbitrary shapes and textures, but it is very time consuming.

Polygon-based representation is a wave-oriented approach [33–35]. The object is a collection of P planar segments of a polygonal shape (**Figure 7**). Each polygon is a tilted surface source of a light field calculated by propagation of its angular spectrum of plane wave decomposition [27] using a fast Fourier transform (FFT). An angular-dependent rotational transformation in the spectral domain is applied to find the spectrum in a plane parallel to the hologram in the global coordinate system from the spectrum in the tilted plane of the local coordinate system $(x_p, y_p, z_p), p = 1, 2...P$ for each polygon [36, 37]. The z-axis in the local coordinate system is along the vector to the polygon surface. The object field is found after FFT of the final angular spectrum which is a sum of the transformed angular spectra of the polygon fields in the global

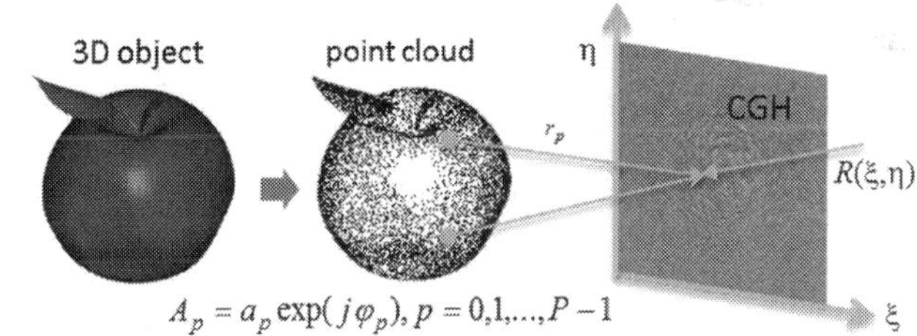

Figure 6. CGH synthesis from a point cloud model.

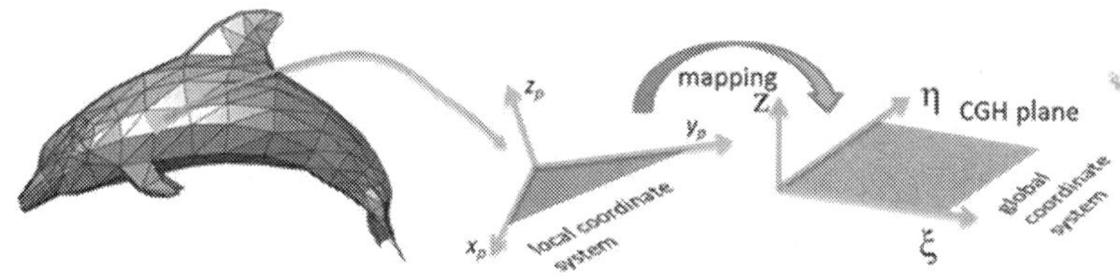

Figure 7. CGH synthesis from a polygon-based model.

coordinate system. Computation of a polygon field is slower than that of a spherical wave emitted by a point light source, but the number of polygons is much smaller than that of point sources and the total computation time is shorter compared to the point cloud approach. The traditional polygon-based method evolved to analytical implementation when the angular spectrum of a triangle of arbitrary size, shape, orientation and location in space is analytically calculated from the known spectrum of a reference triangle [38–40]. The analytical method eliminates the need to apply FFT for each polygon.

The CGH synthesis of real objects can be carried out by 3D capture based on holographic means or structured light methods under coherent or incoherent illumination [41]. The output from, e.g. profilometric/tomographic reconstruction can be converted into a point cloud which allows for CGHs synthesis. The substantial advantage is the option to adapt the captured data to any holographic display. Incoherent capture of multiple projection images to generate holographic data has a lot of advantages such as incoherent illumination, no need of interferometric equipment and display of large objects. The concept was advanced 40 years ago in [42] by generating a holographic stereogram (HS). High quality of large format HSs as a ray-based display, especially those printed by HS printers, are well known [43]. The input data for HS imaging are composed from colour and directional information. This causes a decrease of resolution for deep scenes and blurring. Introduction of a ray-sampling plane close to the object and computation of the light wavefront from this plane to the hologram is proposed in Ref. [44]. Synthesis of a full-parallax colour CGH from multiple 2D projection images captured by a camera scanned along a 2D grid is proposed in Refs. [45, 46]. The approach given in Ref. [46] relies on calculation of the 3D Fourier spectrum and was further improved [47] by developing a parabolic sampling of the spectrum for data extraction and needing only 1D camera scanning. Methods in which directional information from projection images is combined with a depth map are under development [48–50].

Over the last decade, the efforts were focused on improving image quality by different rendering techniques and on accelerating the CGH computation. The holographic data—amplitude and phase—should encode occlusions, materials and roughness of the object surface, reflections, surface glossiness and transparency. It is difficult to create an occlusion effect using 3D object representation as a collection of primitives—points or polygons—due to the independent contribution of all primitives to the light field. To decrease the computational cost of occlusion synthesis, a silhouette mask approach has been proposed in the polygon-based computation [35]. The mask produced by the orthographic projection of the foreground objects blocks the wavefront of light coming from background objects. The method allows for synthesis of a very large CGH [35] but is prone to errors at oblique incidence. Computation is accelerated if occlusion is included in a light-ray rendering process from multiple 2D projection images during the synthesis of a CGH as an HS [51]. As the method suffers from decrease of angular resolution in deep scenes, accuracy is improved by processing occlusion in the light-ray domain along with sampling the angular information from the projection images. This is done in a virtual ray-sampling plane [52, 53]. Furthermore, the sampled data are converted by Fourier transform to the object beam complex amplitude. Considering occlusion as geometric shadowing [54], effective CGH synthesis can be carried out by casting from each sample at the hologram plane, a bundle of rays at uniform angular separation within the diffraction angle given in Eq. (2). Such approaches are described in Refs. [54–56] with representing the 3D objects as composed from planar segments parallel to the hologram plane [55] or performing a lateral shear of the 3D scene to use the z-buffer of the graphic processing unit (GPU) for the rays with the same direction to accelerate computation [54]. Occlusion, texture and illumination issues can be handled by computer graphics techniques. Their effective use is possible when the ray casting is applied by spatially dividing the CGH into a set of sub-holograms and building different sets of points or polygons for them [57–59].

At specular reflection, the viewer is able to see only part of the object while the diffuse reflection sends light rays in all directions. Both types of reflections must be encoded in a CGH by adopting different reflection models to represent texture of the objects [60–62]. In the CGH synthesis, the luminance is encoded in the amplitude while reflectance is incorporated as a phase term. The task of representing reflection becomes rather complicated at non-plane wave illumination or in the case of background illumination [60]. A perfect diffuse reflection is achieved by adding a uniformly distributed random phase. Unfortunately, this causes speckle noise at reconstruction [63]. A variety of methods have been proposed for fast synthesis of CGHs as look-up table methods with pre-computed fringes [63, 64], recurrence relation methods instead of directly calculating the optical path [65], introduction of wavefront recording plane [66], HS methods and many others. Hardware solutions as special-purpose computers like 'Holographic ReconstructioN (HORN)' [67] or GPU computing [32, 68–70] are very effective for fast calculation because the pixels on a CGH can be calculated independently.

3.2. Phase-added holographic stereogram as a fast computation approach

Effective acceleration of computation is achieved in coherent stereogram (CS) algorithms when the CGH is partitioned into segments and the directional data for each segment are sampled (**Figure 8**). A similar idea has been advanced in the diffraction-specific fringe computation by Lucente [71] with partitioning the hologram into holographic elements called hogels and each hogel having a linear superposition of weighted basic fringes corresponding to the points in a point cloud. Each segment in the CS emits a bundle of light rays that form a wavefront as a set of patches of mismatched plane waves due to lack of depth information. This drawback was overcome by adding a distance-related phase [72]. The phase-added stereogram (PAS) is

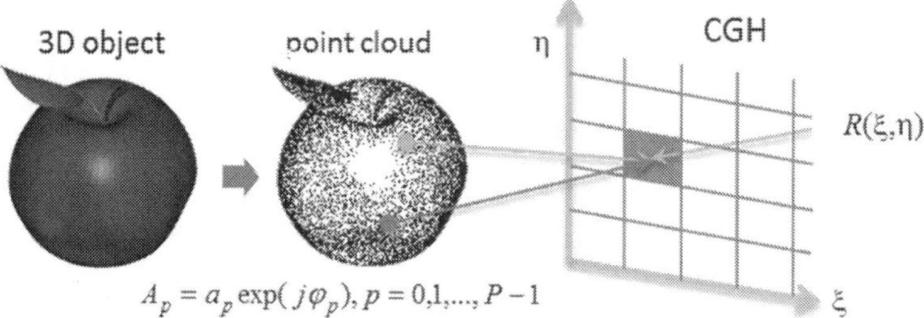

Figure 8. Synthesis of a CGH as a coherent stereogram with partitioning the hologram plane into square segments and sampling the directional information.

computationally effective if implemented by FFT. To clarify this point, we depict schematically the PAS computation with FFT in **Figure 9**.

In CS and PAS algorithms, the hologram is partitioned into $M \times N$ equal square segments with $S \times S$ pixels. The object is described by a point cloud with P points. The segment size, $\Delta_d S \times \Delta_d S$, where Δ_d is the pixel period at the hologram plane, is chosen small enough to approximate the spherical wave from a point as a plane wave given by a 2D complex harmonic function within the segment. This approximation means that the contribution from a point source is constant across the segment and is determined with respect only to its central pixel. In this way, the input data and computation time are substantially reduced; for the segment $(m, n), m = 1..M, n = 1..N$ the contribution from the point 'p' comprises spatial frequencies (u^p_{mn}, v^p_{mn}) of the plane wave at a wavelength λ_d, the distance between the point 'p' and the central point, r^p_{mn}, the initial phase of the sinusoid, Φ^p_{mn}. The spatial frequencies are determined by the illuminating angles, $(\Theta^p_{mn}, \Omega^p_{mn})$, of the ray coming from the point 'p' to the central point of the segment (m, n) and angles $\theta_{R\xi}$ and $\theta_{R\eta}$ of the plane reference wave with respect to ξ and η axes at the hologram plane as follows: $u^p_{mn} = (\sin \Theta^p_{mn} - \sin \theta_{R\xi})/\lambda_d$, $v^p_{mn} = (\sin \Omega^p_{mn} - \sin \theta_{R\eta})/\lambda_d$. The phases $\Phi^p_{mn}, m = 1..M, n = 1..N$ ensure matching of the wavefronts of the plane waves diffracted from all segments and may contain the initial phase ϕ_p and also the distance-related phase $2\pi r^p_{mn}/\lambda_d$. For all object points, the fringe pattern across the segment is approximated as a superposition of 2D complex sinusoids. Computation of this pattern is carried out by placing the amplitudes of the sinusoids to the corresponding frequency locations in the spatial frequency domain and by applying an inverse Fourier transform to the spectrum. FFT implementation is the second step for acceleration of CGH computation (**Figure 9**). The FFT step moves the spatial frequencies to the nearest allowed values in the discrete frequency domain. The complex amplitudes remain the same. The two-step procedure is repeated for each segment to compute the CGH.

The PAS approximation should yield a wavefront close to the wavefront provided by the Rayleigh-Sommerfeld diffraction model that treats the propagating light from a point as a spherical wave. The complex amplitude in the reference model is given by:

$$O_O^{RS}(\xi, \eta) = \sum_{p=1}^{P} \frac{A_p}{r_p} \exp\left(j\frac{2\pi}{\lambda_d} r_p\right), A_p = a_p \exp(j\phi_p) \tag{6}$$

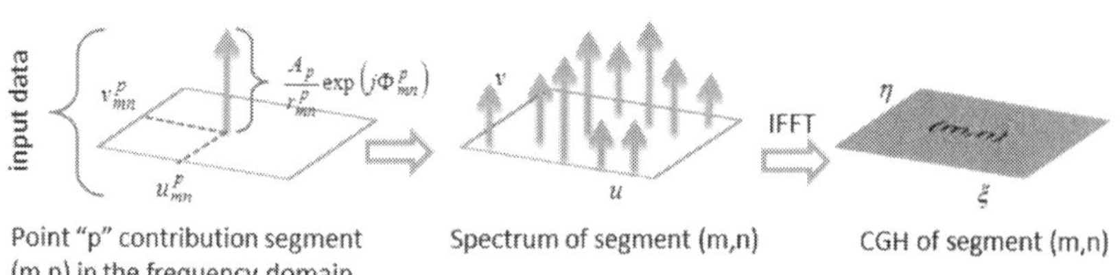

Figure 9. Schematic representation of the synthesis of a CGH within a segment.

We applied PAS computation to generate digital input contents for a wavefront printer developed by us for printing a white-light viewable full-parallax reflection hologram [73, 74]. The printed hologram was recorded as a 2D array of elemental holograms. The CGH for each elemental hologram was fed to amplitude SLM with 1920 × 1080 pixels. The object beam encoded in the CGH was extracted by spatial filtering and demagnified using a telecentric lens system. Unlike the HS printers [43], the wavefront printer uses full holographic data. That is why the synthesis of a large number of elemental holograms, e.g. 100 × 100, takes a very long time. This requires a fast computation method that provides quality of imaging close to the reference model. We solved this task by developing a fast PAS (FPAS) method [75] as a further elaboration of the already existing PAS methods. Usage of the FFT is crucial for fast PAS implementation, but this may affect negatively the quality of imaging due to spatial frequencies mapping to a predetermined coarse set of discrete values. The sampling step, $1/S\Delta_d$, in the frequency domain could not be made small due to necessity to approximate the reference model. Thus, the fringe pattern generated by the PAS with FFT inaccurately steers the diffracted light. The improvements developed to compensate the error caused by the frequency mapping are based on the two possible ways for steering control—phase compensation and finer sampling of the spectrum attached to each segment. The functional form of the developed approximations is shown in **Table 1** which gives the fringe pattern at a single spatial frequency in the segment (m, n); $(\xi^c_{mn}, \eta^c_{mn})$ is the central point of the segment and the following notation is introduced for the complex sinusoid:

$$F(u^p_{mn}, v^p_{mn}) = (A_p/r^p_{mn}) \exp\left\{ j2\pi[u^p_{mn}(\xi-\xi^c_{mn}) + v^p_{mn}(\eta-\eta^c_{mn})] \right\} \tag{7}$$

The first improvement CPAS (compensated PAS) [76] performed some steering correction by adding the phase, which includes the difference between the spatial frequencies in the continuous and the discrete domains. The CPAS provided a better reconstructed image than the PAS with FFT at almost the same calculation time. Finer sampling was proposed in the accurate PAS (APAS) [77] by computing the FFT in an area which exceeds the segment and by properly truncating the larger-size IFFT output. Phase compensation and directional error reduction by

---

Fringe pattern of the method

CS: $F(u^p_{mn}, v^p_{mn})$

PAS (no FFT): $F(u^p_{mn}, v^p_{mn}) \exp(jkr^p_{mn})$

PAS (FFT): $F(\hat{u}^p_{mn}, \hat{v}^p_{mn}) \exp(jkr^p_{mn})$

CPAS: $F(\hat{u}^p_{mn}, \hat{v}^p_{mn}) \exp(jkr^p_{mn}) \times \exp\left\{ j2\pi[(\hat{u}^p_{mn}-u^p_{mn})(\xi^c_{mn}-x_p) + (\hat{v}^p_{mn}-v^p_{mn})(\eta^c_{mn}-y_p)] \right\}$

APAS: $F(\hat{u}'^p_{mn}, \hat{v}'^p_{mn}) \exp(jkr^p_{mn})$

ACPAS: $F(\hat{u}'^p_{mn}, \hat{v}'^p_{mn}) \exp(jkr^p_{mn}) \times \exp\left\{ j2\pi[(\hat{u}'^p_{mn}-u^p_{mn})(\xi^c_{mn}-x_p) + (\hat{v}'^p_{mn}-v^p_{mn})(\eta^c_{mn}-y_p)] \right\}$

FPAS: $F(\hat{u}'^p_{mn}, \hat{v}'^p_{mn}) \exp(jkr^p_{mn}) \times \exp\left\{ j2\pi[u^p_{mn}(\xi^c_{mn}-x_p) + v^p_{mn}(\eta^c_{mn}-y_p)] \right\}$

Spatial frequencies: $\hat{u}^p_{mn} = \frac{l_u}{S\Delta_d}, \hat{v}^p_{mn} = \frac{l_v}{S\Delta_d}; -\frac{S}{2}\leq l_u, l_v \leq \frac{S}{2}; \hat{u}'^p_{mn} = \frac{l_u}{S'\Delta_d}, \hat{v}'^p_{mn} = \frac{l_v}{S'\Delta_d}; -\frac{S'}{2}\leq l_u, l_v \leq \frac{S'}{2}, S' < S$

Table 1. Single frequency fringe pattern in the segment.

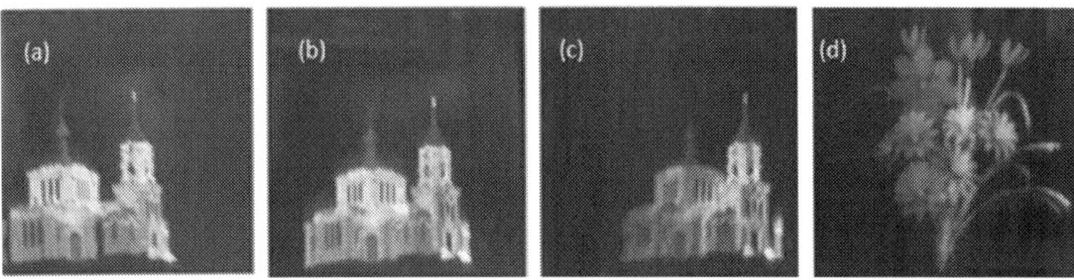

Figure 10. Photographs of reconstruction from printed holograms: (a)–(c): different views of a church model; (d): 9 cm × 9 cm printed hologram of a bunch of flowers.

finer sampling were merged into a single step in the algorithm ACPAS [57] which yielded quality of reconstruction very close to the reference model. The best results are provided by the FPAS algorithm which is characterized with better phase compensation than the previous methods. This was confirmed by quality assessment with conventional image-based objective metrics as intensity distribution and peak signal-to-noise ratio [75] for reconstruction of a single point and also by good quality of reconstruction from white-light viewable colour holograms (**Figure 10**) printed by our wavefront printing system [73] on an extra-fine grain silver-halide emulsion Ultimate08 [78]. The CGH computed by the FPAS algorithm for each elemental hologram was displayed on an amplitude type SLM. The demagnified pixel interval was 0.42 μm at the plane of the hologram and gives a diffraction angle of ± 39.3°. For uniform illumination of the CGH on the SLM without decreasing too much the laser beam intensity we used only 852 × 852 pixels in the SLM to project CGHs. Thus, the size of the elemental hologram became equal to 0.38 mm by 0.38 mm. The printed holograms are shown in **Figure 10**; their size is 5 cm × 5 cm and 9 cm × 9 cm. The smaller hologram consisted of 131 × 131 elemental holograms. The segment size for calculating the CGH fed to a given elemental hologram was 32 × 32 pixels while the FFT computation area was 128 × 128 pixels, and each elemental hologram comprised more than 700 segments.

4. Conclusion

Holographic imaging is a 3D imaging with all depth cues and inherent vision comfort for the viewer. That is why the last decade was marked by rapid development of methods of 3D capture and 3D content generation for holographic display, holographic projection and holographic printing. In the chapter, we considered implementation of the holographic imaging by digital means when the input data are in the form of a 2D real-valued matrix, which should encode the light wavefront coming from the 3D scene. This wavefront can be extracted from optically recorded holograms or synthesized numerically using various 3D scene descriptions. Holographic recording by digital photo-sensors or computer generation of holograms for pixelated SLMs imposes severe limitations on the space-bandwidth product of the capture/display system. We discussed two cases of data mapping from holographic capture to holographic display to show that holographic data transfer from optically recorded digital holograms to the data format of a given display is not a trivial task due to inevitable distortions introduced as a result of different capture and display parameters. Representing 3D contents as computer-generated holograms seems more flexible and promising way to create input data for holographic displays. The main requirements are to improve the quality of imaging and computational efficiency. We presented an algorithm for fast computation of holograms and showed the good quality of imaging it provided in holographic printing of white-light viewable reflection holograms.

Acknowledgements

This work was supported by the Ministry of Science, ICT and Future Planning (Cross-Ministry Giga KOREA Project) and Bulgarian National Science Fund, project H 08/12 "Holographic imaging, beam shaping and speckle metrology with computer generated holograms".

Author details

Elena Stoykova[1]*, Hoonjong Kang[2], Youngmin Kim[2], Joosup Park[2], Sunghee Hong[2] and Jisoo Hong

*Address all correspondence to: elena.stoykova@gmail.com

1 Institute of Optical Materials and Technologies to Bulgarian Academy of Sciences, Sofia, Bulgaria

2 VR/AR Research Center, Korea Electronics Technology Institute, Mapo-gu, Seoul, Korea

References

[1] Sainov V, Stoykova E, Onural L, Ozaktas H: Trends in development of dynamic holographic displays. Proceedings of SPIE. 2006;6252: 62521C. DOI: 10.1117/12.677056.

[2] Kim YM, Hong KH, Lee BH: Recent researches based on integral imaging display method. 3D Research. 2010; 1(1): 17–27. DOI: 10.1007/3DRes.01(2010)2.

[3] Takaki Y: Development of super multi-view displays. ITE Transactions on Media Technology and Applications. 2014; 2(1): 8–14.DOI: 10.3169/mta.2.8.

[4] Gabor D: A new microscopic principle. Nature. 1948; 161: 777–778. DOI: 10.1038/161777a0.

[5] Leith E, Upatnieks J: Reconstructed wavefronts and communication theory. Journal of the Optical Society of America. 1962;52;1123–1130.DOI: 10.1364/JOSA.52.001123.

[6]   Sainov V, Stoykova E: Display holography – status and future. In: Osten W, Reingand N, editors. Optical Imaging and Metrology: Advanced Technologies, 1st ed. Weinheim: Wiley-VCH Verlag GmbH & Co. KGaA; 2012. p. 93117. DOI: 10.1002/9783527648443.ch4.

[7]   Schnars U, Jueptner W: Direct recording of holograms by a CCD target and numerical reconstruction. Applied Optics 1994; 33(2):179–181.DOI: 10.1364/AO.33.000179.

[8]   Onural L, Gotchev A, Ozaktas H, Stoykova E: A survey of signal processing problems and tools in holographic 3DTV. IEEE Transactions on Circuits and Systems for Video Technology. 2007;17 (11): 1631–1646.DOI: 10.1109/TCSVT.2007.909973.

[9]   Cuche E, Marquet P, Depeursinge C: Simultaneous amplitude-contrast and quantitative phase-contrast microscopy by numerical reconstruction of Fresnel off-axis holograms. Applied Optics. 1998; 38: 6994–7001.DOI: 10.1364/AO.38.006994.

[10]   Kim M: Digital Holographic Microscopy: Principals, Techniques and Applications. New York, NY: Springer; 2011. 230 p. DOI: 10.1007/978-1-4419-7793-9.

[11]   Jericho M, Kreuzer H: Point-source digital in-line holographic microscopy. In: Ferraro P, Wax A, Zaevsky Z, editors. Coherent Light Microscopy. Berlin, Heidelberg: Springer Series; 2011. pp. 3–30. DOI: 10.1007/978-3-642-15813-1_1.

[12]   Charrière F, Marian A, Montfort F, Kuehn J, Colomb T, Cuche E, Marquet P, Depeursinge C: Cell refractive index tomography by digital holographic microscopy. Optics Letters. 2006; 31: 178–180.DOI: 10.1364/OL.31.000178.

[13]   Pelagotti A, Locatelli M, Geltrude A, Poggi P, Meucci R, Paturzo M, Miccio L, Ferraro P: Reliability of 3D imaging by digital holography at long IR wavelength. Journal of Display Technology. 2010; 6(10): 465–471. DOI: 10.1007/3DRes.04(2010)06.

[14]   Gire J, Denis L, Fournier C, Thiébaut E, Soulez F, Ducottet C: Digital holography of particles: benefits of the inverse problem approach. Measurement Science and Technology. 2008;19:074005. DOI: 10.1088/0957-0233/19/7/074005.

[15]   Stern A, Javidi B: Theoretical analysis of three-dimensional imaging and recognition of micro-organisms with a single-exposure on-line holographic microscope. Journal of the Optical Society of America A. 2007; 24, 163–168.DOI: 10.1364/JOSAA.24.000163.

[16]   Stoykova E, Kang H, Park J: Twin-image problem in digital holography-a survey. Chinese Optics Letters. 2014; 12: 060013. DOI: 10.3788/COL201412.060013.

[17]   Lohmann A: A pre-history of computer-generated holography. Optics and Photonics News. 2008; February: 36–41. DOI: 10.1364/OPN.19.2.000036.

[18]   Slinger C, Cameron C, Stanley M: Computer-generated holography as a generic display technology. IEEE Computer. 2005; 38(8): 46–53. DOI: 0018-9162/05/$20.00.

[19]   Shimobaba T, Kakue T, Endo Y, Hirayama R, Hiyama D, Hasegawa S, Nagahama Y, Sano M, Oikawa M, Sugie T, Ito T: Improvement of the image quality of random phase-free holography using an iterative method. Optics Communications. 2010, 355: 596–601. DOI: 10.1016/j.optcom.2015.07.030.

[20] Chang NIY, Chung JK: Design and implementation of computer-generated hologram and diffractive optical element. In: Chung JK, Tsai M, editors. Three-Dimensional Holographic Imaging. John Wiley & Sons, Inc., New York. 1st ed. 2003; pp. 167–189. DOI: 10.1002/0471224545.ch9.

[21] Onural L, Yaras F, Kang H: Digital holographic three-dimensional video displays. Proceedings of the IEEE. 2011;**99** (4): 576–589. **DOI:** 10.1109/JPROC.2010.2098430.

[22] Yaras F, Kang H, Onural L: Multi-SLM holographic display system with planar configuration. In: Proceedings of the IEEE International Conference on 3DTV: The True Vision—Capture, Transmission and Display of 3D Video.7–9 June. 2010. DOI: 10.1109/3DTV.2010.5506332.

[23] Mishina T, Okui M, Okano F: Viewing-zone enlargement method for sampled hologram that uses high order diffraction. Applied Optics. 2002; **41**: 1489–1499. DOI: 10.1364/AO.41.001489.

[24] Hahn J, Kim H, Lim Y, Park G, Lee B: Wide viewing angle dynamic holographic stereogram with a curved array of spatial light modulators. Optics Express. 2008; **16**(16): 12372–12386. DOI: 10.1364/OE.16.012372.

[25] Yaras F, Kang H, and Onural L: ircular holographic video display system, Optics Express **19**: 9147–9156 (2011). DOI: 10.1364/OE.19.009147.

[26] Kozacki T, Finke G, Garbat P, Zaperty W, Kujawinska M: Wide angle holographic display system with spatiotemporal multiplexing. Optics Express. 2012; **20**(25): 27473–27481. DOI: 10.1364/OE.20.027473.

[27] Goodman J: Introduction to Fourier Optics. 3rd ed. USA: Robert & Company Publishers; 2005. 491 p.

[28] Paturzo M, Pelagotti A, Finizio A, Miccio I, Locatelli M, Gertrude A, Poggi P, Meucci R, Ferraro P: Optical reconstruction of digital holograms recorded at 10.6 μm: route for 3D imaging at long infrared wavelengths. Optics Letters. 2010; **35**: 2112–2114. DOI: 10.1364/OL.35.002112.

[29] Stoykova E, Yaras F, Kang H, Onural L, Geltrude A, Locatelli M, Paturzo M, Pelagotti A, Meucci R, Ferraro P: Visible reconstruction by a circular holographic display from digital holograms recorded under infrared illumination. Optics Letters. 2012; **37**(15): 3120–3122 DOI: 10.1364/OL.37.003120.

[30] Meier R: Magnification and third-order aberrations in holography. Journal of the Optical Society of America. 1965;**55**: 987–992. DOI: 10.1364/JOSA.55.000987.

[31] Stoykova E, Yaras F, Yontem A, Kang H, Onural L, Hamel P, Delacrétaz Y, Bergoënd I, Arfire C, Depeursinge C: Optical reconstruction of transparent objects with phase-only SLMs. Optics Express. 2013; **21**: 28246–28257. DOI: 10.1364/OE.21.028246.

[32] Chen RH-Y, Wilkinson T: Computer generated hologram from point cloud using graphics processor. Applied Optics. 2009; **48**: 6841–6850. DOI: 10.1364/AO.48.006841.

[33] Leseberg D, Frère C: Computer-generated holograms of 3-D objects composed of tilted planar segments. Applied Optics. 1988; **27**: 3020–3024. DOI: 10.1364/AO.27.003020.

[34] Matsushima K: Computer-generated holograms for three-dimensional surface objects with shade and texture. Applied Optics. 2005; **44**(22): 4607–4614. DOI: 10.1364/AO.44.004607.

[35] Matsushima K, Nakahara S: Extremely high-definition full-parallax computer-generated hologram created by the polygon-based method. Applied Optics. 2009; **48**: H54–H63. DOI: 10.1364/AO.48.000H54.

[36] Matsushima K, Schimmel H, Wyrowski F: Fast calculation method for optical diffraction on tilted planes by use of the angular spectrum of plane waves. Journal of the Optical Society of America A. 2003; **20**: 1755–1762. DOI: 10.1364/JOSAA.20.001755.

[37] Matsushima K: Formulation of the rotational transformation of wave fields and their application to digital holography. Applied Optics. 2008; **47**: D110–D116.DOI: 10.1364/AO.47.00D110.

[38] Kim H, Hahn J, Lee B: Mathematical modeling of triangle-mesh-modeled three-dimensional surface objects for digital holography. Applied Optics. 2008; **47**: D117–D127. DOI: 10.1364/AO.47.00D117.

[39] Ahrenberg L, Benzie P, Magnor M, Watson J: Computer generated holograms from three dimensional meshes using an analytic light transport model. Applied Optics. 2008; **47**:, 1567–1574. DOI: 10.1364/AO.47.001567.

[40] Pan Y, Wang Y, Liu J, Li X, Jia J: Fast polygon-based method for calculating computer-generated holograms in three-dimensional display. Applied Optics. 2013; **52**: A290-A299. DOI: 10.1364/AO.52.00A290.

[41] Stoykova E, Alatan A, Benzie P, Grammalidis N, Malassiotis S, Ostermann J, Piekh S, Sainov V, Theobalt C, Thevar T, Zabulis X: 3D time-varying scene capture technologies—a survey. IEEE Transactions on Circuits and Systems for Video Technology. 2007; **17** (11): 1568–1586. DOI: 10.1109/TCSVT.2007.909975.

[42] Yatagai T: Stereoscopic approach to 3-D display using computer-generated hologram. Applied Optics. 1976; **15** (11): 2722–2729. DOI: 10.1364/AO.15.002722.

[43] Bjelkhagen H, Brotherton-Ratcliffe D: Ultra-Realistic Imaging – Advanced Techniques in Analogue and Digital Color Hoography. 1st ed. London, New York: Taylor & Francis; 2013. 664 p. DOI: 10.1080/00107514.2014.907347.

[44] Wakunami K, Yamaguchi M: Calculation for computer generated hologram using ray-sampling plane. Optics Express. 2011; **19**: 9086–9101. DOI: 10.1364/OE.19.009086.

[45] Abookasis D, Rosen J: Computer-generated holograms of three-dimensional objects synthesized from their multiple angular viewpoints. Journal of the Optical Society of America A 2003; **20**: 1537–1545. DOI: 10.1364/JOSAA.20.001537.

[46] Sando Y, Itoh M, Yatagai T: Color computer-generated holograms from projection images. Optics Express. 2004; **12**: 2487–2493. DOI: 10.1364/OPEX.12.002487.

[47] Sando Y, Itoh M, Yatagai T: Full-color computer-generated holograms using 3-D Fourier spectra. Optics Express. 2004; **12**(25): 6246–6251. DOI: 10.1364/OPEX.12.006 246.

[48] Hayashi N, Sakamoto Y, Honda Y: Improvement of camera arrangement in computer-generated holograms synthesized from multi-view images. Proceedings of SPIE. 2011; **7957**: 795711. DOI: 10.1117/12.874444.

[49] Senoh T, Wakunami K, Ichihashi Y, Sasaki H, Oi R, Yamamoto K: Multiview image and depth map coding for holographic TV system. Optics Engineering. 2014; **53**(11), 112302–112302. DOI: 10.1117/1.OE.53.11.112302.

[50] TakakiY, Ikeda K: Simplified calculation method for computer generated holographic stereograms from multi-view images. Optics Express. 2013; **21**(8): 9652–9663. DOI: 10.1364/OE.21.009652.

[51] Smithwick QYJ, Barabas J, Smalley D, Bove VM Jr: Real-time shader rendering of holographic stereograms. Proceedings of SPIE. 2009; **7233**: 723302 DOI: 10.1117/12.808999.

[52] Wakunami K, Yamashita H, Yamaguchi M: Occlusion culling for computer generated hologram based on ray wavefront conversion. Optics Express. 2013; **21**: 21811–21822. DOI: 10.1364/OE.21.021811.

[53] Symeonidou A, Blinder D, Munteanu A, Schelkens P: Computer-generated holograms by multiple wavefront recording plane method with occlusion culling. Optics Express 2015; **23**: 22149–22161. DOI: 10.1364/OE.23.022149.

[54] Chen RHY, Wilkinson T: Computer generated hologram with geometric occlusion using GPU-accelerated depth buffer rasterization for three-dimensional display. Applied Optics. 2009;**48**: 4246–4255. DOI: 10.1364/AO.48.004246.

[55] Janda M, Hanak I, Onural L: Hologram synthesis for photorealistic reconstruction. Journal of the Optical Society of America A. 2008; **25**: 3083–3096. DOI: 10.1364/JOSAA.25. 003083.

[56] Zhang H, Collings N, Chen J, Crossland B, Chu D, Xie J: Full parallax three-dimensional display with occlusion effect using computer generated hologram. Optics Engineering. 2011; **50** (7): 074003. DOI: 10.1117/1.3599871.

[57] Kang H, Yamaguchi T, Yoshikawa H, Kim S-C, Kim E-S: Acceleration method of computing a compensated phase-added stereogram on a graphic processing unit. Applied Optics. 2008; **47**: 5784–5789. DOI: 10.1364/AO.47.005784.

[58] Ichikawa T, Yamaguchi K, Sakamoto Y: Realistic expression for full-parallax computer-generated holograms with the ray tracing method. Applied Optics. 2013; **52**: A201–A209. DOI: 10.1364/AO.52.00A201.

[59] Zhang Y, Peng W, Chen H, Xu Y, Chen W, Xu W: Computer-generated-hologram-accelerated computing method based on mixed programming. Chinese Optics Letters. 2014; **12**: 030902 . DOI: 10.3788/COL201412.030902.

[60] Yamaguchi K, Sakamoto Y: Computer generated hologram with characteristics of reflection: reflectance distributions and reflected images. Applied Optics. 2009; **48:** H203–H211. DOI: 10.1364/AO.48.00H203.

[61] Yamaguchi K, Ichikawa T, Sakamoto Y: Calculation method for computer-generated holograms considering various reflectance distributions based on microfacets with various surface roughnesses. Applied Optics. 2011; **50:** H195-H202. DOI: 10.1364/AO.50.00H195.

[62] Ichikawa T, Sakamoto Y, Subagyo A, Sueoka K: Calculation method of reflectance distributions for computer-generated holograms using the finite-difference time-domain method. Applied Optics. 2011; **50:** H211–H219. DOI: 10.1364/AO.50.00H211.

[63] Shimobaba T, Makowski M, Nagahama Y, Endo Y, Hirayama R, Hiyama D, Hasegawa S, Sano M, Kakue T, Oikawa M, Sugie T, Takada N, Ito T: Color computer-generated hologram generation using the random phase-free method and color space conversion. Applied Optics. 2016; **55:** 4159–4165. DOI: 10.1364/AO.55.004159.

[64] Lucente M: Interactive computation of holograms using a look-up table. Journal of Electronic Imaging. 1993; **2**(1): 28–34. DOI: 10.1117/12.133376.

[65] Kim S, Kim J, Kim E: Effective memory reduction of the novel look-up table with one-dimensional sub-principle fringe patterns in computer-generated holograms. Optics Express. 2012; **20:** 12021–12034. DOI: 10.1364/OE.20.012021.

[66] Matsushima K, Takai M: Recurrence formulas for fast creation of synthetic three-dimensional holograms. Applied Optics. 2000; **39**(35): 6587–6594. DOI: 10.1364/AO.39.006587.

[67] Shimobaba T, Masuda N, Ito T: Simple and fast calculation algorithm for computer-generated hologram with wavefront recording plane. Optics Letters. 2009; **34:** 3133–3135. DOI: 10.1364/OL.34.003133.

[68] Murano K, Shimobaba T, Sugiyama A, Takada N, Kakue T, Oikawa M, Ito T: Fast computation of computer-generated hologram using Xeon Phi coprocessor. Computer Physics Communications. 2014; **185**(10): 2742–2757. DOI: 10.1016/j.cpc.2014.06.010.

[69] Ahrenberg L, Benzie P, Magnor M, Watson J: Computer generated holography using parallel commodity graphics hardware. Optics Express. 2006; **14:**7636–7641. DOI: 10.1364/OE.14.007636.

[70] Yaras F, Kang H, Onural L: Real-time Multiple SLM Color Holographic Display Using Multiple GPU Acceleration. In: Advances in Imaging, OSA Technical Digest (CD) (Optical Society of America, 2009), paper DWA4. DOI: 10.1364/DH.2009.DWA4.

[71] Lucente M: Holographic bandwidth compression using spatial subsampling. Optics Engineering. 1996; **35**(6): 1529–1537. DOI: 10.1117/1.600736.

[72] Yamaguchi M, Hoshino H, Honda T, Ohyama N: Phase-added stereogram: calculation of hologram using computer graphics technique. Proceedings of SPIE. 1993; **1914:** 25–31. DOI: 10.1117/12.155027.

[73] Kang H, Stoykova E, Kim YM, Hong SH, Park JS, Hong JS: Color wavefront printer with mosaic delivery of primary colors. Optics Communications. 2015; **350**: 47–55. DOI: 10.1016/j.optcom.2015.02.041.

[74] Kim Y, Stoykova E, Kang H, Hong S, Park J, Park JS, Hong J: Seamless full color holographic printing method based on spatial partitioning of SLM. Optics Express. 2015; **23** : 172–182. DOI10.1364/OE.23.000172.

[75] Kang H, Stoykova E, Yoshikawa H: Fast phase-added stereogram algorithm for generation of photorealistic 3D content. Applied Optics. 2016; **55**: A135–A143. DOI: 10.1364/AO.55.00A135.

[76] Kang H, Fujii T, Yamaguchi T, Yoshikawa H: Compensated phase-added stereogram for real-time holographic display. Optics Engineering. 2007; **6**: 095807. DOI: 10.1117/1.2784463.

[77] Kang H, Yamaguychi T, Yoshikawa H: Accurate phase added stereogram to improve the coherent stereogram. Applied Optics. 2008; **47**: D44–D54. DOI: 10.1364/AO.47.000D44.

[78] Gentet Y, Gentet P: Ultimate emulsion and its applications: a laboratory-made silver halide emulsion of optimized quality for monochromatic pulsed and full-color holography. Proceedings of SPIE. 2000; **4149**: 56–62. DOI: 10.1117/12.402459.

Multiwavelength Digital Holography and Phase-Shifting Interferometry Selectively Extracting Wavelength Information: Phase-Division Multiplexing (PDM) of Wavelengths

Tatsuki Tahara, Reo Otani, Yasuhiko Arai and Yasuhiro Takaki

Additional information is available at the end of the chapter

http://dx.doi.org/10.5772/67295

Abstract

In this chapter, we introduce multiwavelength digital holographic techniques and a novel multiwavelength imaging technique. General multiwavelength imaging systems adopt temporal division, spatial division, or space-division multiplexing to obtain wavelength information. Holographic techniques give us unique multiwavelength imaging systems, which utilize temporal or spatial frequency-division multiplexing. Conventional multiwavelength digital holography systems have been combined with one of the methods listed above. We have proposed phase-shifting interferometry selectively extracting wavelength information, characterized as a multiwavelength three-dimensional (3D) imaging technique based on holography and called phase-division multiplexing (PDM) of multiple wavelengths. In PDM, wavelength-multiplexed phase-shifted holograms are recorded, and multiwavelength information is separately extracted from the holograms in the space domain. Phase shifts are introduced for respective wavelengths to separate object waves with multiple wavelengths in the polar coordinate plane, and multiple object waves are selectively extracted by the signal processing based on phase-shifting interferometry. Additionally, the system of equations needed to obtain a multiwavelength 3D image is solved with less wavelength-multiplexed images using two-step phase-shifting interferometry-merged phase-division multiplexing (2π-PDM), which makes the best use of 2π ambiguity of the phase and two-step phase-shifting method. The PDM techniques are reviewed and color 3D imaging ability is described with numerical and experimental results.

Keywords: digital holography, holography, interferometry, holographic interferometry, phase-shifting interferometry, multiwavelength interferometry, color holography, multiwavelength 3D imaging, color 3D imaging, multiwavelength imaging, phase-division multiplexing of wavelengths, 2π-PDM

1. Introduction

Holography [1–4] is a technique to record a wavefront of an object wave by utilizing interference of light as well as reconstruct a three-dimensional (3D) image of an object. The medium containing the information of an interference fringe image is called a "hologram", which contains both the amplitude and phase information of an object wave. 3D image information is reconstructed using a hologram and diffraction theory. One of the most remarkable features in holography is that 3D motion-picture recording of any ultrafast physical phenomenon can be achieved, even for light propagation in 3D space [3]. Digital holography [5–8] is a technique to record a hologram digitally using an image sensor, and reconstruct both the 3D and quantitative phase images of an object using a computer or spatial light modulator. This technique has been researched for not only the observation of ultrafast phenomenon, but also for microscopy [9, 10], quantitative phase imaging [11, 12], and multimodal imaging [13, 14].

In recent years, there has been an increase in demand for multispectral imaging techniques. Multiwavelength information helps us to perceive, analyze, and recognize an object such as body tissue or a tumor. Wavelength of light has the ability to clarify color and material distributions of an object [15], visualize the localization and dynamics of molecules with Raman scattering [16, 17], and analyze the health of human skin [18]. In digital holography, the information of multiple wavelengths and 3D space is obtained by recording waves with multiple wavelengths that are irradiated from light sources, called multiwavelength/color digital holography [19, 20]. Multiwavelength digital holography has the ability for not only color 3D imaging [19, 20], but also dispersion imaging [21] and 3D shape measurement with a wide range by using multiwavelength phase unwrapping [22], due to the recording of quantitative phase information with multiple wavelengths. Temporal division [23–25], spatial division [26–28], and space-division multiplexing [19, 20, 29], which are generally adopted for multiwavelength imaging in an imaging system, can be merged into digital holography to record multiple wavelengths. In general imaging systems, wavelength information is temporally or spatially separated when recording image(s), as shown in **Figure 1(a)–(e)**. However, holographic techniques make it possible to record multiwavelength/ color information using a monochromatic image sensor and to reconstruct it from wavelength-multiplexed image(s). In holography, multiple wavelength information is obtained also by utilizing temporal frequency-division multiplexing (**Figure 1(f)**) [30, 31] and spatial frequency-division multiplexing (**Figure 1(g)**) [32, 33]. In these techniques, Fourier and inverse Fourier transforms are required to separate wavelength information. In the former, many wavelength-multiplexed images and an image sensor with a high frame rate are needed. In the latter, the spatial bandwidth available for recording an object wave at a wavelength is restricted as the number of wavelengths is increased.

Since 2013, we have presented a novel multiwavelength imaging technique utilizing holography and wavelength-multiplexed images [34–39]. The presented technique gives phase-shifting interferometry [40–51] the function to extract wavelength information such as wavelength dependencies of amplitude, phase, and polarization state selectively from wavelength-multiplexed phase-shifted holograms. It is especially important to record not only phase images but also amplitude distributions of object waves at multiple wavelengths in order to achieve multicolor and multispectral 3D imaging of multiple objects. By making use of holography for multiwavelength imaging, 3D space information is simultaneously captured. In this chapter, we explain the proposed technique, phase-shifting interferometry selectively extracting wavelength information: phase-division multiplexing (PDM) of multiple wavelengths and two-step phase-shifting interferometry-merged phase-division multiplexing (2π-PDM).

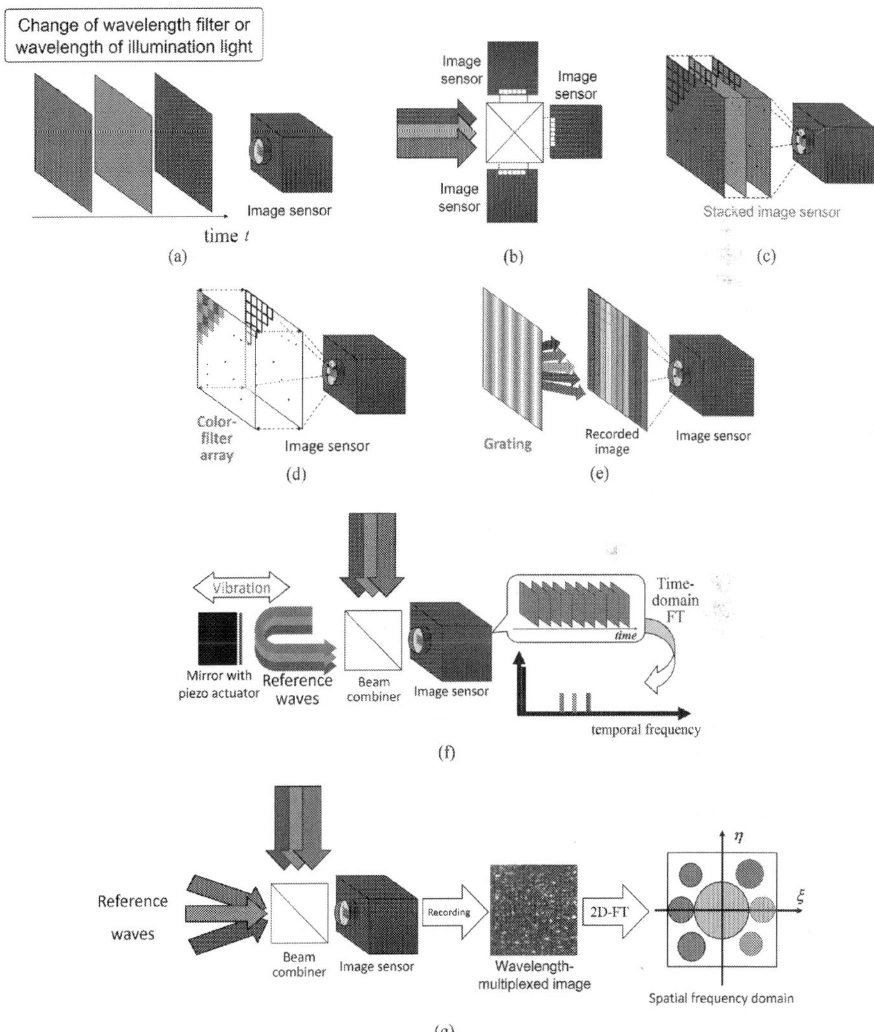

Figure 1. Multiwavelength imaging systems. (a) Temporal division, spatial division with (b) multiple image sensors and a prism and (c) a stacked image sensor, space-division multiplexing with (d) a color image sensor and (e) a grating, (f) temporal frequency-division multiplexing, and (g) spatial frequency-division multiplexing.

2. Phase-shifting interferometry selectively extracting wavelength information: phase-division multiplexing (PDM) of wavelengths

Figure 2 illustrates the schematic of the proposed multiwavelength 3D imaging technique in the case where the number of wavelengths N is two, which was initially presented in 2013 [34–36]. Optical setup is based on phase-shifting digital holography with multiple lasers. Multiple object and reference waves with multiple wavelengths illuminate a monochromatic image sensor simultaneously. The sensor records wavelength-multiplexed phase-shifted holograms $I(x,y:\alpha_1,\alpha_2)$ by changing the phases of the reference waves. Phase shifts for respective wavelengths α_1 and α_2 are introduced. An object wave at the desired wavelength is selectively extracted from the holograms by the signal processing based on phase-shifting interferometry. As a result, a color 3D image is reconstructed from the selectively extracted object waves. Thus, color 3D imaging can be achieved with grayscale wavelength-multiplexed images. When the number of wavelengths is N, $2N + 1$ variables are contained in a wavelength-multiplexed hologram: the number N of object waves, N of conjugate images, and the sum of the 0th-order diffraction waves. Therefore, five holograms are required to solve the system of equations when $N = 2$. It is noted that no Fourier transform is essentially required.

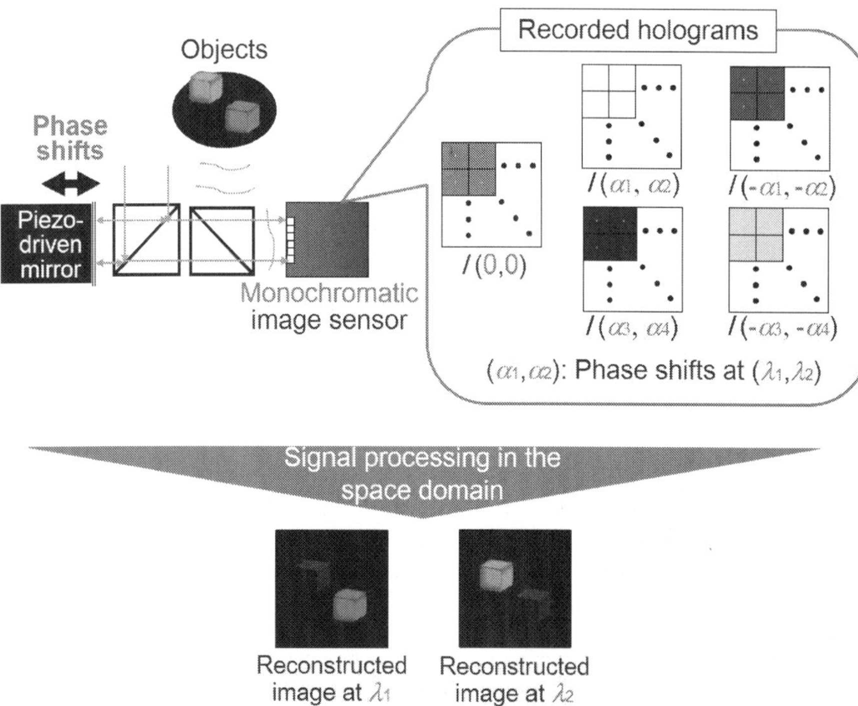

Figure 2. Schematic representation of the proposed multiwavelength 3D imaging technique.

Figure 3 describes the principle that wavelength information is selectively extracted by the signal processing in the space domain. As seen in **Figure 3**, different phase shifts for respective wavelengths are given to object waves with multiple wavelengths, and then wavelength information is separated in the polar coordinate plane. Although this separation is used to extract an object wave from a hologram in general phase-shifting interferometry, in the proposed technique, the separation is utilized to remove not only the conjugate images and 0th-order diffraction wave, but also undesired wavelength information. This means phase-division multiplexing (PDM) of wavelengths. **Figure 3** shows the case where specific phase shifts are used [34–36], but this concept is also applicable to the case where arbitrary phase shifts are introduced [39].

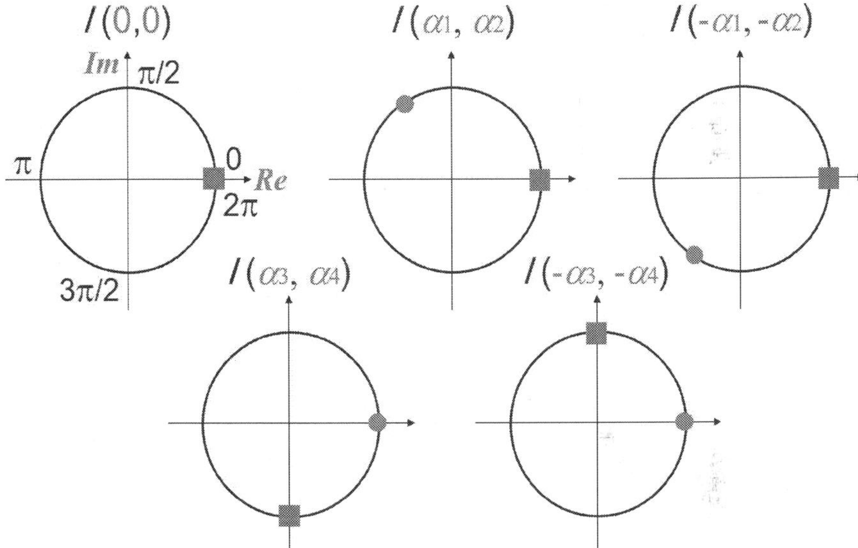

Figure 3. Principle of phase-division multiplexing (PDM) of wavelengths: separation of multiple wavelengths in the polar coordinate plane.

Figure 4 illustrates optical implementations of the proposed digital holography. Multiple lasers irradiate laser beams with multiple wavelengths simultaneously. A device for shifting the phase of light, such as a mirror with a piezo actuator, a spatial light modulator, or wave plates, is placed in the path of the reference arm. A monochromatic image sensor records the required wavelength-multiplexed phase-shifted holograms sequentially. An optical system based on PDM has the following features: the spectroscopic sensitivity of the optical system can be extended in comparison to the system with a color image sensor; full space-bandwidth product of an image sensor can be used to record object waves with multiple wavelengths; a bright color image can be obtained due to no spectroscopic absorption, while wavelengths filters required in conventional systems absorb light to obtain a color image; and measurement time is shortened by the wavelength-multiplexed recording in comparison with temporal division technique.

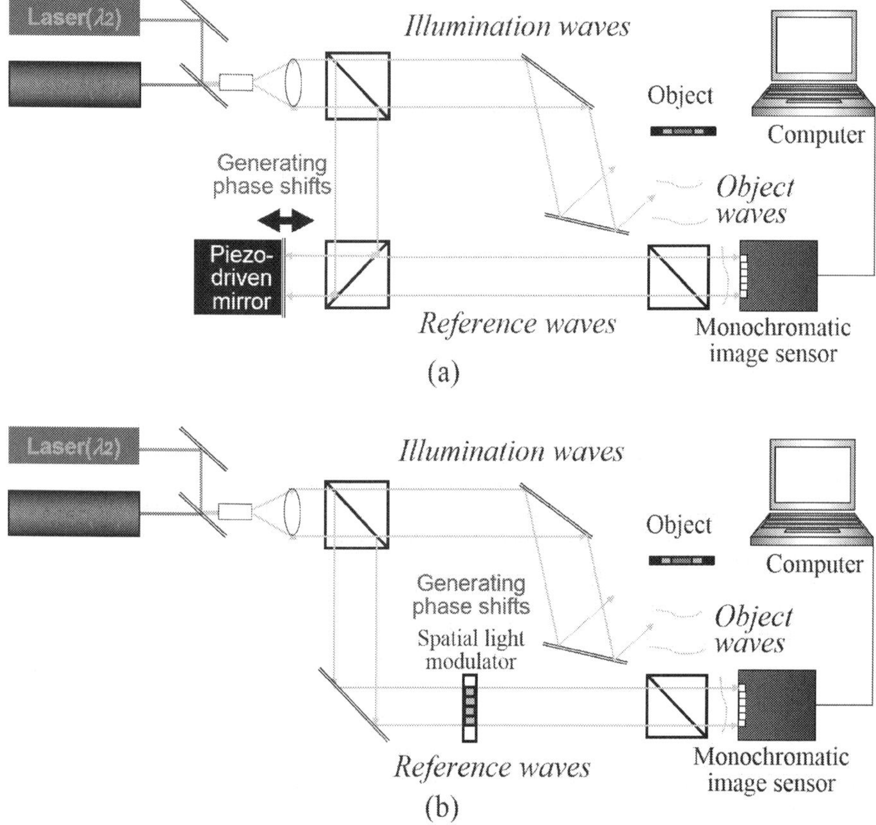

Figure 4. Optical implementations of PDM. Optical setups with (a) a mirror with a piezo actuator and (b) a spatial light modulator that has wavelength dependency in phase modulation.

Figure 5 illustrates the image reconstruction algorithm [34–36]. A wavelength-multiplexed phase-shifted hologram $I(x,y{:}\alpha_1,\alpha_2)$ is expressed as follows,

$$I(x,y:\alpha_1,\alpha_2) = I_{\lambda 1}(x,y:\alpha_1) + I_{\lambda 2}(x,y:\alpha_2), \tag{1}$$

here $I_{\lambda 1}(x,y{:}\alpha_1)$ and $I_{\lambda 2}(x,y{:}\alpha_2)$ are holograms at the wavelengths of λ_1 and λ_2, respectively. Eq. (1) means that a recorded monochromatic image is the sum of $I_{\lambda 1}(x,y{:}\alpha_1)$ and $I_{\lambda 2}(x,y{:}\alpha_2)$. When the complex amplitude distributions of object waves with different wavelengths are $U_{\lambda 1}(x,y)$ and $U_{\lambda 2}(x,y)$, $0th(x,y)$ is the 0th-diffraction wave, $Ar(x,y)$ is the amplitude distribution of the reference wave, j is imaginary unit, * means complex conjugate, and L and M are integers, then $I(x,y{:}\alpha_1,\alpha_2)$ can be rewritten as follows,

$$I(x,y:\alpha_1,\alpha_2) = 0th_{\lambda 1}(x,y) + Ar_{\lambda 1}(x,y)\{U_{\lambda 1}(x,y)\exp(-j\alpha_1) + U_{\lambda 1}{}^*(x,y)\exp(j\alpha_1)\}$$
$$+\, 0th_{\lambda 2}(x,y) + Ar_{\lambda 2}(x,y)\{U_{\lambda 2}(x,y)\exp(-j\alpha_2) + U_{\lambda 2}{}^*(x,y)\exp(j\alpha_2)\}. \tag{2}$$

Only the complex amplitude distributions of object waves with dual wavelengths $U_{\lambda 1}(x,y)$ and $U_{\lambda 2}(x,y)$ are derived from five wavelength-multiplexed phase-shifted holograms $I(x,y:0,0)$, $I(x,y:\alpha_1,\alpha_2)$, $I(x,y:-\alpha_1,-\alpha_2)$, $I(x,y:\alpha_3,\alpha_4)$, and $I(x,y:-\alpha_3,-\alpha_4)$ because five variables are contained in Eq. (2). If the system shown in **Figure 4(a)** is used to implement the proposed technique by moving the mirror in the reference arm with a piezo actuator at a distance Z in the depth direction, the phase shifts are

$$\alpha_1 = \frac{4\pi Z}{\lambda_1}, \tag{3}$$

$$\alpha_2 = \frac{4\pi Z}{\lambda_2}. \tag{4}$$

Here, when Z is equal to $L\lambda_1/2$, α_1 is $2\pi L$ and α_2 is $2\pi L\lambda_1/\lambda_2$. As a result, the intensity distribution $I_{\lambda 1}(x,y:\alpha_1)$ is not changed and $I_{\lambda 2}(x,y:\alpha_2)$ is changed, unless $L\lambda_1/\lambda_2$ is an integer. In the case where an integral multiple of 2π is utilized for phase shifts, meaning $\alpha_2 = 2\pi M$ and $\alpha_3 = 2\pi L$, $U_{\lambda 1}(x,y)$ and $U_{\lambda 2}(x,y)$ are separately derived by the following expressions.

$$U_{\lambda 1}(x,y) = [2I(x,y:0,0)-\{I(x,y:\alpha_1,2\pi M) + I(x,y:-\alpha_1,-2\pi M)\}]/\{4Ar_{\lambda 1}(x,y)(1-\cos\alpha_1)\}$$
$$+\, j\{I(x,y:-\alpha_1,-2\pi M) - I(x,y:\alpha_1,2\pi M)\}/(4Ar_{\lambda 1}(x,y)\sin\alpha_1), \tag{5}$$

$$U_{\lambda 2}(x,y) = [2I(x,y:0,0)-\{I(x,y:2\pi L,\alpha_4) + I(x,y:-2\pi L,-\alpha_4)\}]/\{4Ar_{\lambda 2}(x,y)(1-\cos\alpha_4)\}$$
$$+\, j\{I(x,y:-2\pi L,-\alpha_4) - I(x,y:2\pi L,\alpha_4)\}/(4Ar_{\lambda 2}(x,y)\sin\alpha_4). \tag{6}$$

As shown in Eqs. (5) and (6), subtraction between holograms, which is based on phase-shifting interferometry, is calculated and the unwanted wavelength component $I_{\lambda 1}(x,y)$ or $I_{\lambda 2}(x,y)$ is removed. Thus, dual-wavelength information is extracted selectively from five phase-shifted holograms. In this way, multiwavelength information can be separately extracted from $2N+1$ holograms when the number of wavelengths is N. From the extracted complex amplitude distributions on the image sensor plane, a multiwavelength 3D object image is reconstructed by the calculations of diffraction integrals and color synthesis.

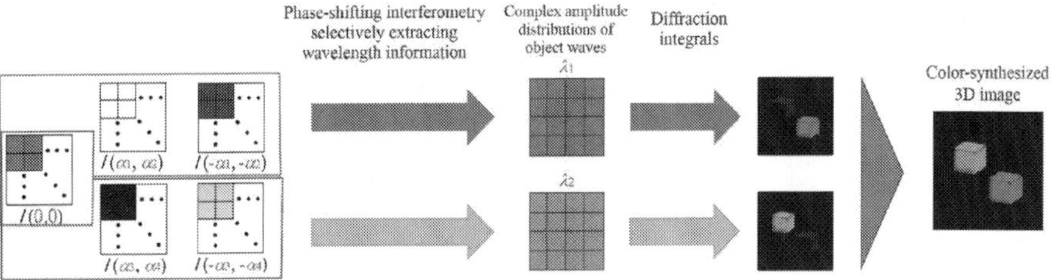

Figure 5. Image-reconstruction procedure.

3. Numerical simulation

Numerical simulations were conducted to verify the effectiveness of the proposed technique. **Figure 6** shows the amplitude and phase distributions of the object wave at each wavelength. As shown in **Figure 6(b)**, a color object with rough surface was assumed. 640 and 532 nm were assumed as the wavelengths of the light sources. Red and green color components of a standard image "pepper" were used as amplitude images at 640 and 532 nm, respectively. In these simulations, the distance between the object and image sensor was assumed as 200 mm, pixel pitch was 5 μm, resolution was 10 bits, and number of pixels was 512 × 512. **Figure 7** shows the images reconstructed by the proposed technique. Faithful images were reconstructed at each wavelength, and crosstalk between object waves with different wavelengths was not seen. The color synthesized image in **Figure 7(c)** indicates color 3D imaging ability. Thus, the validity of the proposed technique was numerically confirmed. Detailed numerical analyses and an experimental demonstration using an image sensor with 12-bit resolution were reported in Ref. [36].

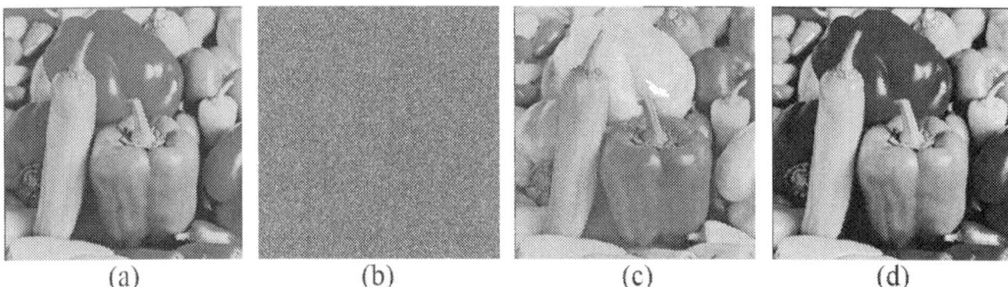

Figure 6. Object wave for a numerical simulation. (a) Amplitude and (b) phase distributions of the object wave. Assumed amplitude images at the wavelengths of (c) 640 nm and (d) 532 nm.

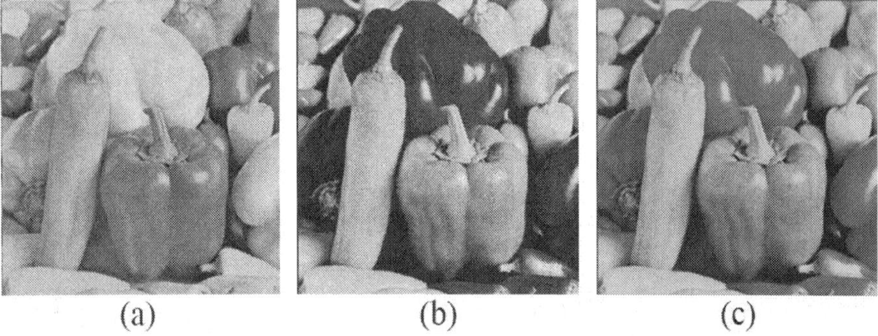

Figure 7. Numerical results. Reconstructed images at the wavelengths of (a) 640 nm and (b) 532 nm. (c) Color synthesized image.

4. Two-step phase-shifting interferometry-merged phase-division multiplexing (2π-PDM)

In a wavelength-multiplexed hologram, $2N + 1$ variables are contained. Therefore, $2N + 1$ images are needed to extract object waves separately in a general PDM technique. However, $2N$ wavelength-multiplexed holograms are sufficient to selectively extract object waves with N wavelengths, with the two-step phase-shifting interferometry-merged phase-division multiplexing (2π-PDM) technique [38]. **Figure 8** illustrates the basic concept of 2π-PDM. Two main points of 2π-PDM are the utilization of 2π ambiguity of the phase [34, 35] and merger of two-step phase-shifting interferometry [52–56]. As described in section 2, an intensity distribution at a wavelength is not changed when a phase shift is an integral multiple of 2π. We make the best use of this nature to decrease the required number of wavelength-multiplexed images. Also, merging PDM and two-step phase-shifting interferometry is important to satisfy high-quality multiwavelength 3D imaging and acceleration of a recording simultaneously. When recording three wavelengths, six holograms are sufficient with 2π-PDM, as described with an optical implementation in Ref. [38].

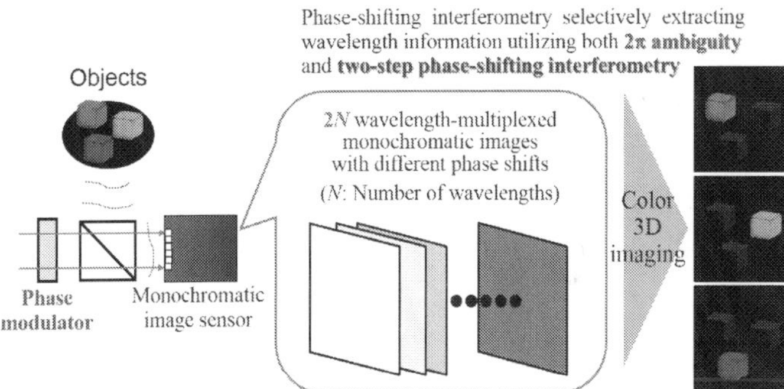

Figure 8. Basic concept of 2π-PDM.

The optical setup required for 2π-PDM is the same as that for other PDM techniques. Therefore, the systems in **Figure 4** are applicable to 2π-PDM. In 2π-PDM, various types of two-step phase-shifting methods [52–56] can be employed. When merging Meng's two-step method [53] into 2π-PDM, intensity distributions of reference waves $Ir_{\lambda 1}(x,y) = Ar_{\lambda 1}{}^2(x,y)$ and $Ir_{\lambda 2}(x,y) = Ar_{\lambda 2}{}^2(x,y)$ are sequentially recorded before the measurement by inserting a shutter in the path of the object arm. **Figure 9** describes an algorithm for selectively extracting wavelength information in 2π-PDM adopting Meng's technique. In the case of $N = 2$, a monochromatic image sensor records four wavelength-multiplexed phase-shifted holograms $I(x,y:0,0)$, $I(x,y:\alpha_1,\text{arb.})$, $I(x,y:2\pi M,\alpha_2)$, and $I(x,y:-2\pi M,-\alpha_2)$, and intensity distributions of reference waves $Ir_{\lambda 1}(x,y)$ and $Ir_{\lambda 2}(x,y)$. By making use of 2π ambiguity, both a 0th-order diffraction wave $0th_{\lambda 2}(x,y)$ and an intensity distribution of a hologram at an undesired wavelength $I_{\lambda 1}(x,y)$ are removed simultaneously by the subtraction procedure. Therefore, an object wave $U_{\lambda 2}(x,y)$ is extracted from three holograms, although five variables are contained in each hologram. In the case where α_1 and $\alpha_2 > 0$, $U_{\lambda 2}(x,y)$ is derived by

$$U_{\lambda2}(x,y) = [2I(x,y:0,0) - \{I(x,y:2\pi M,\alpha_2) + I(x,y:-2\pi M,-\alpha_2)\}]/\{4Ar_{\lambda2}(x,y)(1-\cos\alpha_2)\}$$

$$+ j\{I(x,y:2\pi M,\alpha_2) - I(x,y:-2\pi M,-\alpha_2)\}/(4Ar_{\lambda2}(x,y)\ \sin\alpha_2).$$

$$(7)$$

From the extracted object wave $U_{\lambda2}(x,y)$ and the amplitude distribution of the reference wave at λ_2, the intensity distribution at only λ_2 component $I_{\lambda2}(x,y:\alpha_2)$ is numerically generated by a computer,

$$I_{\lambda2cal}(x,y:\alpha_2) = |U_{\lambda2}(x,y)|^2 + Ar_{\lambda2}(x,y)^2 + Ar_{\lambda2}(x,y)\{U_{\lambda2}(x,y)\exp(-j\alpha_2)$$

$$+ U_{\lambda2}{}^*(x,y)\exp(j\alpha_2)\}.$$

$$(8)$$

If the sum of the intensities of the 0th-order diffraction waves is equal to $|U_{\lambda1}(x,y)|^2 + Ir_{\lambda1}(x,y) + |U_{\lambda2}(x,y)|^2 + Ir_{\lambda2}(x,y)$, noiseless multiwavelength 3D imaging can be achieved with 2π-PDM adopting Meng's two-step phase-shifting interferometry, according to the procedures described from here. By using the numerically generated images $I_{\lambda2cal}(x,y:0)$ and $I_{\lambda2cal}(x,y:arb.)$, intensity distributions at only λ_1 component $I_{\lambda1}(x,y:0)$ and $I_{\lambda1}(x,y:\alpha_1)$ are obtained from $I(x,y:0,0)$ and $I(x, y:\alpha_1,arb.)$ as the following expressions:

$$I_{\lambda1}(x,y:0) = I(x,y:0,0) - I_{\lambda2cal}(x,y:0)$$

$$= |U_{\lambda1}(x,y)|^2 + Ar_{\lambda1}(x,y)^2 + Ar_{\lambda1}(x,y)\{U_{\lambda1}(x,y) + U_{\lambda1}{}^*(x,y)\},$$

$$(9)$$

$$I_{\lambda1}(x,y:\alpha_1) = I(x,y:\alpha_1,arb.) - I_{\lambda2cal}(x,y:arb.)$$

$$= |U_{\lambda1}(x,y)|^2 + Ar_{\lambda1}(x,y)^2 + Ar_{\lambda1}(x,y)\{U_{\lambda1}(x,y)\exp(-j\alpha_1) + U_{\lambda1}{}^*(x,y)\exp(j\alpha_1)\}.$$

$$(10)$$

From the obtained $I_{\lambda1}(x,y:0)$ and $I_{\lambda1}(x,y:\alpha_1)$ and amplitude distribution of the reference wave at λ_1, the object wave at λ_1 $U_{\lambda1}(x,y)$ can be analytically extracted by using two-step phase-shifting interferometry.

$$U_{\lambda1}(x,y) = [\{I_{\lambda1}(x,y:0) - s(x,y)\}$$

$$+ j\{I_{\lambda1}(x,y:\alpha_1) - I_{\lambda1}(x,y:0)\cos\alpha_1 - (1-\cos\alpha_1)s(x,y)\}]/2Ar_{\lambda1}(x,y),$$

$$(11)$$

where,

$$s(x,y) = |U_{\lambda1}(x,y)|^2 + Ar_{\lambda1}(x,y)^2 = \left(\frac{v - \sqrt{v^2 - 4uw}}{2u}\right),$$

$$(12)$$

$$u = 2(1-\cos\alpha_1),$$

$$(13)$$

$$v = 2\big[(1-\cos\alpha_1)\{I_{\lambda1}(x,y:0) + I_{\lambda1}(x,y:\alpha_1)\} + 2Ir_{\lambda1}(x,y)\sin^2\alpha_1\big],$$

$$(14)$$

$$w = I_{\lambda 1}(x,y:0)^2 + I_{\lambda 1}(x,y:\alpha_1)^2 - 2I_{\lambda 1}(x,y:0)I_{\lambda 1}(x,y:\alpha_1)\cos\alpha_1 + 2Ir_{\lambda 1}(x,y)^2\sin^2\alpha_1. \quad (15)$$

Thus, the object waves at the desired wavelengths are extracted selectively from four wavelength-multiplexed phase-shifted holograms and intensity distributions of the reference waves. In this way, in the case where the number of wavelengths is N, multiwavelength information can be separately extracted from $2N$ holograms. By applying diffraction integrals to the object waves, amplitude and phase distributions of the object on the desired depth are reconstructed at multiple wavelengths. Therefore, a 3D image and wavelength dependency of the object can be obtained simultaneously.

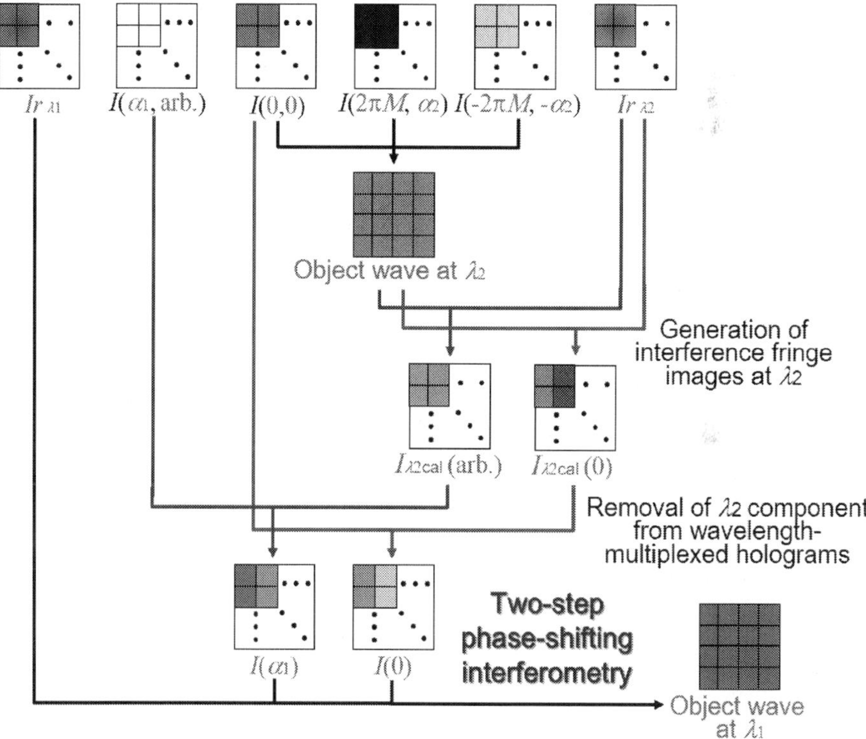

Figure 9. Algorithm for selectively extracting wavelength information in 2π-PDM.

Note that an arbitrary phase shift at λ_2 is allowable in one of the wavelength-multiplexed, phase-shifted, and monochromatic holograms $I(x,y:\alpha_1,\text{arb.})$ in a 2π-PDM algorithm described above. Therefore, 2π-PDM conducts asymmetric phase-shifting and belongs to partially generalized phase-shifting interferometry.

5. Experimental demonstration of 2π-PDM

We have demonstrated 2π-PDM experimentally to show color 3D imaging ability [38]. **Figure 10** shows a completed model of the optical system illustrated in **Figure 4(a)**. Four wavelength-multiplexed phase-shifted holograms were recorded sequentially by using a mirror with a piezo actuator. Before/after that, two intensity images of two reference waves were sequentially recorded only once. The wavelengths of the lasers were $\lambda_1 = 640$ and $\lambda_2 = 473$ nm. A monochromatic CMOS image sensor was used to record the holograms and reference intensities. The sensor has 12-bit resolution, 2592 × 1944 pixels, and the pixel pitch of 2.2 μm. The mirror with a piezo actuator moved $Z = 0$, 237, and ±320 nm sequentially to generate phase shifts that were required for 2π-PDM. Phase shifts (α_1, α_2) at (λ_1, λ_2) were $(0,0)$, $(2\pi(\lambda_2/\lambda_1), 2\pi)$, $(2\pi, 2\pi(\lambda_1/\lambda_2))$, and $(-2\pi, -2\pi(\lambda_1/\lambda_2))$. To investigate the phase shifts at their respective wavelengths, interference fringe patterns at the wavelengths were observed before the experimental demonstration, and details were explained in Ref. [38]. Two transparency sheets were set as a color 3D object. The logo of the International Year of Light (IYL) and the characters "2015" were printed on the sheets, and blue and red color films were attached to the logo and characters, respectively. The red "2015" sheet and blue logo sheet were set on the depths of 250 and 320 mm from the image sensor plane, respectively. Opaque sheets were also attached on blue and red color sheets to scatter the object illumination light. Therefore, the 3D color object had a rough surface and scattered object waves illuminated the image sensor. The object wave at the wavelength $\lambda = 473$ nm was extracted from three holograms and the object wave at $\lambda = 640$ nm was obtained by the procedures of Eqs. (7)–(15). For comparison, a colored object image was also reconstructed from a wavelength-multiplexed hologram.

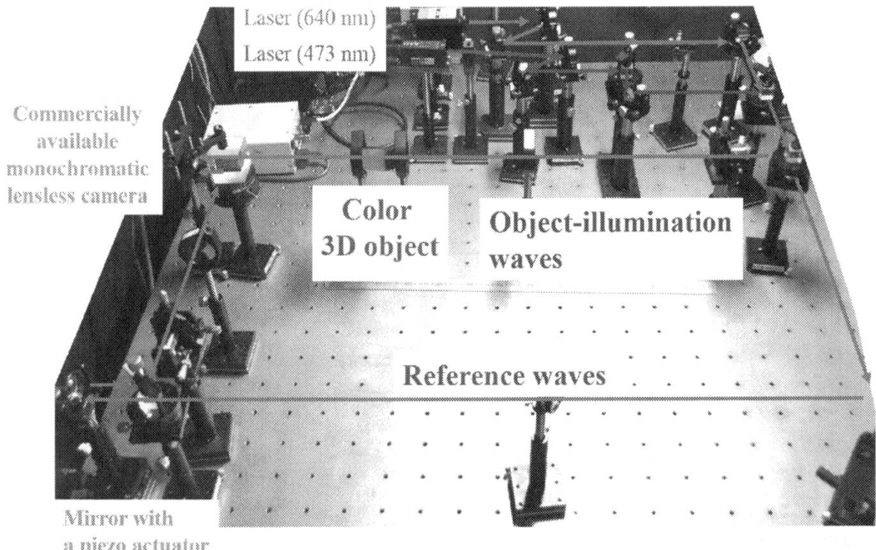

Figure 10. Photograph of the constructed dual-wavelength optical system of 2π-PDM.

Figure 11 shows the experimental results. Wavelength-multiplexed monochromatic images such as **Figure 11(a)** were captured, and wavelength information was superimposed on space and spatial frequency domains as seen in **Figure 11(a)** and **(b)**. **Figure 11(c)** and **(d)** were the images focused digitally at a distance of 320 mm from the image sensor plane and reconstructed by diffraction integral alone and 2π-PDM, respectively. Blue and red color films attached to the sheets absorbed red and blue light, respectively. However, **Figure 11(c)**, which was obtained from a wavelength-multiplexed hologram, indicated the superimpositions of not only the 0th-order diffraction wave and the conjugate image but also image components given by the crosstalk between $I_{\lambda1}(x,y{:}\alpha_1)$ and $I_{\lambda2}(x,y{:}\alpha_2)$. As a result, color information was not retrieved adequately. In contrast, **Figure 11(d)** showed the removal of the unwanted images, the crosstalk components, and the successful experimental demonstration of clear color imaging by 2π-PDM. **Figure 11(e)** and **(f)** were the object images focused on 250 and 320 mm depths from the sensor plane, which were obtained by an image-reconstruction procedure of 2π-PDM. Thus, we validated 2π-PDM in the imaging of wavelength dependency of absorption for a 3D object and high-quality color 3D imaging ability.

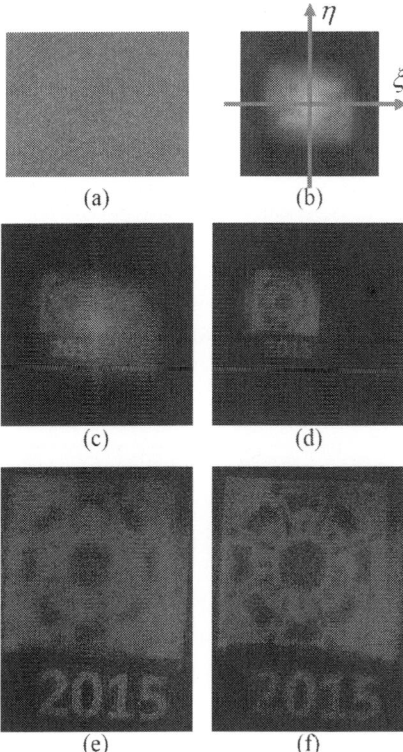

Figure 11. Experimental results of 2π-PDM. (a) One of the recorded holograms and (b) its 2D Fourier transformed image. (c) Image reconstructed from the hologram of (a). (d) Whole image reconstructed by 2π-PDM. (c) and (d) are the images digitally focused on 250 mm depth from the image sensor plane. Object images numerically focused on (e) 250 mm and (f) 320 mm depths, which were reconstructed by 2π-PDM.

6. Discussions and summary

We have proposed phase-shifting interferometry selectively extracting wavelength information as a novel multiwavelength imaging technique. In this technique, not only multiwavelength images but also the information of 3D space are simultaneously captured by the combination with holography. The technique is characterized as phase-division multiplexing (PDM) of wavelengths, and wavelength information is separately extracted in the space domain from the information of multiple wavelength-multiplexed images. 2π-PDM is the technique to analytically and completely solve the system of equations with $2N$ holograms against $2N + 1$ variables contained in each hologram. An experimental demonstration was conducted and clear color 3D imaging ability was successfully shown. Note that detailed analyses against both the experimental demonstration and the theory in 2π-PDM were reported in Ref. [38].

As future works, constructions of three-color digital holography and multidimensional holography systems are important to realize full-color 3D imaging and multidimensional holographic sensing. **Figure 12** shows an example of the required holograms in three-wavelength 2π-PDM [38] and numerical results for theoretical validation. Phase shifts indicated in **Figure 12(a)** mean that three-color 3D imaging with 2π-PDM is capable, when a spatial light modulator or wave plates are used as phase shifter(s) as described in Ref. [38]. Also, a combination of a piezo and a wave plate or a spatial light modulator will be applicable as another implementation. **Figure 12(b)–(i)** shows the results of a numerical simulation for three-

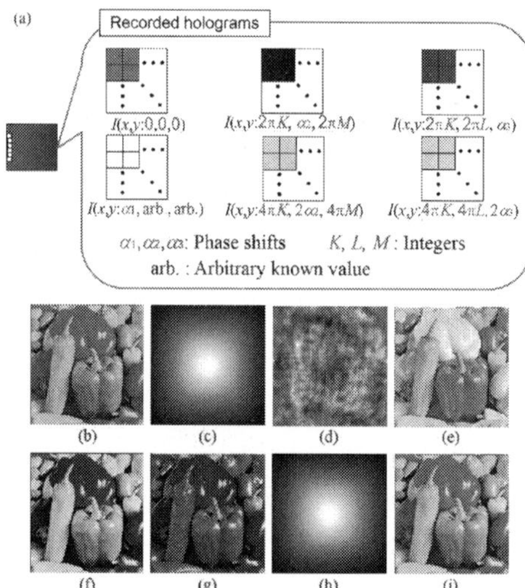

Figure 12. (a) An example of holograms required for three-wavelength 2π-PDM and (b)–(i) its numerical results. (b) Amplitude and (c) phase distributions of the assumed object wave and (d) one of three-wavelength-multiplexed phase-shifted holograms. Reconstructed amplitude images at the wavelengths of (e) 640 nm, (f) 532 nm, (g) 473 nm, and (h) phase image at 640 nm. (i) Color synthesized image obtained from (d)–(f). In the results, wave plates are assumed as phase shifters as described in Ref. [38]. The image-reconstruction procedure is in the same manner of dual-wavelength 2π-PDM, which is explained in Section 4.

wavelength 2π-PDM. In this simulation, a three-color object "pepper" with a smooth surface shape, red, green, and blue color wavelengths of 640, 532, and 473 nm, and 200 mm distance between image sensor and object planes, an image sensor with the pixel pitch of 5 μm, 512 × 512 pixels, ideal bit resolution, and α_1, α_2, $\alpha_3 = \pi/2$ were assumed. These assumptions can be satisfied with the optical system with five quarter wave plates, which is illustrated in Ref. [38]. Numerical results indicate that multiwavelength holographic 3D imaging can be done with high image quality from grayscale wavelength-multiplexed images, if successfully constructed. Improvements on the measurement principle and/or an image-reconstruction algorithm are important to simplify the construction; this is one of the main issues to be solved. From the viewpoint of multidimensional holographic imaging, PDM and 2π-PDM have the potential for not only multiwavelength, but also polarization-imaging digital holography [37] and instantaneous measurement [35], as implementations are described in these references. It is expected that simultaneous imaging of 3D structures, multiple wavelengths, and polarization distribution can be demonstrated with 2π-PDM.

The next step of the PDM techniques is the extension to multicolor holographic 3D image sensing, simultaneous imaging of color and 3D shape with multiwavelength phase unwrapping, dispersion imaging of a 3D specimen, and multidimensional holographic imaging. This technique has prospective applications to multispectral microscopy to observe 3D specimens with a wide field of view, quantitative phase imaging, multicolor lensless 3D camera, multidimensional holographic image sensors, and other multiwavelength 3D imaging applications.

Acknowledgements

We appreciate Kris Cutsail-Numata for checking the English grammar in this chapter of the book. One of the authors would like to sincerely thank Shu Tahara for encouragement. This research was supported by Japan Science and Technology Agency (JST), PRESTO, Konica Minolta Science and Technology Foundation, The Okawa Foundation, Research Foundation of Tokyo Institute of Technology, the Japan Society for the Promotion of Science (JSPS), MEXT-Supported Program for the Strategic Research Foundation at Private Universities (from 2013 to 2018), and Research Foundation for Opt-Science and Technology.

Author details

Tatsuki Tahara[1,2*], Reo Otani[3], Yasuhiko Arai[1] and Yasuhiro Takaki[4]

*Address all correspondence to: tahara@kansai-u.ac.jp

1 Faculty of Engineering Science, Kansai University, Suita, Osaka, Japan

2 PRESTO, Japan Science and Technology Agency, Kawaguchi, Saitama, Japan

3 SIGMA KOKI CO., LTD., Hidaka-shi, Saitama, Japan

4 Institute of Engineering, Tokyo University of Agriculture and Technology, Tokyo, Japan

[31] D. Barada, T. Kiire, J. Sugisaka, S. Kawata, and T. Yatagai. Simultaneous two-wavelength Doppler phase-shifting digital holography. Appl. Opt. 2011;**50**:H237–H244.

[32] A. W. Lohmann. Reconstruction of vectorial wavefronts. Appl. Opt. 1965;**4**:1667–1668.

[33] R. Onodera and Y. Ishii. Two-wavelength interferometry that uses a Fourier-transform method. Appl. Opt. 1998;**37**:7988–7994.

[34] T. Tahara, S. Kikunaga, Y. Arai, and Y. Takaki. Phase-shifting interferometry capable of selectively extracting multiple wavelength information and color three-dimensional imaging using a monochromatic image sensor. In: Optics and Photonics Japan 2013 (OPJ); Nov. 13; Nara, Japan. Optical Society of Japan (OSJ); 2013. p. 13aE9 (2 pages). (in Japanese)

[35] T. Tahara, S. Kikunaga, Y. Arai, and Y. Takaki. Phase-shifting interferometry capable of selectively extracting multiple wavelength information and its applications to sequential and parallel phase-shifting digital holography. In: Digital Holography and Three-Dimensional Imaging 2014 (DH), OSA Technical Digest (online); July 14; Seattle, USA. Optical Society of America (OSA); 2014. p. DM3B.4 (3 pages).

[36] T. Tahara, R. Mori, S. Kikunaga, Y. Arai, and Y. Takaki . Dual-wavelength phase-shifting digital holography selectively extracting wavelength information from wavelength-multiplexed holograms. Opt. Lett. 2015;**40**:2810–2813.

[37] T. Tahara, S. Kikunaga, Y. Arai. Digital holography apparatus and digital holography method. Application number PCT/JP2014/067556. Filing date July 1, 2014.

[38] T. Tahara, R. Mori, Y. Arai, and Y. Takaki. Four-step phase-shifting digital holography simultaneously sensing dual-wavelength information using a monochromatic image sensor. J. Opt. (IOP Publishing). 2015;**17**(12):125707 (10 pages).

[39] T. Tahara, R. Otani, Y. Arai, and Y. Takaki. Multiwavelength digital holography based on phase-division multiplexing using arbitrary symmetric phase shifts. In: Digital Holography and Three-Dimensional Imaging 2016 (DH), OSA Technical Digest (online); July 27; Heidelberg, USA. Optical Society of America (OSA); 2016. p. DW5E.2 (3 pages).

[40] J. H. Bruning, D. R. Herriott, J. E. Gallagher, D. P. Rosenfeld, A. D. White, and D. J. Brangaccio. Digital wavefront measuring interferometer for testing optical surfaces and lenses. Appl. Opt. 1974;**13**:2693–2703.

[41] Y. Ishii and R. Onodera. Two-wavelength laser-diode interferometry that uses phase-shifting techniques. Opt. Lett. 1991;**16**:1523–1525.

[42] R. Onodera and Y. Ishii. Two-wavelength phase-shifting interferometry insensitive to the intensity modulation of dual laser diodes. Appl. Opt. 1994;**33**:5052–5061.

[43] I. Yamaguchi and T. Zhang. Phase-shifting digital holography. Opt. Lett. 1997;**31**:1268–1270.

[44] S. Tamano, Y. Hayasaki, and N. Nishida. Phase-shifting digital holography with a low-coherence light source for reconstruction of a digital relief object hidden behind a light-scattering medium. Appl. Opt. 2006;**45**:953–959.

[45] A. Stern and B. Javidi. Improved-resolution digital holography using the generalized sampling theorem for locally band-limited fields. J. Opt. Soc. Am. A. 2006;**23**:1227–1235.

[46] J. Rosen and G. Brooker. Non-scanning motionless fluorescence three-dimensional holographic microscopy. Nat. Photon. 2008;**2**:190–195.

[47] D. Naik, T. Ezawa, Y. Miyamoto, and M. Takeda. Phase-shift coherence holography. Opt. Lett. 2010;**35**:1728–1730.

[48] Y.-C. Lin, C.-J. Cheng, and T.-C. Poon. Optical sectioning with a low-coherence phase-shifting digital holographic microscope. Appl. Opt. 2011;**50**:B25–B30.

[49] Y. Lim, S.-Y. Lee, and B. Lee. Transflective digital holographic microscopy and its use for probing plasmonic light beaming. Opt. Express. 2011;**19**:5202–5212.

[50] R. Horisaki and T. Tahara. Phase-shift binary digital holography. Opt. Lett. 2014;**39**:6375–6378.

[51] W. Li, C. Shi, M. Piao, and N. Kim. Multiple-3D-object secure information system based on phase shifting method and single interference. Appl. Opt. 2016;**55**:4052–4059.

[52] S. Almazán-Cuellar and D. Maracala-Hernandez. Two-step phase-shifting algorithm. Opt. Eng. 2003;**42**:3524–3531.

[53] X. F. Meng, L. Z. Cai, X. F. Xu, X. L. Yang, X. X. Shen, G. Y. Dong, and Y. R. Wang. Two-step phase-shifting interferometry and its application in image encryption. Opt. Lett. 2006;**31**:1414–1416.

[54] T. Kiire, S. Nakadate, and M. Shibuya. Digital holography with a quadrature phase-shifting interferometer. Appl. Opt. 2009;**48**:1308–1315.

[55] J. -P. Liu and T.-C. Poon. Two-step-only quadrature phase-shifting digital holography. Opt. Lett. 2009;**34**:250–252.

[56] J. Vargas, J. Antonio Quiroga, T. Belenguer, M. Servín, and J. C. Estrada. Two-step self-tuning phase-shifting interferometry. Opt. Express. 2011;**19**:638–648.

Chapter 10

Dynamic Imaging with X-ray Holography

Felix Büttner

Additional information is available at the end of the chapter

http://dx.doi.org/10.5772/66689

Abstract

X-ray holography is a type of coherent diffractive imaging where the phase information is physically encoded in the diffraction pattern by means of interference with a reference beam. The image of the diffracting specimen is obtained by a single Fourier transform of the interference pattern. X-ray holography is particularly well-suited for high resolution dynamic imaging because, intrinsically, the reconstructed image does not drift and the images show high contrast. Therefore, the motion of features between two images can be determined with a precision of better than 3 nm, as demonstrated recently. In this chapter, the technical aspects of X-ray holography are discussed from an end user perspective, focusing on what is required to obtain a high quality image in a short time. Specifically, the chapter discusses the key challenges of the technique, such as sample design and fabrication, beam requirements, suitable end stations, and how to implement pump-probe dynamic imaging. Good imaging parameters were found using simulations and experiments, and it is demonstrated how a deviation from the optimum value affects the image quality.

Keywords: X-ray holography, high resolution imaging, dynamic imaging, magnetic imaging, soft X-ray imaging

1. Introduction

X-ray imaging is one of the work horses of modern science, at least since the availability of brilliant and coherent light at accelerator radiation sources of the third and fourth generation. X-ray imaging can yield excellent spatial resolution due to the short wavelength of the light and provides a great depth of information of the electronic state of the imaged specimen via spectroscopy. In addition, synchrotron X-ray photons typically come in short pulses, which facilitates time-resolved imaging. Manifold techniques exist for X-ray imaging, each with its merits and constraints. X-ray holography is one of these techniques for imaging of the real space electronic structure with particular strengths in applications requiring drift-free

imaging (a merit that is derived from Fourier space imaging because drift in Fourier space translates to phase shifts in real space) and in situ sample manipulations.

Using holography for soft X-ray imaging, first demonstrated in a lensless setup in 2004 [1], is a rather novel approach that is still under heavy development and significant improvements have been made in the past few years [2–12]. Still, permanent holography end stations with user support, as common for more established techniques such as (scanning) transmission X-ray microscopy (STXM) or photo emission electron microscopy (PEEM), are not yet available. Therefore, the following chapter discusses the key ingredients and solutions for the main challenges of X-ray holography from an end user perspective. Specifically, the content of this chapter is organized as follows: The basic theory of how to obtain a hologram and how to reconstruct the real space information is presented in Section 2; the tricks of time resolved measurements and how to measure time zero in Section 3; some of the most important considerations for efficient imaging in Section 4; a suggested end station for magnetic imaging in Section 5; steps of how to fabricate suitable samples in Section 6; and finally, an outlook of anticipated future developments in Section 7. For those interested in more fundamental and technical aspects of X-ray holography, I suggest the other specialized literature, for example [9, 13].

2. How to obtain a real space image

A typical and convenient realization of X-ray holography is in a lensless off-axis geometry as depicted in **Figure 1**. Here, the entire optics of the imaging process constitutes of a mask in the X-ray beam with two circular apertures, the so-called object and reference holes. The object hole is typically approximately 1 µm in diameter and the reference hole is roughly 50 nm in diameter. The two holes are separated by 2–5 µm (at least three times the object hole radius) in the direction transverse to the incident beam. The specimen that is to be imaged is placed behind the object hole, ideally rigidly attached to the mask to exclude drift of the reconstructed image. The beam is transmitted through both holes and the specimen and is diffracted due to absorption and phase modulation during the transmission process. The hologram, that is, the interference pattern of the two diffracted beams, is recorded using a camera. For details regarding the wave propagation, see Refs. [9, 13]. Here, we consider the typical application where the camera is placed in the far field of the scattering process. Therefore, the scattering amplitude is conveniently described by the Fourier transform of the total transmission function of sample and mask.

The camera detects the intensity of the scattered light. Mathematically, the intensity is the absolute square of the scattering amplitude. An inverse Fourier transform of this intensity pattern yields the so-called reconstruction, which is the autocorrelation of the original total transmission function. The reconstruction can be written as a sum of the autocorrelations of object hole transmission function and reference hole transmission function plus the cross-correlations between these two transmission functions. When pictured, the autocorrelation is located in the center of the reconstruction and the cross-correlation terms are displaced by the vector from object hole to reference and vice versa, see **Figure 1**. Hence, there is no spatial overlap between these terms. Since the reference is small, the cross-correlation yields an image of the transmission function of the specimen with a resolution determined mainly by the reference hole diameter [1, 13].

In theory, reconstructing the real space image of a specimen from a hologram is just a simple Fourier transform. However, in practice, a number of post-processing steps are required to obtain a high quality image, as briefly discussed subsequently. First, a hologram is seldom recorded without artifacts. For instance, cosmic rays, stray light, pixel defects, and particles on the camera chip lead to overly bright or dark pixels in the hologram and to wave-like noise in the reconstruction. Such artifacts can be eliminated by statistical analysis (e.g., identifying artifacts as pixels deviating from the local average intensity by many standard deviations and by much more than a single photon count) and by subtracting a dark image. Other artificial artifacts, such as a central beam stop and the wire holding it, can be smoothed to avoid high intensity noise in the reconstruction due to sharp edges in the hologram. Best results are obtained when using high quality camera chips (typically 2048×2048 pixels) with a low noise readout electronics and by carefully eliminating sources of stray light.

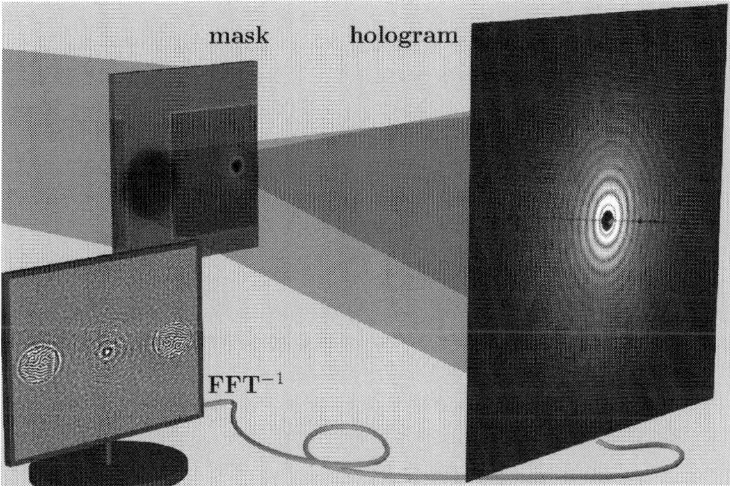

Figure 1. Schematic illustration of X-ray holography. The sample (labeled mask) is illuminated with a coherent plane wave from the left. The sample consists of a transparent SiN membrane. On the back side is an opaque Au layer with two holes, a larger one (the object hole, typically 1 μm in diameter and a smaller one (the reference hole, typically 50 nm in diameter). These holes are visible as dark shadows in the scanning electron micrograph overlaid on the mask. On the front side of the SiN membrane is the specimen that is to be imaged: In the present example, a magnetic film patterned into a wire. The incident beam is transmitted through the two holes and gets scattered. In the far field, the interference of the two scattered beams forms the hologram, which is recorded with a camera. The direct beam is blocked via a circular beam stop (typically made by a drop of glue on a thin wire, both of which are visible as a black circle and a black line in the hologram) so that the dynamic range of the camera can be optimized to detect the diffracted beam. The hologram can be digitally reconstructed via an inverse Fourier transform FFT $^{-1}$ to obtain the local transmission function of the sample, here showing the out-of-plane magnetization of the sample as black and white contrast. The image of the sample appears twice, a phenomenon known as twin image formation.

In a second step, the center of the hologram has to be found. This will be the center for the Fourier transform. At least one pixel precision should be aimed for to avoid strong wavy modulations of the reconstruction. However, by Fourier identities, a displacement in the hologram is equivalent to a phase shift in the reconstruction. Therefore, centering can also be performed in the reconstruction by multiplication with a plane wave $exp^{(i(k_x x + k_y y)}$, where x and y are coordinates in the reconstruction and k_x and k_y measure the center displacement in the hologram, both in pixels. With this method, sub-pixel centering can be achieved.

The third manipulation of the hologram is a numerical correction for the fact that specimen and reference typically have a finite relative shift in the propagation direction of the beam. In **Figure 1**, the reference exit wave is formed approximately 1 μm upstream of the specimen due to the finite thickness of mask, SiN membrane, and the specimen itself. Also, the reference itself acts as a focusing optics, introducing another in-line displacement between the smallest spot of the reference beam (i.e., the best resolution for the reconstruction) and the specimen [14]. The hologram contains the full wave field information (intensity and phase). Therefore, the reference focus can be numerically moved along the beam direction until both reference focus and specimen are in a common plane perpendicular to the beam [6]. Using this reference propagation algorithm often significantly improves the reconstruction quality and resolution and allows to obtain depth information of three dimensional specimen [4].

Strictly speaking, the hologram is the Fourier transform of the transmission function only if measured on a spherical detector. In practice, however, detectors are planar. For very close camera distances, an inverse gnomonic projection of the hologram is required to correct for this geometrical artifact [15]. In our measurements, such a correction has only been required if scattering angles exceeding 5° were recorded.

The reconstruction is in general complex valued. In theory, real and imaginary part of the reconstruction measure the refracting and absorptive part of the refractive index of the specimen, respectively [16]. However, such a quantitative correlation requires excellent centering, patching of the intensity blocked by the beam stop, a very low noise hologram, and a homogeneous phase across the reference beam. In most applications, it is therefore more practical to artificially shift all the relevant information into the real part by multiplying a constant phase factor to the reconstruction. The real part can subsequently be displayed as an image.

With an optimized sample design (see Section 4) and after following the previously described reconstruction steps, a high quality reconstruction of a magnetic sample as shown in **Figure 1** can be obtained from two camera accumulations (each with a maximum of 1500 photons per pixel), one for left-circular polarized light and one for right-circular polarized light. The total acquisition time, excluding camera readout and polarization change, can be as low as 1 s at a high intensity, high coherence beamline such as P04 at PETRA III in Hamburg, Germany.

3. Time-resolved measurements

In general, there are two ways of time-resolved imaging: The first way is single-shot imaging, where images are acquired on a time scale much shorter than the dynamics that is to be observed. Here, the dynamics is recorded as it is happening, without any need of reproducibility. However, when temporal resolution in the nanosecond regime or below and simultaneous spatial resolution in the nanometer regime is needed, the intensity of the light required to obtain a single image becomes so large that the sample evaporates on a picosecond time scale. X-ray holography is unique in being capable of recording single shot videos with only a few femtoseconds between the frames [17], that is, before the atoms of the sample start to move, but the approach is limited to a few frames and to sub-picosecond imaging.

For longer time scales or more frames, pump-probe imaging needs to be employed. Here, the intensity in a single shot is so low that the sample remains unperturbed. However, in order to obtain an image, many such shots need to be accumulated and the sample needs to be in an identical state during every shot. Besides a perfect reproducibility of the dynamics in the specimen, two steps are critical to enable such a pump-probe experiment: First, the excitation that triggers the dynamics must be periodic with a repetition that exactly matches the repetition rate of the incident photon pulses. And second, it is crucial to know the time at which the excitation should be applied in order to arrive simultaneously with the photons at the sample. Details of how to realize this precise timing are discussed in the appendix.

Once the excitation is in sync with the probing X-rays, images can be acquired at every delay of interest between pump and probe. That is, videos are recorded in a frame-by-frame mode: The delay between pump and probe is fixed for one image. After the acquisition of each image, the delay is changed and the accumulation of a new frame starts.

4. Efficient imaging

There are a great number of parameters that can be tweaked in X-ray holography in order to optimize the imaging for the specific scientific question. These parameters include the following: (i) object hole diameter; (ii) reference hole diameter; (iii) distance between object hole and reference hole; (iv) contrast of the specimen (e.g., thickness of a magnetic material); (v) camera-specimen distance; (vi) number of pixels of the camera and pixel size (changed by, e.g., binning and region of interest); (viii) camera gain or sensitivity; (ix) beam stop diameter; (x) an absorptive layer in or before the specimen (a parameter that is called here object linear transmission); and many more. Optimizing these parameters can yield orders of magnitude better contrast in the reconstructed image, and it is strongly recommended to use simulations to determine the optimum parameters.

Figure 2 illustrates how the contrast of a magnetic stripe domain image depends on some of the aforementioned parameters. The reconstructions were obtained from simulations of a purely two dimensional sample with a circular reference and a Co-containing magnetic specimen in a stripe domain phase. Contrast is generated exploiting the X-ray magnetic circular dichroism of the Co magnetic domains, that is, in absorption lengths of 13.7 nm for up domains and 23.4 nm for down domains [18]. For the simulations, the specimen is modeled as a magnetic layer with a total Co thickness of 2 nm, a hexagonal lattice of 125-nm diameter bubble domains, and a object linear transmission of 25%. The object hole has a diameter of 1.5 μm, the reference hole a diameter of 50 nm, and the distance between the two is fixed to 4 μm. The camera is a chip of 2048 × 2048 pixels of 13.5 × 13.5 μm² size at a distance of 24 cm to the sample. The sensitivity is assumed to be 50 counts per photon and the readout noise is 3 counts per pixel in average. The camera saturates at 64,000 counts. The model includes a beam stop of 1 mm diameter, a coherence of 80.00% and sample vibrations relative to the camera of 300 nm.

The simulations in **Figure 2** demonstrate how significantly the contrast is determined by the intensity ratio of object and reference, the overall coherence, and the dynamic range of the camera. Within a reasonable range and assuming that the intensity of the incoming flux is not a limiting factor, more absorption of the object and a smaller object hole improve the intensity ratio of reference to object and yield better contrast. That is, the image quality can be improved by coating the specimen with some absorptive layer.

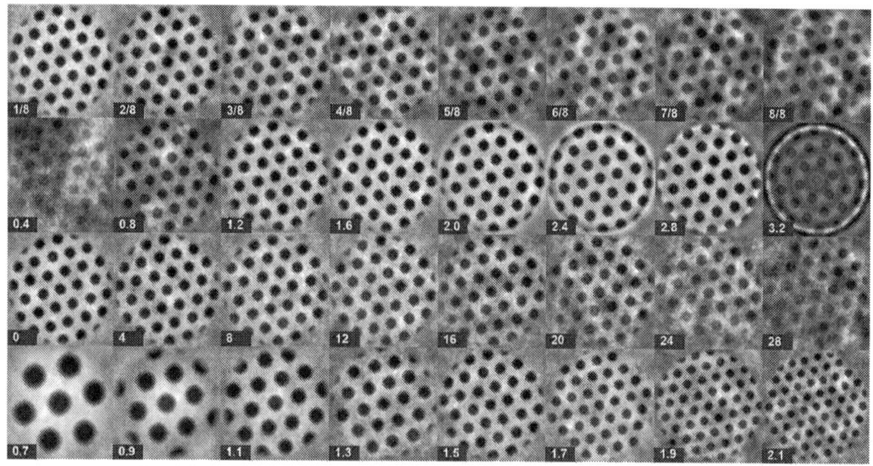

Figure 2. Contrast of the reconstruction as a function of imaging parameters. Top row: Object linear transmission, from 0.125 (left) to 1.0 (right) in steps of 0.125. Second row: Beamstop diameter, from 0.4 mm (left) to 3.2 mm (right) in steps of 0.4 mm. Third row: Vibrations (sigma of a Gaussian distribution), from 0 (left) to 28 µm (right) in steps of 4 m. Bottom row: Object hole size, from 700 nm (left) to 2100 nm (right) in steps of 200 nm.

The presence of a beam stop allows for using the dynamic range of the camera to detect signals at high scattering angles, which generally increases the contrast. However, if the beam stop becomes too large, the missing small scattering angle signals (corresponding to constant or low frequency modulations in the hologram) offset the intensity level of the reconstruction. The effect can be seen in **Figure 2** for a beam stop diameter of 2.4 mm. The white domains have now a color comparable to the background. For an even larger beam stop, the effect of ringing can be observed, as illustrated for the 3.2 mm beam stop. The optimum size of the beam stop depends on most of the other imaging parameters and has to be determined from simulations.

Finally, vibrations between the sample and the camera have a similar effect as a reduced coherence of the incoming beam [19]: Speckles and interference modulations become blurred and the image contrast reduces. Similar to the beam stop size, the question of at which magnitude the vibrations negatively effect the contrast can be answered only through simulations. In the present case, vibrations of as much as 8 µm have almost no effect on the image quality. However, for other geometries, the threshold may be as low as 300 nm.

Experimentally, the following parameters have been verified to yield full black-white contrast of magnetic domains in a single camera acquisition per helicity and a spatial resolution of better than 20 nm: (almost) fully coherent photons with energy at the Co L_3 edge (778 eV); an object hole with 800 nm field of view; a 50 nm reference that has its most constricted part on the camera side of the mask (considering that most references are conical); a center-to-center distance of 3 µm between object and reference holes; a specimen with a total of 9 nm of Co and a nonmagnetic absorption of 75%; a camera with 2048 × 2048 pixels of 13.5 µm size at a distance of 17 cm to the sample operated using 1 MHz low noise readout; a beam stop diameter of 0.75 mm diameter blocking just the central part of the object hole's airy disk; and a rigid mounting of the sample and the camera. The relatively small size of the object hole and the absorptive layer lead to a favorable total intensity ratio of object and reference beams, which manifests in a clear interference modulation of the entire hologram, including the center, as visible in **Figure 1**. Fine speckle patterns can be distinguished in the hologram due to the good coherence and the reduction in relative transverse vibrations between camera and sample. The excellent resolution is obtained due to a focus formed by a cylindrical reference in a thick mask material [14] and the large numerical aperture associated with a close camera distance.

5. Experimental setup

The design of a holographic end station should be tailored to the actual scientific question of the experiment. In contrast to many other imaging techniques, holography gives the user a large flexibility for instrumentation in the vicinity of the sample. Because of the absence of optical elements, an area of typically 20 cm radius around the sample is freely available and can be used to apply electromagnetic fields or temperature to the sample. Even optical excitations are possible when using a filter of, e.g., aluminum to shield the camera from this form of stray light. To reduce the effect of vibrations, it is recommended to mount the sample on a rigid holder and fix it onto the vacuum chamber.

Figure 3 illustrates an example of a chamber optimized for magnetic imaging. The beam first passes through a 1 mm aperture to facilitate a vacuum pressure gradient of two orders of magnitude between the two sides of the aperture. This way the chamber can be operated in pressures of as high as 5×10^{-6} mbar, thus avoiding restrictions to ultra high vacuum components and enabling quick venting and pumping. Carbon deposition on the sample was found to be negligible, even when imaging a single sample for more than one week in such a poor vacuum, at least when using photon energies exceeding 700 eV. The suggested chamber has a quadrupole magnet that can produce fields of larger than 1T at a gap of 2 mm, a shutter to stop the illumination during camera readout, a camera with a beam stop, and a sample held by a rigid mounting.

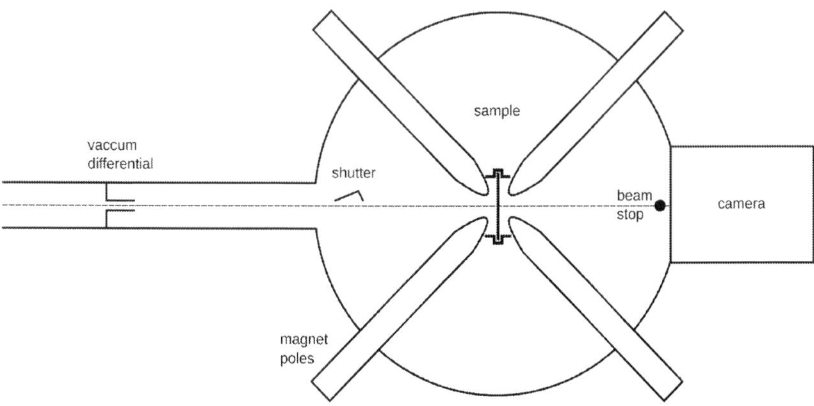

Figure 3. Top-view schematic of a holographic imaging chamber.

6. Sample fabrication

In the conventional approach, X-ray holography samples are integrated with the holographic masks, leading to the unique advantage of inherently drift-free imaging at the price of exceptionally complex sample fabrication. There is a concept to separate mask and specimen [2, 3], but it requires giving up drift-free imaging and hence the main argument for using X-ray holography instead of, e.g., STXM. Therefore, in the foreseeable future, the fabrication of advanced integrated samples will remain one of the main challenges of X-ray holography from an end users perspective. A detailed recipe has been published in [10], which will be briefly reviewed here.

Despite some demonstration of X-ray holography in reflection geometry [8], most present day applications of the technique rely on transmission measurements of transparent samples. Soft X-rays have a sub-micrometer penetration depth in any solid material. Hence, free standing films, the so-called membranes, are required to support the specimen, which itself needs to be thin. The most wide-spread approach is to use commercially available silicon nitride (SiN) membranes. The thickness of the membrane needs to be adapted to the specific imaging conditions, in particular to the photon energy. For instance, for magnetic imaging at the transition metal M edges (around 60 eV), anything more than a few tens of nanometers would already be opaque. For measurements at energies exceeding 500 eV, thicknesses of 500 nm and more are feasible and often even advisable because of the increased stability and robustness against various fabrication hardships. For the same reason, membranes should not be unnecessarily large, that is, their size should be just enough to fit the object and reference holes.

Figure 4 illustrates the steps to fabricate a sophisticated sample that is suitable for time-resolved imaging of field-induced magnetic domain dynamics [10, 20]. Not all of these steps are required for every sample. However, all holographic samples start with a membrane (step a) with an opaque layer on the back side (step b). $[Cr(5)/Au(55)]_{20}$ has proven suitable for imaging at 778 eV, where the transmission of this stack is below 10^{-9}. The absorption is mainly due to the gold. The chrome layers prevent the formation of large Au grains, which significantly eases focused ion beam (FIB) milling of the material. Steps c, g, and h, that is, FIB milling of the object and reference holes, are also required in any holography sample process. In principle, any process can be used to prepare a specimen on the front side of the membrane as long as ultrasonic exposure is avoided. In **Figure 4**, the remaining steps are marker fabrication (step d), material deposition and shaping (step e), and patterning of a microcoil (step f).

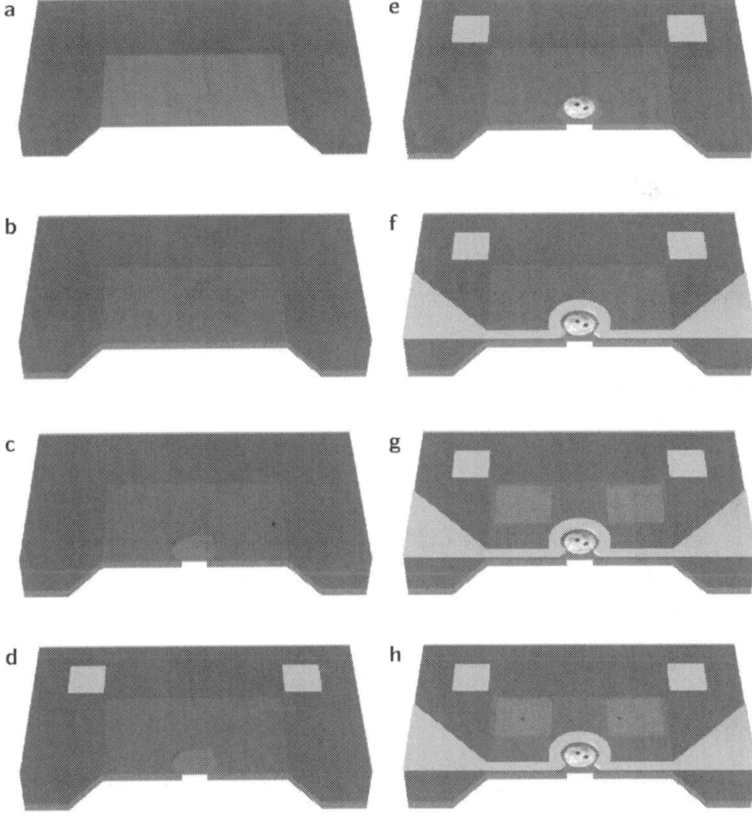

Figure 4. Steps for fabrication of a holographic sample. (a) Starting with a commercially available SiN membrane of a few micro meters in lateral dimensions. (b) An opaque Cr/Au multilayer is deposited on the topographic side of the membrane. (c) The Cr/Au is removed in a circular region, defining the object hole. The SiN is not removed. (d) Alignment markers are fabricated to align subsequent steps with respect to the object hole. (e) A disk-shaped magnetic specimen is fabricated behind the object hole. (f) A microcoil is wrapped tightly around the magnetic specimen to generate short magnetic field pulses. (g) The SiN is removed in large squarish areas where the references are supposed to be located. The removal of SiN makes the fabrication of small references significantly easier. (h) References are prepared in the previously designated areas. Reproduced from Ref. [10].

The result of this process can be seen in **Figure 5**. Note that optical lithography or even simple shadow-masking can be used to considerably simplify the overall process if sub-micrometer alignment precision is not required.

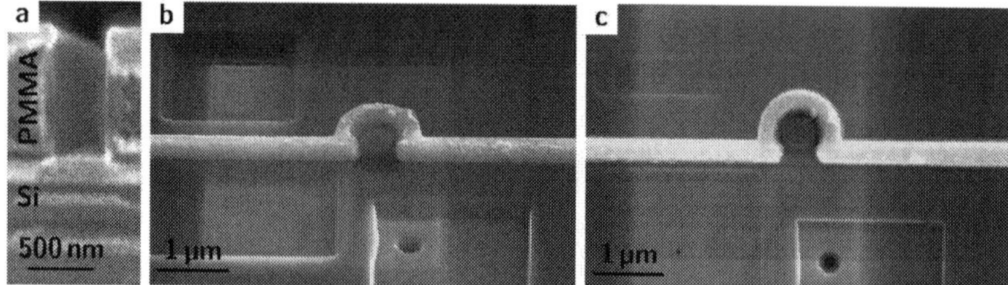

Figure 5. Scanning electron micrographs of a holographic sample. (a) Cross section of the PMMA resist used to fabricate the microcoil. Steep walls are required to prepare the coil in close vicinity to the magnetic specimen. (b) View of the final sample under 52°. The disk-shaped element in the center is the magnetic specimen. The black halo around it is the object hole visible through the SiN membrane. Wrapped around the sample is a gold microcoil. Three large square pads are milled into the SiN membrane to facilitate the fabrication of reference holes. One of the reference holes was milled from this side of the sample, here visible as a large conical aperture. (c) Top view of the same sample, now also showing the second reference in the bottom-left pad. This reference was milled from the other side of the sample and the exit is much more constricted then the entrance. The properties of the reference wave depend significant on whether the beam first passes the conical part or first the constricted part [14]. Reproduced from [10].

7. Outlook

So far, most reports using X-ray holography are improving the technique itself. Only a few studies exist where X-ray holography has been used to answer a scientific question not related to optics or imaging, and most of those where published in collaboration with the same groups that developed the technique (e.g. [20–26]). It is still a long way before X-ray holography will be a standard imaging tool, available to a similarly large community as STXM or PEEM. Above all, permanent end stations with full user support are needed. The new soft X-ray synchotron MAX IV in Lund, Sweden, will probably be the first to provide such an end station. However, even now, imaging times and quality are at least competitive to other soft X-ray imaging techniques and the parameters to achieve such performance have been discussed in this chapter. The perspective of improved cameras with readout times of sub-milliseconds (compared to the present 4 s) and single pixel adjustable gain in concert with even higher X-ray intensities and fast helicity switches suggest that almost live imaging will be possible in the future.

Acknowledgements

I thank my colleagues and coworkers for help and support during the beamtimes, their preparation and analysis. These include in particular B. Pfau, M. Schneider, C. M. Günther, J.

Geilhufe, P. Hessing, I. Lemesh, L. Caretta, S. Eisebitt, and the team of beamline P04 at PETRA III for the latest imaging experiments, A. Bisig and M. Kläui for valuable advice regarding the time-resolved measurements, and M. Mondol, J. Daley, B. Lägel, V. Guzenko and the LMN group at PSI, Switzerland, for help with the sample fabrication. Finally, I acknowledge financial support by the German Science Foundation.

Appendix

Here, we discuss the electronics to realize time-resolved X-ray holographic imaging using the example of electrical excitations and imaging in the 1.25 MHz repetition rate single bunch mode of BESSY II in Berlin, Germany [20, 27, 28]. The following discussion is largely adapted from Ref. [28].

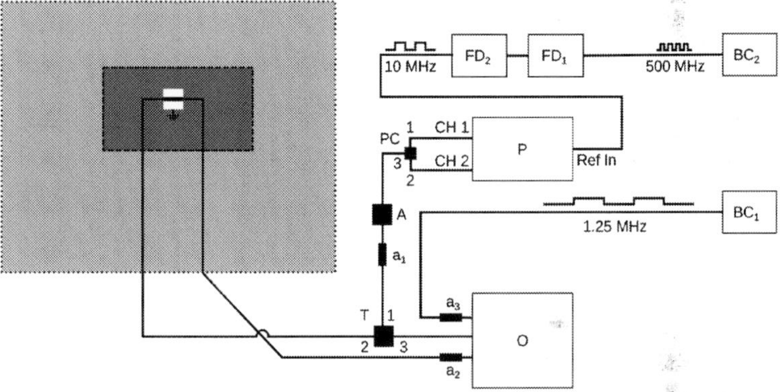

Figure 6. Electrical schematics for pump-probe X-ray holography. The outer light gray rectangle symbolizes the vacuum chamber and the inner dark gray rectangle the sample board. The sample itself is depicted as a white square with a horizontal wire on top. The thick black lines denote high frequency cables with SMA connectors. The acronyms represent the following: a stands for attenuator, T for pick-off tee, A for amplifier, O for oscilloscope, P for pulse generator, PC for power combiner, CH for channel, FD for frequency divider, and BC for bunch clock. A more detailed discussion of the figure is provided in the text. Reproduced from Ref. [28].

A schematic of the electrical circuit for the synchronized pulse injection is drawn in **Figure 6**. We use a Picosecond Pulse Labs 12080 800 MHz pulse generator (P in **Figure 6**) that has two individually programmable output channels, each with two SMA-type output connectors: one for the normal and one for the inverted signal. Each channel can create rectangular pulses with sub-100 ps rise time with up to 2 V bipolar amplitude and up to 800 MHz repetition rate. Both outputs provide adjustable time delays. The pulse generator has an internal 10 MHz clock, which can be replaced by an external clock signal (at Ref In). To ensure that the pulse generator injects pulses with the same repetition rate as that of the incident photon pulses (which is slightly less than 1.25 MHz in the single bunch mode of BESSY II), the eightfold multiple of the synchrotron pulse repetition rate (which is slightly <10 MHz) is fed into the pulse generator as a 10 MHz clock signal. With respect to this external clock, a 1.25 MHz signal has the exact same repetition rate as the photon pulses.

To create such a 10 MHz signal from the synchrotron, we use the 400-fold single bunch frequency (approximately 500 MHz), because such a signal is provided by the synchrotron (at bunch clock BC_2) and because it is much easier to reduce the frequency of a signal than multiplying it. That is, we use frequency dividers (FD_1 and FD_2 in **Figure 6**), where the first one (FD_1) divides the frequency by 25, and the second one (FD_2) divides by another factor 2%. The reason for not using directly a division factor of 50% is that this would result in a rectangular pulse pattern with a duty cycle of 2 (1/50), whereas our setup with two frequency dividers provides the 50 duty cycle signal expected by the pulse generator.

We can use this pulse generator to create bipolar rectangular pulses with variable amplitudes in both polarities. For this purpose, we use channel 1 (CH 1) of the pulse generator for the positive pulse and the inverted channel two ($\overline{CH2}$) for the negative pulse. The relative delay between the pulses is set to the duration of the first pulse, thus creating an uninterrupted succession of both pulse polarities, which is often useful because this pulse shape provides the strongest change of excitation at a given ohmic heat load. The signal from both outputs is combined using a power combiner (PC) that combines the input signals on connectors 1 and 2 in the output connector 3. The combined signal is amplified by 32 dB (power gain factor of 1600, voltage increase by a factor of 40) using a built-to-order Kuhne KU PA BB 5030 A amplifier (A) with a band width of 10–1500 MHz. To protect the amplifier against reflected signals, an attenuator of −3 dB (a_1) is mounted at its output. Any reflection will pass the attenuator twice and will thus be attenuated by −6 dB.

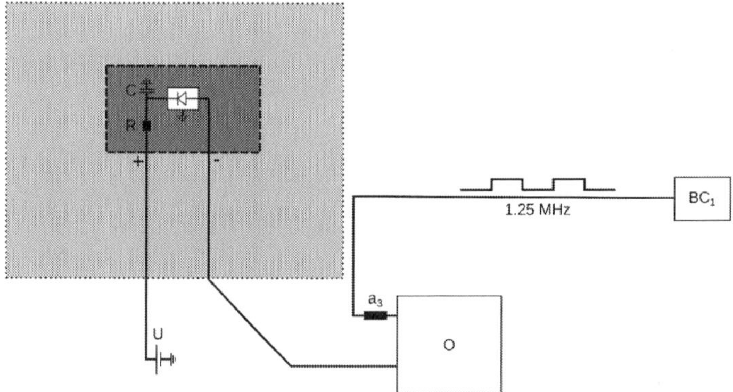

Figure 7. Electrical schematics for the time zero determination with an APD. The outer light gray rectangle symbolizes the vacuum chamber and the inner dark gray rectangle the APD board. The APD itself is depicted as a white diode symbol on the APD board. On the positive contact side of the APD, a 1 MΩ resistor R and a 1nF capacitor C are integrated in the APD board. A source meter is used to supply a voltage of 100 V on the positive input of the APD. The negative side is connected with cables of well-known length with the oscilloscope O. This oscilloscope is triggered by the 1.25 MHz bunch clock signal BC_1 provided by the synchrotron. Reproduced from [28].

Before being injected into the sample, part of the amplified signal is picked off to be monitored with a LeCroy WavePro 735ZI 3.5 GHz real time oscilloscope (O). This splitting of the signal is performed using a built-to-order Kuhne KU DIV 0112 A−371 pick-off tee (T), which splits the input signal on connector 1 in two parts, one almost unperturbed (power reduced by −2 dB) on output 2 and the other one attenuated by −20 dB on output 3. The signal from output 3 is monitored on the oscilloscope, whereas the signal from output 2 is injected into a microcoil on the sample, creating a magnetic field pulse (for details of the sample geometry, see **Figures 4 and 5**). Part of the pulse is transmitted and subsequently recorded with the oscilloscope (optionally attenuated at a_2), another part is absorbed by heating the microcoil, and the rest is reflected and sent through the pick-off tee again with −20 dB attenuation to the oscilloscope. The current transmitted through the microcoil can be calculated from the voltage of the transmitted signal recorded on the oscilloscope (if present, corrected by the damping of a_2) divided by its 50 Ω input impedance.

We now send bipolar pulses with a repetition rate synchronized to the incident photon pulses through the microcoil. The remaining challenge is to have both pulses simultaneously on the sample. For this purpose, we use the rising edge of the 1.25 MHz bunch clock signal (BC_1) provided by the synchrotron as a reference time zero, that is, we record this bunch clock signal on the oscilloscope (attenuated by −20 dB (at a_3) because its voltage is too large for the oscilloscope) and set its trigger to the respective channel. The temporal position of the photon pulse with respect to the same trigger is determined by mounting a Hamamatsu S9717-05K fast Avalanche Photo Diode (APD) on the position at which the sample is during the measurement, and using cables to transport the signal from the APD to the oscilloscope of precisely the same length as in the excitation scheme. The circuit used for this measurement is sketched in **Figure 7**. One side of the APD is connected to the oscilloscope, which is triggered by the BC_1 bunch clock signal. That is, this side is electrically on ground potential. The other side is lifted

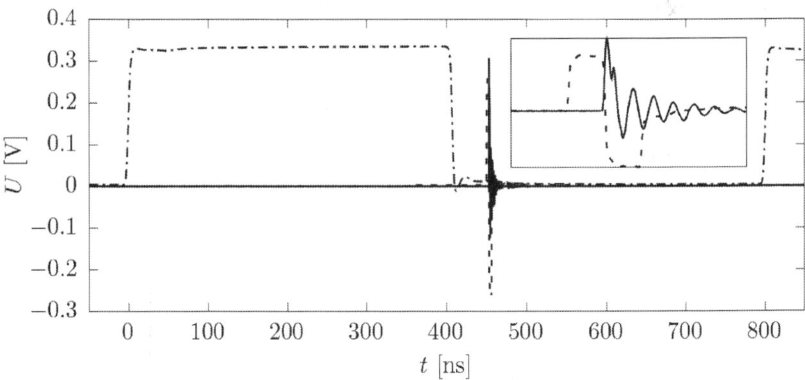

Figure 8. Signal measured with the oscilloscope. The dash-dotted line is the bunch clock BC_1 that serves as a trigger for the oscilloscope. The 50% level of the rising edge of this signal defines the time zero of the oscilloscope. The solid line is the signal from the APD (multiplied by 5), and the dashed line is the transmitted pulse (divided by 10). The latter two signals are plotted enlarged in the inset. Reproduced from Ref. [28].

to 100 V, and part of this potential drops on a 1 MΩ resistor placed in series before the APD. In this configuration, the diode is operated in reverse bias mode, that is, the depletion zone is increased by the electric field gradient. The resistance of the diode is much larger than 1 MΩ, such that almost the whole 100 V drop at the APD. A 1nF capacitor couples this side of the APD to ground; in the static case, however, this capacitor is insulating. As soon as a photon is absorbed in the diode, the situation changes significantly. The photons create free electrons that are accelerated in the external potential and create an avalanche of new charge carriers by collisions during their motion (hence the name APD). The capacitor acts as a sink for the (temporarily) generated charges. The holes are filled by a current from the oscilloscope, which is detected as a positive voltage peak. The avalanche stops because the voltage at the APD decreases immediately as the device becomes conducting (then most of the voltage drops at the 1 MΩ resistor). The signal decays in oscillations characteristic of the complicated RLC equivalent internal circuit of the diode [29]. The time of the photon event is reconstructed from the start of the pulse on the oscilloscope.

The signal recorded with the oscilloscope is plotted in **Figure 8**. The dash-dotted line depicts the 1.25 MHz bunch clock signal BC_1. The 50.00% level of its rising edge defines the time zero of the oscilloscope. The photon pulse found on the APD (solid line) starts at $t=452.7$ ns with respect to the oscilloscope trigger. After changing to the sample setup, the pulse send through the sample (dashed line) arrives at the same time delay at the oscilloscope. In this example, the magnetic state is probed at the transition between positive and negative pulse.

Author details

Felix Büttner

Address all correspondence to: felixbuttner@gmail.com

Department of Materials Science and Engineering, Massachusetts Institute of Technology, Cambridge, MA, USA

References

[1] Eisebitt S, Lüning J, Schlotter WF, Lorgen M, Hellwig O, Eberhardt W, Stöhr J. Lensless imaging of magnetic nanostructures by X-ray spectro-holography. Nature. 2004;**432**:885–888. doi:10.1038/nature03139

[2] Tieg C, Frömter R, Stickler D, Stillrich H, Menk C, Streit-Nierobisch S, Stadler LM, Gutt C, Leupold O, Sprung M, Grübel G, Oepen HP. Overcoming the field-of-view restrictions in soft x-ray holographic imaging. Journal of Physics: Conference Series. 2010;**211**:012024. doi:10.1088/1742-6596/211/1/012024

[3] Stickler D, Frömter R, Stillrich H, Menk C, Tieg C, Streit-Nierobisch S, Sprung M, Gutt C, Stadler LM, Leupold O, Grübel G, Oepen HP. Soft x-ray holographic microscopy. Applied Physics Letters. 2010;**96**:042501. doi:10.1063/1.3291942

[4] Geilhufe J, Tieg C, Pfau B, Günther CM, Guehrs E, Schaffert S, Eisebitt S. Extracting depth information of 3-dimensional structures from a single-view X-ray Fourier-transform hologram. Optics Express. 2014;**22**:24959–24969. doi:10.1364/OE.22.024959

[5] Geilhufe J, Pfau B, Schneider M, Büttner F, Günther CM, Werner S, Schaffert S, Guehrs E, Frömmel S, Kläui M, Eisebitt S. Monolithic focused reference beam X-ray holography. Nature Communications. 2014;**5**:3008. doi:10.1038/ncomms4008

[6] Guehrs E, Günther CM, Pfau B, Rander T, Schaffert S, Schlotter WF, Eisebitt S. Wavefield back-propagation in high-resolution X-ray holography with a movable field of view. Optics Express. 2010;**18**:18922–18931. doi:10.1364/OE.18.018922

[7] Martin AV, D'Alfonso AJ, Wang F, Bean R, Capotondi F, Kirian RA, Pedersoli E, Raimondi L, Stellato F, Yoon CH, Chapman HN. X-ray holography with a customizable reference. Nature Communications. 2014;**5**:4661. doi:10.1038/ncomms5661

[8] Roy S, Parks D, Seu KA, Su R, Turner JJ, Chao W, Anderson EH, Cabrini S, Kevan SD. Lensless X-ray imaging in reflection geometry. Nature Photonics. 2011;**5**:243–245. doi:10.1038/nphoton.2011.11

[9] Pfau B, Günther CM, Schaffert S, Mitzner R, Siemer B, Roling S, Zacharias H, Kutz O, Rudolph I, Treusch R, Eisebitt S. Femtosecond pulse x-ray imaging with a large field of view. New Journal of Physics. 2010;**12**:095006. doi:10.1088/1367-2630/12/9/095006

[10] Büttner F, Schneider M, Günther CM, Vaz CAF, Lägel B, Berger D, Selve S, Kläui M, Eisebitt S. Automatable sample fabrication process for pump-probe X-ray holographic imaging. Optics Express. 2013;**21**:30563–30572. doi:10.1364/OE.21.030563

[11] Duckworth TA, Ogrin FY, Beutier G, Dhesi SS, Cavill SA, Langridge S, Whiteside A, Moore T, Dupraz M, Yakhou F, van der Laan G. Holographic imaging of interlayer coupling in Co/Pt/NiFe. New Journal of Physics. 2013;**15**:023045. doi:10.1088/1367-2630/15/2/023045

[12] Duckworth TA, Ogrin F, Dhesi SS, Langridge S, Whiteside A, Moore T, Beutier G, van der Laan G. Magnetic imaging by x-ray holography using extended references. Optics Express. 2011;**19**:16223. doi:10.1364/OE.19.016223

[13] Pfau B, Eisebitt S. X-Ray Holography. In: Jaeschke EJ, Khan S, Schneider JR, Hastings JB, editors. Synchrotron Light Sources and Free-Electron Lasers. Cham: Springer International Publishing. 2016; p. 1093–1133.

[14] Geilhufe J. High resolution soft X-ray Fourier transform holography [thesis]. Berlin: TU Berlin; 2015.

[15] Schaffert S, Pfau B, Geilhufe J, Günther CM, Schneider M, von Korff Schmising C, Eisebitt S. High-resolution magnetic-domain imaging by Fourier transform holography at 21 nm wavelength. New Journal of Physics. 2013;**15**:093042. doi:10.1088/1367-2630/15/9/093042

[16] Scherz A, Schlotter WF, Chen K, Rick R, Stöhr J, Lüning J, McNulty I, Günther CM, Radu F, Eberhardt W, Hellwig O, Eisebitt S. Phase imaging of magnetic nanostructures

using resonant soft x-ray holography. Physical Review B. 2007;**76**:214410. doi:10.1103/PhysRevB.76.214410

[17] Günther CM, Pfau B, Mitzner R, Siemer B, Roling S, Zacharias H, Kutz O, Rudolph I, Schondelmaier D, Treusch R, Eisebitt S. Sequential femtosecond X-ray imaging. Nature Photonics. 2011;**5**:99–102. doi:10.1038/nphoton.2010.287

[18] Stöhr J, Siegmann HC. Magnetism — From Fundamentals to Nanoscale Dynamics. Berlin, Heidelberg: Springer-Verlag; 2006.

[19] Thibault P, Menzel A. Reconstructing state mixtures from diffraction measurements. Nature. 2013;**494**:68–71. doi:10.1038/nature11806

[20] Büttner F, Moutafis C, Schneider M, Krüger B, Günther CM, Geilhufe J, von Korff Schmising C, Mohanty J, Pfau B, Schaffert S, Bisig A, Foerster M, Schulz T, Vaz CAF, Franken JH, Swagten HJM, Kläui M, Eisebitt S. Dynamics and inertia of skyrmionic spin structures. Nature Physics. 2015;**11**:225–228. doi:10.1038/nphys3234

[21] Wang T, Zhu D, Wu B, Graves C, Schaffert S, Rander T, Müller L, Vodungbo B, Baumier C, Bernstein DP, Bräuer B, Cros V, de Jong S, Delaunay R, Fognini A, Kukreja R, Lee S, López-Flores V, Mohanty J, Pfau B, Popescu H, Sacchi M, Sardinha AB, Sirotti F, Zeitoun P, Messerschmidt M, Turner JJ, Schlotter WF, Hellwig O, Mattana R, Jaouen N, Fortuna F, Acremann Y, Gutt C, Dürr HA, Beaurepaire E, Boeglin C, Eisebitt S, Grübel G, Lüning J, Stöhr J, Scherz AO. Femtosecond single-shot imaging of nanoscale ferromagnetic order in Co/Pd multilayers using resonant x-Ray holography. Physical Review Letters. 2012;**108**:267403. doi:10.1103/PhysRevLett.108.267403

[22] Günther CM, Hellwig O, Menzel A, Pfau B, Radu F, Makarov D, Albrecht M, Goncharov A, Schrefl T, Schlotter WF, Rick R, Lüning J, Eisebitt S. Microscopic reversal behavior of magnetically capped nanospheres. Physical Review B. 2010;**81**:064411. doi:10.1103/PhysRevB.81.064411

[23] Hauet T, Günther CM, Pfau B, Schabes ME, Thiele JU, Rick RL, Fischer P, Eisebitt S, Hellwig O. Direct observation of field and temperature induced domain replication in dipolar coupled perpendicular anisotropy films. Physical Review B. 2008;**77**:184421. doi:10.1103/PhysRevB.77.184421

[24] Pfau B, Günther CM, Guehrs E, Hauet T, Hennen T, Eisebitt S, Hellwig O. Influence of stray fields on the switching-field distribution for bit-patterned media based on pre-patterned substrates. Applied Physics Letters. 2014;**105**:132407. doi:10.1063/1.4896982

[25] Pfau B, Günther CM, Guehrs E, Hauet T, Yang H, Vinh L, Xu X, Yaney D, Rick R, Eisebitt S, Hellwig O. Origin of magnetic switching field distribution in bit patterned media based on pre-patterned substrates. Applied Physics Letters. 2011;**99**:062502. doi:10.1063/1.3623488

[26] von Korff Schmising C, Pfau B, Schneider M, Günther CM, Giovannella M, Perron J, Vodungbo B, Müller L, Capotondi F, Pedersoli E, Mahne N, Lüning J, Eisebitt S. Imaging ultrafast demagnetization dynamics after a spatially localized optical excitation. Physical Review Letters. 2014;**112**:217203. doi:10.1103/PhysRevLett.112.217203

[27] Büttner F, Moutafis C, Bisig A, Wohlhüter P, Günther CM, Mohanty J, Geilhufe J, Schneider M, von Korff Schmising C, Schaffert S, Pfau B, Hantschmann M, Riemeier M, Emmel M, Finizio S, Jakob G, Weigand M, Rhensius J, Franken JH, Lavrijsen R, Swagten HJM, Stoll H, Eisebitt S, Kläui M. Magnetic states in low-pinning high-anisotropy material nanostructures suitable for dynamic imaging. Physical Review B. 2013;**87**:134422. doi:10.1103/PhysRevB.87.134422

[28] Büttner F Topological mass of magnetic Skyrmions probed by ultrafast dynamic imaging [thesis]. Mainz: University of Mainz; 2013.

[29] Dai D, Chen HW, Bowers JE, Kang Y, Morse M, Paniccia MJ. Equivalent circuit model of a Ge/Si avalanche photodiode. In: Group IV Photonics, 2009. GFP'09. 6th IEEE International Conference on, 9–11 September 2009.

Chapter 11

Indirect Off-Axis Holography for Antenna Metrology

Ana Arboleya, Jaime Laviada, Juha Ala-Laurinaho,

Yuri Álvarez, Fernando Las-Heras and

Antti V. Räisänen

Additional information is available at the end of the chapter

http://dx.doi.org/10.5772/67294

Abstract

Phase acquisition in antenna measurement, especially at millimeter- and submillimeter-wave frequencies, is an expensive and challenging task. The need of a steady phase reference demands not only a very stable source but unvarying temperature conditions and strong positioning accuracy requirements. Indirect off-axis holography is an interferometric technique that allows for characterization of an unknown field by means of a simple filtering process of the hologram or intensity interference pattern in the spectral domain, provided that the reference field, employed to interfere with the unknown field, is known in amplitude and phase. This technique can be used to avoid the effect of the errors related to the phase acquisition and to further develop new efficient and robust techniques capable of phase retrieval from amplitude-only acquisitions allowing for cost and complexity reduction of the measurement setup. A short review of the state-of-the-art in antenna metrology is presented in this chapter, as well as a description of conventional indirect off-axis techniques applied to this field. Last sections are devoted to the description of novel measurement techniques developed by the authors in order to overcome the main limitations of the conventional methods.

Keywords: antenna measurement, antenna diagnostics, amplitude-only, interferometry, off-axis holography, indirect holography, phaseless, microwave holography, millimeter-wave, submillimeter-wave

1. Introduction

Antenna measurement techniques are devoted to obtaining the main radiation parameters (radiation pattern, antenna gain, polarization, etc.) in the antenna far-field (FF) region[1] from the acquisition of the fields radiated by the antenna under test (AUT). Novel methods for antenna measurement [1] and postprocessing techniques [2] are constantly emerging to cope with the requirements needed to provide efficient and accurate characterization of new types of antennas, mainly at high frequency bands. Additionally, antenna diagnostics enables non-destructive inspection of the antennas for detection of design or fabrication failures by means of the analysis of their extremely near fields or their equivalent currents [3–6].

First, antenna measurements were performed in outdoor ranges at FF distances. Those tests were highly affected by weather conditions, interference, and multipath from multiple reflections mainly caused by the floor. Anechoic chamber testing was sooner adopted as the standard method for antenna metrology. Anechoic chambers have an electromagnetic absorber lining to reduce electromagnetic reflections and to control the measurement environment [7].

Advances in fabrication technologies have contributed to the development of new components and antennas at millimeter (mm-) and submillimeter (submm-) wave frequency bands.[2] At these frequencies, measurement of directive antennas would require extremely large anechoic chambers to fulfill the FF condition. Hence, other types of measurement ranges such as near-field (NF) measurement ranges have been developed to avoid the previous shortcoming [1].

In NF measurement systems, the field is acquired over a surface in the vicinity of the AUT. Planar, cylindrical, or spherical surfaces are the most common acquisition surfaces, with recent extensions to arbitrary geometry [9] or noncanonical domains [10, 11]. The acquired NF can be employed to obtain the FF radiation pattern of the antenna by means of mathematical NF-FF transformations based either in wave expansions [1, 12, 13] or integral equation methods such as the sources reconstruction method (SRM) [3, 9]. Diagnostics applications can also be developed from NF data using backpropagation techniques toward the AUT aperture [1, 13] or the SRM [3, 9]. After several decades of research and development, NF ranges have become the preferred approach for antenna testing.

Special attention must be given to the probe pattern and positioning accuracy [1] as well as to the effects that error sources in NF acquisitions, such as truncation of the measurement plane, cable flexing, stray signals, leakage, etc., can introduce in the FF pattern of the AUT [1, 2, 13, 14].

---

[1]The far-field distance is defined by $R = 2D^2/\lambda$ ($R >> \lambda$), being D the maximum dimension of the antenna and λ the wavelength [1].

[2]The mm-wave band is defined according to the IEEE Standard 521-2002 from 110 to 300 GHz. This standard is a review of the standard published in 1984 that also considered the lower bands defined from 30 to 110 GHz (Ka, V, and W bands) as part of the mm-wave band. This older definition is still commonly accepted. Frequency bands above 300 GHz are not included in the standard; the submm-wave or Terahertz band corresponds, depending on the author, to the fraction of the spectrum from 300 GHz to either 3 or 10 THz in the lower limit of the far-infrared spectrum [8].

NF techniques for both NF-FF transformation and antenna diagnostics generally require the knowledge of amplitude and phase of the radiated electric field by the AUT [1–5]. Nevertheless, phase acquisition, particularly at mm- and submm-wave bands, is a challenging task that requires sophisticated and expensive equipment due to the high thermal stability requirements and the effect of the errors, mostly resulting from thermal drift and cable flexing [1, 13–16].

Nowadays research is focused on the development of new measurement systems [17, 18] and techniques that allow reducing the acquisition time and costs and preventing or correcting the effect of errors in NF measurements [2–7, 19]. Among these techniques, amplitude-only measurements, commonly referred to as phaseless or scalar measurements (in contrast to vector, also referred to as complex measurements involving amplitude and phase), are frequently employed due to their multiple advantages such as the use of simpler and less expensive receivers and robustness to errors related to phase acquisition. Amplitude-only techniques can be indistinctly applied to antenna measurements and diagnostics and are divided into two main groups depending on the implementation approach: iterative and noniterative techniques.

On the one hand, most of the iterative techniques [3, 19, 10] are based on the acquisition of the field intensity in two or more surfaces. Then, an iterative process is employed to propagate the field from one surface to another after guessing an initial phase, until certain condition is satisfied for all the surfaces. This kind of technique is popular because they involve minor changes in the measurement setup, nevertheless they can suffer from stagnation and their convergence is strongly related to the first guess solution. On the other hand, and belonging to noniterative techniques, most of the interferometric approaches [5, 20–23] rely on the use of a reference field, previously known in amplitude and phase, used to interfere the field of the AUT and allowing an easy and iteration-free phase retrieval by means of a filtering process in the spectral domain.

Indirect off-axis holography, also known as Leith-Upatnieks holography [24], is an interferometric technique adapted from optical holography to amplitude-only antenna metrology in the early 1970s [25, 26]. During the last years, great efforts have been made to improve aspects such as sampling [22] and overlapping reduction [27] or reference signal calibration [28, 29]. The rest of the chapter is divided as follows: Section 2 contains an introduction to conventional off-axis holography techniques applied to antenna metrology. Novel techniques that allow for the use of synthesized reference waves with mechanical phase shifts [5, 30] will be introduced in Section 3. A new efficient method for amplitude-only characterization of broadband antennas [23] compatible with nonredundant sampling techniques [31] will be described in Section 4. Finally, main conclusions regarding the advantages and disadvantages of the proposed methods will be drawn in Section 5. Numerical validation of the proposed techniques in Sections 3 and 4, performed in Planar NF (PNF) measurement ranges [32, 33], will be given for each method and, thus, although easily translatable to other geometries, formulation will be particularized for planar acquisition systems.

2. Conventional indirect off-axis holography review

The word holography comes from the Greek words hólos (whole) and gráphō (written or represented) and was first coined by Gabor in 1948 to define a new technique in the optics field for retrieving the amplitude and phase of an unknown field after recording the intensity of a coherent wave disturbance [34] with a reference field, whose amplitude and phase could be properly characterized. The technique was later adapted by Leith and Upatnieks to use an off-axis reference [24].

The term holography has been subsequently employed in the context of antenna metrology and electromagnetic imaging to refer to another technique in which the phase information is directly acquired with the amplitude and a cable reference is employed (direct holography) [35, 36]. Thus, to avoid confusion, the methods described in this chapter will be referred to as *indirect off-axis holography*, since the phase is indirectly measured.

2.1. Indirect off-axis holography

Indirect off-axis techniques are based on two-step procedures: (1) recording the intensity of the interference pattern formed by the AUT and the reference field and (2) performing the phase retrieval of the unknown field (AUT's field) by means of a filtering process of the recorded pattern or hologram in the spectral domain. Conventional setup is usually implemented as shown in **Figure 1** employing a radiated reference field [21, 25] that is obtained from a sample of the source by means of a directional coupler. A variable attenuator (or amplifier) is usually included in the AUT or reference branches in order to balance the power between both branches and to increase the dynamic range of the hologram.

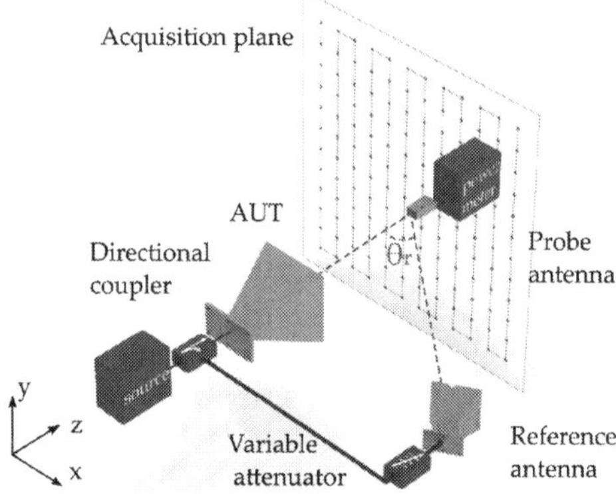

Figure 1. Basic setup for conventional indirect off-axis holography antenna measurement.

Another option is to create a plane reference wave by means of a shaped plane mirror which is employed as the collimator in compact antenna ranges [37]. Nevertheless, correctly shaping the mirror for high frequency indirect holography requires accurate and expensive machining.

The hologram is recorded at each point of the acquisition plane as the squared sum of the fields of the AUT E_{aut} and the reference antenna E_{ref} as:

$$H(\vec{r}) = |E_{\text{aut}}(\vec{r}) + E_{\text{ref}}(\vec{r})|^2. \tag{1}$$

The expression of the hologram can be further developed into

$$H(\vec{r}) = |E_{\text{aut}}(\vec{r})|^2 + |E_{\text{ref}}(\vec{r})|^2 + E_{\text{aut}}(\vec{r})E_{\text{ref}}^*(\vec{r}) + E_{\text{aut}}^*(\vec{r})E_{\text{ref}}(\vec{r}), \tag{2}$$

where the asterisk is used to denote complex conjugate.

If the expression in Eq. (2) is Fourier-transformed to the spatial frequency domain or k-space, the spectrum of the hologram can be expressed as

$$h(\vec{k}) = |e_{\text{aut}}(\vec{k})|^2 + |e_{\text{ref}}(\vec{k})|^2 + e_{\text{aut}}(\vec{k}) \otimes e_{\text{ref}}^*(-\vec{k}) + e_{\text{aut}}^*(-\vec{k}) \otimes e_{\text{ref}}(\vec{k}), \tag{3}$$

being e_{aut} and e_{ref} the Fourier transform (FT) of E_{aut} and E_{ref}, respectively, and $\otimes$ is the convolution operator.

As it is depicted in **Figure 2**, the spectrum of the hologram is composed of four different terms: the two zero-frequency harmonics in the center, known as autocorrelation terms, and the cross-correlation or image terms, which contain shifted and distorted (in case of using a nonplanar wave reference field) information about the complex field of the AUT.

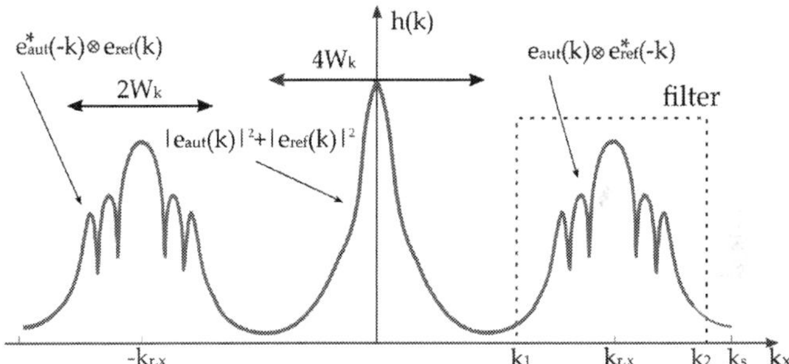

Figure 2. Schematic representation of the spectrum of the hologram for an off-axis angle in the x-axis.

Providing no overlap between the autocorrelation terms and the image term corresponding to $e_{\text{aut}}(\vec{k}) \otimes e_{\text{ref}}^*(-\vec{k})$ exists, the latter can be bandpass-filtered as

$$h_{\text{filtered}}(\vec{k}) = \Pi(\vec{k}_1, \vec{k}_2)\{e_{\text{aut}}(\vec{k}) \otimes e_{\text{ref}}^*(-\vec{k})\}, \tag{4}$$

where $\Pi(\vec{k}_1, \vec{k}_2)$ is a rectangular window defined by its corners at the spectral points $\vec{k}_1$ and $\vec{k}_2$ to filter the desired image term.

From the filtered term, the unknown field of the AUT can be easily retrieved back in the spatial domain by removing the effect of the complex conjugate of the reference field as

$$E_{\text{aut,retrieved}}(\vec{r}) = \frac{FT^{-1}\{h_{\text{filtered}}(\vec{k})\}}{E^{*}_{\text{ref}}(\vec{r})}.\tag{5}$$

It is relevant to remark that $E^{*}_{\text{ref}}(\vec{r})$ is a term whose amplitude usually suffers small changes along the spatial domain and, consequently, Eq. (5) can be evaluated without the risk of divisions by zero.

Quality of the phase retrieval will mostly depend on the degree of overlapping between the autocorrelation and cross-correlation terms, which for radiated reference fields is related to the off-axis position of the reference antenna, as it will be addressed next.

At this point it is worth noting two facts: first, the retrieved field corresponds to one of the tangential components of the electric field. In order to obtain the FF pattern of the AUT, both tangential fields are needed [1] and, thus, the process has to be repeated after turning the AUT 90° to acquire the other component [23]. Second, for the sake of simplicity, the offset of the reference antenna has only been introduced in the x-axis (as shown in **Figure 1**) without loss of generality.

2.1.1. Overlapping control: off-axis reference and sampling requirements

Central position of the image terms is defined by the off-axis angle of the reference antenna as

$$k_{r,x} = \pm k_0 \sin(\theta_r)\tag{6}$$

being k_0 the propagation vector in vacuum, defined as $k_0 = 2\pi/\lambda$, with λ the wavelength of the fields, and θ_r the off-axis angle formed by the reference antenna and the normal to the acquisition plane (see **Figure 1**).

According to Ref. [1], the maximum spatial bandwidth[3] of a radiated field in a planar acquisition is $W_k = k_0$. On the other hand, since the autocorrelation terms are the FT of a squared field, their bandwidth doubles the bandwidth of the original field [21, 28, 38] and, thus, the no overlapping condition is given by

$$k_{r,x} \geq 3k_0.\tag{7}$$

Nevertheless, due to the limitations imposed by the topology of the setup, the maximum off-axis angle is limited to 90°, yielding a maximum value of $k_{r,x\max} = k_0$. Therefore, although overlapping can be reduced by employing certain techniques (e.g., filtering after backpropagation of the planar wave spectrum (PWS) of the hologram toward the aperture or employing the so-called modified hologram, described later), it cannot be completely avoided in these setups with radiated reference waves.

---

[3]Bandwidth is defined for the positive half-space of the spectrum. Since the spectrum of the hologram is symmetric, the total bandwidth is twice the defined bandwidth.

On the other hand, sampling in the spatial domain is related to the extension of the k-space and has to be carefully selected in order to avoid aliasing. According to the *Nyquist* theorem, the extension of the k-space is related to the sampling step Δx by Ref. [12]:

$$k_s = \frac{\pi}{\Delta x} \tag{8}$$

As previously mentioned, the image terms are centered in k_0 ($k_{r,x} = k_{r,xmax}$) and have a bandwidth of $W_k = k_0$, yielding a total extension of $k_s = 2k_0$. Therefore, sampling in the spatial domain can be calculated from Eq. (8) as

$$\Delta x = \frac{\pi}{k_s} = \frac{\pi}{2k_0} = \frac{\lambda}{4} \tag{9}$$

In practice, the off-axis angle is lower than 90° and the sampling step can be slightly larger. Furthermore, overlapping degree varies depending on the type of reference antenna and the measured AUT. Directive antennas have narrower spectra [28] and the part of the spectrum associated to the squared signals often decays faster as it is computed for the convolution of two signals of bandwidth k_0 [5].

2.2. Modified hologram

The modified hologram technique was first employed for setups with radiated reference fields in Refs. [21, 38] and successively adapted for synthesized reference fields (see Section 2.3) in Refs. [27–29]. The technique consists in the removal of the autocorrelation terms of the hologram prior to the filtering process and can be implemented by means of two different approaches. First of them requires an extra measurement to characterize the amplitude of E_{aut} (the amplitude of E_{ref} is *a priori* known) [21, 23, 29, 30, 39]. Second approach, commonly known as *opposite-phase* holography [28, 40], introduces a *hybrid-T* component in the setup, which provides simultaneously the complete hologram in the sum port and the autocorrelation terms in the difference port. Another approach, used in imaging applications, is to increase the reference level several times above the level of the AUT's field in order to reduce the autocorrelation terms of the hologram [41, 42].

Thanks to the removal of the autocorrelation terms, separation between the image terms can be reduced, meaning that physical separation between the AUT and the reference antenna can also be reduced yielding the following advances:

- Overlapping is diminished and thus quality of the phase retrieval is improved.

- The extension of the k-space can also be reduced, involving larger sampling steps and less acquisition time [21, 28].

- Since the antennas can be placed close to each other and the off-axis angle can be reduced, the size of the setup is decreased and the paths of the reference and AUT fields are similar, resulting in less sensitive setups to scanning errors and source instability [21, 43].

Another advantage of this technique is that since the intensity of E_{aut} is measured, the final field can be composed with the measured amplitude and the retrieved phase rather than retrieving both, amplitude and phase, from the interferometric pattern as supposed so far. Thus, the quality of the phase retrieval is improved.

Main disadvantage for the modified hologram technique is that an extra measurement for the characterization of the amplitude of the AUT is required.

2.3. Synthesized reference field off-axis holography

Main differences between optical and microwave holography are stated in Ref. [27]. One of the most important remarks is that in microwave (and mm- and submm-wave bands) the hologram can be (coherently) recorded by scanning the probe across the acquisition plane, meaning that, instead of using radiated reference waves, they can be electronically synthesized and added to the field of the AUT.

Conventional approach to implement synthesized wave setups is schematically shown in **Figure 3**. A plane wave is synthesized by means of a phase shifter by cyclically modifying the phase of the sample of the field in the output of the directional coupler for each point of the acquisition plane. The synthesized wave is added to the acquired field of the AUT by means of a power combiner in the receiver's end.

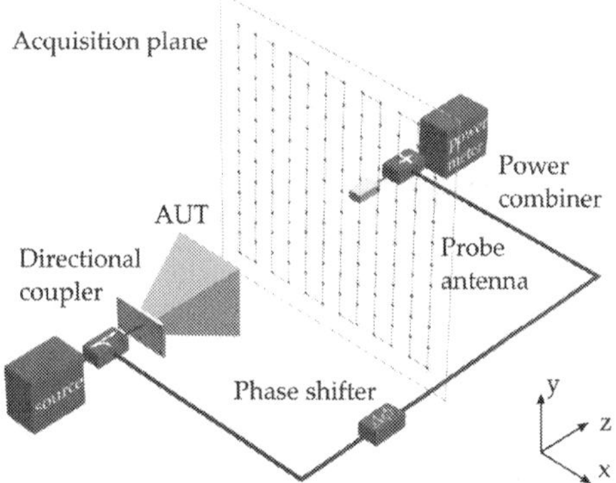

Figure 3. Conventional setup for synthesized wave off-axis holography.

In synthesized reference wave setups, position of the image terms is no longer related to the physical position of the reference antenna but to spatial sampling and the phase shifts $\Delta\phi$, between each point of the acquisition plane, and can be defined as:

$$k_{r,x} = \frac{\pm\Delta\phi}{\Delta x}. \tag{10}$$

The use of electrically synthesized waves removes the limitation imposed by the off-axis angle and makes possible to displace the image terms to the nonvisible part of the spectrum defined by $k_x^2 + k_y^2 < k_0^2$ [1].

Considering the nonoverlapping condition imposed in Eq. (7), the sampling step has to be selected depending on the value of the introduced phase shifts, which are typically selected as $\pi/2$, $2\pi/3$, or $3\pi/4$, yielding sampling steps of $\lambda/4$, $\lambda/6$, or $\lambda/8$, respectively [5, 28, 29].

This technique has several advantages:

- Overlapping can be controlled by selecting the phase shifts and the corresponding sampling rate.

- Modified hologram approaches can also be applied, thus sampling rate can also be relaxed.

- Since the reference wave is synthesized, it is not necessary to previously characterize it in amplitude and phase and its analytical expression can be employed in Eq. (5) for the phase retrieval. Hence, completely scalar acquisitions are made. Nevertheless, the nonideal behavior of the phase shifter and the rest of the components introduce modulations in the signal and, thus, its characterization is recommended [44].

However, synthesized reference field indirect off-axis holography also presents the following limitations:

- The sampling rate has to be increased in order to displace the image terms to the non-visible part of the spectrum and to extend its limits. Thus, the acquisition time is increased and so it is the required system stability.

- The increased sampling step can also be a problem at mm- and submm-wave bands if too dense sampling grids are required, due to the positioning accuracy of the system.

- Two new components have to be included in the setup which can also pose a problem at high frequency bands due to the cost and complexity of those types of devices.

2.4. Main drawbacks and limitations of indirect off-axis holography

Despite the multiple advantages of conventional indirect off-axis techniques versus complex field measurements, such as robustness and cost reduction [21, 43], and also versus other amplitude-only techniques based on iterative approaches, conventional indirect off-axis techniques exhibit several limitations, which are summarized next:

- The reference field needs to be characterized in amplitude and phase at least once, and thus, the technique cannot be implemented only by means of scalar acquisitions since an initial vector calibration is required. Nevertheless, the use of synthesized waves [28, 29, 40] solves this problem, since the phase can be obtained analytically. Other methods to avoid the phase acquisition of the reference antenna such as the use of well-known antennas whose phase behavior can be modeled have also been proposed [21, 45].

- Setups based on synthesized waves solve the previous drawback and also allows to control overlapping of the image terms. However, implementation of this type of setups involves the use of more radiofrequency (RF) components, i.e., phase shifters and power combiners. Implementation of these types of devices is not trivial at high frequency bands and the cost of the system can be highly increased.

- In addition, as shown in **Figure 3**, the reference signal has to be conveyed from the output of the directional coupler and phase shifter to the power combiner, located at the receiver's end. Nevertheless, high frequency equipment (e.g., over 110 GHz) usually requires the use of waveguide sections to convey the signal. In general, these waveguides cannot be arbitrarily bent. Other choice is to convey, by means of flexible cables, a low-frequency signal as reference and, at the end of the cable, resort to a frequency multiplier. However, this approach can suffer from phase inaccuracies due to cable flexing and temperature drift; also the use of frequency multipliers can increase the cost of the measurement system.

- The use of the modified hologram technique can alleviate the dense sampling demanded at the expenses of an extra measurement for the characterization of the amplitude of the AUT.

- Conventional indirect off-axis holography is a monochromatic technique. Thus, its use for broadband antennas characterization might be unfeasible if each frequency analysis requires an independent spatial acquisition.

Other phase retrieval approaches have been proposed in order to overcome the dense sampling requirements. In Refs. [41] and [46], a new approach, known as *phase-shifting*, derived from digital inline microscopy, employs three different holograms recorded after introducing phase shifts in the reference field to perform the phase retrieval in the spatial domain; in this case, the phase can be retrieved point-by-point. The method presented in Ref. [47] for a bistatic imaging setup can also be directly employed in antenna measurement setups. In this case, the phase retrieval is performed by solving a set of equations formed by the modified hologram expression and the expression that relates $\|E_{\text{aut}}(\vec{r})\|^2$ to its real and imaginary parts. For both cases the phase is retrieved directly in the spatial domain and, therefore, a sampling rate of $\lambda/2$ can be used. An added advantage is that there is no restriction in the position of the reference antenna.

3. Indirect off-axis holography with mechanical phase shifts

In order to overcome some of the above-mentioned limitations of conventional techniques, two methods allowing either to substitute the phase shifter for mechanical displacements or to control the position of the image terms in setups with radiated reference waves are described in this section.

3.1. Synthesized reference field by means of mechanical shifts

As mentioned before, main advantages of the use of synthesized reference waves are overlapping control of the image terms and that the reference field can be analytically obtained by means of a phase shifter from a sample of the field. Nevertheless, phase shifters can increase the cost of the measurement system or simply not be available for a specific frequency band.

The proposed method aims for the substitution of the phase shifter (see **Figure 3**) with mechanical displacements of the probe to create the interference-like pattern. The reference branch will provide a constant sample of the source added to the field recorded by the probe by means of a power combiner.

The expression of the hologram in Eq. (2) can be particularized for the case of using synthesized plane waves ($E_{\text{ref}}(\vec{r}) = Ae^{-jk_0r}$) as:

$$H(\vec{r}) = |E_{\text{aut}}(\vec{r})|^2 + A^2 + AE_{\text{aut}}(\vec{r})e^{+jk_0r} + AE^*_{\text{aut}}(\vec{r})e^{-jk_0r}. \tag{11}$$

On the other hand, the recorded hologram, over a planar conventional acquisition grid, in the setup of **Figure 3**, when no phase shifter is employed, could be expressed in the following way:

$$H(\vec{r}) = |E_{\text{aut}}(\vec{r}) + C|^2, \tag{12}$$

where C is the constant reference level added to the power combiner.

If small mechanical displacements $\vec{d} = d\vec{r}/\|\vec{r}\|_2$ are added between each of the points of that conventional acquisition grid, the field of the AUT can be approximated in those new points, disregarding the amplitude variation and taking into account only the phase change by

$$E_{\text{aut}}(\vec{r} + \vec{d}) \approx E_{\text{aut}}(\vec{r})e^{-jk_0d}. \tag{13}$$

For those new points, the hologram in Eq. (12) can be rewritten as in Eq. (14), yielding an equivalent expression to Eq. (11):

$$H(\vec{r} + \vec{d}) = |E_{\text{aut}}(\vec{r})e^{-jk_0d} + C|^2 = |E_{\text{aut}}(\vec{r})|^2 + C^2 + CE_{\text{aut}}(\vec{r})e^{-jk_0d} + CE^*_{\text{aut}}(\vec{r})e^{+jk_0d}. \tag{14}$$

Therefore, if the mechanical displacements are selected so that the term e^{-jk_0d} in Eq. (13) introduces appropriate phase shifts, the use of phase shifters can be avoided.

The new grid will be a three-dimensional layered grid with as many layers as number of considered phase shifts $N_\phi = 2\pi/\Delta\phi$. N_ϕ is fixed together with the sampling rate to control the position of the image terms of the hologram, see Eq. (10), and of course, the *modified hologram* technique (Section 2.2) can also be applied.

Figure 4 shows two different views of the measurement grid generated for the experimental validation of the setup presented next. For those examples, the mechanical displacements are selected to introduce a phase shift of $\pi/2$ and thus, $N_\phi = 4$, as it can be clearly seen in **Figure 4(a)**. **Figure 4(b)** shows the top view of the grid in which the cyclically repeated pattern can be observed. The orange dots represent the top layer with regular sampling of $\lambda/2$, whereas the blue ones are those corresponding to the modified points introduced to generate the phase shifts, yielding a final sampling step of $\lambda/8$. The solid line interconnecting the dots indicates the sweep direction. The grid creation process can equivalently be seen as a modification of $N_\phi - 1$ of every N_ϕ points in the sweep axis of a regular grid to introduce the desired phase shifts.

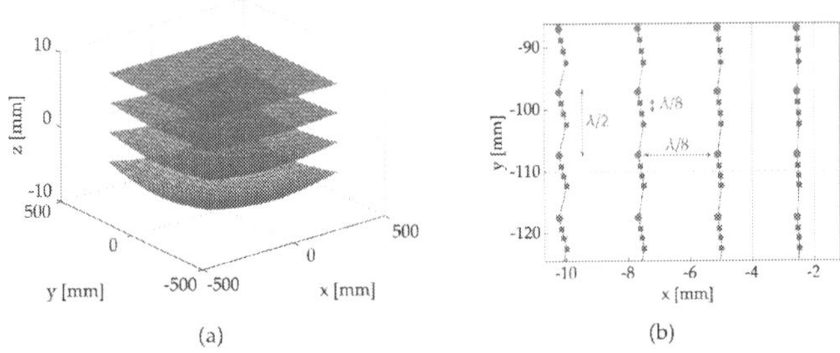

Figure 4. Three-dimensional acquisition grid for the proposed method. Note that a different scale has been used for all the axes: (a) complete grid and (b) detail of the top view.

For the phase retrieval, there are two different options: (i) either Eq. (4) is transformed back to the spatial domain and only the points corresponding to the top layer of the grid are selected, or (ii) the field is retrieved as in Eq. (5) analytically modeling the phase of the reference field. A compensation for the $e^{+jk_0 r}$ term introduced in the modified acquisition points (see Eq. (13)) has to be considered for the latter case.

Despite the approximation in Eq. (13), it is only valid in the FF of the AUT, the maximum phase shift that can be considered is π. This phase shift is associated to a displacement of $\lambda/2$, which does not have an influence in the amplitude level; therefore, as it will be proven in the experimental validation, the method provides good results when applied to NF acquisitions.

3.1.1. Experimental validation in the Ku-band for antenna measurement and diagnostics

A small 15 dB standard gain horn (SGH) antenna is characterized at 15 GHz. The measurements are repeated for the case in which a metallic plate blocks part of the antenna aperture as shown in **Figure 5**. In order to perform antenna diagnostics, in both cases, the retrieved field on the measurement plane is backpropagated to the aperture plane of the AUT. The setup is equivalent to those for imaging applications measured in transmission [41, 45].

The regular acquisition grid is a XY rectangular grid of 700 mm $\times$ 700 mm with 10 mm sampling ($\lambda/2$ at 15 GHz) in the y-axis and 2.5 mm ($\lambda/8$) in the x-axis, placed at $z_0 = 620$ mm of the aperture of the AUT. As $\pi/2$ phase shifts are being considered, three more layers of modified points, as shown in **Figure 4**, are considered, being the sampling step considering all the points in the y-axis also of $\lambda/8$.

If Eq. (10) is applied for the proposed configuration, the central position of the image terms is $\pm 2k_0$. **Figure 6(a)** shows the recorded NF hologram while its spectrum is shown in **Figure 6(b)**. Since the sweep (and the phase shifts) is made along the y-axis direction, the image terms will appear shifted in the k_y axis of the spectrum. The abrupt decay of the autocorrelation terms makes possible to correctly filter the desired image term between $0.4\,k_0$ and $3.6\,k_0$, and correctly retrieve the field of the AUT.

Figure 5. Ku band SGH with blocked aperture.

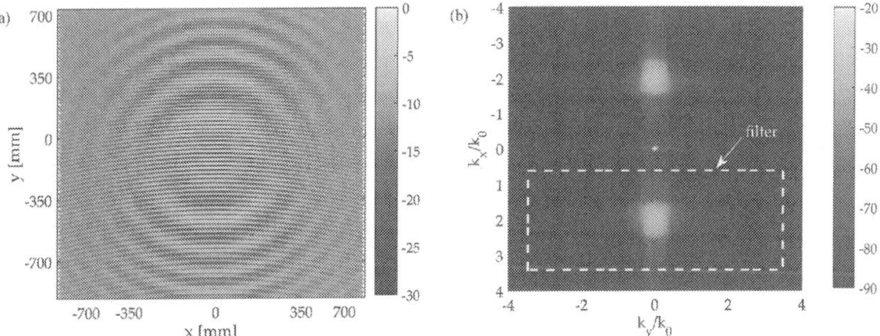

Figure 6. (a) Recorded hologram in the modified three-dimensional grid, normalized amplitude in dB. (b) Spectrum of the hologram, normalized amplitude in dB.

The retrieved amplitude and phase of the acquired NF are shown in **Figure7(a)** and, respectively, for the case in which the horn is not blocked. The backpropagated field in the aperture is shown in **Figure 7(c)** together with the size of the aperture. The retrieved amplitude and phase for the case of the blocked aperture are shown in **Figure 7(d)** and. Some discrepancies with respect to the first case can be observed and when the field is backpropagated to the aperture of the AUT, **Figure 7(f)**, the blockage can be clearly detected.

Thus, the proposed method can be successfully applied to antenna measurement and diagnostics with equivalent results to the conventional indirect off-axis method with synthesized reference wave.

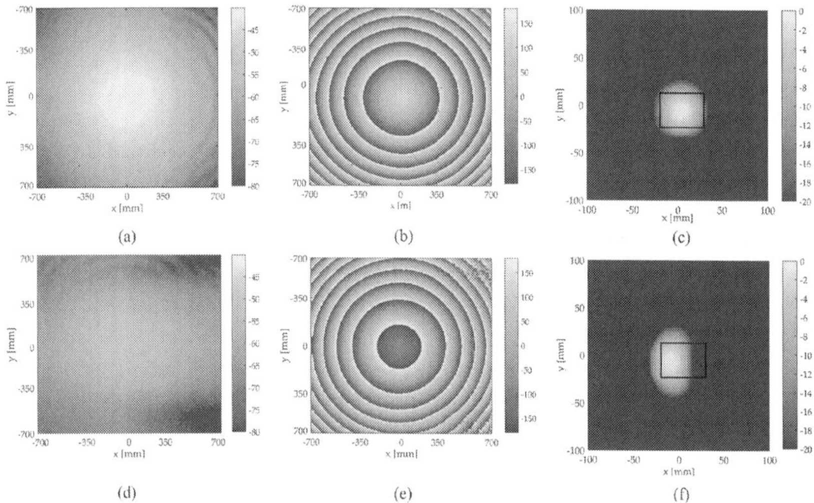

Figure 7. Retrieved NF of the AUT without blocking metallic plate (a)–(c) and with blocking metallic plate (d)–(f): (a) and (d) normalized amplitude in dB, (b) and (e) phase in degrees, and (c) and (f) backpropagation of the retrieved field toward the aperture, normalized amplitude in dB.

3.2. Multiplexed holograms with radiated reference field

As explained in Section 2.4, setups with synthesized reference waves for antenna characterization are challenging at high frequency bands, being necessary to resort to setups with radiated reference waves [21, 30]. The main limitation of these setups is that the position of the image terms is determined by the off-axis angle of the reference antenna, see Eq. (6), and will always be below $\pm k_0$, that is, in the visible part of the spectrum. This separation might not be enough to avoid overlapping for certain types of antennas such as nondirective antennas, which have wider spectra [28]. Overlapping can also be observed when the level in the AUT branch is higher than the reference level, due to the differences between the level of the autocorrelation and image terms [30].

The previously presented technique with mechanical phase shifts of the probe cannot be applied when radiated reference waves are employed because the displacements of the probe antenna will introduce the phase shifts in both the reference and the AUT fields, leading to an erroneous approach of the off-axis holography technique.

In order to control the position of the image terms and displace it to the nonvisible part of the spectrum as with synthesized reference waves, this subsection describes a new method for the case of using radiated reference waves. The method consists in multiplexing two subsampled holograms, Eq. (1), obtained from two 180° phase-shifted reference waves. The phase shift can be generated by means of a phase shifter or displacing the reference antenna a distance of $\lambda/2$.

The first subsampled hologram, blue grid in **Figure 8(a)**, is acquired in a grid with $2\Delta x$ and Δy sampling. The samples are stored in the odd columns of the multiplexed hologram. Then, a displacement of $\lambda/2$ is introduced in the reference antenna and the second subsampled hologram, which is stored in the even columns of the multiplexed hologram (orange grid in **Figure 8(b)**) is acquired over a grid identical to the first one but with an offset of Δx.

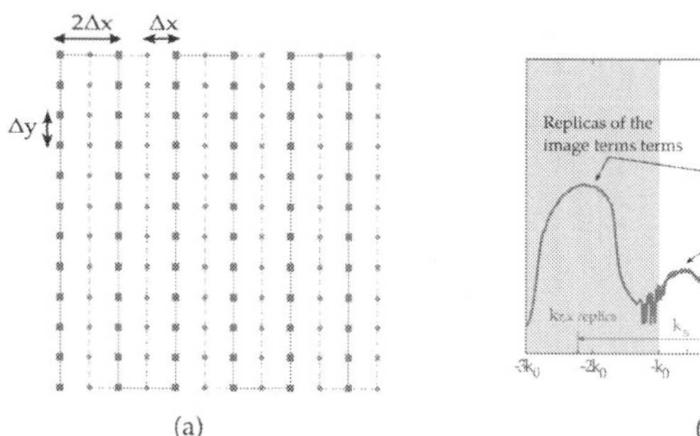

(a)   (b)

Figure 8. (a) Spatial multiplexation of the subsampled grids for the hologram formation. (b) Spectrum of the hologram for the proposed method for an example with $\Delta x = \lambda/6$ sampling.

By combining the two subsampled holograms with 180° phase-shifted references, the amplitude of the final hologram remains almost unchanged with respect to a hologram acquired in the complete grid, while the phase steps of the reference field ($\Delta\phi$) in the acquisition plane will be increased by a factor of π (see Ref. [30] for a step-by-step proof), leading to the following position of the image terms (see Eqs. (8) and (10)):

$$k'_r = \pm\frac{\Delta\phi + \pi}{\Delta x} = \pm\frac{\Delta\phi}{\Delta x} + \frac{\pi}{\Delta x} = \pm k_r + k_s. \tag{15}$$

Two replicas of the image terms of the hologram appear at a distance of $k_s = \frac{\pi}{\Delta x}$ of the original image terms as shown in **Figure 8(b)**. The replicas are in the nonvisible part of the spectrum, shaded in gray, and have the same information than the original image terms, which are overlapped with the autocorrelation terms. Hence, the field can be retrieved by filtering the desired replica without the need to resort to the modified hologram technique. It has been demonstrated that if the reference field is a plane wave, the original terms are completely canceled allowing a cleaner filtering [30].

Position of the image terms depends on the off-axis angle of the reference antenna, Eq. (6). A common option to convey the reference signal in holography setups is to use mirror reflection (see **Figure 9**). This option has multiple advances since it is possible to increase the path of the reference field and interfere with a quasi-plane wave. Furthermore, by modifying the position and orientation of the reflector it is possible not only to control the off-axis angle but also to modify the shape of the pattern of the reference field in the acquisition plane, which also influences the shape and the width of the image terms and their replicas in the k-space.

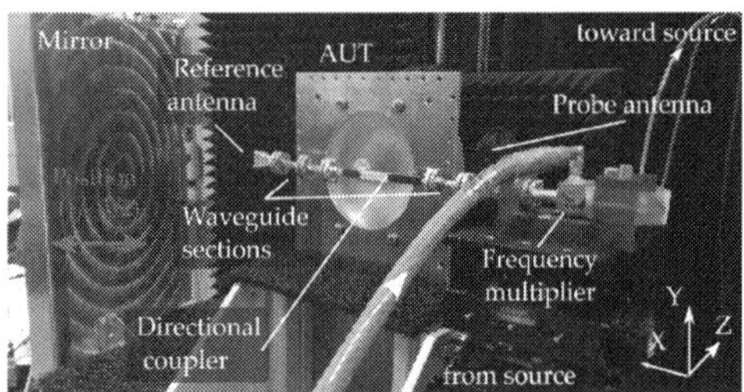

Figure 9. Measurement setup for the lens antenna characterization at 94 GHz. Rear view.

3.2.1. Corrections

Two small corrections have to be applied to the retrieved field to compensate the effect that the high frequency replicas introduce in the retrieved field. First, the retrieved phase is contaminated with high frequency noise that can be eliminated by low-pass filtering. Second, since only a fraction of the spectral density of the image term is being considered (the replica), the retrieved amplitude of the AUT is slightly smaller than the one directly acquired. A correction factor can be obtained from the analysis of the reference field, which is known. The spectrum of the reference field is filtered using the same filter that will be used to filter the image term of the complete hologram; then, that filtered part is transformed back to the spatial domain and its amplitude level is compared to the initial amplitude of the reference field. The difference can be used as a correction factor for the retrieved amplitude of the AUT.

3.2.2. Experimental validation: 94 GHz lens antenna NF characterization

The measurement setup shown in **Figure 9** has been implemented for the experimental validation of the method. A 64 mm circular lens fed with a horizontally polarized WR10 open-ended waveguide (OEWG) is characterized at 94 GHz. A 20 dB SGH is employed as reference antenna. A plane metallic mirror with a tilt of 22° is placed at 270 mm of the aperture of the reference antenna and used to direct the reference field toward the acquisition plane, at 200 mm of the AUT.

The NF is acquired for a 200 mm cut at $y = 0$ with $\lambda/2$ sampling for the first position of the mirror. Then, the mirror is displaced $\lambda/2$ toward the acquisition plane by means of a micropositioner and the second subsampled hologram is acquired. Direct acquisition of the phase and acquisition with conventional off-axis holography with $\lambda/4$ sampling have also been made to compare the results to those obtained with the proposed method.

Figure 10(a) shows the hologram for the proposed method and for conventional indirect off-axis holography. An off-axis angle of 22° produces two image terms centered in $\pm 0.38k_0$ and two replicas at $\mp 2.38k_0$, which means that, in the $[-2k_0, 2k_0]$ interval, the replicas are swapped and centered at $\mp 1.64k_0$, as it can be clearly seen. While the replicas for the proposed method can be filtered, there is some overlapping between the image term and the autocorrelation terms for the conventional case. This is due to the high amplitude level of the AUT, which produces a large autocorrelation term, highly above the level of the image terms of the spectrum.

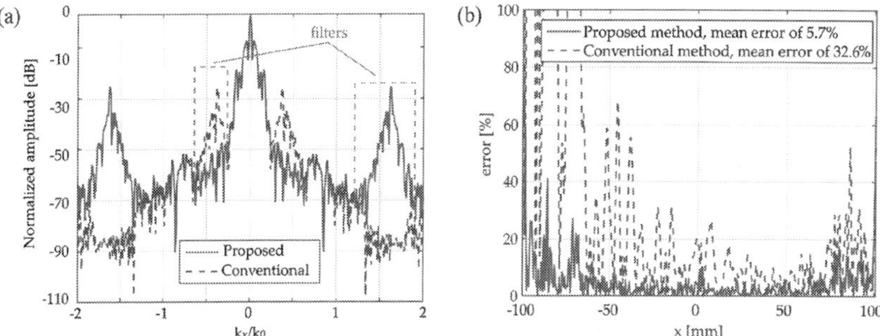

Figure 10. (a) Spectrum of the hologram and filtering windows, normalized amplitude in dB and (b) percentual error of the phase retrieval.

Figure 10(b) depicts the error of the phase retrieval process calculated as

$$error[\%] = 100\,\frac{\|\mathbf{E}_{measured} - \mathbf{E}_{retrieved}\|_2}{\|\mathbf{E}_{measured}\|_2},\tag{16}$$

where $\mathbf{E}_{measured}$ and $\mathbf{E}_{retrieved}$ are vectors containing the samples of the measured (with amplitude and phase) and the retrieved field (from amplitude-only acquisitions) at the acquisition points, and $\|\cdot\|_2$ denotes the Euclidean norm. Due to the overlapping with the autocorrelation term, the mean error of the conventional method is 32.8% while the error achieved with the proposed method is only of 5.70%.

Figure 11(a) shows the retrieved amplitude in the acquisition plane with both methods compared to the amplitude directly acquired, whereas in **Figure 11(b)** the same data are shown for the phase. It can be clearly observed that, while with the proposed method, the retrieved amplitude and phase are in very good agreement with the data from the direct acquisition the retrieved fields with the conventional method exhibit some discrepancies, especially in the areas with larger error (see **Figure 10(b)**) due to the overlapping of the spectrum.

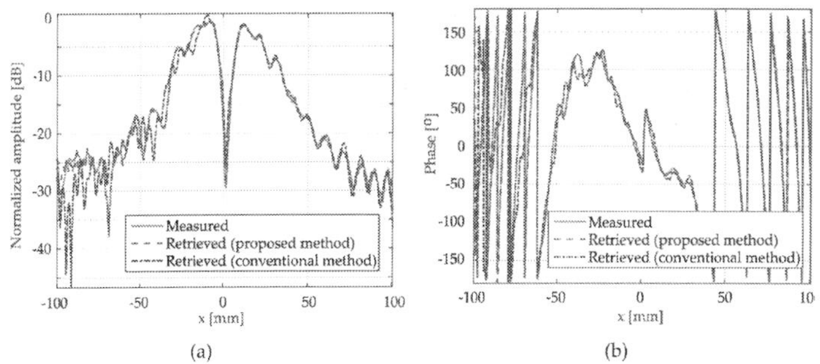

Figure 11. (a) Amplitude of the AUT, normalized in dB and (b) phase of the AUT in degrees.

4. Broadband indirect off-axis holography

Previous techniques are monochromatic techniques that might not be suitable for characterization of broadband antennas, for whose measurement it is usual to resort to time-domain (TD) techniques [48, 49].

The herein presented technique is an extrapolation of conventional off-axis holography that allows for efficient characterization of broadband antennas by means of amplitude-only acquisitions. Although the data acquisition and phase retrieval are different to the previous methods, as they are carried out in the TD, the physical layout of the elements is identical to the one already presented in **Figure 1**. This layout is presented in **Figure 12(a)** again in order to define some relevant distances that will be discussed later.

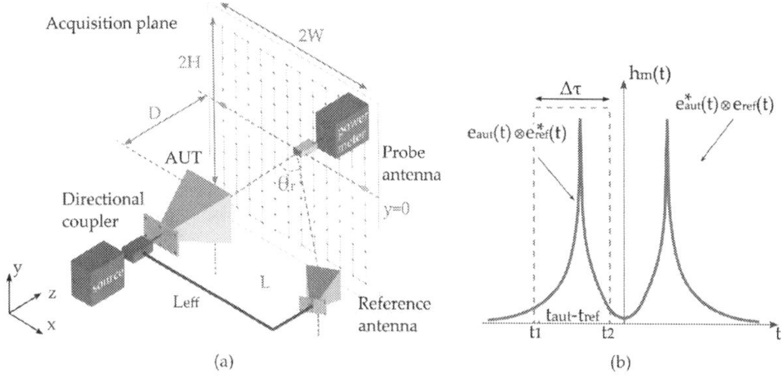

Figure 12. Broadband indirect off-axis holography: (a) layout of the measurement setup and (b) spectrum of the modified hologram.

During the acquisition process, a frequency sweep is made for each point of the spatial grid and the hologram is acquired over the studied frequency band, Eq. (17); then the spectrum is computed in the TD by means of an inverse FT, Eq. (18):

$$H(\vec{r},\omega) = |E_{aut}(\vec{r},\omega)|^2 + |E_{ref}(\vec{r},\omega)|^2 + E_{aut}(\vec{r},\omega)E^*_{ref}(\vec{r},\omega) + E^*_{aut}(\vec{r},\omega)E_{ref}(\vec{r},\omega) \tag{17}$$

$$h(\vec{r},t) = |e_{aut}(\vec{r},t)|^2 + |e_{ref}(\vec{r},t)|^2 + e_{aut}(\vec{r},t) \otimes e^*_{ref}(\vec{r},t) + e^*_{aut}(\vec{r},t) \otimes e_{ref}(\vec{r},t) \tag{18}$$

After filtering the desired image term in the TD by means of a time window Π, defined from t_1 to t_2:

$$h_{filtered}(\vec{r},t) = \Pi(t_1,t_2)\{e_{aut}(\vec{r},t) \otimes e^*_{ref}(\vec{r},t)\}, \tag{19}$$

the phase retrieval is performed at each spatial point, simultaneously for all the acquired frequencies as

$$E_{\text{aut,retrieved}}(\vec{r},\omega) = \frac{FT_t\{h_{\text{filtered}}(\vec{r},t)\}}{E^*_{\text{ref}}(\vec{r},\omega)}. \tag{20}$$

The subindex t in the FT indicates that the spectrum is computed in the TD.

This allows to retrieve one of the components of the tangential field in the acquisition plane, in order to obtain the FF of the AUT, as in the previous methods, the second tangential component also needs to be retrieved for NF-FF transformation. To do that, the process has to be repeated after a turn of 90° of the AUT to change the acquired polarization.

Main advantages of this method are that position of the image terms can be controlled with the distance between the AUT and the reference antenna, the physical length of the AUT and reference branches, and the separation between the antennas and the acquisition plane, as it will be addressed next. Furthermore, as the phase is retrieved point-by-point in the spatial grid, the technique is compatible with array thinning techniques that allow to drastically reduce the number of acquisition points with the consequent time reduction [22, 31, 50].

On the other hand, the method also presents some disadvantages. As in conventional indirect off-axis holography, the reference antenna has to be previously known in amplitude and phase, also all the components of the setup, mainly the AUT, must be broadband; otherwise their time responses will be spread and may cause overlapping in the spectrum of the recorded hologram [23].

4.1. Main parameter constraints

As in the previous methods, quality of the retrieved fields depends on how clean the filtering process is. Since the spectrum of the hologram is computed in the TD, position of the image terms is dependent on the starting times of the signals coming from the AUT t_{aut} and from the reference antenna t_{ref}, and thus, it can be controlled with the distance and the length L_{eff} of the transmission lines employed in the setup.

In order to avoid overlapping two main restrictions have to be fulfilled:

- The length of the elements in the reference branch must be selected so that the image terms of the spectrum are swapped, $t_{\text{aut}} - t_{\text{ref}} + \Delta\tau < 0$. Thus, the desired term can be easily filtered, as shown in **Figure 12(b)**.

  In terms of the distances between elements in the setup, as defined in **Figure 12(a)**, the previous condition yields the following expression considering the worst-case scenario (points in the corners of the acquisition plane closer to the reference antenna for whose $t_{\text{ref}} > t_{\text{aut}}$):

$$\sqrt{D^2 + W^2 + H^2} - \left(\sqrt{D^2 + (W-L)^2 + H^2} + L_{\text{eff}}\right) + c\Delta\tau < 0, \tag{21}$$

$$L_{\text{eff}} - L > c\Delta\tau. \tag{22}$$

- The frequency sampling must be selected according to the *Nyquist* rule:

$$\Delta f < \frac{1}{2T} = \frac{1}{2(t_{\text{ref}} - t_{\text{aut}})}. \tag{23}$$

4.2. Numerical validation for the characterization of a horn antenna in the Ka-band

For the numerical validation of the method, a 25 dB SGH is characterized in the Ka-band from 26.5 to 40 GHz. The physical layout is shown in **Figure 13**. The acquisition plane is a square grid of 300 mm side with spatial sampling of 3.7 mm in both directions, that is, $\lambda/2$ at 40 GHz, and is located at a distance of $D = 260$ mm of the aperture of the AUT. A 15 dB horn is employed as reference antenna placed at $L = 200$ mm from the center of the aperture of the AUT with an off-axis angle of $\theta_r = 37.5°$. A coaxial cable of $L_{\text{eff}} \approx 48$ cm is employed to connect the directional coupler to the reference antenna.

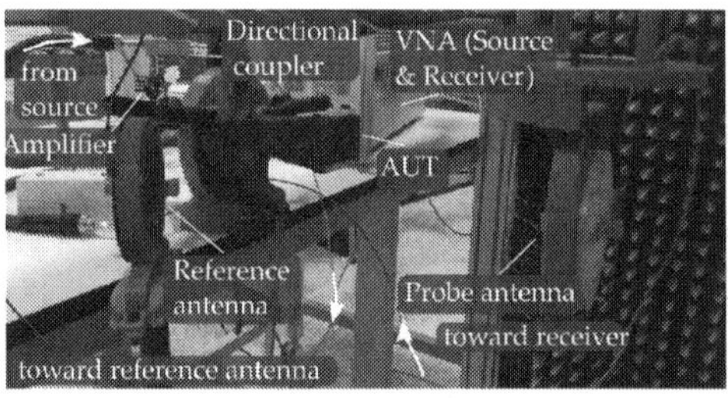

Figure 13. Setup for the 25 dB SGH antenna characterization in the Ka-band.

Figure 14(a) shows the modified hologram for the three points highlighted in **Figure 12(a)**. The position of the image terms varies depending on the position of the probe in the acquisition plane. **Figure 14(b)** shows a detail of the retrieved phase in the central part of the frequency band for the worst-case scenario. Apart from some 180° phase shifts, the agreement between the retrieved and directly measured phase is almost complete. Finally, **Figure 14(c)** depicts the error computed as in Eq. (16). Mean value of the error in the complete frequency band is 2.24%. The large values above 37 GHz are due to the signal level of the reference antenna, which decays in that part of the band.

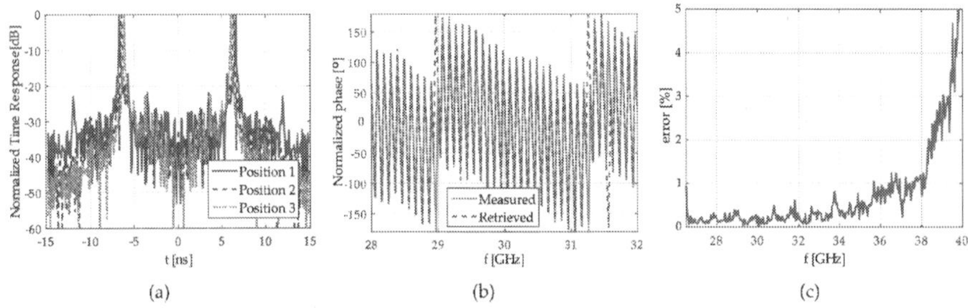

Figure 14. Phase retrieval process: (a) spectrum of the modified hologram for three different acquisition points, (b) detail of the retrieved phase in the central frequency band, and (c) error for the phase retrieval in the complete frequency band.

The retrieved phase in the acquisition plane at 30 GHz is shown in **Figure 15** compared to the phase directly acquired at that frequency. For this frequency, the error of the phase retrieval is 0.25%; thus, the retrieved phase is practically identical to the measured one.

After the phase is retrieved simultaneously for all the frequencies at each point of the acquisition plane, conventional NF-FF transformation and backpropagation techniques can be applied for the computation of the FF pattern and the fields in the aperture of the AUT [1]. **Figure 15(a)** shows the copolar pattern of the FF at 30 GHz, while the E_x component of the field in the aperture is shown in **Figure 15(b)**. The black rectangle depicts the position of the aperture whose size is 700 mm × 500 mm.

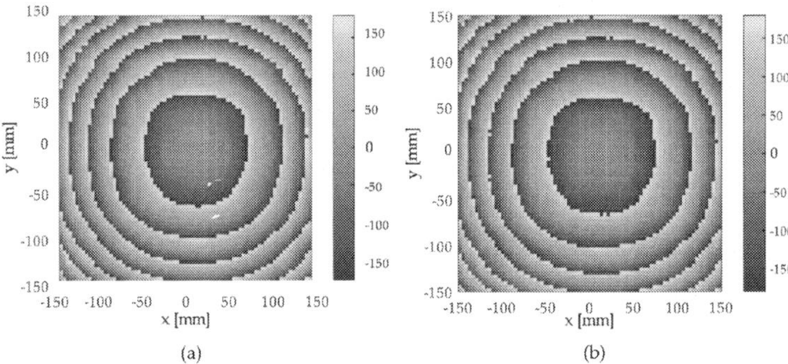

(a)   (b)

Figure 15. Retrieved phase of the AUT at 30 GHz compared to the direct measurement: (a) directly acquired phase in the NF, degrees, and (b) retrieved phase, degrees.

Finally, **Figure 16** shows the main cuts for $\phi= 0°$ and $\phi= 90°$ of the copolar pattern in **Figure 15(a)** (blue line labeled as *Retrieved NF*) compared to the cuts of a direct FF acquisition in an spherical anechoic chamber (labeled as *Measured FF*) and the cuts obtained for a NF-FF transformation of a field acquired with amplitude and phase (labeled as *Measured NF*). The valid margin of the NF-FF transformation, in which the data are comparable, is ±25° [1]. High level of coincidence

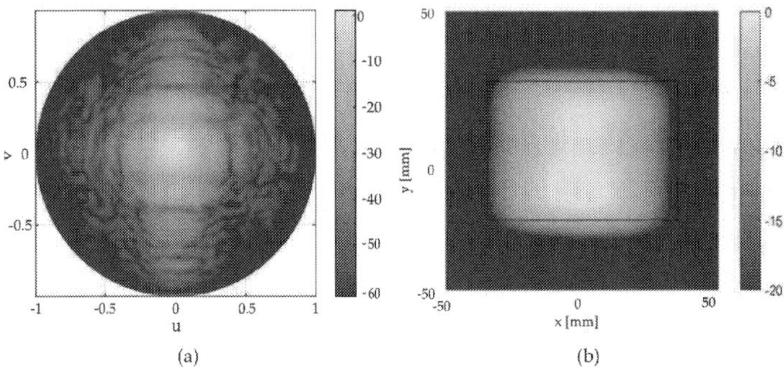

(a)   (b)

Figure 16. AUT characterization at 30 GHz from the retrieved data: (a) normalized FF copolar pattern in dB and (b) normalized E_x component of the field in the aperture of the AUT in dB.

can be observed between the three measurements. The small differences between the data directly acquired in FF and the transformed data are attributed to the lack of application of probe correction techniques during the NF-FF transformation (**Figure 17**) [1].

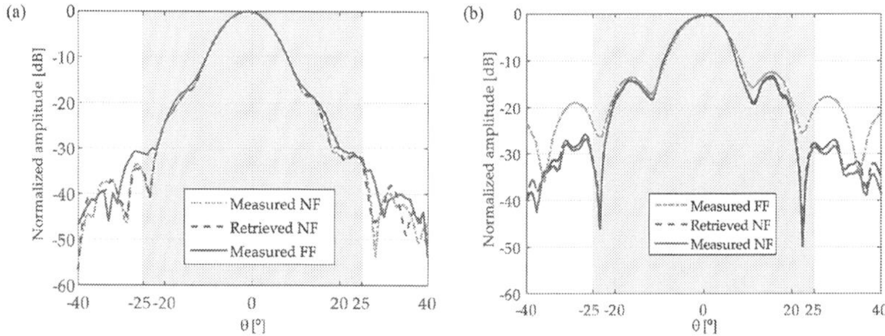

Figure 17. Comparison of the main cuts of the normalized amplitude of the AUT: (a) $\phi = 0°$ and (b) $\phi = 90°$. The gray shaded areas indicate the valid margin of the NF-FF transformation [23].

5. Conclusion

Indirect off-axis holography is a method that allows for phase retrieval of an unknown field from amplitude-only acquisitions. This technique has been widely employed for antenna measurement and diagnostics for which phase acquisition is challenging, especially at high frequency bands, where very accurate positioning and high environmental stability are required.

Several modifications such as the *modified hologram* technique and the use of *synthesized reference waves* have been discussed, in order to overcome known disadvantages of the conventional technique regarding the required sampling rates or the spectral overlapping issues. Nevertheless, even with these modifications, indirect off-axis holography exhibits some limitations, and thus, three novel methods developed in order to overcome them are proposed.

Two of the presented techniques employ mechanical shifts, the first one to avoid the use of phase shifters and reduce the cost of the measurement system, and the second to control the position of the image terms in the same way that it is controlled with synthesized reference waves but with radiated reference fields. This enables to apply synthesized reference-like techniques in high frequency bands. The last technique is an extrapolation of the conventional technique employed for efficient phase retrieval of broadband antennas in which the phase is retrieved point-by-point in the acquisition plane and simultaneously for all frequency bands, by filtering the hologram in the TD instead of the k-space. **Table 1** summarizes the main advantages and disadvantages of the conventional and novel indirect off-axis techniques employed for antenna metrology.

Experimental validation has been presented for each of the proposed methods with very good agreement with the reference results obtained from acquisitions performed directly with amplitude and phase.

Method	Advantages	Disadvantages
Conventional [24–26]	Amplitude-only measurement (applicable to all methods)	Complex characterization: $E_{\mathrm{ref}}(\vec{r})$ Image terms: visible part of the spectrum
Modified hologram [5, 21, 23]	No autocorrelation terms: overlapping reduction	Extra acquisition: $|E_{\mathrm{aut}}(\vec{r})|^2$
	Less dense sampling than conventional technique	
	Only phase retrieved: $|E_{\mathrm{aut}}(\vec{r})|$ is measured	
Synthesized reference [27, 28, 43, 44]	Image terms: nonvisible region	More dense sampling
	Further overlapping reduction that modified hologram	Not implementable at high frequency bands with waveguide sections
	No need to measure $E_{\mathrm{ref}}(\vec{r})$: scalar acquisition	
Mechanical phase shifts [5]	No phase shifter	Three-dimensional positioner
	The other advantages and disadvantages are the same as in *Synthesized reference*	
Multiplexed holograms [30]	Image terms in the nonvisible region	
	Radiated reference fields	Need of quasi-planar reference field,
	Implementable at high frequency bands	the path of the reference field has to be
	Less dense sampling than *Synthesized reference*	increased (higher sensitivity to errors)
Broadband holography [23, 31]	Efficient broadband characterization	Acquisition: frequency sampling capabilities
	Standard antenna measurement sampling $(\lambda/2)$	
	Phase retrieval point-by-point	

Table 1. Main features of the presented indirect off-axis holography techniques for antenna metrology.

Acknowledgements

This work has been partially supported by the Ministerio de Ciencia e Innovación of Spain/ FEDER under projects TEC2014-55290-JIN (PortEMVision) and TEC2014-54005-P (MIRIIEM); by the Gobierno del Principado de Asturias through PCTI 2013-1017 GRUPIN14-114 and by grant LINE 525-002; and by the Academy of Finland through DYNAMITE project. The authors would like to thank M.Sc. Luis Díaz for his help with 3D modeling.

Author details

Ana Arboleya[1]*, Jaime Laviada[1], Juha Ala-Laurinaho[2], Yuri Álvarez[1],
Fernando Las-Heras[1] and Antti V. Räisänen[2]

*Address all correspondence to: aarboleya@tsc.uniovi.es

1 Departamento de Ingeniería Eléctrica, Escuela Politécnica de Ingeniería, Universidad de Oviedo, Gijón, Spain

2 Department of Radio Science and Engineering and MilliLab, Aalto University, Espoo, Finland

References

[1] A.D. Yaghjian. An overview of near-field antenna measurements. *IEEE Trans. Antennas Propag.*, 34(1):30–45, Jan. 1986.

[2] M.S. Castaner, A. Munoz-Acevedo, F. Cano-Fácila, and S. Burgos. Overview of novel post-processing techniques to reduce uncertainty in antenna measurements. In Md. Zahurul Haq, editor, *Advanced Topics in Measurements*, Chapter 9. Intech, 2012.

[3] F. Las-Heras and T.K. Sarkar. A direct optimization approach for source reconstruction and NF-FF transformation using amplitude-only data. *IEEE Trans. Antennas Propag.*, 50 (4):500–510, Apr. 2002.

[4] C. Cappellin, A. Frandsen, S. Pivnenko, G. Lemanczyk, and O. Breinbjerg. Diagnostics of the SMOS radiometer antenna system at the DTU-ESA spherical near-field antenna test facility. In *2007 2nd European Conf. on Antennas and Propag. (EuCAP)*, pages 1–6, Edinburgh, UK, Nov. 2007.

[5] J. Laviada Martínez, A. Arboleya-Arboleya, Y. Álvarez López, C. García-González, and F. Las-Heras. Phaseless antenna diagnostics based on off-axis holography with synthetic reference wave. *IEEE Antennas Wireless Propag. Lett.*, 13:43–46, 2014.

[6] B. Fuchs, L.L. Coq, and M.D. Migliore. Fast antenna array diagnosis from a small number of far-field measurements. *IEEE Trans. Antennas Propag.*, 64(6):2227–2235, Jun. 2016.

[7] C.A. Balanis. *Antenna Theory: Analysis and Design*. John Wiley Sons, 2nd edition, New York, 1997.

[8] Std 521-2002 (revision of IEEE std 521-1984). IEEE standard letter designations for radar-frequency bands. Technical report, Institute of Electrical and Electronics Engineers, 2003.

[9] Y. Álvarez, F. Las-Heras, and C. García. The sources reconstruction method for antenna diagnostic and imaging applications. In Prof. Ahmed Kishk, editor, *Solutions and Applications of Scattering, Propagation, Radiation and Emission of Electromagnetic Waves*, Chapter 6. Intech, 2012.

[10] Y. Rahmat-Samii, V. Galindo-Israel, and R. Mittra. A plane-polar approach for far-field construction from near-field measurements. *IEEE Trans. Antennas Propag.*, 28(2):216–230, Mar. 1980.

[11] F. D'Agostino, F. Ferrara, C. Gennarelli, R. Guerriero, and M. Migliozzi. An effective NF-FF transformation technique with planar spiral scanning tailored for quasi-planar antennas. *IEEE Trans. Antennas Propag.*, 56(9):2981–2987, Sept. 2008.

[12] J.J.H. Wang. An examination of the theory and practices of planar near-field measurement. *IEEE Trans. Antennas Propag.*, 36(6):746–753, Jun. 1988.

[13] S. Gregson, J. McCormick, and C. Parini. *Principles of Planar Near-field Antenna Measurements. Electromagnetic Waves.* Institution of Engineering and Technology (IET), London, 2007.

[14] A.C. Newell. Error analysis techniques for planar near-field measurements. *IEEE Trans. Antennas Propag.*, 36(6):754–768, Jun. 1988.

[15] IEEE recommended practice for near-field antenna measurements. *IEEE Std 1720-2012*, pages 1–102, Institute of Electrical and Electronics Engineers, Dec. 2012.

[16] J. Säily, P. Eskelinen, and A.V. Räisänen. Pilot signal-based real-time measurement and correction of phase errors caused by microwave cable flexing in planar near-field tests. *IEEE Trans. Antennas Propag.*, 51(2):195–200, Feb. 2003.

[17] J.A. Gordon, D.R. Novotny, M.H. Francis, R.C. Wittmann, M.L. Butler, A.E. Curtin, and J.R. Guerrieri. Millimeter-wave near-field measurements using coordinated robotics. *IEEE Trans. Antennas Propag.*, 63(12):5351–5362, Dec. 2015.

[18] L.J. Foged, G. Barone, and F. Saccardi. Antenna measurement systems using multi-probe technology. In *2015 IEEE Conf. on Antenna Measurements Applications (CAMA)*, pages 1–3, Chiang Mai, Thailand, Nov. 2015.

[19] Y. Álvarez, F. Las-Heras, and M.R. Pino. The sources reconstruction method for amplitude-only field measurements. *IEEE Trans. Antennas Propag.*, 58(8):2776–2781, Aug. 2010.

[20] M.D. Migliore and G. Panariello. A comparison of interferometric methods applied to array diagnosis from near-field data. *IEE Proc. Microwaves Antennas Propag.*, 148(4):261–267, Aug. 2001.

[21] G. Junkin, T. Huang, and J.C. Bennett. Holographic testing of terahertz antennas. *IEEE Trans. Antennas Propag.*, 48(3):409–417, Mar. 2000.

[22] J. Laviada and F. Las-Heras. Phaseless antenna measurement on non-redundant sample points via Leith-Upatnieks holography. *IEEE Trans. Antennas Propag.*, 61(8):4036–4044, Aug. 2013.

[23] A. Arboleya, J. Laviada, J. Ala-Laurinaho, Y. Álvarez, F. Las-Heras, and A.V. Räisänen. Phaseless characterization of broadband antennas. *IEEE Trans. Antennas Propag.*, 64(2):484–495, Feb. 2016.

[24] E.N. Leith and J. Upatnieks. Reconstructed wavefronts and communication theory. *J. Optical Soc. Am.*, 52(10):1123–1128, Oct. 1962.

[25] P.J. Napier and R.H.T. Bates. Antenna - aperture distributions from holographic type of radiation-pattern measurement. *Proc. Inst. Elect. Eng.*, 120(1):30–34, Jan. 1973.

[26] J.C. Bennett, A.P. Anderson, P. McInnes, and A.J.T. Whitaker. Microwave holographic metrology of large reflector antennas. *IEEE Trans. Antennas Propag.*, 24(3):295–303, May 1976.

[27] G.A. Deschamps. Some remarks on radio-frequency holography. *Proc. IEEE*, 55(4):570–571, Apr. 1967.

[28] M.P. Leach, D. Smith, S.P. Skobelev, and M. Elsdont. An improved holographic technique for medium-gain antenna near field measurements. In *2007 2nd European Conf. on Antennas and Propag. (EuCAP)*, pages 1–6, Edinburgh, UK, Nov. 2007.

[29] V. Schejbal, V. Kovarik, and D. Cermak. Synthesized-reference-wave holography for determining antenna radiation characteristics. *IEEE Antennas Propag. Mag.*, 50(5):71–83, Oct. 2008.

[30] A. Arboleya, J. Ala-Laurinaho, J. Laviada, Y. Álvarez, F. Las-Heras, and A.V. Räisänen. Millimeter-wave phaseless antenna measurement based on a modified off-axis holography setup. *J. Infrared Millimeter Terahertz Waves*, 37(2):160–174, 2016.

[31] A. Arboleya, J. Laviada, J. Ala-Laurinaho, Y. Álvarez, F. Las-Heras, and A.V. Räisänen. Reduced set of points in phaseless broadband near-field antenna measurement: Effects of noise and mechanical errors. In *2016 10th European Conf. on Antennas and Propag. (EuCAP)*, pages 1–5, Davos, Switzerland, Apr. 2016.

[32] A. Arboleya, Y. Álvarez, and F. Las-Heras. Millimeter and submillimeter planar measurement setup. In *2013 IEEE Antennas and Propag. Soc. Int. Symp. (APSURSI)*, pages 1–2, Orlando, FL, Jul. 2013.

[33] A.V. Räisänen, J. Ala-Laurinaho, A. Karttunen, J. Mallat, A. Tamminen, and M. Vaaja. Measurements of high-gain antennas at THz frequencies. In *2010 4th European Conf. on Antennas and Propag. (EuCAP)*, pages 1–3, Barcelona, Spain, Apr. 2010.

[34] D. Gabor. Microscopy by reconstructed wave-fronts. *Proc. R. Soc. London A: Math., Phys. Eng. Sci.*, 197(1051):454–487, Jul. 1949.

[35] A.P. Anderson. Microwave holography. *Proc. Inst. Elect. Eng.*, 124(11):946–962, Nov. 1977.

[36] G. Tricoles and N.H. Farhat. Microwave holography: Applications and techniques. *Proc. IEEE*, 65(1):108–121, Jan. 1977.

[37] A.V. Räisänen and J. Ala-Laurinaho. Holographic principles in antenna metrology at millimeter and submillimeter wavelengths. In *2015 9th European Conf. on Antennas and Propag. (EuCAP)*, pages 1–2, Lisbon, Portugal, Apr. 2015.

[38] P.H. Gardenier. *Antenna Aperture Phase Retrieval*. PhD thesis, Electrical and Electronic Engineering School, University of Canterbury, Christchurch, New Zealand, Apr. 1980.

[39] P.J. Napier. *Reconstruction of Radiating Sources*. PhD thesis, Electrical and Electronic Engineering School, University of Canterbury, Christchurch, New Zealand, Apr. 1971.

[40] D. Smith, M. Leach, M. Elsdon, and S.J. Foti. Indirect holographic techniques for determining antenna radiation characteristics and imaging aperture fields. *IEEE Mag. Antennas Propag.*, 49(1):54–67, Feb. 2007.

[41] J. Marín García. *Off-axis Holography in Microwave Imaging Systems*. PhD thesis, Departament de Telecomunicació i Enginyeria de Sistemes, Universitat Autònoma de Barcelona, 2015.

[42] M.S. Heimbeck, M.K. Kim, D.A. Gregory, and H.O. Everitt. Terahertz digital holography using angular spectrum and dual wavelength reconstruction methods. *Opt. Express*, 19 (10):9192–9200, May 2011.

[43] V. Schejbal, J. Pidanic, V. Kovarik, and D. Cermak. Accuracy analyses of synthesized-reference-wave holography for determining antenna radiation characteristics. *IEEE Mag. Antennas Propag.*, 50(6):89–98, Dec. 2008.

[44] A. Arboleya, J. Laviada, Y. Álvarez, and F. Las-Heras. Versatile measurement system for imaging setups prototyping. In *2015 9th European Conf. Antennas Propag. (EuCAP)*, pages 1–5, Lisbon, Portugal, Apr. 2015.

[45] A. Tamminen, J. Ala-Laurinaho, and A.V. Räisänen. Indirect holographic imaging at 310 GHz. In *2008 European Radar Conf. (EuRAD)*, pages 168–171, Amsterdam, The Netherlands, Oct. 2008.

[46] G. Junkin. Planar near-field phase retrieval using GPUs for accurate THz far-field prediction. *IEEE Trans. Antennas Propag.*, 61(4):1763–1776, Apr. 2013.

[47] A. Enayati, A. Tamminen, J. Ala-Laurinaho, A.V. RÃ¤isÃ¤nen, G.A.E. Vandenbosch, and W. De Raedt. THz holographic imaging: A spatial-domain technique for phase retrieval and image reconstruction. In *2012 IEEE MTT-S Int. Microw. Symp. Digest (MTT)*, pages 1–3, Montreal, Canada, Jun. 2012.

[48] J. Young, D. Svoboda, and W.D. Burnside. A comparison of time- and frequency-domain measurement techniques in antenna theory. *IEEE Trans. Antennas Propag.*, 21(4):581–583, Jul. 1973.

[49] Y. Huang, K. Chan, and B. Cheeseman. Review of broadband antenna measurements. In *2006 1st European Conf. on Antennas and Propag. (EuCAP)*, pages 1–4, Nice, France, Nov. 2006.

[50] O. Bucci, C. Gennarelli, and C. Savarese. Fast and accurate near-field far-field transformation by sampling interpolation of plane polar measurements. *IEEE Trans. Antennas Propag.*, 39:48–55, Jan. 1991.

Chapter 12

Surface Characterization by the Use of Digital Holography

Dahi Ghareab Abdelsalam, Takeshi Yasui,
Takayuki Ogawa and Baoli Yao

Additional information is available at the end of the chapter

http://dx.doi.org/10.5772/66082

Abstract

Digital holography (DH) is an attractive measuring optical technique in the fields of engineering and science due to its remarkable accuracy and efficiency. The holograms are recorded by an interferometer and reconstructed by numerical methods such as Fresnel transform, convolution approach, and angular spectrum. Because harmful coherent noise often arises when long coherent lengths are used, bright femtosecond pulse light with ultrashort coherent length may be the solution to reduce both spurious and speckle noises. Since the usual DH uses a visible light, it is difficult to visualize 3D internal structure of visibly opaque objects due to their limited penetration depth. The terahertz (THz) radiation has a good penetration capability; thus, 3D visualization of both surface shape and internal structure in visibly opaque object can be achieved via THz-DH technique.

Keywords: digital holography, numerical reconstruction, 3D surface metrology, femto-second DH, terahertz DH

1. Introduction

Various optical techniques have been developed for measuring 3D shape from a single position. The height distribution of the surface of the object is encoded into a deformed fringe pattern, and then shape is directly decoded by one of those optical techniques. DH is considered one of those optical techniques that have received much interest for surface characterization. DH has been heavily developed over recent years because of newly available high-resolution charge-coupled device (CCD) cameras and advances in digital and automated image processing techniques. Performing Fourier transforms and spectral filtering without the need for additional optical

components for reconstruction has given advantages of digital holography over conventional optical holography. DH enables the extraction of both amplitude and phase information of objects in real time with high resolution. DH technique is less sensitive to external perturbations and has long-term stability in object measurement. DH has merits of wide applications covering particles, living cells, and 3D profiling and tracking of micro-objects or nano-objects. In this chapter, we present recent developments in DH techniques carried out by the author. In Section **2**, the principle of holography with highlights on three numerical reconstruction methods, namely, Fresnel approximation, convolution approach, and angular spectrum, is explained. In Section **3**, the impact of slightly imperfect collimation of the reference wave in off-axis DH is presented. In Section **4**, low-coherence, off-axis digital holographic microscope (DHM) by the use of femtosecond pulse light for measuring fine structure of in vitro sliced sandwiched biological sarcomere sample is described. In Section **5**, off-axis terahertz DH using continuous-wave radiation generated from cascade laser source for testing a letter T from paper is described. Section **6** gives concluding discussions and remarks.

2. The principle of holography

The word holography is derived from the Greek words "holos," which means whole or entire, and graphein, which means to write. Holography is a method that records and reconstructs both irradiance of each point in an image and the direction in which the wave is propagating at that point. Holography consists of two procedures: recording as shown in **Figure 1(a)** and reconstruction as shown in **Figure 1(b)**. Because of the development of digital recording process for recording and computer technology for numerical reconstruction, the optical

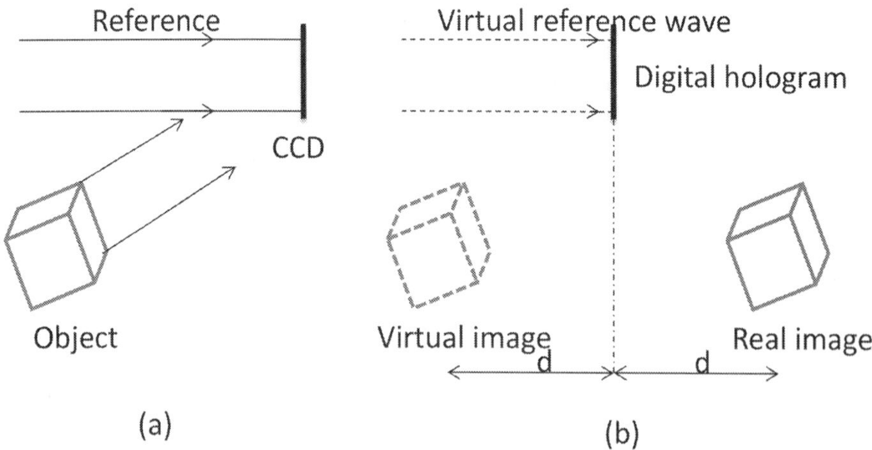

Figure 1. Principle of digital holography: (a) recording and (b) reconstruction with reference wave.

holography has been replaced by digital holography. The idea of numerical reconstruction was proposed by Goodman and Lawrence [1]. In 1993, Schnars and Juptner [2] used a CCD camera to record a hologram and performed numerical reconstruction in order to reconstruct this digital hologram.

2.1. Numerical reconstruction in digital holography

In digital holography, the CCD or Complementary Metal-Oxide Semiconductor (CMOS) camera captures the image and transfers it to the computer. This image is saved digitally as a digital hologram. This hologram is digitally accessed and numerically reconstructed by a virtual reference wave, which effectively simulates the reference wave used in the process of recording. The speed of reconstruction procedure depends on the implementation of the numerical reconstruction algorithm and the speed of the computer processing. Because the reference wave has to be generated virtually in the computer, a plane wave or a spherical wave is usually used in the recording process. **Figure 1** shows the typical setup of digital holography and the reconstruction with virtual reference wave. Let us consider the coordinate system as shown in **Figure 2**; then the diffraction by the aperture or hologram in the distance of d along the propagation direction of the wave can be quantitatively described by Fresnel-Kirchhoff integral [3].

If the reference wave is set up to be nominally normal incident to the hologram, then the diffracted light is approximated by the Fresnel-Kirchhoff integral as

$$\Gamma(\eta',\xi') = \frac{i}{\lambda} \int\limits_{-\infty}^{\infty} \int\limits_{-\infty}^{\infty} U_h(x,y)U_r(x,y)\frac{\exp\left(-i\frac{2\pi}{\lambda}\rho'\right)}{\rho'}dxdy \tag{1}$$

where $\Gamma(\eta', \xi')$ is the diffraction pattern, $U_h(x, y)$ is the digital hologram captured by the CCD camera, λ is the wavelength of the light in the virtual reference beam used in the reconstruction, ρ' is the distance between a point in the hologram plane and a point in the reconstruction plane, which has the form $\rho' = \sqrt{(x-\xi')^2 + (y-\eta')^2 + d^2}$, and $U_r(x, y)$ is the function describing the reference wave. In Eq. (1), $\Gamma(\eta', \xi')$ is the diffraction pattern calculated at a distance d behind the CCD plane (see **Figure 2**), which means it reconstructs the complex amplitude in the plane of the real image. Therefore, both the intensity and the

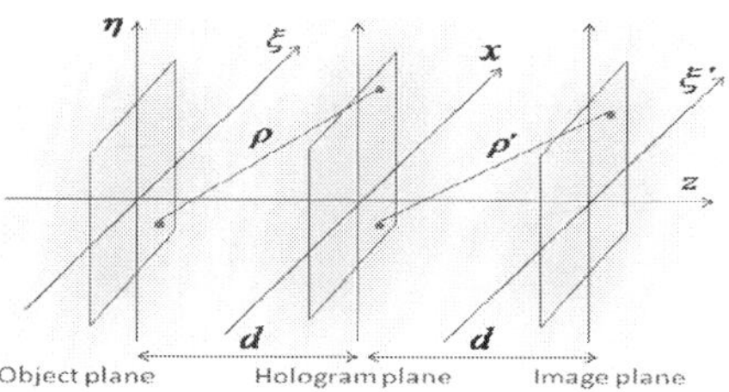

Figure 2. Coordinate system for numerical hologram reconstruction.

phase information can be obtained after numerical reconstruction. The reconstructed intensity is written as

$$I(\eta',\xi') = \left|\Gamma(\eta',\xi')\right|^2 \tag{2}$$

And the reconstructed phase is

$$\varphi(\eta',\xi') = \arctan\frac{\mathrm{Im}\left[\Gamma(\eta',\xi')\right]}{\mathrm{Re}\left[\Gamma(\eta',\xi')\right]} \tag{3}$$

where Re denotes the real part and Im denotes the imaginary part. The calculated diffraction pattern is the complex amplitude at a distance d behind the CCD plane where the real image is reconstructed. However, the real image could be distorted by the reference wave. To avoid this effect and ensure that an undistorted real image is left, a conjugate reference wave has to be introduced in the reconstruction. Then the calculated diffraction pattern is rewritten as

$$\Gamma(\eta,\xi) = \frac{i}{\lambda}\int_{-\infty}^{\infty}\int_{-\infty}^{\infty} U_h(x,y)U_r^*(x,y)\frac{\exp\left(-i\frac{2\pi}{\lambda}\rho\right)}{\rho}dxdy \tag{4}$$

with

$$\rho = \sqrt{(x{-}\xi)^2 + (y{-}\eta)^2 + d^2} \tag{5}$$

where $U_r^*(xy)$ is conjugate to the original reference wave $U_r(x, y)$. Both results from Eq. (1) and Eq. (4) are equivalent because $U_r(xy) = U_r^*(xy)$. As illustrated above, Eq. (4) is the key formula of digital holography, and it is essential to calculate it numerically to perform numerical reconstruction of a digital hologram. The direct approach of Eq. (4) is not feasible in terms of the calculation complexity and computer run time. Some approximations have to be applied in order to calculate the double integral to make the numerical reconstruction effective and efficient. According to the approximation used in the algorithm, the numerical reconstruction can be classified into three types: Fresnel approximation, convolution approaches, and angular spectrum.

2.1.1. Reconstruction by the Fresnel approximation

In digital holography, the values of the coordinates x and y as well as ξ and η are very small compared to the distance d between the reconstruction plane and the CCD or CMOS device. If now the right hand side of Eq. (5) is expanded to a Taylor series and the fourth term is smaller than the wavelength,

$$\frac{\left[(x{-}\xi)^2 + (y{-}\eta)^2\right]^2}{8d^3} << \lambda \tag{6}$$

the effect of it and the terms after it are negligible, and they can be removed. Thus the distance ρ can be approximated as

$$\rho = d + \frac{(\xi-x)^2}{2d} + \frac{(\eta-y)^2}{2d} \tag{7}$$

Replacing the denominator in Eq. (4) with d and inserting Eq. (7) into it, the following expression results in the reconstruction of the real image:

$$\Gamma(\eta,\xi) = \frac{i}{\lambda d}\exp\left(-i\frac{2\pi}{\lambda}d\right)\exp\left(-i\frac{\pi}{\lambda d}(\xi^2+\eta^2)\right)$$
$$\times \int\limits_{-\infty}^{\infty}\int\limits_{-\infty}^{\infty} U_r^*(x,y)U_h(x,y)\exp\left(-i\frac{\pi}{\lambda d}(x^2+y^2)\right)\exp\left(-i\frac{2\pi}{\lambda d}(x\xi+y\eta)\right)dxdy \tag{8}$$

This equation is known as the Fresnel approximation or Fresnel transformation due to its mathematical similarity with the Fourier transform.

The intensity is calculated by squaring

$$I(\eta,\xi) = |\Gamma(\eta,\xi)|^2 \tag{9}$$

And the phase is calculated by

$$\varphi(\eta,\xi) = \arctan\frac{\mathrm{Im}[\Gamma(\eta,\xi)]}{\mathrm{Re}[\Gamma(\eta,\xi)]} \tag{10}$$

To convert the discrete Fresnel transformation in Eq. (8) to a digital implementation, two substitutions are applied [4]:

$$v = \frac{\xi}{\lambda d}; \quad \mu = \frac{\eta}{\lambda d}; \tag{11}$$

Therefore Eq. (8) turns into

$$\Gamma(v,\mu) = \frac{i}{\lambda d}\exp\left(-i\frac{2\pi}{\lambda}d\right)\exp\left(-i\pi\lambda d(v^2+\mu^2)\right)$$
$$\times \mathfrak{F}^{-1}\left\{U_r^*(x,y)U_h(x,y)\exp\left(-i\frac{\pi}{\lambda d}(x^2+y^2)\right)\right\} \tag{12}$$

Because the maximum frequency is determined by the sampling interval in the spatial domain according to the theory of the Fourier transform, the relationships among Δx, Δy, Δv, and $\Delta\mu$ are

$$\Delta v = \frac{1}{N\Delta x}; \quad \Delta\mu = \frac{1}{N\Delta y} \tag{13}$$

With Eq. (13), Eq. (12) can be rewritten as

$$
\Gamma(m,n) = \frac{i}{\lambda d} \exp\left(-i\frac{2\pi}{\lambda}d\right) \exp\left(-i\pi\lambda d\left(\frac{m^2}{N^2 \Delta x^2} + \frac{n^2}{N^2 \Delta y^2}\right)\right) \\
\times \mathfrak{I}^{-1}\left\{U_r^*(k,l)U_h(k,l)\exp\left(-i\frac{\pi}{\lambda d}\left(k^2\Delta x^2 + l^2\Delta y^2\right)\right)\right\}
\tag{14}
$$

Eq. (14) is known as the discrete Fresnel transform. The matrix Γ is calculated by applying an inverse discrete Fourier transform to the product of $U_r^*(k,l)$ with $U_h(k, l)$ and $\exp(-i\pi(k^2\Delta x^2 + l^2\Delta y^2)/(\lambda d))$. The calculation can be done very effectively using the fast Fourier transform (FFT) algorithm.

2.1.2. Reconstruction by the convolution approach

This method makes use of the convolution theorem. This approach was introduced to digital holography by Kreis and Juptner [5]. Eq. (4) can be interpreted as a superposition integral:

$$
\Gamma(\eta,\xi) = \int\limits_{-\infty}^{-\infty} \int\limits_{-\infty}^{-\infty} U_h(x,y)U_r^*(x,y)g(\eta,\xi,x,y)dxdy
\tag{15}
$$

where the impulse response $g(\eta,\xi,x,y)$ is given by

$$
g(\eta,\xi,x,y) = \frac{i}{\lambda}\frac{\exp\left[-i\frac{2\pi}{\lambda}\rho\right]}{\rho}
\tag{16}
$$

Eq. (15) can be regarded as a convolution and the convolution theorem can be applied. The convolution theorem states that the Fourier transform of the convolution of two functions is equal to the product of the Fourier transforms of the individual functions. In other words, the convolution of two functions in the spatial domain can be easily obtained through the multiplication of them in another domain, namely, spatial frequency domain.

Applying the convolution theorem to Eq. (4), it is converted to

$$
\Gamma(\eta,\xi) = \mathfrak{I}^{-1}\left\{\mathfrak{I}\left(U_h(x,y).U_r^*(x,y)\right).\mathfrak{I}(g(x,y))\right\}
\tag{17}
$$

Eq. (17) includes two forward Fourier transformations and one inverse Fourier transformation, all of which can be practically implemented via the FFT algorithm. Both Fresnel and convolution methods are practically implemented via the FFT algorithm. In the Fresnel approximation, only a forward FFT is performed. However, two or three FFTs are performed in the convolution approach. In the convolution approach, the pixel sizes in the reconstructed image are equal to that of the hologram. It would seem that a higher resolution could be achieved if a CCD or CMOS device with a smaller pixel size was used in the recording process. For applications that detect very small objects, the convolution approach has more advantages and is more accurate than the Fresnel approximation algorithm.

2.1.3. Reconstruction by the angular spectrum method

Both the Fresnel approximation and the convolution approach suffer the same limitation, i.e., that the object under observation must be placed farther away than some minimum distance. If it is placed inside this distance, the spatial frequency of the detector is too low and aliasing occurs. This minimum distance is given [6]:

$$d_{\min} = \frac{(N\Delta x)^2}{N\lambda} \tag{18}$$

where N and Δx are the number and the size of the pixels. However, the angular spectrum method [7] is able to overcome this disadvantage. It is comparable with the other methods in terms of computational efficiency but has the potential of higher accuracy. If the wave field at the plane $d = 0$ is $U_0(x,y;0)$, the angular spectrum $A(k_x,k_y;0)$ at this plane is obtained by taking the Fourier transform:

$$A(k_x, k_y; 0) = \int\int U_0(x, y; 0)\exp\{-i(k_x x + k_y y)\}dxdy \tag{19}$$

where k_x and k_y are the corresponding spatial frequencies of x and y. The angular spectrum at the distance d, i.e., $A(k_x,k_y;d)$, is calculated from $A(k_x,k_y;0)$ as given by

$$A(k_x, k_y; d) = A(k_x, k_y; 0)\exp(ik_z d) \tag{20}$$

where $k_z = \sqrt{k^2 - k_x^2 - k_y^2}$. The reconstructed complex wave field at any plane perpendicular to the propagating z axis is found by

$$U(\xi, \eta; d) = \int\int A(k_x, k_y; d)\exp[i(k_x\xi + k_y\eta)]dk_x dk_y = \Im^{-1}[\Im(U_0)\exp(ik_z d)] \tag{21}$$

The resolution of the reconstructed images from the angular spectrum method is the same as that in the hologram plane, which means that the pixel size does not vary with changes of wavelength or reconstruction distance.

3. Impact of imperfect collimation of the reference wave in off-axis DH

In digital holography, the simulation of the plane wave is essential for performing a numerical reconstruction. Conventionally, a shear interferometer is used for producing perfect collimation and hence producing a perfect plane wave. In Section 3, we show that using a slightly imperfect plane wave in digital holography experiments is acceptable [8]. We experimentally proved that by using the Mickelson interferometer, no influence of imperfect collimation of the reference wave in an off-axis digital holography exists, as has been previously claimed. We applied perfect and imperfect collimations to three different surface (flat, spherical, and step height) shapes for height inspection, and the results were almost in good agreement. The samples being tested were mounted in the Michelson interferometer one by one, as shown in

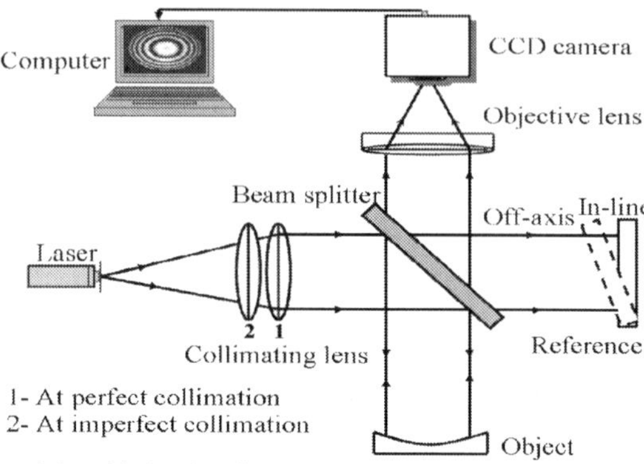

Figure 3. Schematic diagram of the Michelson interferometer.

Figure 3. A laser diode beam passed through a collimating lens of focal lens 100 mm and expanded. The beam splitter splits the collimated beam into two equal beams: one for reference (optical flat of $\lambda/20$ flatness) arm and the other for the object (flat, spherical, and step height surfaces) arm. The beam reflected from the reference and the object is recombined at the beam splitter to produce an interference pattern. The perfect collimation that produced a perfect plane wave impinging on the reference was adjusted by a shear interferometer placed between the collimating lens and the beam splitter.

The slightly imperfect collimations were seven equidistance displacements of the collimating lens with 1.5 mm from the perfect collimation and between two successive displacements. The off-axis holograms for the samples under test at perfect and slightly imperfect plane waves were captured and then reconstructed. Details of the reconstruction process are explained in reference [8]. The reconstructed phase for perfect **Figure 4(a)** and slightly imperfect collimations **Figure 4(2–8)** and the height line profile for both along the central x-axis are shown in **Figure 4(1(b)–1(c))**, respectively.

The wrapping phase for the spherical surface for perfect collimations and slightly imperfect collimations is shown in **Figure 5(a)** and **(2–8)**, respectively. The unwrapping phases of **Figure 5b(1–8)** are shown in **Figure 5c(1–8)**, and the height line profiles along the central x-axis of **Figure 5b(1–8)** are shown in **Figure 5d(1–8)**, respectively.

For the third object (step height surface), the off-axis holograms at the perfect and slightly imperfect collimations were captured and reconstructed. The height line profiles along the central x-axis of the reconstructed heights at perfect and slightly imperfect collimations at imaging and Fresnel transform are shown in **Figure 6a** and **b**, respectively.

As seen from **Figures 4–6**, for flat, spherical, and step surfaces, the measured height values of the three tested surfaces were almost consistent at perfect and imperfect collimations. Very small variations may be observed due to noise, which is commonly observed in interferometry measurements. We claim that the variations may be due to the mechanical imperfection of the collimating lens as shown in **Figure 7**. We claim that when the lens mounting was ideally

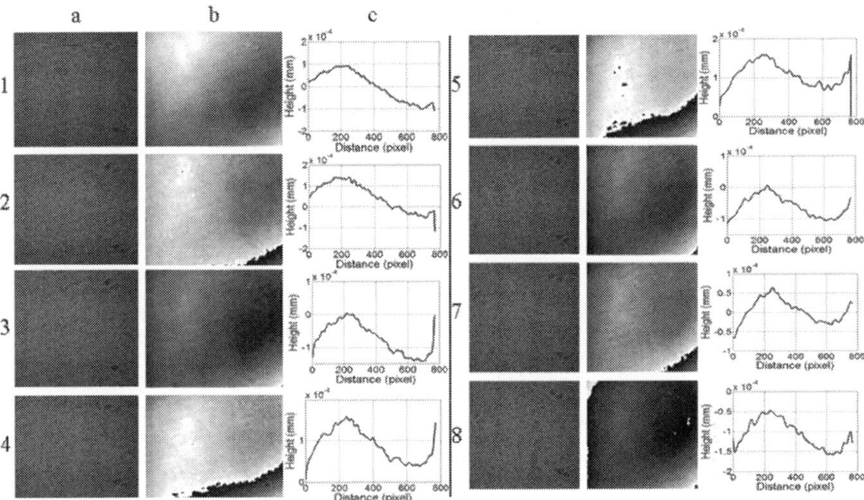

Figure 4. (a) Off-axis interferograms. (b) Reconstructed phases of (a). (c) Line height profiles along the central x-axis of the tested flat surface produced at (1) perfect collimation and (2–8) slightly imperfect collimations.

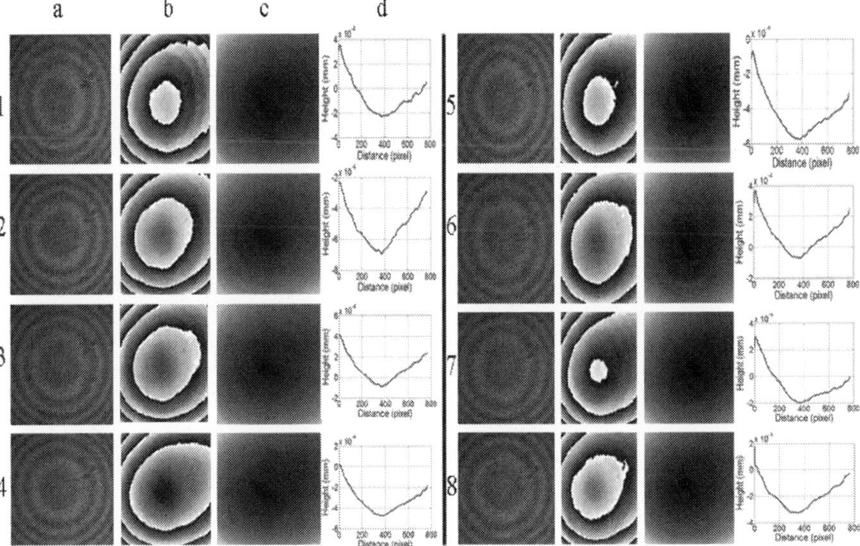

Figure 5. (a) Off-axis interferograms. (b) Reconstructed phases of (a). (c) Unwrapping phases of (b). (d) Line height profiles along the central x-axis of the tested spherical surface produced at (1) perfect collimation and (2–8) imperfect collimations.

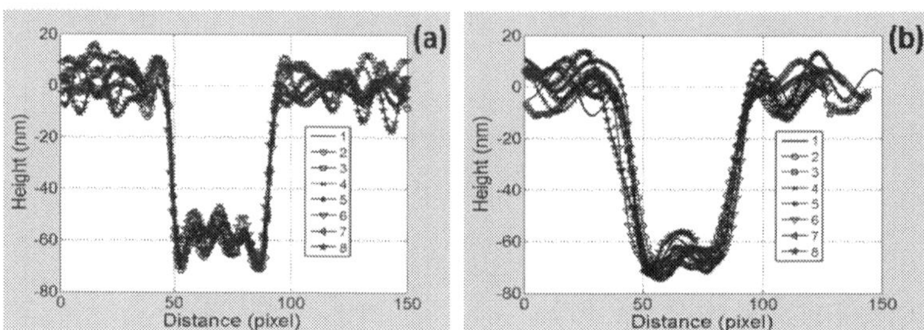

Figure 6. Line height profiles of the tested step surface at perfect (1) and imperfect (2–8) collimations produced at (a) $d = 0.0$ mm (imaging scheme) and (b) $d = -500.0$ mm (Fresnel transform).

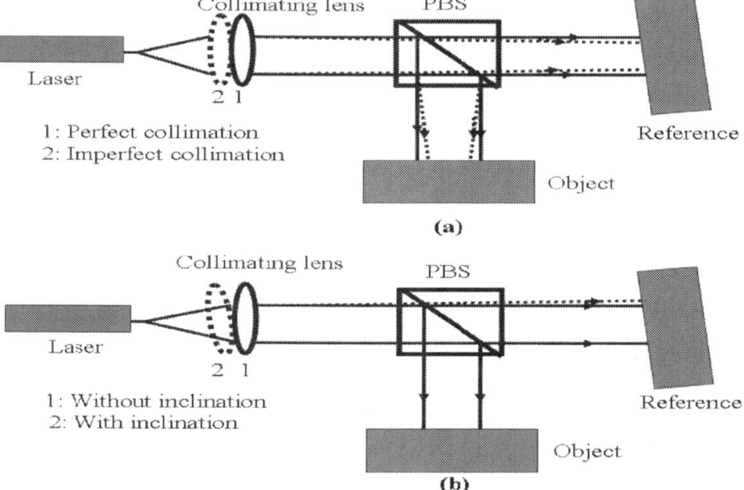

Figure 7. The effect of design of mounting and the adjustment of the collimation lens on the very small height variations: (a) ideal mounting, (b) nonideal mounting.

displaced as shown in **Figure 7(a)** at position 2 (slightly imperfect collimation), the beams converge toward the reference and the object. The convergent beams would then be canceled out and subsequently have no impact on the height variations. However, it is hard to achieve ideal mounting mechanically. Thus we expect that the effect of nonideal mounting as shown in **Figure 7(b)** may be the reason of small height variations as shown in **Figure 7(b)**.

4. Low coherence, off-axis DHM for in vitro sandwiched biological samples investigation

In digital holographic microscopy (DHM), optical sources with long coherent lengths such as He-Ne laser have been widely used to feature the sample. Because of the high degree of coherence of the He-Ne laser light, harmful coherent noise often arises. This noise affects the quality of the holograms and hence leads to error in phase measurement. The larger the phase noise is, the lower the measurement precision will be. The harmful coherent noise is mainly classified into two types. The first is the random diffraction patterns (speckle noise) due to scattered light. The second is the formation of unwanted interference fringes (spurious noise) due to stray light. The spurious noise is formed when light reflected or scattered from various surfaces in the optical path is coherent with the main beam. The amplitude of the scattered light a_s adds vectorially to the amplitude of the main beam, resulting in a phase error $\Delta\phi$ as illustrated in **Figure 8(a)**. Some practical solutions such as introducing a wedged beam splitter, a rotating diffuser, and antireflection coating to the optical surfaces, in the optical system setup, were proposed to minimize the unwanted coherent noise. Although these practical solutions are effective and may circumvent to suppress the coherent noise to some amount, they have some drawbacks in terms of blurring the fringe visibility and hindering the fringe formation in DHM, which require perfect alignment. Optical sources with short coherent lengths such as LEDs were proposed in order to avoid the harmful coherent noise. However, the limited coherence length of LED and its insufficient brightness hinder its application in an off-axis DHM, since just a limited number of interference fringes with poor visibility appear in the field of view (FOV). In Section 4, we present an off-axis DHM configuration using bright femtosecond pulse light with ultrashort coherent length, which makes possible to feature sandwiched biological samples with no coherent noise (speckle and spurious) in the reconstructed object wave [9].

A typical configuration of the sandwiched biological sample is shown in **Figure 8(b)**, where the specimen is mounted in between two thin glass plates to avoid dehydration. Investigating such biological samples using conventional DHM with long coherent He-Ne laser light is challenging because of existence of the harmful coherent noise. Photograph of the investigated sample taken by the proposed DHM system (see **Figure 9**) with blocking the reference arm is shown in **Figure 8(c)**. The DHM experimental setup is schematically shown in **Figure 9**. The configuration is comprised of two parts: generation of femtosecond pulse light in near-infrared region and a Mach-Zehnder interferometer in transmission. A mode-locked Er-doped fiber laser light (center wavelength λ_c = 1550 nm, spectral bandwidth $\Delta\lambda$ = 73 nm, pulse duration $\Delta\tau$ = 100 fs, mean power P_{mean} = 380 mW, and repetition frequency f_{rep} = 250 MHz) was focused on a periodically poled lithium niobate (PPLN) crystal to convert the wavelength by second

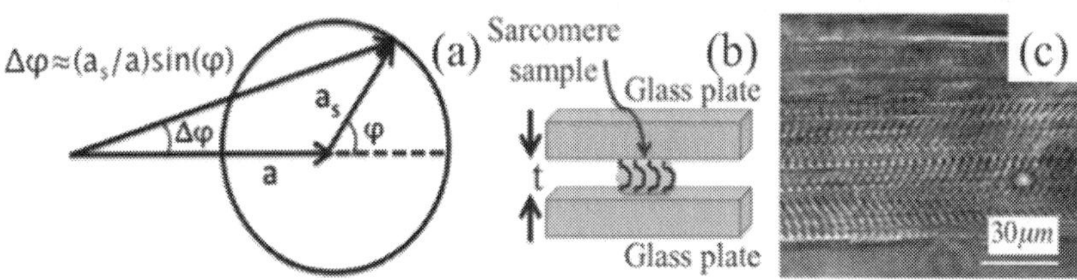

Figure 8. (a) Phase error $\Delta\phi$ produced by scattered long coherent light a_s, (b) sliced biological specimen mounted in between two thin glass plates to avoid dehydration, and (c) photograph of the investigated sarcomere sample taken by the proposed setup with blocking the reference arm.

harmonic generation (SHG) into the operating wavelength region of a charge-coupled device (CCD) camera used. To extract the SHG light, we used a narrow band-pass optical filter (F, passband wavelength = 775 ± 5 nm). The extracted SHG light has λ_c of 777.8 nm, $\Delta\lambda$ of 10 nm, $\Delta\tau$ of 120 fs, and P_{mean} of 14 mW (left inset of **Figure 9**).

The output power was sufficient to illuminate the sample and produce off-axis holograms with high contrast in the entire field of the CCD camera. The coherence length of the SHG pulse light was 30 μm. The SHG beam was expanded to a diameter of 20 mm by a telescope system. In the Mach-Zehnder off-axis setup in transmission, a pair of non-polarized beam splitters (NPBS1 and NPBS2) was used to separate the two SHG beams into reference (R) and object (O) beams and combine them again. Difference of optical path length in the two arms was precisely adjusted within the coherence length of 30 μm by a scanning mirror, equipped with a mechanical translation stage, in the reference arm. The interfering object beam and the reference beam were tilted at small angle with respect to each other to produce off-axis hologram at the plane of the beam splitter NPBS2. The off-axis hologram was transferred via a microscope lens MO3 (20 × , NA = 0.1) to a black-and-white CCD camera (640 pixels by 480 pixels, pixel size = 4.3 μm). We conducted the experiment on microstructured sarcomere sample, which was isolated fibers dissected from rabbit muscle and mounted in between two thin glass plates to avoid dehydration (gap distance t = 15 μm) as shown in **Figure 8(c)**. The off-axis hologram was recorded by making the reference wave (instead of the object wave) subtending the off-axis angle with the optical axis. Such arrangement is not only easier to align but also makes the image plane parallel to the sensor surface.

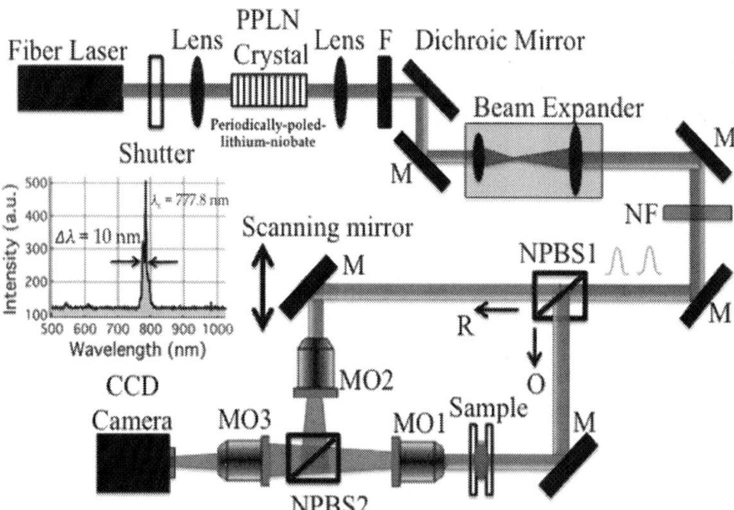

Figure 9. Experimental setup: PPLN is periodically poled lithium niobate (PPLN) crystal; F is a band bass filter at 775 nm; M is mirror; NF is neutral density filter; NPBS1 and NPBS2 are nonpolarizing beam splitters; MO1, MO2, and MO3 are microscope objectives with (50 × , NA = 0.45), (20 × , NA = 0.45), and (20 × , NA = 0.1), respectively.

The off-axis digital hologram recorded by the CCD camera was reconstructed using convolution-based Fresnel method. Three spectra were obtained when 2D-FFT was implemented to the off-axis hologram as shown in **Figure 10**. Only one filtered spectrum from the three spectra in 2D-FFT is used. The inverse 2D-FFT was applied after filtering out the spectrum, and the calculation result gives a complex object wave (amplitude and phase). The obtained complex amplitude was multiplied by the digital reference wave $R_D(m,n)$ to generate the final amplitudes and phases. An amplitude-contrast image and a phase-contrast image can be obtained by using the following intensity $[Re(\Gamma)^2 + Im(\Gamma)^2]$ and the argument $\arctan[Re(\Gamma)/Im(\Gamma)]$, respectively. The digital reference wave $R_D(m,n)$ can be calculated as $R_D(m,n) = A_R \exp[i(2\pi/\lambda)(k_x m\Delta x + k_y n\Delta y)]$, where A_R is the amplitude, λ is the wavelength of the light source(777.8 nm for the femtosecond pulse light), and k_x and k_y are the two components of the wave vectors, which are adjusted such that the propagation direction of $R_D(m,n)$ matches as closely as possible with that of the experimental reference wave. The reconstructed amplitude and phase were recorded by selecting the appropriate values of the two components of the wave vector $k_x = 0.02145$ mm^{-1} and $k_y = -0.51570$ mm^{-1}. In order to see the effectiveness of our method compared to the conventional DHM, the femtosecond pulse light and PPLN crystal were replaced by long coherent He-Ne laser light source ($\lambda = 632.8$ nm).

The obtained off-axis hologram was reconstructed with the same procedure of **Figure 10** and the final amplitude and phase obtained at $k_x = 0.00999$ mm^{-1} and $k_y = -0.5239$ mm^{-1}. **Figure 11** **(a)** and **(d)** shows the off-axis holograms of the sarcomere sample obtained by a He-Ne laser light and femtosecond pulse light, respectively. A layered structure of around 15 sarcomeres

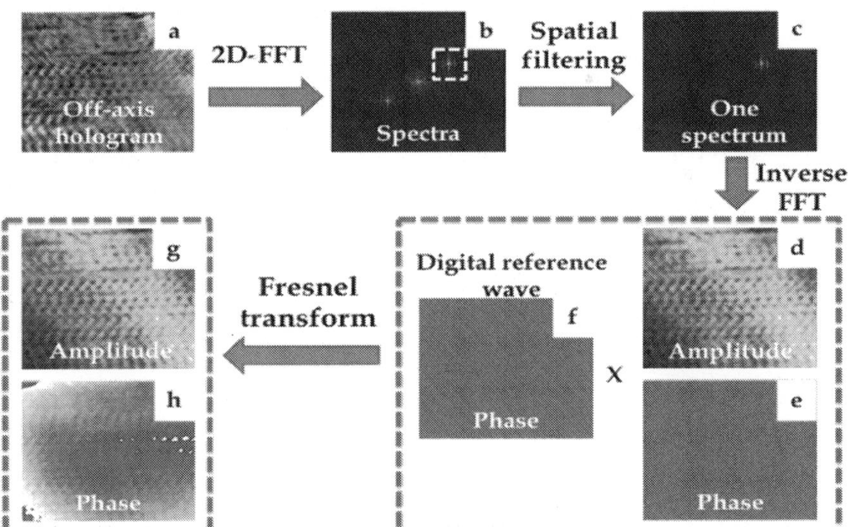

Figure 10. Sequential reconstruction steps (a) off-axis hologram, (b) Fourier transformed spatial frequency domain data, (c) filtered one spectrum, (d) and (e) reconstructed amplitude and phase before removing the fringes in the observation plane, (f) digital reference wave, and (g) and (h) final amplitude and phase maps.

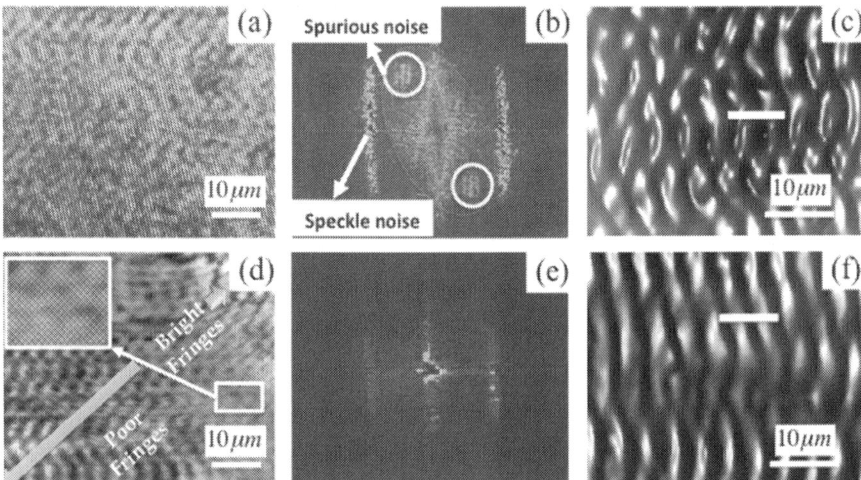

Figure 11. Off-axis holograms of layered structure of sarcomeres taken by (a) He-Ne laser light and (d) femtosecond pulse light. (b) and (e) are filtered 2D-FFT spectrum of (a) and (b), respectively. (c) and (f) are 3D pseudocolor reconstructed phase-contrast image of stripy sarcomere with He-Ne laser light and femtosecond pulse light, respectively.

was captured at nearly same region of FOV. Comparison of these images indicated that the image brightness of DHM with the femtosecond pulse light was higher than that of the He-Ne laser light due to temporally localized energy of the femtosecond pulse light. **Figure 11(b)** and **(e)** shows one filtered spectrum from the three spectra in frequency domain when two-dimensional fast Fourier transform (2D-FFT) has been used for the off-axis interferogram as shown in **Figure 11(a)** and **(d)**, respectively. Note that the three spectra appearing in the filtered one spectrum are due to the off-axis fringes of the sarcomere sample itself. **Figure 11(b)** shows the appearance of both spurious and speckle noises, while such noise was totally disappearing by using our setup as shown in **Figure 11(e)**. In order to see the effectiveness of our setup compared to the conventional DHM with He-Ne laser light, we have not applied any of the numerous image enhancement techniques, to significantly improve the perceived image quality for biological applications. **Figure 11(c)** and **(f)** shows 3D pseudocolor reconstructed phase-contrast images of stripy sarcomere of **Figure 11(a)** and **(d)**, respectively. Although phase images tend to suffer from the coherent noise to a significantly less degree compared to the amplitude images, the sarcomeres are hardly viewed in **Figure 11(c)** because of the existence of coherent noise at the background. In contrast, **Figure 11(f)** shows that the stripe structures of 10 sarcomeres are clearly viewed in the phase-contrast image because of no coherent noise in the background image. The phase profiles extracted along white lines in the phase-contrast image of **Figure 11(c)** and **(f)** are shown in **Figure 12**, indicating the cross-sectional profile of two sarcomeres. As shown from **Figure 12**, the phase profile of the proposed technique (red color) is free from noise, and the sarcomere cross section can be calculated precisely with no need of image enhancement techniques, which in turn takes time to enhance the image to some amount.

The phase profiles have been measured at different locations, and the average phase profile of the proposed method was found to be in good agreement with nominal values of the sarcomere depth. The contrast (axial resolution) of the proposed method is estimated from **Figure 12** to be two times better than the contrast of He-Ne phase-based result. It is noted that the mismatching in the peaks of the phase profiles shown in **Figure 12** is due to difference in magnifications of the captured off-axis holograms of both He-Ne and femtosecond pulse light. To enhance the differentiation of the sarcomere structure within the reconstructed amplitude map, the 3D reconstructed amplitude maps of both He-Ne laser light and femtosecond pulse light may be displayed in a false color representation as shown in **Figure 13(a)** and **(b)**, respectively.

It is noted that these 3D reconstructed amplitude maps were flipped upside down to see the sarcomeres from different views. In **Figure 13(a)**, existence of coherent noise in the background image makes it difficult to visualize the structure of the sarcomeres. On the other hand, **Figure 13(b)** shows the high quality and contrast of structure detail on the sarcomeres and

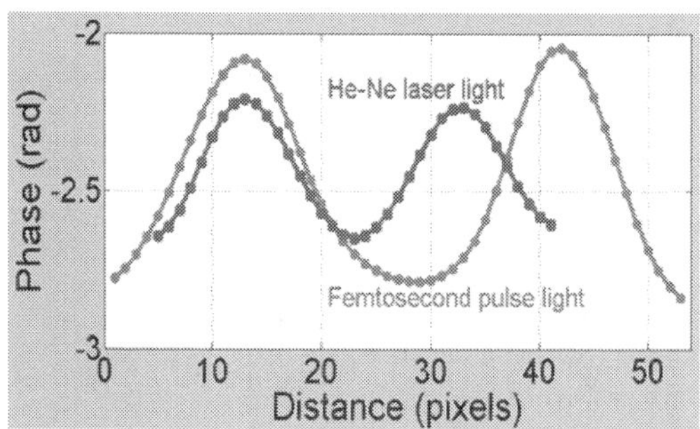

Figure 12. Phase profiles extracted along white lines of two sarcomeres in phase-contrast images of both **Figure 11(c)** (blue color) and **Figure 11(f)** (red color).

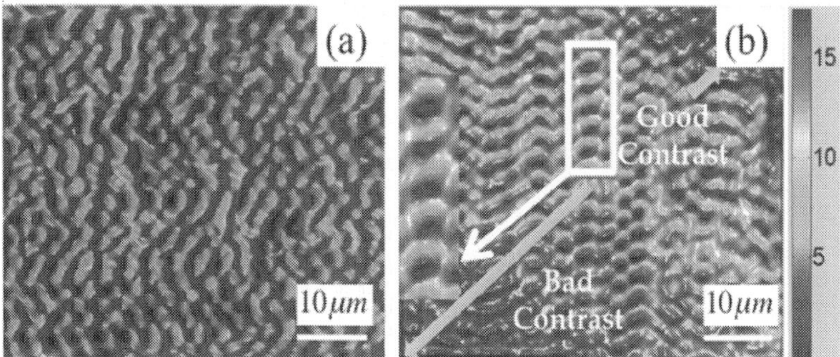

Figure 13. 3D pseudocolor reconstructed amplitude-contrast image of (a) He-Ne laser light and (b) femtosecond pulse light.

provides accurate profile edges of hexagonal shape of the sarcomeres. This makes our technique preferable in featuring such sandwiched biological samples, which is quite difficult to investigate using atomic force microscope (AFM).

Our deductions were verified by applications of apodization technique [10], to estimate the coherent noise level in the reconstructed amplitude maps of the off-axis holograms generated by both He-Ne and femtosecond pulse light, respectively. Apodization is the same topic as windowing in signal processing. The transmission of the apodized aperture function is completely transparent in the large central part of the profile. At the edges, the transmission varies from zero to unity following a curve defined by a cubic spline interpolation. The 2D transmission size of (480 × 480) pixels of the apodized aperture function is multiplied with the off-axis holograms (480 × 480) pixels of both He-Ne laser light and femtosecond pulse light, respectively. Normalization of intensity distribution of four sarcomeres at the middle of the off-axis hologram of the He-Ne laser light before and after application of apodization is shown in the left side of **Figure 14**. Normalization of intensities distribution of four sarcomeres at the middle of the off-axis hologram of the femtosecond laser light before and after application of apodization is shown in the right side of **Figure 14**.

As seen from the left figure, the variation in intensities before and after application of apodization function indicates that there is a coherent noise in the reconstructed amplitude of He-Ne off-axis hologram. Such coherent noise is totally disappearing in the right figure, whereas no variation in intensities before and after application of apodization. This confirms that the reconstructed amplitude of femtosecond pulse light off-axis hologram is free from coherent noise. Due to the short coherence length of the pulsed light, only fraction of hologram shows high-contrast fringe, resulting in a good reconstruction in this region as shown in **Figure 13(b)** which is corresponding to the off-axis hologram of **Figure 11(d)**. The contrast of the fringes in **Figure 11(d)** reduces from center to two sides diagonally, which indicates the zero-path-difference point is nearly in the middle of the sensor. To obtain a high-brightness full-field image, we can move the center of the fringes diagonally and collect holograms with different zero path difference. Twelve off-axis holograms were generated diagonally by varying the optical path length of the interferometer to cover a sarcomere sample of around 45 × 45 micrometers in the field of view (FOV) with high-contrast fringes at different regions in the

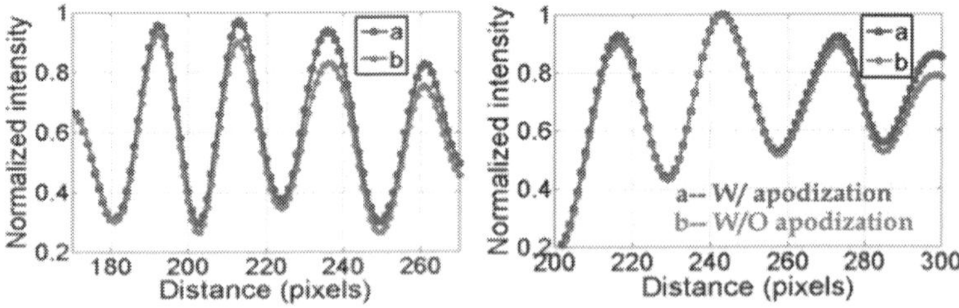

Figure 14. Normalization of intensities distribution of four sarcomeres with (a) and without (b) apodization taken at the middle of the off-axis holograms of He-Ne laser light (left) and femtosecond pulse light (right).

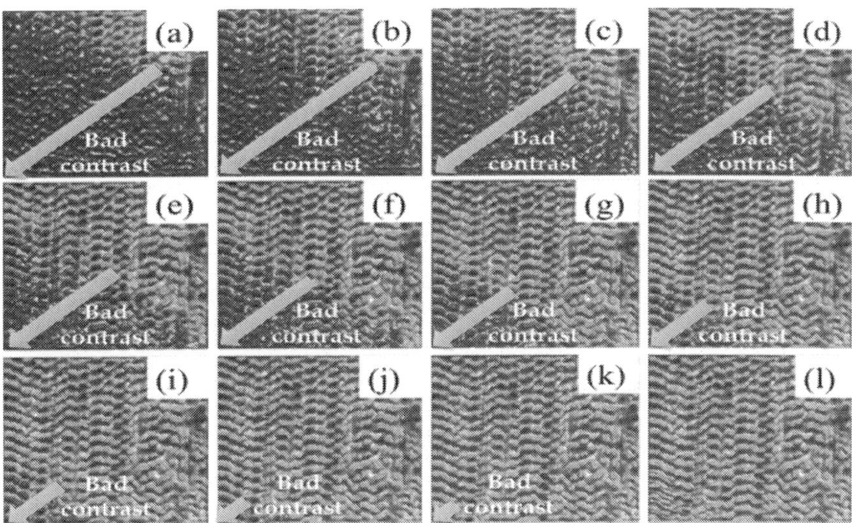

Figure 15. 3D pseudocolor reconstructed amplitude-contrast image from superimposing of (a) 1 hologram, (b) 2 holograms, (c) 3 holograms, (d) 4 holograms, (e) 5 holograms, (f) 6 holograms, (g) 7 holograms, (h) 8 holograms, (i) 9 holograms, (j) 10 holograms, (k) 11 holograms, and (l) 12 holograms produced by femtosecond pulse light by using linear direct method.

image. The full-field image can be obtained by adding multiple such single reconstructions on the intensity basis as shown in **Figure 15(a)–(l)**. The synthesized image map is shown in **Figure 15(l)**. Because of the holograms' shifting process, the reference and object beam will have some phase shifts when the second hologram is recorded. When the second hologram is subtracted from the first hologram, the zero order is removed. Subtractions among successive holograms were superimposed using a direct linear addition method to constitute a full-field, high-quality synthesized hologram as shown in **Figure 9**. The intensity of the synthesized hologram I can be written as follows:

$$I_{synth} = \sum_{i=1}^{N/2} (h_N - h_i) + \sum_{i=1}^{N/2} (h_i - h_N), \tag{22}$$

where i takes from 1 to N, whereas N is the total number of off-axis holograms = 12.

5. Off-axis terahertz DH using continuous-wave THZ radiation

Terahertz (THz) radiation is an electromagnetic radiation lying between the microwave and infrared portions of the spectrum as shown in **Figure 16**. THz radiation can be produced by many techniques such as quantum cascade lasers (QCLs). QCLs are semiconductor heterostructures that can emit continuous-wave (CW) THz radiation [10]. QCLs are electron-only

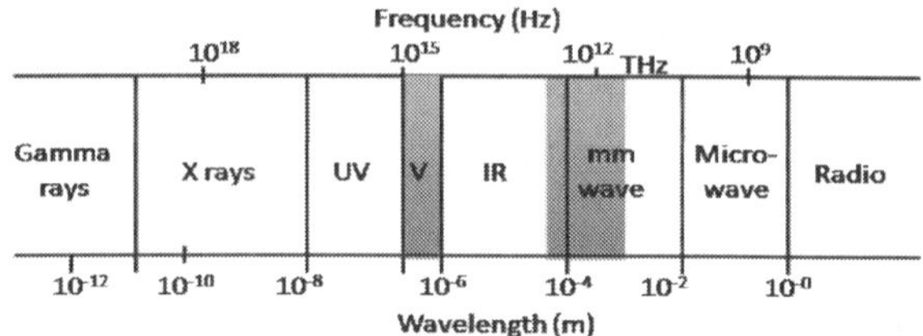

Figure 16. Spectrum of waves showing the location of THz radiation.

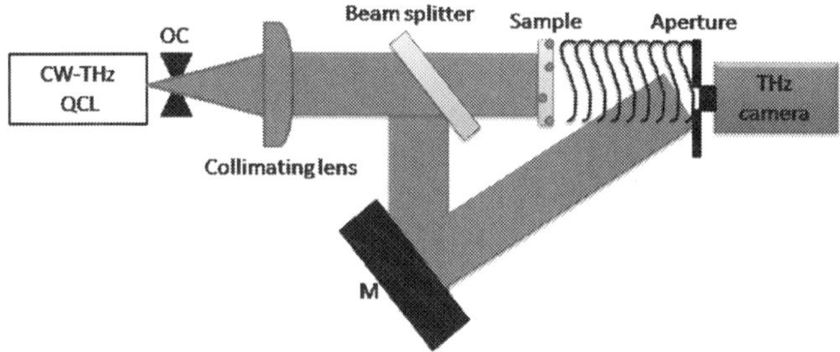

Figure 17. Experimental setup of CW THz-DH: OC is optical chopper and M is a mirror.

devices that exploit transitions between conduction band states. The conduction band offsets between neighboring materials in the superlattice create a series of quantum wells and barriers. The most widely used QCL designs are based on GaAs/AlGaAs superlattices. The word cascading means that one electron can produce many photons in the superlattice periods. A significant advantage of THZ radiation is that it can easily inspect sealed packages for contrasting metal and plastic objects, testing pharmaceutical tablets for integrity, detecting skin cancers, etc.

In Section 5, we present the usage of THz radiation for 3D surface characterization via a digital holography (DH) technique [11]. Since the usual DH uses a visible light, it is difficult to visualize 3D internal structure of visibly opaque objects due to their limited penetration depth. The compelling advantage of THz radiation is that it has a good penetration capability; thus, 3D visualization of both surface shape and internal structure in visibly opaque object can be achieved [12]. We constructed off-axis THz digital holography (THz-DH) system equipped with CW-THz radiation generated by QCL, and the THz digital hologram is captured by a THz camera.

Figure 17 illustrates a schematic diagram of off-axis THz-DH system. An optical chopper (OC) is positioned in front of the QCL to reduce the noise. The radiation was collimated by a Teflon lens (f = 300 mm). The collimated THz beam of diameter around 60 mm is divided into a signal THz beam and a reference one by a silicon beam splitter (BS). **Figure 18(a)** shows 2D intensity distribution of the THz beam without the sample. **Figure 18(b)** shows the dark frame captured

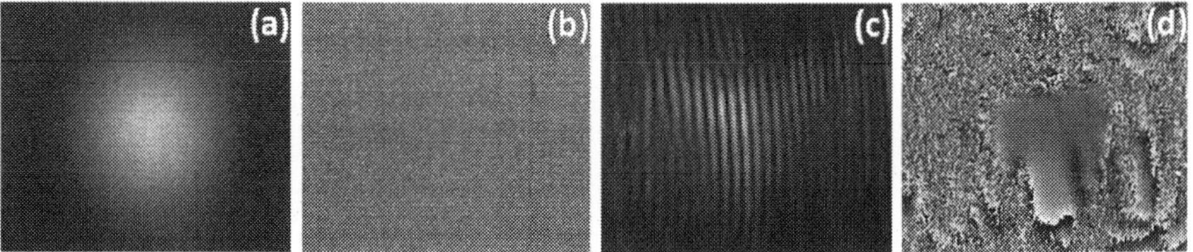

Figure 18. (a) A 2D intensity distribution of the THz beam without the sample, (b) dark frame captured by the THz camera when there is no illumination, (c) off-axis hologram, and (d) 3D phase-contrast image reconstructed by angular spectrum method.

by the THz camera when there is no illumination. The signal THz beam passed through a sample (here, the sample is a letter T from paper), while a reference THz beam is reflected by a mirror (M). Then, these two THz beams were spatially overlapped at a certain off-axis angle to generate 2D fringe of THz beams. Finally, the off-axis THz digital hologram is captured by a THz camera as shown in **Figure 18(c)**. The off-axis THz hologram has been reconstructed with angular spectrum method to extract both amplitude and phase. **Figure 18(d)** shows the 3D reconstructed phase of the sample.

6. Conclusion

In conclusion, we have presented the recent developments of digital holography techniques for surface characterization. In this chapter, the principle of digital holography with focus on numerical reconstruction algorithms is presented. Also, influence of slightly imperfect collimation of the reference wave in off-axis DH is discussed. Finally, we have described two different DH techniques for surface characterization: the first technique by using short coherent length, namely, high-brightness DHM, and the second technique by using long coherent length, namely, THz-DH. Experimental results are presented to verify the principles.

Author details

Dahi Ghareab Abdelsalam[1]*, Takeshi Yasui[2], Takayuki Ogawa[2] and Baoli Yao[3]

*Address all correspondence to: shosho_dahi@yahoo.com

1 Engineering and Surface Metrology Laboratory, National Institute for Standards, Egypt

2 Graduate School of Science and Technology, Tokushima University, Japan

3 State Key Laboratory of Transient Optics and Photonics, Xi'an Institute of Optics and Precision Mechanics, Chinese Academy of Sciences, China

References

[1] Goodman, J.W.; & Lawrence, R.W.: Digital image formation from electronically detected holograms, Applied Physics Letters. 1967; **11**: 77-79.

[2] Schnars, U.; & Juptner, W.: Direct recording of holograms by a CCD target and numerical reconstruction, Applied Optics. 1994; **33**: 179-181.

[3] Juptner, W.; & Schnars, U.: Digital Holography: Digital Hologram Recording, Numerical Reconstruction, and Related Techniques, Springer-Verlag, Berlin. (2005).

[4] Yaroslavsky, L.P.; & Merzlyakov, N.S.: Methods of Digital Holography, Consultants Bureau, New York (1980).

[5] Kreis, T.M.; & Juptner, W.: Principles of digital holography. In Juptner, W. & Osten, W. (Eds.) Fringe '97, Proceeding of 3rd International Workshop on Automatic Processing of Fringe Patterns. Akademie, Berlin. (1997).

[6] Hecht, E.: Optics, Addison Wesley Longman, Inc., San Francisco, United States of America (1998). p. 485.

[7] Kim, M.K.; Yu, L.; & Mann, C.J.: Interference techniques in digital holography. Journal of Optics A: Pure and Applied Optics. 2006; **8**: 518-523.

[8] Abdelsalam, D.; Baek, B.; & Kim, D.: Influence of the collimation of the reference wave in off-axis digital holography. Optik. 2012; **123**: 1469-1473.

[9] Abdelsalam, D.; Yamamoto, H.; & Yasui, T.: High Contrast Digital Holographic Microscopy by use of Femtosecond Pulse light. JSAP-OSA Joint Symposia, paper 15p_2F_3. (2015).

[10] D.G. Abdelsalam, and Daesuk Kim, "Coherent noise suppression in digital holography based on flat fielding with apodized apertures", Optics Express, 19, pp. 17951-17959, (2011).

[11] Takayuki, O.; Abdelsalam, D.; Masuoka, T.; Yasui, T.; & Yamamoto, H.: Off-Axis Terahertz Digital Holography using Continuous-Wave Terahertz radiation. Conference on Lasers and Electro-Optics Pacific Rim, paper 27P_99. (2015).

[12] Li, Q.; Xue, K.; Li, Y.-D.; & Wang, Q.: Experimental research on terahertz Gabor inline digital holography of concealed objects. Applied Optics. 2012; **51**, 7052-7058.

Digital Holographic Interferometry for Analysing High-Density Gradients in Fluid Mechanics

Jean-Michel Desse and François Olchewsky

Additional information is available at the end of the chapter

http://dx.doi.org/10.5772/66111

Abstract

Digital holographic interferometry has been developed by ONERA for analysing high refractive index variations encountered in fluid mechanics. First, the authors present the analysis of a small supersonic jet using three different optical techniques based on digital Michelson holography, digital holography using Wollaston prisms and digital holography without reference wave. A comparison of the three methods is given. Then, two different interferometers are described for analysing high-density gradients encountered in high subsonic and transonic flows. The time evolution of the gas density field around a circular cylinder is given at Mach 0.7. Finally, a digital holographic method is presented to visualize and measure the refractive index variations occurring inside a transparent and strongly refracting object. For this case, a comparison with digital and image holographic interferometry using transmission and reflection holograms is provided.

Keywords: digital holography, holographic interferometry, real-time holography, phase measurement

1. Introduction

In-line and off-axis digital holographic interferometry is now became an optical metrological tool more and more used in the domain of fluid mechanics [1]. For instance, it is widely developed in macro- or microscopy for measuring in the flow the location or size of particles [2, 3] or for measuring the temperature or the thermal exchanges in the flames [4, 5]. Other authors have developed digital colour holographic interferometry by using three different wavelengths (one red, one green and one blue) as a luminous source. Qualitative results have

---

been obtained for visualizing convective flows induced by the thermal dissipation in a tank filled with oil [6]. Quantitatively, the feasibility of three-wavelength digital holographic interferometry has been demonstrated for analysing the variations in the refractive index induced by a candle flame [7] and the technique has been applied in wind tunnel on two-dimensional unsteady flows where the time evolution of the gas density field has been determined on the subsonic near wake flow downstream a circular cylinder [8]. But, when the flow regime reaches the transonic or supersonic domain, problems appear because refractive index gradients become very strong and a shadow effect is generated by the shock waves, for instance, superimposes to the micro-fringes of interferences. Phase shifts appear and limit the interferogram analysis. In order to solve these different problems, the authors propose to study three different cases of flows presenting high-density gradients using specific optical techniques based on digital holography. The first one concerns a small supersonic jet analysed by Michelson colour digital interferometry, colour holographic interferometry using Wollaston prisms and monochromatic digital holography without reference wave. The second case is to compare Michelson and Mach-Zehnder interferometers for analysing the unsteady wake flow around a circular cylinder at transonic Mach number. And finally, digital and image holographic methods are presented to visualize and measure the refractive index variations, convection currents or thermal gradients occurring inside a transparent and strongly refracting object. In the case of image holographic interferometry, a comparison with transmission and reflection holograms is provided.

2. Fundamental

Digital holography has been widely developed for analysing diffusive objects since the digitally reconstructing of the optical wavefront was shown by Goodman and Lawrence [9]. But, in fluid mechanics, the objects under analysis are very often transparent because it is the field of refractive index of the flow which is measured. There are two ways to measure variations in the refractive index by digital holography. The first one, presented in **Figure 1**, is comparable to the technique used for measuring diffusive objects in structural mechanics.

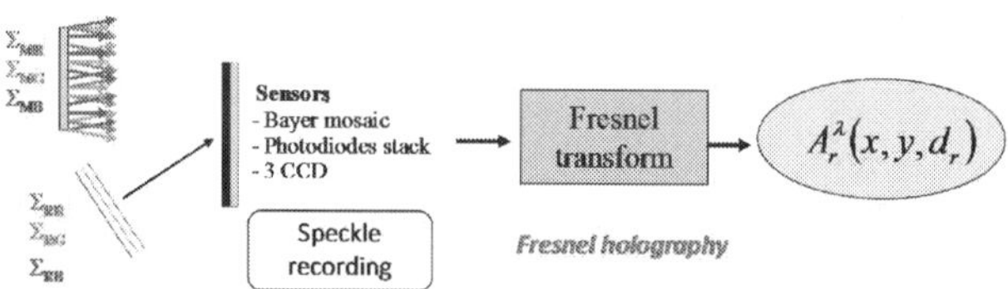

Figure 1. Fresnel holography for measuring transparent objects.

For example, if three different wavelengths are considered, $\sum$MR for the red line, $\sum$MG for the green line and $\sum$MB for the blue line, the wavefronts of measurement which cross the transparent object in the test section can be sent on a ground plate and each point of the plate diffracts and interferes on the sensor with the three reference waves, $\sum$RR, $\sum$RG and $\sum$RB. In this case, the sensor can be a Bayer mosaic, a stack of photodiodes or a 3CDD. The recorded image is a speckle image which can be processed using Fresnel transform and the field $A_r^\lambda(x, y, d_r)$ diffracted at the distance d_r and at the coordinates (x, y) of the observation plane is given by the propagation of the three object waves to the recording plane. The second technique is shown in **Figure 2**. The three wavelengths $\sum$MR, $\sum$MG and $\sum$MB interfere directly onto the sensor with the three reference waves, $\sum$RR, $\sum$RG and $\sum$RB. As the three measurement waves are smooth waves, the interferences with the three reference waves on the sensor produce three gratings of interference micro-fringes which can be used as spatial carrier frequencies, one for each wavelength. By using direct and inverse 2D Fast Fourier Transform (FFT), the amplitude and the phase of the analysed field is obtained.

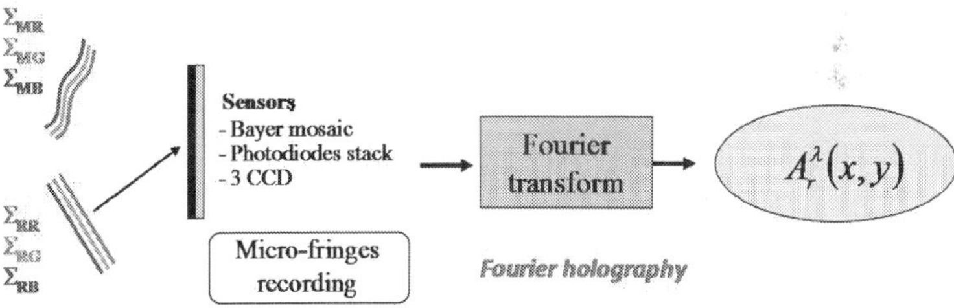

Figure 2. Fourier holography for measuring transparent objects.

All details and basic fundamentals of these two techniques can be found in the study of Picart et al. [10].

3. Digital holography for analysing supersonic jet

In this part, the supersonic flow of a small vertical jet has been analysed using three different techniques based on digital holography. The first one is based on Michelson digital holographic interferometer using three wavelengths as a luminous source [8], the second one uses the same source (three wavelengths) and Wollaston prisms to separate the reference waves and the measurement waves [11] and the last one is a little bit particular because a specific diffraction grating is manufactured to obtain several different diffractions of measurement waves and to avoid having the reference wave [12].

3.1. Michelson holographic interferometry

The optical set-up presented in **Figure 3** is very simple and looks like a conventional Michelson interferometer in which a beam splitter cube (7) is inserted between the spatial filter (6) and the aerodynamic phenomenon under analysis (11). The light source consists of three diode-pumped solid-state lasers, one red (R), one green (G) and one blue (B), emitting respectively at 660, 532 and 457 nm. A half wave plate (1) is used to rotate by 90° the polarization of the blue line (S to P) and a flat mirror (2) and two dichroic plates (3) allow the superimposing of the three wavelengths. An acousto-optical cell (4) deflects the parasitic wavelengths in a mask (5) and diffracts the three wavelengths RGB using three characteristic frequencies injected into the crystal. The spatial filter (6), composed of microscope objective (60×) and a small hole of 25 μm, is placed at the focal length of the achromatic lens (9) in order to illuminate the phenomenon with a parallel beam. On-going, 50% of the light is returned towards the concave mirror (8) to form the three reference beams and 50% of the light passes through the test section (between (9) and (12) to form the measuring waves. The flat mirror (12) placed behind the test section (11) returns the beams in the beam splitter cube (7). 25% of the light focused on the diaphragm which is placed in front of the achromatic lens (13). It is the same for the 25% of the reference beam which is focused on the same diaphragm by the concave mirror (8).

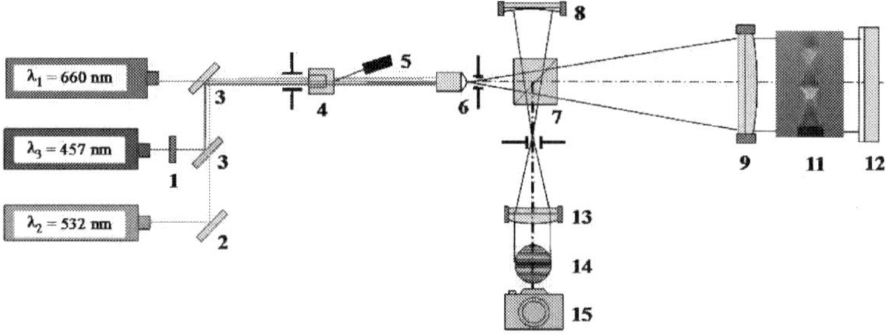

Figure 3. Michelson digital holographic interferometer.

Michelson digital holographic interferometer has been implemented around the ONERA wind tunnel and two optical tables isolate the optical set-up from external vibrations. **Figure 4** shows the generation of micro-fringes used as spatial carrier frequencies.

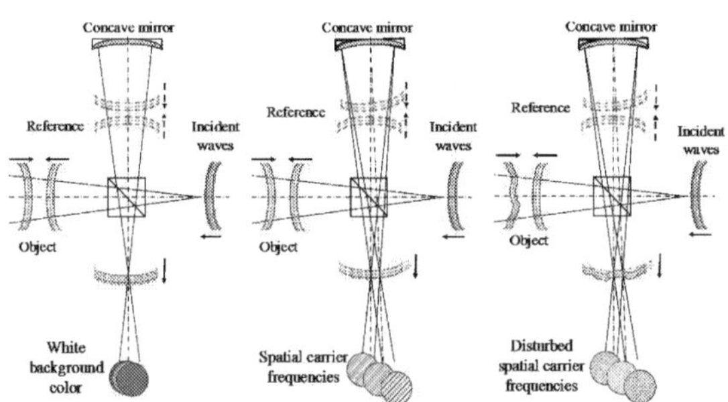

Figure 4. Micro-fringes formation by the transparent object.

When the focal points of the reference and object waves are superimposed in the diaphragm which is placed in front of the lens (13), see **Figure 3**, a uniform background colour is observed on the screen for each colour. The combination of three background colour (R, G and B) produces a white colour on 3CCD camera. If the focusing point of the three reference waves is moved in the plane of the diaphragm, straight interference fringes are introduced into the field of visualization. This is achieved very simply by rotating the concave mirror (8). Without flow, these micro-fringes are recorded on the 3CCD to calculate the three reference phase maps. Then, the wind tunnel is running and the three object waves are distorted by the aerodynamic phenomenon. Micro-fringe interferences are again recorded to enable calculation of the phase maps related to the object. For maps of phase difference, the reference phase is subtracted from the phase object. This optical technique was tested for analysing the supersonic flow of a small vertical jet, 5.56 mm in inner diameter at different pressures of injection. The location of the vertical jet in the middle of the test section is shown in **Figure 3**. The exposure time (10 ms) is given by the acousto-optical cell noted (4) in **Figure 3**. The fringe space introduced in the field is much narrowed, about four or five pixels between two successive fringes, in order to generate three high spatial carrier frequencies. With this configuration, the sensitivity is increased. Each interferogram is processed with 2D fast Fourier transform and **Figure 5** shows the spectra computed for the reference and measurement for each colour plane. One can see that the generated spatial frequencies are respectively equal to 40.5, 30.9 and 28.4 lines per millimetre for the blue, green and red lines. Then, a filtering window is selected to cover the useful signal of the +1 order localized in the spectrum and an inverse 2D FFT is applied to reconstruct the amplitude and the phase of the signal.

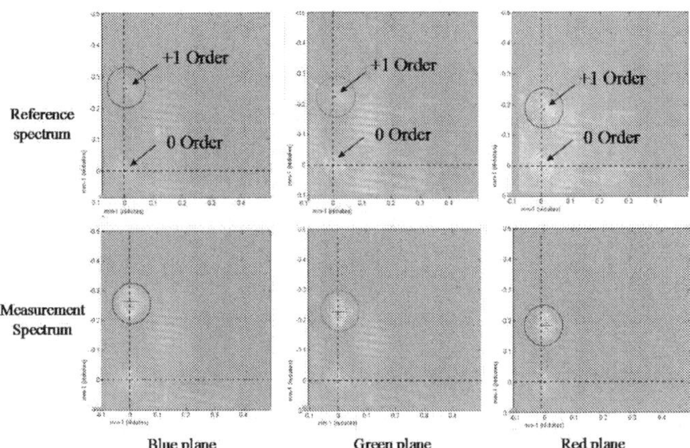

Figure 5. 2D spectra computed from the reference and the measurement interferograms.

First, the phase maps are calculated from the three reference and three measurement spectra so that the modulo 2π phase difference maps shown in **Figure 6**. One can see that the structures of shocks and decompression appear in the jet. As the difference phase maps are computed modulo 2π, a phase unwrapping has to be conducted and the results given the unwrapped phase maps are also presented in **Figure 6**. At a pressure of 3 bar, we can note a phase variation of 12 rad.

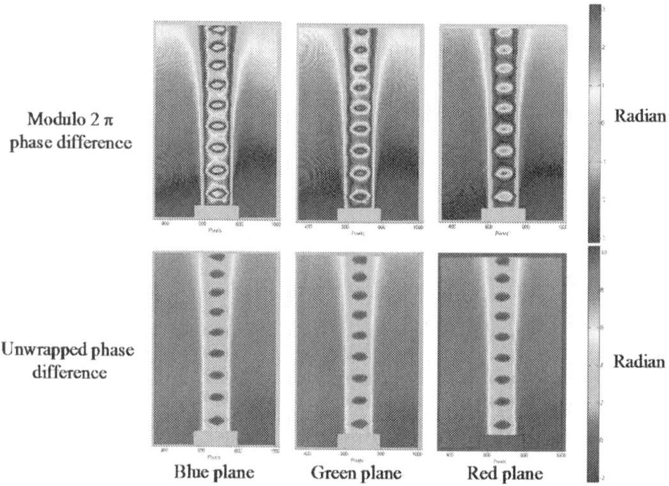

Figure 6. Maps of RGB phase difference (modulo 2π and unwrapped), P = 3 bar.

Finally, the maps of light intensity and optical thickness difference are calculated from the phase difference maps. They are presented in **Figure 7** for pressures ranging from 2 to 5 bar.

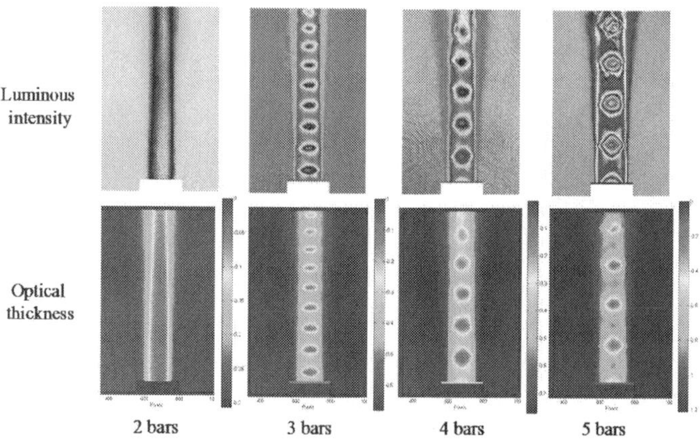

Figure 7. Evolution of the luminous intensity and the optical thickness with the pressure.

Concerning the maps of the luminous intensity, they are corresponding to figures which will be obtained if a technique of image holographic interferometry using panchromatic plates has been used. Knowing the wavelength and the phase, the maps of optical thickness can be deduced. They are also presented in **Figure 7** from 2 to 5 bar. At 2 bar and in the middle of shock structures, the optical thickness varies up to 0.2 µm and at 5 bar, it varies up to 1µm.

3.2. Three-wavelength holographic interferometry using Wollaston prisms

This part proposes an optical set-up based on digital holographic interferometry using two widely shifting Wollaston prisms and a single crossing of the phenomenon. Each Wollaston prism is located at the focal point of 'Z' astigmatic optical set-up. The second Wollaston is located in front of the camera and between the two sagittal and transverse focal lines so that a rotation around the optical axis generates interference micro-fringes which are used as spatial carrier frequency.

3.2.1. Definition of Wollaston prism characteristics

Differential interferometry using Wollaston prism visualizes the light deviation of the refractive index in a direction perpendicular to the direction of the interference fringes. Indeed, in the case of quartz prism having a very weak pasting angle, the gradient of the refractive index is measured because the birefringence angle is very weak and the distance between the two interfering beams is of the order of a few tenths of a millimetre or a few millimetres in the test section. Data integration is necessary to obtain the absolute refractive index. To avoid this integration, it was decided to manufacture two Wollaston prisms having a very high birefringence angle so that the distance between the two interfering beams is greater than the dimension of the measuring field (jet size). The interference measurement will be made between a beam which does not pass through the phenomenon (reference beam) and one which crosses the phenomenon under analysis. If $(n_e - n_o)$ is the crystal birefringence and α, the pasting angle of prisms, the birefringence angle ϵ can be expressed using the following equation:

$$\varepsilon = \varepsilon(\lambda) = 2(n_e - n_o)\tan(\alpha) \tag{1}$$

If a very high birefringence angle is sought, the pasting angle and the crystal birefringence have to be as high as possible. To remember, the Δn birefringence values for quartz and calcite are, respectively, equal to +0.009 and −0.172. It can be seen that calcite birefringence is basically twenty times greater than quartz birefringence.

If R is the radius curvature of the spherical mirror used in the optical set-up, the shift dx between the two interfering beams can be written as:

$$dx = \varepsilon R = 2R(n_e - n_o)\tan(\alpha) \tag{2}$$

Thus, for a spherical mirror of 400 mm in diameter and 4 m in the radius of curvature, dx has to be near to 200 mm. By choosing calcite crystal, the pasting angle can be found from the following relationship:

$$\alpha = \arctan\left(\frac{dx}{2R\Delta n}\right) = \arctan\left(\frac{0.2}{8x0.172}\right) = 8.27° \tag{3}$$

Calcite Wollaston prisms with 8° pasting angle have been manufactured.

3.2.2. Optical set-up with single crossing of the test section

Figure 8 shows the principle of Z optical set-up using Wollaston prisms. Here also, three different DPSS lasers (red, green and blue) constitute the luminous light source and the optical set-up uses two spherical mirrors, 250 mm in diameter and 2.5 m in radius of curvature.

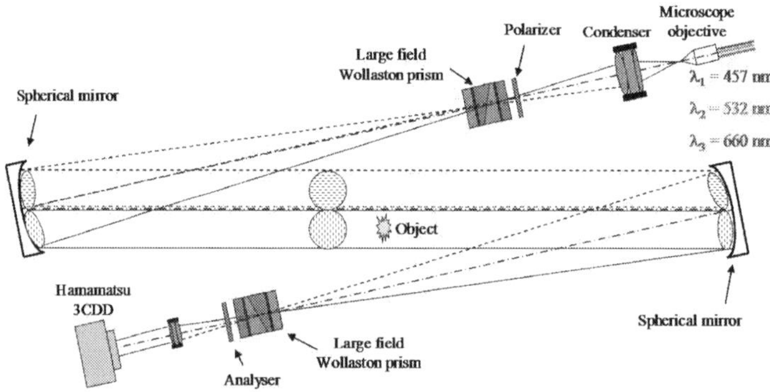

Figure 8. Digital holographic interferometer using very large Wollaston prisms in 'Z' set-up.

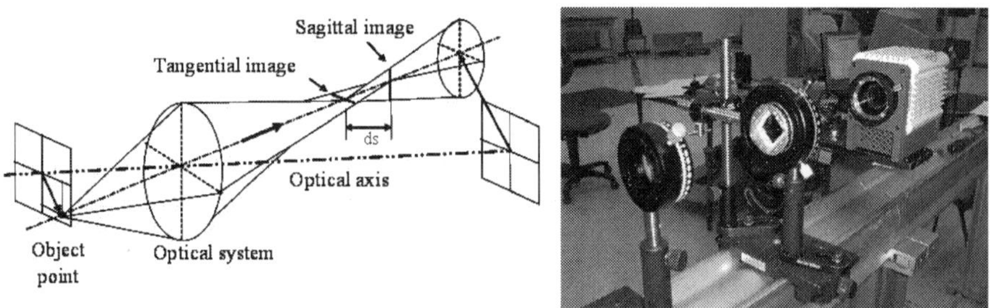

Figure 9. Astigmatism represented by sectional views and Wollaston prism in the front of the camera.

As all optical pieces are not exactly on the optical axis of spherical mirrors, we can observe astigmatism in the optical arrangement. The first prism located at the focal length of the first spherical mirror produces two optical rays which are returned by parallel light beams onto the second spherical mirror. This one refocuses the light beam into the second Wollaston prism which is mounted 'tumble' with the first one. An analyser located behind the second prism allows visualizing the interference fringes in colour. The image of the object under analysis is formed by a field lens placed in front of the 3CCD sensor. Here, the advantage of astigmatic set-up is used because the focusing point in the front of the camera is not unique. **Figure 9** shows this particularity: the optical beams are focused on the two focal images successively separated by a few millimetres. The first one gives the tangential image encountered when the beam focuses in the horizontal plane, and the second one, called the sagittal image, is obtained when the beam focuses in the vertical plane.

Figure 10 shows, on the reception side, the different figures of interference observed when the second Wollaston prism is moved along the optical axis from the tangential image (TI) towards the sagittal image (SI). The interference fringes which were horizontal and much narrowed, spread. When the interference fringes spread again, we can observe a rotation of 90° by them to give a quasi-uniform vertical background colour, at half distance between the tangential and sagittal images. Then, they continue to rotate by 90° up to the sagittal image and they narrow to become horizontal. Interference fringes stay horizontal above the sagittal image and narrow more and more. Knowing this property, we can adjust the spatial carrier frequency by the axial displacement of the prism for its amplitude and by rotating the prism for its orientation. In our tests, the Wollaston prism is located at half distance between the tangential and sagittal images, so that the interference fringes are generated in the same direction as the direction of the two interfering beams (vertical shift and vertical fringes). Gontier et al. [13] has widely described this feature. If the number of fringes in the visualized field has to be increased, the Wollaston prism has to be turned on itself in the plane perpendicular to the optical axis. **Figure 10** shows two positions of rotation of the Wollaston prism (20 and 45°) with a maximum number of fringes obtained for the rotation of 45°.

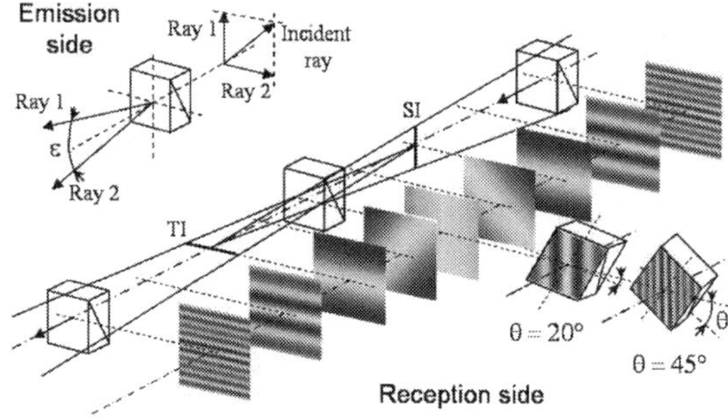

Figure 10. Evolution of interference fringes when the second Wollaston is moved from the sagittal image to the tangential image.

3.2.3. Results obtained

First, **Figure 11** shows the interferograms for the reference and the measurement with an enlarged view near the injection. For a pressure of 4 bar, for instance, one can see the horizontal interference fringes disturbed by the flow. The interferograms of **Figure 10** also show that the field is reduced on the right and left sides: this is the result of the rotation of the Wollaston prism at return which has a limited size (15 mm²). The polarization fields which were completely separated on the way interfere with each other as the prism placed in front of the camera is rotated. It is also noteworthy that the polarizer is rotated exactly to the same amount as the Wollaston prism. The tightening of the fringes is maximal when the prism is rotated by 45°.

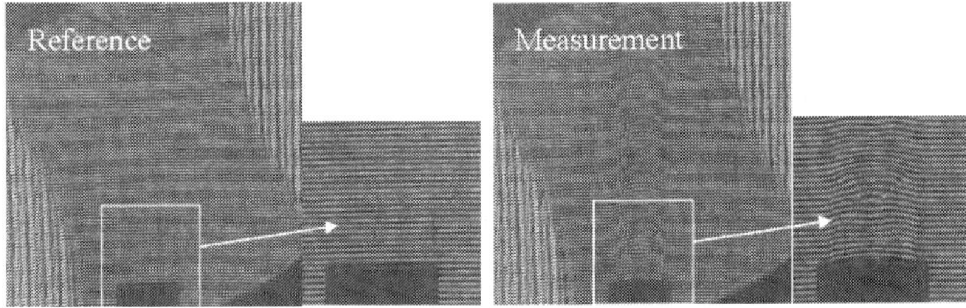

Figure 11. Interference micro-fringes recorded for the reference and the measurement, $P = 4$ bar.

Then, 2D fast Fourier transform is applied to filter the zero and -1 orders on the three channels for the reference and the measurement interferograms. In **Figure 12**, one sees that the different window filtering size can be taken on the three channels and that the reduced frequencies are equal to 0.12, 0.10 and 0.9 mm⁻¹ for the blue, green and red channels that correspond to resolution of 18.6 lines/mm, 15.5 lines/mm and 13.9 lines/mm. The spatial resolution used is lower than that used in the technique of Michelson interferometry.

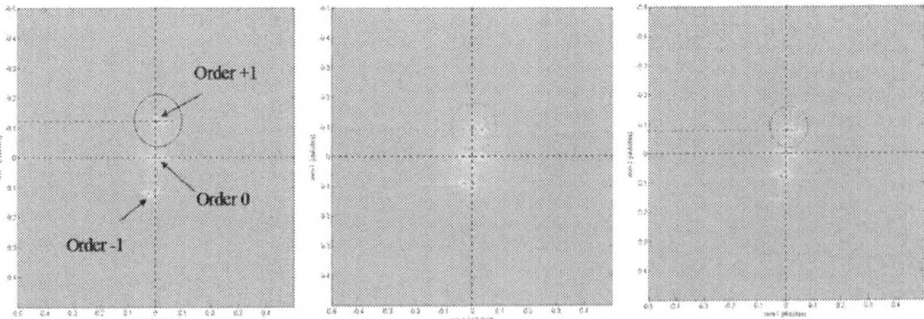

Figure 12. 2D spectra computed on the three channels for the reference interferogram, $P = 4$ bar.

Figure 13 shows the spectrum of the measurement for P = 3 bar, the modulo 2π phase map, the superimposition of the three red, green and blue luminous intensities deduced from the phase difference maps and also the optical thickness map computed from the phase difference map. These maps are concerning the red channel. Moreover, a deconvolution of the optical thickness maps based on the assumption that the jet is axisymmetric has been applied. Thus, it is possible to obtain the radial distribution of the refractive index and the density in the jet according to the relation proposed by Gladstone-Dale. This method is widely described by Rodriguez et al. [14]. In the treatment process, the optical thickness of maps calculated for each jet pressure is split into two parts, on either side of the axis of symmetry of the jet. If the results found by both sides of the jet are identical to the symmetry axis, the assumption of the axial jet symmetry is verified and the results can be considered correct. In **Figure 12**, the radial gas density is presented at 3 bar, and the density values found on the axis are very close, the analysis being done on the right or on the left.

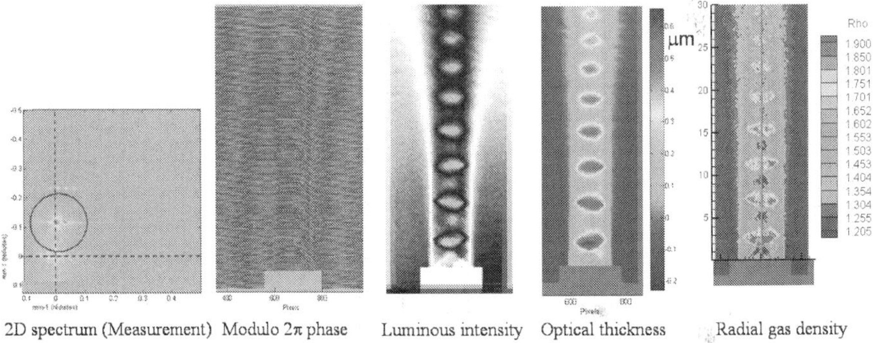

2D spectrum (Measurement)   Modulo 2π phase   Luminous intensity   Optical thickness   Radial gas density

Figure 13. Analysis of the case for red channel P = 3 bar (from spectrum to gas density).

3.3. Digital holography without reference wave

Digital holography without reference wave allows quantitative phase imaging by using a high-resolution holographic grating for generating a four-wave shearing interferogram. The high-resolution holographic grating is designed in a 'kite' configuration so as to avoid parasitic mixing of diffraction orders. The selection of six diffraction orders in the Fourier spectrum of the interferogram allows reconstructing phase gradients along specific directions. The spectral analysis yields the useful parameters of the reconstruction process. The derivative axes are exactly determined whatever the experimental configurations of the holographic grating. The integration of the derivative yields the phase and the optical thickness [12].

3.3.1. Base of digital holography without reference

Figure 14 shows the principle of the hologram recording of pure phase modulation where an incident plane crosses the phenomenon under analysis. This wave, disturbed by the phenomenon, is simultaneously diffracted in several directions by a diffraction grating operating in reflection. The different images diffracted by the grating interfere with each other at a δz distance of the diffraction plane.

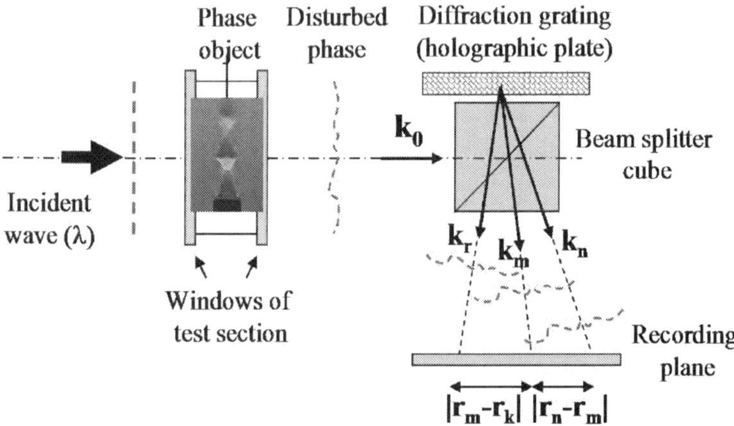

Figure 14. Principle of self-referenced digital holography by reflection.

The sensor therefore records a digital hologram produced by the coherent superimposition of all the diffraction orders. Let $A(r')$ the complex object wave front in the object plane, and $O(r) = A_o(r)\exp(i\varphi_o(r)(i = \sqrt{-1})$ the wave front diffracted from the object plane to the recording plane (**r** is the vector of the Cartesian coordinates $\{x, y\}$ in the plane perpendicular to the z direction). The reflection of the incident wave on the holographic grating produces a set of replicated waves, whose propagation direction is given by their wave vector $k_n = 2\pi/\lambda e_n$ (e_n is the unit vector of the propagation direction). The amplitude of the diffracted wave front at the recording plane is expressed as:

$$O(r, k_n) = A_o(r - r_n)\exp(ik_n r + i\varphi_o(r - r_n))$$

(4)

In Eq. (4), r_n is the spatial shift produced by propagation along distance δz from the holographic plane and in the direction of unit vector e_n. Due to the holographic grating, $P = 4$ wave fronts (n varying from 1 to $P = 4$) are diffracted in different directions. The interferogram recorded in the sensor plane is written as:

$$H(r) = \sum_{n=1}^{n=P} A_o^2(r - r_n) + 2\Re\left\{\sum_{n=1}^{P-1}\sum_{m=n+1}^{P} O(r, k_n)O^*(r, k_m)\right\}$$

(5)

In Eq. (5), the first term is related to the zero order, and the last one is related to coherent cross-mixing between the P diffracted orders. The last term includes the useful data related to the phase at the object plane. Noting $\Delta\varphi_{nm}$ the phase of cross-mixing $O(r, k_n)O^*(r, k_m)$, we get:

$$\Delta\varphi_{nm}(r) = (k_n - k_m)r + \varphi_0 - r - r_n) - \varphi_0(r - r_m) \tag{6}$$

Eq. (6) can be simplified by considering spatial derivatives of the object phase according to:

$$\Delta\varphi_{nm}(r) \cong (k_n - k_m)r + |s_{nm}| \frac{\partial\varphi_0(r)}{\partial re_{nm}} \tag{7}$$

In Eq. (7), e_{nm} is the unit vector of vector $s_{nm} = r_n - r_m$ and $(k_n - k_m)r$ is the spatial carrier phase modulation. In the Fourier plane of the interferogram, the diffraction orders are separated from the zero-order diffraction and localized by the spatial frequency vector $(k_n - k_m)/2\pi$. Since they are localized at different spatial frequencies in the Fourier domain, they can be filtered in the same way as for off-axis interferometry. Then, the spatial carrier frequency is removed. Note that spatial derivatives of the object phase are provided along an axis given by the scalar product re_{nm}. The scaling of each spatial derivative is related to $|s_{nm}|$. Thus, it appears that the method provides spatial derivatives with different sensitivities, which depend on the geometric configuration of the diffraction orders. After extracting each useful order, the term $|s_{nm}|\partial\varphi_0/\partial re_{nm}$ is extracted from the argument of the inverse Fourier transform of the filtered interferogram spectrum. We note $\partial\varphi_0/\partial re_{nm} = \partial\varphi_0/\partial x_q$, $|s_{nm}| = \alpha_q$ and $D_q = (1/\alpha_q)|s_{nm}|\partial\varphi_0/\partial re_{nm}$, with q varying from 1 to Q, Q being the number of really independent axis re_{nm} amongst the set of the useful orders included in the spectrum. So, the spatial variable x_q is simply the direction of the axis along which the derivative operator operates. In the spatial frequency domain, this axis has a corresponding axis which will be referred as u_q. Note that, from a computational point of view, x_q and u_q are 2D vectors. In case that D_q exceeds 2π, phase jumps occur and phase unwrapping is required. The scaling coefficient α_q depends on the distance δz and on the couple of involved wave vectors (k_n, k_m). Then, the spatial integration of terms D_q has to be carried out to get the quantity ψ. The wave-front reconstruction problem has already been discussed by many authors and the methods are based on least-square estimations or modal estimations. Note that in these works the wave front differences are defined at each point according to the sensor sampling geometry. In the modal approach, the wave front and its differences are expanded in a set of functions and the optimal expansion coefficients are determined (for example, using Zernike and Legendre polynomials). Here, the numerical method is based on the weighted least square criterion and according to Refs. [15, 16], quantity ψ can be recovered.

3.3.2. Design of diffraction grating

First, a holographic grating is recorded with the optical set-up shown in **Figure 15**. The holographic plates are single-layer silver-halide holographic plates from Gentet (http://www.ultimate-holography.com/). The spatial resolution reaches 7000 lines per mm and the holographic plate has been preferred to the photopolymer which has lower spatial resolution (1000–2000 lines per mm).

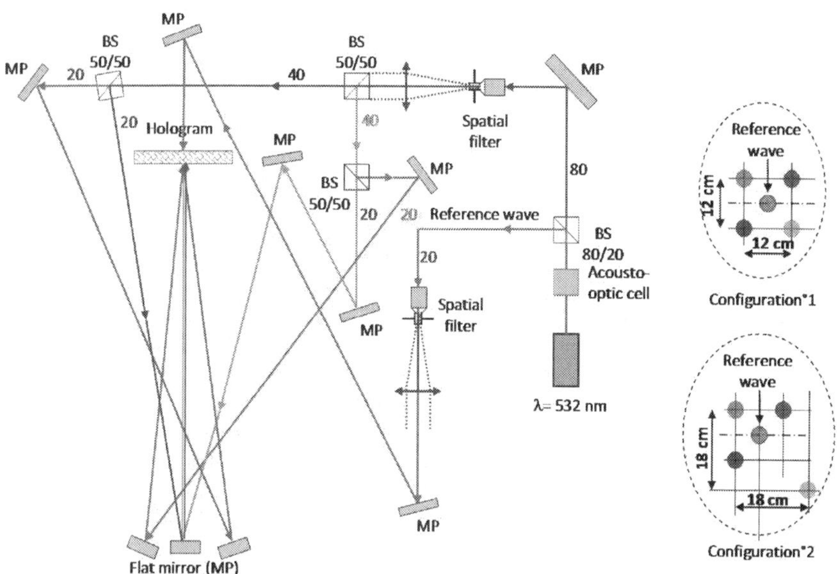

Figure 15. Optical set-up defined for recording of reflection holographic grating.

A first beam splitter cube (80/20) forms a reference beam (blue beam) with 20% of the incident light and 80% of the light is used to form the four-object beams. Plane waves are obtained with two lenses and two spatial filters. Object waves are generated by three-beam splitter cubes (50/50) so that the luminous intensities of each beam (reference and object) are all equal to 20% of the initial laser power. After several reflections on flat mirrors (MP), four small mirrors located around a square (configuration no. 1) and around a kite (configuration no. 2) returns each object beams towards the holographic plate. As the reference wave and the four object waves are incoming on each side of the hologram, the hologram is recorded by reflection and the angle θ formed by the reference and the object waves are equal to 27 mrad for configuration no. 1. After four sequential exposures, one for each object wave, the holographic plate is developed and bleached. Then, the grating is inserted in the optical set-up which is used for analysing the small supersonic jet from a nozzle. **Figure 16** shows the optical set-up with a single crossing of the phenomenon at the distance δz between the sensor and the image of the high-resolution holographic grating (HRHG).

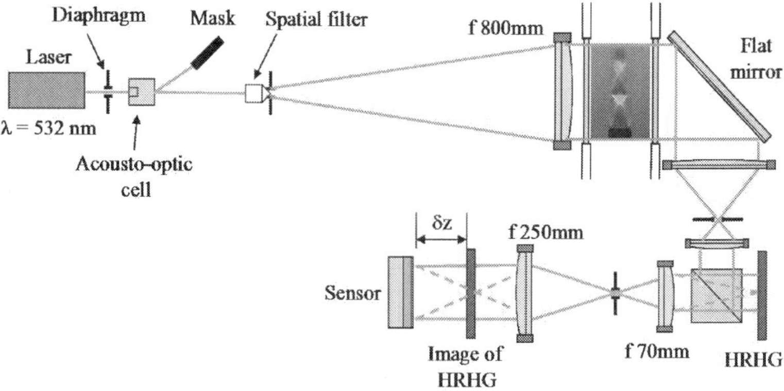

Figure 16. Digital holographic interferometer without reference.

An interferogram without flow and another with flow are directly recorded on the sensor (2000 × 1500 pixels, 365 mm²), then analysed in delayed time by 2D fast Fourier transform in order to localize the different interference orders. For configuration no. 1, **Figure 17** shows the location of four mirrors used at the recording (square). Order 1 results of interaction of the beams incoming from M1 and M2 mirrors and the order 1' between M3 and M4. Similarly, order 2 is generated by the interference between the waves incoming from M1 and M3 mirrors and order 2' those issuing from M2 and M4. Order 3 is only produced by the interference between M1 and M4 and order 4 between M2 and M3. For configuration no. 1, order 1 or 2 has been enlarged in order to show that order 1 and 1' or 2 and 2' are not quite superimposed.

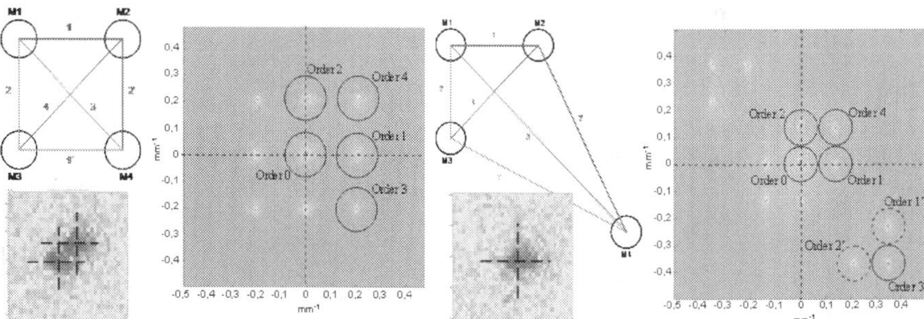

Figure 17. Position of four mirrors (square and kite) at the recording, localization of different diffraction orders in 2D FFT plane and zoom of +1 order.

In fact, one obtains two spectral signatures slightly shifted. It is not possible to separate them by filtering and to reconstruct the phase derivative map induced by only order 1. For this reason, the four mirrors have been set at the four tops of a kite configuration (no. 2). The problem encountered with configuration no. 1 does not exist and 2D FFT shows that it is very easy to localize all the different diffraction orders (on right in **Figure 17**). There is no spectral overlap and all orders useful for the reconstruction are well separated. Each order of interference is then selected successively and separately with a circular mask (0.05 mm^{-1} radius). Then, the phase gradient of reference image is calculated for each order of interference (**Figure 18**). Subtracting the reference image to the measurement image gives a modulo 2π map of phase gradient difference caused by the flow. Then, difference phase maps have to be unwrapped and results are presented in **Figure 18** for the six diffracted orders and for a value of the generating pressure equal to 5 bar. Finally, knowing the phase gradient difference in the six directions, a reconstruction of the absolute phase map is possible. For this processing of integration calculation, one can use one of integration methods proposed in the literature, for instance that proposed by Frankot and Chellappa [15]. The modulus of complex amplitude and the optical phase of the diffracted field by the object can be combined for obtaining the complex wave diffracted in the sensor plane.

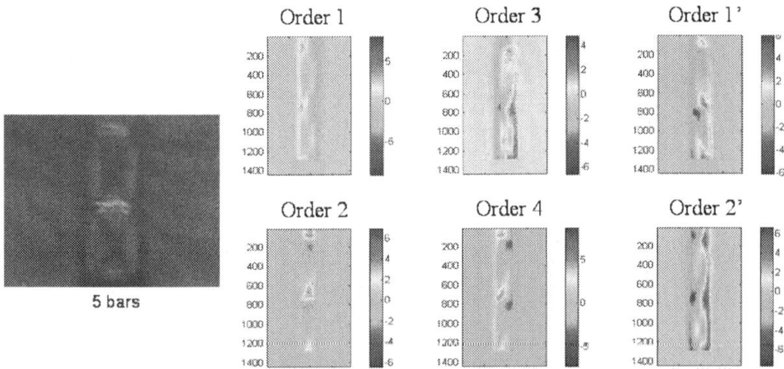

Figure 18. Recorded interferogram and gradient phase maps obtained for the six interference orders.

3.4. Comparisons with digital holographic interferometry using a reference wave

Figure 19 shows results obtained with digital holographic interferometry without reference and two other results obtained with digital holographic interferometry using a reference wave. The comparison is made by taking into account the difference of optical thickness.

The scale level is basically the same for the three results (from 0 up to 1.2 μm), and **Figure 19** shows at 5 bar that they are in good agreement because spatial locations of the structures of compression and expansion waves are similarly positioned in the three measurements. From a point of view of easiness and accuracy of results, the optical set-up without reference is complicated to implement and must achieve a kite-type reference hologram. It is also difficult to obtain a hologram with high diffraction efficiency. In addition, the data obtained must be integrated, which cause a certain imprecision in the measurement. For the optical set-up using Wollaston prisms, it is very bulky and costly because the Wollaston prisms of 'large field' type are expensive and difficult to manufacture. On the other hand, the measured values are absolute values as those obtained with Michelson interferometer that seems the least restrictive optical arrangement of the three set-ups tested.

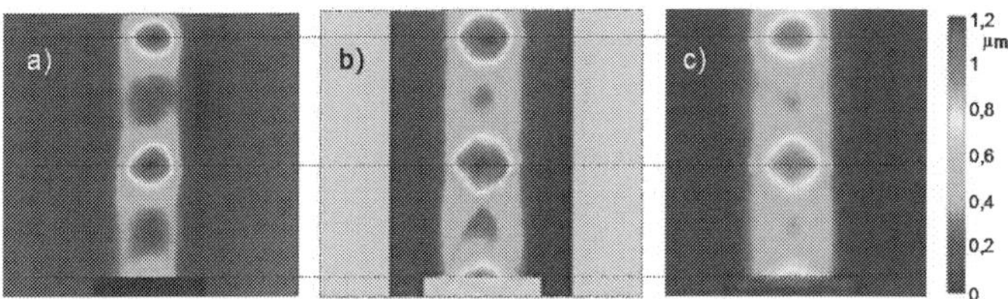

Figure 19. Comparison of experimental results obtained for three different interferometric techniques for a pressure at P=5 bar. (a) Without reference set-up, (b) Michelson set-up, (c) Wollaston set-up.

4. Digital holography for analysing unsteady wake flows

The unsteady wake flows generated in wind tunnel present a large scale of variations in refractive index from subsonic to supersonic domain. The feasibility of three-wavelength digital holographic interferometry has been shown on two-dimensional unsteady flows and the time evolution of the gas density field has been determined on the subsonic near wake flow downstream a circular cylinder [8]. But, when the flow regime reaches the transonic or supersonic domain, problems appear because refractive index gradients become very strong and a shadow effect superimposes to the micro-fringes of interferences. Moreover, the displacement of vortices is very high compared to the exposure time (300 ns given by the acousto-optical cell, **Figure 3**) what leads to blurred zones in interferograms and limits the interferograms analysis (**Figure 20**).

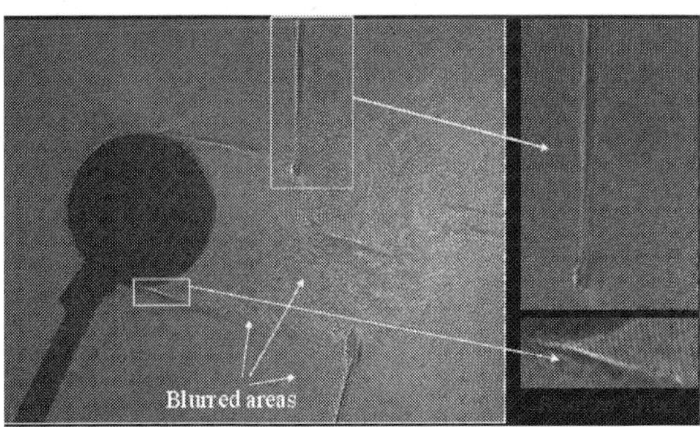

Figure 20. Highlighting of blurred areas and shadow effect—Mach 0.73.

4.1. Michelson holographic interferometry

At first, an ORCA Flash 2.8 camera from Hamamatsu with a matrix of 1920 × 1440 pixels, 3.65 μm^2, has been bought to increase the spatial resolution and, for the temporal resolution, the continuous laser light source of the interferometer has been replaced by a Quanta-Ray pulsed laser, Model Lab 170-10 Hz from Spectra-Physics. This laser is injected through a 1064 nm laser diode and outputs a wavelength at 1064 nm having 3 m in coherence length (TEM00 mode). Here, the first harmonic is used (532 nm) and delivers about 400 mJ in 8 ns. The beam diameter is about 8–9 mm. **Figure 21** shows how the laser was installed in Michelson interferometer presented in **Figure 3**. The output beam is equipped with two sets 'λ/2-polarizing beam splitter cube' to significantly reduce the laser energy sent to the camera. It is seen in **Figure 21** that the beam splitter cube forms the reference wave which is reflected by the concave mirror on the camera and the measurement wave which passes through the test section. The second achromatic lens, 70 mm in focal length of 70 mm yields the magnification of the image on the CCD.

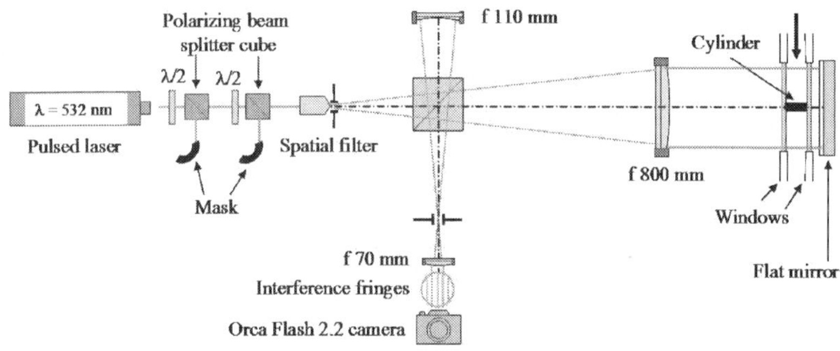

Figure 21. Digital Michelson holographic interferometer using a pulsed laser.

If L_1 is the distance between the beam splitter cube and the concave mirror, and L_2 the distance between the same beam splitter cube and the flat mirror located behind the test section, the laser coherence length must be greater than twice the difference $(L_2 - L_1)$ for the interference fringes may be formed on the CCD. This difference is here of the order of 2.5 m.

Figure 22 shows an interferogram of unsteady wake flow around a circular cylinder at Mach 0.73 with Michelson interferometer, the 2D FFT spectrum with the +1 order used to reconstruct the map of the modulo 2π phase difference. The interferogram exhibits a good quality indicating that vortex structures and small shock waves are well frozen. But, in the modulo 2π phase difference map shown on the right of **Figure 22**, phase jumps are still present. They are surrounded by black ellipses on the figure and they will cause phase shifts during the unwrapping of the modulo 2π phase map. To decrease the sensitivity of the measurement by a factor of 2, the optical bench has been modified to create a Mach-Zehnder type bench.

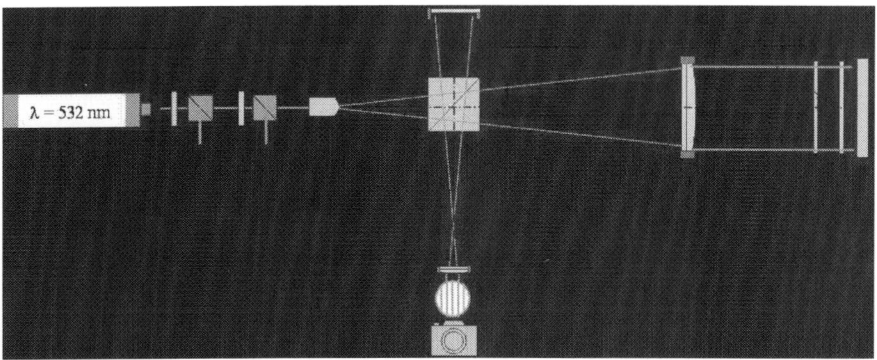

Figure 22. Interferogram analysis at Mach 0.73 — residual phase shifts.

4.2. Mach-Zehnder holographic interferometry

In Mach-Zehnder interferometer, shown in **Figure 23**, the measuring beam crosses only once the test section and the reference beam passes outside the test section so that the sensitivity is decreased by a factor 2.

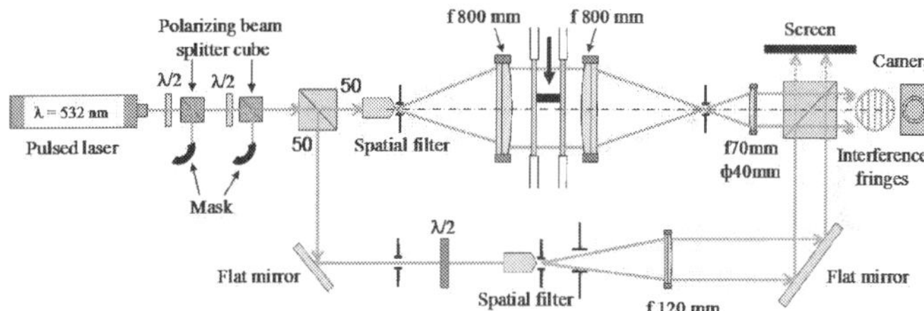

Figure 23. Digital Mach-Zehnder holographic interferometer using a pulsed laser.

In this optical set-up, the reference beam is reflected successively by several little flat mirrors. That produces a polarization rotation of the reference wave which must be corrected by inserting a $\lambda/2$ plate in front of the spatial filter of the reference wave. The contrast of the interference fringes can thus be optimized on the interferogram. The cylinder is equipped with an unsteady pressure transducer at a 90° azimuth to the flow axis in order to correlate the laser pulse with the signal of unsteady pressure. In this manner, one period of the phenomenon can be sampled by 20° step with several different tests. First, in the enlarged part of reference and measurement interferograms of **Figure 24**, one can see the straight interference micro-fringes distorted by the shear layer incoming from the upper of the cylinder. 2D FFT spectra show that the spatial carrier frequency (vertical fringes) is localized on horizontal axis (order +1 of hologram). After applying a spatial filter around the first order and subtracting the reference to the measurement phase map, one obtains the modulo 2π phase difference map where no phase shifts appear.

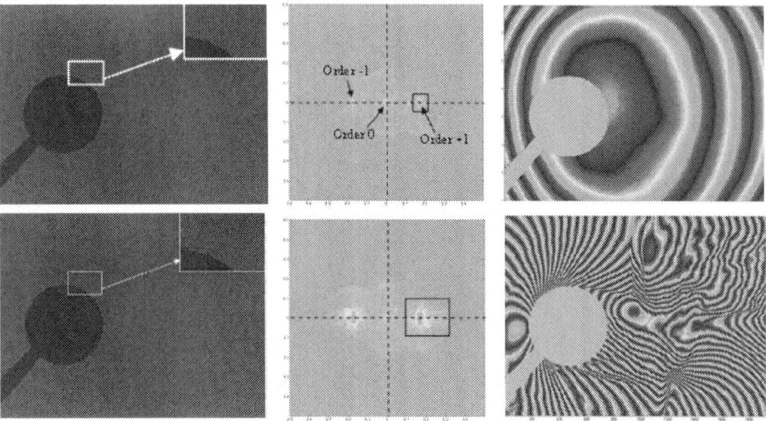

Figure 24. Interferograms analysis at Mach 0.73.

Then, an unwrapping has to be applied to obtain the phase difference map $\Delta\theta$ and the gas density field ρ/ρ_0 presented in **Figure 25** is deduced from the Gladstone-Dale relationship and Eq. (8) is obtained:

$$\frac{\rho}{\rho_0} = 1 - \left(\frac{\rho_s}{\rho_0} \frac{\lambda \Delta \phi}{2\pi e K} \right) \tag{8}$$

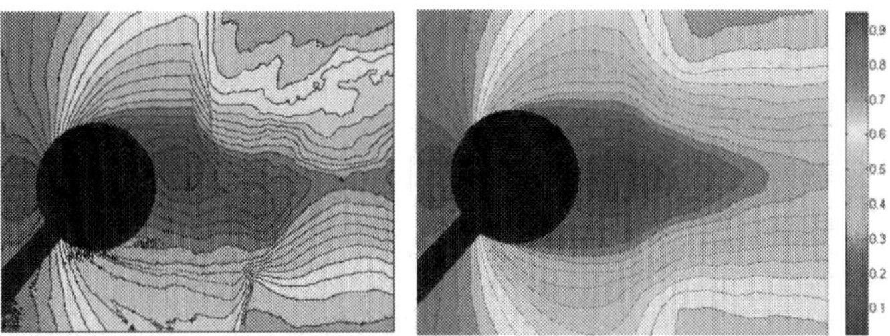

Figure 25. Instantaneous and averaged gas density fields (ρ/ρ_o) — Mach 0.73.

where ρ_s is the standard gas density computed at 1 atm and 0°C, ρ_0 the stagnation gas density, λ the wavelength of the interferometer, e the width of the test section and K the Gladstone-Dale constant: 296×10^{-6}.

The instantaneous interferogram of **Figure 25** shows that shock waves emitted by the vortices of the vortex shading are very well analysed (no phase shift) and the averaged gas density field exhibits a strong decreasing of the gas density just behind the cylinder up to 90% of ρ_0.

For information, the shadow effect can be easily reduced. If the beam of the reference arm is blocked (see **Figure 23**), the Mach-Zehnder interferometer looks like to shadowgraph optical set-up. In these conditions, the sensor can be adjusted along the optical axis to focus and image the middle of the test section on the sensor. As this condition is reached, the shadow effect is minimized.

5. Digital holography for visualizing inside strongly refracting transparent objects

High-density gradients can also exist inside strongly refracting objects and the visualization and the measurement of these phenomena remain an open problem. For example, objects as a glass ball, a light bulb, a glass container, a glass flask, etc. are not opaque but they are strongly refracting light and measuring inside is not straightforward. It follows that observing phenomena, such as refractive index variations, convection currents, or thermal gradients, occurring inside the object requires specific methods. Different experimental methods are usually used to investigate fluids and to visualize/measure dynamic flows [7, 8, 17]. Nevertheless, these approaches are appropriated when the envelope including the flow is relatively smooth and transparent (i.e. not strongly refracting). A suitable experimental method should be able to exhibit the phase changes inside the object without suffering from any image distortion. The experimental approach described here is based on stochastic digital holography to investigate flows inside a strongly refracting envelope [18]. It leads to the measurement of the phase change inside the object, so as to get a quantitative measurement. Experimental results are provided in the case of the visualization of refractive index variations inside a light bulb and a comparison with image transmission and reflection holography is also provided.

5.1. Proposed method

The approach adapted to visualize inside a strongly refracting object is described in **Figure 26**. The sensor includes $N \times M = 1920 \times 1440$ pixels with pitches $p_x = p_y = 3.65$ μm. The main feature is that a diffuser is used to illuminate the object to provide a back illumination. The set-up exhibits some similarity compared to a classical transmission microscope, although, no microscope objective is used and the illuminating wave is quite a speckled wave. A negative lens is put in front of the cube to virtually reduce the object imaged by this lens. This leads to a more compact system compared to the case where the lens is not used. For example, for an object size of 10–15 cm, the distance d_0 in **Figure 26** has to be greater than 2 m. The use of the negative lens produces a smaller image of the image, whose position is close to the sensor [19, 20]. Thus, the distance that has to be used in the algorithm is d'_0 (see **Figure 25**). The optimization of the off-axis the set-up has to follow the basic rules about the Shannon conditions [21].

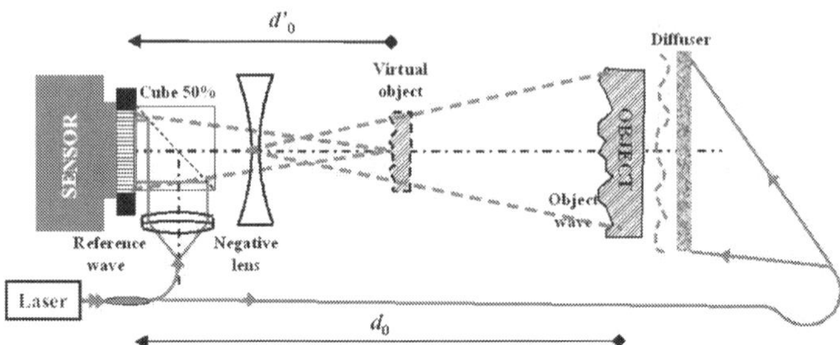

Figure 26. Stochastic digital holographic set-up.

In particular, the focal length of the lens has to be judiciously chosen. Especially, the criterion is the observation angle θ_{max} from the sensor, which has to fulfil this condition:

$$\theta_{max} = \frac{\lambda}{(4-2\alpha)\max(p_x,p_y)} \qquad (9)$$

where α is the accepted tolerance in the superposition of the useful +1 order and the 0 order. Here, the diffuser (considered here as a 'stochastic screen') is sized 10 cm × 20 cm and a superposition tolerance of $\alpha = 20\%$ is accepted. The evaluation of the focal length and distance leads to $d_0 = 800$ mm, $d'_0 = 100$ mm and $f = -150$ mm. Holograms can be reconstructed by the adjustable magnification method described in [22] or by the discrete Fresnel transform [19–21]. After reconstruction of the complex amplitude in the virtual object plane, an amplitude image and a phase image can be calculated. The amplitude image is related to the image of the object given by the lens, whereas the phase is useful to investigate refractive index variations, convection currents, or thermal gradients, occurring inside the object. For this, one has to evaluate the temporal phase difference at different instants. A quantitative measurement can be obtained after unwrapping the phase differences. Since the refractive index variations are encoded in the unwrapped phase, the use of the Gladstone-Dale relation allows determining density variations.

5.2. Proof of principle

The proposed method has been applied to the visualization and analysis of light bulb during its lighting. This bulb was submitted to a current to produce light and holograms were recorded at different instants after its lighting. **Figure 27** shows the recorded hologram when the bulb is off (a) and when the bulb is lighting (b). The speckle nature of the hologram is clearly observed. **Figure 27c** shows the amplitude image obtained with the discrete Fresnel transform. The stochastic screen and the ampoule can be clearly seen so that the strand of the bulb. **Figure 27d** and **e** shows respectively the modulo 2π digital fringes and unwrapped phase differences obtained between two instants (light off and light on). One can note a very large amplitude variation since the phase values are in the range 10–50 rad (see the colour bar in **Figure 27e**). This measurement includes the contribution due to the refractive index change in the bulb and also a contribution due to the dilatation of the envelope and its refractive index variation due to the temperate increase inside the lamp (≈ 500°C). The 'numerical fringes' observed in **Figure 27d** exhibits the refractive index variations integrated in the glass container.

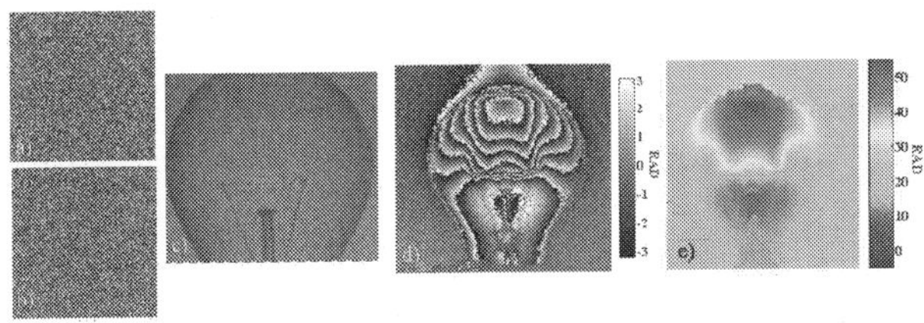

Figure 27. Quantitative measurement inside the bulb, (a) virtual phase extracted from numerical reconstruction (bulb off), (b) bulb lighting, (c) image amplitude of the strand, (d) modulo 2π phase computed from (a) and (b), (e) unwrapping of (d).

5.3. Comparison with silver-halide plate holographic interferometry

In order to check for the quality of the results obtained with the proposed method, the results obtained were compared with analogue image-holography [23]. The two possible set-ups are described in **Figure 28** and can be either transmission or reflection holographic interferometry. **Figure 28a** shows the transmission holography mode and **Figure 28b** that for reflection holography. Note that the set-ups require the use of photographic plates and that the diffuser is also used to get a stochastic screen to illuminate the object. The process is as follows: record a transmission or reflection hologram, apply the chemical treatment to the plate to develop and bleach, dry the plate, put the holographic plate in the set-up anew (exactly at the same location), at this step the holographic image of the ampoule is observable, adjust the camera lens to produce a focused image, then record real-time interferences between the initial bulb and that currently submitted to the current. Note that only the luminous intensity of interference fringes can be obtained, and not the phase image as it is the case for the digital holographic approach.

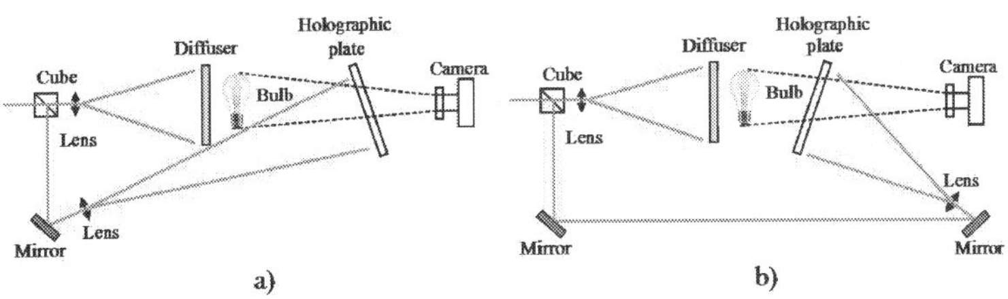

Figure 28. Image transmission holography (a) and image reflection holography (b).

Figure 29 shows a comparison between results obtained with digital holography and those obtained with image holography. **Figure 29a** shows the image obtained with the amplitude and phase change measured by digital holography, after calculating the intensity $I = A(1 + \cos(\Delta\varphi))$, where $\Delta\varphi$ is the phase change and A the amplitude image. **Figure 29b** shows the interference fringes obtained with the set-up of **Figures 28a** and **29c** shows those obtained with the set-up of **Figure 28b**. A very good agreement can be observed. Furthermore, the image quality given by each method can be appreciated. Image holography provides the best spatial resolution: the strand of the lamp can be clearly seen in **Figure 29b** and **c**. However, digital holography is more flexible since no chemical processing is required and a phase image can be obtained.

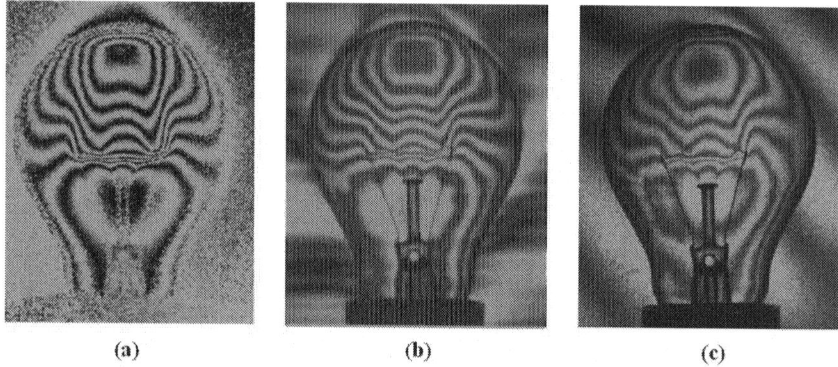

Figure 29. Comparison between intensity of fringes (a) fringes calculated with digital holography, (b) fringes obtained with transmission holography and (c) fringes obtained with reflection holography.

6. Conclusion

This chapter has shown several possibilities of digital holographic interferometry for analysing high-density gradients encountered in transonic and supersonic flows. Concerning the analysis of a small supersonic jet, a comparison is given between three different techniques, two techniques use reference waves: Michelson holographic interferometry and digital holography using Wollaston prisms; the last one uses a specific diffraction grating to obtain several different diffractions of measurement waves and to avoid having the reference wave.

For analysing transonic flows in wind tunnel, two types of interferometer have been developed. The first one is very simple to implement because it is a Michelson interferometer with double crossing of the test section for increasing the sensitivity and the second one is a Mach-Zehnder interferometer, more difficult to adjust, with a single crossing of the test section. These two interferometers are equipped with a pulsed laser and interferograms obtained have a very good quality and, basically, no phase shift.

Finally, a digital holographic method is proposed to visualize and measure refractive index variations, convection currents, or thermal gradients, occurring inside transparent but a strongly refracting object. The principle of this technique is provided through the visualization of refractive index variation inside a lighting ampoule. Comparisons with image transmission and reflection holographic interferometry demonstrate the high image and phase quality that can be extracted from the stochastic digital holographic set-up.

Currently, digital holographic interferometry is developed by ONERA for studying 3D flows from multi directional tomographic interferograms recorded in several directions. The aim is first to compare this method with other techniques yielding the gas density field as differential interferometry, back-oriented schlieren (BOS) and colour BOS; and secondly, to find the best compromise between the number of sight of view, the computation time and the results accuracy.

Acknowledgements

The authors thank the French National Agency for Research (ANR) for funding this work under grant agreement no. ANR-14-ASTR-0005-01.

Author details

Jean-Michel Desse* and François Olchewsky

*Address all correspondence to: Jean-Michel.Desse@onera.fr

ONERA, The French Aerospace Lab, Lille, France

References

[1] Katz J, Sheng J. Applications of holography in fluid mechanics and particle dynamics. Annu. Rev. Fluid Mech. 2010;42 p. 531–555.

[2] Atlan M, Gross M, Desbiolles P, Absil E, Tessier G, Coppey-Moisan M. Heterodyne holographic microscopy of gold particles. Opt. Lett. 2008;33(5) p. 500–502.

[3] Müller J, Kebbel V, Jüptner W. Characterization of spatial particle distributions in a spray-forming process using digital holography. Meas. Sci. Technol. 2004;15 p. 706–710.

[4] Sharma S, Sheoran G, Shakher C. Investigation of temperature and temperature profile in axi-symmetric flame of butane torch burner using digital holographic interferometry. Opt. Lasers Eng. 2012;50 p. 1436–1444.

[5]   Dolocek R, Psota P, Ledl V, Vit T, Vaclavik J, Kopecky V. General temperature field measurement by digital holography. Appl. Opt. 2013;52(1) p. A319–A325.

[6]   Demoli N, Vukicevic D, Torzynski M. Dynamic digital holographic interferometry with three wavelengths. Opt. Express. 2003;11(7) p. 767–774.

[7]   Desse JM, Picart P, Tankam P. Digital Three-color holographic interferometry for flow analysis. Opt. Express. 2008;16(8) p. 5471–5480.

[8]   Desse JM, Picart P, Tankam P. Digital three-color holographic interferometry applied to fluid and structural mechanics. Opt. Lasers Eng. 2012;50 p. 18–28.

[9]   Goodman JW, Lawrence RW. Digital image formation from electronically detected holograms. Appl. Phys. Lett. 1967;11 p. 77–79.

[10]   Picart P, Gross M, Marquet P. Basic fundamentals of digital holography. In: Picart P., editor. New Techniques in Digital Holography. ISTE Wiley, London; 2015 ISBN 978-1-84821-773-7.

[11]   Desse JM, Picart P. Quasi-common path three-wavelength holographic interferometer based on Wollaston prisms. Opt. Lasers Eng. 2015;68 p. 188–193.

[12]   Desse JM, Picart P, Olchewsky F. Quantitative phase imaging in flows with high resolution holographic diffraction grating. Opt. Express. 2015;23(18) p. 23726–23737.

[13]   Gontier G, Carr P, Henon G. On differential interferometric device to arbitrarily rotate the fringes compared to the direction of the beams shift. Compt. Rend. Acad. Sci. 1966; 262 p. 674–677.

[14]   Rodriguez O, Desse JM, Pruvost J. Interaction between a supersonic jet and a coaxial supersonic flow. Aerosp Sci Technol. 1997;11(6).

[15]   Frankot RT, Chellappa R. A method for enforcing integrability in shape from shading algorithms. IEEE Trans. Pattern Anal. Mach. Intell. 1988;10(4) p. 439–451.

[16]   Velghe S, Primot J, Guérineau N, Cohen M, Wattelier B. Wave-front reconstruction from multidirectional phase derivatives generated by multilateral shearing interferometers. Opt. Lett. 2005;30(3) p. 245–247.

[17]   Kakue T, Yonesaka R, Tahara T, Awatsuji Y, Nishio K, Ura S, Kubota T, Matoba O. High-speed phase imaging by parallel phase-shifting digital holography. Opt. Lett. 2011;36(21) p. 4131–4133.

[18]   Desse JM, Picart P. Stochastic digital holography for visualizing inside strongly refracting transparent objects. Appl. Opt. 2015;54(1) A1–A8.

[19]   Schnars U, Kreis TM, Jüptner WO. Digital recording and numerical reconstruction of holograms: reduction of the spatial frequency spectrum. Opt. Eng. 1996;35 p. 977–982.

[20]   Mundt J, Kreis T. Digital holographic recording and reconstruction of large scale objects for metrology and display. Opt. Eng. 2010;49 p. 125–801.

[21] Picart P, Leval J. General theoretical formulation of image formation in digital Fresnel holography. J Opt Soc Am A. 2008;25(7) p. 1744–1761.

[22] Li JC, Tankam P, Pen Z, Picart P. Digital holographic reconstruction of large objects using a convolution approach and adjustable magnification. Opt. Lett. 2009;34(5) p. 572–574.

[23] Desse JM, Tribillon JL. Real-time three-color reflection holographic interferometer. Appl. Opt. 2009;48(36) p. 6870–6877.

Chapter 14

Holography: The Usefulness of Digital Holographic Microscopy for Clinical Diagnostics

Zahra El-Schich, Sofia Kamlund, Birgit Janicke,
Kersti Alm and Anette Gjörloff Wingren

Additional information is available at the end of the chapter

http://dx.doi.org/10.5772/66042

Abstract

Digital holographic (DH) microscopy is a digital high-resolution holographic imaging technique with the capacity of quantification of cellular conditions without any staining or labeling of cells. The unique measurable parameters are the cell number, cell area, thickness, and volume, which can be coupled to proliferation, migration, cell cycle analysis, viability, and cell death. The technique is cell friendly, fast and simple to use and has unique imaging capabilities for time-lapse investigations on both the single cell and the cell-population levels. The interest for analyzing specifically cell volume changes with DH microscopy, resulting from cytotoxic treatments, drug response, or apoptosis events has recently increased in popularity. We and others have used DH microscopy showing that the technique has the sensitivity to distinguish between different cells and treatments. Recently, DH microscopy has been used for cellular diagnosis in the clinic, providing support for using the concept of DH, e.g., screening of malaria infection of red blood cells (RBC), cervix cancer screening, and sperm quality. Because of its quick and label-free sample handling, DH microscopy will be an important tool in the future for personalized medicine investigations, determining the optimal therapeutic concentration for both different cancer types and individual treatments.

Keywords: cell death, cell volume, digital holographic microscopy, individual treatment

1. Introduction

Digital holographic (DH) microscopy is a digital high-resolution holographic imaging technique with the capacity of quantification of cellular status without any staining or labeling of cells [1–3]. Various cellular parameters can be visualized and calculated from the particular hologram, including individual cell area, thickness, volume, and population confluence and cell counts [4–10]. One of the advantages of studying cells with DH microscopy is that they can be grown and analyzed in their normal growth medium during the entire study. The culture vessel will be placed on the microscope for imaging and then replaced in the 37°C incubator, or placed on a heating plate to retain 37°C, during the analysis. Since the first studies on living cells, DH microscopy has been used to study a wide range of different cell types, e.g., protozoa, bacteria, and plant cells, mammalian cells such as nerve cells, stem cells, various tumor cells, bacterial-cell interactions, red blood cells (RBC), and sperm cells [11–15].

2. Technique

DH microscopy is based on the interference between two, preferably coherent, beams that differ in phase (**Figure 1**). The beams usually originate from the same source, which are split before the sample. One of the beams, the reference beam, will remain undisturbed, while the other, the object beam, will be shifted in phase by the sample. The optical set-up can be either transmissive or reflective, providing no difference in the principle only in the configuration of the optical elements [16]. When the object beam has traveled through or been reflected by the object, the two beams merge. A light detector (e.g., a CCD-sensor) will capture the interference pattern and computer algorithms will convert the signal into a holographic image based on the light phase shifting properties of the cells, the refractive index [17]. The three-dimensional holographic image is then a representation of the real objects [18]. The technique is cell friendly, fast, and simple to use and has unique imaging capabilities for time-lapse investigations on

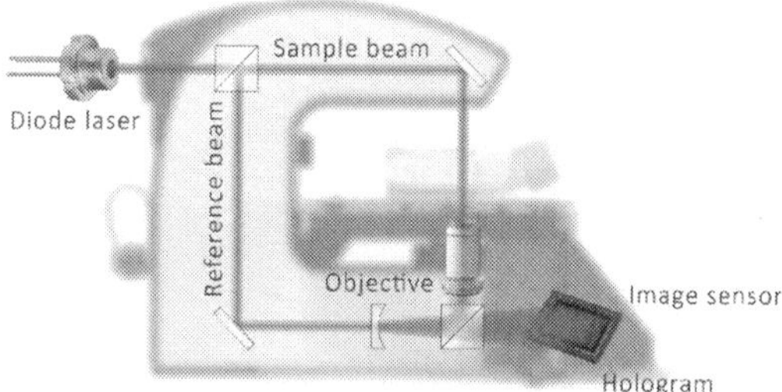

Figure 1. Schematic view of the DH microscopy technique. A digital holographic setup with a laser beam is split into two identical beams. The sample beam passes through the cells, while the reference beam travels undisturbed. The two beams merge and the image sensor will capture an interference image, which display a 3D-image after reconstruction (www.phiab.se).

both the single cell and the cell-population levels. The reconstructed image contains information about the entire depth of the field of view. For reconstruction to be accurate, the sample has to be transparent and homogenous, where the differences in refractive index between the background and the cells create the tomography of the image [19].

After recording, the hologram consists of the phase and the amplitude of the entire image field. Reconstruction of the image is dependent on the optical configuration, possibly to get rid of optical elements as zero order image and images of other diffraction order. Mathematical algorithms as Fourier transforms or Fresnel transform are usually performed on the wave front [20] .

3. Morphological changes connected to cellular events

3.1. Cell death of adherent cells

Cell volume changes, resulting from cytotoxic treatments or apoptosis events, have recently been investigated with DH microscopy [11, 21–25]. When cells go in to early apoptosis, the first discernible indication is an increase in the cell phase shift followed by a decrease as the cell eventually dies [21]. Pavillon et al. recognized early apoptotic cells within minutes by their DH phase signal, while it took several hours to identify dead cells using trypan blue staining [21].

We have previously demonstrated that death-induced cells can be distinguished from untreated cells by the use of DH microscopy [25]. Morphological analyses of the two adherent cell lines L929 and DU145, treated with the anti-tumor agent etoposide for 1–3 days, were performed in cell culture flasks. Etoposide causes errors in the DNA synthesis and promotes apoptosis of the cancer cell by forming a ternary complex with DNA and the enzyme topoisomerase II [26]. Measurements revealed significant differences in the average cell number, the confluence, cell volume, and cell area when comparing etoposide-treated cells with untreated cells. The cell volume of the treated cell lines was initially increased at early time points. By time, cells decreased in volume, especially when treated with high doses of etoposide [25]. Moreover, this analysis was confirmed by a MTS assay. With DH microscopy, small differences between the two cell lines were clarified. Mouse fibroblast L929 cells showed a lower sensitivity for etoposide at the lowest concentrations, while for the human prostate cancer cell line DU145, the confluence, cell area, and volume increased at first, and then decreased over time.

In another study, we selected two suspension cell lines, a diffuse large B-cell lymphoma (DLBCL) cell line, U2932 and the T-cell acute lymphoblastic leukemia cell line Jurkat. The cell lines were treated with dimethyl sulfoxide (DMSO), 100 µM etoposide or left untreated as a control, and were incubated for 24 h. Unpublished work by us shows that the average cell area and cell volume decreased significantly for the Jurkat cell line compared with control. For the U2932 cell line, the average cell area did not change, whereas the average cell volume significantly decreased after etoposide treatment (**Figure 2**). Interestingly, the results may indicate cell line sensitivity, which also has been shown in the earlier studies [25, 27]. In conclusion, cell death experiments performed with DH microscopy reveal that small differences between two cell lines can be clarified.

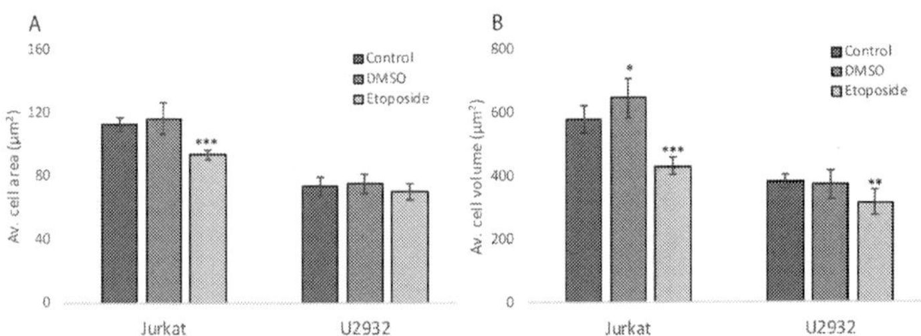

Figure 2. Etoposide induces a loss of cell area and volume in the cell lines Jurkat and U2932. Jurkat and U2932 cells were treated with etoposide (100 µM), or left untreated, for 24 h, and holograms were captured by the Holomonitor™ M4. The mean cell area (A) and the mean cell volume (B) were calculated using holographic microscopy images. Error bars are based on the total number of images.

Human α-lactalbumin made lethal to tumor cells (HAMLET) is based on a natural protein present in human breast milk [28]. HAMLET induces cell death in tumor cells and immature cells, but not in normal differentiated cells [29]. As monitored by DH, 15 min of incubation, with 35 µM of HAMLET, was enough for a reduction in cell area and increase in thickness, with evidence of membrane blebbing in human lung carcinoma A549 cells [26]. After 60 min, the cells became even smaller in area and thicker [30]. Puthia et al. examined how HAMLET affects β-catenin and Wnt-signaling in the treated human colon cancer cell line DLD1. Already after 30 min, the cell morphology changed with HAMLET treatment. A time-dependent decrease in cell area and an increase in maximum thickness was seen [31]. DH microscopy was also used to analyze the effect of the cell death-inducing curcumin analog C-150 [32]. Four different glioblastoma cell lines were treated with 1 µM of the analog for 24 h. The results showed significantly increased cell volume and average thickness and decreased cell area for the cell lines investigated.

DH microscopy has been applied for the analysis of chemokinetic responses, selective cytotoxic, adhesion, and migration modulator effects on two different melanoma cell lines, HT168-M1 and A2058, after treatment with di- and trihydroxyanthraquinones [33]. Alizarin and purpurin have been reported to have activity against cancer cells. Their results showed that no basic parameter was influenced by alizarin or purpurin as a cytotoxic or apoptotic substance in HT168-M1 cells. In the case of A2058 cells, alizarin could induce positive effects in the average cell area and volume as measured by DH.

3.2. Cell cycle of adherent cells

Our earlier results on etoposide, colcemid, or staurosporine treated cells showed changes in average cell volume [34]. Mouse fibroblasts were treated and analyzed with DH microscopy after 24 h of incubation. The results showed comparable accuracy to flow cytometry measurement of cell cycle distribution, where staurosporine induced G1 arrest and colcemid or etoposide induced G2/M arrest. The results with DH microscopy showed that the cells decreased in cell size in response to staurosporine treatment, while the cell size increased in response to colcemid or etoposide treatment. Etoposide was further used in a dose-dependent manner in order to investigate how well DH microscopy was able to record a change in the cell cycle profile, as compared to flow cytometry. Etoposide reduced average cell number, decreased average cell confluence, and increased average cell volume. Indeed, using immortalized murine fibroblast cells, this first proof-of-concept study suggests that DH microscopy is a possible alternative tool for analysis of cell cycle alterations [34]. In another study, treated SKOV3-TR cells were visualized for 24 h until cell cycle arrest and characterized by the presence of rounded cells that were unable to complete mitosis [35]. After 44 h, the cells had undergone apoptosis. Higher concentrations of treatment

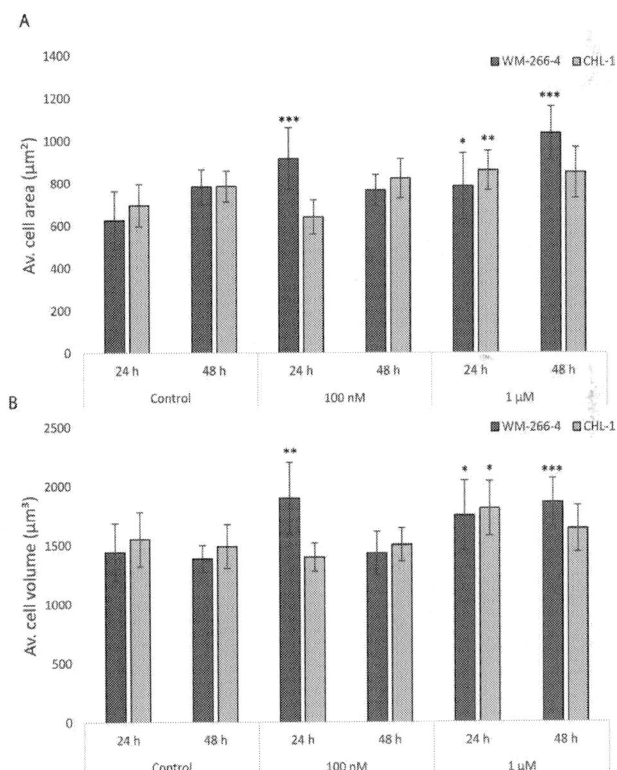

Figure 3. The drug PLX4032 influences cell area and volume differently in the human melanoma cell lines WM-266-4 and CHL-1. WM-266-4 and CHL-1 cells were treated with PLX4032 (100 nM and 1 μM), or left untreated, and holograms were captured by Holomonitor™ M4 after 24 and 48 h, respectively. The mean cell area (A) and the mean cell volume (B) were calculated using holographic microscopy images. Error bars are based on the total number of images.

showed early cell cycle arrest, and the cell population started to undergo apoptosis after 14 h. Indeed, by using time-lapse DH imaging, cell cycle arrest followed by progression to apoptosis was clearly visualized.

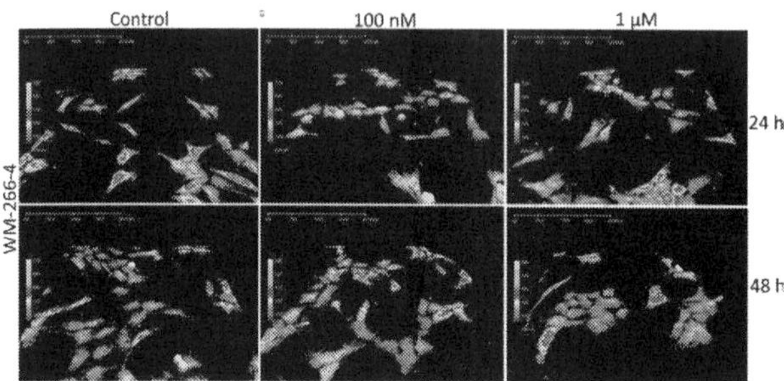

Figure 4. 3D-images of WM-266-4 cells. The human skin melanoma cell line WM-266-4 treated with PLX4032 (100 nM and 1 µM), or left untreated. Holograms of the cells were captured using holographic microscopy after 24 and 48 h, respectively. Hologram pictures show the morphology changes over time with the different concentrations of PLX4032.

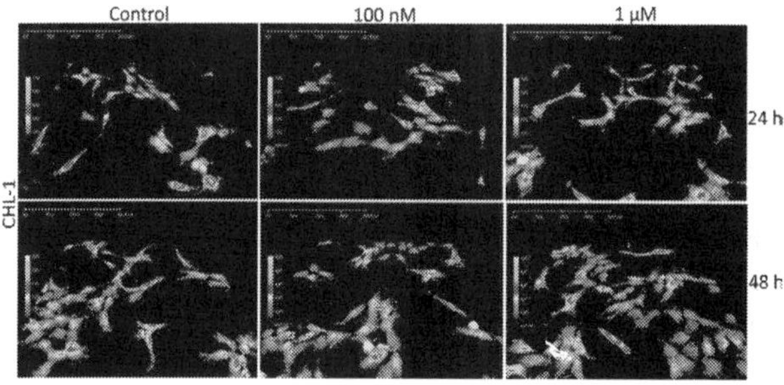

Figure 5. 3D-images of CHL-1 cells. 3D holograms showing the human skin melanoma cell line CHL-1 treated with PLX4032 (100 nM and 1 µM), or left untreated. Holograms of the cells were captured using holographic microscopy after 24 and 48 h, respectively. Hologram pictures show the morphology changes over time with the different concentrations of PLX4032.

We have treated two human melanoma cell lines, WM-266-4 and CHL-1, with different sensitivity for the drug PLX4032, also called vemurafenib [36]. PLX4032 induces cell cycle arrest in lower doses and apoptosis in higher doses in melanoma cells with a certain *BRAF* gene mutation. It has previously been shown that CHL-1 cells are not inhibited by the drug due to lack of this mutation. In our study, PLX4032 treatment increased the average cell area and cell volume for the WM-266-4 cell line compared with untreated control cells, while the CHL-1 cell line was less affected (**Figure 3**). Morphological cell changes are presented in 3D holograms for WM-266-4 cells (**Figure 4**) and CHL-1 cells (**Figure 5**). The cells become more flat, with increased area, after PLX4032 treatment. Indeed, with DH microscopy, even small differences between treated cells were clarified.

The effect of the novel anti-cancer drug ISA-2011B, etoposide, and docetaxel was monitored with DH microscopy in real-time for up to 48 h by Semenas et al. ISA-2011B treatment led to a reduction in cell size and changes in morphology, which was also achieved by docetaxel treatment [37].

3.3. Cell death of suspension cells on antibody-based microarray

We have introduced antibody-based microarrays [38] to the experimental DH microscopy set-up. By using single-chain variable antibody fragments (scFv) [39], directed against some of the most common cell membrane proteins on T- and B-lymphocytes, suspension cells can be analyzed with DH. Antibody-based microarray techniques have been used to determine phenotypic protein expression profiles for human B cell sub-populations [39] and to detect soluble antigens [40]. In our study [27], we combined DH microscopy and antibody-based microarray to introduce a powerful tool to measure morphological changes in specifically etoposide-treated antibody-captured cells, U2932, and Jurkat (**Figure 6**). We demonstrated that the cell number, mean area, thickness, and volume could be noninvasively measured by using DH microscopy. The cell number was stable over time, but the two cell lines used showed changes of cell area and cell irregularity after treatment. The cell volume in etoposide-treated cells was decreased, whereas untreated cells showed stable volume [27]. In conclusion, cell death of suspension cells investigated with the help of antibody-based microarrays and DH demonstrated that morphological parameters can be investigated of different cell lines and treatments.

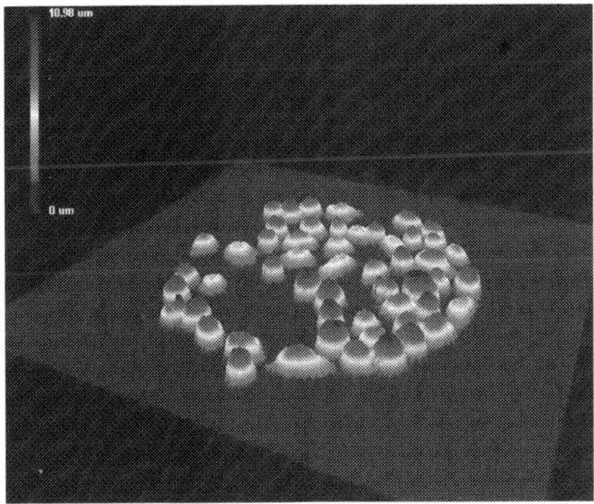

Figure 6. Jurkat cells on an antibody-based microarray captured with DH microscopy. A 200,000 Jurkat cells in 100 µl of phosphate-buffered saline (PBS)-0.5% bovine serum albumin were applied to an antibody array and incubated at room temperature for 30 min. The array was thereafter washed manually, until the cell binding areas were clearly visible. A 3D-image was thereafter captured with DH microscopy.

In conclusion, several independent studies now show the feasibility of DH microscopy to demonstrate cell-death induced morphological changes after compound addition.

4. Clinical applications

Lately, DH microscopy is being developed for clinical applications in widely different areas of medicine such as transmembrane water flux, cancer screening, sperm motility, blood cell analysis, and inflammation.

4.1. Transmembrane water flux

In some cases, current imaging techniques are not very well developed. One such example is the measurement of transmembrane water fluxes in epithelial cells directly linked to the activity of a protein involved in cystic fibrosis [41]. DH microscopy was used to quantify the transmembrane water fluxes in situ by determining the phase shift associated with activation of chloride channels. This opens up for the usage of DH microscopy to screen drugs acting on water transporter molecules.

4.2. Cancer screening

Recently, Benzerdjeb et al. reported a preliminary study with DH microscopy as a screening tool for cervical cancer. The study is based on materials from three randomly chosen laboratories, which was analyzed and subjected to DH microscopy. The sensitivity and specificity of DH microscopy was calculated for the detection of neoplasia. The results demonstrated for the first time that the DH microscopy technique is suitable for the processing of gynecologic cervical samples [42].

4.3. Sperm analysis

DH has been used to characterize sperm cells, supplying data for both morphology, motility, and the concentration of the sperm cells, without affecting the sperm reviewed in Ref. [43]. The morphology of the sperm head has often been correlated with the outcome of in vitro fertilization and has been shown to be the sole parameter in semen of value in predicting the success of intracytoplasmic sperm injection and intracytoplasmic morphologically selected sperm injection [44, 45]. Indeed, DH microscopy generates useful information on the dimensions and structure of human sperm, not revealed by conventional phase-contrast microscopy, in particular the volume of vacuoles. This suggests its use as an additional prognostic tool in assisted reproduction technology to better underline the differences between normal and abnormal sperm morphology.

4.4. Blood cell screening

The function of RBCs is strongly connected to their shape, related to different diseases [46]. Therefore, a robust classification method would be of great advantage when analyzing RBC for medical diagnosis and therapeutics. DH microscopy has allowed several investigators to determine vital erythrocyte parameters including morphology and cell counting [15, 47, 48]. Indeed, a DH microscopy-based automated RBC classification method could have the potential for use in drug testing and the diagnosis of RBC-related diseases. Malaria parasites induce morphological, biochemical, and mechanical changes in RBC. Main clinical diagnostics of malaria is based on microscopic inspection of blood smears, treated with reagents, which stains the malarial parasites. In developing countries, visual identification of malarial RBCs may become unreliable due to lack of sufficiently trained technicians and poor-quality microscopes and reagents. Anand et al. describe the use of quantitative DH microscopy for automatic identification of malaria-infected RBCs by comparing their shape profiles at different axial planes [49]. A correlation algorithm discriminates between the shapes of the cells and determines whether the cell is infected by malaria parasite. Shape comparison is fast and was found to yield fairly accurate discrimination. This technique is mostly advantageous for healthcare personnel working in developing countries. Similarly, other RBC infecting microbes can be investigated, such as *Babesia microti*, which is an obligate parasite in humans, hamster, and mouse. To find alternatives to methods requiring experience of professional technicians, usually based on optical microscope with Giemsa-stained blood smears, DH methodology was exploited [50]. The authors found the technique to be useful for determining morphological modifications in host RBCs, quantifying contents, and concentration of the cellular dry mass, as well as dynamic membrane fluctuations measured at the individual cell level, which are in turn strongly correlated with the mechanical deformability of cell membrane. An automatic compact diagnostic tool will be advantageous especially for healthcare personnel working in developing countries, which lack trained professionals and high-quality equipments.

Platelet spreading and retraction play a pivotal role in the platelet plugging and the thrombus formation. In routine laboratory, platelet function tests include exhaustive information about the role of the different receptors present at the platelet surface without information on the 3D-structure of platelet aggregates. Boudejltia et al. used DH microscopy to develop a convenient method to characterize the platelet and aggregate 3D shapes [51]. This is the first report on analysis of platelets aggregates by DH microscopy. According to the authors, the method is particularly well suited for the study of the platelet physiology, the physiopathology in clinical practice, and the development of new drugs.

4.5. Quantification of inflammation

Lenz et al. have utilized DH microscopy for investigation of inflammatory bowel diseases including Crohn's disease and ulcerative colitis [52]. Dextran sodium sulfate-induced colitis was performed and colonic sections were subsequently examined by histological analyses and by DH microscopy. With DH microscopy, optical path length delay including refractive index was monitored, and thereby tissue density assessment could be performed. Indeed, the average refractive index was an accurate marker to distinguish between different layers of the intestinal wall of the colitis induced murine model.

Furthermore, DH microscopy reliably detects inflamed colonic segments with a strong correlation between the severity of inflammation and the refractive index. In conclusion, DH microscopy analysis opens a novel diagnostic option for optical quantification of inflammation in murine models of colitis. Moreover, the same research group assessed cellular growth and motility in epithelial wound healing in vitro using DH microscopy [53]. Interestingly, phase images quantifying cell thickness, dry mass, and tissue density were demonstrated. The study concluded that the technique can assist in the evaluation of potential therapeutics in, for example, helping to elucidate the specific role of certain cytokines for wound healing.

5. Conclusion

The correlation between cellular morphological changes and cellular events is rather well documented. In several studies, researchers have shown how holographic cell morphology analysis can be connected to pathological diagnostics. Although the experiments in some cases have been performed ex vivo or in animal models, the analysis of humans is just one small step ahead. For other of the abovementioned applications, experiments are performed with human tissues, and the methods are already beginning to be developed for clinical use. As DH microscopy is noninvasive, the same patient sample can often be used for other analyses, thus adding further benefit to the method.

6. Further research

Future applications could include real-time monitoring of holographic microscopy parameters in human clinical cell samples in response to a broad range of clinically relevant compounds.

Acknowledgements

We are grateful to Mekdam Fadhil, Gillian Dao, Anna Mölder, and Maria Falck Miniotis for performing experiments. This work was supported by grants from the following foundations: Åke Wibergs stiftelse, Kungliga fysiografiska sällskapet, Allmänna Sjukhusets i Malmö stiftelse för bekämpande av cancer and Malmö University.

Author details

Zahra El-Schich[1], Sofia Kamlund[2], Birgit Janicke[2], Kersti Alm[2] and Anette Gjörloff Wingren[1*]

*Address all correspondence to: anette.gjorloff-wingren@mah.se

1 Biomedical Science, Health and Society, Malmö University, Malmö, Sweden

2 Phase Holographic Imaging AB, Lund, Sweden

References

[1] Alm K., Cirenajwis H., Gisselsson L., Gjörloff Wingren A., Janicke B., Mölder A., Oredsson S., Persson J. Digital holography and cell studies. In: Rosen, J., editors. Holography, Research and Technologies. In Tech; Rijeka, Croatia: 2011, pp. 237–252. DOI: 10.5772/15364

[2] Marquet P., Rappaz B., Magistretti P. J., Cuche E., Emery Y., Colomb T., Depeursinge C. Digital holographic microscopy: a noninvasive contrast imaging technique allowing quantitative visualization of living cells with sub wavelength axial accuracy. Optical Society of America. 2005;30(5):468–470. DOI: 10.1364/OL.30.000468

[3] Rappaz B., Marquet P., Cuche E., Emery Y., Depeursinge C., Magistretti P. Measurement of the integral refractive index and dynamic cell morphometry of living cells with digital holographic microscopy. Optical Society of America. 2005;13(23): 9361–9373. DOI: 10.1364/OPEX.13.009361

[4] Carl D., Kemper B, Wernicke G., Bally von G. Parameter-optimized digital holographic microscope for high-resolution living-cell analysis. Applied Optics. 2004;43(36):6536–6544. DOI: 10.1364/AO.43.006536

[5] Chalut K.J., Ekpenyong A.E., Clegg W.L., Melhuisha I.C., Gucka J. Quantifying cellular differentiation by physical phenotype using digital holographic microscopy. Intergrative Biology. 2012;4(3):208–284. DOI: 10.1039/C2IB00129B

[6] Ferraro P., Grilli S., Alfieri D., Nicola S.D., Finizio A., Pierattini G., Javidi B., Coppola G., Striano V. Extended focused image in microscopy by digital holography. Optics Express. 2005;13(18):6738–6749. DOI: 10.1364/OPEX.13.006738

[7] Kemper B., Carl D., Schnekenburger J., Bredebusch I, Schäfer M, Domschke W., Bally von G. Investigation of living pancreas tumor cells by digital holographic microscopy. Journal of Biomedical Optics. 2006;11(3):34005. DOI: 10.1117/1.2204609

[8] Lenart T., Gustafsson M., Öwall V. A hardware acceleration platform for digital holographic imaging. Journal of Signal Processing Systems. 2008;52(3):297–311. DOI: 10.1007/s11265-008-0161-2

[9] Mann C.J., Yu L., Lo C.M., Kim M.K. High-resolution quantitative phase-contrast microscopy by digital holography. Optics Express. 2005;13(22):8693–8698. DOI: 10.1364/OPEX.13.008693

[10] Khmaladze A., Matz R.L., Epstein T., Jasensky J., Banaszak Holl M.M., Chen Z. Cell volume changes during apoptosis monitored in real time using digital holographic microscopy. Journal of Structural Biology. 2012;178(3):270–278. DOI: 10.1016/j.jsb.2012.03.008

[11] Alm K., El-Schich Z, Miniotis M.F., Gjörloff Wingren A., Janicke B., Oredsson S. Cells and holograms–holograms and digital holographic microscopy as a tool to study the

morphology of living cells. In: Mihaylova E., editor. Holography: Basic Principles and Contemporary Applications. In Tech; Rijeka, Croatia: 2013. pp. 335–351. DOI: 10.5772/54505

[12] Marquet P., Depeursinge C., Magistretti P.J .Review of quantitative phase-digital holographic microscopy: promising novel imaging technique to resolve neuronal network activity and identify cellular biomarkers of psychiatric disorders. Neurophotonics. 2014;1(2):020901-1–020901-15. DOI: 10.1117/1.NPh.1.2.020901

[13] Rappaz B., Breton B., Shaffer E., Turcatti G. Digital holographic microscopy: a quantitative label-free microscopy technique for phenotypic screening. Combinatorial Chemistry & High Throughput Screening. 2014;17(1):80–88. DOI: 10.2174/1386207311 3166660062

[14] Nadeau L.J., Cho Y.B., Kühn J., Liewer K. Improved tracking and resolution of bacteria in holographic microscopy using dye and fluorescent protein labeling. Frontiers in Chemistry. 2016;4(17):1–10. DOI: 10.3389/fchem.2016.00017

[15] Yi F., Moon I., Javidi B. Cell morphology-based classification of red blood cells using holographic imaging informatics. Biomedical Optics Express. 2016;7(6):2385-2399. DOI: 10.1364/BOE.7.002385

[16] Kim. M.K. Principles and techniques of digital holographic microscopy. SPIE Reviews. 2010;1:018005. DOI: 10.1117/6.0000006

[17] Xiao X., Puri I.K. Digital recording and numerical reconstruction of holograms: an optical diagnostic for combustion. Applied Optics. 2002;41(19):3890–3899. DOI: 10.1364/AO.41.003890

[18] Sebesta M., Gustafsson M. Object characterization with refractometric digital fourier holography. Optics Letters. 2005;30(5):471–473. DOI: 10.1364/OL.30.000471

[19] Palacios, F., Ricardo, J., Palacios, D., Goncalves, E., Valin, J.L., De Souza, R. 3D image reconstruction of transparent microscopic objects using digital holography. Optics Communications. 2005;248(1–3):41–50. DOI: 10.1016/j.optcom.2004.11.095

[20] Liebling M., Unser M. Comparing algorithms for reconstructing digital off-axis Fresnel holograms. SPIE Proceedings. 2005;6016:6016M. DOI: 10.1117/12.631039

[21] Pavillon N., Kühn J., Moratal C., Jourdain P., Depeursinge C., Magistretti P.J., Marquet P. Early cell death detection with digital holographic microscopy. PloS One. 2012;7(1): 1–9. DOI: org/10.1371/journal.pone.0030912

[22] Wang Y., Yang Y., Wang D., Ouyang L., Zhang Y., Zhao J., Wang X. Morphological measurement of living cells in methanol with digital holographic microscopy. Computational and Mathematical Methods in Medicine. 2013;2013:1–7. DOI: org/ 10.1155/2013/715843

[23] Trulsson M., Yu H., Gisselsson L., Chao Y., Urbano A., Aits S., Mossberg A.K., Svanborg C. HAMLET binding to α-actinin facilitates tumor cell detachment. PloS One. 2011;6(3): 1–16. DOI: 10.1371/journal.pone.0017179

[24] Kühn J., Shaffer E., Mena J., Breton B., Parent J., Rappaz B., Chambon M., Emery Y., Magistretti P., Depeursinge C., Marquet P., Turcatti G. Label-free cytotoxicity screening assay by digital holographic microscopy. ASSAY and Drug Development Technologies. 2013;11(2):101–107. DOI: 10.1089/adt.2012.476

[25] El-Schich Z., Mölder A., Tassidis H., Härkönen P., Miniotis M.F., Gjörloff Wingren A. Induction of morphological changes in death-induced cancer cells monitored by holographic microscopy. Journal of Structural Biology. 2015;189(3):207–212. DOI: 10.1016/j.jsb.2015.01.010

[26] Montecucco A., Biamonti G. Cellular response to etoposide treatment. Cancer Letters. 2007;252(1):9–18. DOI: 10.1016/j.canlet.2006.11.005

[27] El-Schich Z., Nilsson E., Gerdtsson A.S, Wingren C., Gjörloff Wingren A. Interfacing antibody-based microarrays and digital holography enables label-free detection for loss of cell volume. Future Science OA. 2015;1(3):1–11. DOI: 10.4155/fso.14.2

[28] Fischer W., Gustafsson L., Mossberg A.K., Gronli J., Mork S., Bjerkvig R., Svanborg C. Human α-lactalbumin made lethal to tumor cells (HAMLET) kills human glioblastoma cells in brain xenografts by an apoptosis-like mechanism and prolongs survival. Cancer Research. 2004;64(6):2105–2112. DOI: 10.1158/0008-5472.CAN-03-2661

[29] Svensson M., Håkansson A., Mossberg A.-K., Linse S., Svanborg C. Conversion of alpha-lactalbumin to a protein inducing apoptosis. PNAS. 2000;97(8):4221–4226. DOI: 10.1073/pnas.97.8.4221

[30] Ho J.C.S., Storm P., Rydström A., Bowen B., Alsin F., Sullivan L., Ambite I., MoK K.H., Northen T., Svanborg C. Lipids as tumoricidal components of human alpha-lactalbumin made lethal to tumor cells (HAMLET): unique and shared effects on signaling and death. The Journal of Biological Chemistry. 2013;288(24):17460–17471. DOI: 10.1074/jbc.M113.468405

[31] Puthia M., Storm P., Nadeem A., Hsiung S., Svanborg C. Prevention and treatment of colon cancer by peroral administration of HAMLET (human α-lactalbumin made lethal to tumour cells). Gut. 2014;63(1):131–142. DOI: 10.1136/gutjnl-2012-303715

[32] Hackler Jr. L., Ózsvári B., Gyuris M., Sipos P., Fábián G., Molnár E., Marton A., Faragó N., Mihály J., Nagy L.I., Szénási T., Diron A., Párducz A., Kanizsai I., Puskás L.G. The curcumin analog C-150, influencing NF-κB, UPR and akt/notch pathways has potent anticancer activity in vitro and in vivo. PloS One. 2016;11(3):1–16. DOI: 10.1371/journal.pone.0149832

[33] Lajkó E., Bányai P., Zámbó Z. Targeted tumor therapy by *Rubia tinctorum* L.: analytical characterization of hydroxyanthraquinones and investigation of their selective cyto-toxic, adhesion and migration modulator effects on melanoma cell lines (A2058 and

HT168-M1). Cancer Cell International. 2015;15(119):1–15. DOI: 10.1186/s12935-015-0271-4

[34] Miniotis M.F., Mukwaya A., Gjörloff Wingren A. Digital holographic microscopy for non-invasive monitoring of cell cycle arrest in L929 cells. PloS One. 2014;9(9):1–6. DOI: 10.1371/journal.pone.0106546

[35] Zhang Y., Sriraman S.K., Kenny H.A., Luther E., Torchilin V., Lengyel E. Reversal of chemoresistance in ovarian cancer by co-delivery of a P-glycoprotein inhibitor and paclitaxel in a liposomal platform. Molecular Cancer Therapeutics. 2016;15(10);2282–2293. DOI: 10.1158/1535-7163

[36] Yaktapour N., Meiss F., Mastroianni J., Zenz T., Andrlova H., Mathew N. R., Claus R., Hutter B., Fröhling S., Brors B., Pfeifer D., Milena P.M., Bartsch I., Spehl T.S., Meyer P.T., Duyster J., Zirlik K., Brummer T., Zeiser R. BRAF inhibitor-associated ERK activation drives development of chronic lymphocytic leukemia. The Journal of Clinical Investigation. 2014;24(11):5074–5084. DOI: 10.1172/JCI76539

[37] Semenas J., Hedblom A., Miftakhova R.R., Sarwaa M., Larsson R., Shcherbina L., Johansson M.E., Härkönen P., Sterner O., Persson J.L. The role of PI3K/AKT-related PIP5K1alpha and the discovery of its selective inhibitor for treatment of advanced prostate cancer. PNAS. 2014;111(35):E3689–E3698. DOI: 10.1073/pnas.1405801111

[38] Wingren C., James P., Borrebaeck C.A.K. Strategy for surveying the proteome using affinity proteomics and mass spectrometry. Proteomics. 2009;9(6):1511–1517. DOI: 10.1002/pmic.200800802

[39] Borrebaeck C.A.K., Wingren C. Recombinant antibodies for the generation of antibody arrays. In: Protein Microarrays. Korf U., editor. Humana Press; New York City, USA: 2011. pp. 247–262. DOI: 10.1007/978-1-61779-286-1_17

[40] Belov L., Mulligan S.P., Barber N., Woolfson A., Scott M., Stoner K., Chrisp J.S, Sewell W.A., Bradstock K.F., Bendall L., Pascovici D.S., Thomas M., Erber W., Huang P., Sartor M., Young G.A.R., Wiley J.S., Juneja S., Wierda W.G., Green A.R., Keating M.J., Christopherson R.I. Analysis of human leukaemias and lymphomas using extensive immunophenotypes from an antibody microarray. British Journal of Haematology. 2006;135(2):184–197. DOI: 10.1111/j.1365-2141.2006.06266.x

[41] Jourdain P., Becq F., Lengacher S., Boinot C., Magistretti P.J., Marquet P. The human CFTR protein expressed in CHO cells activates aquaporin-3 in a cAMP-dependent pathway: study by digital holographic microscopy. Journal of Cell Science. 2014;127:546–556. DOI: 10.1242/jcs.133629

[42] Benzerdjeb N., Garbar C., Camparo P., Sevestre H. Digital holographic microscopy as screening tool for cervical cancer preliminary study. Cancer Cytopathology. 2016;124(8):573–580. DOI: 10.1002/cncy.21727

[43] Di Caprio G., Ferrara M.A., Miccio L., Merola F., Memmolo P., Ferraro P., Coppola G. Holographic imaging of unlabelled sperm cells for semen analysis: a review. Journal of Biophotonics. 2015;8(10):779–789. DOI: 10.1002/jbio.201400093

[44] Chra I., Zakova J., Huser M., Ventruba P., Lousova E., Pohanka M. Digital holographic microscopy in human sperm imaging. Journal of Assisted Reproduction and Genetics. 2011;28:725–729. DOI: 10.1007/s10815-011-9584-y

[45] Coppola G., Di Caprio G., Wilding M., Ferraro P., Esposito G.T., Di Matteo L., Dale R., Coppola G., Dale B. Digital holographic microscopy for the evaluation of human sperm structure. Zygote. 2014;22(4):446–454. DOI: 10.1017/S0967199413000026

[46] Yi F., Moon I., Javidi B., Boss D., Marquet P. Automated segmentation of multiple red blood cells with digital holographic microscopy. Journal of Biomedical Optics. 2013;18(2):26006. DOI: 10.1117/1.JBO.18.2.026006

[47] Jaferzadeh K., Moon I. Quantitative investigation of red blood cell three-dimensional geometric and chemical changes in the storage lesion using digital holographic microscopy. Journal of Biomedical Optics. 2015;20(11):111228. DOI: 10.1117/1.JBO. 20.11.111218

[48] Yi F., Moon I., Lee Y.H. Three-dimensional counting of morphologically normal human red blood cells via digital holographic microscopy. Journal of Biomedical Optics. 2015;20(1):016005. DOI: 10.1117/1.JBO.20.1.016005

[49] Anand A., Chhaniwal V.K., Patel N.R., Javidi B. Automatic identification of malaria-infected RBC with digital holographic microscopy using correlation algorithms. IEEE Photonics Journal. 2012;4(5):1456–1464. DOI: 10.1109/JPHOT.2012.2210199

[50] Park H.J., Hong S.H., Kim K., Cho S.H., Lee W.J., Kim Y., Lee S.E., Park Y.K. Characterizations of individual mouse red blood cells parasitized by Babesia microti using 3-D holographic microscopy. Nature Scientific Reports. 2015;5:10827. DOI: 10.1038/srep10827

[51] Boudejltia K.Z., Ribeiro de Sousa D., Uzureau P., Yourassowsky C., Perez-Morga D., Courbebaisse G., Chopard B., Dubois F. Quantitative analysis of platelets aggregates in 3D by digital holographic microscopy. Biomedical Optics Express. 2015;6(9):3556–3563. DOI: 10.1364/BOE.6.003556

[52] Lenz P., Bettenworth D., Krausewitz P., Brückner M., Ketelhut S., von Bally G., Domagka D., Kemper B. Digital holographic microscopy quantifies the degree of inflammation in experimental colitis. Integrative Biology. 2013;5(3):624–630. DOI: 10.1039/C2IB20227A

[53] Bettenworth D., Lenz P., Krausewitz P., Brückner M., Ketelhut S., Domagk D., Kemper B. Quantitative stain-free and continuous multimodal monitoring of wound healing in vitro with digital holographic microscopy. PloS One. 2014;9(9):e107317. DOI: 10.1371/journal.pone.0107317

Chapter 15

Unlabeled Semen Analysis by Means of the Holographic Imaging

Giuseppe Coppola, Maria Antonietta Ferrara, Giuseppe Di Caprio, Gianfranco Coppola and Brian Dale

Additional information is available at the end of the chapter

http://dx.doi.org/10.5772/67552

Abstract

The morphology, the motility, and the biochemical structure of the spermatozoon have often been correlated with the outcome of *in vitro* fertilization and have been shown to be the sole parameters of the semen analysis in predicting the success of intracytoplasmic sperm injection and intracytoplasmic morphologically selected sperm injection. In this context, digital holography has demonstrated to be an attractive technique to perform a label-free, noninvasive, and high-resolution technique for characterization of live spermatozoa. The aim of this chapter is to summarize the recent achievements of digital holography in order to show its high potentiality as an efficient method for healthy and fertile sperm cell selection, without injuring the specimen and to explore new possible applications of digital holography in this field.

Keywords: holographic imaging, label-free techniques, human sperm structure, *in vitro* fertilization

1. Introduction

Following the advent of human *in vitro* fertilization [1], much attention has been given to understand both the spermatozoa morphological alterations and the kinematics/dynamics of the swimming spermatozoa [2–11]. In fact, semen analysis is commonly employed both in human and in the zoo-technic field. In the first case, the analysis is mainly applied to study the couple's infertility or to confirm success of male sterilization procedures. Moreover, several studies have shown that for infertile men, the risk for developing a testicular cancer is slightly higher-than-average. So, independently of the will to have children, male fertility is a good

indicator for general health. On the other hand, in the zoo-technic field, animal semen analysis is commonly used in animal production laboratories and reproductive toxicology.

The main requirements for the development of techniques used for an accurate semen analysis are the following:

- avoid any alteration of the health of the spermatozoa under test;

- use a label-free approach to eliminate all adverse effects of the probe labeling;

- obtain results independent on the technician's experience and/or the laboratory environmental conditions (such as temperature, humidity, and duration).

The sperm cell is almost transparent in conventional bright field microscopy, as its optical proprieties differ slightly from the surrounding liquid, generating little contrast. On the other hand, a light beam that passes through a spermatozoon undergoes a phase change, in comparison with the surrounding medium, the amplitude of which depends on the light source, the thickness, and the integral refractive index of the object itself. A qualitative visualization of this phase contrast may be obtained by contrast interference microscopy (phase contrast or Nomarski/Zernicke interferential contrast microscopy). However, it is difficult and time-consuming to obtain a quantitative morphological imaging. In fact, a fine z-movement of the biological sample is required in order to acquire a collection of different planes in focus. This collection of acquired images is used in postelaboration to produce a 3D image of the object under investigation [12]. The same approach has been used to obtain information about sperm motility. Nevertheless, this 2D intrinsic analysis implies a partial in-plane representation of the motility features due to difficulty to track the 3D spatial motion of spermatozoa that quickly move out of focus. In order to overcome these intrinsic limitations, several approaches have been recently developed. In this contest, the optical approaches are deeply investigated.

In particular, over the last few years, holographic imaging in microscopy has been established as a valid noninvasive, quantitative, label-free, high-resolution, and phase-contrast imaging technique. So this chapter tries to summarize the state-of-art on the semen analysis and recent achievements obtained by a holographic imaging [13–17]. We will show that the unique potentialities of the holographic imaging have been used to provide structural information on both the morphology and the motility of sperm cells [18]. Moreover, the combination of the holographic technique with others approaches, such as the Raman spectroscopy, will be described, too. In fact, spermatozoa from infertile men could present a variety of alterations (such as alterations of chromatin organization [19], aneuploidy [20], and DNA fragmentation [21]) that can decrease reproductive capacity of men. Current methods of DNA assessment are mainly based on fluorescence microscopy, and thus samples are unusable after the analysis [22–25]. Therefore, the ability to simultaneously analyze, in a nondestructive and noninvasive way, both the morphology and biochemical functionalities of the spermatozoa could bring greater understandings [26]. Thus, the chapter will allow a bird's-eye view into the potentiality of the semen analysis performed by means of the holographic imaging, showing that this approach is extremely important for the intracytoplasmic sperm injection (ICSI) procedure, where it is highly required the development of a method that allows characterizing and directly select the best spermatozoon to inject into the oocytes [9, 27].

2. Principle of the holographic imaging

An optical field consists of amplitude and phase distributions; if this field interacts with the object under test, the morphology of the object alters the phase distribution. The holographic approach employs the interference between two optical beams to transform the phase information (i.e., the morphological information) into a recordable intensity distribution [28]. A sketch of an experimental set up for holographic imaging is shown in **Figure 1**. It consists in a coherent laser beam splits into a reference and an object beam.

The object beam intensity is always set well below the level for causing any damage to the spermatozoa structure and functionality. A microscope objective lens is used to collect the object beam. The reference and the object beam are then recombined by a beam splitter onto a CCD (Charge-Coupled Device) or CMOS (Complementary Metal-Oxide Semiconductor) detector, which acquires the interference pattern. According to the angle θ between the reference and object beams, either on-axis ($\theta = 0°$) or off-axis configuration can be adopted. Besides, the hologram of the sample under investigation, a second hologram is acquired on a reference surface in proximity to the object in order to numerically compensate all the aberrations introduced by the optical components, including the defocusing due to the microscope objective. The image reconstruction

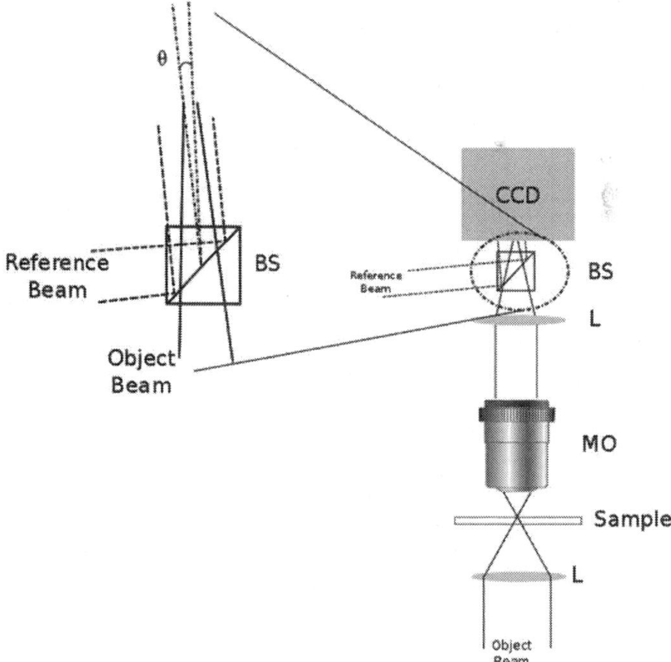

Figure 1. Sketch of the principle of hologram formation (L: lens, MO: microscope objective, BS: beam splitter).

procedure allows retrieving a discrete version of the complex optical wavefront (amplitude and phase) present on the surface of the specimen under test. This optical wavefront is obtained multiplying the recorded hologram by a numerical replica of the reference beam and numerically backpropagating this product. Actually, this product generates three diffraction terms: zeroth order, real image, and conjugate image. In an on-axis configuration, unless a partially coherent light is adopted that allows reducing the speckle and multi-reflection interference noise [29], all terms are superimposed. Thus, in order to recover only the real image, i.e., an exact replica of the object wavefront, either a spatial or temporal phase-shifting methods has to be employed. However, in this way the complexity and capture time increase [13]. On the other hand, by introducing a small angle between the object and reference beam (off-axis configuration), a spatial separation between the three terms is obtained, at the expense of suboptimal use of camera sensor space-bandwidth product. Thus, this separation allows selecting and retrieving only the real image. The possibility offered by DH to numerically retrieve the phase distribution of the object wavefront allows not only the possibility to evaluate the object morphology but also to remove and/or compensate the unwanted wavefront variation (such as optical aberrations and slide deformations) [30–32].

3. Morphological imaging

Coppola's group [33] investigated the possibility to better understand the sperm behavior by means of a quantitative analysis of the 3D spermatozoa's morphology. In particular, experiments on bovine sperm cells were performed. The recorded hologram is illustrated in **Figure 2**, whereas the intensity of the fringe pattern generated by the interference between the object and reference beam is highlighted into the inset.

In **Figure 3**, the reconstructed images of abnormal bovine spermatozoa are reported [33]. For the reported analysis, the spermatozoa were fixed and without the surrounding liquid. In particular, the retrieved image shown in **Figure 3(a)** is relative to a spermatozoon with a cytoplasmatic droplet along the tail. Cytoplasm surrounding the sperm cell is accumulated during maturation, and it is extruded from the cell in the last phases of this maturation. However, cytoplasmatic residues may persist in the cell and, in particular, are retained in the tail as a droplet [34]. Thus, the presence of drops along the tail is connected to the degree of cell maturation and may indicate an excessive utilization of a donor.

In **Figure 3(b)**, an image of a spermatozoon with a bent tail is shown. Generally, when this defect is present in the semen either before or after the freezing process, the donor may be afflicted with a reproductive problem. On the other hand, if this anomaly appears with high frequency only in frozen semen, it can indicate that the spermatozoa have been subjected to hypoosmotic stress possibly due to an improper use of freezing extender and to an extremely low concentration of solutes. Finally, the reconstructed image of a spermatozoon with broken acrosome is illustrated in **Figure 3(c)**. In particular, the loss of acrosomal substances indicates premature acrosome activation far from the site of fertilization. This defect is present with high percentage in frozen semen samples due to incorrect sperm handling during the freezing process. The great advantage of managing quantitative information allows carrying out different numerical analysis, such as estimation area/volume, profiles along particular

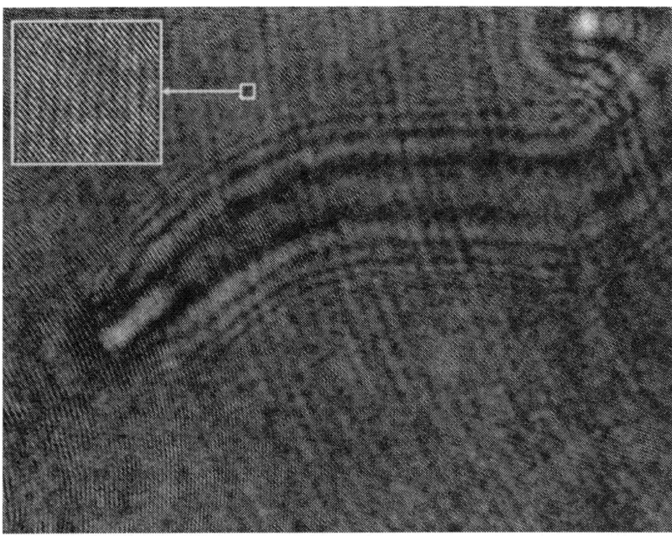

Figure 2. Acquired hologram, a region is enhanced in order to show the interference pattern (inset). Ref. [33] (by permission of IEEE Society).

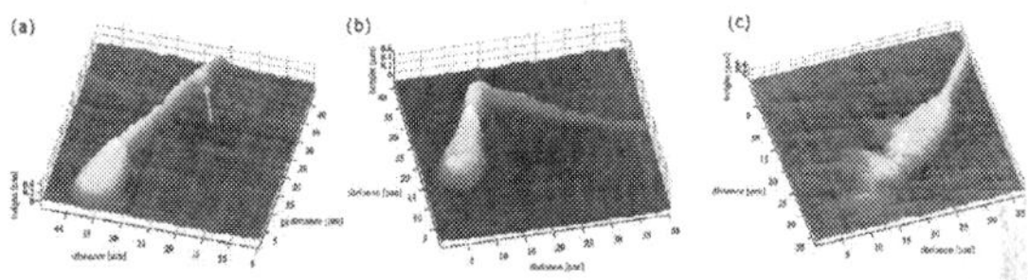

Figure 3. Pseudo 3D representation of the thickness of a spermatozoon with: (a) a cytoplasmatic droplet along the tail; (b) a bent tail; (c) an acrosome broken. Ref. [33] (by permission of IEEE Society).

directions, and selection of different zones. The 3D analysis can add further information to the data provided by the traditional bi-dimensional optical techniques, allowing to better understand the relationship between the male infertility and the abnormal morphology. Due to this potentiality, the holographic approach has been also employed to analyze the human sperm characteristics [35, 36]. Crha et al. [35] tested about 3000 sperm cells to individuate a phase difference between spermatozoa in normo-zoospermia (NZ) and oligoasthenoterato-zoospermia (OAT). **Table 1** summarizes the obtained results in terms of mean, median, standard deviation (SD), and confidence intervals (CI).

The Dale's group performed a comparison between the results of spermatozoa analyzed both by a semiautomated digitally enhanced Nomarski microscopy (DESA) and by the holographic imaging [36]. In **Table 2**, the values relative to five primary parameters (length, width, perimeter, area, and volume) for normal human spermatozoa are compared. Results shows that no significant differences were observed in the gross morphometric values of the sperm cells analyzed.

Sperm group	Median	Mean	SD	CI
NZ	2.90	2.91	0.61	2.94
OAT	2.00	2.10	0.38	2.13

Table 1. Descriptive statistics for statistically significant ($\rho < 0.001$) phase shifts according to the NZ/OAT group [35].

Imaging	Length [μm]	Width [μm]	Perimeter [μm]	Area [μm²]	Volume [μm³]
DESA	5.1 ± 0.6	3.5 ± 0.4	13.8 ± 1.4	14.1 ± 2.0	-
Holography	5.6 ± 0.3	2.9 ± 0.5	14.3 ± 1.2	13.0 ± 1.2	8.0 ± 0.8

Table 2. Mean morphometric values of normal human sperm heads obtained by DESA and holographic techniques [36].

It is important to note that the volume estimation could not be performed by the DESA technique. Due the great influence of nuclear vacuoles in the sperm head on the fertilization capacitance of sperm cell [9], the volumetric analysis was performed to analyze vacuolated human spermatozoa. In **Figure 4(a)**, a conventional differential interference contrast (DIC) image of a vacuolated human sperm is reported. The holographic 3D reconstruction of the vacuolated spermatozoon is illustrated in **Figure 4(b)**. From this figure, it is clear that spermatozoa with vacuole had a reduced volume, and this reduction could be probably be due to variation of the inner structure of the sperm head with a loss of material.

Table 3 summarizes the volumetric analysis carried out for three different groups of spermatozoa defined by the length and width of the head. Mean values of the total volume of the spermatozoa minus the vacuoles volume are also reported.

Memmolo et al. [37] proposed to use DH in order to identify and measure specific region-of-interest of spermatozoa. **Figure 5** shows some steps of the applied method that starts from a filtered version of the reconstructed spermatozoon image and is able to identify the head region.

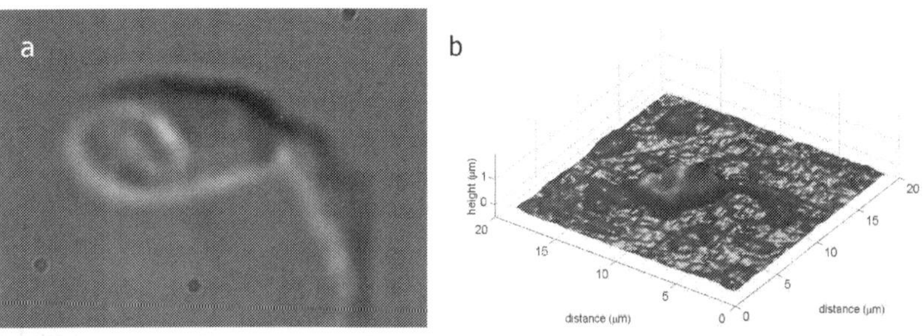

Figure 4. Differential interference contrast image (a) and pseudo 3D holographic reconstruction (b) of a vacuolated sperm head. Ref [36] (by permission of Cambridge University Press).

Sperm dimensions	Volume [μm^3]	
	Total	Total vacuoles
Length < 2.9 μm, width < 4.2 μm	5.8 ± 0.7	4.0 ± 0.8
2.9 < length < 3.7μm; 4.2 < width < 5.3 μm	8.2 ± 0.8	6.4 ± 0.8
Length > 3.7 μm, width > 5.3μm	10.1 ± 0.8	8.4 ± 0.8

Table 3. Mean volumetric values of vacuolated sperm clustered in three different subpopulations [36].

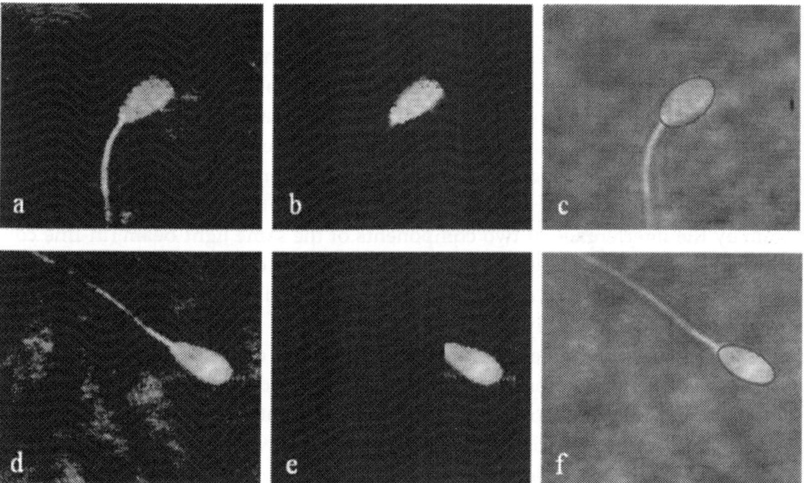

Figure 5. Detection of sperm head by the algorithm proposed by Memmolo et al. [37] (by permission of The Optical Society): (a) and (d) are the results of the denoising, (b) and (e) are the results of extraction algorithm, (c) and (f) are the best fit ellipses.

The proposed algorithm could be very useful to retrieve noisy holograms due to the impurity of the liquid surrounding the spermatozoa.

4. Tracking analysis

One of the main advantages of the holographic approach is the possibility to retrieve a quantitative 3D image by means of a numerical refocusing of only one bi-dimensional image at different object planes. Thus, the realigning of the optical imaging system with mechanical translation can be eliminated. This peculiarity enables the characterization of live specimen [38], and in particular, to track the 3D spatial motion of spermatozoa that quickly move out of focus. The tracking approach allows estimating many quantitative parameters useful for a semen analysis [39], such as:

Advanced Materials and Optical Systems for Holographic Recording

Chapter 16

One-Step Holographic Photoalignment for Twisted Nematic Liquid Crystal Gratings

Kotaro Kawai, Moritsugu Sakamoto, Kohei Noda,
Tomoyuki Sasaki, Nobuhiro Kawatsuki and
Hiroshi Ono

Additional information is available at the end of the chapter

http://dx.doi.org/10.5772/67293

Abstract

Liquid crystal gratings, in which liquid crystal molecules are periodically aligned, are fabricated by highly efficient and practical one-step holographic photoalignment method using a photocrosslinkable polymer liquid crystal (PCLC). This method is an innovative fabrication technique for liquid crystal grating containing a twisted nematic alignment, which does not require a conventional complex fabrication process. In this chapter, three types of liquid crystal gratings with twisted nematic alignment are fabricated. Periodic director distributions of these liquid crystal gratings are analyzed based on the elastic continuum theory and observed experimentally using a polarized light optical microscope. Furthermore, the polarization diffraction properties were measured by illumination with a visible laser beam. The resultant liquid crystal gratings exhibit various polarization diffraction properties depending on the director distributions and the polarization states of the incident beams. These polarization diffraction properties are well explained by theoretical analysis based on Jones calculus. These resultant liquid crystal gratings exhibit great potential for application as a diffractive optical element that can simultaneously control the various parameters of the light wave, such as amplitude, polarization states, and propagation direction.

Keywords: diffraction gratings, liquid crystals, polarization, Jones calculus, photocrosslinkable polymer liquid crystals

1. Introduction

Control of the various parameters, such as amplitude, polarization states, wavelength, and propagation direction of the light wave, is of great importance in a wide range of fields,

including the optoelectronics field. In particular, diffractive optical elements, in which light wave propagation is controlled by diffraction phenomena, are expected to realize such a function. Generally, light propagating inside the diffractive optical element is diffracted by inducing a phase difference to the light propagating through a medium whose shape or isotropic refractive index is periodically modulated. In addition, anisotropic diffractive optical elements in which the optical anisotropy is periodically modulated have been reported [1–10]. Anisotropic diffractive optical elements show the polarization controllability which the diffraction efficiency and polarization states depend on the polarization states of the incident beams. This is because various modulations of an effective refractive index along a grating vector depend on incident electric field vectors.

Structures, fabrication techniques, and materials of anisotropic diffraction gratings are wide ranging. In particular, polarization holographic recordings on an azobenzene-containing material are a typical fabrication technique and materials [1]. When two orthogonally (i.e., the product of the electric field vector and the complex conjugate of the other electric field vectors is zero) polarized beams interfere with each other, the polarization state is periodically modulated in the interference field; however, the intensity is not modulated. Therefore, with simultaneously induced photoisomerization reactions depending on a direction of incident polarized light, a periodically modulated anisotropic structure is fabricated by exposure of azobenzene polymer films to the orthogonal polarization interference field. In addition, liquid crystal (LC) gratings, in which LC directors are periodically modulated by periodically aligned films, are mentioned as an example of anisotropic diffractive optical elements [2–10]. Photoalignment by holographic exposure [2, 4, 8, 9], photo-masking exposure [3], microrubbing method [5], and using an interdigitated electrode [6] are the common methods of the fabrication methods of LC gratings. Photoreactive polymer LCs are mentioned as materials to use for alignment films other than azobenzene-containing material [2–4, 7–10]. LC gratings can be applied to optical switching elements by applying a voltage [2, 4–6]. Moreover, control of diffraction properties and wavelength selection properties is realized by birefringence control in LC gratings using temperature control [10]. In addition, diffraction efficiencies of each diffraction order (i.e., the direction of propagation) can be controlled by the incident polarization in LC gratings in which the LC directors continuously rotate along the grating vector [2, 4, 7, 8]. LC grating is not limited to a transmission type; there is also a reflection type [4]. The diffraction efficiency of LC grating is higher than the anisotropic diffractive optical elements of thin film type. This is because the thickness of the structure LC grating induces a large phase difference due to a thick structure. Based on these, LC gratings are suitable to be applied to optical elements that can simultaneously control the parameters of a light wave. However, fabricating an LC grating requires periodically and finely alignment processing in two alignment films and accurate fabrication technique so as not to shift the two alignment patterns.

In this chapter, we propose the efficient yet practical method for fabricating LC gratings containing a twisted nematic (TN) alignment structure using polarization holographic photoalignment and photocrosslinkable polymer LC (PCLC) synthesized by us as alignment films. First, as a preliminary experiment, we experimentally demonstrate that different patterns between two alignment substrates can be applied by one-step linearly polarized UV beam irradiation to an empty glass cell whose inner walls are coated with PCLC films. In addition, we show that fabrication of three types of LC gratings by one-step exposure of the empty glass cells to polarized interference UV fields. The periodic director distributions of the resultant LC gratings are observed experimentally by polarized light microscopy and are analyzed based on the elastic continuum theory. Furthermore, the polarization diffraction properties are measured experimentally by the incident of a visible laser and analyzed theoretically by Jones calculus.

2. One-step photoalignment for fabricating a TN-LC cell

2.1. Materials

In this chapter, a PCLC with 4-(4-methoxycinnamoyloxy)biphenyl side groups (P6CB) is adopted as materials of alignment substrates. The chemical structure of P6CB is shown in **Figure 1**. The synthetic method and the details of the characteristics can be found in reference [11]. In the P6CB alignment films after linearly polarized UV light exposure, axis-selective cross-linked LC mesogens act as a trigger, the cooperative reorientation of the side chains is induced during the annealing process as shown in **Figure 2**. The LC mesogen alignment due to the cross-linking reaction is thermally and long-term stable. P6CB shows the absorption in the ultraviolet light; however, it does not show absorption in the visible region. Therefore, P6CB is suitable for application to optical elements. In addition, the order parameter of P6CB depends on cross-linking density, which is proportional to the exposure dose. When the exposure dose is greater than 100 mJ/cm^2, mesogens of P6CB are oriented parallel to the polarization direction of linearly polarized UV after the annealing process. However, when the exposure dose is less than 100 mJ/cm^2, mesogens are oriented perpendicularly to the polarization direction of the linearly polarized UV.

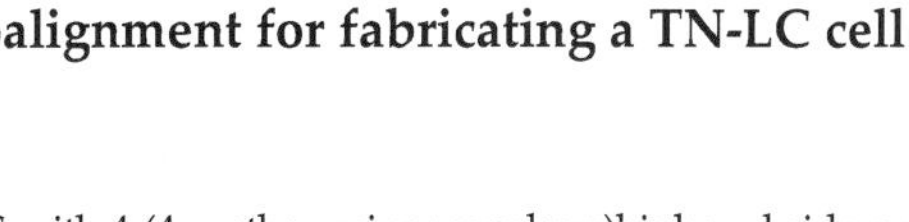

Figure 1. Chemical structure of PCLC with 4-(4-methoxycinnamoyloxy)biphenyl side groups (P6CB).

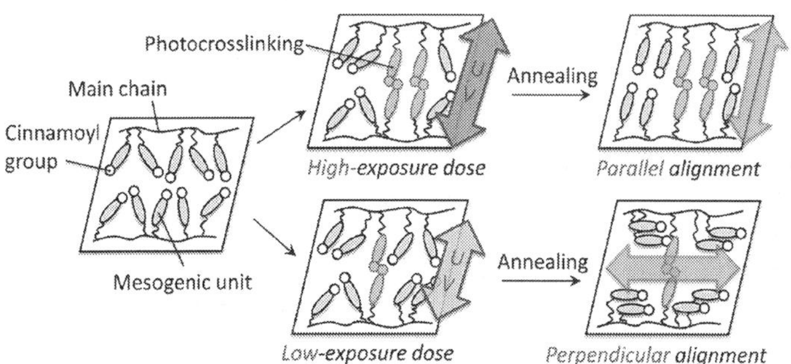

Figure 2. Schematic illustration of alignment mechanism and dependence of alignment direction on exposure dose in the P6CB.

2.2. Experiment and results

By applying the feature of P6CB described above, we propose a one-step photoalignment method as shown in **Figure 3**. In this one-step photoalignment method, orthogonal alignment direction between the two P6CB substrates is applied by linearly polarized UV beam irradiation to an empty glass cell whose inner walls are coated with P6CB. The one-step photoalignment method is realized by leveraging the phenomenon that the exposure dose between the two P6CB films is different due to the light absorption in the front P6CB film as shown in **Figure 3**. Therefore, a TN-aligned LC cell can be fabricated by injecting low-molecular-mass LCs in the empty glass cell. The experimental procedure and results of the demonstration experiment of the one-step photoalignment are described below.

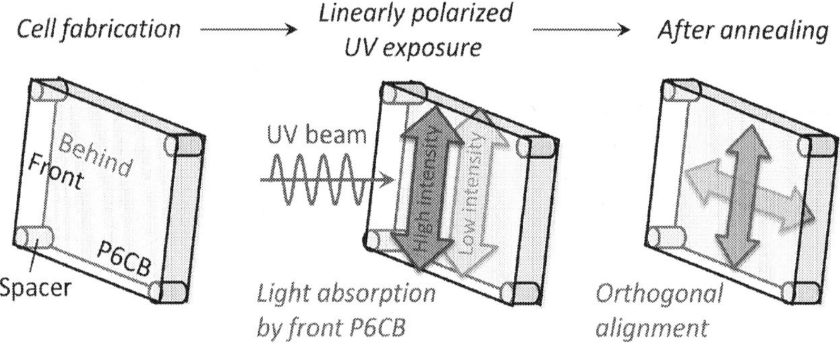

Figure 3. Schematic illustration of fabrication procedure of TN-LC cell by one-step photoalignment method.

P6CB substrates were prepared by spin coating, a solution of 1.5 wt% P6CB in methylene chloride on cleaned glass substrates. The spin coating in the first step is carried out for 3.0 s at 500 rpm, and then the second step is carried out for 40.0 s at 1500 rpm; these steps are continuous. The thickness of the resultant P6CB films on the glass substrates was 0.3 μm. An empty glass cell was fabricated by interposing 12 μm-thick spacers between two P6CB substrates, and then these were adhered using an epoxy-based adhesive. The empty glass cell was exposed to the linearly polarized UV beam as shown in **Figure 3**. A 325 nm wavelength He-Cd laser, which operates in TEM_{00} mode and emits a linear polarization, was used as the light source. The cross-sectional area of the beam was set to 0.04 cm^2 using two planoconvex lenses with different focal lengths. The beam intensity was set to 50 mW/cm^2. In this experiment, the exposure dose varied from 90 to 525 mJ/cm^2 in 72.5 mJ/cm^2 steps by changing the exposure time from 1.8 to 10.5 s. After laser irradiation, the empty glass cell was annealed at 150°C for 15 min. After cooling to room temperature, the empty glass cell was filled with the nematic LC 4-pentyl-4′-cyanobiphenyl (5CB, Merck Japan K-15) through capillary action. The transmitted light from the resultant LC cell was observed by crossed Nichols method when a white light was used as the light source. In addition, the polarization state of the transmitted light was measured by the rotation-analyzer method using a Glan-Thompson prism as the analyzer. A 633 nm wavelength linearly polarized He-Ne laser, which was incident normal to the plane of the P6CB substrates, was used as the probe beam.

Figure 4 shows the photograph of the resultant LC cell under crossed Nicol polarizers and the polarization states of the incident and transmitted beams. The polarization direction of the irradiated linearly polarized UV beam in the photoalignment process is parallel to the transmission axis of the analyzer as shown in **Figure 4(a)**. Therefore, the bright fields and the dark fields are 90° TN alignment and 0° planar alignment, respectively. The 0° planar alignment structure can be also fabricated. This is because the sufficient exposure dose to align the P6CB along the polarization direction of the irradiated UV beam in the behind substrates can be given by increasing the exposure dose to the empty glass cell. The transmittance of the 325 nm wavelength UV beam in the front P6CB substrate is approximately 30%; however, the transmittance increases gradually during UV irradiation. The alignment structures are different between the inside and the outside of the exposed spots because the transverse mode of the irradiated UV laser is TEM_{00} (i.e., an intensity distribution in accordance with a Gaussian function exists in the beam cross section). **Figure 4(b)** shows the polarization states of the incident and transmitted beams which through the spots are exposed at 235 mJ/cm^2 (TN, the third spot from the left) and 525 mJ/cm^2 (planar, the rightmost) in the photoalignment process. The polar plot represents the azimuthal distribution of the measured light intensity. The polarization azimuth of the probe beam which was transmitted through the TN alignment regions rotates 90°. Note that, the probe beam is not completely rotated 90° because the resultant LC cell does not strictly satisfy Morgan condition. Moreover, in the 0° planar alignment regions, the polarization states do not vary. These results indicate that the 90° TN and 0° planar alignment can be fabricated by one-step photoalignment method.

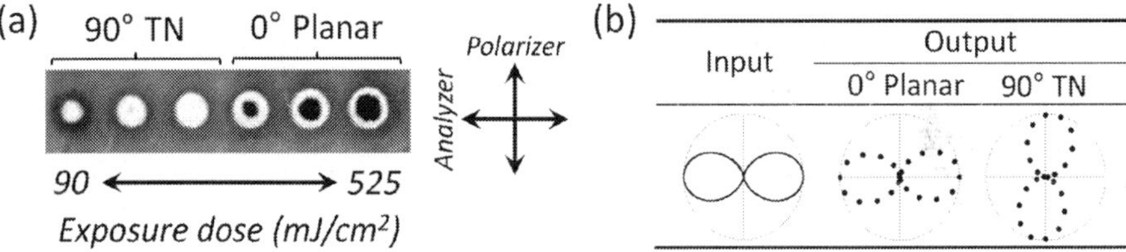

Figure 4. (a) Photograph of the resultant LC cell fabricated by one-step photoalignment under crossed Nicol polarizers. (b) Polarization states of the input and the output beams.

3. TN-LC gratings fabricated by one-step holographic photoalignment

3.1. Holographic photoalignment

LC gratings containing the TN alignment can be fabricated by extended to an interference exposure from the single beam one-step photoalignment described above. By exposure of the empty glass cell to UV interference beam in which polarization states are periodically modulated, LC gratings are fabricated accurately and efficiently. In the present study, three types of LC gratings, which hereafter referred to as the "continuous," "binary," and "planar TN," are fabricated. These LC gratings are fabricated using the common two-beam interference optical system shown in **Figure 5**. The light source was He-Cd laser which was the same as that used in the previous experiment of the one-step photoalignment. The cross-sectional area of the beam was expanded to 0.04 cm^2. The crossing angle was 0.3°, and the resultant modulation period of the electric field was 60 µm. The polarization states of the interfering beams were adjusted using the half-/quarter-wave plates. The intensity ratio of the interfering beams can be controlled by adjusting the polarization azimuth, which was an incident on the polarization beam splitter, using the half-wave plate. The one-step holographic photoalignment for the fabrication of the three types of LC gratings is described below individually. The empty glass cells used in the present experiment were the same as that described in Section 2.2. Moreover, the annealing process after the UV exposure and the injection process of nematic LCs were also the same.

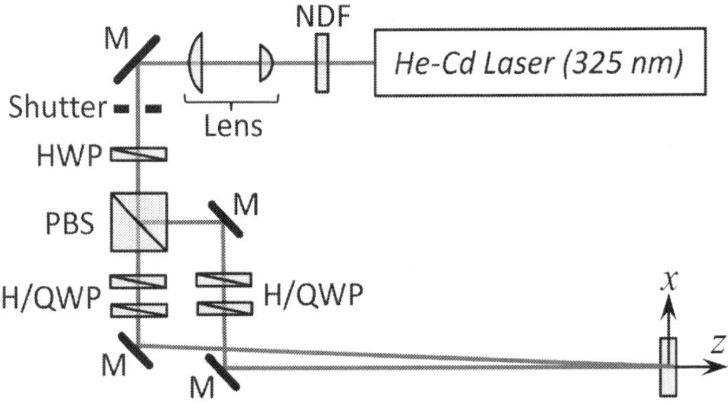

Figure 5. Optical system for two-beam interference exposure. NDF, M, PBS, and H/QWP represent the neutral-density filter, mirror, polarization beam splitter, and half-/quarter-wave plates.

3.1.1. Continuous LC gratings

Figure 6 shows the fabrication procedure for the continuous LC grating with 0° planar or with 90° TN alignment. In the continuous LC grating, LC directors are constantly rotated along the grating vector. These were fabricated by one-step circular polarization interference exposure. When two orthogonally circular polarized beams interfere with each other, the polarization azimuth of the linear polarization in the interference field is continuously modulated; however, the polarization ellipticity and the intensity are not modulated. Therefore, the periodic alignment process, in which alignment directions are continuously rotated along the grating vector, can be simultaneously applied to two P6CB alignment films in the empty glass cell. Moreover, the same alignment pattern and the orthogonal pattern with each other (i.e., the period of the pattern is shifted by a half period with each other) can be applied into the empty glass cell by adjusting the exposure dose as shown in **Figure 6(b)**. In this experiment, the beam powers of both interfering two beams were set to 2 mW. The exposure doses to fabricate the continuous LC grating with planar and with TN alignment were set to 400 mJ/cm^2 and 200 mJ/cm^2, and the exposure times were set to 8.0 s and 4.0 s, respectively. The self-diffraction from the front P6CB substrate during the photoalignment process does not occur because the optical anisotropy of P6CB is induced after annealing. The continuous LC gratings with planar or with TN alignment were fabricated by injecting the nematic LC after annealing process as shown in **Figure 6(c)**.

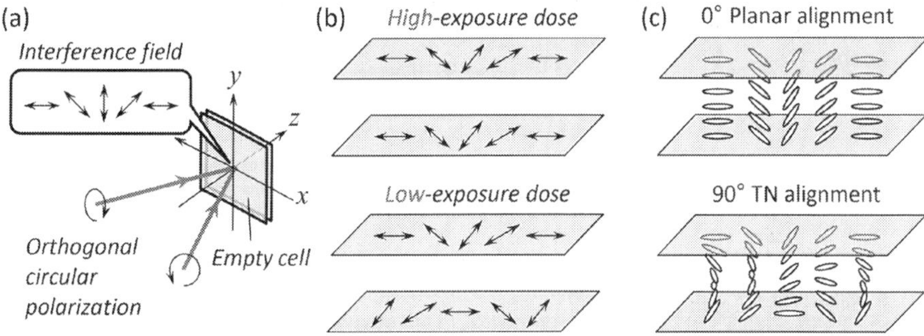

Figure 6. Schematic of the fabrication procedure for the continuous LC grating. (a) One-step exposure of an empty glass cell to a UV interference beam obtained by interfering reverse rotated circularly polarized beams with each other, (b) periodic alignment patterns after annealing in the P6CB films, and (c) director distributions after injecting with a nematic LC (5CB).

3.1.2. Binary LC gratings

Figure 7 shows the fabrication procedure for the binary LC grating with 0° planar or with 90° TN alignment. In the binary LC grating, LC directors are changed periodically and discretely by 90° in the grating vector. These were fabricated by one-step exposure of the empty glass cells to the UV interference field obtained by the interference of linearly polarized beams which were inclined +45° and −45° from the x-axis. The interference field periodically modulates the polarization states only because the +45° and −45° linear polarizations are orthogonality relation. The polarization ellipticity in the interference field is continuously modulated in the range from 0.0 to 1.0, and the polarization azimuth is discretely changed by 90° at the boundary point where the polarization ellipticity is 1.0; the polarization state changes between $\pm S_3$ via $\pm S_1$ in Poincaré sphere. Considering that the alignment direction of P6CB in the alignment films is predominantly in the longitudinal direction of the irradiated elliptical polarization, the alignment direction in the alignment films is periodically and discretely changed by 90° after annealing as shown in **Figure 7(b)**. However, the regions in the alignment films which were irradiated elliptical or circular polarization involve the decline in the anchoring energy. In this experiment, the exposure doses to fabricate the continuous grating with planar and with TN alignment were set to 600 mJ/cm^2 and 200 mJ/cm^2. Other experimental conditions and fabrication procedure were identical to those for the previously described continuous LC gratings.

fitting parameter, and the optimum cell gap in the planar-TN-LC grating obtained by fitting was 14.8 μm. The diffraction properties in the positive and negative diffraction orders were the same.

4. Conclusions

We demonstrated the efficient yet practical method for fabricating the LC gratings containing a TN alignment using one-step polarization holographic photoalignment. In addition, the director distributions of the resultant LC gratings are analyzed based on the elastic continuum theory and observed experimentally using a polarized light optical microscope. Furthermore, the polarization diffraction properties were measured experimentally by the incident of a visible laser and analyzed theoretically by Jones calculation. This study is of significance in that the various LC gratings containing TN alignments can be fabricated by simultaneous exposure of two P6CB substrates to the polarization interference beams. In the resultant continuous gratings, the polarization conversion properties to the circular polarization and the dependence of the propagation direction on the polarization states of the probe beams are obtained. In the resultant binary LC grating, the polarization azimuth of the diffracted beam changed ranging from 0° to 90° depending on the polarization azimuth of the probe beam. Moreover, when the probe beam is elliptical or circularly polarized, the rotation direction of the diffracted beam is converted. In the resultant planar-TN-LC grating, the polarization azimuth of both the probe beam and the diffracted beam showed an inverse relationship. In addition, the polarization ellipticity varied depending on the polarization azimuth of the probe beam. These polarization diffraction properties are well explained by theoretical analysis based on Jones calculus. These resultant LC gratings exhibit great potential for application as a diffractive optical element that can simultaneously control the various parameters of the light wave, such as amplitude, polarization states, and propagation direction.

Author details

Kotaro Kawai[1], Moritsugu Sakamoto[1], Kohei Noda[1], Tomoyuki Sasaki[1], Nobuhiro Kawatsuki[2] and Hiroshi Ono[1]*

*Address all correspondence to: onoh@nagaokaut.ac.jp

1 Department of Electrical Engineering, Nagaoka University of Technology, Nagaoka, Niigata, Japan

2 Department of Applied Chemistry, University of Hyogo, Himeji, Hyogo, Japan

References

[1] Todorov, T., Nikolova, L., Tomova, N. Polarization holography. 2: Polarization holographic gratings in photoanisotropic materials with and without intrinsic birefringence. Applied Optics. 1984;**23**(24):4588–4591. DOI: 10.1364/AO.23.004588

[2] Crawford, G.P., Eakin, J.N., Radcliffe, M.D., Callan-Jones, A., Pelcovits, R.A. Liquid-crystal diffraction gratings using polarization holography alignment techniques. Journal of Applied Physics. 2005;**98**(12):123102. DOI: 10.1063/1.2146075

[3] Yu, C.-J., Kim, D.-W., Kim, J., Lee, S.-D. Polarization-invariant grating based on a photoaligned liquid crystal in an oppositely twisted binary configuration. Optics Letters. 2005;**30**(15):1995–1997. DOI: 10.1364/OL.30.001995

[4] Komanduri R.K, Escuti M.J. High efficiency reflective liquid crystal polarization grating. Applied Physics Letters. 2009;**95**(9):091106. DOI: 10.1063/1.3197011

[5] Honma, M., Nose, T. Highly efficient twisted nematic liquid crystal polarization gratings achieved by microrubbing. Applied Physics Letters. 2012;**101**(4):041107. DOI: 10.1063/1.4737945

[6] Zhu, J.-L., Lu, J.-G., Qiang, J., Zhong E.-W, Ye Z.-C, He Z, et. al. 1D/2D switchable grating based on field-induced polymer stabilized blue phase liquid crystal. Journal of Applied Physics. 2012;**111**(3):033101. DOI: 10.1063/1.3680875

[7] Kuzuwata, M., Sasaki, T., Kawatsuki, N., Ono, H. Fabrication of twisted nematic structure and vector grating cells by one-step exposure on photocrosslinkable polymer liquid crystals. Optics Letters. 2012;**37**(6):1115–1117. DOI: 10.1364/OL.37.001115

[8] Kawai, K., Sasaki, T., Noda, K., Kawatsuki, N., Ono, H. Simple fabrication of liquid crystalline grating cells with homogeneous and twisted nematic structures and effects of orientational relaxation on diffraction properties. Applied Optics. 2014;**53**(17):3679–3686. DOI: 10.1364/AO.53.003679

[9] Kawai, K., Sasaki, T., Noda, K., Sakamoto, M., Kawatsuki, N., Ono H. Holographic binary grating liquid crystal cells fabricated by one-step exposure of photocrosslinkable polymer liquid crystalline alignment substrates to a polarization interference ultraviolet beam. Applied Optics. 2015;**54**(19):6010–6018. DOI: 10.1364/AO.54.006010

[10] Kawai, K., Sakamoto, M., Noda, K., Sasaki, T., Kawatsuki, N., Ono, H. Design and fabrication of a tunable wavelength-selective polarization grating. Applied Optics. 2016;**55**(26):6269–6274. DOI: 10.1364/AO.55.006269

[11] Kawatsuki, N., Goto, K., Kawakami, T., Yamamoto, T. Reversion of alignment direction in the thermally enhanced photoorientation of photo-cross linkable polymer liquid crystal films. Macromolecules. 2002;**35**(3):706–713. DOI: 10.1021/ma011439u

[12] Scharf, T. Polarized light in liquid crystals and polymers. Hoboken, New Jersey: John Wiley & Sons, Inc.; 2007. 400 p. DOI: 10.1002/047007437X

Application of High Performance Photoinitiating Systems for Holographic Grating Recording

C. Ley, C. Carré, A. Ibrahim and X. Allonas

Additional information is available at the end of the chapter

http://dx.doi.org/10.5772/66073

Abstract

In this chapter, a compilation of different systems able to photogenerate active radicals toward polymerization reaction(type I, type II and three component photoinitiating systems) for application in holographic grating recording when associated to monomers is reviewed. In particular, the visible curable system is associated to fluorinated acrylate monomers formulation for creation of transmission gratings. The PIS efficiencies are presented in term of diffraction grating yields and compared to photopolymerization experiments. The special case of photocyclic initiating systems is described in details, its influence on the grating built up being discussed on the basis of selected mixtures using visible dyes, electron donors (e.g. amines), electron acceptors (e.g. iodonium salts) or hydrogen donors as coinitiators. The role of the photochemical properties of dye on the performance of the holographic recording material is investigated through time resolved and steady state spectroscopic studies of the PIS (e.g. nanosecond laser flash photolysis), to highlight the photochemistry underlying active radicals photogeneration. In order to get more insight into the hologram formation, grating formation curves were compared to those of monomer to polymer conversion obtained by real time Fourier transform infrared spectroscopy (RTFTIR). This work outlines the importance of the coupling between the photoinitiating system (i.e. the photochemical reactions) and the holographic resin.

Keywords: free radical photopolymerization, photoinitiating systems, holographic recording, polymer material, diffraction gratings

1. Introduction

Photopolymerization is a chemical reaction where organic molecules exposed to UV or visible photons react to form macromolecules corresponding to high molecular weight molecules, i.e.,

the polymer. Photopolymerizable resins usually contain a photoinitiating system (PIS) which converts light into chemical energy, a mixture of monomers, oligomers and additives [1]. The most versatile process is the free radical photopolymerization (FRPP) which offers the most important choice of materials and potential PIS. The efficiency of the PIS is determined by the light absorption properties of the photosenzitizer (PS, the molecules that absorb photons, like organic dyes), given by Beer-Lambert's law, the quantum yield of initiating radicals and the reactivity of these radicals towards the monomer. It is recognized that the photoinitiating systems is the corner stone of photopolymerization process. One application of photopolymerization is holographic recording [2, 3], for example, for information storage [4–7]. Holography also represents an interesting and growing field due to an increasing demand in security. The development of such applications is directly governed by the characteristics of the material available for holographic recording. Photopolymerizable media are promising candidates. In that case, the performance of the material is related to the photosensitivity of the photopolymer and the diffraction efficiency which could be obtained. Therefore, the design of systems for highest performances is still an interesting challenge. For instance, Acrylic monomers, which are currently used in these recording systems, have opened up in this field interesting possibilities, due to their attractive features (the complete absence of wet processing, high flexibility of the formulation, high diffraction efficiencies) [8, 9].

2. Basics of photoinitiating systems

Historically, two classes of photoinitiating systems were defined depending on the mechanisms of light conversion into chemical potential (i.e., radicals). In the first class, the photoinitiating system contains one molecule (the photoinitiator PI) which is promoted into a dissociative excited state after light absorption and undergoes a homolytic (or heterolytic) cleavage through a Norrish I photoreaction [10–12]. These type I photoinitiators produce two radicals that could be both reactive toward free radical photopolymerization (FRPP) (**Figure 1a**).

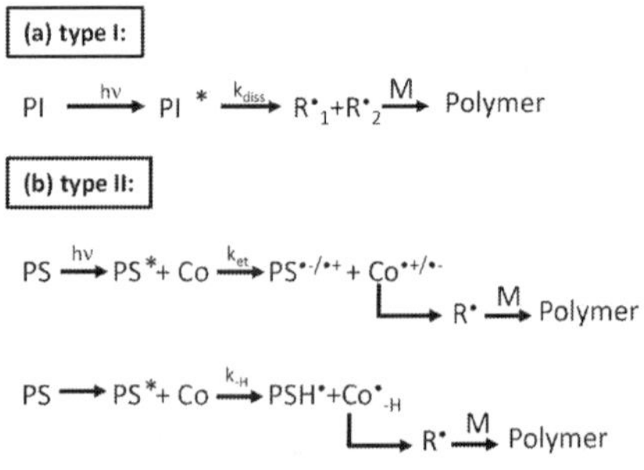

(a) type I:

$$PI \xrightarrow{h\nu} PI^* \xrightarrow{k_{diss}} R^{\bullet}_1 + R^{\bullet}_2 \xrightarrow{M} Polymer$$

(b) type II:

$$PS \xrightarrow{h\nu} PS^* + Co \xrightarrow{k_{et}} PS^{\bullet-/\bullet+} + Co^{\bullet+/\bullet-}$$
$$\longmapsto R^{\bullet} \xrightarrow{M} Polymer$$

$$PS \longrightarrow PS^* + Co \xrightarrow{k_{-H}} PSH^{\bullet} + Co^{\bullet}_{-H}$$
$$\longmapsto R^{\bullet} \xrightarrow{M} Polymer$$

Figure 1. Type I and type II photoinitiating systems (PIS), PI: photoinitiator, PS: photosensitizer, Co: coinitiator, R$^{\bullet}$: initiating radical, M: monomer, k_{diss}: rate constant of dissociation, k_{et}: electron transfer rate constant, k_{-H}: hydrogen abstraction rate constant.

Among type I photoinitiators, one can find hydroxylalkylphenones, benzylketals, benzoin ether derivatives, α-aminoketones and acylphosphine oxides (**Figure 2**). In these compounds, the cleavage rate constants are high, leading to very good quantum yields of radical generation Φ_R. The quantum yield of radical generation is defined as the number of radicals formed divided by the number of absorbed photons. Some type I photoinitiating systems exhibit quantum yield as high as 0.8–1.0 [13, 14]. However, the vast majority of type I photoinitiators is only reactive under UV light [14, 15]. Only a limited set of available type I photoinitiating systems absorbs in the blue or green region. For instance, a bisbenzoylphosphine oxide derivative (Irgacure 819) exhibits an absorption spectrum extending up to around 410–420 nm. The great advantage of this class of acylphosphine is the efficient photobleaching ability that increases the photoinitiation efficiency. This is especially useful when high thickness of photopolymer is needed. However, oxygen inhibition impacts the efficiency of this class of acylphosphine oxide, which limits their applications [10]. A titanocene derivative (CG-784) absorbing in the green region was applied to the photopolymerization of some high-index organic monomers and incorporated into acrylate oligomer-based formulations, which enables irradiation at 546-nm light source [16]. Unfortunately, it seems that this compound does not produce enough initiating radicals to achieve the appropriate monomer conversion [17]. Recently, a visible light photoinitiator based on acylgermanium structure was developed, exhibiting high reactivity under 550-nm irradiation. However, its main drawback relies on the availability of the molecule (proprietary structure and synthesis) [18].

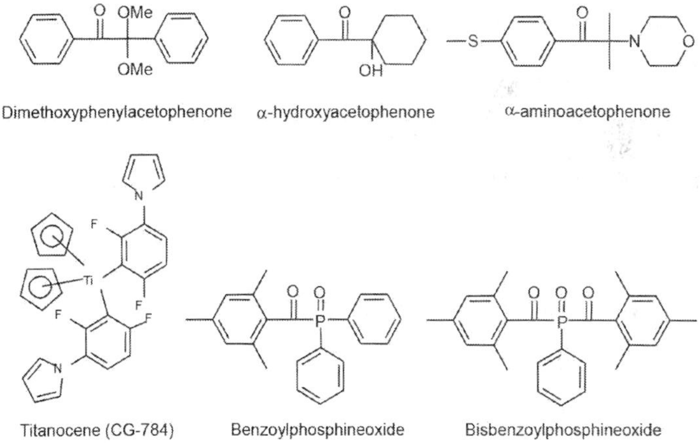

Dimethoxyphenylacetophenone   α-hydroxyacetophenone   α-aminoacetophenone

Titanocene (CG-784)   Benzoylphosphineoxide   Bisbenzoylphosphineoxide

Figure 2. Examples of commercially available type I photoinitiators.

Even if type I photoinitiators can exhibit high quantum yields of radicals, their main drawback is their limited spectral sensitivity to the UV—blue region of the electromagnetic spectrum. By contrast, type II PIS are versatile initiators for UV curing systems and visible light photopolymerization. Indeed, the combination of organic dyes and coinitiators provides tremendous flexibility in the selection of irradiation wavelength from the UV to the near infra-red region.

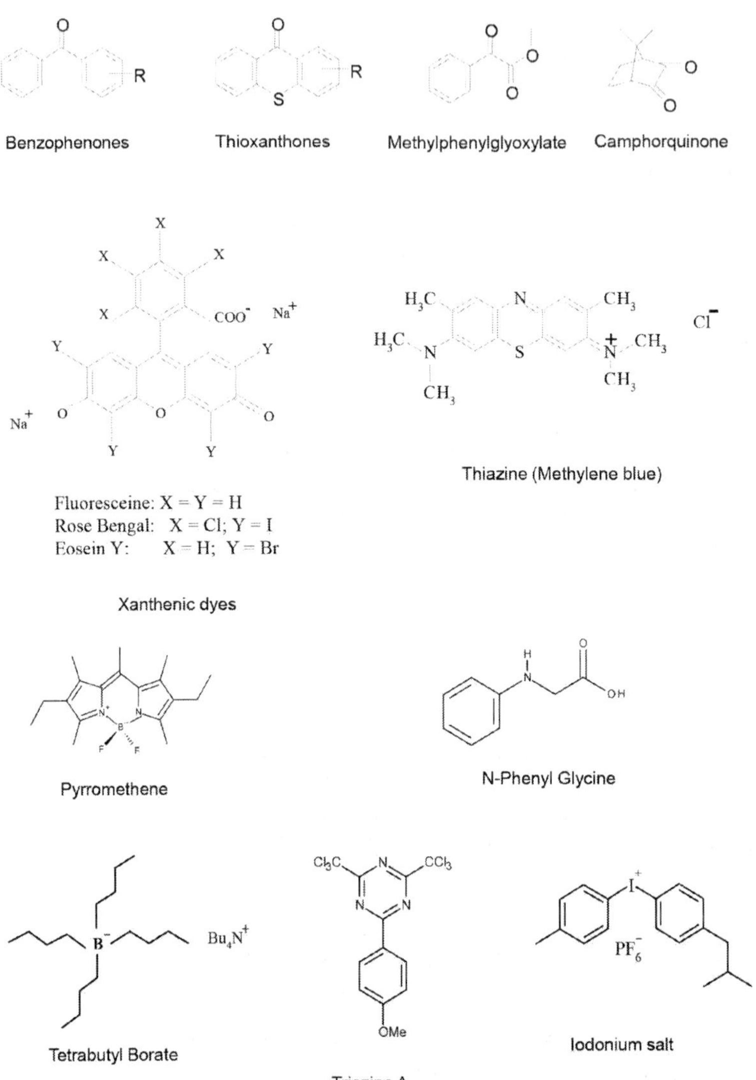

Figure 3. Examples of commercially available type II photosensitizers (PS) and coinitiators (Co).

Thus, on the contrary to type I PIs which are monomolecular, type II photoinitiating systems rely on the combination of two molecules (see **Figure 1b**). The first molecule absorbs the photon. It is the chromophore and is often called the photoinitiator (PI) or the photosensitizer (PS). The second one could be an electron donor, an electron acceptor or a hydrogen donor (see **Figure 1b**), the so-called coinitiator (Co), which gives the initiating radicals R$^{\bullet}$ through photoreaction [19, 20]. After light absorption, the photosensitizer (PS) is promoted into one of its electronic excited states (singlet and/or triplet) from which the photochemical reaction occurs with the coinitiator (Co). One important feature of type II PIS is that the photosensitizer (PS) and the coinitiator (Co) must be selected to prevent any dark thermal reaction. Thus, photopolymerization occurs only in irradiated zones allowing a full control of the polymerization in time and space. In typical type II PIS, photosensitizers with good absorption features in the UV-blue region can be selected among benzophenones [21–28], thioxanthones [29–34], camphorquinone [35–37], benzyls [22, 38] and ketocoumarin derivatives [39–41]. For visible light PIS, the PS can be selected in whole panel of organic dyes such as, coumarins [41], xanthenic dyes [42–44], cyanine dyes [45], thiazine dyes [42], phenazine dyes and pyrromethene dyes [46–48]. The hydrogen donor coinitiators are generally amines [36, 49–54], ethers [55–57], sulfides [57–61] and thiols [61–63](see **Figure 3**). However, the ketyl radical formed on the PS moiety is generally unreactive with respect to the double bonds and could even act as a terminating agent towards the growing chain [17, 49, 64, 65]. Coinitiators reacting through electron transfer are borate salts [66, 67], iodonium salts [68–70] or triazine derivatives [47] which lead to the production of radical after a photodissociative electron transfer reaction with excited PS. However, these two components systems have limited efficiency compared to type I systems.

3. Photocyclic initiating systems

One of the reasons that could be responsible for the lower sensitivity of type II photoinitiating systems (PIS) compared to type I is their inherent chemical mechanisms. In type I PIS, the molecules are cleaved after light absorption: this is an intramolecular fast reaction. On the other side, for type II PIS, the reactions are bimolecular and can be limited by diffusion process of the photosensitizer (PS) and coinitiator (Co) (see **Figure 4**). The actual reaction rate constants of electron transfer (or H-abstraction) in such conditions can be evaluated from a simple encounter complex kinetic model (see [45] and ref. herein for more details) and is generally lowered when the viscosity of the resin increases. As a result, the efficiency of reaction is greatly impacted and the PIS becomes inefficient with low radical quantum yields.

One way to overcome the lack of reactivity of conventional type II photoinitiating systems (PIS) is to develop one molecule type II PIS where the PS and the coinitiator (Co) are chemically linked together (see **Figure 4b**). In this case, reaction rates are independent of the diffusion process and highly sensitive systems can be obtained [71–74]. However, such kind of single molecule type II photoinitiating systems (PIS) suffer of proprietary structure and synthesis costs which makes them tricky to use.

In order to enhance type II sensitivity, many groups have developed more complex photoinitiating systems by adding a third component into the PIS formulation leading to the so-called three-component photoinitiating system. Indeed, the photopolymerization efficiency of type II PIS can be greatly improved by introducing an additive, which yields to an additional radical

this thermodynamic approach covers also the type II photoinitiating systems requirements. Finally, if ever the fourth electron transfer reaction occurs (**Figure 5** [4]), the reduced PS is oxidized by the third component and the PS is regenerated while a second initiating radical is produced. This leads to the so-called photocyclic (or photocatalytic) initiating systems (PCIS) (vide infra). Detailed explanation of PCIS kinetics and thermodynamics can be found in Ref. [95]. However, obtaining a photocyclic behavior in three-component systems is not straighforward and great care must be taken when combining dyes and coinitiators.

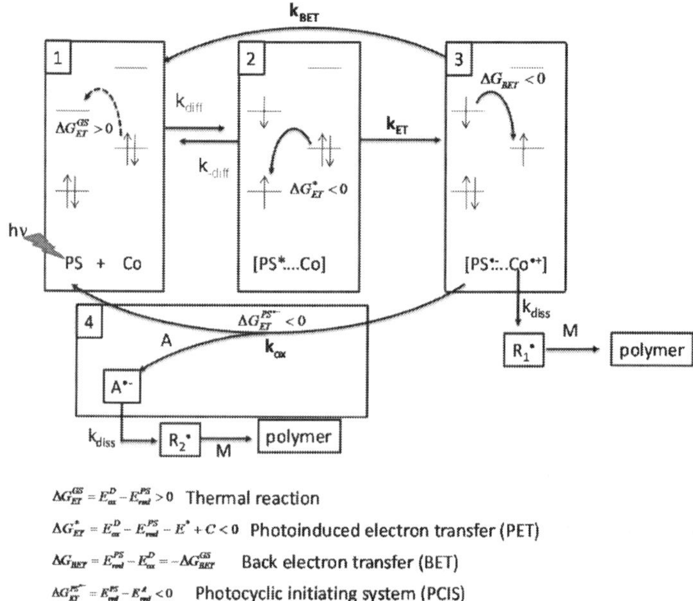

$$\Delta G_{ET}^{GS} = E_{ox}^{D} - E_{red}^{PS} > 0 \quad \text{Thermal reaction}$$

$$\Delta G_{ET}^{*} = E_{ox}^{D} - E_{red}^{PS} - E^{*} + C < 0 \quad \text{Photoinduced electron transfer (PET)}$$

$$\Delta G_{BET} = E_{red}^{PS} - E_{ox}^{D} = -\Delta G_{BET}^{GS} \quad \text{Back electron transfer (BET)}$$

$$\Delta G_{ET}^{PS⁻} = E_{red}^{PS} - E_{red}^{A} < 0 \quad \text{Photocyclic initiating system (PCIS)}$$

Figure 5. Thermodynamics of an oxidative three-components PCIS [1], ground state reaction (ΔG_{ET}^{GS}) [2], excited state reaction (ΔG_{ET}^{*}) [3], back electron transfer (BET, ΔG_{BET}) [4], PS regeneration ($\Delta G_{ET}^{PS^{\bullet+}}$) in photocyclic initiating system (PCIS vide infra).

Thus, in the case of three-components PIS, two mechanisms have been observed leading to two general classes (see **Figure 6**):

a. Parallel reactions in which the coinitiators Co and the additive A react with the excited state of the dye independently (**Figure 6a**);

b. (b) Sequential reactions in which, for example, the Co reacts first through PET with the dye excited state (**Figure 6b**) leading to reduced PS and a first initiating radical. Then, the reduced PS can react with the additive A to regenerate the PS and give a second initiating radical.

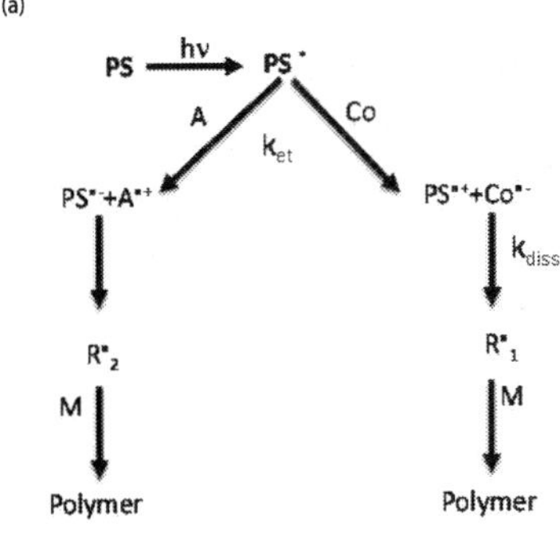

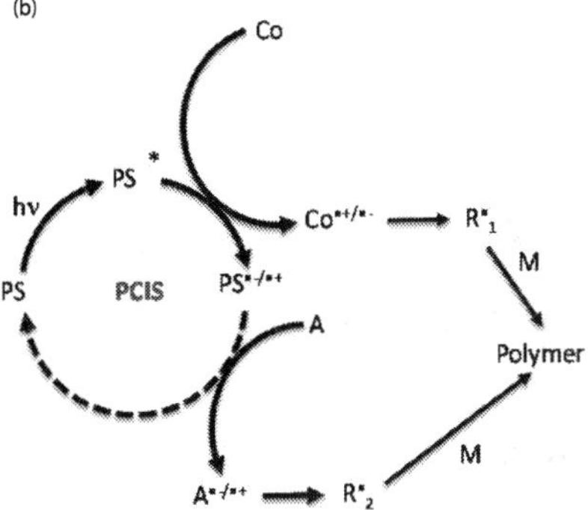

Figure 6. General reaction mechanism occurring in three-component photoinitiating systems, (a) parallel mechanisms, (b) photocyclic initiating system (PCIS).

In parallel (i.e., independent and competitive) reactions, the total yield of radicals depends on the reactivity of each coinitiator with the excited state and is not very interesting. The sequential reactions present more attractive features. This mechanism yields two advantages: the additive (A) leads to the formation of supplementary initiating radical, and the ground state dye is recovered and can be involved in further photoreactions. Therefore, a real cyclic photoreaction occurs until complete depletion of reactants. Moreover, the maximum theoretical quantum yields of PCIS are two, meaning that one absorbed photon can give two initiating radicals.

4. Photoinitiating systems for holographic recording

Holographic polymerization recording is a very particular application of photopolymerization: a three-dimensional image is built through inhomogeneous polymerization when the interference pattern illuminates the photosentive medium [5–7]. Indeed, photopolymerization is ideally suited for such application as the reaction can be spatially and temporally controlled. Holographic elements, reversible holograms and switchable holographic gratings have been created by this method [5, 96–99]. Since the 1970s, photopolymers were developed in holography as media able to record an interference pattern or small series of pattern, through building-up of refractive index variations or relief profiles [100–102]. During volume hologram recording in a photopolymer, a complex fringe pattern with small features at the micrometer scale is recorded. The local incident variations of irradiance induce inhomogeneous photopolymerization of the photosensitive recording medium at the sub-micrometer scale leading to refractive index modulations in the hologram. Many physical and chemical processes are involved in the holographic recording: photochemical conversion of the sensitizer, of the monomer, mass transport (being a consequence of the formation of spatial concentration gradients of monomer and sensitizer), hardening of the polymer matrix, etc. Therefore, formulating the material requires a fair knowledge of all these processes, which is not a straightforward way as many parameters must be taken into account [4, 103, 104].

Many PIS can be used for holographic recording applications. Titanocene derivative Bis(η5-2,4-cylcopentadien-1-yl)-bis (2,6-difluoro-3-(1H-pyrrol-1-yl)-phenyl) titanium, Irgacure®784, was used for the optimization of several high index organic monomers into high optical quality acrylate oligomer-based formulation and compared to the type II PIS [105]. However, even if it is a one molecule process by-products that can alter recoding are formed [106]. Moreover, by introducing with these type I titanocene compounds, nanoparticles in the holographic polymer, the effect of nanoparticles concentration and size, as well as the benefic effect of chain transfer agent were studied [107, 108]. Triphenylphosphine (TPO) type I PIS was used for initiating thiol-ene photopolymerization in a composite holographic resin containing nanoparticles in a way to reduce shrinkage and enhance Δn_{sat} [109]. Near UV type I photoinitiator Irgacure 1700 was used to study the effect of surface modified ZrO_2 and TiO_2 nanoparticles, allowing high refractive index modulation and better stability against UV light [110].

A widely used type II PIS is the combination of phenanthrenequinone (PQ) with methacrylates (MA) monomers and oligomers (PMMA) [111–116]: in this case, the PQ is supposed to directly react with PMMA in its triplet state by hydrogen abstraction [112, 113]. Among other Type II PIS, methylene blue (MB) and rose Bengal (RB) have been tested in crylamide and polyvinylalcohol films [42] under 633 or 514 nm irradiation, diffraction efficiencies of 65 and 35%, and sensitivities of 30 and 100 mJ cm^{-2} have been, respectively, reached, with a spatial resolution of *ca.* 1000 lines mm^{-1}.

The influence of photonic and chemical parameters on the holographic recording capabilities and photochemical bleaching process of a series of xanthene dyes such as RB, eosin Y (EY), erythrosin B (ErB), fluorescein (F) and rhodamine B (RoB) has been investigated with triethanolamine (TEA) as electron donor Co [117, 118]. The photobleaching efficiency, i.e., the ability of the PS to lose their tint, followed the order ErB > EY > RB > RoB > F. The highest photobleaching rate constant of ErB PIS was invoqued to explain the higher diffraction efficiency obtained compared to EY, RB, RoB and F under the same experimental conditions. More recently, the same family of xanthenic dyes was theoretically and experimentally investigated [119].

A system using EY, F, MB and thionine (TH) as photosensitizers with morpholine, dimethylaminoethanol and piperidine as electron donors, and an oligourethane-acrylates resin has been used for holographic applications such as interferometry and pattern recognition systems [120]. A sufficiently high speed of recording in the 460–540 nm range has been noticed. Despite higher absorbance in the longer wavelength, holographic experiment in the red light with the MB systems outlined low reactivity and slow recording rates. More recently, combination of MB and trimethylamine (TEA) as coinitiator was still used as type II PIS in holographic recording systems bearing metallic ions as dopers to enhance holographic sensitivity efficiency [121, 122].

If type II photoinitiating systems (PIS) are widely used in holographic recording, the use of three-components PIS is less common. The efficiency of a three-component PIS based on hexaarylbisimidazole derivative (HABI), associated to a chain transfer agent 2-mercaptobenzooxazole (MBO) and 2,5-bis[[(4-diethylamino)phenyl] methylene] cyclopentanone (DEAW) as the PS incorporated into high optical quality acrylate oligomer-based formulations was reported [105] (see **Figure 7**).

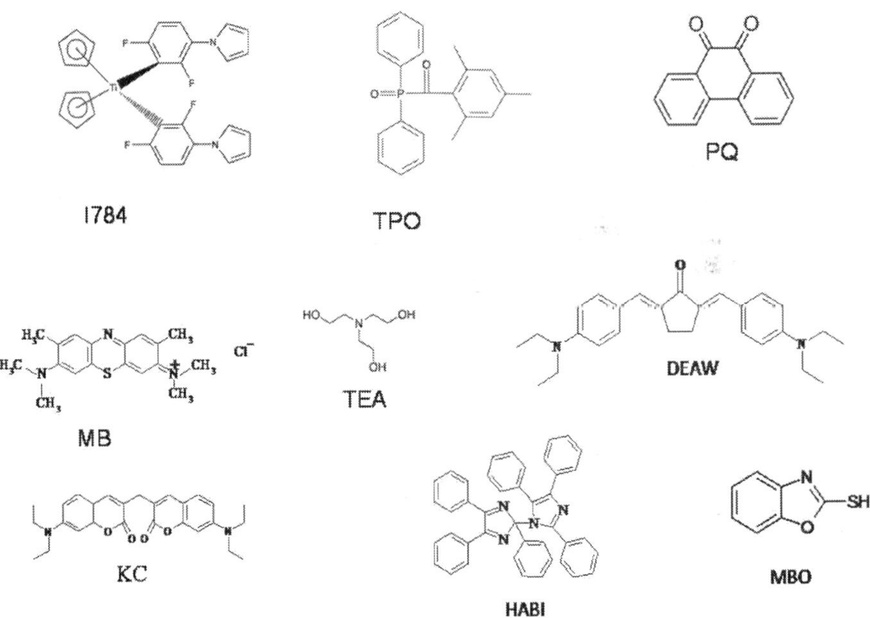

Figure 7. Structures of some PIS compounds; Bis(η5-2,4-cylcopentadien-1-yl)-bis (2,6-difluoro-3-(1H-pyrrol-1-yl)-phenyl) titanium: Irgacur®784, 2,4,6-Trimethylbenzoyl-diphenylphosphine oxide: Darocur® TPO, phenanthrenequinone: PQ, methylene blue: MB, triethanolamine: TEA; 2-mercaptobenzooxazole: MBO, 2,5-bis[[(4-diethylamino)phenyl] methylene] cyclopentanone: DEAW, hexaarylbisimidazole: HABI, 3-3′-carbonyl-bis-7-diethylaminocoumarin: KC.

Another three-component photosensitive resin, based on a 3-3′-carbonyl-bis-7-diethylamino-coumarin (KC) PS, N-phenylglycine (NPG) and diphenyl iodonium chloride (DPI) has been used to record holograms at 488 nm (Ar⁺ laser). A diffraction efficiency around 51% corresponding to a refractive index modulation of 0.013 was obtained [123]. The efficiency of PIS based on new original synthesized dyes that could be sensitive to He-Ne laser line (632.8 nm), a HABI derivative and 3-mercapto-4-methyl-4H-1,2,4-triazole (MTA), was studied [124]. A 80% diffraction efficiency was obtained, with good physical and chemical stability under ambient conditions. The singlet excited state reactivity of bipyrromethene-BF_2 complexes (also known as BODIPY) was used in amine-free photosensitive hydrophobic binder resin as an alternative to xanthene dyes-based redox PIS [125]. The unbleached final gratings showed diffraction efficiency of 85% with good sensitivity in the 457–520 nm range.

5. Influence of photoinitiating system on holographic recording

In summary, this survey of the literature shows that most of the photoinitiating systems used for holographic recording are simple classical type I or type II PIS. Three components combination in holographic resins are less common. Moreover, the exact photochemistry underlying the initiating radical generation is not very well-known, and the effect of the PIS photochemistry on hologram formation was rarely questioned [126–128]. Furthermore, it is difficult to compare and gather holographic recording resin results, many different PIS systems are available and can be associated to various polymerizable resin, with or without binders, for use in different optical setup with diverse photonic parameters.

However, in a recent work, the influence of photochemistry on the holographic recording efficiency was performed by our group in collaboration with Bayer material science team [129]. It was shown that the prediction and interpretation of the holographic performance of a photosensitive resin containing a type II photo initiating systems is directly related to the reactivity of the dyes excited states involved and to the intrinsic properties of the photopolymerizable medium. Indeed the radical quantum yield of the dyes (RB and SFH⁺) coupled to borates salt electron donor coinitiator was fixed by the viscosity of the holographic resin matrix and the redox properties of the dyes and borates. A method was proposed to calculate the initial yield of initiating radicals. It was found that this radical formation quantum yield directly governs not only the maximum rate constant of photopolymerization, but also the final diffraction efficiency.

With this in mind, we have recently tailored different three-components photoinitiating systems for holographic recording with the advantage that all measurements were performed on the same holographic resin formulation, under fixed experimental conditions in a given holographic recording setup [130–132]. Furthermore, the holographic results were compared to the visible curing of the holographic resin formulation followed by real-time FTIR spectroscopy [130–134]. RT-FTIR allowed the study of free radical polymerization (FRP) by following the disappearance of C-C double bonds in monomer (see Ref. [131–133] for more detail): it permitted to measure the final monomer conversion into polymer and the rate of double bond consumption during the polymerization reaction R_c (s^{-1}) (see **Figure 8a**). The IR spectra were recorded during sample irradiation using a green laser diode emitting at 532 nm (Roithner Lasertechnik, 50 mW) which was adapted to the FTIR spectrometer by a light guide (see **Figure 8a**). The irradiation intensity was adjusted at 25 mW/cm^2 on the sample. To prevent the diffusion of oxygen into the sample during the irradiation, experiments were carried out by laminating the resin between two polypropylene films and two CaF$_2$ windows. The thickness of the sample was adjusted using a 25-μm Teflon spacer. The spectra were recorded between 600 and 3900 cm^{-1}. The kinetics of the polymerization were measured by following the disappearance of the C-C bond stretching signal at 1637 cm^{-1}. The degree of conversion was directly related to the decrease in peak area at 1637 cm^{-1} according to:

$$C = \frac{\left(A_{1637}\right)_0 - \left(A_{1637}\right)_{t0}}{\left(A_{1637}\right)_0} \tag{1}$$

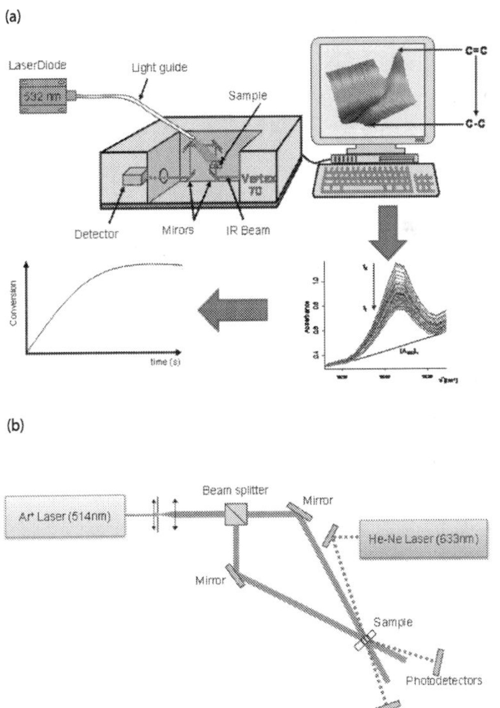

Figure 8. RT-FTIR (a) and Holographic grating recording (b) setup.

where $(A_{1637})_0$ and $(A_{1637})_t$ were the area of the IR absorption band at 1637 cm^{-1} of the sample before exposure and at time t, respectively.

Holographic gratings were recorded in transmission at 514 nm for a spatial frequency of 1000 lines mm^{-1} transmission grating in the resin with a 514 nm actinic laser. For that purpose, the samples are prepared by embedding the photopolymerizable formulation between two glass-substrates. Calibrated glass beads were used as spacers to guarantee the thickness of the system around 20 µm. The photopolymerizable system was irradiated by the sinusoidal interference pattern of two incident s-polarized beams of equal intensity, corresponding to a total power density of 25 mW/cm^2 on the photosensitive sample with a beam diameter of 2.5 cm (**Figure 8b**). Inhomogeneous polymerization reaction and dye bleaching took place leading to a modulation of the refractive index, giving rise to thick phase volume diffraction gratings. The fact that no chemical posttreatment was needed for this recording medium used, allowed the continuous follow up of the process during exposure with an inactinic reading light beam (HeNe laser at 633 nm) which was more or less diffracted (see **Figure 8b**). The diffraction efficiency at 633 nm (η) was defined by the ratio of the intensity of the first diffraction order to the diffracted plus transmitted light intensities.

The holographic resin was a mixture of different monomers and additives: the choice of the formulation was governed by earlier experiments performed in the field of visible curable systems and use of fluorinated acrylate monomers for the recording of holographic polymer-dispersed liquid crystals (LC) transmission gratings. This self-developing formulation contained:

- 45 wt% of a hexafunctional aliphatic urethane acrylate oligomer (Ebecryl 1290, Cytec) acting as primary oligomer;

- 22.5 wt% of 1,1,1,3,3,3-hexafluoroisopropyl acrylate and 22.5 wt% of vinyl neononanoate, both from Sigma-Aldrich (France). The vinyl ester monomer is known to copolymerize very easily with acrylic monomers;

- 5 wt% of N-vinyl-2-pyrrolidinone (Sigma-Aldrich, France) which is a standard additive introduced in photopolymerizable systems here to favor compounds solubility;

- 5 wt% of Trimethylpropane tris (3-mercaptopropionate) (Sigma-Aldrich, France) which is a trifunctional thiol able to increase the photopolymerization rate in air and leading to higher monomer conversion. These compounds were used as received. The chemical structures of the reagents used for the preparation of holographic resin can be found in Ref [132].

An example of RT-FTIR monomer conversion of the holographic resin as a function of irradiation time is given on **Figure 9b**. The photoinitiaitng system was based on Safranine O (SFH$^+$) as photosensitizer (PS), EDB as an electron donor and Triazine A electron acceptor (see **Figure 3** for molecular structures) as the third component. It can be seen that going from two components type II to three-components PIS increases both the rate of conversion R_c and the final conversion C_f. The same observation is valid for measured diffraction yield as a function of irradiation time (**Figure 9a**): both the formation building up time of the diffraction grating and the final diffraction efficiency increase.

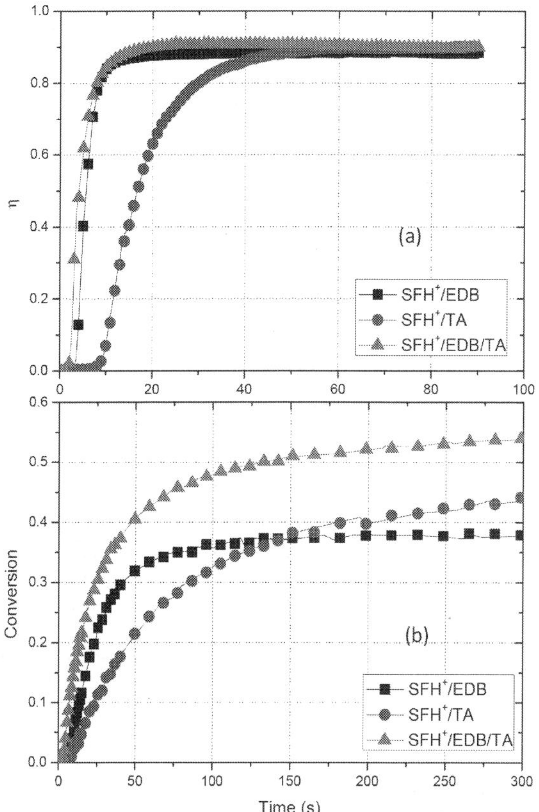

Figure 9. Evolution of the diffraction efficiency η during grating writing (a) of SFH⁺ PIS and corresponding monomer conversion curves as a function of irradiation time (b).

Moreover, besides RT-FTIR and holographic measurements, a complete and detailed study of the photochemical reaction of the PIS was performed. For this purpose, steady state (UV-Vis, fluorescence) and time resolved (laser flash photolysis, time correlated single photon counting, etc.) spectroscopies were used. The first system was based on the singlet excited state reactivity of Bipyrromethene-BF$_2$ complexes (EMP) combined with an amine (EDB) and two electron acceptor (TA, I250) [130]. The two other systems were based on the reactivity of the triplet excited state of two dyes, RB and Safranine O (SFH⁺) [131, 132]. In the first one, the reactivity of RB was compared to the reactivity of SFH⁺ when combined to NPG electron donor coinitiator and HABI as additive third component [131]. In the last system, SFH⁺ was combined with one electron donor (EDB) and one electron acceptor. However, it was demonstrated that no photocycle occurred in these PIS (see **Figure 9** [2, 3]). [133] Indeed, besides the nature of the excited state involved in the radical photogeneration process, it was shown that EMP PIS exhibited a photocyclic behavior (i.e., forms a PCIS) while RB and SFH⁺ PIS presented a parallel behavior (see **Figure 10**).

In order to understand correctly Scheme 2 in **Figure 10**, Hexaarylbiimidazole (HABI) derivatives deserve a little more explanations. HABI (Scheme 1 in **Figure 10**) was first synthesized by Hayashi and Maeda (see [134] and ref. Herein). It was proved that the two imidazolyl rings are twisted almost 90° relative to each other [134]. The bond energy of C-N in ClHABI is very low, which easily leads to the homolytic cleavage of ClHABI when exposed to the UV light or heated [135] to a pair of triarylimidazolyl radicals (lophyl radicals = L•). The lophyl radical (L•) is known to be a poor initiator of free radical polymerization, because of both high stability [135–137]. However, the lophyl radical is an excellent hydrogen atom abstractor, and this can be exploited in initiation using a hydrogen donor coinitiator (Scheme 2 in **Figure 10**).

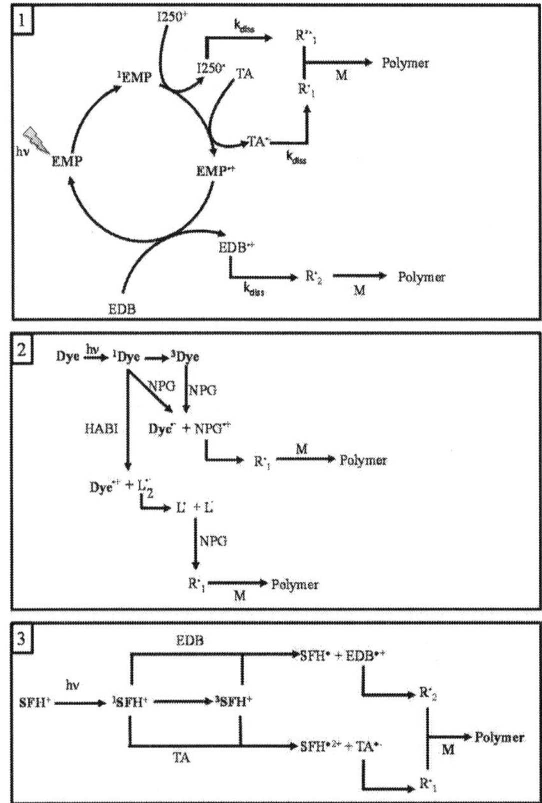

Figure 10. Photochemical mechanism underlying the radical photogeneration of [1] pyrromethene-based photocyclic initiating system (PCIS) [2], RB and SHF⁺ where L• stands for lophyl radical, i.e., the moiety of a HABI molecule (see text) [3], SFH⁺ with one reductant and one oxidant coinitiators.

PIS	C_f	η_f	$R_\eta (s^{-1})$	$R_c (s^{-1})$
RB-NPG	0.52	0.78	0.25	6.0
RB-ClHABI	0.22	0	0	0.3
RB-NPG-ClHABI	0.63	0.4	0.27	8.0
SFH$^+$-NPG	0.3	0.95	0.41	16
SFH$^+$-ClHABI	0.39	0.88	0.12	1.6
SFH$^+$-NPG-ClHABI	0.34	0.95	0.55	20
EMP-EDB	0.44	0	0	0.8
EMP-TA	0.52	0.32	0.025	1.2
EMP-EDB-TA	0.55	0.66	0.033	1.4
EMP-I 250	0.54	0.94	0.21	2.3
EMP-EDB-I 250	0.55	0.40	0.23	2.5
EMP-NPG		0	0	0.9
EMP-NPG-I250		0.25	0.25	6.3
SFH+-EDB	0.37	0.89	0.26	1.3
SFH+-TA	0.37	0.88	0.08	0.42
SFH+-EDB-TA	0.51	0.91	0.31	2.1

Table 1. Holographic and RT-FTIR characterization of the 16 PIS combination [131–133]. η_f: final diffraction yield, C_f: final conversion in FRP, R_η: maximum rate of grating formation, R_c: maximum rate of monomer conversion.

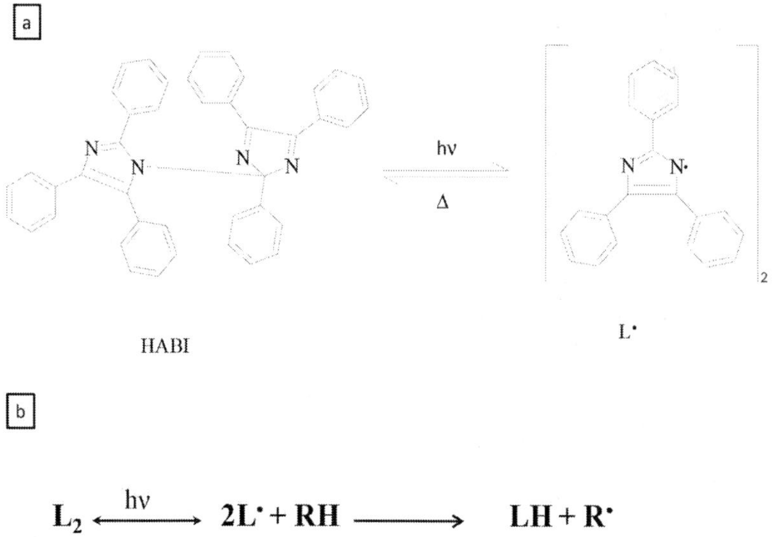

$$L_2 \xrightleftharpoons{h\nu} 2L^\bullet + RH \longrightarrow LH + R^\bullet$$

Figure 11. (a) Reversible photodissociation of HABI (L_2) into two lophyl radicals L$^\bullet$; (b) reaction of lophyl radical with hydrogen donor (RH).

Indeed, we have here a very unique combination of photosensitzers, coinitiators and third components showing very different mechanisms of radical photogeneration. With the three PIS presented here, 16 different combinations of PS-Co, PS-additive and PS-Co-additive were measured both in real-time FTIR (RT-FTIR) and holographic recording. The results in term of both FRP and holographic recording of these combinations are summarized in **Table 1**. The performance of the PIS toward homogeneous-free radical photopolymerization are given by the final conversion C_f and maximum rate of conversion R_c (s^{-1}), while the gratings are characterized by their final diffraction yield η_f and maximum rate of grating formation R_η (s^{-1}).

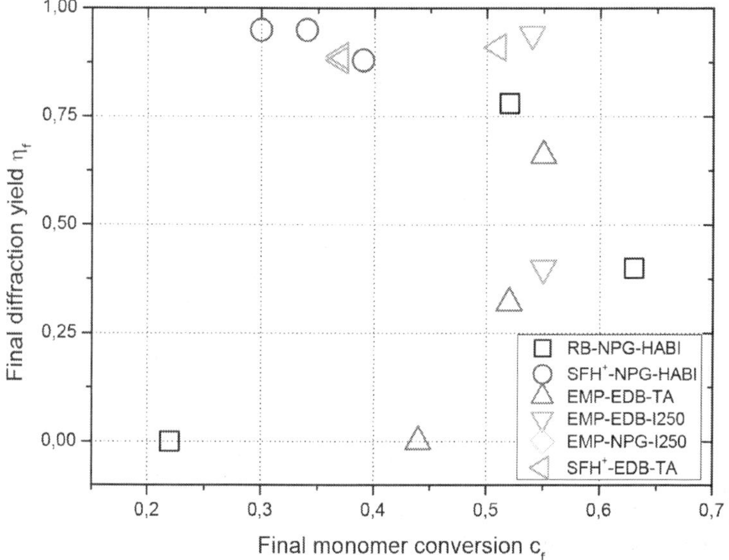

Figure 12. Final diffraction efficiency of grating recording η_f as a function of final monomer conversion C_f.

The existence of a relationship between the evolution of monomer conversion under uniform irradiation (FRP) and that of diffraction efficiency under holographic exposure is not straightforward. In **Figure 11**, the final diffraction yield η_f is plotted as a function of the final monomer conversion C_f.

Figure 12 shows that no clear correlation exists between the final conversion C_f achieved in homogeneous FRP and grating efficiency η_f.

The picture is completely different when the maximum rate of grating formation R_η are plotted as a function of the corresponding maximum rate of monomer conversion R_c. As can be seen in **Figure 13**, a monotonic curve is obtained despite the various photochemical reactions and photopolymerization kinetics of the 16 PS-Co combinations.

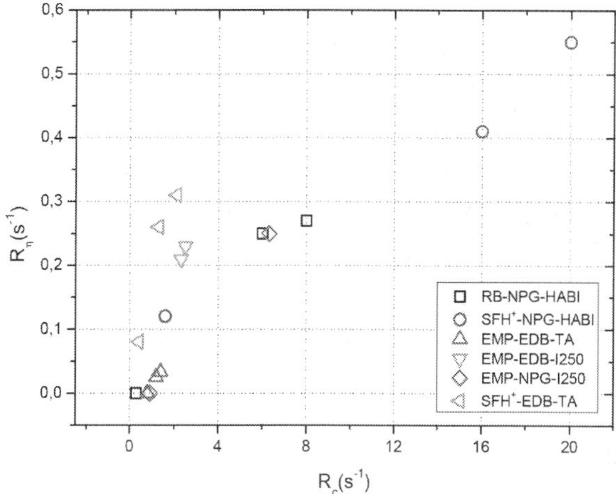

Figure 13. Maximum rate of grating formation R_η as a function of the maximum rate of conversion R_c.

The faster is the monomer conversion R_c, the faster is the building up of the diffraction grating R_η. Therefore, as the holographic resin is always the same for all these experiments, the key role in the grating formation is the number of active radicals locally created and capable of initiating the polymerization. Indeed, the fast polymerization of the monomer mixture in the bright fringes of the interference pattern results in the fast formation of refractive index modulation in the medium. On **Figure 13**, it is clearly seen that two regimes are present, each one showing a quasi linear relation between R_η and R_c with a saturation effect occurring for R_c higher than around 4 s^{-1}. At low R_c, i.e., lower than 4 s^{-1}, the mass transport of reactants (PIS, monomers, fillers, etc.) needed to build the index modulation is not limited by a too fast jellification of the medium during polymerization and high refractive index modulation can be obtained. While at higher R_c (i.e., >4 s^{-1}), the faster polymerization of the resin in the bright areas leads to a sooner freezing of the resin, preventing the mass transport effect needed for high index modulation building up, resulting in lower grating efficiency.

Thus, the coupling between PIS and holographic grating recording is not easy, and a fine tuning of the photonic parameters, holographic material, with a good comprehension of the photochemistry underlying the radical photogeneration is needed to tailor photopolymerizable systems to holographic recording, i.e., PIS-resin couple. Moreover, during our work [131–133], it appears that holographic recording reveals differences in photoinitiating system reactivity that are not detected with classical RT-FTIR measurements.

6. Conclusion

In this chapter, it was shown that many photoinitiating systems are usable for holographic polymerization. Type I and type II are widely exploited even if they are not the most efficient in term of radical quantum yields (especially, visible type I PIS). If in the UV-vis curing and photopolymerization field, three-components systems are widely described and used, because they proved high reactivity in photopolymerization reactions, their application is not so much developed for holographic recording through polymerization. This can be due to higher complexity of the photochemistry and choice of components, as described in this chapter. However, it was shown that three-component photoinitiating systems can be great choice for application in holographic recording: high diffraction grating building rates with high final diffraction yields were obtained paving the way toward highly sensitive holographic materials. Even if photopolymerization and holographic recording is not straightforward, the challenge is worth and the need to improve both photosensitivity and diffraction efficiency of a photo-polymerizable recording medium is certainly the driving force to pay more attention on the development of three-components and photocyclic initiating systems specifically designed for such application. As many different physical and chemical processes (photochemistry of the PIS, monomer, mass transport and gelation of the polymer matrix) are taking place in the medium to give rise to index modulation. Optimizing the material requires a fair knowledge of all these processes, which is tricky as many parameters are involved. This insight is needed to tailor the material combinations to meet the specifications required by the user.

Author details

C. Ley[1*], C. Carré[2], A. Ibrahim[1] and X. Allonas[1]

*Address all correspondence to: christian.ley@uha.fr

1 Laboratory of Macromolecular Photochemistry and Engineering (LPIM), University of Haute Alsace, ENSCMu, Mulhouse, France

2 CNRS, FOTON Laboratory, UMR 6082, Lannion Cedex, France

References

[1] Decker, C. (1987) UV-curing chemistry: past, present and future. J. Coat. Technol. 59, 97–106.

[2] Kloosterboer, J.G. (1988) Network formation by chain crosslinking photopolymeriza-tion and its applications in electronics. In: Electronic applications, Springer Berlin Heidelberg, Series Advances in Polymer Science, vol. 84, pp. 1–61.

[3] Calixto, S. (1987) Dry polymer for holographic recording. Appl. Opt. 26, 3904–3910.

[4] Guo, J., Gleeson, M.R., Sheridan, J.T. (2012) A review of the optimization of photopol-ymer materials for holographic data storage. Phys. Res. Int. 16 (ID 803439).

[5]   Jurbergs, D., Bruder, F.-K., Deuber, F., Fäcke, T., Hagen, R., Hönel, D., Rölle, T., Weiser, M.-S., Volkov, A. (2009) New recording materials for the holographic industry. Proc. SPIE 7233, Practical Holography XXIII: Materials and Applications pp. 72330.

[6]   Smith, D.M., Li, C.Y., Bunning, T.J. (2014) Light-directed mesoscale phase separation via holographic polymerization. J. Polym. Sci. Part B Polym. Phys. 52, 232–250.

[7]   Bruder, F.-K., Hagen, R., Rölle, T., Weiser, M.-S., Fäcke, T. (2011) From the surface to volume: concepts for the next generation of optical–holographic data-storage materials. Angew. Chem. Int. Ed. 50, 4552–4573.

[8]   Jradi, S., Croutxé-Barghorn, C., Carré, C. (2005) Expanding the spatial resolution of acrylic films for data storage applications. Proc. SPIE Photonic Eng. 5827, 410–417.

[9]   Hocine, M., Fressengeas, N., Kugel, G., Carré, C., Lougnot, D.J., Bachelot, R., Royer, P. (2006) Modelling the growth of a polymer micro-tip on an optical fiber end. J. Opt. Soc. Am. B 23, 611–20.

[10] Dietliker, K. (2002) A compilation of photoinitiators commercially available for UV today. SITA Technology Limited, Edinburgh.

[11] Allonas, X., Morlet-Savary, F. Lallevee, J., Fouassier, J.P. (2006) A photodissociation reaction: experimental and computational study of 2-hydroxy-2,2-dimethylacetophenone. Photochem. Photobiol., 82, 88–94.

[12] Jockusch, S., Turro, N.J. (1998) Phosphinoyl radicals: structure and reactivity. A laser flash photolysis and time-resolved ESR investigation. J. Am. Chem. Soc. 120, 11773–11777.

[13] Lalevee, J., Allonas, X., Jradi S., Fouassier J.P. (2006) Role of the medium on the reactivity of cleavable photoinitiators in photopolymerization reactions, Macromolecules. 39, 1872–1879.

[14] Crivello, J.V. Dietliker, K. (1999) Photoinitiators for free radical cationic & anionic photopolymerisation. John Wiley & Sons, Chichester.

[15] Green, W.A. (2010) Industrial photoinitiators: a technical guide. Boca Raton FL, CRC Press.

[16] Chan, C.M., Ko T.M., Hiraoka H. (1996) Polymer surface modification by plasmas and photons. Surf. Sci. Rep. 24, 1–54.

[17] Fouassier, J.P. (1995) Photoinitiation, photopolymerization, and photocuring: fundamentals and applications. Hanser Gardner Publications , Cincinnati.

[18] Moszner, N., Fischer, U.K., Ganster, B., Liska, R., Rheinberger, V. (2008) Benzoyl germanium derivatives as novel visible light photoinitiators for dental materials. Dent. Mater. 24, 901–907.

[43] Mauguière-Guyonnet, F., Burget, D., Fouassier, J.P. (2007) The role of the photoinitiating systems towards the inhibiting effect of phenolic compounds in the photopolymerization of acrylates. Prog. Org. Coat. 59, 37–45.

[44] Mallavia, R., Amat-Guerri, F., Fimia, A., Sastre, R. (1994) Synthesis and evaluation as a visible-light polymerization photoinitiator of a New Eosin Ester with an O-Benzoyl-.alpha.-oxooxime group. Macromolecules 27, 2643–2646.

[45] Ley, C., Ibrahim, A., Allonas, X. (2016). Isomerization controlled photopolymerization: effect of dye photophysics on photoinitiation efficiency. Photochem. Photobiol. Sci. 15(8), 1054–1060.

[46] Ibrahim, A., Ley, C., Tarzi, O. I., Fouassier, J. P., Allonas, X. (2010) Visible light photoinitiating systems: toward a good control of the photopolymerization efficiency. J. Photopolym. Sci. Technol. 23, 101–108.

[47] Tarzi, O.I., Allonas, X., Ley, C., Fouassier, J.P. (2010) Pyrromethene derivatives in three-component photoinitiating systems for free radical photopolymerization. J. Polym. Sci., Part A: Polym. Chem. 48, 2594–2603.

[48] Costela, A., García, O., Garcia-Moreno, I., Sastre, R. (2004) Pyrromethene 567 dye as visible light photoinitiator for free radical polymerization. Macromol. Chem. Phys. 204, 2233–2239.

[49] Hageman, H.J. (1985) Photoinitiators for free radical polymerization. Prog. Org. Coat. 13, 123–150.

[50] Cook, W.D. (1992) Photopolymerization kinetics of dimethacrylates using the camphorquinone/amine initiator system. Polymer 33, 600–609.

[51] Mateo, J.L., Bosch, P., Lozano, A.E. (1994) Reactivity of radicals derived from dimethylanilines in acrylic photopolymerization. Macromolecules 27, 7794–7799.

[52] Hoyle, C.E., Cranford, M., Trapp, M., No, Y.G., Kim, K.J. (1988) Photopolymerization of 1,6-hexanediol diacrylate with deoxybenzoin as photoinitiator. Polymer 29, 2033–2040.

[53] Hoyle, C.E. Kim, K.-J. (1987) The effect of aromatic amines on the photopolymerization of 1,6-hexanediol diacrylate. J. Polym. Sci., Part A: Polym. Chem. 33, 2985–2996.

[54] Hoyle, C.E., Keel, M. Kim, K.-J. (1988) Photopolymerization of 1,6-hexanediol diacrylate: the effect of functionalized amines. Polymer 29, 18–23.

[55] Buback, M., Gilbert, R.G., Russell, G.T., Hill, D.J.T., Moad, G., O'Driscoll, K.F., Shen, J., Winnik, M.A. (1992) Consistent values of rate parameters in free radical polymerization systems. II. Outstanding dilemmas and recommendations. J. Polym. Sci., Part A: Polym. Chem. 30, 851–863.

[56] Soh, S.K. Sundberg, D.C. (1982) Diffusion-controlled vinyl polymerization. I. The gel effect. J. Polym. Sci., Part A: Polym. Chem. 20, 1299–1313.

[57] Andrzejewska, E. (1996) Sulfur-containing polyacrylates: V. Temperature effects on the photoinitiated polymerization of diacrylates. Polymer 37, 1039–1045.

[58] Andrzejewska, E. (1993) The effect of aliphatic sulfides on the photopolymerization of diacrylates. Polymer 34, 3899–3904.

[59] Guttenplan, J.B., Cohen, S.G., (1973) Quenching and reduction of photoexcited benzophenone by thioethers and mercaptans. J. Org. Chem. 38, 2001–2007.

[60] Andrzejewska, E. (1992) The influence of aliphatic sulfides on the photoinduced polymerization of butanediol-1,4 dimethacrylate. J. Polym. Sci., Part A: Polym. Chem. 30, 485–491.

[61] Lalevée, J., Morlet-Savary, F., Roz, M.E., Allonas, X., Fouassier, J.P. (2009) Thiyl radical generation in thiol or disulfide containing photosensitive systems. Macromol. Chem. Phys. 210, 311–319.

[62] Hoyle, C.E., Bowman, C.N. (2010) Thiol–ene click chemistry. Angew. Chem., Int. Ed. 49, 1540–1573.

[63] Morgan, C.R., Kyle, D.R. (1983) UV Generated Oxygen Scavengers and Method for Determining Their Effectiveness in Photopolymerizable Systems. Technology Marketing Corporation, Norwalk, CT, ETATS-UNIS.

[64] Padon, K.S., Scranton, A.B. (2000) A mechanistic investigation of a three-component radical photoinitiator system comprising methylene blue, N-methyldiethanolamine, and diphenyliodonium chloride. J. Polym. Sci., Part A: Polym. Chem. 38, 2057–2066.

[65] Block, H., Ledwith, A., Taylor, A.R. (1971) Polymerization of methyl methacrylate photosensitized by benzophenones. Polymer 12, 271–288.

[66] Kabatc, J., Celmer, A. (2009) An argon laser induced polymerization photoinitiated by both mono- and bichromophoric hemicyanine dye–borate salt ion pairs. The synthesis, spectroscopic, electrochemical and kinetic studies. Polymer 50, 57–67.

[67] Kabatc, J., Kucybała, Z., Pietrzak, M., Ścigalski F., Paczkowski, J. (1999) Free radical polymerization initiated via photoinduced intermolecular electron transfer process: kinetic study 3. Polymer 40, 735–745.

[68] Kabatc, J., Paczkowski, J. (2004) The photophysical and photochemical properties of the oxacarbocyanine and thiacarbocyanine dyes. Dyes Pigm. 61, 1–16.

[69] Kabatc, J., Zadrużyńska, A., Czech, Z., Kowalczyk, A. (2012) The synthesis, spectroscopic and electrochemical properties, and application of new dyeing photoinitiator systems for acrylate monomers polymerization. Dyes Pigm. 92, 724–731.

[70] Padon, S.K., Scranton, A.B. (2000) The effect of oxygen on the three-component radical photoinitiator system: methylene blue, N-methyldiethanolamine, and diphenyliodonium chloride. J. Polym. Sci., Part A: Polym. Chem. 38, 3336–3346.

[71] Kawamura, K., Schmitt, J., Barnet, M., Salmi, H., LEY, C., Allonas, X. (2013) Squarylium-triazine dyad as a highly sensitive photoradical generator for red light. Chem. Eur. J. 19, 12853–12858.

[72] Kawamura, K., Ley, C., Schmitt, J., Barnet, M., Allonas, X. (2013) Relevance of linked dye-coinitiator in visible three-component photoinitiating systems: application to red light photopolymerization. J. Pol. Sci. A 51, 4325–4330.

[73] Nergis, A., Esen, D.S., Temel, G. et al. (2014). One-component thioxanthone acetic acid derivative photoinitiator for free radical polymerization. Photochem. Photobiol. 90(2), 463–469.

[74] Karaca, N., Karaca Balta, D. et al. (2014). Mechanistic studies of thioxanthone–carbazole as a one-component type II photoinitiator. J. Lumin. 146, 424–429.

[75] Fouassier, J.P., Allonas. X., Burget, D. (2003) Photopolymerization reactions under visible lights: principle, mechanisms and examples of applications. Prog. Org. Coat. 47, 16–36.

[76] Fouassier, J.P., Chesneau E. (1991) Polymérisation ***induite sous irradiation laser visible, 5. Le système éosine/amine/sel de iodonium. Makromol. Chem. 192, 1307–1315.

[77] Fouassier, J.P., Morlet-Savary, F., Yamashita, K., Imahashi, S. (1997) The role of the dye/iron arene complex/amine system as a photoinitiator for photopolymerization reactions. Polymer 38, 1415–1421.

[78] Fouassier, J.P., Wu, S.K. (1992) Visible laser lights in photoinduced polymerization. VI. Thioxanthones and ketocoumarins as photoinitiators. J. Appl. Polym. Sci. 44, 1779–1786.

[79] Fouassier, J.-P., Lalevee, J. (2012) Three-component photoinitiating systems: towards innovative tailor made high performance combinations. RSC Adv. 2, 2621–2629.

[80] Allonas, X., Fouassier, J.P., Kaji, M., Murakami, Y. (2003) Excited state processes in a four-component photosensitive system based on a bisimidazole derivative. Photochem. Photobiol. Sci. 2, 224–229.

[81] Roffey C.G. (1997) Photogeneration of reactive species for UV curing. John Wiley & Sons, Chichester.

[82] Burget, D., Fouassier, J.P. (1998) Laser flash photolysis studies of the interaction of Rose Bengal with an iron arene complex. J. Chem. Soc., Faraday Trans. 94, 1849–1854.

[83] Kaneko, Y., Neckers, D.C. (1998) Simultaneous photoinduced color formation and photoinitiated polymerization. J. Phys. Chem. A 102, 5356–5363.

[84] Gao, F., Yang, Y.Y. (1999) Dye-sensitized phoropolymerization of methyl methacrylate by coumarin dye/iodonium salt system. Chin. J. Polym. Sci. 17, 589–594.

[85] Wang, E.J., He, J.H., LI, M.Z., Song, H.H., Li, J. (1992) A novel intra-ion-pair electron transfer sensitization system for visible photopolymerization. J. Photopolym. Sci. Technol. 5, 505–513.

[86] Erddalane, A., Fouassier, J.P., Morlet-Savary, F., Takimoto, Y. (1996) Efficiency and excited state processes in a three-component system, based on thioxanthene derived dye/amine/additive, usable in photopolymer plates. J. Polym. Sci. Part A Polym. Chem. 34, 633–642.

[87] Kabatc, J., Jurek, K. (2012) Free radical formation in three-component photoinitiating systems. Polymer 53, 1973–1980.

[88] Kabatc, J. (2011) The three-component radical photoinitiating systems comprising thiacarbocyanine dye, n-butyltriphenylborate salt and N-alkoxypyridinium salt or 1,3,5-triazine derivative. Mater. Chem Phys. 125, 118–124.

[89] Bi, Y., Neckers, D.C. (1994) A visible light initiating system for free radical promoted cationic polymerization. Macromolecules 27, 3683–3693.

[90] Zhou, W., Wang, E. (1996) Photoinduced electron transfer in the ion pair compound (XTOn): influence of ionic association. J. Photochem. Photobiol. A Chem. 96, 25–29.

[91] Kavarnos, G.J., Turro, N.J. (1986) Photosensitization by reversible electron transfer: theories, experimental evidence, and examples. Chem. Rev. 86, 401–449.

[92] Kabatc, J. (2010) High speed three-component photoinitiating systems composed of cyanine dyes borate salt and heteroaromatic thiols. Polymer 51, 5028–5036.

[93] Kabatc, J., Pączkowski, J. (2006) Acceleration of the free radical polymerization by using N-alkoxypyridinium salt as co-initiator in hemicyanine dye/borate salt photoinitiating system. J. Photochem. Photobiol., A 184, 184–192.

[94] Rhem, D., Weller, A. (1970) Kinetics of fluorescence quenching by electron and H-atom transfer. Israel Journal of Chemistry 8, 259–271.

[95] Ley, C., Christmann, J., Ibrahim, A., di Stefano, L.H., Allonas Beilstein, X. (2014) Tailoring of organic dyes with oxidoreductive compounds to obtain photocyclic radical generator systems exhibiting photocatalytic behaviour. J. Org. Chem. 10, 936–947.

[96] Ghailane, F., Manivannan, G., Lessard, R.A. (1995) Spiropyran-doped poly(vinyl carbazole): a new photopolymer recording medium for erasable holography. Opt. Eng. 34, 480–485.

[97] Weiser, M.-S., Bruder, F.-K., Fäcke, T., Hönel, D., Jurbergs, D., Rölle, T. (2010) Self-processing, diffusion-based photopolymers for holographic applications. Macromol. Symp. 296, 133–137.

[98] De Sarkar, M., Qi, J., Crawford, G.P. (2002) Influence of partial matrix fluorination on morphology and performance of HPDLC transmission gratings. Polymer 43, 7335–7344.

[99] Massenot, S., Chevallier, R., de Bougrenet de la Tocnaye, J.L., Parriaux, O. (2007) Tunable grating-assisted surface plasmon resonance by use of nano-polymer dispersed liquid crystal electro-optical material. Opt. Commun. 275, 318–323.

[100] Colburn, W.S., Haines, K.A. (1971) Volume hologram formation in photopolymer materials. Appl. Opt. 10, 1636–1641.

[101] Coufal, H.J., Psaltis, D., Sincerbox, G.T. (2000) Holographic data storage, Springer Series in Optical Sciences 76, Springer Verlag, New-York.

[102] Lawrence, J.R., O'Neill, F.T., Sheridan, J.T. (2001) Photopolymer holographic recording material. Optik 112, 449–463.

[103] Qi, Y., Sheridan, J.T. (2015) Dyes and photopolymers. Dyes and chromophores in polymer science. John Wiley & Sons, Inc. pp. 251–277.

[104] Kowalski, B.A., McLeod, R.R. (2016) Design concepts for diffusive holographic photopolymers. J. Polym. Sci. Part B Polym. Phys. 54(11), 1021–1035.

[105] Schilling, M.L., Colvin, V.L., Dhar, L., Harris, A.L., Schilling, F.C., Katz, H.E., Wysocki, T., Hale, A., Blyler, L.L., Boyd, C. (1999) Acrylate oligomer-based photopolymers for optical storage applications. Chem. Mater. 11, 247–254.

[106] Sabol, D., Gleeson, M.R. et al. (2010) Photoinitiation study of Irgacure 784 in an epoxy resin photopolymer. J. Appl. Phys. 107(5), 053113.

[107] Suzuki, N., Tomita, Y. et al. (2006) Highly transparent ZrO_2 nanoparticle-dispersed acrylate photopolymers for volume holographic recording. Opt. Express 14(26), 12712–12719.

[108] Guo, J., Fujii, R. et al. (2015) Volume holographic recording in nanoparticle–polymer composites doped with multifunctional chain transfer agents. Opt. Rev. 22(5), 832–836.

[109] Kawana, M., Takahashi, J.-I. et al. (2015) Characterization of volume holographic recording in photopolymerizable nanoparticle-(thiol-ene) polymer composites at 404 nm. J. Appl. Phys. 117(5), 053105.

[110] Sakhno, O. V., Goldenberg, L.M. et al. (2007) Surface modified ZrO_2 and TiO_2 nanoparticles embedded in organic photopolymers for highly effective and UV-stable volume holograms. Nanotechnology 18(10), 105704.

[111] Veniaminov, A.V., Mahilny, U.V. (2013) Holographic polymer materials with diffusion development: principles, arrangement, investigation, and applications. Opt. Spectrosc. 115(6), 906–930.

[112] Liu, H., Yu, D. et al. (2012) Enhancement of photochemical response in bulk poly(methyl methacrylate) photopolymer dispersed organometallic compound. Opt. Commun. 285(24), 4993–5000.

[113] Liu, H., Li, Y. et al. (2013) Determination of kinetics parameters using holographic scattering strategy in glass like bulk photopolymer. Opt. Commun. 311, 207–211.

[114] Lin, C.-H., Cho, S.-L. et al. (2014) Two-wavelength holographic recording in photopolymer using four-energy-level system: experiments and modeling. Opt. Eng. 53(11), 112303–112303.

[115] Li, C., Cao, L. et al. (2014) Holographic kinetics for mixed volume gratings in gold nanoparticles doped photopolymer. Opt. Express 22(5), 5017–5028.

[116] Liu, Y., Li, Z. et al. (2015) The optical polarization properties of phenanthrenequinone-doped poly(methyl methacrylate) photopolymer materials for volume holographic storage. Opt. Rev. 22(5), 837–840.

[117] Gong, Q., Wang, S., Huang, M., Dong, Y., Gan, F. (2005) A novel CuTCNQ derivative for rewritable optical storage. Seventh Int. Symp. Optical Storage (ISOS 2005) 5966, 59660–59665.

[118] Gong, Q., Wang, S., Huang, M., Gan, F. (2005) A humidity-resistant highly sensitive holographic photopolymerizable dry film. Mat. Lett. 59, 2969–2972.

[119] Qi, Y., Li, H. et al. (2014) Material response of photopolymer containing four different photosensitizers. Opt. Commun. 320, 114–124.

[120] Smirnova, T.N., Sakhno, O.V., Tikhonov, E.A., Ezhov, P.V., Shibanov, V.V. (2000) New self-developing photopolymers for holographic recording in the 500–700 nm range. J. Appl. Spectrosc. 67, 34–39.

[121] Aswathy, G., Rajesh, C.S. et al. (2016) Improving the performance of methylene blue sensitized photopolymer by doping with nickel ion. Opt. Mater. 55, 27–32.

[122] Pramitha, V., Das, B. et al. (2016) High efficiency panchromatic photopolymer recording material for holographic data storage systems. Opt. Mater. 52, 212–218.

[123] Fouassier, J.P., Ruhlmann, D., Graff, B., Takimoto, Y., Kawabata, M., Harada, M. (1993) A new three-component system in visible laser light photo-induced polymerization. J. Imaging Sci. Technol. 37, 208–210.

[124] Zhang, C., Zhao, J., He, J., Li, L., Yang, Y. (1998) Photoinitiating systems and photopolymer materials for holography. In: Hsu, D., Hong, J.H. (Eds.) Proceedings of the holographic displays and optical elements II, Beijing, China, vol. 3559, pp. 81–87.

[125] Ortuño, M., Márquez, A., Gallego, S., Neipp, C., Fernández, E. (2007) Pyrromethene dye and non-redox initiator system in a hydrophilic binder photopolymer. Opt. Mater. 30, 227–230.

[126] Peng, H., Bi, S. et al. (2014) Monochromatic visible light "Photoinitibitor": Janus-faced initiation and inhibition for storage of colored 3D images. J. Am. Chem. Soc. 136(25), 8855–8858.

[127] Ni, M., Peng, H. et al. (2015) 3D image storage in photopolymer/ZnS nanocomposites tailored by "Photoinitibitor". Macromolecules 48(9), 2958–2966.

[128] Li, H., Qi, Y. et al. (2015) Analysis of the absorptive behavior of photopolymer materials. Part I. Theoretical modeling. J. Modern Opt. 62(2), 143–154.

[129] Ibrahim, A., Allonas, X. et al. (2014) High performance photoinitiating systems for holography recording: need for a full control of primary processes. Chem. A Eur. J. 20(46), 15102–15107.

[130] Ibrahim, A., Ley, C. et al. (2012) Optimization of a photopolymerizable material based on a photocyclic initiating system using holographic recording. Photochem. Photobiol. Sci. 11(11), 1682–1690.

[131] Ibrahim, A., Ley, C. et al. (2014) Tailoring 3-component photoinitiating systems for use as efficient photopolymerizable holographic material. J. Display Technol. 10(6), 456–463.

[132] Ibrahim, A., Fouhaili, B.E. et al. (2015) Optimization of a safranine O three-component photoinitiating system for use in holographic recording. Can. J. Chem. 93(12), 1345–1353.

[133] Decker, C., Moussa, K. (1989) Real-time kinetic study of laser-induced polymerization. Macromolecules 22(12), 4455–4462.

[134] Qin, X.Z., Liu, A., Trifunac, A.D., Krongauz, V.V. (1991) Photodissociation of hexaaryl-biimidazole. 1. Triplet-state formation. J. Phys. Chem. 95, 5822–5826.

[135] Jinqi, X., Fang, G., Yong-Yuan, Y. (1999) Study of Biimidazole Ultraviolet Photosensitive Initiating Systems in Presensitized Printing Plate. J. Photopolym. Sci. Technol 12, 343–346.

[136] Fang, G., Zhao, C.Y., Li, L.D., Feng, S.J., Yong-Yuan, Y (2000) Dye-sensitized photolysis of o-Cl-Hexaarylbiimidazole and photopolymerization kinetics study of the long-wavelength dye/Hexaarylbiimidazole systems. Chin. J. Polymer Sci. 18, 493–500.

[137] Zammit, M.D., Davis, T.P., Willett, G.D.(1997) Visible light pulsed-laser polymerization at 532 nm employing a Julolidine dye photosensitizer initiation system. Macromolecules 30(19), 5655–5659.

Chapter 18

Fluorite Crystals with Color Centers: A Medium for Recording Extremely Stable but Broadly Transformable Holograms

Aleksandr I. Ryskin, Aleksandr E. Angervaks and
Andrei V. Veniaminov

Additional information is available at the end of the chapter

http://dx.doi.org/10.5772/66114

Abstract

The mechanisms of (i) forming the photochromic color centers in fluorite crystals ("additive coloring") and (ii) recording and transforming holograms through the use of their photochromism are described here. The diffusion-drift mechanism of hologram recording in additively colored fluorite crystals determines the recording kinetics and properties of holograms. An important feature of holograms recorded in additively colored fluorite is an opportunity to perform the photothermal transformation of color centers under the incoherent optical radiation that results in nondestructive switching of the hologram between the amplitude, amplitude-phase (in-phase or counter-phase), and phase types at a given readout wavelength. Possible applications of holographic elements based on the additively colored fluorite crystals are discussed.

Keywords: fluorite crystal, additive coloring, color center, colloids, transformation, holography, diffraction efficiency, kinetics, profile

1. Introduction

Holographic elements are broadly used in the laser technique for spectral narrowing, stabilizing, and tuning the laser emission, phase locking in resonators, angular narrowing and steering the laser beams, stretching, compressing, and shaping the laser pulses, and also in combining laser beams. These applications impose specific requirements in holographic media. One of important requirements is their stability to the effects of optical radiation and temperature. Another useful feature is the transparency in the infrared because IR lasers are

widely used in the modern techniques. In this paper, a holographic medium is described that satisfies both these requirements: it is extremely stable and allows for reading out holograms in the IR up to ~10 μm. This medium is calcium fluoride crystals (CaF_2, fluorite) with color centers. Color centers in fluorite are the combination of anion vacancies and electrons trapped by the latter; the centers exhibit the absorption bands in the visible region and, thus, color the crystal. To form the centers in the crystal bulk, heating the crystal in the reducing atmosphere of calcium vapor is used (so-called "additive coloring" of the crystal). Color centers can also be created in the crystal volume under the impact of γ-radiation or high-energy electron beams; however, such coloration is less stable.

The photochromism of colored crystals that allows for their use as a holographic medium is due to the transformation of color centers under the illumination of the crystal in the absorption band of specific center at an elevated temperature.

In this paper, the technique of additive coloring of fluorite crystals is described. The types of color centers are discussed as well as their photochromic transformations. Special attention is paid to the mechanism of hologram recording because it is this mechanism that determines the most important features of holograms recorded in this medium. The phenomenon of self-organization of color centers under hologram recording is considered. In conclusion, possible applications of the medium are discussed.

2. Additive coloring of fluorite crystals

As mentioned above, the color centers in fluorite crystals are anion vacancies that capture electrons. The additive coloring procedure is executed in gas-controlled heat pipe [1, 2]. The essence of heat-pipe method that implies the use of furnace and water-cooled refrigerator (**Figure 1**) is in the spatial separation of a buffer inert gas (He) and metal vapor due to vertically directed metal diffusion at the temperature gradient formed by the furnace and the refrigerator. The metal vapor is condensed on the manipulator rod at a dew point temperature in a zone above the container with the crystal, drains to the hot zone and evaporates in it. As a result, the vapor-gas mixture pressure is determined by the pressure of He that is in equilibrium with the metal vapor, thus being almost independent of the temperature of a sample under coloration.

The dynamic mode of the heat pipe—continuous circulation of metal vapor within it—is implemented at a fairly low pressure of saturating metal vapor at its freezing temperature. This condition is not satisfied for calcium, but is fulfilled for alkali metals. Therefore, a calcium-lithium mixture (*10*) is used to implement the aforementioned mode. In this case, the dew point is determined by lithium that dominates in the mixture composition (~99%), and the coloring agent is calcium vapor.

Thus, the heat-pipe method allows one to control the calcium vapor pressure, p, and temperature, T, of the colored crystal almost independently. The ranges of the parameter magnitudes are as follows: $p = 10^{-4}$–1 Torr, $T = 730$–870°C.

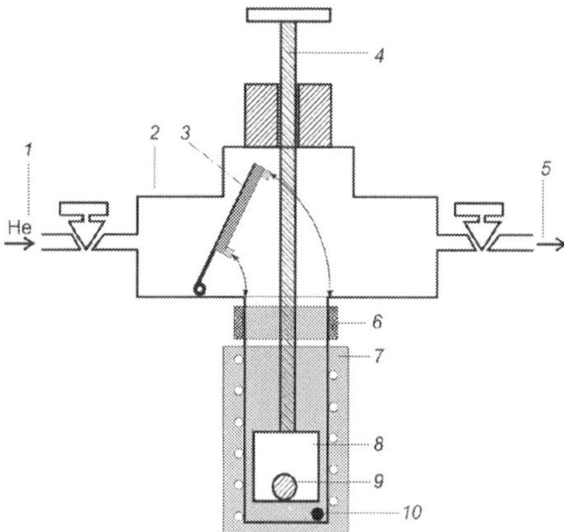

Figure 1. Schematic representation of the heat-pipe system: (*1*) helium supply, (*2*) stainless steel vacuum chamber, (*3*) vacuum valve, (*4*) manipulator for displacing the container with a sample, (*5*) line to the vacuum pump, (*6*) water-cooled refrigerator, (*7*) furnace, (*8*) container, (*9*) sample, and (*10*) metal weight.

About several tens of coloring procedures can be implemented, with reproducible results, using the same lithium-calcium weight.

The formation of color centers under the additive coloring is related to the deviation of the crystal from stoichiometry. The crystal surface builds up when interacting with metal vapor and using anions borrowed from the crystal bulk. In other words, the anion vacancies diffuse into the crystal simultaneously with electrons supplied by calcium to support the charge neutrality of the colored sample. One should note that, at sufficiently high coloring temperature, the surface undergoes decomposition (erosion). During this process, the metal cations pass to the gas phase at a low vapor pressure and remain on the crystal surface at pressures close to the saturation vapor pressure. Fluorine that evolved during the surface layer decomposition recombines with anion vacancies formed as a result of the interaction with the metal film on the surface. Thus, from the viewpoint of crystal stoichiometry violation, these two reactions, namely, the surface building up and decomposition, are oppositely directed. One should note that, for CaF_2 crystal, the process of building-up the surface prevails over its decomposition.[1]

The recombination of anion vacancies and electrons diffusing into the crystal bulk produces a variety of color centers. The method used allows for the uniform coloring of CaF_2 crystals of a large size (**Figure 2**).

After the furnace is switched off in the end of the coloring procedure, the crystal cools down to the room temperature; a minute quantity of oxygen present in helium penetrates, because

---

[1] This is not the general case; for example, in CdF_2 crystal that has the fluorite structure, the rates of both processes are comparable and the surface of additively colored crystals turns out to be greatly eroded.

of absence of Ca vapor, into the surface layers of colored crystal and substitutes fluorine ions for the O_2^- ions with electrons borrowed from the color centers. So, the surface layers of the crystal become partially discolored. For hologram recording, plates of uniformly colored inner part should be cut out and polished.

Figure 2. Samples of fluorite crystals 12 mm in diameter and 6 mm thick: initial (right) and additively colored (left).

To form color centers that consist of anion vacancies and electrons, it is necessary to use high-purity and high-quality fluorite crystals. Luckily, fluorite is an important material of photolithography optics used together with excimer lasers for semiconductor chip production, which is why the technology of growing such crystals is well elaborated. So, such crystals are available and not expensive.

3. Color centers and their photothermal transformation

Color centers in fluorite crystals may be separated into three groups. "Simple" centers are those comprising 1–4 anion vacancies and equal number of trapped electrons (F-, M-, R-, and N-centers, respectively); the structure and energy levels of simple centers in fluorite crystals are well studied [3]. "Colloidal" centers (colloids) are the giant agglomerates of vacancies and electrons converted, at the coloring temperature, into the metal calcium drops less than ~50 nm in diameter (its value depends on the coloring mode). "Quasi-colloidal" centers occupy, by the number of vacancies/electrons, an intermediate position between simple and colloidal centers; probably, they are more or less large agglomerates of simple centers.

All centers are characterized by the specific absorption bands. The bands of simple centers are located in the $\lambda < 550$ nm wavelength range. The extinction of colloidal centers is well described by Mie theory [4–6]; the visible band of these centers is located in the 500 nm $< \lambda <$ 600 nm range depending on the coloring mode (the second band of colloidal centers is located at ~200 nm). There is a lot of quasi-colloidal centers, their bands covering a wide spectral range, 550 nm $< \lambda < 10$ μm. The bigger the quasi-colloidal center, the closer its absorption band to the band of colloids [7].

The modification of coloring conditions (calcium-vapor pressure and temperature) determines the composition of color centers in the colored crystal. The higher the calcium pressure the larger the amount of colloidal particles formed (**Figure 3**); their size increases with an increase in their concentration in the colored crystal. Only a minute quantity of quasi-colloidal centers arises during the coloring process because they are less stable compared to the simple and colloidal centers and cannot exist at the coloring temperature.

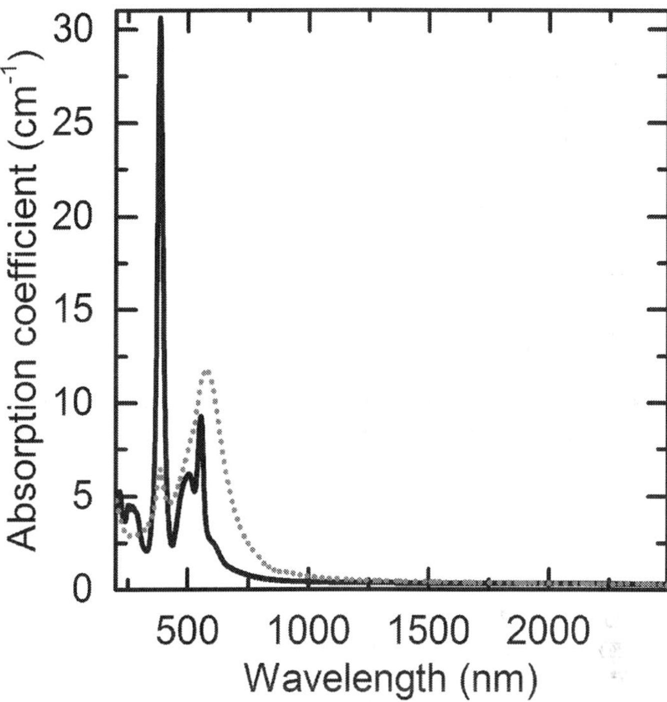

Figure 3. Absorption spectra of 2.4 mm-thick CaF_2 crystals colored at temperature $T = 830°C$ and pressure p equal to (i) 3 × 10^{-4} Torr ("weakly colored," solid line) and (ii) 8 × 10^{-3} Torr ("strongly colored," dotted line).

Temperature determines the coloring time, but it also plays an important role in determining the composition of color centers present in the crystal in another aspect. The illumination of crystal by radiation resonant to the absorption band of a specific center at elevated temperature results in the destruction of this center and formation of another type of centers. This type crucially depends on temperature. $T > 300°C$ is favorable for the simple center formation because of high entropy of these centers. At $T = 150–200°C$, the colloidal centers arise. The 70–150°C temperature range is favorable for the quasi-colloidal center formation. The lower temperatures of this range correspond to the formation of long-wavelength quasi-colloids; at higher temperatures, the short-wavelength quasi-colloids arise (**Figure 4**).

Photochromism of color centers in additively colored CaF_2 crystals allows for hologram recording on the crystals.

5. Hologram profile

Due to the diffusion-drift recording mechanism, the hologram profile does not reproduce the sinusoidal distribution of light intensity in the fringe pattern. The flows of electrons and vacancies off their maxima to minima result in the compression of holographic planes. As a result, several diffraction orders are observed. Below, the profile of a hologram recorded by 532 nm laser with a moderate DE of ~10% in the first order (the readout wavelength being the same) is discussed [13].

Figure 7 shows images of the $15 \times 15\ \mu m^2$ area of this sample obtained using the confocal laser scanning microscope (LSM) in (i) the light of the crystal luminescence excited by argon ion laser operating at 514.5 nm and (ii) the transmitted excitation light. The luminescence is due to M and M_A^+ color centers (the M_A^+-center is the M-center in which the Na^+ ion present in the crystal as a trace impurity is incorporated). The transversal profiles of the grating obtained from the images shown in **Figure 7** are presented in **Figure 8**. The transmittance profile is close to the sine curve, whereas the luminescence profile deviates substantially from this shape.

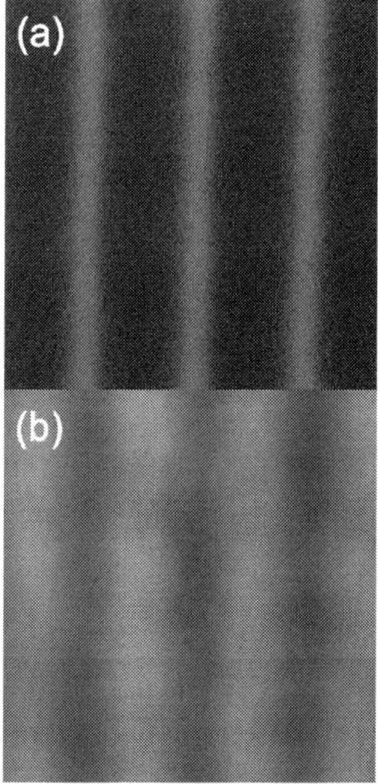

Figure 7. Images of the 15 μm × 15 μm area of the sample with a holographic grating obtained using confocal LSM: (a) in the light of the crystal luminescence excited by an argon ion laser operating at 514.5 nm and (b) in the transmitted excitation light.

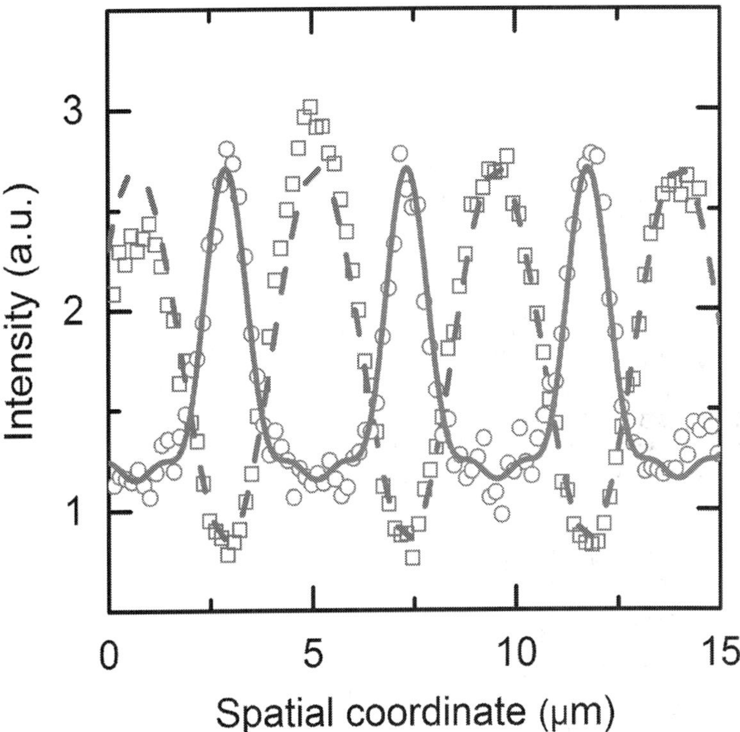

Figure 8. Transversal profiles of the grating obtained from the images shown in **Figure 7**: the transmittance profile (squares) and its sine-approximation (dashed curve); the luminescence profile (circles) and its best fit with the sum of the first three harmonic components, the amplitude ratio being 100:50:19 (solid curve).

Due to spatial filtering of optical signals with the pinhole diaphragm, confocal microscopy provides enhanced selectivity and contrast of fluorescent and reflection images: only light emitted (or scattered) within a tiny focal volume is collected at the photodetector. 3D images are constructed of "optical slices" obtained by layer-by-layer scanning of an object at different focal positions. Contrastingly, the transmitted-light images of the same thin layers include signal coming from the light cone passing through entire thickness of the sample, and the major contribution to the resulting picture is given by a number of defocused images of hologram sections. Summation of such patterns results in a nearly sinusoidal distribution, even if the original grating consisted of sharp thin lines.

Higher diffraction orders of a volume holographic grating observed at the Bragg angles θ_m corresponding to spatial frequencies $K_m = 2\pi m/d$, where d is the spatial period of the pattern, imply its nonsinusoidal shape. In order to reconstruct the spatial dependences of the refractive index $n(x)$ and absorption coefficient $\alpha(x)$ of the grating (spatial profiles), we apply partial

Fourier series with harmonic coefficients δn_m and $\delta\alpha_m$ obtained from measured angular dependences of diffraction efficiencies for respective orders and alternating signs by analogy with Fourier expansion of the truncated cosine function:

$$\delta n(x) = \sum_m (-1)^{m+1}\, \delta n_m \cos\left(\frac{2\pi mx}{d}\right), \tag{2}$$

$$\delta\alpha(x) = \sum_m (-1)^{m+1}\, \delta\alpha_m \cos\left(\frac{2\pi mx}{d}\right) \tag{3}$$

Here, x is the spatial coordinate along the grating vector K.

To determine the values of harmonic components, the angular dependences of the hologram response for three (most intense) diffraction orders can be used. The angular dependences of the zeroth and ±1st diffraction orders read out at $\lambda = 532$ nm are symmetric with respect to the normal incidence as well as those of the higher diffraction orders (**Figure 9**).

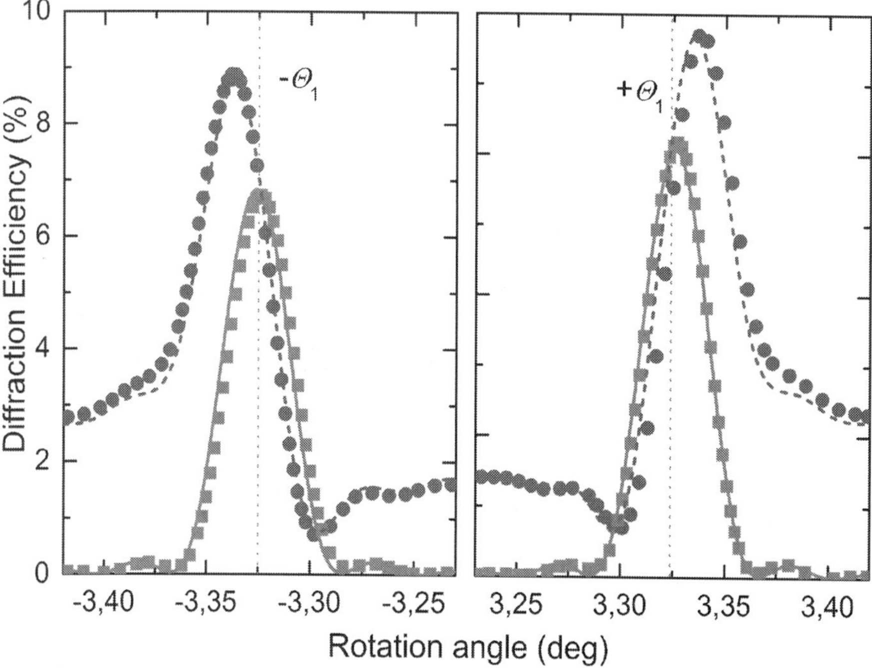

Figure 9. Angular dependences of the zeroth and ±1 diffraction orders for the grating when read out at 532 nm. Circles (η_0) and squares ($\eta_{\pm1}$) are referred to the experimental data; dashed, and solid curves correspond to the theoretical approximation using Eqs. (5) and (4), respectively.

Using a criterion given in Refs. [14, 15], namely, that of the effectively equal values of diffraction efficiencies in the +1 and -1 diffraction orders, one can conclude that the hologram has an amplitude-phase nature with the amplitude and refractive index gratings being in phase. Therefore, to fit the experimental angular dependences, the following expressions can be used for the angular dependences of the diffraction efficiencies η_m, η_0 in the mth ($m \neq 0$) and zero orders.

$$\eta_m(\theta) = 2 \exp\left(-\frac{2\alpha_0 t}{\cos\theta}\right)\frac{\kappa_1^2 + \kappa_2^2}{z_0}\left\{\cosh\left[\frac{\sqrt{z_0}\, t \cos(\psi/2)}{\cos\theta}\right] - \cos\left[\frac{\sqrt{z_0}\, t \sin(\psi/2)}{\cos\theta}\right]\right\}, \tag{4}$$

$$\eta_0(\theta) = \frac{\exp\left(-\frac{2\alpha t}{\cos\theta}\right)}{z_0}\left\{\begin{array}{l}\dfrac{\vartheta^2 + z_0}{2}\cosh\left[\dfrac{\sqrt{z_0}\, t \cos(\psi/2)}{\cos\theta}\right] - \dfrac{\vartheta^2 - z_0}{2}\cos\left[\dfrac{\sqrt{z_0}\, t \sin(\psi/2)}{\cos\theta}\right] \\[2ex] +\vartheta\sqrt{z_0}\sin(\psi/2)\sinh\left[\dfrac{\sqrt{z_0}\, t \cos(\psi/2)}{\cos\theta}\right] - \vartheta\sqrt{z_0}\cos(\psi/2)\sin\left[\dfrac{\sqrt{z_0}\, t \sin(\psi/2)}{\cos\theta}\right]\end{array}\right\} \tag{5}$$

Here $\alpha_0 = 3.29$ cm^{-1} is the mean absorption coefficient of the crystal at readout wavelength, $n_0 = 1.43$ is its mean refractive index, t is the thickness of the grating in n_m, and α_m are the modulation amplitudes of the mth harmonics of the refractive index and absorption coefficients, $\kappa_1 = \pi n_m/\lambda$, $\kappa_2 = \alpha_m/2$,

$$\vartheta = \frac{4\pi n_0 \sin\theta_m}{\lambda}(\sin\theta - \sin\theta_m), \tag{6}$$

$$z_0 = \left[(\vartheta^2 + 4(\kappa_1^2 - \kappa_2^2))^2 + (8\,\kappa_1\,\kappa_2)^2\right]^{1/2}, \tag{7}$$

$$\psi_0 = \mathrm{acos}\left\{-\frac{[\vartheta^2 + 4(\kappa_1^2 - \kappa_2^2)]}{z_0}\right\} \tag{8}$$

Modulation amplitudes for the mth harmonics of the absorption coefficient and refractive index found as the fit parameters are shown in **Table 1**.

Using data given in the second and third columns of **Table 1**, one may determine the ratios of amplitudes for the first three harmonic components of the hologram. These ratios are 100:58:22 and 100:42:14 for the absorption coefficient and refractive index, respectively. A difference between the ratios is probably caused by the presence of several types of color centers in the crystal and disproportionality of the spatial distributions of different type centers along the grating vector. Accordingly, the relative magnitudes of modulation amplitudes of the absorption coefficient and refractive index for different spatial harmonics appear to be similar but unequal.

Harmonic number	Modulation amplitude of the absorption coefficient, $\delta\alpha_m$ (cm^{-1})	Modulation amplitude of the refractive index, δn_m
1	2.13	2.6×10^{-5}
2	1.24	1.1×10^{-5}
3	0.47	0.36×10^{-5}

Table 1. Grating parameters.

The hologram profile determined from the luminescence measurements (i.e., the spatial distribution of luminescent color centers) is adequately described by the sum of three harmonic components (amplitude ratio 100:50:19, **Figure 8**). This ratio does not differ strongly from the harmonics ratio for the absorption profile 100:58:22 that follows from the angular dependences of diffraction efficiency and represents the spatial distribution of all color centers forming the grating. This confirms that both the spatial profiles reconstructed from holographic and microscopic measurements are determined by the same spatial distribution of color centers.

The modulation amplitude of absorption coefficient found from the analysis of angular dependences shows that the concentration of colored centers between the holographic planes is small as compared to the average absorption of the crystal with the hologram. At the saturation value of DE, this concentration does not exceed several percents of the total amount of the centers. The overwhelming majority of color centers present in the crystal with hologram are located in the holographic planes.

6. Hologram convertibility under the photothermal treatment using the incoherent radiation

The small amount of color centers (electron traps) between the holographic planes is a premise for the hologram stability with respect to the optical radiation and temperature. When the crystal with hologram is illuminated by incoherent radiation, most of the photoionized electrons arising in the holographic planes cannot be captured by these centers and be localized between the holographic planes. They return to the planes under the effect of electric field generated by their removal from centers subjected to the ionization. However, if the optical radiation is resonant with respect to the color centers dominating in the planes, the recombination of returning electrons with photoionized centers results in the formation of other centers, the type of these centers depending on the crystal temperature. This process opens up a unique possibility for the hologram reconstruction with the incoherent radiation [16, 17].

In **Figure 10**, the absorption spectra of additively colored CaF_2 crystal and sample cut of this crystal with hologram (Hologram *1*) are shown. One may see that hologram recording leads to increased absorption of colloidal centers (the shoulder at ~600 nm) at the expense of simple centers. This sample was subjected to the series of successive photothermal transformations that converted Hologram *1* to Holograms *2–5* (**Table 2**). The spectra of the samples with these holograms are shown in **Figure 11**. All holograms were read out using the DPSS laser (532 nm), and Holograms *2–5* were also read out with diode Thorlabs S3FC1550 laser (1.55 μm). The types of holograms and their DE values are shown in **Table 2**.

As seen (**Figure 12**), noticeable narrowing of the profile of the treated holograms and an accompanying increase in the intensity of the higher diffraction orders occur.

These facts can be explained by spatial redistribution of various center types in Hologram *1*. The highly aggregated color centers are located predominantly in the immediate vicinity of the

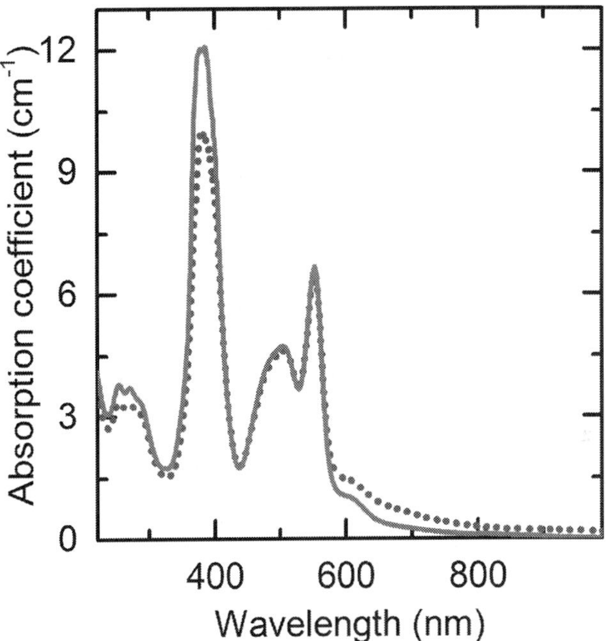

Figure 10. Absorption spectra of CaF$_2$ sample with color centers before (solid line) and after (dotted line) recording Hologram *1*.

Stage of treatment	Hologram number	T (°C)	Impact λ (μm)	Impact time (h)	Exposure (kJ cm^{-2})	Hologram type at 532 nm readout	+1st order DE at 532 nm readout	Hologram type at 1.55 μm readout	+1st order DE at 1.55 μm readout
Hologram recording	1	-	-	-		Amplitude-phase (in-phase)	7.8	Not measured	-
(1)	2	82	0.365	36.8	10	Phase	26.0	Amplitude-phase (antiphase)	6.0
(2)	3	202	-	84.4	-	-	-	-	-
		190	>1	24.4	1	Amplitude-phase (antiphase)	12.0	Amplitude-phase (in-phase)	29.0
(3)	4	186	0.578	49.3	10	Amplitude-phase (in-phase)	6.5	Phase	4.2
(4)	5	193	0.365	6.0	1	Amplitude	14.1	Phase	14.2

Table 2. Sample treatment parameters and hologram characteristics.

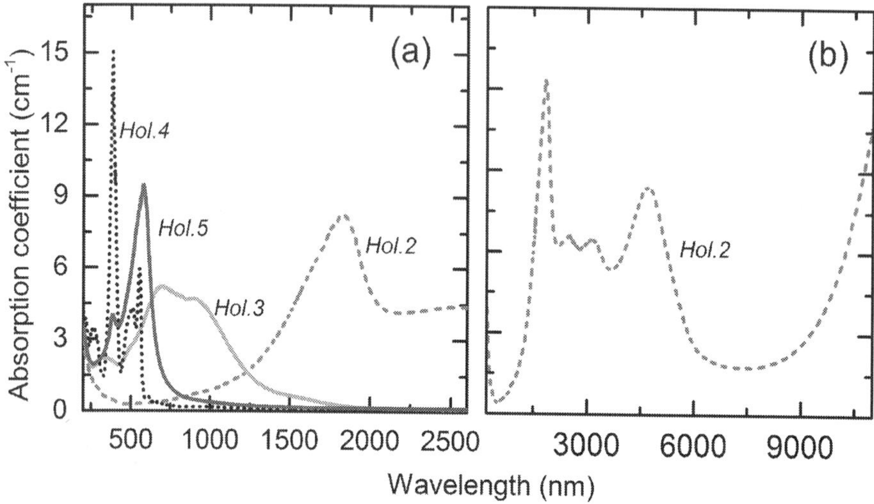

Figure 11. Absorption spectra of samples with Holograms *2–5* (a) and Hologram *2* in the extended wavelength range (b).

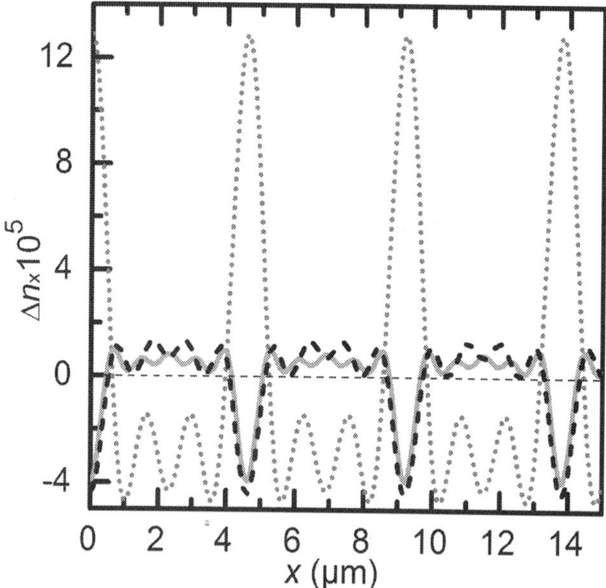

Figure 12. Refractive index profiles of Hologram *1* (dotted line), Hologram *2* (solid line), and Hologram *3* (dashed line) as reconstructed from the angular dependences of the diffraction response at 532 nm. The half-widths of the profiles are 1.00 μm (Hologram *1*), 0.65 μm (Hologram *2*), and 0.70 μm (Hologram *3*).

fringe pattern minima, where the density of vacancies/electrons is relatively high, whereas the peripheral areas of these minima contain mainly simple centers. During Stage (1), the 365 nm radiation effectively destroys the simple centers because all of them have the absorption bands located near this wavelength. However, this radiation just weakly affects the highly aggregated centers. Electrons arising under the photoionization of simple centers move towards the central areas of holographic planes, where the concentration of color centers (traps) is higher than that at the peripheral areas and localize there generating an electric field that attracts vacancies. This increases somewhat the center concentration in the central areas and forms the quasi-colloidal centers stable at temperature of about 80°C. This results in narrowing the Hologram 2 profile that becomes more meander-like. As shown in **Figure 11**, the transformation of the long-wavelength quasi-colloidal centers into the predominantly short-wavelength quasi-colloidal and colloidal ones does not result in a noticeable change of the profile. It should be noted that, at elevated temperatures, the color centers of various types are in equilibrium with each other. The equilibrium state can shift toward a certain type of color centers depending on temperature and, on illuminating the sample, on the wavelength and intensity of the light. At Stages (1) and (2), both heating and the illumination play the same role in facilitating the concentration of the centers and their transforming into the long-wavelength quasi-colloidal centers during Stage (1) and into the short-wavelength and colloidal centers during Stage (2); this is the reason for narrowing the profiles of Holograms 2 and 3. During Stage (3), in contrast, these factors act in the opposite directions. The temperature of 186°C favors the colloidal center formation; however, the 578 nm radiation destroys them, as well as the short-wavelength quasi-colloidal centers present in Hologram 3, thus hindering the accumulation of color centers, which results in some broadening the Hologram 4 profile.

The sample with the hologram under above transformations was maintained at 80–190°C for more than 8 days and ~2/3 of this period the sample was under the impact of actinic radiation with the total exposure of 22 kJ cm^{-2}. Such treatment does not result in the hologram erasure. It should be noted that (i) the absorption spectrum of the sample with Hologram 4 thus treated practically coincides with the spectrum of the initial sample and (ii) DE of the hologram is reduced only by ~1.3% as compared to that of Hologram 1 (it should be taken into account that these two holograms are similar but not wholly identical). As seen, one can state an extremely high stability of holograms in this medium with respect to the optical radiation and temperature.

The read out of Hologram 5 with 532 nm laser shows the equality of intensities of diffracted and transmitted radiation (Borrmann effect) due to a large absorption at the readout wavelength.

The above considerations allow for managing the hologram type (amplitude-phase, mostly amplitude, or mostly phase one), characteristics, and diffraction efficiency. Such changes can be implemented throughout the visible and IR spectral ranges up to the CaF$_2$ transparency limit (10 μm). It should be noted that **Figure 11** shows only the examples of center-type transformation. Actually, one can perform the finer "tuning" of the center type by modifying the wavelength of incoherent radiation and temperature. The other ruling parameter is the concentration of color centers in the crystal (the additive coloring mode).

7. Self-organization of color centers in the course of hologram recording

The investigation of weakly colored samples with holograms recorded under various power densities of laser radiation, exposure, temperature, and grating period revealed structuring the holographic planes with an increase in the colloidal center concentration: the holographic planes became thinner and were pierced by fragmentary spiral-like bundles that consisted of colloids.

Figure 13 shows the 3D view of such hologram composed with the confocal LSM. One may conclude that, under hologram recording, (i) the above self-organization of color centers took place and (ii) the colloidal centers played an important role in this process [18, 19].

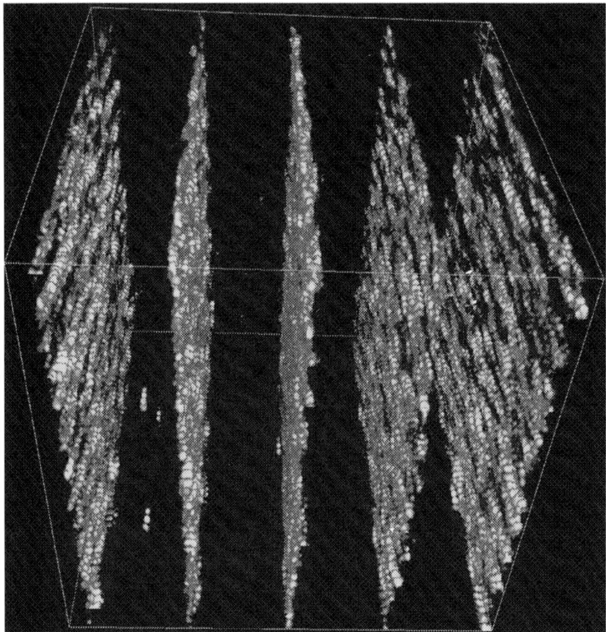

Figure 13. 3D LSM image of the sample with bundles in the holographic planes seen in the reflected light of 405 nm laser.

The colloidal particles can be considered as the second phase inclusions in the fluorite lattice. It should be noted that, though metallic calcium and fluorite have the same Bravais lattice and mismatch of their lattice parameter, a, is very small ($a_{Ca} = 0.556$ nm, $a_{CaF_2} = 0.545$ nm), the mutual orientation of the matrix and colloids is not expected to be cube-on-cube [5]. Thus, the colloidal centers disturb the fluorite lattice. This disturbance displays itself in broadening the absorption bands with the growth of the colloid content.

It was stated above that the color centers including colloids both form and decay in the hologram recording process. So, recording a hologram on the CaF_2 crystals with color centers is accompanied by continuous phase transitions.

The internal self-consistency (self-organization) arises in complex systems due to the interaction of various subsystems [20]. Their interaction is the most effective near the phase transition; when a subsystem that experiences the transition becomes soft and weak, an external perturbation can cause the strong modification of the subsystem state and, in particular, its order parameter. In the case under consideration, such perturbations could be the fluctuations of concentrations of simple centers, vacancies, and electrons. These fluctuations could, in turn, trigger the formation of large-scale stable spatially inhomogeneous states in the subsystem of colloidal centers located in the holographic planes. Such states are bundles. The bundles arise in the recording conditions and turn out to be frozen on cooling the crystal after finishing the recording process.

The bundle formation is probably governed by (i) bi-directional "compression" of holographic planes by vacancy flows emanating from the neighboring fringe pattern maxima (the bundle thickness is about the thickness of the holographic planes) and (ii) the direction of the Poynting vector of the interference field that determines successive recording of the hologram deeply into the sample (the bundle orientation coincides with this direction).

Within the framework of the synergetic theory [20], a CaF_2 crystal in the process of hologram recording may be considered as an open system that is in the heat exchange with a heat source having temperature of 150–200°C. From this standpoint, the formation of bundles (dissipative structures) is the result of importing the negative entropy into the crystal.

At some colloid content, the bundles become continuous and correlated with each other, thus forming the 2D superlattice of a symmetry very close to *cmm* plane symmetry group [21] with the lattice parameters as follows: a is the doubled period of the hologram and b is a separation between the neighboring bundles along the holographic plane (**Figure 14**). For the sample shown in **Figure 13**, $a = 9$ μm and $b \approx 4.2$ μm. Under further increase in the colloid concentration, however, the correlation between bundles breaks and they tear off.

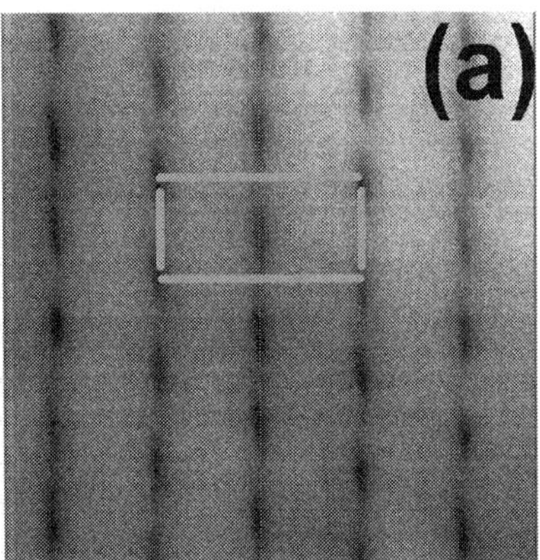

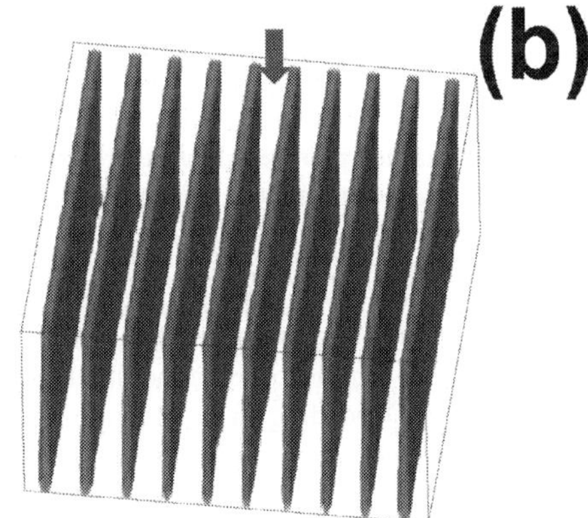

Figure 14. Absorption image of a hologram with 2D superlattice in one of orthogonal projections resulted from postprocessed series of their optical slices recorded using LSM at 405 nm (a). The schematic drawing of hologram (b); an arrow indicates the projection shown in (a). The green rectangle in (a) shows the superlattice elementary cell.

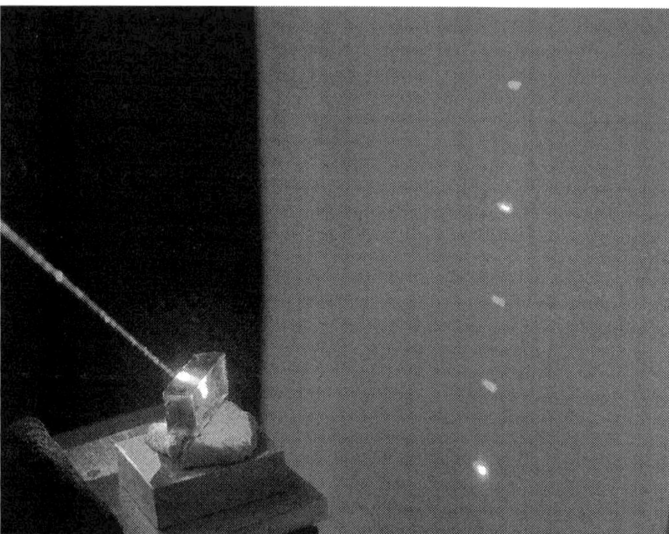

Figure 16. Fan of diffracted beams emerging from HP-II.

The uniquely small mass and dimensional characteristics of this angular measure (10 g and 0.5–1 cm³, respectively) make it possible to use such HP as a basis for developing devices for measuring/setting rotation angles that will combine two antinomic requirements such as the mobility and high accuracy of angular measurements (see [25] for details).

8.2. Volume holographic elements for mid-IR spectral range

The specific features of holograms listed above allow for taking the holographic elements based on additively colored CaF_2 crystals to be quite promising as the transmission and reflection filters in the mid-IR spectral range. Below, the expected characteristics of holographic filters based on CaF_2 crystals with photothermally transformed holograms are discussed.

The absorption spectrum of CaF_2 crystal after special photothermal treatment is shown in **Figure 17**. An absorption band attributed to the short-wavelength quasi-colloidal centers ($\lambda_{max} \cong 2$ μm) is present in the spectrum.

Under suggestions that (a) the absorption spectrum of the sample with a hologram is similar to that shown in **Figure 17**, (b) the holographic grating plane width is about 0.2 of the grating period d (e.g., 1 μm width at 4.5 μm period [13]), and (c) ~90% of color centers are located within the holographic planes (and, hence, the same fraction of the sample absorption originates from the planes), it is possible to estimate the expected characteristics of transmission and reflection holograms read out with 3.5 μm radiation.

The absorption spectrum shown in **Figure 17** ensures recording of efficient transmission and reflection holograms in the crystal samples of several millimeters thick. When neglecting the absorption of readout radiation, it is possible to use the Kogelnik theory to calculate the phase hologram parameters [27].

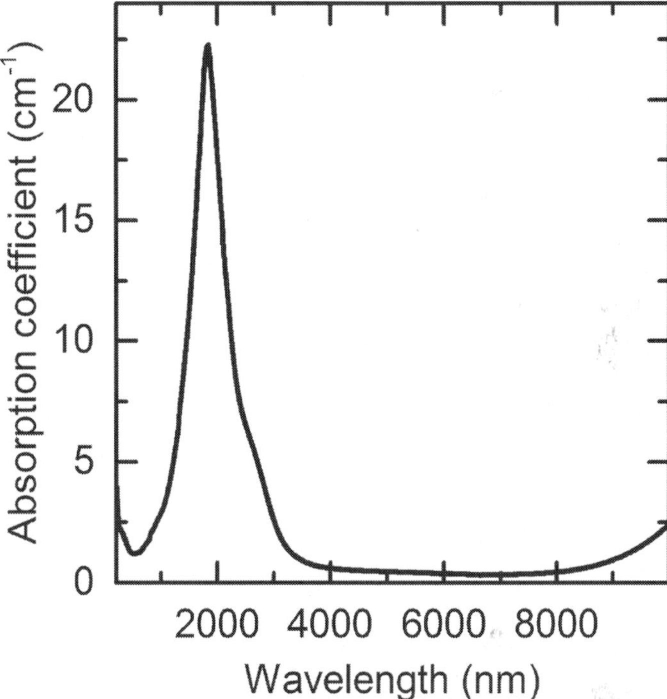

Figure 17. Absorption spectrum of the photothermally treated sample.

According to suggestions (b) and (c), the spectral dependence of the modulation amplitude of the absorption coefficient $\delta a(v)$ of the crystal with a hologram can be calculated by multiplication of the absorption spectrum shown in **Figure 17** by coefficient such as (4.5 μm/1 μm) × 0.9. Kramers-Kronig relation (1) allows the estimation of the corresponding spectral dependence of the modulation amplitude of the refractive index $\delta n(v)$ shown in **Figure 18**.

The modulation amplitude of the refractive index δn at the readout wavelength $\lambda = 3.5$ μm equals to 6.82×10^{-4}. The hologram thickness T is determined by the phase incursion $v_t = \pi/2$ that provides the 100% diffraction efficiency of the phase hologram. To calculate the optimum thickness of the hologram, an expression can be used as follows:

$$T = v_t \lambda \cos \theta_0 / \pi \delta n, \tag{9}$$

where θ_0 is the Bragg angle for the readout radiation inside the holographic medium ($\theta_0 = 15°$ for the grating period $d = 4.5$ μm). The thickness of a hologram with the above parameters equals to 2.45 mm.

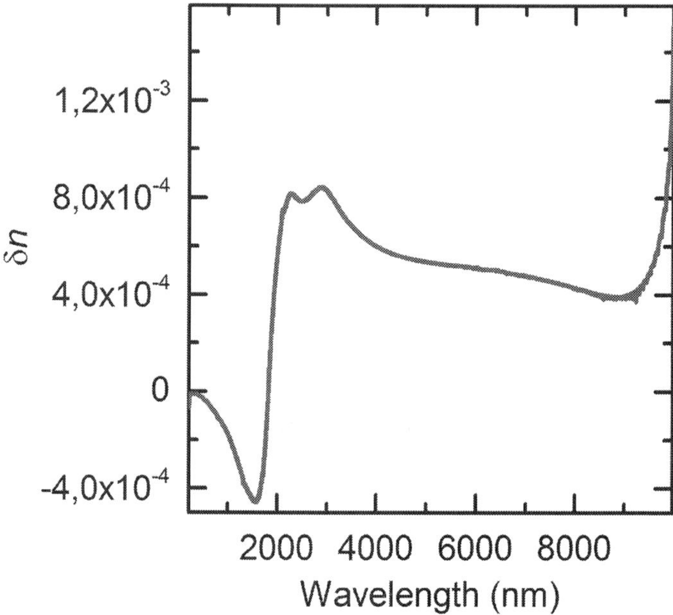

Figure 18. Spectral dependence of the modulation amplitude of the refractive index for a crystal with the hologram.

It should be noted that the nonsinusoidal nature of the hologram profile in this crystal results in the appearance of several diffraction orders from the recorded hologram (the diffraction from several spatial harmonic components). The fraction of the first diffraction order that can be used for holographic filtering at the Bragg angle is about 65% of the total diffraction efficiency of the hologram [13].

The spectral selectivity of the transmission hologram, $\delta\lambda$, can be approximately calculated using an equation as follows:

$$\delta\lambda \approx \frac{\lambda d \operatorname{ctg} \theta_0}{T} \tag{10}$$

At the above values of grating parameters, $\delta\lambda = 24$ nm.

Angular selectivity of the hologram $\delta\theta$ is given by

$$\delta\theta = \lambda \, \xi_t / \left(2\pi n T \sin \theta_0\right), \tag{11}$$

where $n = 1.43$ is the refraction index of CaF_2 crystal at the readout wavelength. The misalignment parameter ξ_t is proportional to the deviation of the readout angle (in the medium) from θ_0. The ξ_t value of ~2.7 corresponds to DE equal to zero. Under these conditions, the angular selectivity equals to 0.13° according to Eq. (11).

When using the sample with hologram as a reflection-type filter, the wavelengths of recording (λ_{rec}) and reflected (λ_{read}) radiations are different but connected—according to the Bragg condition—via the hologram period d:

$$d = \frac{\lambda_{rec}}{2 \sin \theta_{rec}} = \frac{\lambda_{read}}{2 \sin \theta_{read}} \tag{12}$$

For the actual case $\theta_{read} = 90°$ at $\lambda_{read} = 3.5$ µm, the period of reflection grating d equals to 1.22 µm.

Recording of the reflection hologram readout with 3.5 µm radiation can be executed with the 532 nm radiation in the symmetric transmission scheme with the $2\theta_{rec} = 25.2°$ angle between the recording beams (**Figure 19**).

The assumption that relation between grating period and holographic plane thickness is the same for both transmission and reflection grating allows using the same $\delta n(\nu)$ dependence (**Figure 18**) to calculate the phase incursion for the reflection hologram.

The DE of the reflection hologram increases with an increase in the phase incursion, ν_r:

$$\eta = \mathrm{th}^2(\nu_r), \tag{13}$$

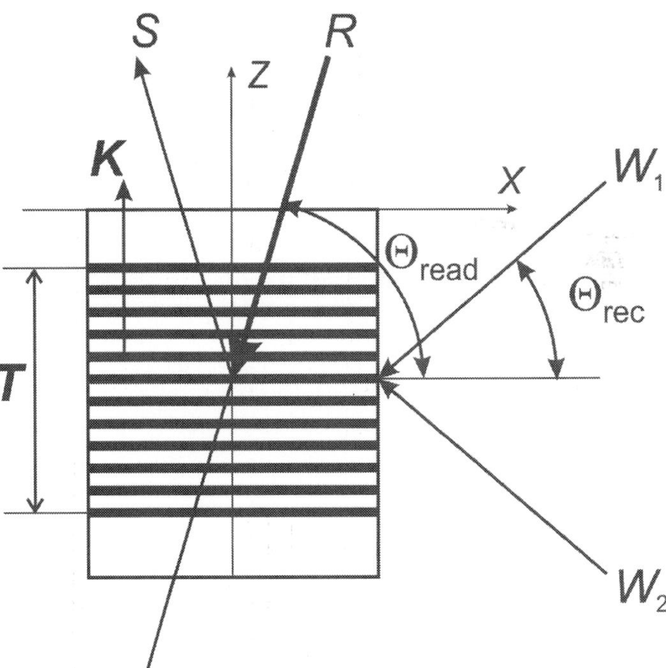

Figure 19. The scheme of recording/readout the reflection hologram. W_1 and W_2 are the recording beams, R and S are readout and diffracted beams, respectively, $K = 2\pi/d$ is the grating vector.

where $v_r = \frac{\pi \Delta n T}{\lambda \sin \theta_0}$. For $\delta n = 6.82 \times 10^{-4}$, the thickness of a hologram with DE = 100% equals to 6 mm. Absorption in such sample does not exceed 3%.

The spectral and angular selectivity of the reflection hologram can be expressed through the misalignment parameter ξ_r. The ξ_r value of 3.5 corresponds to the deviation of pitch angle θ_0 from its magnitude of 90°; at the latter, DE $\cong$ 0 and the ξ_r parameter and the spectral selectivity are connected through a relation as follows:

$$\delta \lambda = -\frac{\xi_r \lambda^2}{\left(2 \pi n T \sin \theta_0\right)} \tag{14}$$

At the above ξ_r value, the spectral $|\delta \lambda|$ and angular $\delta \varphi$ selectivities are equal to 1.3 nm and 0.02°, respectively.

These estimates demonstrate the possibility of using the holographic elements based on CaF_2 crystals with color centers as the volume narrow-band transmission and reflection filters for the mid-IR spectral range.

9. Conclusions

The fluorite crystal with color centers is a promising holographic medium. The technology of its preparation allows for producing reproducibly large-size samples and enables the modification of color center concentration in a wide range. There exists the set of color centers whose absorption bands overlap with each other, thus covering the entire transparency region of fluorite. The photochromism of color centers enables hologram recording in the fluorite crystals. The diffusion-drift mechanism of recording that causes not only the color center transformation but also their redistribution over the crystal bulk determines the holographic features of this medium such as (i) the nonsinusoidal hologram profile, (ii) a high hologram stability with respect to temperature and optical radiation, and (iii) an opportunity to change the type of readout hologram (amplitude, amplitude-phase, or phase) using postexposure incoherent radiation. The highly stable volume holograms with high angular and spectral selectivities can be used as metrological elements and narrow-band transmission and reflection filters for the mid-IR spectral range.

Acknowledgements

The authors are grateful to Yurii I. Terekhin for preparing all CaF_2 samples, Tatiana S. Semenova, Lyudmila F. Koriakina, and Marina A. Petrova for additive coloring the samples, and also Evgenii B. Verkhovskii and Anatolii K. Kupchikov for a technical assistance (all of them, ITMO University).

The paper is dedicated to the memory of our colleague, Aleksandr S. Shcheulin (1955–2016), who was an active participant of this study.

Research was funded by Russian Science Foundation (Agreement #14-23-00136).

Author details

Aleksandr I. Ryskin, Aleksandr E. Angervaks* and Andrei V. Veniaminov

*Address all correspondence to: angervax@mail.ru

ITMO University, St. Petersburg, Russian Federation

References

[1] Shcheulin AS, Semenova TS, Koryakina LF, Petrova MA, Kupchikov AK, Ryskin AI. Additive coloration of crystals of calcium and cadmium fluorides. Opt. Spectrosc. 2007;**103**:660–664. DOI: 10.1134/S0030400X07100219

[2] Shcheulin AS, Semenova TS, Koryakina LF, Petrova MA, Angervaks AE, Ryskin AI. Additive coloring rate and intensity for pure and doped fluorite crystals. Opt. Spectrosc. 2011;**110**:617–623. DOI: 10.1134/S0030400X11040205

[3] Hayes W, editor. Crystals with Fluorite Structure. Electronic, Vibrational, and Defect Properties. 1st ed. Oxford: Clarendon Press; 1974. 448 p.

[4] Orera VM, Alkala E. Optical properties of cation colloidal particles in CaF_2 and SrF_2. Phys. Status Solidi. 1977;**44**:717–723. DOI: 10.1002/pssa.2210440239

[5] Cramer LP, Schubert BE, Petite PS, Langfort SC, Dickinson JT. Laser interactions with embedded Ca metal nanoparticles in single crystal CaF_2. J. Appl. Phys. 2005;**97**:074307. DOI: 10.1063/1.1862758

[6] Rix S, Natura U, Loske F, Letz M, Felser K, Reichling M. Formation of metallic colloids in CaF_2 by intense ultraviolet light. Appl. Phys. Lett. 2011;**99**:261909. DOI: 10.1063/1.3673301

[7] Shcheulin AS, Angervaks AE, Aksenova KA, Gainutdinov RV, Ryskin AI. Photothermal transformation of color centers in CaF_2 crystals. Opt. Spectrosc. 2015;**118**:542–546. DOI: 10.1134/S0030400X15040189

[8] Belous VM, Mandel VE, Popov AY, Tyurin AV. Mechanism of holographic recording based on photothermal transformation of color centers in additively colored alkali halide crystals. Opt. Spectrosc. 1999;**87**:305–310.

[9] Popov AY, Belous VM, Mandel VE, Shugailo VB, Tyurin AV. Drift model of photo-induced processes in alkali-halide crystals during hologram recording. Proc. SPIE. 1999;**3904**:195–200. DOI: 10.1117/12.370402

[10] Shcheulin AS, Veniaminov AV, Korzinin YuL, Angervaks AE, Ryskin AI. A highly stable holographic medium based on CaF_2:Na crystals with colloidal color centers: III. Properties of holograms. Opt. Spectrosc. 2007;**103**:655–659. DOI: 10.1134/S0030400X07100207

New Photo-Thermo-Refractive Glasses for Holographic Optical Elements: Properties and Applications

Nikonorov Nikolay, Ivanov Sergey,
Dubrovin Victor and Ignatiev Alexander

Additional information is available at the end of the chapter

http://dx.doi.org/10.5772/66116

Abstract

This chapter presents a survey of recent achievements of the ITMO University (St. Petersburg, Russia) in developing new holographic media such as fluoride, chloride, and bromide silicate photo-thermo-refractive (PTR) glasses as well as the holographic diffractive optical elements that are the volume Bragg gratings recorded in the glasses for improving dramatically the parameters of laser systems of different types. The photo-thermo-induced crystallization process and the properties of fluoride, chloride, and bromide PTR glasses are demonstrated. This new technology enabled recording high-efficiency phase volume holograms in the optical quality silicate glass. These holograms are used for developing a number of unique diffractive optical elements that provide new opportunities for the laser technique. Some examples of designing and fabricating of holographic optical elements such as the super-narrowband filters for solid-state lasers and laser diodes, laser beam combiners, and collimator sights are demonstrated in this chapter. It is shown that the PTR glass doped with rare earth ions can be used for designing lasers with Bragg reflectors and distributed feedback.

Keywords: PTR glass, photo-thermo-refractive glass, photo-thermo-induced crystallization, volume Bragg grating, beam combining, refractive index, photosensitive glass

1. Introduction

Photo-thermo-refractive (PTR) glasses are a new class of photosensitive materials intended for recording three-dimensional (3D) phase holograms. This class was developed based on photo-sensitive sodium zinc aluminosilicate glasses that were first put into practice by

---

Corning, Inc., in 1977 and were referred to as polychromatic (PC) glasses [1–3]. In Russia, similar photosensitive glasses [4, 5] were denoted by multichromatic (MC) ones. PC/MC glasses are known to contain, in addition to Na_2O, Al_2O_3, ZnO, and SiO_2, some other ingredients such as (i) photosensitive dopants playing the roles of electron donors (Ce^{3+}) and acceptors (Ag^+, Sb^{5+}, and Sn^{4+}) and also (ii) halogen ions (F^- and Br^-) that participate in the formation of the crystalline phases. The main specific feature of PC/MC glasses is the selective absorption in the visible. Namely, PC glasses can acquire, under the effects of the UV exposure and subsequent heat treatment, a wide variety of colors. In brief, the final stages of photochemical and diffusion processes responsible for this coloration were assumed to be as follows. The colloidal silver particles formed under the above effects play the role of nucleation centers. Around such centers, the growth of NaF and (Ag, Na)Br nano- or microcrystals occurs. Under particular growth conditions, the microcrystals acquire complicated anisotropic shapes such as the elongated pyramid-like structures stretched along an axis [1, 3, 6]. Additional multistage UV irradiation and heat treatment lead to the photolytic precipitation of silver layer on the surfaces of these anisotropic structures (so-called "decoration of the latter with silver"). The anisotropy of metallic silver shells thus formed results in a certain shift of the corresponding absorption band into the visible. So the substantial anisotropy of metallic silver particles was considered to be the principal condition for the occurrence of "PC/MC coloration" in PC/MC glasses.

In the late 1980s–early 1990s [7–10], it was proposed first in Vavilov State Optical Institute to apply PC/MC glasses for recording the 3D phase holograms. Unlike the case of PC/MC coloration, only a single stage of photo-thermo-induced crystallization was used, and this stage included the UV irradiation and subsequent heat treatment. When developing the corresponding procedures, the principal attention was paid to a difference obtainable in the refractive indices of vitreous and crystalline phases rather than the anisotropic shapes of microcrystals. As a result, a new class of materials was developed in Vavilov State Optical Institute, this class was denoted [10] by a specific term such as "photo-thermo-refractive (PTR) glasses" (i.e., glasses whose refractive index varies due to the UV irradiation and subsequent heat treatment). Later [11, 12], this term started to be used widely in other countries as well. Now, there is an increased interest in PTR glasses because the volume Bragg gratings recorded on these glasses reveal a unique combination of working characteristics such as the high angle and spectral selectivity, high diffraction efficiency, high mechanical and optical strength, and also high thermal and chemical durability. Based on PTR glasses, a broad variety of optical devices are developed including extra narrow-band filters, wavelength division multiplexing (WDM) devices, combiners of high-intensity light beams, chirped gratings for compressing the light impulses, filters for increasing the spectral brightness of laser diodes, etc.

The given paper is a survey of recent achievements of ITMO University (St. Petersburg, Russia) in developing new holographic media such as fluoride, chloride, and bromide silicate photo-thermo-refractive (PTR) glasses as well as the holographic diffractive optical elements that are the volume Bragg gratings recorded in the glasses for improving dramatically the parameters of laser systems of different types.

2. Properties of fluoride PTR glasses

The fluoride PTR glass was designed and synthesized in ITMO University, Russia [12]. The fluoride PTR glass is a photosensitive multicomponent sodium-zinc-alumino-silicate one containing fluorine (6 mol%) and small amount of bromine (0.5 mol%) and also doped with additives (cerium, antimony, and silver) that are responsible for the photo-thermo-induced precipitation of silver nanoparticles and sodium fluoride crystals—see for example [1, 13, 14]. Untreated fluoride PTR glasses are transparent in a wide spectral range of 250–2500 nm (**Figure 1(a)**). The selective UV irradiation into the Ce^{3+} absorption band in the spectra of these glasses results in the formation of neutral silver molecular clusters. The subsequent heat treatment of UV-irradiated PTR glasses near the glass transition temperature (T_g) induces the silver nanoparticle formation [1] (**Figure 1(b)**). The thermal treatment of these glasses at temperatures above T_g leads to the growth of silver bromide shell on a silver nanoparticle [15] and then to the precipitation of sodium fluoride cone on it [1, 16]. Image of XRD pattern of UV-exposed and thermal-treated PTR glass sample is shown in **Figure 2**.

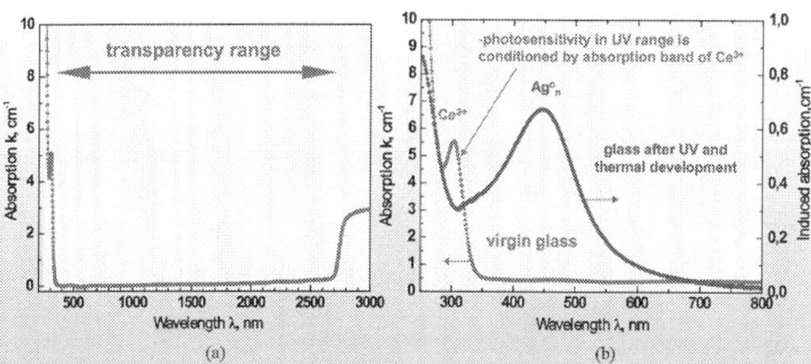

Figure 1. Absorption spectra of (a) virgin PTR glass and (b) the glass sample after the UV irradiation and subsequent heat treatment.

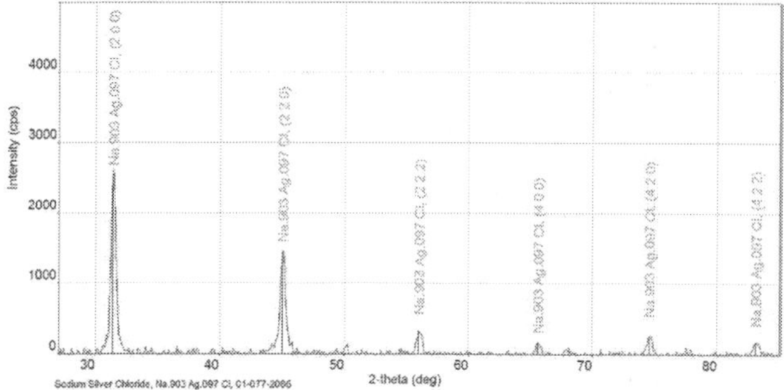

Figure 2. X-ray diffraction pattern of UV-irradiated and thermal-treated PTR glass.

In Ref. [13], authors showed, for the first time, the dramatic effect of bromine on the process of NaF crystal growth in fluoride PTR glasses. The paper has demonstrated that the growth of sodium fluoride crystals is possible only in the presence of bromide additives in the PTR glass composition. A generalized NaF crystallization mechanism that consists of three stages is proposed in Refs. [1, 17].

The process of photo-thermo-induced crystallization of fluoride PTR glass is shown schematically in **Figure 3**.

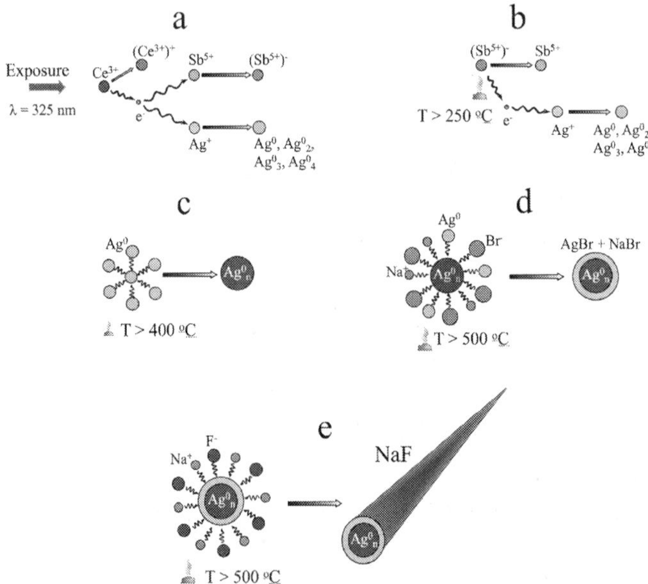

Figure 3. Photo-thermo-induced crystallization of fluoride PTR glass. (a) Cerium photoionization and trapping the photoelectrons by Sb; (b) Releasing electrons Sb and trapping them by Ag ions with the formation of neutral silver atoms and clusters; (c) Formation of colloidal particles under heating up to 400°C; (d) Growth of (Ag, Na)Br shell on colloidal silver particles at $T > 500°C$; (e) Growth of NaF microcrystals at $T > 500°C$.

At the first stage, the trivalent cerium ion donates an electron under the effect of the UV irradiation, thus increasing its own valency in accordance with the following reaction **(Figure 3(a))**

$$Ce^{3+} + h\nu \rightarrow e^- + \left[Ce^{3+}\right]^+ \tag{1}$$

Released photoelectrons can be trapped partially by silver ions (~20%) with subsequent neutral silver atom and molecular cluster formation (Ag^0, Ag_2^0, Ag_2^+, Ag_3^{2+}), but most photoelectrons are trapped by antimony ions according to the following reaction **(Figure 3(b))**:

$$e^- + Sb^{5+} \rightarrow \left[Sb^{5+} \right]^- \tag{2}$$

At the second stage, the heat treatment at relatively low temperatures (300–450°C) leads to releasing the trapped electrons from antimony (**Figure 3(c)**) with further formation of silver molecular clusters and colloidal nanoparticles (**Figure 2(b)**):

$$\left[Sb^{5+} \right]^- \rightarrow Sb^{5+} + e^- \tag{3}$$

$$nAg^+ + ne^- \rightarrow nAg^0 \tag{4}$$

At the third stage, the heat treatment at temperatures above T_g results, first, in the growth of mixed silver bromide-sodium bromide shell on a silver nanoparticle (**Figure 3(e)**) and, further, in the coaxial growth of sodium fluoride crystalline phase on this shell (**Figure 3(g)**).

In Ref. [15], authors showed that the UV irradiation and subsequent heat treatment of fluoride PTR glass induces the refractive index change only in the UV-irradiated area. There is still some uncertainty in the origin of refractive index change in PTR glass, and several presumable mechanisms of the change are discussed. Classically, this effect is assumed to be caused by difference in the refractive indices between the NaF crystal phase ($n \sim 1.33$) sedimented in the UV-irradiated area and the unexposed glass area ($n \sim 1.49$) so that the precipitation of sodium fluoride leads to the negative refractive index increment. Although a difference between the refractive indices of sodium fluoride and vitreous phase is rather big, the negative refractive index change in the UV-irradiated area does not exceed 1×10^{-3} [15, 18]. This can probably be due to the fact that, in addition to the NaF phase precipitation, there is also the silver bromide shell with a high refractive index value ($n \sim 2.3$) on the silver nanoparticle. As shown in many sources (see for example Refs. [14, 19, 20]), the maximum of surface plasmon resonance of silver nanoparticles in fluoride PTR glasses shifts to the greater wavelengths owing to the silver bromide shell growth.

On the other hand, the authors of [21] proposed another possible mechanism of photo-thermo-induced refractive index change in PTR glass. They assumed that the transformation of Na^+ and F^- distributed in the PTR glass matrix into the crystalline NaF (a chemical change) and structural relaxation process are not the main causes of photo-thermo-induced refractive index change and assigned this change to high residual stresses around the NaF crystals. According to calculations presented in the paper, these stresses are the most important cause for the photo-thermo-induced refractive index change in PTR glass.

Also, fluoride PTR glasses have outstanding mechanical, optical, and chemical properties. In particular, they show a high photosensitivity, high thermal stability of the recorded phase holograms, and high tolerance to the optical and ionizing irradiation. The basic optical and spectral properties of PTR glass are described in Refs. [14, 22–24]. The holographic optical elements (HOE)s recorded on the PTR glass demonstrate high chemical stability, thermal, mechanical and optical strength and also reveal, from this point of view, practically no difference with the commercial optical glass BK7 (Schott). The optical and spectral parameters of the HOEs and gradient index (GRIN)-elements do not change after its multiple heating to high enough temperature (500°C). The important advantages of PTR glass as the optical medium are as follows:

i.   High optical homogeneity (the refraction index fluctuations across the glass bulk are of the order of 10^{-5}).

ii.   Reproducibility of its parameters from one glass synthesis to another and also in the course of the photo-thermo-induced crystallization.

iii.   PTR glass can be subjected, similar to optical glass BK7, to various kinds of both the mechanical processing such as grinding and polishing and the formation technologies such as molding, aspheric surface production, and drawing fiber.

iv.   One can fabricate PTR glass both in the laboratory conditions (hundreds of grams) and industrial ones (hundreds of kilograms) using a simple and nontoxic technology. The chemical reagents required for the glass fabrication are commercially available and not too expensive.

Transparency range, nm	350–3000
Photosensitivity spectral range, nm	280–350
Photosensitivity, mJ/cm²	50
RI change, Δn, ppm	1000
RI modulation amplitude, δn, ppm	500
Induced optical loss, cm⁻¹	
• visible range	0.1
• near IR range	0.01
Optical resistance (laser-induced damage threshold):	
• CW regime, kW/cm²	10
• Nanosecond pulse regime, J/cm²	40 (Data of University of Central Florida)
Mechanical and thermal resistance, chemical durability	Close to commercial optical glass BK7
Spatial frequency VBGs, mm⁻¹	up to 10,000 (Data of University of Central Florida)
Diffraction efficiency, %	95
Hologram thickness, mm	0.1–10
Angular selectivity, ang. min	<1
Bandwidth FWHM, nm	0.1
Size, mm	up to 25 × 25
VBGs are completely stable at temperature, °C	500
VBGs are completely stable at temperature, °C	500

Table 1. Characteristics of PTR glass and VBGs recorded on the glass.

One should also note some features of PTR glass that are unusual for other recording media. For example, PTR glass can be processed with the ion exchange technology, which provides possibilities (i) to fabricate the ion-exchanged optical [25] or plasmonic waveguides and (ii) to implement the surface strengthening, thus improving the mechanical strength, chemical stability, and thermal and also optical strength.

Some characteristics and advantages of fluoride PTR glasses and also of holographic volume Bragg gratings (VBG) recorded on the glasses are presented in **Table 1** [26].

3. Properties of chloride PTR glasses

The chloride PTR glasses are photosensitive multicomponent glasses based on Na_2O-ZnO-Al_2O_3-SiO_2-NaF system doped with variable batch concentration of Cl (0–2.2 mol%), a photosensitizer such as CeO_2 (0.01 mol%), a reducer such as Sb_2O_3 (0.05 mol%), and also Ag_2O (0.15 mol%). The chloride PTR glass was designed and synthesized in ITMO University, Russia [24].

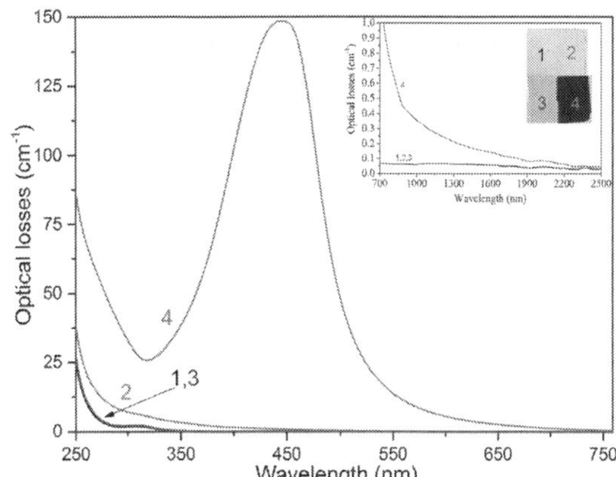

Figure 4. The evolution of the absorption spectra of PTR glass containing 2.2 mol% Cl during photo-thermo induced cristallization (1) is the spectrum for initial untreated glass, (2) is that for glass after the UV irradiation for 50 s alone, (3) is the spectrum for glass after the heat treatment alone at 550°C for 3 h, and (4) is the spectrum for glass after the UV irradiation for 50 s and subsequent heat treatment at 550 °C for 3 h. An inset shows the photos and absorption spectra (700–2500 nm) of treated chloride PTR glass samples containing 2.2 mol% Cl. Here (1) is initial untreated glass, (2) is glass after the UV irradiation for 50 s alone, (3) is glass after the heat treatment alone, and (4) is glass after the UV irradiation for 50 s and subsequent heat treatment.

With changing the type of halide (fluoride to bromide or chloride) in the PTR glass composition, it is possible to control the sign of the RI increment. As mentioned above, for the case of fluoride PTR glass, thermal treatment at temperatures higher than T_g results in a decrease in the RI of the UV-irradiated area in comparison with that of nonirradiated area. On the other hand, the substitution of fluorine by chlorine leads to the precipitation of nano-crystalline phases of mixed silver and sodium chlorides in glass host and to the positive increment of RI (Δn up to 1.0×10^{-3}) [24].

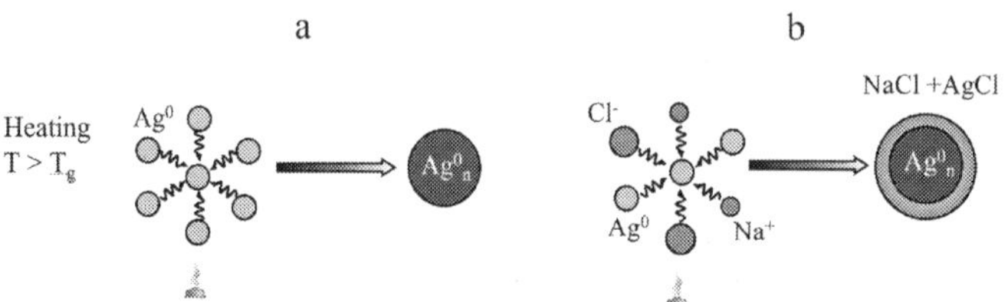

Figure 5. Scheme for the photo-thermo-induced crystallization mechanism inherent in chloride PTR glasses for various Cl concentrations (0–2.2 mol%). (a) Is the growth of shell-free silver nanoparticles in glasses containing 0–1.0 mol% Cl. (b) Is the growth silver nanoparticles with a shell composed of mixed silver and sodium chlorides in glasses containing 0–2.2 mol% Cl.

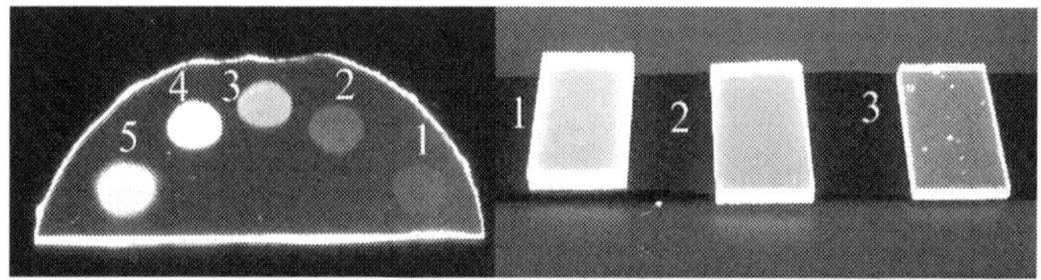

Figure 6. Photos of chloride PTR glass luminesce under UV (λ = 365 nm) excitation (a) is the photo of PTR glass containing 1 mol% Cl after the UV irradiation with various doses. The exposure duration (sec) that sets a dose is (1) 0.5 s, (2) 1 s, (3) 5 s, (4) 50s, (5) 500 s; (b) is the photo of the UV-irradiated and heat treated (1 h 400°C) chloride PTR glasses differing in the chlorine concentration. The chlorine concentrations (mol%) being (1) 0, (2) 1, and (3) 2.

Initially, chloride PTR glasses are transparent in a wide spectral range. 250–2500 nm (**Figure 4**). The UV irradiation of chloride PTR glasses results in the Ce^{3+} ion photoionization and the resultant formation of silver molecular clusters (SMC), the latter playing the role of crystallization centers (**Figures 4** and **5**). Heating all studied chloride PTR glasses at temperatures above 250°C and less than T_g results, as shown in **Figure 5(b)**, in releasing electrons from Sb and capturing them by Ag ions with further formation of an extra amount of neutral silver atoms and molecular clusters [19]. The latter provide, according to Refs. [27, 28], a broadband luminescence in the visible and NIR ranges (**Figure 6**). Further, the heat treatment of PTR glasses containing 0–1.0 mol% Cl at temperatures above T_g leads to the precipitation of silver nanoparticles with no shell (**Figure 5**). At the same time, such treatment of PTR glasses containing >1.0–2.2 mol% Cl results in the precipitation of silver nanoparticles with a shell consisting, according to Ref. [24], of mixed sodium and silver chlorides in a varied proportion (**Figures 4** and **5**). The evolution of absorption spectra during the photo-thermo-induced crystallization is shown in **Figure 4**. It can be seen that the heat treatment of nonirradiated chloride PTR glass has no measurable effect on the absorption spectra. According to calculations described in Ref.

[24], the sizes of silver nanoparticles and silver and sodium chloride nanocrystals are relatively small (about 3 nm [**Figure 7**] for silver nanoparticles, NPs, and 27 nm for nanocrystals). This is why chloride PTR glasses exhibit a rather low level of scattering.

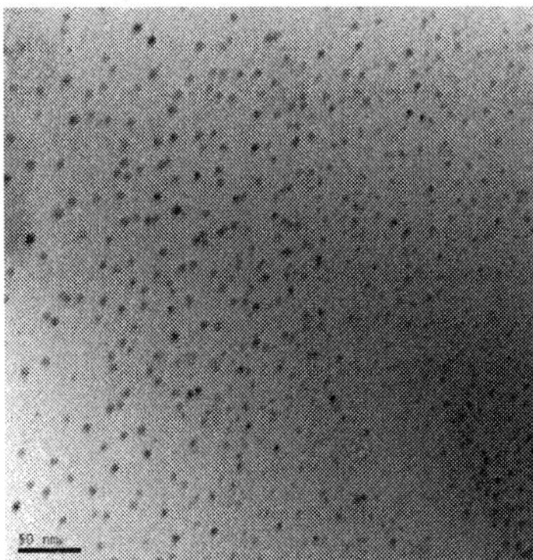

Figure 7. TEM image of silver nanoparticles in chloride PTR glass. Scale – 50 nm.

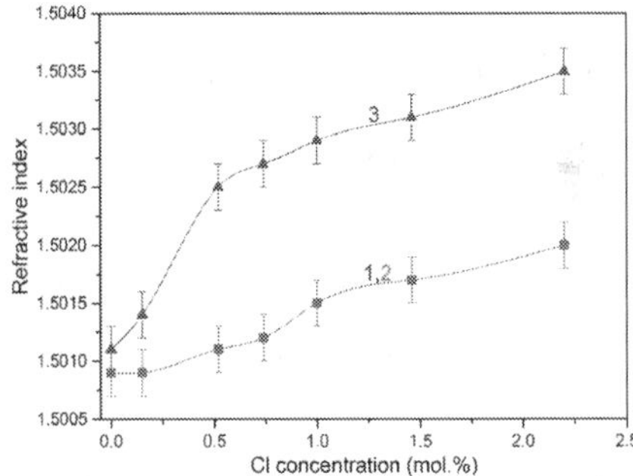

Figure 8. Effect of chlorine concentration on the refractive index (n_d) of PTR glass. 1—untreated glass samples, 2—glass samples after the heat treatment, 3—glass samples after the UV irradiation and subsequent heat treatment.

Figure 8 shows the evolution of the refractive index of PTR glass with an increase in the chlorine concentration for initial, heat-treated, and UV-irradiated and then heat-treated glasses (curves 1–3). As seen, the incorporation of Cl results in a consecutive increase in the refractive index of glass irrespective of treatment applied. In particular, Curves 1 and 2 coincide with each other, i.e., the heat treatment of nonirradiated chloride PTR glasses does not change their refractive index [24]. On the contrary, the UV irradiation and subsequent heat treatment of chloride PTR glasses result in a significant increase in their refractive index. For the maximum chlorine concentration, a difference Δn between the refractive index values of the UV-irradiated and nonirradiated glasses after the heat treatment reaches magnitudes up to 1.0×10^{-3}. The positive increment of refractive index as well as high value of Δn in chloride PTR glasses can be used for recording VBGs and optical waveguides.

4. Properties of bromide PTR glasses

The bromide PTR glasses are photosensitive multicomponent glasses based on Na_2O-ZnO-Al_2O_3-SiO_2-NaF system doped with variable batch concentration of Br (0–1.5 mol%), photosensitizer, such as CeO_2 (0.01 mol%), reductant, such as Sb_2O_3 (0.05 mol%), and Ag_2O (0.1 mol %). The bromide PTR glass was designed and synthesized in ITMO University, Russia [17].

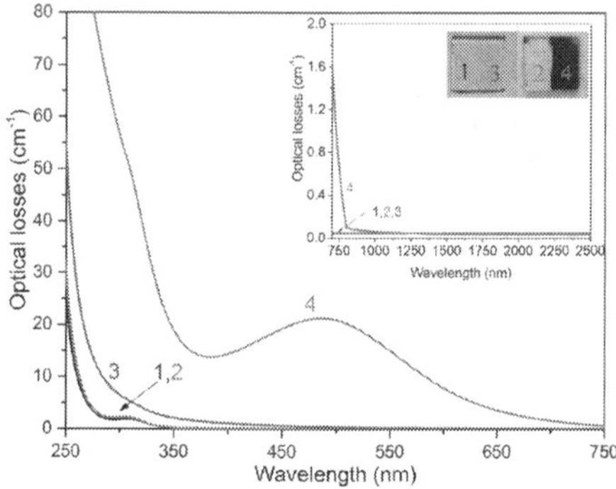

Figure 9. Absorption spectra of PTR glass containing 0.7 mol% Br (1) is the spectrum of initial untreated glass, (2) is the spectrum for glass after the UV irradiation for 50 s alone, (3) is the spectrum for glass after the heat treatment alone, and (4) is the spectrum for glass after the UV irradiation for 50 s and subsequent heat treatment. An inset shows the photos and absorption spectra (700–2500 nm) of treated bromide PTR glass samples containing 0.7 mol% Br. Here (1) is initial untreated glass, (2) is glass after the UV irradiation for 50 s alone, (3) is glass after the heat treatment alone, and (4) is glass after the UV irradiation for 50 s and subsequent heat treatment.

Initially, bromide PTR glasses are transparent in a wide range: 250–2500 nm (**Figure 9**). The substitution of chlorine by bromine in PTR glass composition affects the crystallization mechanism (**Figure 10**). The UV irradiation of bromide PTR glasses results in the Ce^{3+} ion photoionization and SMC formation (**Figure 9**); the latter playing the role of crystallization centers (**Figure 3(a)**). Heating all the studied bromide PTR glasses at temperatures above 250 C and less than T_g results, as shown in **Figure 3(b)**, in releasing electrons from Sb and capturing them by Ag ions with further formation of an extra amount of neutral silver atoms and molecular clusters [19]. The latter provides, according to Refs. [27, 29], a broadband luminescence in the visible and NIR ranges. Further, the heat treatment of PTR glasses containing 0.25–0.7 mol% Br at temperatures above T_g leads to the precipitation of silver nanoparticles with a silver bromide-based shell varying in thickness [20] and/or composition [30]; namely, mixed silver and sodium bromides can occur (**Figure 10(a)**). Moreover, the above heat treatment can result in shifting the plasmon resonance absorption band toward the greater wavelengths (**Figure 9**); such a treatment of PTR glasses containing from 1.0 to 1.5 mol% Br results in the precipitation of small silver nanonoparticles without a perceptible plasmon resonance peak in the absorption spectrum (**Figure 11**) — the nanoparticles being covered by a shell consisting of silver bromide (**Figure 10(b)**). The sizes of silver nanoparticles and silver bromide nanocrystals are relatively small (<3 nm for silver NPs and <11 nm for nanocrystals).

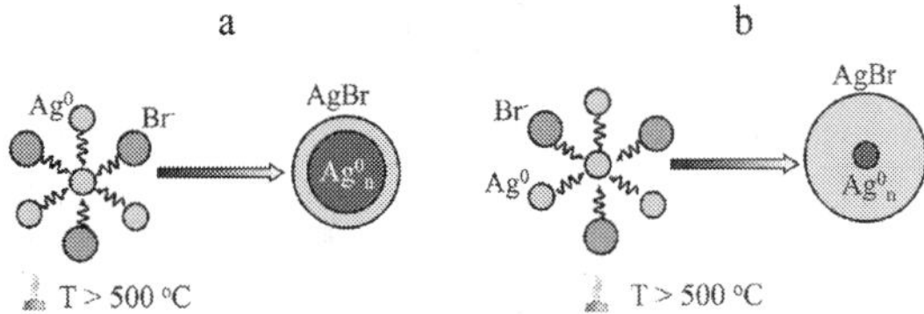

Figure 10. Scheme for the photo-thermo-induced crystallization mechanism inherent in bromide PTR glasses for various Br concentrations (0–1.5 mol%). (a) The photoactivation of PTR glass (Ce^{3+} ion photoionization), formation of neutral silver molecular clusters, and capturing electrons by Sb^{5+} valence states. (b) Releasing electrons by Sb and capturing them by Ag ions with the formation of neutral silver atoms and clusters, and (c) The growth of (i) silver nanoparticles with a shell composed of silver bromide in glasses containing 0.25–0.7 mol% Br or (ii) small silver nanoparticles characterized by broad plasmon resonance peak with a shell made of silver bromide nonocrystals in glasses containing 1–1.5 mol% Br.

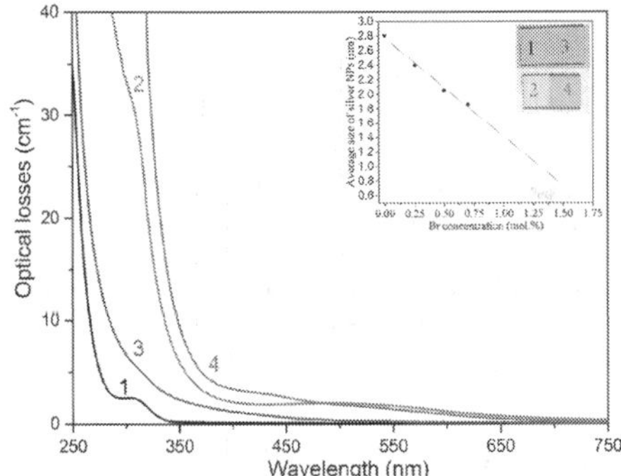

Figure 11. Absorption spectra of PTR glass containing 1 mol% Br (1) is the spectrum for initial untreated glass, (2) is the spectrum for glass after the heat treatment alone, (3) is that for glass after the UV irradiation for 50 s alone, and (4) is the one for glass after the UV irradiation for 50 s and subsequent heat treatment. An inset shows the effect of bromine concentration on the average size of silver nanoparticles (NP) calculated using Mie theory and the photos of bromide PTR glass containing 1 mol% Br at all stages of photo-thermo-induced crystallization (1) initial untreated glass, (2) glass after the heat treatment alone, (3) glass after the UV irradiation for 50 s alone and (4) is the one after the UV irradiation for 50 s and subsequent heat treatment.

Figure 12 shows the evolution of the PTR glass refractive index with an increase in the bromine concentration for initial, heat-treated, and UV-irradiated and then heat-treated glasses (curves 1–3). As is shown, the incorporation of Br leads to a consecutive increase in the refractive index of glass irrespective of treatment applied. In particular, curves 1 and 2 coincide with each other up to reaching the bromine concentration of 0.7 mol%. In other words, the heat treatment of nonirradiated bromide PTR glasses with bromine concentration <1 mol% does not change their refractive index [13]. On the contrary, the UV irradiation and subsequent heat treatment of bromide PTR glasses result in a significant increase in their refractive index. For the maximum bromine concentration, a difference Δn between the refractive indices of the UV-irradiated and nonirradiated glasses after the heat treatment reaches magnitudes up to 0.8×10^{-3}.

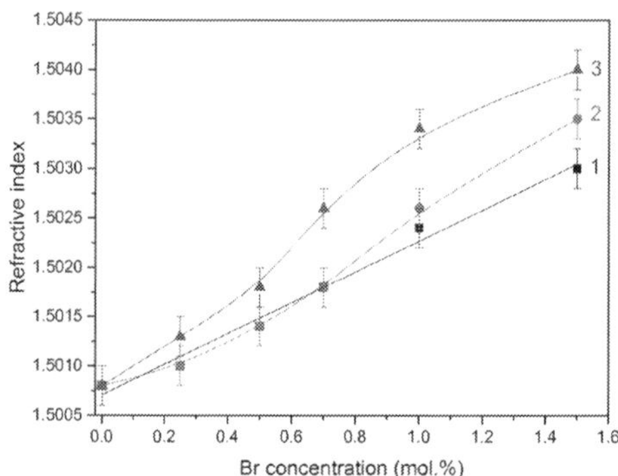

Figure 12. Effect of bromine concentration on the refractive index (n_d) of PTR glass. 1—untreated glass samples, 2—glass samples after the heat treatment, 3—glass samples after the UV irradiation and subsequent heat treatment.

5. Holographic properties of PTR glasses

Since the main purpose of the material is to serve as a holographic media, study of the refractive index dynamic range was held by utilizing holographic technique. For this purpose, Bragg gratings with period of 775 nm were recorded with UV radiation of He-Cd laser ($\lambda = 325$ nm). Conditions of thermal treatment as well as exposure schedule differed depending on glass type, due to the difference in the mechanism responsible for refractive index change. After UV exposure and thermal treatment, gratings were measured and analyzed using Collier [31] and Carretero [32] equations. All measurements were performed at the wavelength of He-Ne laser ($\lambda = 632.8$ nm). Analysis was made with respect to the form of the angular dependence contour either in the zero order or in the first-order of diffraction. Even though the gratings are quasi-sinusoidal, we confine our analysis and therefore material characterization with first harmonic of the refractive index modulation amplitude (RIMA). In this chapter, we will show the exposure dependencies of the RIMA for each glass and its behavior connected with thermal treatment schedule.

5.1. Fluoride PTR glass

In **Figure 13**, typical dependence of the RIMA on the UV exposure for our fluoride PTR glass is shown. One can see that there is a quite wide range of the exposures in which the RIMA is at maximum. Therefore, we assume that an optimum exposure for this glass lies within 0.4–0.65 J/cm^2. Decreasing the RIMA with an increase in the exposure, we explain by the effect of the stray scattering of neutral silver clusters that appears during the recording process. This scattering affects the contrast of the interference pattern, thus lowering the RIMA in the grating.

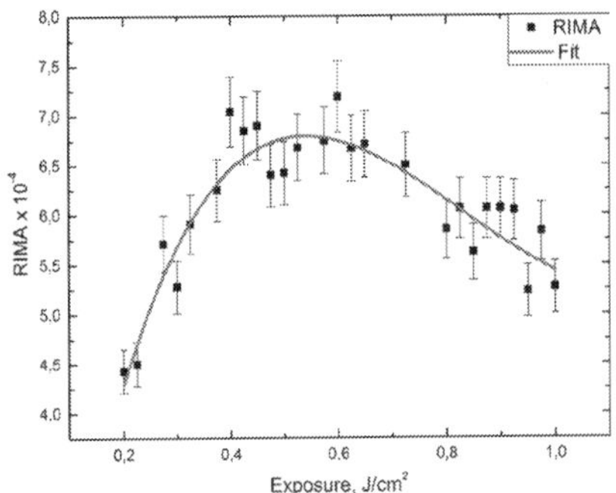

Figure 13. Dependence of the RIMA on exposure.

In **Figure 14**, the dependence of RIMA value on the duration of the thermal treatment is shown. One can see that this dependence is not linear. Basically, we can vary the duration together with temperature and obtain the same effect. For example, the RIMA value of 1.3×10^{-3} can be achieved for 8 h of thermal treatment at temperature of 500 C or for 130 h of heat treatment at temperature of 470°C.

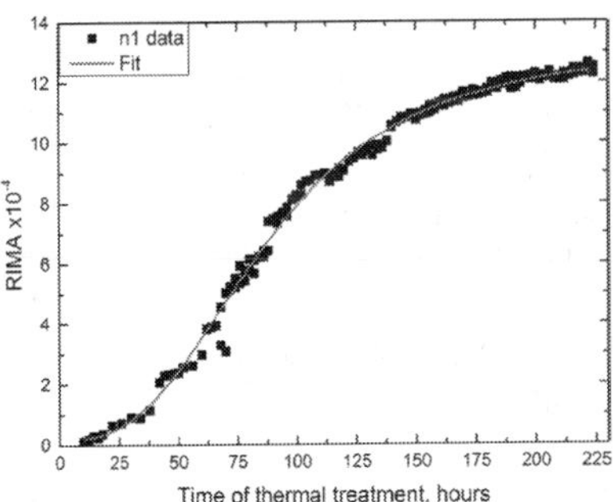

Figure 14. Refractive index modulation amplitude of the grating in the fluorine PTR glass with respect to duration of the thermal treatment.

Additional studies of glass chemical composition allowed for implementing the complex optimization of components, the main goal being to decrease optical losses in the visible spectral range caused by the absorption band of colloidal silver [12]. Components that had undergone the concentration optimization were as follows: halides (fluorides and bromides) responsible for the growth of microcrystalline shell and crystalline phase; antimony that plays a key role in capturing and donating the photoelectrons arising upon the irradiation of cerium and subsequent thermal treatment of PTR glass; also, the concentration of impurities capable of capturing photoelectrons was lowered. As a result, a number of parameters were improved, thus exceeding those of commercially produced material. First of all, the problem of undesirable absorption in the visible spectral range was solved, which resulted in a great decrease in the induced optical losses caused by colloidal silver. PTR glass with the renewed composition shows, after the FTI crystallization process, no absorption band related to the colloidal particles in the optical loss spectra of a sample with a hologram recorded (**Figure 15**).

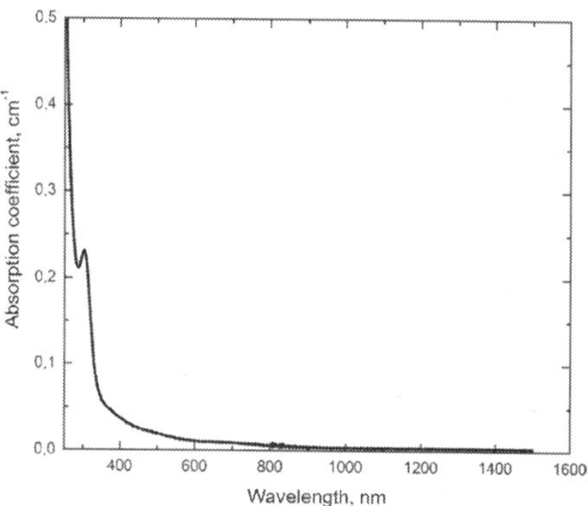

Figure 15. Absorption coefficient spectra of modified PTR glass with a hologram recorded.

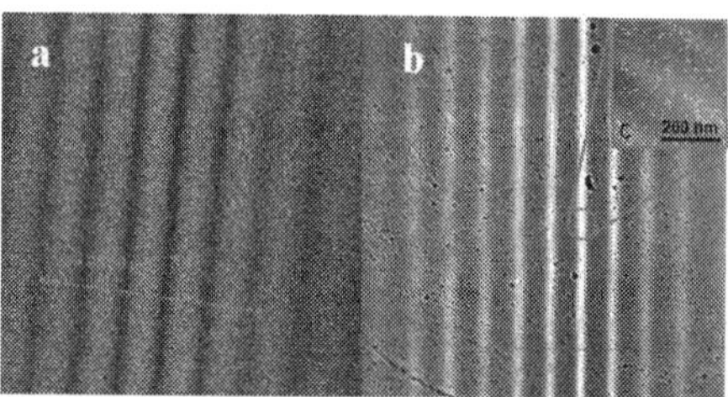

Figure 16. Microscope image of the grating (a) right after the UV exposure and (b) after the heat treatment, and TEM image of the grating fringe (c).

Nowadays, the maximum RIMA for the fluoride PTR glass can be as high as 1.5×10^{-3}. If we neglect scattering by the crystalline phase inside the glass, the maximum RIMA magnitude can be even greater (like 2.5×10^{-3}).

Also, we performed the visualization of the recorded gratings right after an exposure with the UV radiation (**Figure 16(a)**) and after the heat treatment (**Figure 16(b)**). In **Figure 16(a)**, one can see the luminescence of the silver clusters in accord with the interference pattern, whereas, in **Figure 16(b)**, there is the grating itself only formed with NaF crystals.

5.2. Chloride PTR glass

We only started studying the holographic characteristics of this type of PTR glasses. By now, investigations carried out were intended, by analogy with similar studies performed earlier for fluoride glasses, to estimate the maximum possible changes in the RIMA for these glasses.

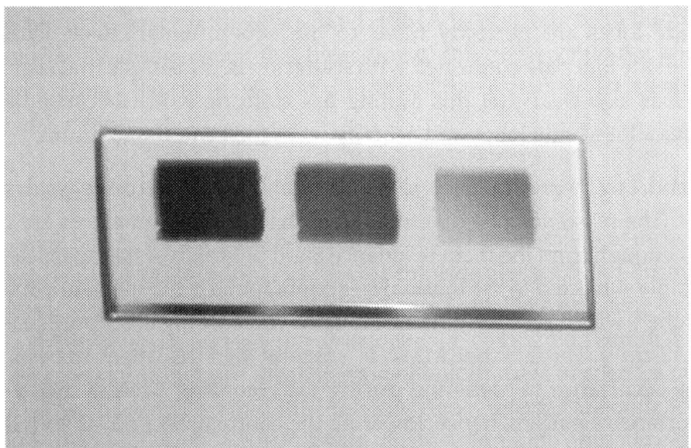

Figure 17. Image of the sample with gratings recorded.

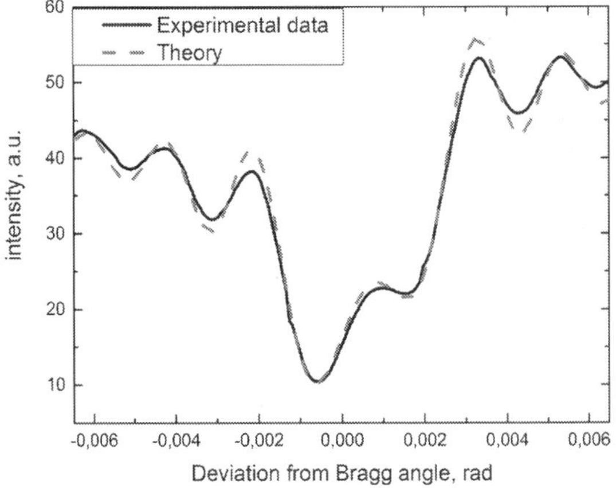

Figure 18. Example of the angular response of the mixed absorption—the phase holographic grating recorded in chloride PTR glass.

does not exceed 1×10^{-4}, though this value differs from that obtained with absolute measurements, $\sim 8 \times 10^{-4}$.

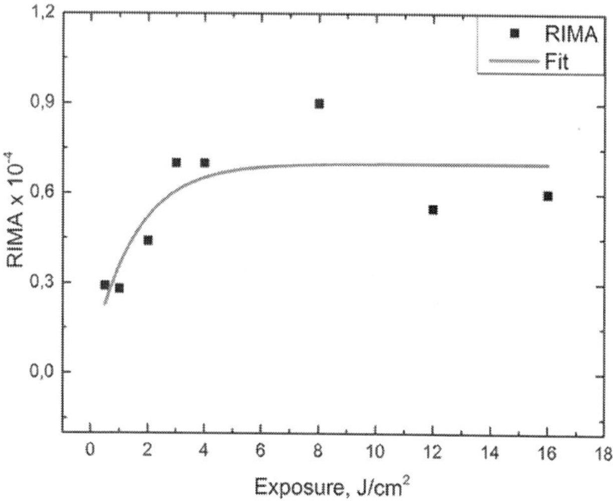

Figure 20. Typical dependence of the RIMA on exposure for bromide PTR glass.

6. Holographic optical elements

PTR glass is a bulk material that is characterized by high homogeneity. Therefore, it is possible to manufacture gratings with high efficient thickness (say, about 1 mm and more). The use of high thickness of the material opens up a possibility to manufacture spatial and spectral filters with outstanding parameters. As known, the selectivity of the Bragg grating depends on its thickness; therefore, it is possible to create gratings with sub nm spectral selectivity and with angular selectivity of <1 angular min.

6.1. Super narrow-band filters for laser diodes and their temperature stabilization of radiation

The widespread use of semiconductor lasers is stimulated by a number of their advantages [33–35] such as the high efficiency (75–80%), small sizes, simplicity of operation, and relatively low cost. An important advantage of semiconductor lasers is also the possibility of fabricating emitters operating at different wavelengths in the visible, near-infrared, and mid-infrared spectral ranges. Apart from the above beneficial features, the semiconductor lasers have certain drawbacks: their emission is quasi-monochromatic and spectrally unstable. This is caused by a number of factors. The broadening of the lasing spectrum under an increase in the injection current stems from the fundamental aspects of charge-carrier transport and captures into the quantum-confined active region. The lasing spectrum is also affected by the multimode design of the laser cavity. A shift of the spectrum occurs as a result of heating the active region with an increase in the injection current, which causes a reduction in the band gap and, thus, the shift of the lasing spectrum to the longer wavelengths.

This problem can be solved by means of VBG recorded in photo-thermo-refractive glass. Due to high spectral selectivity of recorded holograms, the implementation of such grating inside the external cavity of laser diode can significantly narrow the output spectra. This idea was used widely and proved its advantages. External cavity design based on the VBG can vary (see **Figure 21**), as well as both reflecting or transmitting Bragg grating can be used [26].

The simplest implementation of VBG as an external cavity element is shown in **Figure 21(a)**, where a radiation after being passed through the collimating lens falls normally on the VBG element. Unfortunately, due to a high divergence along the fast axis of the LD output radiation, it is impossible to create the reliable external cavity of LD without additional collimation optics. **Figure 21(b)** shows typical design of external cavity using transmission Bragg grating. The grating works backward and forward, and its diffraction efficiency has to be lower than 80% to couple output radiation efficiently. So there is a need for an additional mirror in the cavity setup to reduce the power loss through the nondiffracted radiation on backward cavity trip. The position of mirrors can be changed, but the number of output channels will remain the same. Also, the cavity designs for coupling the higher-order modes of the LD are also possible. Such designs require the high diffraction efficiency of the grating to provide the maximum output performance and are suitable for wide stripe emitting diodes. Stabilized by means of VBG, the laser diodes show a stable output in the temperature range from 15°C to 75°C [36].

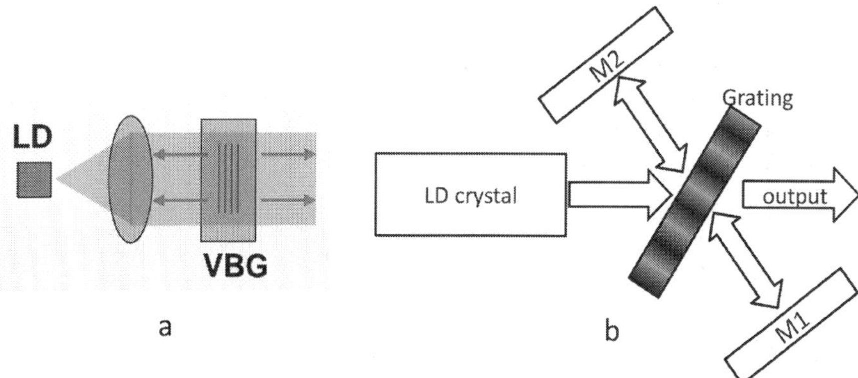

Figure 21. Examples of design of external cavity of a diode laser based on VBGs (a) is an example of reflecting VBG implementation and (b) is an example of cavity based on transmitting VBG.

Recent studies of VBG-based external cavity LD show that the implementation of the grating inside cavity significantly increases its selective properties. For example, a grating used in our experiment [37] was recorded with estimated spectral selectivity as great as ~2 nm. We used a cavity shown in **Figure 21(b)** with the transmitting VBG. The emission spectra from such cavity show us two longitudinal modes with the separation of 100 pm and bandwidth of 4–8 pm (**Figure 22**).

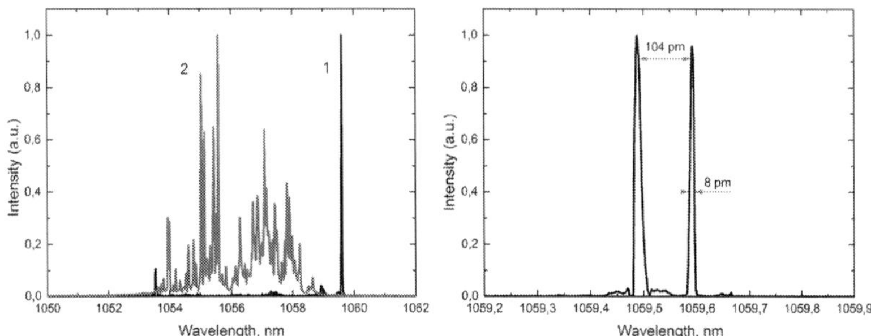

Figure 22. Emission spectra of laser diode source. Left: spectra recorded with (1) and without (2) grating. Right: the detailed view of the emission line [36].

Similar to the conventional ways of LD stabilization such as Littrow scheme and Litman-Metcalf configurations, using the standard diffraction gratings based on the VBG in the external cavities can provide tuning of the output emission of the source. Merely by the rotation of the grating, we can achieve a tunability along all the gain spectra of the semiconductor crystal that can be really huge, up to 60 nm. An example of such tuning is shown in **Figure 23**.

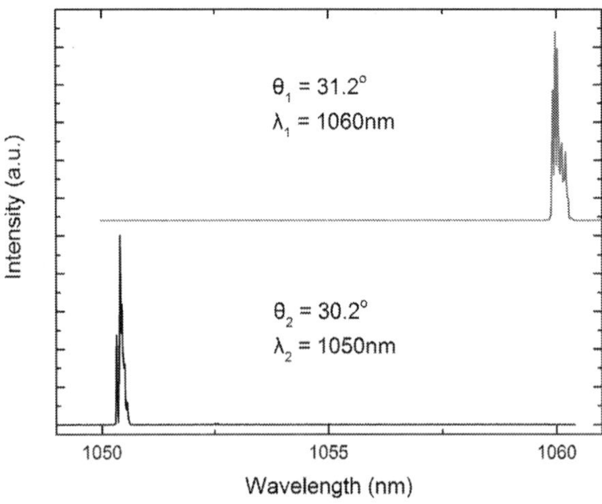

Figure 23. Emission spectra of the external cavity laser diode with different angles of VBG.

6.2. Laser beam combiners

The diffraction efficiency directly depends on the thickness and RIMA, and as shown, this glass has quite a big inflicted refractive index change. Therefore, it is also possible to record multiple gratings inside the single volume of the glass (**Figure 24**).

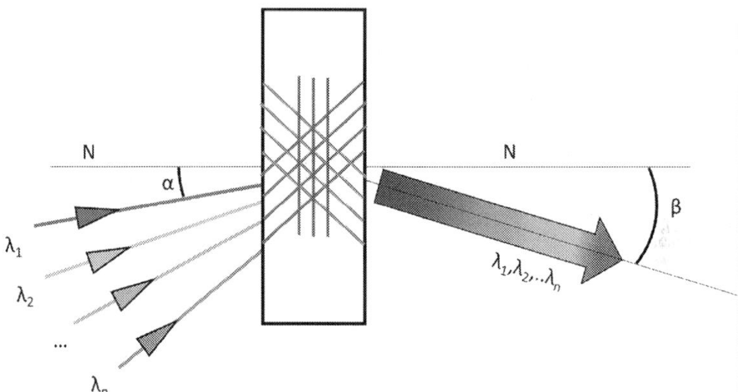

Figure 24. Example of multiple gratings recorded in the single volume of the glass for spectral beam combining.

There is much interest in the use of spectral beam combining (SBC) to combine multiple high-power laser beams into a single high-power one with a narrow spectral linewidth and good beam quality [38]. This idea can be implemented by using several volumes of Bragg gratings for each channel multiplexed in the single volume of PTR glass. Recently, a two and four channel combiner based on the multiplexed reflective Bragg gratings was reported [39]. This approach allows one to develop a combining system with low complexity and better robustness.

6.3. Collimator sights

The holographic collimator sights are the development of the classical collimator sights. This new kind of design provides the greater transparency of the working aperture compared with the classical collimator and greater parallax suppression. This kind of sights has an open design, which means that the sight can be aimed with both eyes. So a shooter can use the peripheral vision and engage more effectively. Also, due to the properties of a hologram, such sight is very resistant to various injuries and pollution. The hologram is recorded over the entire area of the aperture, which is why the sight remains in the working condition even after a partial pollution and/or damage. Also, one of the main advantages over the conventional sights is the absence of a flare toward a target, which is crucial in a combat.

Basic elements of a holographic sight are shown in **Figure 25**. The operation principle of holographic collimator sights can be briefly described as follows. A radiation from the light source falls on the recorded hologram that creates an image of the recorded mark in the image plane. The high transparency of PTR glass in the visible range (above 90% without AR coating) opens up this field of applications.

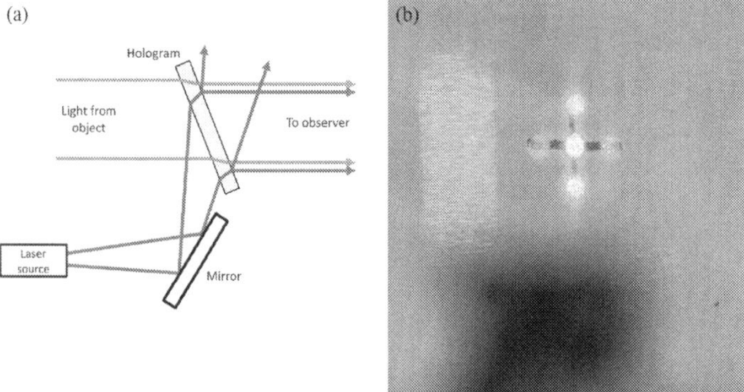

Figure 25. Holographic sight (a) is the basic scheme of the sight and (b) is the observable image of a mark recorded on PTR glass.

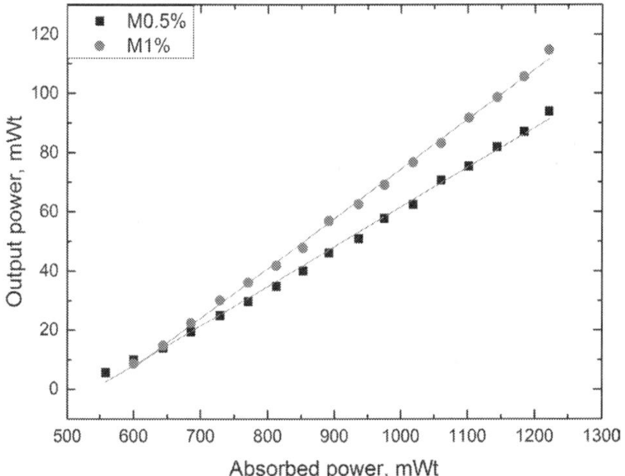

Figure 26. Laser action of Nd^{3+} heavily doped (N_{Nd} = 2.5 × 10^{20}) PTR glass measured for mirrors with the reflection of 1% (red curve) and 5% (black curve) [34].

The application of PTR glass can solve the problem of image stabilization, which is necessary due to the instability of laser diode source used in such sights. To date, this problem is solved by adding, into the optical scheme, the achromatizing diffraction elements such as thin gratings, complex two-cavity mirrors, or compound objectives. The wavelength shift caused by laser diode temperature changes can be nullified by spectral selectivity of thick hologram recorded on PTR glass. Because the diffraction efficiency of holograms on PTR glass can reach values of ~95%, an intensity required for the mark observation is rather low. In **Figure 25**, the observable image of holographic mark recorded on PTR glass is demonstrated.

6.4. Distributed feedback (DFB) and distributed Bragg reflector (DBR) lasers

The concept of DFB lasers was originally demonstrated in 1971 [40] when the laser output from a gelatin film on a glass substrate was obtained for the first time. Two years later [41], a generation from a similar structure on GaAs at nitrogen temperatures was demonstrated. Benefits of such a laser design are pretty obvious: Bragg grating acts as a selective mirror with very narrow reflection bandwidth and, thus, provides a narrow spectral emission output. Since then, DFB lasers had a lot of development, but yet there were no results in creating DFB solid-state lasers.

Doping PTR glass with rare earth elements provides an access to the construction of DFB and DBR lasers because such medium possesses both the laser and holography properties. Recently, first results on laser action on PTR glass were obtained [42, 43]. Later, a generation on heavily Nd-doped PTR glass was obtained in ITMO University [44]. Laser performance is shown in **Figure 26**. Our calculation shows that PTR glass itself is characterized, due to its outstanding homogeneity, by relatively low round trip loss estimated to be ~0.26%, which is comparable to that of commercially fabricated Nd:YAG crystals.

Further investigations of DFB/DBR effect on PTR glass showed that recording a grating inside PTR glass does not affect its lasing properties. For instance, the laser action in the DFB/DBR configuration on Nd- and Yb-doped PTR glasses was demonstrated [45]. In these experiments, the output radiation from both setups (DFB/DBR) and on both types of PTR glasses (Nd and Yb) was obtained. The emission spectra observed show a narrow line with 30 pm bandwidth.

7. Conclusions

Recent achievements of ITMO University (St. Petersburg, Russia) in developing new holographic media such as fluoride, chloride, and bromide photo-thermo-refractive (PTR) glasses are demonstrated. PTR glasses change their refractive index after an exposure to the near-UV radiation followed by thermal treatment at temperatures close to the glass transition one. In the case of fluoride PTR glass, the increment of the refractive index is negative and its magnitude reaches 1.5×10^{-3} ppm. In the case of chloride and bromide PTR glasses, the increment of the refractive index is positive and its magnitudes reach 1.0×10^{-3} and 0.8×10^{-3} ppm, respectively. Thus, the fluoride, chloride, and bromide PTR glasses are very promising photosensitive materials for recording the 3D-phase holographic optical elements. Some examples of holographic optical elements based on PTR glasses are demonstrated such as the supernarrow-band spectral filter for laser diodes, laser beam combiners, the holographic marker for the collimating sight, and lasers with Bragg and distributed feedback.

Acknowledgements

Research was funded by Russian Science Foundation (Agreement #14-23-00136)

Author details

Nikonorov Nikolay, Ivanov Sergey*, Dubrovin Victor and Ignatiev Alexander

*Address all correspondence to: ykkapoh@gmail.com

Saint-Petersburg National Research University of Information Technologies, Mechanics and Optics, St. Petersburg, The Russian Federation

References

[1] Stookey SD, Beall GH, Pierson JE. Full-color photosensitive glass. *J Appl Phys*. 1978;49(10):5114. DOI:10.1063/1.324458.

[2] Pierson JE, Stookey SD. United States Patent 4,057,408. 1977.

[3] Pierson EJ, Stookey SD. United States Patent 4,017,318. 1977.

[4] Panysheva EI, Tunimanova IV, Tsekhomskiĭ VA. A Study of Coloring in Polychromatic Glasses. *Fiz Khim Stekla*. 16(2):239–244 (In Russian).

[5] Dotsenko AV, Efimov AM, Zakharov VK, Panysheva EI, Tunimanova IV. On the absorption spectra of polychromatic. *Fiz Khim Stekla*. 1985;11(5):592–595 (in Russian).

[6] Glebov LB, Nikonorov NV, Panysheva EI, et al. New possibilities of photosensitive glasses for the recording of volume phase diagrams. *Opt Spektros*. 1992;73(2):404–412 (in Russian).

[7] Kuchinskii SA, Nikonorov NV, Panysheva EI, Savvin VV, Tunimanova IV. Properties of volume phase holograms on polychromatic glasses. *Opt Spektrosk*. 1991;70(6):1286–1300 (in Russian).

[8] Nikonorov N.V., Panysheva E.I., Savvin V.V., and Tunimanova I.V., Polychromatic Glasses-A New Medium for Optical Data Recording, "Opticheskoe izobrazhenie i registriruyushchie sredy" (Proceedings of All-Union Conference "Optical Image and Recording Media"), Leningrad, Russia, 1990, 2 p. 48.

[9] Glebov LB, Nikonorov NV, Panysheva EI, Tunimanova IV, Savvin VV, Tsekhomskii VA. Photothermorefractive glass. In: IF AN Latv. SSR, ed. *Trudy VII Vsesoyuznoi Konferentsii Po Radiatsionnoi Fizike I Khimii Neorganicheskikh Materialov (Proceedings of VII All-Union*

Conference on Radiation Physics and Chemistry of Inorganic Materials). Riga; 1989:527 (in Russian).

[10] Efimov OM, Glebov LB, Glebova LN, Richardson KC, Smirnov VI. High efficiency Bragg gratings in photo-thermo-refractive glass. *Appl Opt.* 1999;38(2):619–627.

[11] Glebov LB, Glebova LN, Richardson KA, Smirnov VI. Photo-induced processes in photo-thermo-refractive glasses. In: Soc AC, ed. *Proceedings of XV Congress on Glass.* San Francisco; 1998.

[12] Ivanov SA, Ignat AI, Nikonorov NV, Aseev VA. Holographic characteristics of a modified photothermorefractive glass. *J Opt Technol.* 2014;81(6):356–360. DOI:10.1364/JOT.81.000356.

[13] Nikonorov NV, Panysheva EI, Tunimanova IV, Chukharev AV. Influence of glass composition on the refractive index change upon photothermoinduced crystallization. *Glas Phys Chem.* 2001;27(3):241–249. DOI:10.1023/A:1011392301107.

[14] Glebova L, Lumeau J, Klimov M, Zanotto ED, Glebov LB. Role of bromine on the thermal and optical properties of photo-thermo-refractive glass. *J Non-Cryst Solids.* 2008;354(2–9):456–461. DOI:10.1016/j.jnoncrysol.2007.06.086.

[15] Glebov LB, Nikonorov NV, Panysheva EI, et al. New ways to use photosensitive glasses for recording volume phase holograms. *Opt Spectrosc.* 1992;73(2):237–241.

[16] Dyamant I, Abyzov AS, Fokin VM, et al. Crystal nucleation and growth kinetics of NaF in photo-thermo-refractive glass. *J Non-Cryst Solids.* 2013;378:115–120. DOI:10.1016/j.jnoncrysol.2013.06.027.

[17] Nikonorov N, Aseev V, Ignatiev A, Kolobkova E. SA. Novel glasses and nanoglassceramics for photonic and plasmonic applications. In: *Thirteenth International Conference onthe Physics of Non-Crystalline Solids*; 16–20 September 2012; Yichang Three Gorges, China; 201,. p. 89

[18] Cardinal T, Efimov OM, Francois-Saint-Cyr HG, Glebov LB, Glebova LN, Smirnov VI. Comparative study of photo-induced variations of X-ray diffraction and refractive index in photo-thermo-refractive glass. *J Non-Cryst Solids.* 2003;325(1–3):275–281. DOI:10.1016/S0022-3093(03)00310-7.

[19] Mock JJ, Smith DR, Schultz S. Local refractive index dependence of plasmon resonance spectra from individual Nanoparticles. *Nano Lett.* 2003;3(5):485–491. DOI:10.1021/nl0340475.

[20] Nikonorov NV, Sidorov AI, Tsekhomskiĭ VA, Lazareva KE. Effect of a dielectric shell of a silver nanoparticle on the spectral position of the plasmon resonance of the nanoparticle in photochromic glass. *Opt Spectrosc.* 2009;107(5):705–707. DOI:10.1134/S0030400X09110058.

[21] Lumeau J, Glebova L, Golubkov V, Zanotto ED, Glebov LB. Origin of crystallization-induced refractive index changes in photo-thermo-refractive glass. *Opt Mater (Amst).* 2009;32(1):139–146. DOI:10.1016/j.optmat.2009.07.007.

[22] Efimov AM, Ignatiev AI, Nikonorov NV, Postnikov ES. Quantitative UV–VIS spectroscopic studies of photo-thermo-refractive glasses. I. Intrinsic, bromine-related, and impurity-related UV absorption in photo-thermo-refractive glass matrices. *J Non-Cryst Solids*. 2011;357(19–20):3500–3512. DOI:10.1016/j.jnoncrysol.2011.06.031.

[23] Nikonorov N, Dubrovin V, Ignatiev A, Nuryev R, Sidorov A. Effect of halogens on phase separation, spectral and luminescent properties of photothermorefractive glasses. In: *12th International Conference on the Structure of Non Crystalline Materials, Programe and Abstracts*; 7 – 12 Jule 2013; Trento, Italy; 2012, p. 51.

[24] Dubrovin VD, Ignatiev AI, Nikonorov NV. Chloride photo-thermo-refractive glasses. *Opt Mater Express*. 2016;6(5):1701. DOI:10.1364/OME.6.001701.

[25] Sgibnev YM, Nikonorov NV, Vasilev VN, Ignatiev AI. Optical gradient waveguides in photo-thermo-refractive glass formed by ion exchange method. *J. Lightw. Technol.* 2015;33(17):3730–3735.

[26] Nikonorov N, Aseev V, Ignatiev A, Zlatov A. New polyfunctional photo-thermo-refractive glasses for photonics applications. In: Technical Digest of *7th International Conference on Optics-Photonics Design & Fabrication*; 19 – 21 April 2010; Yokohama, Japan; 2010, p. 209–210.

[27] Dubrovin VD, Ignatiev AI, Nikonorov NV, Sidorov AI, Shakhverdov TA, Agafonova DS. Luminescence of silver molecular clusters in photo-thermo-refractive glasses. *Opt Mater (Amst)*. 2014;36(4):753–759. DOI:10.1016/j.optmat.2013.11.018.

[28] Dubrovin VD, Ignat'ev AI, Nikonorov NV, Sidorov AI. Influence of halogenides on luminescence from silver molecular clusters in photothermorefractive glasses. *Tech Phys*. 2014;59(5):733–735. DOI:10.1134/S1063784214050107.

[29] Sgibnev YM, Nikonorov NV, Ignatiev AI. Luminescence of silver clusters in ion exchanged cerium-doped photo-thermo-refractive glasses. J Lumin. 2016;176:292–297. DOI:10.1016/j.jlumin.2016.04.001.

[30] Sinistri C, Riccardu R, Margheritis C, Tittarelli P. Thermodynamic Properties of Solid Systems AgCl + NaCl and AgBr + NaBr from Miscibility Gap Measurements. *Zeitschrift für Naturforsch A*. 1972;21(1):149–154.

[31] Collier R. J., Burckhardt C. B., Lin L. H. in Academic press New York and London. Optical holography Ch. 9; 1971. p. 277–279 DOI:10.1016/B978-0-12-181050-4.50021-4.

[32] Carretero L, Madrigal RF, Fimia a, Blaya S, Beléndez a. Study of angular responses of mixed amplitude—phase holographic gratings: shifted Borrmann effect. *Opt Lett*. 2001;26(11):786–788. http://www.ncbi.nlm.nih.gov/pubmed/18040450.

[33] Hofmann P, Amezcua-correa R, Antonio-lopez E, et al. Strong Bragg gratings in highly photosensitive photo-thermo-refractive-glass optical fiber. *IEEE Photonics Technol Lett*. 2013;25(1):25–28. DOI:10.1109/LPT.2012.2227308.

[34] Crump P, Erbert G, Wenzel H, et al. Efficient high-power laser diodes. IEEE J Sel Top Quantum Electron. 2013;19(4):1501211–150121. DOI:10.1109/JSTQE.2013.2239961.

[35] Tarasov IS. High-power semiconductor separate-confinement double heterostructure lasers. *Quantum Electron.* 2010;40(8):661–681. DOI:10.1070/QE2010v040n08ABEH01 4375.

[36] Pikhtin NA, Slipchenko SO, Sokolova ZN, et al. 16 W continuous-wave output power from 100 μm-aperture laser with quantum well asymmetric heterostructure. *Electron Lett.* 2004;40(22):1413–1414. DOI:10.1049/el:20045885.

[37] Venus GB, Sevian A, Smirnov VI, Glebov LB. High-brightness narrow-line laser diode source with volume Bragg-grating feedback. *Proc SPIE.* 2005;5711:166–176. DOI: 10.1117/12.590425.

[38] Fan TY, Member S. Laser beam combining for high-power. *High-Radiance Sources.* 2005;11(3):567–577. DOI:10.1109/JSTQE.2005.850241.

[39] Ott D, Divliansky I, Anderson B, Venus G, Glebov L. Scaling the spectral beam combining channels in a multiplexed volume Bragg grating. Opt. Express 2013;21(24): 29620–29627. DOI:10.1364/OE.21.029620.

[40] Kogelnik H, Shank CV. Stimulated emission in a periodic structure. *Appl Phys Lett.* 1971;18(4):152–154. DOI:10.1063/1.1653605.

[41] Nakamura M, Yen HW, Yariv A, Garmire E, Somekh S, Garvin HL. Laser oscillation in epitaxial GaAs waveguides with corrugation feedback. *Appl Phys Lett.* 1973;23(5):224–225. DOI:10.1063/1.1654867.

[42] Sato Y, Taira T, Smirnov V, Glebova L, Glebov L. Continuous-wave diode-pumped laser action of Nd^{3+}-doped photo-thermo-refractive glass. *Opt Lett.* 2011;36(12):2257–2259. DOI:10.1364/OL.36.002257.

[43] Ivanov SA, Ignatiev AI, Nikonorov NV. Advances in photo-thermo-refractive glass composition modifications. *Proc SPIE.* 2015;9508:95080E. DOI:10.1117/12.2178651.

[44] Ivanov SA, Lebedev VF, Ignat'ev AI, Nikonorov NV. Laser action on neodymium heavily doped photo-thermo-refractive glass. In Proccedengs of 1st International Symposium on Advanced Photonic Materials; 27 June – 1 July 2016; Saint Petersburg, Russia; p. 29–31.

[45] Ryasnyanskiy A, Vorobiev N, Smirnov V, et al. DBR and DFB lasers in neodymium- and ytterbium-doped photothermorefractive glasses. *Opt Lett.* 2014;39(7):2156–2159. DOI:10.1364/OL.39.002156.

Chapter 20

Active Holography

Zurab V. Wardosanidze

Additional information is available at the end of the chapter

http://dx.doi.org/10.5772/66435

Abstract

The laser active structures with spatial modulation of lasing controlled by the transversely distributed excitation are implemented. The dye-doped cholesteric liquid crystal (DD CLC) and polymer were used as a laser active medium. The interference pattern of two coherent pumping beams was used for excitation of the laser layers. The second harmonic of a Q-switched Nd:YAG laser (532 nm) was used for the pumping. The interference pattern of the pumping light was located in the plane of the laser active layer. The emission of lasers was observed perpendicular to laser active layers from the opposite side of the incidence of the pumping light. The periodical character of the modulation of intensity along cross section of the lasing depends and corresponds to the parameters of the interference pattern of the pumping. So, the emitted light field qualitatively looks like a diffraction from an elementary hologram, and obtained lasers can be called as active elementary hologram.

Keywords: coherence, pumping, DD CLC laser, dye laser, diffraction, holography

1. Introduction

The method of holography has undergone enormous development since the discovery [1] (1948) up to the present time. The holography also has made great strides in the development of many scientific methods and many technological problems starting with the simplest holograms and ending by the digital holograms [2–4]. Especially it should be noted that already is reached the holographic recording and reconstruction of almost all parameters of the light wave—amplitude, phase, wavelength, and polarization characteristics [5–19]. Anyway the main stage of the holographic process is the creation of the diffractive structure corresponding to distribution of relative phase of the object and reference waves. On this basis, it was possible to say that holography has almost exhausted its potential for further development, but it turned out that there are certain prospects in terms of new nonstandard approaches.

where λ_p is the wavelength of lasing of the DD CLC laser cell and d is the period of the inter-ference pattern of pumping. The modulation of the intensity of the emission pattern of lasing disappears when one of the pumping beams is shutting (**Figure 8(c)**).

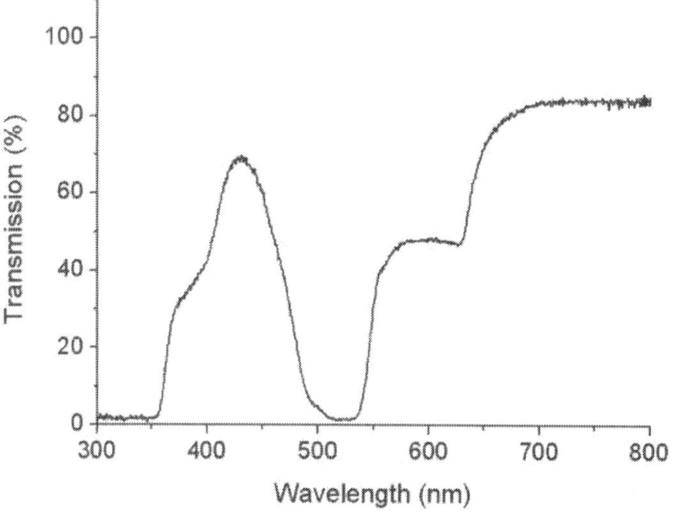

Figure 5. The spectrum of optical transmission of the DD CLC cell along the cholesteric helical axis.

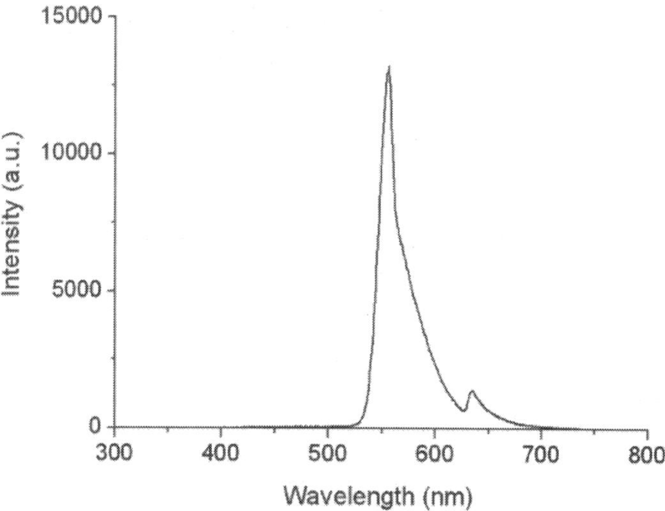

Figure 6. The spectrum of fluorescence of the DD CLC laser cell.

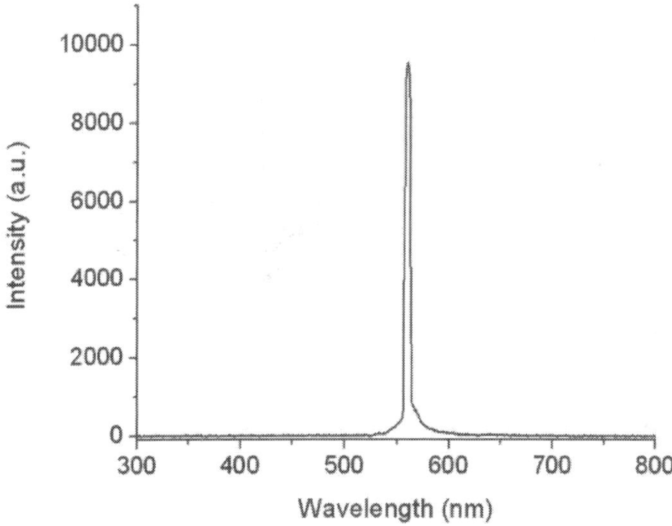

Figure 7. Lasing spectrum of the DD CLC cell.

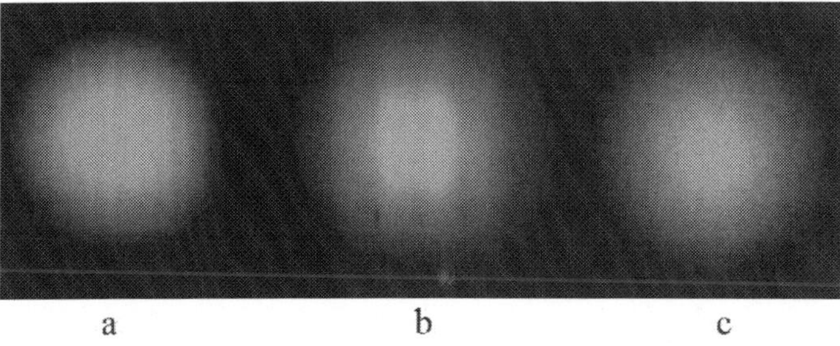

Figure 8. Picture of lasing from DD CLC laser cell at the pumping by interference pattern of two beams (a, b) and at the pumping by one beam (c). The convergence angles of the pumping beams are 1.8° (a) and 0.6° (b). The spatial period of the pumping interference patterns is 17 and 50 μ, respectively.

In author's opinion, the spatial modulation of laser emission field is a result of the mutual correlation between the emitting centers of the individual strips of radiation. Probably, correlation effects, in this case, are of the same nature that provides spatial coherence in the conventional lasers. Thus, the emitting area, of the described laser cell, represents a periodical structure of the mutually coherent microlasers. The total radiation of such a periodical structure, according to the Huygens-Fresnel principle, must form summary interference pattern similar to that shown in **Figure 8(a)** and **(b)**. This phenomenon is similar to the formation of the diffraction pattern from the diffractive grating of the corresponding periodical structure from the point of view of Huygens-Fresnel principle.

Probably, the main factor in reducing the contrast of the spatial modulation of the pattern of lasing is the significant value of the scattering of the light that is characteristic of liquid crystals

(**Figure 8(a)** and **(b)**). The new type of a laser, which combines the properties of a laser and a hologram, was firstly realized on the basis of a DD CLC layer. The field of emission of this laser has a spatial modulation with the periodical distribution of the intensity, controlled by the transversely distributed excitation. Therefore, the spatial distribution of the emission intensity in this case carries out information about the interference pattern of the pumping that makes it similar to the elementary hologram, i.e., holographic diffractive grating. Thus, according to results presented in **Figures 6** and **7** regarding to the spectral.

3. Laser active elementary holographic structure on the basis of dye-doped polymer film

Spatial modulation of laser emission controlled by the structure of the excitation light field was obtained also in the dye-doped polymer film [21–28]. The dye-doped polymer film as an active medium was sandwiched between two laser mirrors forming a laser cavity. The pumping was performed by an interference pattern, formed with two mutually coherent beams of the second harmonic of a Q-switched Nd:YAG laser (532 nm), located in the plane of the laser cell. The laser emission was observed normally to the plane of the laser cell.

The cross section of the obtained laser emission was modulated in intensity with an interval between maximums that depends on the period of the interference pattern of the pumping. Thus, the emitted light field qualitatively looks like a diffraction from an elementary dynamic hologram, i.e., a holographic diffraction grating.

An elementary hologram (holographic grating) usually represents a passive diffractive device. In obtaining information about the recorded holographic structure, an external light source is required.

However, as it is known, diffraction is the result of interference of secondary waves from all lines of the optical heterogeneity of the periodical structure of the grating [29, 30]. Therefore, if we have a periodical structure each strip of which is emitting mutually coherent light waves, the total light field will be analogous to a passive diffraction picture. Such a result was already observed during the study of the coherence of emission of the DD CLC laser. In this case, the excitation also was performed in the form of an interference pattern of pumping beams.

The interference of the laser beams is used in various spheres of science and technology and, among them, for achieving laser emission. In particular, double-beam coherent pumping has long been used for obtaining of the distributed feedback (DFB) in dye lasers [31–36]. In these cases the mutually coherent pumping beams in the active medium form an interference pattern whose bright and dark strips are distributed along generated laser emission (**Figure 9**). But the correlation between the emitting centers in the emitting strips of the active medium allows not only formation DFB in the dye lasers. For instance, as it was shown for the DD CLC laser, the excitation by the interference pattern gives rise to the spatial modulation of the laser emission.

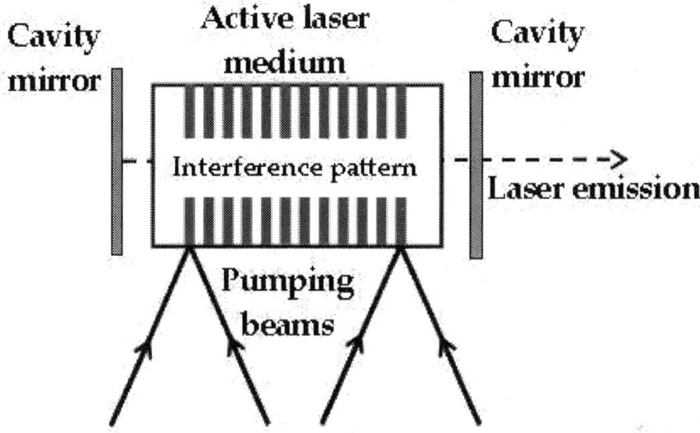

Figure 9. Dye laser with longitudinally distributed excitation.

In this part of chapter, the lasing from the dye-doped polymer film is investigated for the transversely distributed pumping (**Figure 10**). In this case, two mutually coherent pumping beams form in the active medium an interference pattern whose bright and dark strips are distributed perpendicular to the generated laser emission. The luminescent areas of the active medium inside of laser cavity of laser cell can generate laser emission separately. Due to correlation between the emitting centers of different lasing areas, the conditions for interference of the beams from these areas arise.

Therefore, the emission of such a laser should have spatial modulation and will form a pattern similar to the diffraction from the holographic grating. The aim of this study was to obtain and investigate the spatially modulated laser emission from a dye-doped polymer film and to get an improved pattern of lasing by improving the laser emission coherency as compared with DD CLC laser [21].

The experimental setup was the same as that used for holographic recording and for pumping of the DFB lasers which is shown above (**Figure 2**). The second harmonic (532 nm) of a Q-switched Nd:YAG laser with pulse duration of 15 ns was used for the coherent pumping. The repetition frequency of pulses was 12.5 Hz. The laser was ensured a coherence length of approximately 100 mm. With the beam splitter, the beam was divided into two beams of equal intensity. The beam splitter was composed of two interference mirrors 1 and 2 reflecting 50 and 100% accordingly. The distance between the mirrors (15–20 mm) ensured a stable interference pattern. The laser cell consisted of a polyvinyl alcohol (PVA) film doped with Rhodamine-6G and sandwiched between cavity mirrors enough transparent (≈75%) for the pumping emission. The total energy of the pumping radiation was 20–30 mJ, so the real effective energy of the pulse (i.e., the energy incident on the laser cell) was 14–20 mJ. The mirrors were placed with their reflective surfaces inward to the laser cell and by these surfaces have optical contact with the polymer layer. The radius of curvature of the concave mirror was 2 m. The pumping was carried out at the angles of the convergence of the pumping beams **0.6°**, **0.9°**, and **1.8°**. Concentration of the dye was 0.148% and the thickness of the polymer film was 130 μm. The pattern of the laser emission of this laser cell is shown in **Figure 11**. The photos **a, b,** and **c** correspond to the convergence angles of the pumping beams of **0.6°**, **0.9°**, and **1.8°**, respectively. As can be seen, along the cross section of the light bundle here, the smooth distribution of intensity typical for conventional lasers does not take place.

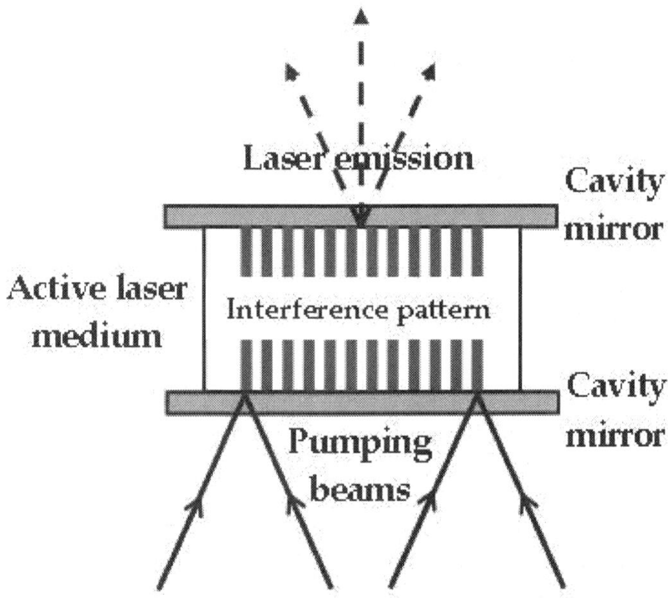

Figure 10. Dye laser with transversally distributed excitation.

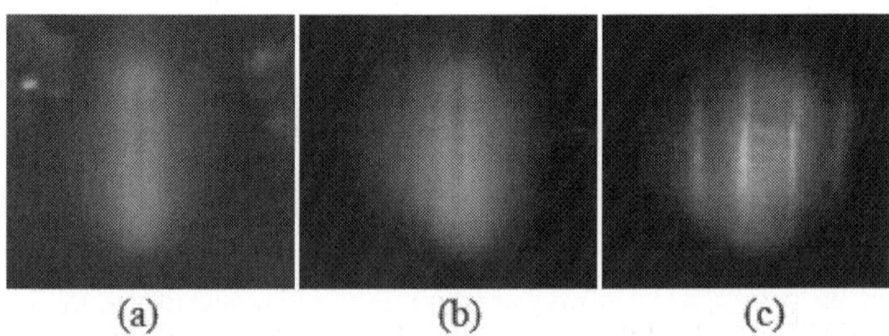

Figure 11. The emission pattern of the dye-doped polymer laser cell with the transverse distribution of the pumping at the convergence angles 0.6°, 0.9°, and 1.8° for the pumping beams—(a), (b), and (c).

But the intensity has a spatially distributed form and qualitatively looks like a diffraction pattern from a diffraction grating. The angles between the intensity maximum directions correspond to the formula (3):

$$\varphi = 2\arcsin\left(\frac{\lambda_p}{2d}\right) \tag{3}$$

where, in our case, λ_p is the wavelength of lasing and d is the period of the interference pattern of the pumping [4, 29, 30]. The diameter of the excited region was 1.5–2.0 mm. In this area, a sufficient number of the lines of interference pattern of the pumping, i.e., microlasers, were located. When shutting one of the pumping beams, the pattern of the spatial modulation, of the laser emission, disappears (**Figure 12**). The elongated shape of the emitted light field in all photos is a result of the plano-concave structure of the laser cavity. To avoid Fabry-Perot interference of the generated emission, the pumping was performed not at the central but at the peripheral part of the resonator.

Figure 12. The emission pattern of the laser cell with single-beam pumping.

Because of pumping, the nonlinear effects can be induced in the polymer film. So the dynamic grating could be formed with enough modulation depth for observation of diffraction. To check this possibility, the area of lasing was tested with a beam of He-Ne laser (632 nm). But no signs of diffraction and, thus, no signs of any grating were detected.

The structure of the emitting spot was investigated under a microscope. In **Figure 13**, the photos of the spot demonstrating the modulated by intensity laser emission are shown. The convergence angles of the pumping beams were **0.6°**, **0.9°**, and **1.8°**, and spatial frequencies of emitting areas were **19, 28,** and **57** lines per millimeter accordingly.

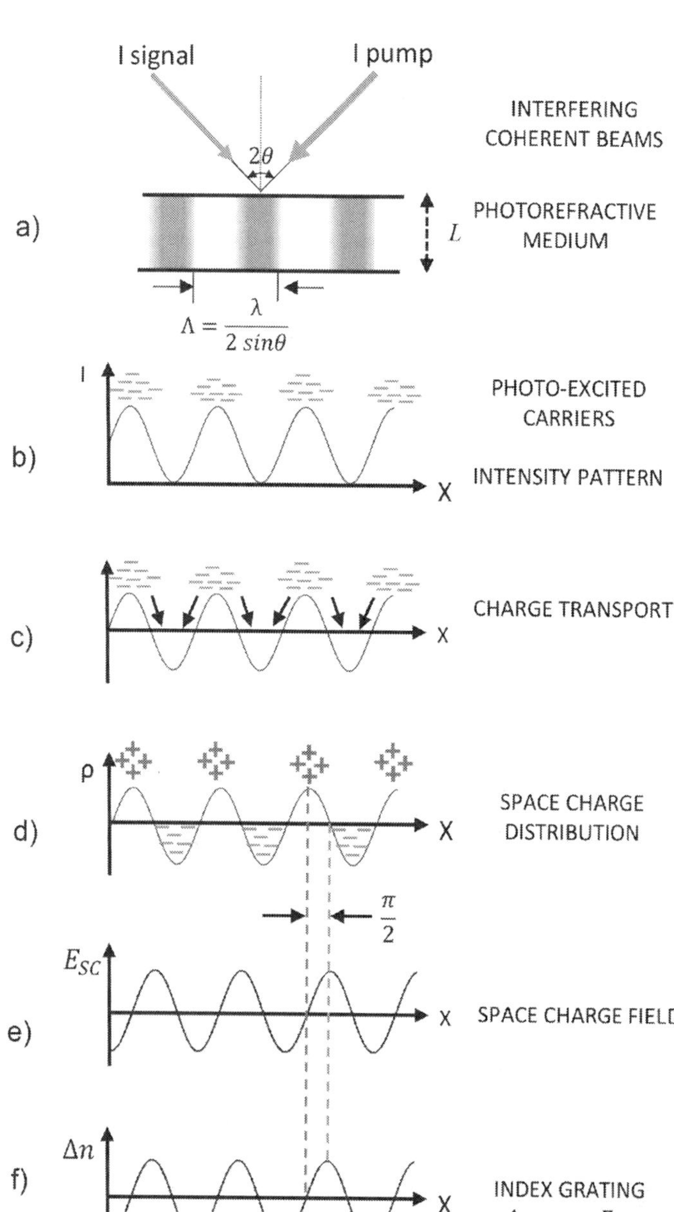

Figure 2. The photorefractive effect: (a) two-beams interference; (b) photo excitation process (intensity pattern); (c) charge transport; (d) space-charge distribution; (e) space-charge field and (f) index grating formation.

$E_D = \frac{KD}{\mu} = \frac{K k_B}{E} T$ is the diffusion field. The magnitude of the E_{sc} depends on several materials parameters, among which the Debye screening length $L_D = \left(\frac{\varepsilon \varepsilon_0 k_B T}{N_{eff} e^2} \right)^{\frac{1}{2}}$ and effective trap density $N_{eff} = \frac{(N_D - N_D^i) N_D^i}{N_D}$.

In liquid crystals, the drift is the dominant mechanism for the charge carrier migration due to the small trap density of organics. In contrast, the diffusion is the dominant mechanism for inorganic materials and the rate at which the recombination happens determine how far the main charge carrier diffuse and how strong is the refractive index modulation. For instance, inorganic crystals offer several orders of magnitude higher concentration of effective trap density in contrast to the LCs and therefore are able to support formation of the small grating spacing and Bragg match regime of diffraction as will be discussed later.

As a result of charge migration and redistribution, the space charge field in combination with the electro-optic effect modulates the refractive index of the media via the Pockel's effect [1, 8, 9]:

$$\Delta\left(\frac{1}{n^2}\right) = r_{ijk} E_{sc} \tag{9}$$

where r_{ijk} is the electro-optic coefficient.

The recorded refractive index grating can diffract light, with the diffraction pattern reconstructing the light-intensity pattern, originally stored in the media. Therefore, the index grating created in the photorefractive material is a "volume phase hologram", which can be written and erased by light, making photorefractive materials fully reversible. Thus, the photorefractive materials have the ability to detect and store spatial distributions of optical intensity in the form of spatial patterns of modulated refractive index.

The most significant consequence from the photorefractive effect is the phase shift between the light-intensity pattern and internal spatial pattern where the later one shifted in respect to the intensity distribution by $\pi/2$ period (see **Figure 2**). This $\pi/2$ phase shift induces an optical energy exchange between the two interacting beams (beam amplification) and refers the photorefractive effect as non-local, non-linear effect [2, 7, 8]. Therefore, when two interfering beams have different intensities noted as respectively I_s "signal" beam (with lower intensity) and I_p "pump" beam (with higher intensity), due to destructive and constructive interference, the unidirectional transfer of optical energy allows a weak beam to grow exponentially with the distance. As a result, at the exit of the medium, the signal beam is not only amplified but also experienced a non-linear phase shift.

The interaction between the two coherent laser beams inside the photosensitive material (assuming the grating wave vector **K** directed along the x axis) gives the total electric field of the two incident beams

$$E = A_1 \exp\left[i\left(k_1 . r - \omega_1 t\right)\right] + A_2 \exp\left[i\left(k_2 . r - \omega_2 t\right)\right] \tag{10}$$

(where $A_{1,2}$ are the beam amplitudes; κ_1 and κ_2 are the wave vectors $\mathbf{K} = |\kappa_2 - \kappa_1|$; r and t are spatial and temporal coordinates; ω_1 and ω_2 are the angular frequency ($\Delta\omega = \omega_2 - \omega_1$) and δ is the frequency detuning between the two beams) and generates a light-intensity fringe pattern of bright and dark regions (sinusoidal light-intensity pattern) described as [1, 7, 8]:

$$I = |A_1|^2 + |A_2|^2 + \{A_1 A_2^* \, exp[i(-Kx + \delta t)] + c.c.\} \tag{11}$$

In fact, Eq. (11) represents the spatial variation of the intensity pattern inside the photosensitive media that generates and redistributes the charge carriers and accumulates the space charge field.

As a result, the refractive index grating, summarized by Refs. [8, 9], can be written by:

$$\Delta n = n_0 + \{\Delta n_0 A_1 A_2^* \, exp[i(-Kx + \delta t + \Phi)] + c.c.\} \tag{12}$$

where Φ is the phase difference between the refractive index grating and interference pattern, n_0 is the refractive index without the light and the Δn_0 is amplitude of index modulation.

By using the couple-mode theory [1, 11], the quantitative measure of the beam-coupling is expressed by the gain coefficient Γ [1, 8, 9]

$$\Gamma = \frac{2\pi\Delta n_0}{\lambda cos\theta} \sin\phi \tag{13}$$

Experimentally, the gain coefficient can be measured by the ratio

$$\Gamma = \frac{1}{L} \ln\left(\frac{I_s' I_p}{I_s I_p'}\right) \tag{14}$$

where $I'_{p(s)}$ is the transmitted intensity of the pump (signal) beam with a coupling, and $I_{p(s)}$ is the transmitted beam intensity without coupling.

The general parameter characterizing the gain is the gain amplification G, given by:

$$G = \frac{1}{L} \log_e |\Gamma| \tag{15}$$

where L is the interaction length of the media.

In last decades, the two-beam coupling effect has been widely investigated in varieties of organic and inorganic compounds [1, 7–13]. In terms of organics, the electro-optic response and the build-up of a refractive index grating in liquid crystals arise from the reorientation of LCs molecules due to an induced space charge field. This effect is known as "orientational photorefractive effect" or "photorefractive-like effect" [12]. For most applications, an external electric field needs to be applied along the grating vector direction, since the drift is the dominant mechanism for the charge migration in LC systems. LCs or PLDCs provide very high amplification gain (up to 2600 cm^{-1} [14]); however, the large grating spacing and small trap density, typical for organics restricted the two-beam coupling to the Raman-Nath regime of diffraction. Therefore, due to the multiple orders of diffracted beams, which accumulate the optical losses, the energy lost limits many of the practical uses.

In terms of inorganic crystals, the direction of the optical energy transfer depends on the sign of the electro-optic coefficient and the sign of the main charge carriers. Up to now, the highest gain coefficient (over 100 cm^{-1}) has been reported in Fe-doped LiNbO$_3$ crystal due to its large refractive index modulation $\Delta n \sim 2 \times 10^{-3}$ [15]. Relatively high beam amplification has been achieved in SBN and BaTiO$_3$ inorganic crystals [7, 10]. In Bi$_{12}$(M = Si,Ti)O$_{20}$ sillenite crystals, the gain coupling is much lower due to the smaller values of the electro-optical coefficient, restricted by the cubic symmetry [16]. However, doped sillenite crystals offer the potential for high-carrier mobility (high photoconductivity) and together with the high-trap density can compensate the small-trap density of LCs when combined into a hybrid structure to support the fine grating spacing and to fulfil the requirements for Bragg-matched regime of diffraction. Furthermore, by selecting the photorefractive substrate sensitivity, the operation interval of the proposed hybrid devices can be easily adjusted. Moreover, doping sillenites with transition metal elements significantly improve their sensitivity and response time at near-infrared spectral range [17–22].

4. Organic-inorganic hybrid structures operating at Raman-Nath regime of diffraction

4.1. Organic-inorganic structure design and principle of operation

This type of organic-inorganic hybrid structure consists of photoconductor substrate (usually an inorganic crystal plate with 0.4–0.6 mm thickness) and electro-optic layer (few microns thickness) arranged into a cell, supported by a glass substrate from another side (see the schematic diagram at **Figure 3(a)**). Selected inorganic crystals stand as photoconductors, whereas a LC layer is used

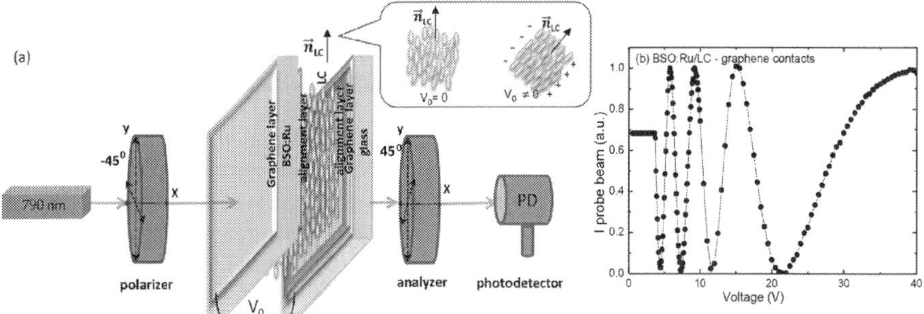

Figure 3. (a) Experimental set-up for voltage-transmittance measurements. The hybrid structure is placed between two crossed polarizes making an angle of 45° with respect to the transmission axis of the polarizer (b) Example of Voltage-Transmittance dependence for BSO:Ru/LC structure with graphene-based electrodes.

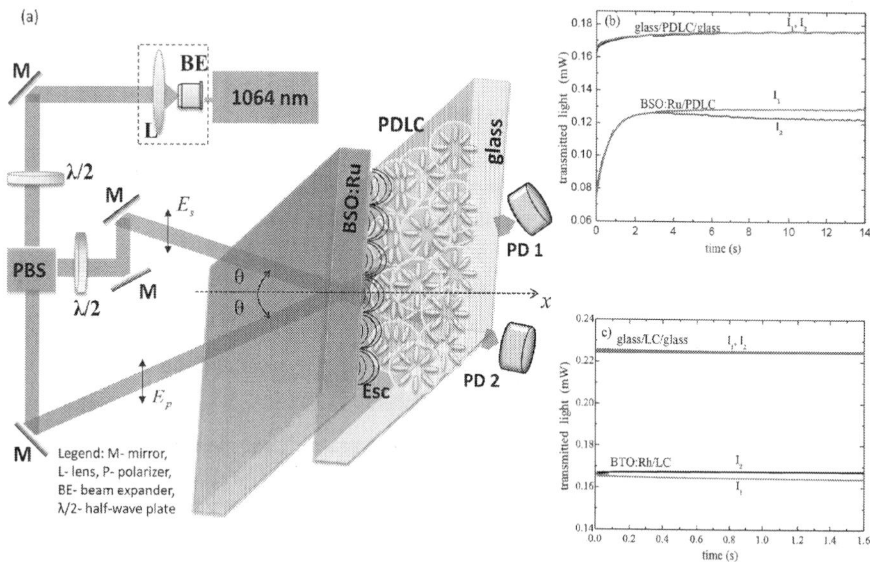

Figure 9. (a) Two-beam coupling experiment in BSO:Ru/PDLC structure and simultaneous behavior of both transmitted beams through the (b) BSO:Ru/PDLC structure and (c) BTO:Rh/LC structure. Comparison with the reference samples as glass/LC/glass and glass/PDLC/glass is also presented.

Type	Symbol	Value	Unit	
LC (MLC type)	$\Delta\varepsilon$ (LC)	$41.6 \times \varepsilon_0$		Anisotropy of NLC's dielectric constant
	K (LC)	5		Elastic constant of NLC
	n_0 (LC)	1.51		O-ray refractive index of LC (nematic)
	n_e (LC)	1.75		E-ray refractive index of LC (nematic)
BTO:Rh and BSO:Ru inorganic crystals	N_D	2×10^{24} for BTO:Rh 6.1×10^{23} for BSO:Ru	cm^{-3}	Donor concentration
	N_A	1×10^{24} for BTO:Rh 5×10^{23} for BSO:Ru	cm^{-3}	Acceptor concentration
	ε	46		Dielectric constant of BTO and BSO crystal
	T	300	K	Temperature

Table 1. Material parameters for theoretical simulations.

high amplification gain (up to 2600 cm^{-1} [14]); however, the large grating spacing and small trap density, typical for organics restricted the two-beam coupling to the Raman-Nath regime of diffraction. Therefore, due to the multiple orders of diffracted beams, which accumulate the optical losses, the energy lost limits many of the practical uses.

In terms of inorganic crystals, the direction of the optical energy transfer depends on the sign of the electro-optic coefficient and the sign of the main charge carriers. Up to now, the highest gain coefficient (over 100 cm^{-1}) has been reported in Fe-doped LiNbO$_3$ crystal due to its large refractive index modulation $\Delta n \sim 2 \times 10^{-3}$ [15]. Relatively high beam amplification has been achieved in SBN and BaTiO$_3$ inorganic crystals [7, 10]. In Bi$_{12}$(M = Si,Ti)O$_{20}$ sillenite crystals, the gain coupling is much lower due to the smaller values of the electro-optical coefficient, restricted by the cubic symmetry [16]. However, doped sillenite crystals offer the potential for high-carrier mobility (high photoconductivity) and together with the high-trap density can compensate the small-trap density of LCs when combined into a hybrid structure to support the fine grating spacing and to fulfil the requirements for Bragg-matched regime of diffraction. Furthermore, by selecting the photorefractive substrate sensitivity, the operation interval of the proposed hybrid devices can be easily adjusted. Moreover, doping sillenites with transition metal elements significantly improve their sensitivity and response time at near-infrared spectral range [17–22].

4. Organic-inorganic hybrid structures operating at Raman-Nath regime of diffraction

4.1. Organic-inorganic structure design and principle of operation

This type of organic-inorganic hybrid structure consists of photoconductor substrate (usually an inorganic crystal plate with 0.4–0.6 mm thickness) and electro-optic layer (few microns thickness) arranged into a cell, supported by a glass substrate from another side (see the schematic diagram at **Figure 3(a)**). Selected inorganic crystals stand as photoconductors, whereas a LC layer is used

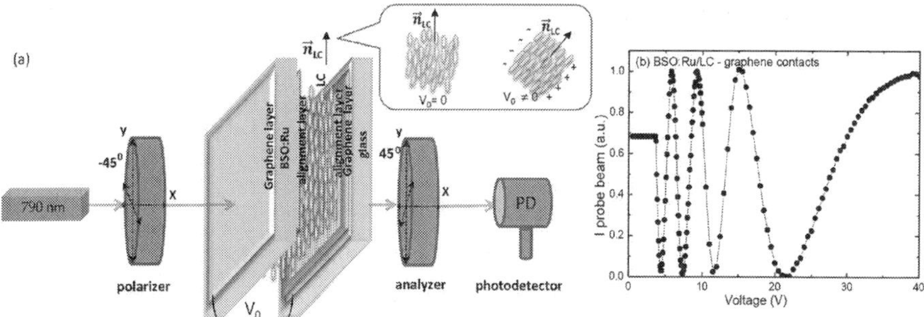

Figure 3. (a) Experimental set-up for voltage-transmittance measurements. The hybrid structure is placed between two crossed polarizes making an angle of 45° with respect to the transmission axis of the polarizer (b) Example of Voltage-Transmittance dependence for BSO:Ru/LC structure with graphene-based electrodes.

as electro-optic material. The proposed configuration is also known as optically addressed spatial light modulator (OASLM) structure. As the read-out process can provide an optical gain, the OASLMs have been also considered as a liquid crystal light valve (LCLV) devices.

$Bi_{12}SiO_{20}$ (BSO) and $Bi_{12}TiO_{20}$ (BTO) crystals are among the perfect components for OASLM devices due to their remarkable photoconductivity and high charge carrier mobility. For a first time, non-doped BSO crystal was assembled with a LC layer into a LCLV, working at transmittance mode by Aubourg et al. [23]. Later on, several devices operating at visible spectral range have been demonstrated [24–26]. Other preferable photoconductor substrates are semiconductors as a-Si:H, crystalline silicon, gallium arsenide, indium phosphate and cadmium tellurite [27, 28]. Usually, transparent indium tin oxide (ITO) conductive layers are preliminary deposited on the outer side of the photoconductive plate and the inner side of glass substrate and coated with polyvinyl alcohol (PVA) for planar alignment of the LC molecules. Recently, owing to the ITO limited transparency at near infrared spectral range and increased cost because of the Indium scarcity in the nature, ITO has been successfully replaced with graphene conductive layers, and several graphene-based devices have been successfully demonstrated [29, 30].

The operation principle of OASLM device relays on the electro-optically controlled birefringence of the LCs molecules where the high sensitivity and photoconductivity comes from the photoconductive plate and high birefringence is provided by the LC layer [2, 31]:

(i)   when an external AC voltage (V_0) is applied across the device (**Figure 3(a)**), the applied voltage acts through the photoconductor substrate because of its high resistance. Since the LCs molecules have different polarizability along their long and short axis, the applied voltage induces a dipole moment in the LC layer, which affects the LC molecules orientation, and they follow the direction of the applied electric field. As the LC nematic phase is characterized by a long-range orientation order, all the LC molecules tend to align along the nematic LC director $\hat{n}_{LC}$. Therefore, when the structure is placed between the crossed polarizers, "on" and "off" illumination states are obtained (**Figure 3**).

(ii) Illumination with the input pump beam activates the photoconductor substrate, and charge carriers are generated at a rate proportional to the pump intensity. Owing to the crystal's high photoconductivity and high dark resistivity, the charge separation decreases the voltage across the photoconductor, and it reduces its impedance. As a consequence, the accumulated voltage is transferred into the LC layer, resulting in a LC molecular reorientation.

Owing to the LC's anisotropy, the output beam obtains a phase shift

$$\varphi = \frac{2\pi}{\lambda}\left(n_e - n_0\right)L \tag{16}$$

which is a function of the applied voltage V_0 and the pump light intensity I:

$$I = \frac{1}{2}sin^2\frac{\Phi}{2} = \frac{1}{2}sin^2\left[\frac{\pi\left(n_e - n_0\right)L}{\lambda}\right] \tag{17}$$

where L is the LC thickness, n_e and n_0 are refractive indexes for a beam polarized along the long or short molecular axis $\Delta n = n_e(I_p) - n_0$ and Φ is the phase retardation [2]. This allows spatial modulation of the amplitude or phase of the incident beam at the exit of device (see **Figure 4(a)**). During the full range, the reorientation angle of the LC molecules can vary from 0 to $\pi/2$, producing a phase shift of several π.

Figure 3 illustrates the experimental set-up and the typical Freedericksz transition character-istics of BSO:Ru/LC device with graphene electrodes, operating at 1064 nm. The modulation behaviour supports the LC molecules alignment in the direction of an applied AC voltage across to the cell. **Figure 4** shows the phase modulation set up and phase difference for the same BSO:Ru/LC device at fixed voltage of 4 V (according to the results at **Figure 3(b)**). The probe-pump intensity dependence is presented as inset at **Figure 4(b)**.

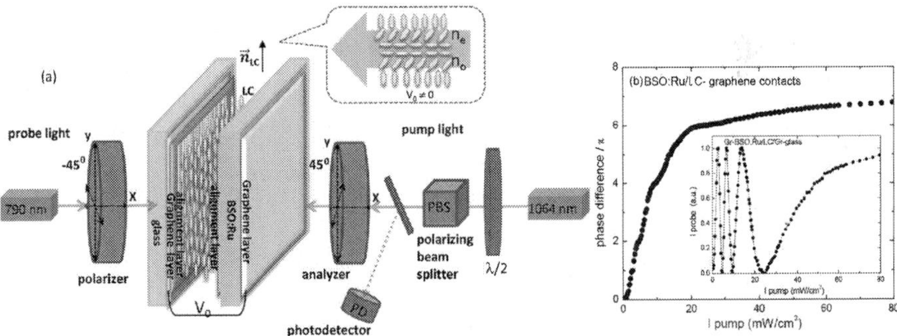

Figure 4. (a) Experimental set-up for phase shift measurements and (b) Phase difference as a function of a pump light intensity (fixed at 4V according to the results from figure 3(b)) for BSO:Ru/LC device. Inset graph shows the probe-pump intensity dependences.

Obviously, the light-induced modulation formed in the photoconductive substrate is the driving force, which affects the LC molecules realignment and spatially modulates the refractive index of LC layer.

4.2. Two-wave mixing and Raman-Nath regime of diffraction

For a first time, energy transfer using two-wave mixing has been demonstrated by Brignon et al. [32] in a device assembled by BSO photoconductive crystal and LC layer. The recorded holographic gratings were not typical local dynamic grating as generally supposed to be cre-ated from the photoconductive substrate. The two-beam interaction has been described as a diffraction of the two beams on a fixed thin local grating (the index grating formed in LC), which is pinned to the conductivity grating [32]. Since the photoconductive and the electro-optic regions are separate, the photo-induced grating is not modified by the interacting beams during their propagation in the LC layer. Later on, beam amplification in LCLV devices has been verified and reported in several papers [19, 21, 23–26, 33]. Recently, significant gain amplification values have been obtained in hybrid structures based on semiconductor crystals as GaAs doped with Cr [33, 34] or CdTe [35].

The interference between the pump and signal beam, expressed by their amplitudes $E_p \exp[i(\kappa_p \cdot r - \omega_p \cdot t)]$ and $E_s \exp[i(\kappa_s \cdot r - \omega_c \cdot t)]$, produced an intensity fringe pattern that induces a space-charge distribution and consequently a molecular re-orientation pattern in the LC layer. The interaction creates a refractive index grating with the same wave vector K, and as a result, the two beams diffracted by the photo-induced grating with spatial grating period of $\Lambda = 2\pi/K$.

In these hybrid structures, the active layer is the LC layer; therefore, the interaction length is sufficiently thin to satisfy the energy and momentum conservation before exiting the medium [1, 2]. As a result, the two-beam coupling occurs in a Raman-Nath regime of diffraction (the LC layer is much thinner in comparison with the grating spacing $L \ll \Lambda$). Consequently, the phase grating recorded in the LC layer acts as a thin hologram with a multiple output beams.

A detailed analysis of the two-wave mixing and expression of the zero and m-output diffracted orders is given in Ref. [24] where the evolution of the amplitude of the refractive index grating and relaxation dynamic of the LC molecules orientation has been considered, using the couple-wave theory [1, 11]. We note that the output signal beam according to Refs. [24, 36] can be written in a form:

$$E_{output} = \sqrt{G\,I_s}\,\exp(i\phi)exp\left[i\left(k_s \cdot r - \omega_s t\right)\right] + c.c. \tag{18}$$

where G is the gain amplification and ϕ is the non-linear phase shift.

Figure 5 demonstrates the two-wave mixing in BTO:Rh/LC hybrid structure using 1064-nm diode laser. The right side of **Figure 5** supports the Raman-Nath diffraction with several diffracted beams (0, ±1, ±2,…) at the output of the hybrid device, detected on the infrared view card.

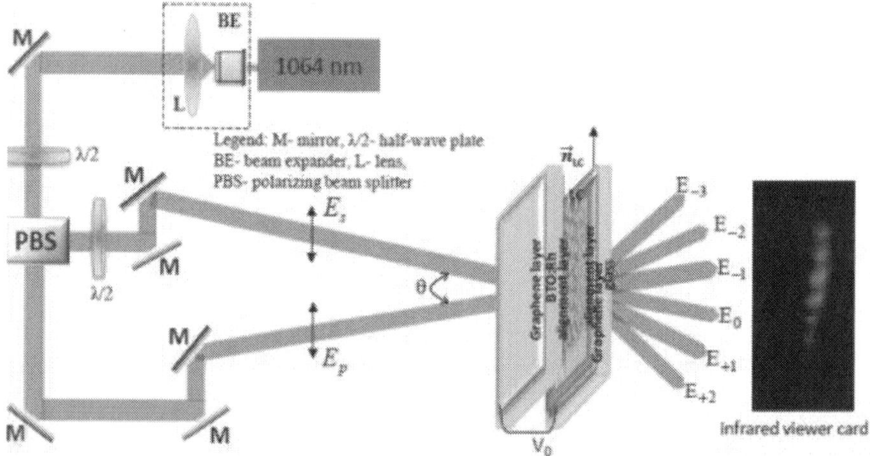

Figure 5. Two-wave mixing at Raman-Nath regime of diffraction (E_s and E_p are the amplitudes of the pump and signal beams) allowing high-gain amplification values (LC layer acts as thin hologram) at 1064 nm. Right side: Raman-Nath orders observed on a view card for BTO:Rh/LC device with graphene electrodes.

Experimentally, the gain parameter G has been measured by monitoring the intensities of two interfering beams as $G = I_0/I_s$, where I_s is the input signal intensity (without pump light) and I_0 is the amplified signal after the device. For example, at an interaction angle of 2.5°θ (12-μm grating period), the gain amplification for BTO:Rh/LC structure is $G = 4.1$ at 1064 nm. The gain coefficient of $\Gamma \sim 1180$ cm^{-1} has been calculated by the relation $I_{(0)} = I_{(s)}e^{\Gamma L}$, which is among the highest value reported until now for hybrid devices, operating at near infrared spectral range. Very recently, a gain amplification of 17 has been achieved at GaAs-based hybrid structure at 1064 nm with optimized thickness of the LC layer [33].

4.3. Applications

Based on the ability to record dynamic phase holograms, the reviewed electro-optically controlled structures found applications as optically addressed spatial light modulator devices, light-valve structures, to control the fast and slow components of light, in adaptive interferometry and metrology, and so forth [33–37].

When the address beam (incoherent image) is projected into photoconductive substrate, due to its high photoconductivity and high dark resistivity, the crystal reduces its impedance and accumulated voltage is transferred to the LC layer, resulting in LC molecular reorientation. Hence, the intensity distribution of the address beam in the photoconductor has a subsequent connection with the voltage distribution in the LC layer. This is the way how the "optical addressing" is realized. Consequently, when the two interfering beams intersect inside the hybrid structure, dynamic phase holograms can be addressed into the liquid crystal layer.

Based on the phase modulation ability, an evolution of image propagating on BTO:Rh/LC device is demonstrated. **Figure 6** shows an image of the character "A" addressed on BTO:Rh/LC device at the beginning of the process and its time evolution at 50 and 100 ms. The response time of the hybrid device is limited by the response of the LC molecules (100–150 ms) since the response of BTO:Rh crystal is much faster (20–30 ms) at the near infrared spectral range [21].

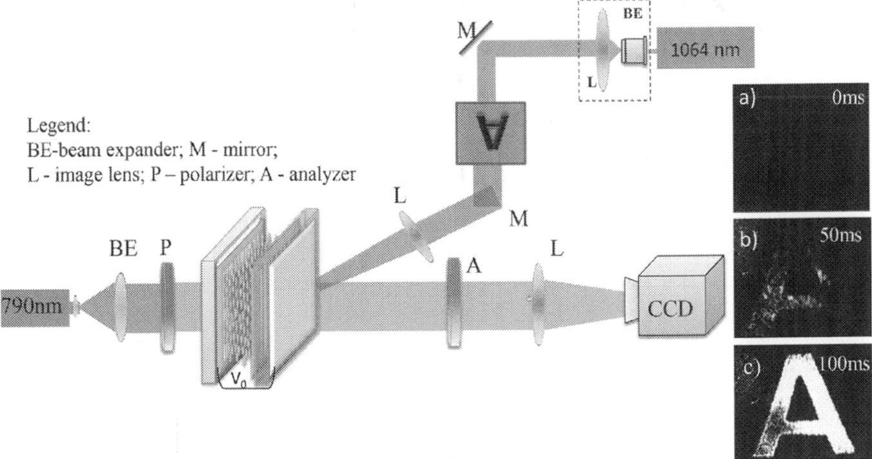

Figure 6. Optical setup for modulated pump light intensity demonstration in BSO:Ru/LC device with graphene electrodes using 1064-nm pump light.

Besides display applications, the Raman-Nath diffraction with multiple output order beams has been successfully applied to control the fast and slow components of light propagation [36]. Different group delays have been obtained depending on the output order and frequency detuning between the pump and signal beam. Varieties of applications in interferometry, optical signal processing, precision metrology and optical sensing are demonstrated [33–37].

5. Organic-inorganic hybrid structures operating at Bragg matched regime of diffraction

5.1. Organic-inorganic hybrid structure design and principle of operation

For most practical realizations, the organic-inorganic structures required to operate at the Bragg matched regime of diffraction, for which the phase matching conditions are satisfied only in one direction. It turns out that selected inorganic photorefractive crystals possesses sufficiently large effective trap density to support efficient space-charge generation necessary to reach the Bragg regime (in comparison with conventional LC cell where the low trap density of LCs is the limitation). In Bragg regime of diffraction, the grating period Λ is comparable with the LC layer thickness ($\Lambda \sim L$) and the hybrid structure acts as a dynamic thick grating.

Generally, this kind of hybrid structure is assembled by photorefractive crystal substrate and a glass substrate, arranged into a cell, filled with liquid crystal or polymer-dispersed liquid crystal layer (PDLC consists of micron-sized droplets of LC molecules randomly dispersed in transparent polymer matrix [38]). The fabrication procedure is very simple and easy, without necessity of conductive layers deposition (external voltage application (and in case of PDLC no need of alignment layers and polarizers)) in contrast to the previously reported devices in Section 4.

The operation principle relays on the unique property of surface-activated photorefractive effect: the photo-generated charge carriers (inside the inorganic substrate) induce a space-charge field, which penetrate into the LC layer and interact with the LC nematic $\hat{n}_{LC}$ director. As a result, the refractive index of LC layer changes which control the light-intensity distribution by producing the diffraction grating. In this hybrid configuration, the two-beam coupling happens at both the photorefractive substrate and LC layer where the charge migration, trap density and space-charge field come from the crystal substrate, whereas the high-beam amplification is provided by the LC layer. Hence, all the processes are controlled only by the action of light.

First, Tabiryan and Umeton theoretically proposed the idea about the surface-localized electromagnetic field in organic-inorganic hybrid structures [39]. In their concept, the photo-generated evanescent electric field combines with the LC director through the LC anisotropy. This electric space charge field plays the essential role as it acts as a driving force for LC molecules re-orientation and subsequent refractive index modulation. **Figure 7** shows the schematic presentation of the above idea.

After Tabiryan and Umeton prediction [39], detailed theory of the beam energy exchange was developed by Jones and Cook [40], according to which the coupling between the space charge field and LC director is caused by the LC static dielectric anisotropy. It predicts that maximal beam coupling occurs when the grating spacing has similar order as LC thickness; however,

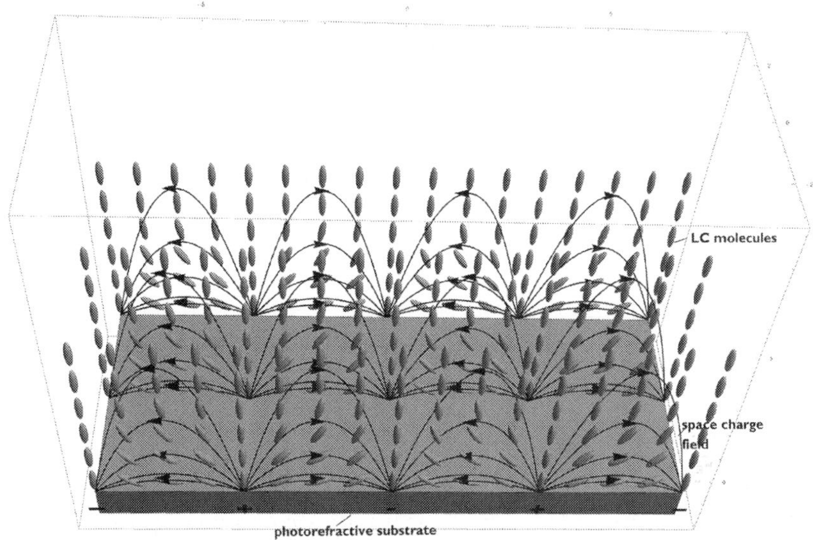

Figure 7. Surface activated photorefractive phenomena [41]. The photo-induced space charge field (indicated with arrows) penetrates into the LC layer and reorient the LC molecules, resulting in a change of the effective refractive index.

experimentally, the maximum coupling happens at much smaller grating spacing than the LC thickness [40]. Later on, Reshetnyak et al. [41] extend the theory summarizing that the exponential gain amplification is a final product of three main components: (i) the beam interference term, (ii) the flexoelectric polarization term of LC (that have upper contribution than the LC static dielectric anisotropy, assumed in Ref. [40]) and (iii) the photo-induced space-charge term. In addition, Evans and Cook [42] performed systematic study and initiate the two necessary conditions to achieve the two-beam coupling at Bragg regime: the LC molecules must be pretilted (asymmetrically aligned) and the LC electrical polarity must be sensitive to the direction of the space-charge field. These conditions enable the refractive index grating to have the same spatial frequency as the interference pattern and make the optical amplification at Bragg regime possible. Afterward, several hybrid configurations based on ferroelectric crystals as $KNbO_3$ and SBN:Ce assembled with nematic LCs, operating at visible spectral range has been realized [42, 43]. For example, Deer [44] demonstrated a structure based on LC layer and $KNbO_3$ substrate, at large beam intersection angle with perfect phase shift between the interference and refractive index gratings. Up to now, only limited numbers of near infrared sensitive structures are designed using semiconductor substrates as CdTe or GaAs. The maximum gain coefficient reported in GaAs/LC cell is 18 cm^{-1} at Λ = 1.2 µm and 16 cm^{-1} at $\Lambda \sim 1$ µm for CdTe/LC cell, both of them operating at 1064 nm [45, 46].

Figure 8 shows the formation of the space-charge field in BSO:Rh/LC structure followed by monitoring the time evolution of the Gaussian laser beam (0.5-mm waist) propagating through the hybrid device (right side) [47]. Owing to the near-infrared absorption and high photoconductivity of the inorganic crystal, illumination with 1064-nm light causes charge carriers generation and formation of photo-induced space-charge field which becomes stronger at the edges of the Gaussian beam.

The numerical simulation of the intensity (I) and the space-charge field (E_{sc}) distributions, as well as time evolution of Gaussian beam shape passing through the hybrid structure are shown at **Figure 8(b** and **c)**. The experimental results are in good agreement with the numerical calculations reported by Stevens and Banerjee [48], which support that Gaussian beam illumination generates notch width which is proportional to the width of the intensity

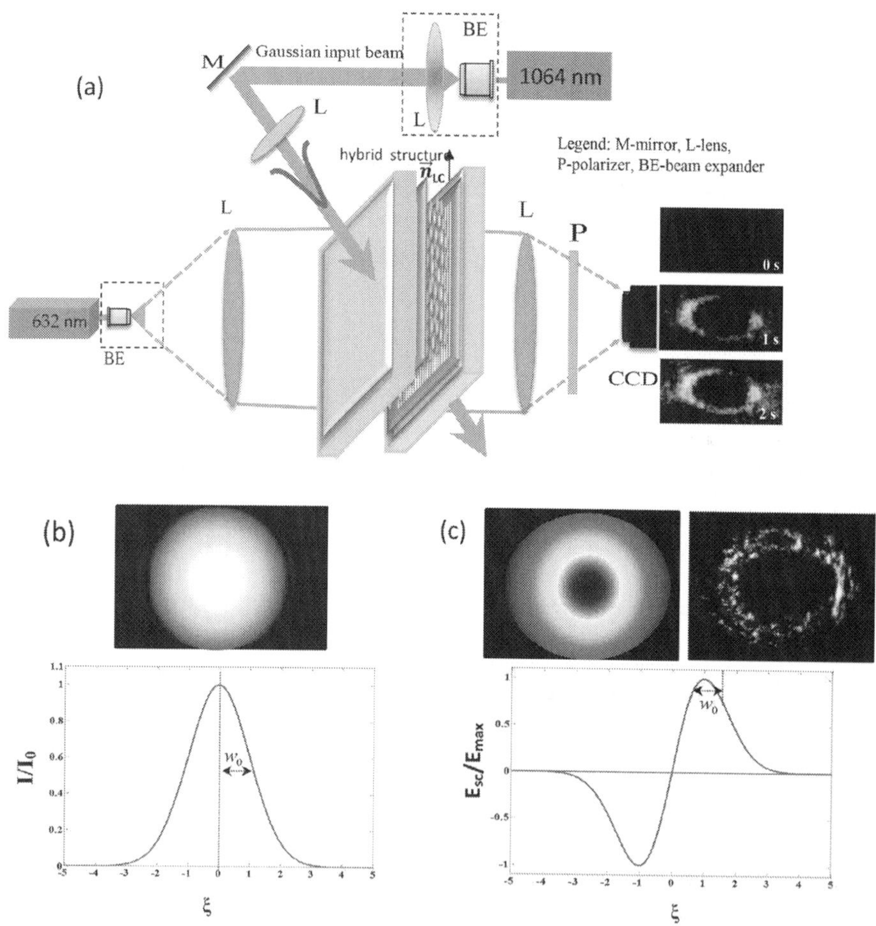

Figure 8. The numerical simulation of the Gaussian intensity beam distribution (a) Gaussian beam propagation through BTO:Rh/LC structure, (b) light intensity numerical distribution and (c) space charge field E_{sc} numerical distribution (left) and experimental propagation of the Gaussian beam (right) through the BSO:Ru/PDLC device.

beam, created by the charge accumulation at the interface between the dark and spurious illumination.

5.2. Two-beam coupling and Bragg-matched regime of diffraction

The evidences of the space charge formation give rise for two-wave mixing experiments. Illumination with two beams leads to light-intensity interference pattern, which induces a space charge field in the photorefractive substrate expressed by [1, 41]:

$$E_{sc} = \frac{i E_D}{1 + \frac{E_D}{E_q}}$$ (19)

where $E_D = K \frac{k_B T}{e}$ is the diffusion field, $E_q = \left(1 - \frac{N_A}{N_D}\right) \frac{e N_D}{\epsilon_0 \epsilon_{PR} K}$ is the saturation field and ϵ_{PR} is the dielectric permittivity of the photorefractive substrate.

Once accumulated in the photorefractive layer, the space-charge field E_{sc} penetrates into the LC layer with decaying evanescent component. In fact, the role of the E_{sc} is to generate electric field, which reorients the nematic LC director $\hat{n}_{LC}$ outside the photorefractive region. Following the couple-wave theory [1, 11], the total electric field obeys the Poisson equation:

$$\nabla \cdot \left(\varepsilon \, \varepsilon_0 \cdot E_{sc} + P_{flex} \right) = 0$$ (20)

where P_{flex} is the flexo-polarization term of LC layer, determined by flexo-electric coefficients according to Refs. [40, 41]. To solve Eq. (20), the authors in Ref. [43] use the relation between the electrical potential in photorefractive substrate $E(x, z)$ and the electrical potential in LC layer $\Psi_{LC}(x, z)$ expressed by $E(x,z) = -\nabla \Psi_{LC}(x, z)$ and the boundary conditions between the $z = -L/2$ to $z = L/2$ planes (where L is the LC thickness). Detailed analysis and analytical solutions have been discussed and presented in Refs. [40–43].

The ability of organic-inorganic structures to operate at Bragg match regime of diffraction is shown at **Figure 9** where two hybrid configurations are discussed: the first one is based on Rh-doped $Bi_{12}TiO_{20}$ crystal and LC layer (BTO:Rh/LC), and the second one consists of Ru-doped $Bi_{12}SiO_{20}$ crystal and PDLC layer (BSO:Ru/PDLC). Examples of simultaneously detected behaviour of two interacting beams (linearly polarized with equal intensity [1:1 ratio]) inside the hybrid structures are shown at **Figure 9(b)** and **(c)**, respectively. As it is seen, during the two-wave mixing, a constructive and deconstructive interference occurs, which is indication for $\pi/2$ phase shift between the light pattern and the index grating pattern. In case of BSO:Ru/ PDLC structure at the beginning of the light illumination, the two beams propagate together since the PDLC layer requires time to reverse its scattering state to the transparent state and after few seconds clear depletion between two beams appear. No changes between the two interfering beams were detected on glass/LC/glass and glass/PDLC/glass reference samples.

The photo-induced space charge field E_{sc} in the photorefractive substrate has been estimated assuming sinusoidal charge density distribution [1] and materials parameters from **Table 1**. By using Eq. (19), the space charge field in BSO:Ru has been estimated as a value of $E_{sc(BSO:Ru)} = 1.6 \times 10^5$ V/m. Taking into account the experimentally measured threshold

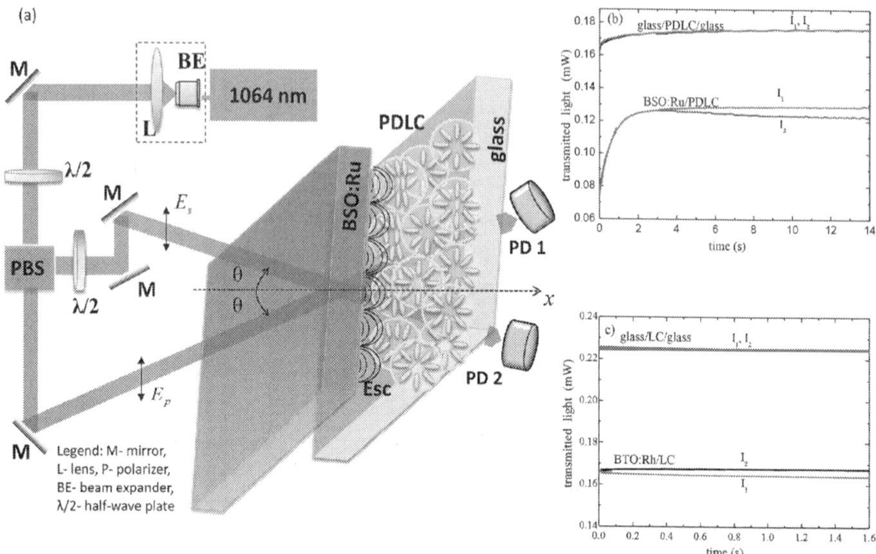

Figure 9. (a) Two-beam coupling experiment in BSO:Ru/PDLC structure and simultaneous behavior of both transmitted beams through the (b) BSO:Ru/PDLC structure and (c) BTO:Rh/LC structure. Comparison with the reference samples as glass/LC/glass and glass/PDLC/glass is also presented.

Type	Symbol	Value	Unit	
LC (MLC type)	$\Delta\varepsilon$ (LC)	$41.6 \times \varepsilon_0$		Anisotropy of NLC's dielectric constant
	K (LC)	5		Elastic constant of NLC
	n_0 (LC)	1.51		O-ray refractive index of LC (nematic)
	n_e (LC)	1.75		E-ray refractive index of LC (nematic)
BTO:Rh and BSO:Ru inorganic crystals	N_D	2×10^{24} for BTO:Rh 6.1×10^{23} for BSO:Ru	cm^{-3}	Donor concentration
	N_A	1×10^{24} for BTO:Rh 5×10^{23} for BSO:Ru	cm^{-3}	Acceptor concentration
	ε	46		Dielectric constant of BTO and BSO crystal
	T	300	K	Temperature

Table 1. Material parameters for theoretical simulations.

voltage of 20 V (for 7.3-µm droplet size) of PDLC layer, the threshold electric field is $E_{th(PDLC)} = 2 \times 10^6$ (V/m). Substituting the known values into the boundary condition $E_{sc(BSO:Ru)} \times \varepsilon_{(BSO)} = E_{sc(PDLC)} \times \varepsilon_{(PDLC)}$, we found the required electric field to re-orient LC molecules in PDLC layer is $E_{sc(PDLC)} = 1.25 \times 10^5$ (V/m). Obviously, the generated E_{sc} field inside BSO:Ru substrate is strong enough to penetrate into the PDLC layer and realign the LCs molecules.

For BTO:Rh/LC structure, similar procedure has been performed. The estimated space charge field in BTO:Rh substrate is about $E_{sc(BTO:Rh)} = 1.9 \times 10^5$ (V/m). Taking into account the experimentally measured driving voltage of LC layer as 2 V (for 12-µm thickness) and the threshold electric field as $E_{th(LC)} = 1.67 \times 10^5$ (V/m), the required space charge field is about $E_{sc(LC)} = 1.5 \times 10^5$ (V/m).

The above two examples verify that the photo-induced space charge field E_{sc} created in photorefractive substrates can grow high enough to exceed the threshold electric field and penetrate into the birefringent layer. The advantage of using PDLC over the LC is no need of alignment layer (since the polymer binder defines the droplets orientations), which permits the photo-generated space-charge field to penetrate directly into the PDLC layer.

Figure 10 shows the experimentally measured gain coefficient Γ (cm^{-1}) dependence on the grating spacing Λ (µm) when the ratio of signal-to-pump beam is 1/70. Besides, **Figure 10** shows the theoretically simulated strength of the space-charge field E_{sc} displayed as a single line. For BSO:Ru/PDLC structure, the measured beam amplification value of $\Gamma = 45$ cm^{-1} is almost three times higher than reported for similar hybrid structures using double-side photorefractive substrates as CdTe (16 cm^{-1}) and GaAs (18 cm^{-1}), operating at near infrared spectral range [46, 47]. In case of BTO:Rh/LC structure, Γ reached almost 10 cm^{-1} at 1-µm grating spacing. It is assumed that large amplification effect comes from suitable doping elements (as Ru and Rh) addition in sillenite crystal structure, which provides enough density of trap levels to support accumulation of high-resolution space charge field.

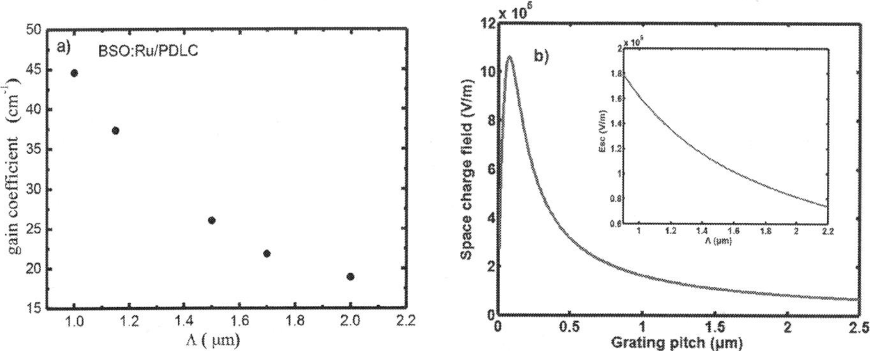

Figure 10. (a) Gain coefficient dependence on the grating spacing Λ(µm) and (b) Theoretical simulation of E_{sc} dependence on Λ(µm) for BSO:Ru/PDLC structure.

As discussed earlier, the Debye screening length in photorefractive material need to be very small to support high concentration of effective trap density. For BSO:Ru crystal, the Debye screening length of 0.08 µm has been calculated from Eq. (7) and materials parameters in **Table 1.** Moreover, as shown in **Figure 10**, the E_{sc} decreases with increasing the grating spacing from 1 to 2 µm. As the gain amplification is controlled by the space charge field, it follows the behaviour of the E_{sc} on the way to decrease with increasing the grating spacing Λ. In that aspect, multi-layer structure may increase the effective interaction length and optimize the E_{sc} penetration depth (however limited by scattering losses).

5.3. Applications

The prime significance of the reviewed hybrid structure is all optically controlled processes. For example, the switching ability BSO:Ru/PDLC structure is demonstrated at **Figure 11**. An image pattern (rectangular mask) is placed into the input plane of 4-f optical system, and the structure is illuminated with 1064-nm Gaussian beam. When the pump light illuminates the device, the PDLC layer transparency is changed due to the induced space charge field in the photorefractive substrate.

Therefore, by controlling the droplet size and consequently the driving voltage of the LC molecules from one side and optimizing the charge carriers' concentration in crystal matrix (providing high enough density for high resolution space charge field), the proposed structure can be further optimized. Moreover, the beam coupling can be significantly improved by addition of nanoparticles in LC layer, which affects the dielectric anisotropy and decreases the driving (threshold) voltage.

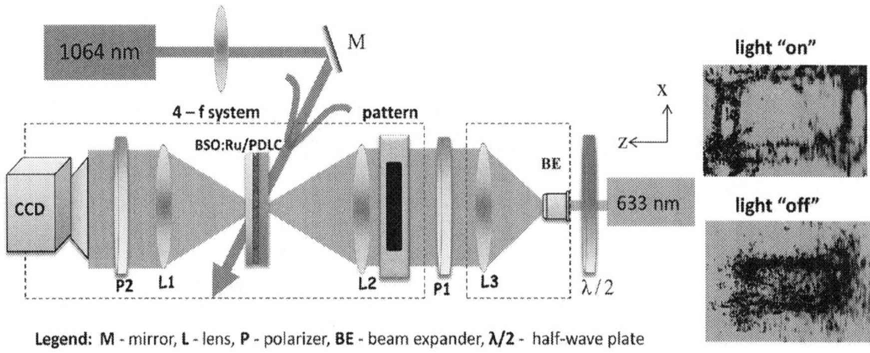

Figure 11. Gaussian laser beam propagating through BSO/PDLC hybrid structure and image mask (rectangular shape) evolution when the light is at "on" and "off" position (right side). All processes are controlled by near infrared light only.

6. Conclusion

The chapter reviewed recent progress of two-wave mixing and beam amplification in novel type of hybrid structures that combine photoconductive and photorefractive properties of inorganic crystals together with the high birefringence and anisotropy of LC (or PDLC) layers. When inorganic crystal acts as photoconductive substrate, the photo-generated charge carriers control the LC molecules alignment and subsequent light modulation. As a result, the two-wave mixing happens in a liquid crystal layer (the active layer) with high amplification values; however, the fringe period of the recorded gratings is limited to few micrometers. When inorganic crystal acts as photorefractive substrate, the two-beam coupling happens at both the photorefractive substrate and LC layer where the space charge field is the driving force for LC molecules reorientation and refractive index modulation. In this configuration, all the processes are controlled by light-permitting submicron resolution.

Depending on the designed structure assembly and operation principle, dynamic holographic gratings at Raman-Nath or Bragg match regimes of diffraction can be recorded. The large trap density and small grating spacing typical for photorefractive materials allow to reach the Bragg matched conditions in all optically controlled structure in contract to the large grating spacing and small trap density typical for LC-based electro-optically controlled structures, which support the Raman-Nath regime of diffraction. Furthermore, by selecting the photosensitivity of inorganic substrate, the spectral interval can be easily adjusted in a regions, where the LC molecules (or PDLC) are not enough sensitive.

The proposed organic-inorganic hybrid structures can control transmission, reflection and scattering of light and are considered in playing an essential role in 3D holographic display technologies and providing sub-micron spatial resolution, large viewing angle and low driving voltage. The reviewed examples can be classified as novel type of non-linear optical components, which exhibit attractive capabilities for light manipulation, coherent image amplification, to control the group velocity of modulated signal beam, in video display technologies. The advantage of simple fabrication and compactness open the way to design varieties of new structures and elements that meet the up-to-date requirements of 3D display technologies and optical information processing.

Acknowledgments

Financial support by the Ministry of Science and Technology, Taiwan under the contracts: MOST 105-2221-E-009-110; 104-2221-E-009-164; 104-2221-E-009-151 and Bulgarian Science Fund under the projects DFNI T-02/26 and H-08/9 are gratefully acknowledged.

Author details

Vera Marinova[1,2]*, Shiuan Huei Lin[3] and Ken Yuh Hsu[1]

*Address all correspondence to: veramarinova@nctu.edu.tw

1 Photonics Department, National Chiao Tung University, Taiwan

2 Institute of Optical Materials and Technologies, Sofia, Bulgaria

3 Department of Electrophysics, National Chiao Tung University, Taiwan

References

[1] Yeh P, Gu C. Optics of Liquid Crystal Displays. 2nd ed. New Jersey: Wiley; 2009. 792 p. ISBN: 978-0-470-18176-8

[2] Yeh P. Introduction to Photorefractive Nonlinear Optics. New York: Wiley; 1993. 491 p. DOI: ISBN: 978-0-471-58692-0

[3] Yariv A, Yeh P. Optical Waves in Crystals: Propagation and Control of Laser Radiation. New York: Wiley; 2002. 604 p. DOI: ISBN: 978-0-471-43081-0

[4] Toal V. Introduction to Holography. Boca Raton: CRC Press; 2011. 502 p. DOI: ISBN: 9781439818688

[5] Klein WR, Cook BD. Unified approach to ultrasonic light diffraction. IEEE Trans Sonics Ultrason. 1967;**SU-14**(3):123–134.

[6] Moharam MG, Young L. Criterion for Bragg and Raman-Nath diffraction regimes. Appl Optics. 1978;**17**(11):1757–1759. DOI: 10.1364/AO.17.001757

[7] Gunter P, Huignard JP, editors. Photorefractive Materials and their Applications I. Berlin: Springer-Verlag; 1988. 441 p.

[8] Yeh P. Two-wave mixing in non-linear media. IEEE J Quant Electron. 1989;**25**(3):484–519. DOI: 10.1109/3.18564

[9] Chi M, Huignard JP, Petersen PM. A general theory of two-wave mixing in non-linear media. J Opt Soc Am B. 2009;**26**(8):1578–1584. DOI: 10.1364/JOSAB.26.001578

[10] Nolte DD, editor. Photorefractive Effects and Materials. New York: Springer Science + Business Media; 1995. 494 p.

[11] Kogelnik N. Coupled wave theory for thick hologram gratings. Bell Syst Tech J. 1969;**48**:2909–2947.

[12] Blanche PA, editor. Photorefractive Organic Materials and Applications. Switzerland: Springer; 2016. 325 p. DOI: 10.1007/978-1-4615-2227-0

[13] Ostroverkhova O, Moerner WE. Organic photorefractives: mechanism, materials and applications. Chem Rev. 2004;**104**:3267–3313. DOI: 10.1021/cr960055c

[14] Kajzar F, Bartkiewicz, Miniewicz A. Optical amplification with high gain in hybrid polymer-liquid-crystal structures. Appl Phys Lett. 1999;**74**(20):2924–2926. DOI: 10.1063/1.123967

[15] Buse K. Light-induced charge transport properties in photorefractive crystals II: materials. Appl Phys B. 1997;**64**:391–407. DOI: 10.1007/s003400050190

[16] Frejlich J. Photorefractive Materials: Fundamental Concepts, Holographic Recording and Materials Characterization. New York: Wiley Interscience; 2007. 336 p. DOI: 10.1002/0470089067

[17] Marinova V, Hsieh ML, Lin SH, Hsu KY. Effect of ruthenium doping on the optical and photorefractive properties of $Bi_{12}TiO_{20}$ single crystals. Opt Comm. 2002;**203**(3–6):377–384. DOI: 10.1016/S0030-4018(02)01127-6

[18] Marinova V, Liu RC, Lin SH, Hsu KY. Real time holography in ruthenium doped bismuth sillenite crystals at 1064 nm. Opt Lett. 2011;**36**(11):1981–1983. DOI: 10.1364/OL.36.001981

[19] Marinova V, Liu RC, Chen MS, Lin YH, Lin SH, Hsu KY. Near infrared properties of Rh-doped $Bi_{12}TiO_{20}$ crystals for photonic applications. Opt Lett. 2013;**38**:495–497. DOI: 10.1364/OL.38.000495

[20] Liu RC, Marinova V, Lin SH, Chen MS, Lin YH, Hsu KY. Near infrared sensitive photorefractive device using PDLC and BSO:Ru hybrid structure. Opt Lett. 2014;**39**:3320–3323. DOI: 10.1364/OL.39.003320

[21] Marinova V, Liu RC, Lin SH, Chen MS, Lin SH, Hsu KY. Near infrared sensitive organic–inorganic photorefractive device. Opt Rev. 2016;**23**(5):811–816. DOI: 10.1007/s10043-016-0249-z

[22] Marinova V, Chi CH, Tong ZF, Berberova N, Liu RC, Lin SH, Lin YH, Stoykova E, Hsu KY. Liquid crystal light valve operating at near infrared spectral range. Opt Quant Electron. 2016;**48**:270. DOI: 10.1007/s11082-016-0546-6

[23] Aubourg P, Huignard JP, Hareng M, Mullen RA. Liquid crystal light valve using bulk monocrystalline $Bi_{12}SiO_{20}$ as the photoconductive material. Appl Opt. 1982;**21**:3706–3712. DOI: 10.1364/AO.21.003706

[24] Residori S, Bortolozzo U, Huignard JP. Slow light using wave mixing in liquid crystal light-valves. Appl Phys B. 2009;**95**:551–557. DOI: 10.1007/s00340-009-3556-2

[25] Bortolozzo U, Residori S, Huignard JP. Beam coupling in photorefractive liquid crystal light valves. J Phys D. 2008;**41**:224007. DOI: 10.1088/0022-3727/41/22/224007

[26] Huignard JP. Spatial light modulators and their applications. J Opt. 1987;**18**:181–186. DOI: 10.1088/0150-536X/18/4/003

[27] Luo S, Wang Y, Tong X, Wang Z. Graphene based optical modulators. Nanoscale Res Lett. 2015;**10**:199. DOI: 10.1186/s11671-015-0866-7

[28] Jung YU, Park KW, Hur ST, Choi SW, Kang SJ. High transmittance liquid-crystal displays using graphene conducting layers. Liq Cryst. 2014;**41**:101–105. DOI: 10.1080/02678292.2013.837517

[29] Fukushima S, Kurokawa T, Ohno M. Real-time hologram construction and reconstruction using a high-resolution spatial light modulator. Appl Phys Lett. 1991;**58**:787–789. DOI: 10.1063/1.104516

[30] White DL, Feldman M. Liquid-crystal light valves. Electron Lett. 1970;**6**:837–839. DOI: 10.1049/el:19700578

[31] Khoo C. Liquid Crystals Physical Properties and Nonlinear Optical Phenomena. 2nd ed. New York: Wiley; 1996. 369 p. DOI: 10.1002/0470084030

[32] Brignon A, Bongrand I, Loiseaux B, Huignard JP. Signal-beam amplification by two-wave mixing in a liquid-crystal light valve. Opt Lett. 1997;**22**(24):1855–1857. DOI: 10.1364/OL.22.001855

[33] Shcherbin K, Gvozdovskyy I, Evans RD. Optimization of the liquid crystal light valve for signal beam amplification. Opt Mat Express. 2016;**6**(11):3670–3675. DOI: 10.1364/OME.6.003670

[34] Bortolozzo U, Residori S, Huignard JP. Transmissive liquid crystal light-valve for near-infrared applications. Appl Opt. 2013;**52**:E73–E77. DOI: 10.1364/AO.52.000E73

[35] Peigine A, Botrolozzo U, Residori S, Molin S, Nouchi P, Dolti D, Huignard JP. Adaptive holographic interferometer at 1.55 μm based on optically addressed spatial light modulator. Opt Lett. 2015;**40**(23):5482–5485. DOI: 10.1364/OL.40.005482

[36] Bortolozzo U, Residori S, Huignard JP. Slow and fast light: basic concepts and recent advancements based on nonlinear wave-mixing processing. Laser Photon Rev. 2009;**4**(4):483–498. DOI: 10.1002/lpor.200910022

[37] Bortolozzo U, Residori S, Huignard JP. Adaptive holography in liquid crystal light valves. Materials. 2012;**5**:1546–1559. DOI: 10.3390/ma5091546

[38] Coates D. Polymer-dispersed liquid crystals. J Mater Chem. 1995;**5**:2063–2072. DOI: 10.1039/JM9950502063

[39] Tabiryan NV, Umeton C. Surface-activated photorefractivity and electro-optic phenomena in liquid crystals. J Opt Soc Am B. 1988;**15**:1912–1917. DOI: 10.1364/JOSAB.15.001912

[40] Jones DC, Cook G. Theory of beam coupling in a hybrid photorefractive liquid crystal cells. Opt Commun. 2004;**232**:399–409. DOI: 10.1016/j.optcom.2003.12.050

[41] Reshetnyak VY, Pinkevych IP, Cook G, Evans DR, Sluckin TJ. Two-beam energy exchange in a hybrid photorefractive-flexoelectric liquid crystal cell. Phys Rev E. 2010;**81**:031705. DOI: 10.1103/PhysRevE.81.031705

[42] Evans DR, Cook G. Bragg-matched photorefractive two-beam coupling in organic-inorganic hybrids. J Nonlinear Optic Phys Mat. 2007;**16**:271–280. DOI: 10.1142/S0218863507003767

[43] Cook G, Carns JL, Saleh MA, Evans DR. Substrate induced pre-tilt in hybrid liquid crystal/inorganic photorefractive. Mol Cryst Liq Cryst. 2006;**453**:141–153. DOI: 10.1080/15421400600651591

[44] Deer MJ. Demonstration of an Fe-doped $KNbO_3$ photorefractive hybrid. Appl Phys Lett. 2006;**88**:254107. DOI: 10.1063/1.2214173

[45] Garcia RR, Rodriguez CB. Enhancement of the coupling gain in GaAs-liquid crystal hybrid devices. Mol Cryst Liq Cryst. 2012;**561**:68–73. DOI: 10.1080/15421406.2012.686713

[46] Gvozdovskyy I, Shcherbin K, Evans DR, Cook G. Infrared sensitive liquid crystal photorefractive hybrid cell with semiconductor substrate. Appl Phys B. 2011;**104**:883–886. DOI: s00340-011-4374-x

[47] MarinovaV, Liu RC, Chen MS, Lin SH, Lin YH, Hsu KY. All optically controlled light valve assembled by photorefractive crystal and PDLC hybrid structure. Proc SPIE. 2015;**9508**:95080O. DOI: 10.1117/12.2178985

[48] Stevens DM, Banerjee PP. Gaussian-beam-induced photorefractive birefringence and its application to radio-frequency signal excision. Opt Lett. 2002;**27**:1333–1335. DOI: 10.1364/OL.27.001333